Post-Wall Berlin

Post-Wall Berlin

Borders, Space and Identity

Janet Ward

First published 2011 by
PALGRAVE MACMILLAN

Palgrave Macmillan in the UK is an imprint of Macmillan Publishers Limited, registered in England, company number 785998, of Houndmills, Basingstoke, Hampshire RG21 6XS.

Palgrave Macmillan in the US is a division of St Martin's Press LLC, 175 Fifth Avenue, New York, NY 10010.

Palgrave Macmillan is the global academic imprint of the above companies and has companies and representatives throughout the world.

Palgrave® and Macmillan® are registered trademarks in the United States, the United Kingdom, Europe and other countries.

ISBN 978–0–230–27657–4   hardback

This book is printed on paper suitable for recycling and made from fully managed and sustained forest sources. Logging, pulping and manufacturing processes are expected to conform to the environmental regulations of the country of origin.

A catalogue record for this book is available from the British Library.

Library of Congress Cataloging-in-Publication Data
Ward, Janet, 1963–
Post-wall Berlin : borders, space and identity / Janet Ward.
p. cm.
Includes index.
ISBN 978–0–230–27657–4 (hardback)
1. Berlin (Germany)—History—1990–   2. Berlin (Germany)—History—
1945–1990.   3. Berlin (Germany)—Social conditions.   4. Boundaries—
Social aspects—Germany—Berlin.   5. Memory—Social aspects—
Germany—Berlin.   6. Group identity—Germany—Berlin.   I. Title.
DD881.3.W37 2011
943'.155088—dc22   2011002019

10   9   8   7   6   5   4   3   2   1
20   19   18   17   16   15   14   13   12   11

Printed and bound in Great Britain by
CPI Antony Rowe, Chippenham and Eastbourne

*For David
and our children
Davey, Ethan and Miranda,
with unbounded love*

Contents

Figures and Sources

Preface and Acknowledgments

Post-Wall Berlin: Borders, Space and Identity appears at a key juncture in the evolution of the reunified German capital. 2011, the fifty-year marker of the construction of the Berlin Wall, provides a moment of reflection regarding the transformations undergone by the iconic city of Berlin and indeed by the world since 13 August 1961. Berlin has spent the last two decades striving toward normal-city status and the overcoming of its division. Yet Berlin is in many respects still a city on the "frontier," marked by post-Cold-War fissures and dividing lines. One reason is that far from being the major site of just one *Wende* following the collapse of communism in 1989, Berlin has known multiple sudden "turning points." Its crisis-ridden past ensures that its contours are not yet entirely fixed, its centers not yet completely filled. A dramatic, often contradictory visual-historical narrative can be decoded on practically every street corner. Given this unsettled legacy, a stabilizing sedimentation below and patina above will need more time to occur. Berlin's multiple kinds of boundaries are interactive acts of construction – not always constructive in the human-to-human sense, but always powerful.

My basic analytical framework for approaching the history of the twentieth century's most contested city is to view Berlin as a "bordered" realm – and not just Berlin in the 1960s, 1970s or 1980s. I study the city's post-Wall years through the lens of its longer-term legacy of boundaries – one with both a pre-story and an afterlife. My book's argument consists of two symbiotically related elements: a discussion of the nature and significance of borders in the modern and postmodern world, and a set of specific urban historical interpretations of the bordered condition of Berlin before, during, and after its literal division during the Cold War.

Appropriately enough, my book offers a *trans-bordering* set of analyses. David Newman knows that it is high time for a "deeper understanding of boundaries ... by recourse to a cross-disciplinary analysis, beyond the exclusive confines of geography," his own discipline. He has called on "boundary scholars to undertake their own form of trans-boundary movement" into other disciplines and discourses where borders have been thematized. For all the academic interest in the globalized and globalizing world and in transnational identities, scholars are still

xiii

learning to "cross to neighboring compartments with ease" when it comes to the challenge of opening up disciplinary training to new ways of asking questions and new patterns of listening to answers.[1] We are just beginning to reach beyond the academic cultures and referential boundaries within which we have been both restrained and nurtured.

One function of this book on Berlin's bordered identities, then, is to help close a few of the gaps between the fields that individually produce the often astonishingly rich scholarship born of the love of cities: anthropology, architectural and art history, economics, geography, history, literary and cultural criticism, planning, political science, and sociology, as well as post-socialist cultural studies.[2] Most scholars of urbanism certainly agree that a multi-faceted approach provides a perspective closest to the lived experience of a city. Berlin is a good case in point because practically all the disciplines have converged on the city in order to articulate responses to the ramifications of the fall of its Wall – yet it still seems as if cross-disciplinary scholarship has been running to catch up with events. Urban spatial environments need to be recognized by humanists not just in terms of competing subjectivities and fields of cultural and aesthetic production but as somewhat more concrete reflections of networked socio-economic and political systems as well. In turn, urbanists trained in the social sciences who extrapolate their theses from empirical case-studies, surveys, and statistical data-analysis may risk falling short if they do not incorporate awareness of a city's most (and least) viscerally powerful sites of representation. With this in mind, *Post-Wall Berlin: Borders, Space and Identity* attempts to fuse the disciplines that seek to unfold aspects of the city, and help the various urban-oriented fields make better sense of each other while making better sense of Berlin.

Part I, "Berlin and the Bordered Condition," serves as an introduction to border studies in relation to Berlin. In Chapter 1, I focus on the epistemological and geopolitical history of borders, especially the growing contemporary public and scholarly interest in how contests over human territorial and collective identity are played out on the urban, national, and transnational levels. Chapter 2 addresses Berlin's long-term "frontier"-status, from its late nineteenth-century rise as the unified Germany's first capital to its unique division during the Cold War and its post-1989 re-suturing. I then relate, in Chapter 3, the city's bordered significance to Europe, specifically in the context of the ongoing changes in European identity which have emerged in the wake of the Schengen Agreement's internal border-opening and external border-hardening for EU member states.

Part II, "Afterlives of the Wall: Reflections and Deflections," provides a series of studies on the Berlin Wall's effect during and after the Cold War. Chapter 4 addresses the joint spatial impact both of the border encircling West Berlin and of the Iron Curtain dividing Germany and Europe from themselves. I suggest that the Cold War's hard geopolitical border was far from static: fuelled by human agency and full of systemic weaknesses, the world's fault-line was in fact full of faults. The visual cultural emphasis of Chapter 5 addresses the contradictions regarding the ex-Wall that have emerged in Berlin since 1989: after several years of thoroughly demolishing the Wall, the reunified capital has evolved toward a belated desire to commemorate it after its demise. In Chapter 6, I interrogate how the voids left behind by the Wall helped foster some of the creatively alternative – and yet also contested – ways in which inhabitants of the post-Wall city have adapted and transformed sites of dereliction.

Part III, "German Geomancy: Power and Planning in Berlin," focuses on urban planning to reveal the intensity of the multiple attempts at defining the city's iconic architecture and infrastructure, its centers and axes. The Wall certainly forced a radical double re-contouring of the city, but it also highlighted what was already considered to be a problem for Berlin. Chapter 7 revisits the modernization projects that planners brought to Berlin during the Weimar German 1920s, Chapter 8 assesses the infrastructural vision of Berlin as the Nazi "world-capital" city of Germania, and Chapter 9 explains the ways in which urban planning has functioned both in divided and re-joined Berlin. I suggest that it is only via this composite picture that the ongoing projects for planning the reunified capital can fully make sense: Berlin has been responding to the re-shaping plans of the entire last century at the same time as trying to bring its two city halves back together.

Part IV, "Holocaust Divides: Memorial Architecture in Berlin," looks at the city's investment in fostering emblematic sites of public memory and national responsibility for Nazi war crimes. Chapter 10, a study of the countermonument, explores how one of the duties that post-Wall Berlin took upon itself was to acknowledge a moral duty of the reunified capital to memorialize the Holocaust. Chapters 11 and 12 offer contrasting discussions in terms of the architectural impact and Holocaust memory-work that have been created, respectively, by the Memorial to the Murdered Jews of Europe designed by Peter Eisenman and located on central former Wall terrain near the Brandenburg Gate; and by Daniel Libeskind's Extension to the Berlin Museum, the Jewish Museum (a project originally entitled "Between the Lines" by the architect). I ask how acts of public urban commemoration may be assisted or impeded by the creation of these significant "memory sites" related to the Shoah.

Finally, Part V, "Rebranding Berlin: Global City Strategies for the Twenty-First Century," investigates how post-Wall Berlin has made intense efforts to be both supremely global and local at the same time. In Chapter 13, I examine how the city's infrastructural and architectural visage was re-engineered in the vain hopes of attaining an economically top global status; the message of a transformed Berlin was part of an attempt to re-rank the former "outpost"-city as the nation's would-be powerhouse. Most of the efforts at global-city-making, however, have produced substitutions and simulations of Berlin's preferred self-imagery instead of a desired return to the modern world city that used to exist before Nazism and the Allied bombing of World War II, Cold War isolation and division. Chapter 14 explores how the high degree of corporate commercial involvement in the large-scale rebuilding of the city became a Mephistophelean pact for Berlin's boosters. The reunified city's planning policy of historical re-enactment, Critical Reconstruction, inadvertently became a corporate (read: "US-style") lackey while ostensibly fostering a return to the values of the European City. Yet as Chapter 15 shows, the virtual realm of city marketing is not without its powers, and some rebranding successes clearly abound in today's Berlin. New urban identities built upon the cultural, high-tech, and media industries may yet follow upon the city's new forms.

While the emphasis of my study is on the still-unfolding re-definition of the reunified German capital, on its sites and structures that have been most transformed since the demise of the socialist state, each part of the book nonetheless emphasizes how Berlin remains indebted to its earlier identities, and also how its struggles may be related further to other cities' recoveries and redefinitions. So even though this book positions Berlin on a forward-looking trajectory, its author spends quite a bit of time looking to see what came before, and what is happening around, as well.

****

From the start of my *Post-Wall Berlin* project I have benefited from generous support from the American Council of Learned Societies, the Fulbright Commission, the German Academic Exchange Service, and the Getty Research Institute, as well as sabbaticals and travel grants from the University of Nevada Las Vegas and the University of Colorado at Boulder. For their skilled help I would like to thank the staff at the Bundesarchiv Koblenz, Bundesarchiv Militärarchiv Freiburg, Getty Research Institute, Landesarchiv Berlin, and the Wende Museum and Archive of the Cold War, as well as the librarians at the University of Nevada Las Vegas. I received very helpful feedback when I gave invited lectures on this material – at the Bard Graduate Center, University of California Los Angeles, University of Cambridge, University of Iowa, University of Pittsburgh, Rice University, and the University of Wisconsin Madison, as well as at the World Congress of Architecture (UIA), the Canadian Association of University Teachers of German (CAUTG), and the conference of "The Space Between: Literature and Culture, 1914–1945"; and when I presented papers at meetings of the German Studies Association and the Modern Language Association. I am grateful to colleagues, both Berliners and *Berlinkenner*, whose stimulating insights have deepened my understanding of the city: Olaf Briese, Jeffry M. Diefendorf, Rolf J. Goebel, Sabine Hake, Nicole Huber, Friedrich Knilli, Brian Ladd, Hubertus Siegert, Marc Silberman, Ralph Stern, Karen E. Till, James Throgmorton, Rasmus Waern, and Andrew J. Webber. To Walter H. Sokel, my former doctoral adviser, I express, as ever, my gratitude for his friendship and intellectual support. I thank the anonymous readers for Palgrave Macmillan and also the editors at the press (Catherine Mitchell, Felicity Plester, and Christobel Scaife), who have provided stellar guidance throughout.

Earlier versions of parts of this book appeared in the following journals and edited volumes, and are reprinted here with kind permission of the publishers: "Berlin-Mahagonny and the Re-Shaping of Post-Wall Borders," *The Brecht Yearbook*, 29 (2004), pp. 406–19; "Berlin, The Virtual Global City," *Journal of Visual Culture*, 3.1 (2004), pp. 239–56; "Monuments of Catastrophe: Holocaust Architecture in Washington and Berlin," in Andreas W. Daum and Christof Mauch, eds, *Berlin–Washington, 1800–2000: Capital Cities, Cultural Representation, and National Identities* (New York: Cambridge University Press, 2005), pp. 155–200; "Las Vegas on the Spree: Americanization in the New Berlin," in Gail Finney, ed., *Visual Culture in Twentieth-Century Germany: Text as Spectacle* (Bloomington: Indiana University Press, 2006), pp. 83–100; and "Recapitalizing Berlin," in Marc Silberman, ed., *The German Wall: Fallout in Europe* (New York: Palgrave Macmillan, forthcoming in 2011). Every effort has been made to identify the copyright holders for the images in this book.

Post-Wall Berlin: Borders, Space and Identity is dedicated to my husband David M. Wrobel as well as to our three young children Davey, Ethan, and Miranda, who were all born during the course of this project and who bring daily wonder into our world. In my writing about the German capital I have been especially guided by my husband's natural ability to understand cities as sites of visitation and transformation. In particular, David has shown me how the urban genius loci is something that natives, newcomers, and sojourners alike can observe, sense, and mould anew.

Notes

1. David Newman, "Boundaries," in John Agnew, Katharyne Mitchell, and Gearóid Ó Tuathail, eds, *A Companion to Political Geography* (Malden: Blackwell Publishers, 2003), pp. 123–37, pp. 124, 135, 124.
2. It is worth mentioning here some of the best research in the various disciplines' attention to post-1989 Berlin and Europe. Anthropological studies by John Bornemann point to the "Wall in the Head": *Belonging in the Two Berlins: Kin, State, Nation* (Cambridge and New York: Cambridge University Press, 1992) and *After the Wall: East Meets West in the New Berlin* (New York: Basic Books, 1990). One of the most incisive readings of post-Wall Berlin's architectural development is by Philipp Oswalt in *Berlin: Stadt ohne Form. Strategien einer anderen Architektur* (Berlin: Prestel, 2000). The Berlin Republic's turn to architecture to symbolically renew the capital city has been analyzed by Deborah Ascher Barnestone, *The Transparent State: Architecture and Politics in Postwar Germany* (New York: Routledge, 2005), as well as journalists Heinrich Wefing, *Kulisse der Macht. Das Berliner Kanzleramt* (Stuttgart and Munich: Deutsche Verlags-Anstalt, 2001) and Michael Z. Wise, *Capital Dilemma: Germany's Search for a New Architecture of Democracy* (Princeton: Princeton Architectural Press, 1998). The "Architects' Debate" in Berlin can best be understood by reading Gavriel Rosenfeld's "The Architects' Debate. Architectural Discourse and the Memory of Nazism in the Federal Republic of Germany, 1977–1997," *History and Memory*, 9.1–2 (1997), in tandem with Daniel Libeskind, *Daniel Libeskind: The Space of Encounter* (New York: Universe, 2000), Wolf Jobst Siedler, *Phoenix im Sand: Glanz und Elend der Hauptstadt* (Berlin: Propyläen Verlag, 1998), and Hans Stimmann, ed., *Berliner Altstadt. Von der DDR-Staatsmitte zur Stadtmitte* (Berlin: Dom, 2009). The urban economy of post-Wall Berlin and post-Iron Curtain Europe forms the focus of work by Stefan Krätke, such as his *Medienstadt. Urbane Cluster und globale Zentren der Kulturproduktion* (Opladen: Leske+Budrich, 2002). Influential books in cultural studies, cultural history, and urban geography focusing on Berlin's relationship to its burdened past include Andreas Huyssen, *Present Pasts: Urban Palimpsests and the Politics of Memory* (Stanford: Stanford University Press, 2003), Lutz Koepnick, *Framing Attention: Windows on Modern German Culture* (Baltimore: Johns Hopkins University Press, 2007), Brian Ladd, *The Ghosts of Berlin: Confronting German History in the Urban Landscape* (Chicago: University of Chicago Press, 1997), and Karen E. Till, *The New Berlin: Memory, Politics, Place* (Minneapolis: University of Minnesota Press, 2005). Berlin's indebtedness to its East European past and future has been convincingly articulated by Karl Schlögel in *Die Mitte liegt ostwärts: Europa im Übergang* (Munich: Carl Hanser Verlag, 2002) and *Promenade in Jalta und andere Städtebilder* (Munich: Carl

Hanser Verlag, 2001), as well as by Uwe Rada, *Berliner Barbaren. Wie der Osten in den Westen kommt* (Berlin: BasisDruck, 2001). Among the many wide-spectrum urban histories of Berlin, two that stand out are David Clay Large's *Berlin* (New York: Basic Books, 2000) and Alexandra Richie's *Faust's Metropolis: A History of Berlin* (New York: HarperCollins, 1998). The literary and visual cultural topoi of (post-Wall and pre-Wall) Berlin have been explored by, for example, Carol-Anne Costabile-Heming, Rachel J. Halverson, and Kristie A. Foell, eds, *Berlin: The Symphony Continues. Orchestrating Architectural, Social, and Artistic Change in the New Capital* (Berlin: Walter de Gruyter, 2004); Katharina Gerstenberger, *Writing the New Berlin: The German Capital in Post-Wall Literature* (Rochester, NY: Camden House, 2008); Susanne Ledanff, *Hauptstadtphantasien. Berliner Stadtlektüren in der Gegenwartsliteratur 1989-2008* (Bielefeld: Aisthesis, 2009); and Andrew J. Webber, *Berlin in the Twentieth Century: A Cultural Topography* (New York: Cambridge University Press, 2008). For the impact of planning on Berliners' diverse ethnicities, see Stephan Lanz, *Berlin aufgemischt: abendländisch – multikulturell – kosmopolitisch? Die politische Konstruktion einer Einwanderungsstadt* (Bielefeld: transcript Verlag, 2007); and for planning histories of Berlin see Harald Bodenschatz, *Städtebau in Berlin. Schreckbild und Vorbild für Europa* (Berlin: Dom, 2010), as well as Bodenschatz's edited comparative compendium, *Renaissance der Mitte. Zentrumsumbau in London und Berlin* (Berlin: Verlagshaus Braun, 2005). Of considerable value have been the urban sociological studies by Hartmut Häußermann and Andreas Kapphan, *Berlin: von der geteilten zur gespaltenen Stadt? Sozialräumlicher Wandel seit 1990* (Opladen: Leske+Budrich, 2000), and Häußermann, Andrej Holm, and Daniela Zunzer, *Stadterneuerung in der Berliner Republik. Modernisierung in Berlin-Prenzlauer Berg* (Opladen: Leske+Budrich, 2002); as well as Uwe Rada, *Hauptstadt der Verdrängung: Berliner Zukunft zwischen Kiez und Metropole* (Berlin: Verlag Schwarze Risse, 1997), Elizabeth A. Strom, *Building the New Berlin: The Politics of Urban Development in Germany's Capital City* (Lanham: Lexington Books, 2001), and Eva Schweitzer, *Großbaustelle Berlin: Wie die Hauptstadt verplant wird* (Berlin: Nicola, 1996). For a selection of the scholarship on the Berlin Wall and inner German border, see Chapter 4, note 2; and on border studies, See Chapter 1, note 8. On the evolution of post-socialist cultural studies, refer to Daphne Berdahl, *Where the World Ended: Re-Unification and Identity in the German Borderland* (Berkeley: University of California Press, 1999); Svetlana Boym, *The Future of Nostalgia* (New York: Basic Books, 2001); Susan Buck Morss, *Dreamworld and Catastrophe: The Passing of Mass Utopia in East and West* (Cambridge, MA: MIT Press, 2000); Tony Judt, *Postwar: A History of Europe since 1945* (New York: Penguin Press, 2005); Charity Scribner, *Requiem for Communism* (Cambridge, MA: MIT Press, 2003); Edith Sheffer, forthcoming: *Burned Bridge: How East and West Germans Made the Iron Curtain* (Oxford University Press, 2011); and Stuart Taberner and Paul Cooke, eds, *German Culture, Politics, and Literature into the Twenty-First Century* (Rochester, NY: Camden House, 2006); see also Magdalena J. Zaborowska, Sibelan Forrester, and Elena Gapova, "Introduction: Mapping Postsocialist Cultural Studies," in Forrester, Zaborowska, and Gapova, eds, *Over the Wall/After the Fall: Post-Communist Cultures Through an East-West Gaze* (Bloomington: Indiana University Press, 2004), pp. 1–35.

Part I

Introduction: Berlin and the Bordered Condition

1
The Berlin Paradigm

"Limit" means: (a) The furthest part of each thing, and the first point outside which no part of a thing can be found, and the first point within which all parts are contained. (b) Any form of magnitude or of something possessing magnitude. (c) The end of each thing ... (d) The reality or essence of each thing ...

(Aristotle)[1]

Wim Wenders' film *Wings of Desire* (1987) suggests how borders define more than a city or a nation – they define humanity. A chauffeur's musings are listened in upon by Cassiel, an angel, and as the man drives his vintage automobile, a ruined, bombed-out Berlin appears through the car windshield. Memories of the Allied air war's all-out destruction of German cities accompany the driver's somber thoughts:

> Are there still borders? More than ever. Every street has its own barrier or border line. There's a no-man's-land strip between the individual properties, camouflaged by a hedge or a ditch. [...] The German population is fragmented into as many small states ... as there are individual people ... and the individual patterns of state are malleable: everyone carries his or her image around with them, and demands an entry fee when someone else wants to cross over.[2]

With moments like this, Wenders' film has become so much more than an unwitting swan song about the Cold War's most famous divided city. The German postwar condition of punitive division into occupied states – which was unilaterally cemented by the country's eastern half

3

with the construction of the Berlin Wall on 13 August 1961 – is shown in emblematic terms to be part of the universal condition of human-to-human separation. Only the panoramic camera-eye of Wenders' angels is able to conquer all boundaries – be they the loneliness, euphoria or despair of people's inner monologues, the firewalls between apartments, the divided terrains of West and East Berlin, and even the entry and exit moments into and out of life itself. Nor was this atomization completely unwa(rra)nted, at least on the nation-state level. For postwar (West) German intellectuals who like Wenders came of age in 1968, divided state identities appeared on a certain level to be preferable to any loss of such borders. It was as if the Nazi past, still decidedly un-"overcome" in both political systems, might set loose a neo-Nazi genie out of the bottle, should German reunification ever occur. In Wenders' film, Nazism could be safely contained within the cinematic imaginary – specifically in this instance, the wartime film set that the chauffeur is driving toward.

If World War II shaped Berlin's division, then Berlin's division shaped not just the city but the estranged double German identities that arose therefrom. Berlin's situation has clearly differed from most border-cities, which are more obviously identified as having a physical edge provided by oceans, rivers, or mountain ranges; by serving as a place for different, neighboring cultures to meet, such as nineteenth-century imperial Vienna; or by being the site of deep religious and ethnic conflicts that divide their peoples, such as Belfast, Jerusalem, or the cities of Bosnia and Croatia. Yet over time, a seemingly "natural" estrangement ensued between the divided German populations, such was the formidable effect of the artificially inserted political schism. The dividing of Berlin began, in fact, before World War II was even over, as the Allies made plans for their subsequent occupation of Germany.[3] Immediately following the end of the war, the city's and indeed country's sectors governed by the occupying Allies began to be defined by their demarcation lines and zones. The Allied forces made the city and the entire divided country serve two distinct functions: a frontier for the West on the one hand, and, simultaneously along with the rest of Eastern Europe, a buffer zone for the Soviet Union on the other. Before the Wall was even built, West Berlin tourism for the international market promoted a form of front-lines-visit that indicated one's loyalty to capitalism (Fig. 1.1). The peripheries of two competing world-systems were imposed upon the center of the defeated capital, affecting all areas of that city's functioning.

Now that this era of separation is over, we are better situated to grasp the greater relevance of Berlin in the history of border-cities. It stands

Figure 1.1 "Don't Miss Berlin – The International City Behind the Iron Curtain." West Berlin promotional brochure (West Germany, c. 1952)

to reason that nowadays, half a century after the construction of the Wall and more than two decades after its fall, Berlin's borders are to some degree still ongoing, since they have lent the city both a specific set of temporal pathways, a structural and infrastructural trajectory. *Post-Wall Berlin: Borders, Space and Identity* investigates these legacies. Berlin's various geographical meanderings – its delayed jump-start into the world-city ranks of Imperial and Weimar modernity, and its subsequent near-fatal marring by Nazi planning, wartime bombing, Cold War division, and now post-Wall reclamation and reinvention – are the reasons why the identity of this city remains so disjointed. They account for how this city has repeatedly failed to live up to the yardsticks of consistent predictability offered by other first-world capital cities and global cities over the course of the twentieth century.

Post-Wall Berlin has been host to one of the world's most dramatic processes of urban re-invention. On 20 June, 1991, the Bundestag (representing states in both the East and West parts of Germany) voted by a mere 337 votes to 320 to move from Bonn, its comfortable, provisional West German capital, back to Berlin – just as the preamble to the postwar West German constitution had stated a reunified Germany would in fact do. By 1999, 7,000 employees constituting most of the sections of the German government finally, if rather reluctantly, had arrived in the rejuvenated capital. It was now being dubbed the "New Berlin" – not for the first time – and over a decade later it is still a work-in-progress. In his landmark study of postwar (and post-Wall) Berlin, historian Brian Ladd suggests that Berlin was selected as the seat of the reunified nation because it alone "had straddled the division of Germany and thus was the best place to heal the wounds of division." Such healing should not preclude memory but rather bring forth scenes of the city's separation from itself: specifically, its myriad "ghosts."[4]

Berlin's post-Wall suturing is not yet an entirely seamless endeavor, and not just for Cold War reasons of a formerly federally subsidized western half essentially taking over an eastern half whose communist capital status was eradicated. Even in its new architectural garb, this city shows us, as if in a magnifying glass, what other urban forms struggle to overcome. Jacques Derrida pointed to the emblematic nature of Berlin's formerly divided territory for all built environments:

> Why is Berlin exemplary? It is a city, has been a city, because of its split, which symbolizes all the division of the world, all the divided cities of the world ... and because the inner differences and the void precisely follow the line or the cut of this difference. Berlin could be considered a noncity, a city whose identity or unity is split along an interrupted line. To the extent that it is so divided and so nonidentical, Berlin could claim to be exemplary.[5]

Berlin, then, became an unintentional urban paradigm. Derrida's advocacy for Berlin recognized it as both an historical crucible and magnet: we are drawn to it in the manner of the problem of a "Humpty Dumpty" city that is perennially being put back together.[6] In the understandable German post-Wall desire to normalize Berlin as much as possible and seek sameness with other cities, multiple temporal and spatial territories still demonstrate the city's legacy of difference and division. Post-Wall instances of boundedness still crop up. Not surprisingly, the socio-economic contrast between the western and eastern parts of the city, the city's relation to most of the surrounding formerly eastern state of Brandenburg, and indeed the capital's difficult relation to the (old, federal) states of West Germany, remain very marked despite all attempts to neutralize those differences.

This book will explore how Berlin's borders have moved on beyond their former roles and gained new contexts. From the boundary *de*-signification of the *Wende*-period, boundary *re*-signification is now well underway. As the reunified city of Berlin and the rest of Europe have been experiencing in the decades since the fall of the Wall, both East and West are not where and not what they were once thought to be.[7] New forms are following new functions, yet echoes remain of the former lines of division.

Beyond Berlin itself, the city's divided and now reunified history has made an inadvertent contribution to the comparative study of borders, be these geographically or phenomenologically understood. The borders that necessarily define our spaces and our places – whether urban, regional, or national, as well as the culturally and ethnically diverse groups who live there – can best be understood not just as a hegemonically linked set of containers, but rather as a series of re-defining, impermanent, and reciprocal engagements between structure and disintegration, stasis and movement, barrier and gateway. This dynamic understanding of border theory reflects a recent repositioning of the "spatial turn" in both the humanities and social sciences toward "low" or "critical" geopolitics – contexts that better fit the postmodern world and defy grand-narrative posturing of nation-states.[8] In this more balanced analysis of territorial desire, fixed borders are recognized for their links to their opposite, namely fluidity; and impermeable walls nonetheless change and are porous. Postmodern border theory thus acknowledges not an unceasing de-territorialization in and by itself, but a continual de- *and* re-territorialization. The ebb and flow of border-making can be traced back to Gilles Deleuze and Félix Guattari, who helped open up the study of socio-spatial structures when they observed that there are two fundamental kinds of dimensions for human engagement: liberatory, nomadic "smooth" space, as well as bordered, sedentary "striated" space. Smooth and striated realms "exist only in mixture" and in transformation one into the other. Thus any spatial striation, once formed, eventually switches into its opposite: "forces at work within space continually striate it," but any newly bordered space "develops other forces and emits new smooth spaces."[9]

Appearances, then, are deceiving: despite their apparent functions to the contrary, borders are fixed neither temporally nor physically. Even the modern world's most visually powerful closed border, as the Berlin Wall (1961–1989) surely was, became a mutable organism through time, first as it was built and then as it evolved, changed, and ended. The Wall, even at its most closed, proved in the end to be not impregnable but permeable and breakable (Fig. 1.2). Even though German division was the cause of significant socio-cultural estrangement for the generations who lived in the two separate political systems, it did not hold. Ultimately, the Wall can be best understood as a highly intangible entity that is outlasting its physical manifestation in unforeseen ways. Its mutability is continuing even in its various stages of memorialized afterlife. The deeper function, then, of the Wall was that despite the global border that it represented, it was fragile and traversable: it could not keep truly separate the two world outlooks that it purportedly marked. Moreover, as an ideology it was far more than its architecture, affecting the *mentalités* of Cold-War East and Cold War West. Nowadays the ex-Wall continues to impact the city as specter and symbol. As unnatural and anti-urban as it first appeared, the Wall in the end – and even more so after its literal, historical end – has become its inverse image: a naturalized urban site. Berlin's ex-Wall is indicative of how borders are a part of the temporal dimension. And they pass just as quickly.

The Berlin Wall brought a literal concretization to the process famously referred to in 1946 by Sir Winston Churchill as an Iron Curtain descending upon Europe.[10] The Wall was a clear and tactile reminder of the power of politics to concomitantly disrupt and challenge that which Paul Virilio terms the emerging electronic era's effects of "drift" and "derealization" upon and "crisis of 'dimension'" for constructed space (Fig. 1.3).[11] Yet even the most hardened of geopolitical boundaries cannot forge a total stasis in the long term. In particular, attempts at the imposition of barriers to migratory movement are destined, eventually, to fail. As the end of the Cold War demonstrated, no borders prove immutable – and certainly not as long-lasting as the colossal US and ex-Soviet nuclear arsenals. Various designations for the immaterial processes of capitalist globalization appear in retrospect to have played a role in defeating the Soviet Bloc countries at the Cold-War game, and eventually helping the disintegration of the Iron Curtain itself – capitalism's technologies as well as its discontents that

Figure 1.2 The Berlin Wall during demolition, Ebertstraße, Berlin, just south of the Reichstag, on 20 February, 1990

10

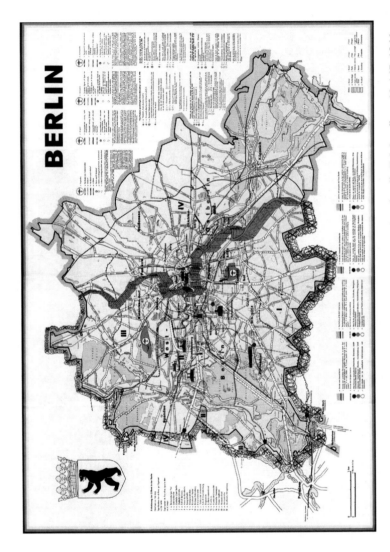

Figure 1.3 "Berlin IRO-Sonderkarte," a special edition from the *Aktuelle IRO-Landkarte* Nr.167, 1966

first conquer and then condense and warp previously established patterns and confines of behavior.[12] Cultural critics like Virilio have tended to translate this unmooring into a boundary-free pan-urbanization (at least of the First World): a geographic drift for the urban centers of the privileged nations, facilitated by electronic communications. The physical site of the postindustrial city has been reconfigured in relation to its role as a global node that is interminably "on." In this vein, some theorists of globalization, particularly in the euphoric post-1989 years, downplayed the significance of social, economic, and geographical boundaries as barriers, and focused on the cross-border flow of distribution networks and migration: the prognosis for city and nation-state alike was that their regular functions were being emptied out.[13]

However, the floodgates began to close again when the post-Cold War era found one rather different self-definition for the West on the tragic 11th day of September 2001. Since the Islamic extremist terrorist attacks on US soil, geo-postmodernism (understood as a temporal-spatial theory of open, globalized borders) has entered a harsher era, one that is full of trepidation. The border-free dreams encouraged by technological advances promising a unifying worldwide web in all areas of postindustrial life have only partially come true. From the vantage point of our current era of global uncertainty, the Cold War seems to have offered certain forms of stability for both sides, after all. We now live in contradictory "global-retro" times that apply biometric border controls for entry and exit, and former military equipment in the surveillance and securitization of everyday life. Multiple fortress metaphors have been re-emerging, symbolizing the USA's political isolation from Europe in the wake of the US-led war in Iraq, and seen in both entities' recent efforts to shore up their perimeters against unwanted immigrants. Such shifts toward less permeable borders unsettle pre-9/11 predictions by economists, planners, philosophers, and geographers alike about the increasing flexibility of international and local boundaries and the interrelated growth of leading cities. This renewed border-emphasis is occurring alongside its apparent opposite, namely fluid globalization, and is impacting the public's perception of the latter. While it did not take 9/11 to foster increases in negative terms for literal (as opposed to virtual or economic) border-crossings as abetting poor migrants, crime, and terrorism, it certainly assisted general acceptance of such fear-mongering images.

Nonetheless, it is possible that a speech by then-US presidential candidate Barack Obama at Berlin's Victory Column in July 2008 before a young crowd of over 200,000 might signify not just a generational but an intercontinental readiness for change beyond the unfortunate fatalism in the Samuel P. Huntington-model of the "clash of civiliza- tions."[14] With a nod to the previous oratories held in Cold War Berlin by both Presidents John F. Kennedy and Ronald Reagan, Obama declared:

> The walls between old allies on either side of the Atlantic cannot stand. The walls between the countries with the most and those with the least cannot stand. The walls between races and tribes, natives and immigrants, Christian and Muslim and Jew cannot stand. These now are the walls that we must tear down.[15]

Obama's call to defuse incendiary barriers between peoples in the post-Wall and now post-9/11 era is timely precisely because of globali- zation's ability to subvert the territorial checkerboard. We are facing a proliferation of boundary transitions and disputes, both on the urban micro- and state macro-levels. Bear in mind that over 4,000 peoples of the Fourth World exist without a nation-state of their own. Yet they are, understandably, striving to get one. Many of these new claims on borders are direct consequences of the devolution – or "dissolution," to use Charles S. Maier's phrase – of the lines of the Cold War.[16]

In short, the terrorist attacks perpetrated by al-Qaeda extremists, themselves practitioners par excellence of (if not believers in) border- free, transnational identities, have impacted the millennial global economy's earlier naivety about an opening-up of patterns of migration and commercial distribution. While such movements are still ineluctably altering the nature of the spatial borders once inherent both to modern statecraft and industrial urban identities, it is also true that the demo- cratic processes of both metropolitan and state entities are in danger of losing ground to the growing need to secure – or, in political terms, to be seen to be securing – those environments.[17] A potential result is that, despite this ostensibly open and globalizing era, freedoms (of speech, movement, and private interaction) can be foreclosed. The radical transformations of international borders since the collapse of the Iron Curtain and the 1990s' initial period of celebration at the opening-up of the Cold War's confined spaces have received their balancing-out with a growing awareness of how counter-terrorist measures citadelize urban spaces and places, and may over-control the people who live there.

Given the above geopolitical trajectories, we may well wonder about the inherently destructive negativity of humankind's need for borders: in short, territoriality. Are there not signs of *ressentiment*-driven Nietzschean herd-mentality here? Do we not make and re-make borders out of fear and insecurity, and could and should the bordering drive be overcome? Since the contours of a state are always engaged in a dialogue with collective memory and identity, state-bound people are thus perennially exposed to the risk of violence as a means of defending or forging at the expense of another group's lives a commemorated or wished-for identity – in short, the downside of belonging to the "imagined communities" detected by Benedict Anderson.[18] Is the era of Berlin's division merely an example of the bordered urban-national condition at its most paranoid, and does its real lesson for us lie in our own present proximity to a compulsive re-engineering and re-enactment of that point of view? Despite globalization's permeation of any national bids to sovereignty, to what degree do we remain inadvertent participants in the tendency toward the "territorial trap"? Our complacency about contained spatial divisions lingers on – even after the end has begun for the era of the nation-state's primacy (from 1815 to the end of the Cold War).[19]

Certainly, in terms of nation-building, the origin of borders has hardly been a democratic process; most national boundaries are born, in fact, of war and colonization. Wholly arbitrary state-boundaries of geopolitical self-interest were superimposed on Africa by the European Great Powers (Belgium, France, Germany, Great Britain, Italy, Portugal, and Spain) at the West African Conference of 1884–1885 that were held in Berlin. The architects of the lines between these colonial territories exhibited no concern for the ethnic and religious groups that they pasted together or split apart. In a myopic re-bordering that protected the interests of the colonial powers, it was simply expected that the colonized peoples would naturally accept and respect the new boundaries that their masters drew up for them. The recent history of African genocides serves as a ghastly testament to the errors of the imperialists' re-ordering of the continent. In opposition to the Organization of African Unity's decision to adhere to the African map that the Europeans once devised, Nobel Laureate Wole Soyinka called for a complete re-drawing of that continent's boundaries.[20]

A cautionary tale in the history of borders can be gleaned from the particularly fraught nature of Germany's relation to space and boundaries in the modern era. The roots of the recurring theme of recovering what were considered rightfully German borders can be traced to nineteenth-century German nationalism, with its aim of re-Germanizing the European East: a pioneer urge as strong as the drive toward the founding of the American West or of the British Empire. This border-recovery theme culminated in Hitler's invasion of Europe. In this sense, the division of Germany after World War II was a fitting punishment for the Nazi expansionist policy of *Lebensraum* ("living space"). Here an uncomfortable intersection occurs between geopolitics and the Holocaust. The *Lebensraum* term was first coined by German geographer Friedrich Ratzel in 1901. He expounded a theory of national organicism that was the application of Darwin's ideas to geography. Ratzel found that a strong, "growing" people (like the Germans) would evolve spatially as well as numerically, by migrating over the land of their weaker neighbors. Essentially, he said, the "struggle for existence" (*der Kampf ums Dasein*) amounts to the extension of borders gained by the territorial "struggle for space" (*der Kampf um Raum*).[21] States hence appeared to have biological functioning, with purer, stronger states taking over from the less pure, or older, less deserving ones.[22]

By the 1920s, the *Lebensraum* concept was featuring in pro-Nazi publications in Germany. Such tracts followed the priorities of the first Nazi party (NSDAP) manifesto by insisting on (Aryan) Germans' need to expand beyond their borders, especially the ones imposed by the Versailles Treaty after World War I which had deprived the country of a quarter of its territory, including its 1815–1918 boundary with Poland. Given the numbers of now-minority Germans left on the other side, the issue of erasing the eastern border became a highly incendiary one. Moreover, the situation would not have required a geopolitical expert like Karl Haushofer to realize that the now-isolated East Prussia, connected to Germany by the "Danzig corridor," could not last ad infinitum in that condition. During the interwar years, Haushofer astutely marketed images of a Germany so "border-oppressed" (*grenzbedrückt*) by its rival imperialist neighbors that it would be justified in stepping over its boundaries.[23] Survival of the state meant purity in order to maintain difference. Thus the border became a stronger concept due to its crucial role in maintaining the claim of German racial cleansing. This is why Haushofer promoted, in his writings, the concept of the border through history and the world, and in so doing paved the way for the Nazi regime's expansionist movement into Eastern Europe. Nazi Propaganda Minister Joseph Goebbels' concept of the "New Order" (*Neue Ordnung*) when Hitler invaded the Soviet Union on 22 June, 1941 was a transformation of spatially contoured Europe into a racially defined Germanic Empire of the German Nation. For Goebbels, German-Aryan blood rights permitted the Slavic realm to be overrun: "Europe is not a geographical term, but one forged by blood ... which is why it is our duty to place [the border] where we want it to be."[24]

It was in this deadly context of Nazified geopolitics that the fate of the most infamous of all border-towns was decided: Auschwitz. The old Holy Roman Empire of the German Nation in the mid-thirteenth century had extended as far east as Auschwitz (originally known, among other names, as Ausswenznis), founded in 1270 and sold as a duchy to the Polish King Casimir IV in 1457. Frederick the Great's expansion of Prussia had led to the re-inclusion of Auschwitz under the Prussian government, and ultimately, by Wilhelmine times, the unified German Reich. By the turn of the twentieth century, Auschwitz was literally located on the aggressively teutonizing edge of what had by then become known as "the German East" between not two but three competing Empires: Russian, Austro-Hungarian, and German.

The role of Auschwitz as a border-town came to an end when the League of Nations redrew Germany's borders in the wake of the Great War – until, that is, its re-Germanizing by Reich Leader-SS Heinrich Himmler into a concentration and death factory for the Jews of Occupied Europe. The *de*-formation of Auschwitz by the Nazis was, in fact, the cruelest *re*-formation of that town as ultra-German. Himmler's reclamation of the town as Auschwitz (from the Polish Oswiecim) was a part of his role as Reich Commissioner for the Consolidation of the German Nation, an exterminationist version of Frederick the Great's expansionism. In making Auschwitz the center of the camp system, Himmler was compensating for the town's non-continuous history of German settlement – an instability witnessed in the linguistic shifting sands of its name over the centuries.[25] A similar biopolitical land-grab was articulated in Goebbels' promise of 1942 that "[t]he [German] East is not just the longing but also the fulfillment of our nation."[26]

Nonetheless, to assert and thus divide social or political space is not always to conquer it or the rights or even lives of those who exist there. Coercion and fearful self-defense are not the only raison-d'être of borders; aggression does not prompt all the stories of the bordering drive, even though it surely accounts for some of the most horrific ones. At the very least, borders help nation-states in their everyday functioning. Most crucially, boundaries are both a highly impermanent construct and yet a quintessential part of human identity-formation and social practice.[27] Like Franz Kafka's stories "Before the Law," "The Burrow," or "The Great Wall of China," walls, borders, and boundaries are in an imperfect but nonetheless vitally needed state of eternal un-building and re-building.[28] As Kafka's prose makes clear, boundaries are a natural part of the temporal-spatial journey of our lives, allowing not just separation but the actual creation and even resurrection of the self. The logic behind such seemingly infinite boundary-making can be extended back to biblical times: the reconstruction of ancient Jerusalem's broken city wall amounts, in the Book of Nehemiah, to a symbolic reclaiming of the city of God and a refortifying of the Jewish people within.[29] While it may be a deeply natural drive for us to delineate our spatial boundaries, no matter how absurdly, such territoriality is more than just primal. It enables us to define who we are – even if that has sometimes meant in the Social Darwinistic service of survival and dominance at the expense of others.

Significantly, in figurative terms a border is the point of creativity: it means the moment or place at which something is about to change or happen. It is being on the brink, or on the verge.[30] This transformative aspect was usefully picked up on by Henri Lefebvre in *The Production of Space* (1974), in which he determined at least four kinds of space emerging from the imposition of boundaries. Of these possibilities, negated space constituted but one variable: 1) "accessible space for normal use"; 2) "boundaries and forbidden territories"; 3) "places of abode"; and 4) "junction points."[31] In the work of Lefebvre, borders and the lives and terrains that they affect are best understood not as absolute barriers but as permeable conditions of temporary impasse.

As an historical social practice, bordering has been with us from the start. River-borders, in particular, have served both as links and divisions of place – a characteristic marking, for example, the river Odra (Oder) between Poland and Germany.[32] Agriculture, one of humankind's first-ever boundary-making activities, constituted a "land-writing" that made possible a spatialized perception of the world.[33] Indeed, the drive to erect a wall is as old as civilization itself. Given the lessons not (yet) learned from Hurricane Katrina in 2005, the Pakistani flood crisis of 2010, and the predictions for global warming, it may well be our last. Yet Holland is leading the way in technologies focusing not on combating but adapting to the impending sea level rise; and a recent "Rising Currents" exhibition at New York's Museum of Modern Art depicted designs for how New York's waterfront could best adapt to flooding.[34]

The original motivation for a pre-modern city wall was that of a protection against danger. Moreover, walls dictated a natural economy of scale for urban settlements. As the dictates of demography, trade, and industrialization altered, Europe's major cities (including Berlin) outgrew first their medieval fortification lines and finally their toll-walls and customs-gates as well.[35] Clearly, the walls and static defense lines that once defined people's lives make little sense in modern military as well as urban terms. In pre-modern times, a fortification line was built to defend an entire empire: among the best-known examples are the wall built by the Roman emperor Hadrian across northern England in 122AD, or the Great Wall by Qin Shi Huangdi in 214BC China. The Iron Curtain was by no means the first line to traverse German territory and make it part West and part East: the longest section of the Upper German-Raetian Roman border wall (*limes*) once stretched for over 340 miles (550 km) from the Rhineland to the Danube, and demarcated the limit of the Roman Empire before the Germanic peoples. The *limes* was in operation from the end of the first century AD until c.260, and was populated by border outposts of watchtowers and fortifications.[36]

Twentieth-century fortified border lines like the French Maginot Line or the Nazi West Wall and Atlantic Wall exposed more than a little fragility. We know now that even if a city were to be walled in, it would be undefendable. A physical barrier for city or country can no longer provide any protection – the air war of World War II, the Cold War's threat of nuclear missile attack, and now the multidirectional threat of terrorism certainly prove as much. The USA's proposed Strategic Defense Initiative (SDI; popularly known as "Star Wars"), introduced in 1983 by President Reagan, was offered up as the ultimate protective barrier with the boast that it would create a fully safe zone for the nation against all future nukes. Perhaps it was the most radical rhetorical-strategic move ever made in the service of the "closed worlds" of the Cold War.[37]

In contrast to the SDI myth, contemporary borders reveal more breaks than solidity. Today's globalized environment shows no clear moral "in" and immoral "out," and the "out" is already well ensconced within. Such contradictory acts of shaping and re-shaping are matched only by the formlessness of transnational terrorism itself. Our new post-9/11 border-checkpoints and ports of entry are far from inviolable. Border-making may continue, but sooner or later one finds oneself back at Kafka's burrow or Wall of China, caught up in building without end. Such gap-ridden fortifications often have no other function than to bond those who fool themselves into thinking that they are protected by such defenses from the dreaded "Other." In the nation-state (of which there are about 200 at present, with an additional 70 dependencies, all linked by almost 310 land boundaries), territorial space that is confined or held in or imposed upon is seen to give a guarantee of ordered identity to those with citizenship within – no matter how the varying technologies of migration, communications, and offense learn to overcome such guarantees.[38] The proliferation of new border terrains goes on, even in the last untouched places left on the planet. These days, global territory includes the as-yet uncharted borders of the sea bed at the earth's poles. With future oil rights in mind, Russia planted an underwater flag at the North Pole in order to demonstrate its purported ownership of the Lomonosov Ridge extending from Russia's continental shelf. Meanwhile, quite literally at the opposite end of the globe, competing claims by seven countries are being made upon the last open continent, Antarctica.[39]

We see, then, that globalization practices, having produced a paradoxically increased focus on localized identities (the "glocal"), are far from leading to a borderless world. Geographers have come to the defense of humankind's bordering drive even in a post-Cold War world.[40] They have also cautioned against our too conveniently subsuming the nation-state tradition within the biological myth of the "territorial imperative." As David Harvey reminds us, just because the 1648 Treaty of Westphalia codified European state sovereignty and fixed state borders (reifying practices that were subsequently extended globally through colonialism), we have tended to forget that states are not "natural" and wars between them are not "inevitable." "Boundaries and borders, like reputations, are not given but made," asserts Harvey: for all their contingencies, borders are made and re-made through time in a veritable "'carving out' of distinctive places" – at least for a while.[41] Our existence has been and still is marked by an intricate series of literal, symbolic, and conceptual borders, even as we become increasingly aware of their destabilizing origins and impermanent ends. Border-making will continue in a post-Wall era because it is, quite simply, a psychosocial necessity. A world without borders would simply signify the end of human identity-formation – which is unlikely.

Notes

1. Aristotle, *Metaphysics*, in *Aristotle in 23 Volumes*, vols. 17–18, trans. Hugh Tredennick (Cambridge, MA: Harvard University Press / London: William Heinemann Ltd, 1933, 1989), V.1022a; www.perseus.tufts.edu/hopper/text?doc=Perseus%3Atext%3A1999.01.0052%3Abook%3D5%3Asection%3D1022a (date accessed 4 June, 2010).
2. Wim Wenders and Peter Handke, *Der Himmel über Berlin. Ein Filmbuch* (Frankfurt am Main: Suhrkamp, 1987), pp. 62–63; Wim Wenders, dir., *Der Himmel über Berlin* (Paris: Road Movies Berlin and Argos Films, 1987). All translations are my own unless otherwise noted.
3. After the Allies met in Tehran in November 1943, a future occupation and division of conquered Germany into zones was in the works. One plan included a corridor linking Berlin with the western-controlled parts of postwar Germany. The London Protocol of September 1944 formalized Berlin's imminent zonal appropriation by the Allies, following the city's own administrative boundaries. A "Committee on Boundaries" was even set

up, part of the Allies' European Advisory Commission. Subsequently, at the Yalta Conference in February 1945, the Big Three agreed to create a French zone out of the US and British ones for Germany. All this was finalized by the Potsdam Conference of August 1945. See Daniel J. Nelson, *Wartime Origins of the Berlin Dilemma* (Huntsville: University of Alabama Press, 1978), pp. 34, 58–60, 171–85; See also Steven Ozment, *A Mighty Fortress: A New History of the German People* (New York: HarperCollins, 2004), p. 290; and Wolfgang Schivelbusch, *In a Cold Crater: Cultural and Intellectual Life in Berlin, 1945–1948*, trans. Kelly Barry (Berkeley: University of California Press, 1998), p. 8.

4. Brian Ladd, *The Ghosts of Berlin: Confronting German History in the Urban Landscape* (Chicago: University of Chicago Press, 1997), p. 225.
5. Jacques Derrida, "Response to Daniel Libeskind," in Daniel Libeskind, *radix-matrix: Architecture and Writings* (Munich and New York: Prestel, 1997), pp. 110–15, p. 111.
6. Derrida's insight is shared by Libeskind in his essay "Out of Line, Berlin" in Libeskind, *radix-matrix*, p. 26.
7. Timothy Garton Ash has suggested that we are witnessing a still-dominant "post-West" and multiple versions of a rising new East. Ash, "What Future for the West? Reflections on an Enlarged Europe and the United States in the Twenty-First Century," *Bulletin of the German Historical Institute*, 37 (Fall 2005), pp. 27–38, p. 35. See also Ash, *Free World: Why a Crisis of the West Reveals the Opportunity of our Time* (New York: Allen Lane, 2004).
8. Edward W. Soja first coined the phrase "spatial turn" in his *Postmodern Geographies: The Reassertion of Space in Critical Social Theory* (New York and London: Verso, 1989), p. 39. At the same time, Peter Sahlins published his landmark history of Catalan borderlands that merged "macro" political and "micro" urban/ethnographic approaches: *Boundaries: The Making of France and Spain in the Pyrenees* (Berkeley: University of California Press, 1989). Geographers have since reconceptualized the study of borders away from the static, ordered nation-state toward multiple bordering practices. See John Agnew and Stuart Corbridge, *Mastering Space: Hegemony, Territory and International Political Economy* (New York: Routledge, 1995); Gearóid Ó Tuathail (Gerard Toal), *Critical Geopolitics* (Minneapolis: University of Minnesota, 1996); David Newman, "The Lines that Continue to Separate Us: Borders in Our 'Borderless' World," *Progress in Human Geography*, 30.2 (2006), pp. 143–61, and Newman, "Boundaries, Borders, and Barriers: Changing Geographic Perspectives on Territorial Lines," in Mathias Albert, David Jacobson, and Yosef Lapid, eds, *Identities, Borders, Orders: Rethinking International Relations Theory* (Minneapolis: University of Minnesota Press, 2001), pp. 137–52; Neil Brenner, "Beyond State Centrism? Space, Territoriality, and Geographical Scale in Globalization Studies," *Theory and Society*, 28 (1999), pp. 39–78, p. 43; and Vladmir Kolossov and John O'Loughlin, "New Borders for New World Orders: Territorialities at the Fin-de-Siècle," *Geojournal*, 44.3 (1998), pp. 259–73. For useful historiographical discussions of border studies, see David Delaney, *Territory: A Short Introduction* (Cambridge, MA: Blackwell Publishing, 2005), pp. 56–69; Vladimir Kolossov, "Theorizing Borders: Border Studies: Changing Perspectives and Theoretical Approaches," *Geopolitics*, 10 (2005), pp. 606–32; Milan Bufon, "From Geopolitics to Political Geography: The New European Challenge," in Marco Antonsich, Vladimar Kolossov, and M. Paola Pagnini,

eds, *Europe Between Political Geography and Geopolitics* (Rome: Società Geografica Italiana, 2001), pp. 335–46; and Raimondo Strassoldo, "The Study of Boundaries: A System-Oriented, Multidisciplinary Bibliographical Essay," *The Jerusalem Journal of International Relations*, 2:3 (1977), pp. 81–107.

9. Gilles Deleuze and Félix Guattari, *A Thousand Plateaus: Capitalism and Schizophrenia*, trans. Brian Massumi (Minneapolis: University of Minnesota Press, 1987), pp. 474, 500.

10. The term originates with Josef Goebbels, regarding an imminent victory of the Soviet Union at the end of World War II. Winston Churchill took up the term and observed on 5 March, 1946: "From Stettin in the Baltic to Trieste in the Adriatic, an iron curtain has descended across the Continent. Behind that line lie all the capitals of the ancient states of Central and Eastern Europe. Warsaw, Berlin, Prague, Vienna, Budapest, Belgrade, Bucharest and Sofia, all these famous cities and the populations around them lie in what I must call the Soviet sphere, and all are subject in one form or another, not only to Soviet influence but to a very high and, in some cases, increasing measure of control from Moscow." See the Churchill Centre for the full text of the speech: http://winstonchurchill. org/i4a/pages/index.cfm?pageid=429 (accessed 15 August, 2007). See also Patrick Wright, *Iron Curtain: From Stage to Cold War* (New York: Oxford University Press, 2007).

11. Paul Virilio, "The Overexposed City" (1984), in K. Michael Hays, ed., *Architecture Theory since 1968* (City of New York: The Trustees of Columbia University/Cambridge, MA: MIT Press, 1998), pp. 542–50, pp. 544, 547, 549.

12. Of considerable influence have been analyses of these processes by cultural critics like David Harvey ("time-space compression"), Gilles Deleuze and Félix Guattari ("de-" and "re-territorialization," or "smooth space" and "striated space"), Saskia Sassen ("global city"), Manuel Castells ("space of flows"), Zygmunt Bauman ("liquid modernity," with the modern:postmodern transition defined as "solid:fluid," "heavy:light," and "hardware: software"), Ulrich Beck ("cosmopolitanism"); and Peter Sloterdijk (theory of "spheres"). See Harvey, *The Condition of Postmodernity: An Enquiry into the Origins of Cultural Change* (Cambridge, MA: Blackwell, 1989); Deleuze and Guattari, *A Thousand Plateaus*, particularly Chapter 14; Sassen, *The Global City* (Princeton: Princeton University Press, 1991); Castells, *The Rise of the Network Society* (Cambridge, MA: Blackwell, 1996), pp. 376–428; Bauman, *Liquid Modernity* (Cambridge, UK: Polity Press, 2000), pp. 113–23; Beck, *The Cosmopolitan Vision*, orig. 2004 (Cambridge, UK: Polity/Blackwell, 2006); and Peter Sloterdijk, "Geometry in the Colossal: The Project of Metaphysical Globalization," trans. Samuel A. Butler, *Environment and Planning D: Society and Space*, 27.1 (2009): pp. 29–40 (from Sloterdijk, *Sphären: Mikrosphärologie*, 3 vols [Frankfurt am Main: Suhrkamp, 1998–2004]: here, vol. 2 *Globen*, pp. 47–72).

13. See, for example, Arjun Appadurai, *Modernity at Large: Cultural Dimensions of Globalization* (Minneapolis: University of Minnesota Press, 1996). For a contextualization of recent globalization theory, see Anssi Paasi's comprehensive analysis of the "'borderless world' discourse" in "The Changing Discourses on Political Boundaries," in Henk van Houtum, Olivier Kramsch, and Wolfgang Zierhofer, eds, *B/ordering Space* (Aldershot: Ashgate, 2005), pp. 17–31, esp. pp. 24–27; Liam O'Dowd and Thomas M. Wilson, "Frontiers

of Sovereignty in the New Europe," in O'Dowd and Wilson, eds, *Borders, Nations and States: Frontiers of Sovereignty in the New Europe* (Aldershot: Avebury, 1996), pp. 1–17, esp. pp. 4–5; and Mathias Albert and Lothar Brock, "What Keeps Westphalia Together? Normative Differentiation in the Modern System of States," in Albert, Jacobson, and Lapid, eds, *Identities, Borders, Orders*, pp. 29–49, p. 38.

14. Tracts like those of Samuel P. Huntington encourage the interpretation of ethno-civilizational "fault lines" as imminent battle lines, all of which are to be drawn and re-drawn in an incessant attempt to defensively separate the existing community from perceived racial threats both within and without. Huntington, *The Clash of Civilizations and the Remaking of World Order* (New York: Simon and Schuster, 1996); and Huntington, *Who Are We? The Challenges to America's National Identity* (New York: Simon and Schuster, 2004). For critiques of Huntington's "clash"-thesis, see John A. Agnew, in *Geopolitics: Re-Visioning World Politics* (New York: Routledge, 1998), pp. 119–20; Gearóid Ó Tuathail, "Samuel Huntington and the 'Civilizing' of Global Space," orig. in *Critical Geopolitics* (1996), in Ó Tuathail, Simon Dalby, and Paul Routledge, eds, *The Geopolitics Reader* (New York: Routledge, 1998), pp. 170–76; and Chris Brown, "Borders and Identity in International Political Theory," in Albert, Jacobson, and Lapid, eds, *Identities, Borders, Orders*, pp. 117–36, p. 117.

15. Jeff Zeleny and Nicholas Kulish, "Obama, in Berlin, Calls for Renewal of Ties with Allies," *The New York Times* (25 July, 2008), A15.

16. Charles S. Maier, *Dissolution: The Crisis of Communism and the End of East Germany* (Princeton: Princeton University Press, 1997). See also Gerald Blake, "Borderlands under Stress: Some Global Perspectives," in Martin Pratt and Janet Allison Brown, eds, *Borderlands under Stress* (The Hague and Boston: Kluwer Law International, 2000), pp. 1–16, p. 8; and the work of Durham University's International Boundaries Research Unit (IBRU) at www.dur. ac.uk/ibru (date accessed 23 June, 2010).

17. In the annual interurban grant contest of the Department of Homeland Security's Urban Areas Security Initiative (UASI), city applicants are required to chart their most significant urban sites in terms of terrorist target-value: "Homeland Security Grant Program," at: www.fema.gov/pdf/government/ grant/2010/fy10_hsgp_kit.pdf, pp. 4–5, 12–15 (accessed 24 March, 2010). On the reinforcing of borders (national, urban, and otherwise) after 9/11, see Michael Sorkin, ed., *Indefensible Space: The Architecture of the National Insecurity State* (New York: Routledge, 2008); Peter Marcuse, "The 'War on Terrorism' and Life in Cities after September 11, 2001," in Stephen Graham, ed., *Cities, War, and Terrorism: Towards an Urban Geopolitics* (Malden, MA: Blackwell Publishing, 2004), pp. 270–75, and Marcuse, "Planners, September 11th and the New Borders of Globalization," in Thomas Geisen and Allen Karcher, eds, *Grenze: Sozial – Politisch – Kulturell: Ambivalenzen in den Prozessen der Entstehung und Veränderung von Grenzen* (Frankfurt am Main: IKO – Verlag für Interkulturelle Kommunikation, 2003), pp. 257–64, p. 257; Peter Andreas, "Redrawing the Line: Borders and Security in the Twenty-First Century," *International Security*, 28.2 (2003), pp. 78–111; Timothy W. Luke, "Postmodern Geopolitics: The Case of the 9.11 Terrorist Attacks," in John Agnew, Katharyne Mitchell, and Gearóid Ó Tuathail, eds,

A Companion to Political Geography (Malden, MA: Blackwell Publishers Ltd, 2003), p. 228; and Susan Buck-Morss on the closing-off of civil liberties in *Thinking Past Terror: Islamism and Critical Theory on the Left* (New York: Verso, 2003).

18. Benedict Anderson, *Imagined Communities: Reflections on the Origin and Spread of Nationalism*, 2nd ed. (New York: Verso, 1991).

19. See John Agnew, "The Territorial Trap: The Geographical Assumptions of International Relations Theory," *Review of International Political Economy*, 1 (1994), pp. 53–80; and Peter Taylor, "The State as Container: Internationality, Interstateness, Interterritoriality," *Progress in Human Geography*, 19 (1995), pp. 1–15.

20. Wole Soyinka, "Blood Soaked Quilt of Africa," *The Guardian* (17 May, 1994). See also Newman, "Boundaries," in Agnew, Mitchell, and Ó Tuathail, eds, *A Companion to Political Geography*, pp. 123–37, p. 125; and Richard Muir, *Political Geography: A New Introduction* (New York: John Wiley & Sons, Inc., 1997), pp. 195–201.

21. Friedrich Ratzel, "Der Lebensraum. Eine biogeographische Studie," in Karl Bücher, ed., *Festgaben für Albert Schäffle zur siebenzigsten Wiederkehr seines Geburtstages am 24. Februar 1901* (Tübingen: Laupp, 1901), pp. 103–89, p. 172, 153. See David M. Smith, "Introduction," in Michael Chisholm and Smith, eds, *Shared Space: Divided Space. Essays in Conflict and Territorial Organisation* (London: Unwin, 1990), pp. 1–21, pp. 3–4; and Muir, *Political Geography*, p. 71. Muir equates Ratzel's statements with proto-Nazi leanings.

22. Wolfgang Natter has identified that Ratzel did in fact balance out his *Lebensraum* concept (that was clearly utilized in the service of German expansionist nationalism) with another new and dynamic notion, namely the "border-edge" (*Grenzsaum*): the border as a non-absolutist, hybrid terrain in constant flux, and in interaction with the center(s) that it both defines and is defined by. Natter, "Friedrich Ratzel's Spatial Turn: Identities of Disciplinary Space and Its Borders Between the Anthropo- and Political Geography of Germany and the United States," in van Houtum, Kramsch, and Zierhofer, eds, *B/ordering Space*, pp. 171–86, pp. 182–84. Ratzel's concept of the *Grenzsaum* appears in his *Ueber allgemeine Eigenschaften der geographischen Grenzen und ueber die politische Grenze*, Berichte der Koenigl. Saechsischen Gesellschaft der Wissenschaft (6 February, 1896).

23. Karl Haushofer, *Grenzen in ihrer geographischen und politischen Bedeutung* (Heidelberg: Kurt Vowinckel Verlag, 1939, orig. 1927), p. 14. Haushofer's extreme rightwing geopolitical sentiment is echoed in one of the Weimar Republic's most popular novels, *A People Without Space* (*Volk ohne Raum* [Munich: Albert Lange, 1926]) by Hans Grimm. On Haushofer see Natter, "Geopolitics in Germany, 1919–45: Karl Haushofer and the *Zeitschrift für Geopolitik*," in Agnew, Mitchell, and Ó Tuathail, eds, *A Companion to Political Geography*, pp. 187–203; Ó Tuathail, "Imperialist Geopolitics: Introduction," in Ó Tuathail, Dalby, and Routledge, eds, *The Geopolitics Reader*, pp. 15–25, pp. 19–21; and Muir, *Political Geography*, pp. 215–20.

24. Cited in Marie-Louise von Plessen, ed., *Idee Europa: Entwürfe zum "Ewigen Frieden"* (Berlin: German Historical Museum, 2003), p. 276. In a related vein, both Jürgen Habermas and Etienne Balibar have traced how legal theorist Carl Schmitt first supported the Nazis' expansion into Eastern Europe, and then

altered his work to suit the postwar period. See Carl Schmitt, *Völkerrechtliche Großraumordnung, mit Interventionsverbot für raumfremde Mächte. Ein Beitrag zum Reichsbegriff im Völkerrecht* (Berlin: Deutscher Rechtsverlag, 1939); and Schmitt, *Der Nomos der Erde im Völkerrecht des Jus Publicum Europäum* (Berlin: Duncker & Humblot, 1950); discussed by Habermas, "Hat die Konstitutionalisierung des Völkerrechts noch eine Chance?", in Habermas, *Der gespaltene Westen* (Frankfurt am Main: Suhrkamp, 2004), p. 191; and Etienne Balibar in *We, the People of Europe? Reflections on Transnational Citizenship*, trans. James Swenson (Princeton: Princeton University Press, 2004), pp. 135–41.

25. In their significant study of Auschwitz, Debórah Dwork and Robert Jan Van Pelt discuss the rivalry between Himmler and Alfred Rosenberg over the right to be in charge of Germanizing the European East. Dwork and Van Pelt, *Auschwitz, 1270 to the Present* (New York: Norton, 1996), pp. 285–99, 383.

26. Josef Goebbels, "Der Osten als Erfüllung," foreword to Heinrich Hoffmann and A.R. Marsani, *Deutscher Osten. Land der Zukunft* (Munich: Heinrich Hoffmann, 1942), p. 4. See also Kristin Kopp, "Cartographic Claims: Colonial Mappings of Poland in German Territorial Revisionism," in Gail Finney, ed., *Visual Culture in Twentieth-Century Germany* (Bloomington: Indiana University Press, 2006), pp. 199–213.

27. In its anthropological origins, bordering constitutes an act of identity-placement, and is as evolving as identity itself. Anthropology's interest in the topic can be traced to Fredrik Barth, ed., *Ethnic Groups and Boundaries: The Social Organization of Culture Difference* (Boston: Little, Brown, and Co., 1969).

28. Franz Kafka, *Erzählungen* (Berlin: Fischer, 1961). Today's Great Wall of China resembles that of Kafka's narrative in several ways: it is crumbling and even being demolished in places, only to be reconstructed, sometimes with the wrong materials or with Disney-effects like giant Buddhas. Elisabeth Rosenthal, "Vandalism and 'Improvements' Mar Great Wall," *The New York Times* (12 June, 2003).

29. "Then I said unto them, Ye see the distress that we are in, how Jerusalem lieth waste, and the gates thereof are burned with fire: come, and let us build up the wall of Jerusalem, that we be no more a reproach." Nehemiah 2.17, *The Holy Bible*, King James Version (Oxford: Oxford University Press, n.d.).

30. A taxonomy of borders reveals that the English language has a vast multitude of terms for the concept and for related sets of associations: boundary, frontier, limen, edge, limit, margin, contact, verge, side, brink, confine, barrier, wall, divide, threshold, filter, bulwark, interstice, seam, line. Edward W. Soja extends the thesaurus list into the potentially "boundless meanings" of borders, and links this very boundlessness to the greater "ontological choreography" of bordering as it engages space, time, and society simultaneously. English multivalencies enjoy many more textures of meaning for the concept of bordering than does the German word for border, *die Grenze*, which is a borrowing from the Slavic (*granica* in Russian and Polish and *hranice* in Czech). The Indo-European root *mar-* is the oldest denotation of a border or buffer zone between nations (English: *march*; German: *mark*; French: *marche*) – hence the term "Mark" Brandenburg, the area surrounding Berlin, which was colonized in the Middle Ages as the easternmost settlement of the Germanic people. The modern geopolitical sense for the word "border"

emerged in the early sixteenth century. While the British have tended to differentiate a *boundary* line between nations from the zone it incorporates (the *border*), Americans use both terms more interchangeably. Frontiers (the lands beyond the border) are usually distinguished from borderlands (the territories each side of the line). Geographers sometimes refer to the spatial broadening of the border as a "border landscape" or "border space" – an appellation entirely befitting not just the terrains impacted by the Berlin Wall, German-German border, and Iron Curtain, but also the entire boundary region between Scotland and England, which is known as "the Borders"; and the European Alps have long facilitated the formation of separate border-peoples of mixed nationalities and languages. Borders tend to be categorized under different terminological headings: Muir, for example, distinguishes boundaries ("vertical interfaces," the lines of the border) from frontiers ("zonal"); and Josef Langer categorizes borders by their characteristics: age, mode, course, semantic (appearance), regime (procedures), permeability, openness (documents), equipment, status, and emotional loading. See René-Marc Pille, "'An unser granizze' – die slawischen Wurzeln des Wortes 'Grenze'," in Barbara Breysach, Arkadiusz Paszek, and Alexander Tölle, eds, *Grenze – Granica: Interdisziplinäre Betrachtungen zu Barrieren, Kontinuitäten und Gedankenhorizonten aus deutsch-polnischer Perspektive* (Berlin: Logos Verlag, 2003), pp. 18–35, p. 22; Soja, "Borders Unbound: Globalization, Regionalism, and the Postmetropolitan Transition," in Houtum, Kramsch, and Zierhofer, eds, *B/ordering Space*, pp. 33–46, p. 34; Muir, *Modern Political Geography*, 2nd ed. (London: Macmillan, 1981), p. 119; Langer, "Towards a Conceptualization of Border: The Central European Experience," in Heikki Eskelinen, Ilkka Liikanen and Jukka Oksa, eds, *Curtains of Iron and Gold: Reconstructing Borders and Scales of Interaction* (Aldershot: Ashgate, 1999), pp. 25–42, pp. 40–41.

31. Henri Lefebvre, *The Production of Space*, trans. Donald Nicholson-Smith (Cambridge, MA: Blackwell, 1991), p. 193.

32. See Karl Schlögel, "Oder, Odra, Oderstromland," *Lettre International. Europas Kulturzeitung* 50 (2000), pp. 19–23; and Uwe Rada, *Die Oder: Lebenslauf eines Flusses* (Berlin: Gustav Kiepenheuer Verlag, 2005).

33. Thomas K. Schippers, "The Border as a Cultural Idea in Europe," in Peter Niedermüller and Bjarne Stoklund, eds, *Europe: Cultural Construction and Reality* (Copenhagen: Museum Tusculanum Press, 2001), pp. 25–30, p. 26.

34. "Rising Currents: Projects for New York's Waterfront," exhibition organized by Barry Bergdoll for the Museum of Modern Art in New York (April 2010).

35. On the fortification and de-fortification of European cities, see, for example, Yair Mintzker, "The Dialectics of Urban Form in Absolutist France," forthcoming in Marc Silberman, Karen E. Till, and Janet Ward, eds, *Walls, Borders, Boundaries: Spatial and Cultural Practices in Europe* (New York: Berghahn Books, 2012). See also Michel Foucault's discussion of how the eighteenth century onwards was witness to cities "opening up" and "resituating" themselves as enlarged spaces of circulation; Foucault, *Security, Territory, Population: Lectures at the Collège de France, 1977–1978*, ed. Michel Senellart, trans. Graham Burchell (New York: Palgrave Macmillan, 2007), p. 13.

36. Historians have emphasized Germany's long history of duality. See, for example, Hagen Schulze, *Germany: A New History*, trans. Deborah Lucas

Schneider (Cambridge, MA: Harvard University Press, 1998), p. 338; and Steven Ozment, *A Mighty Fortress: A New History of the German People* (New York: HarperCollins, 2004), p. 26.

37. As Ronnie D. Lipschutz has noted, the failed "Star Wars" initiative was more a "moral statement" than a practical aide, promising only to redraw national and Cold War borders "between the saved and the damned ... between permitted order and feared disorder." Lipschutz, "(B)orders and (Dis)orders: The Role of Moral Authority in Global Politics," in Albert, Jacobson, and Lapid, eds, *Identities, Borders, Orders*, pp. 73–90, p. 75. See also Paul N. Edwards' comment that SDI, as an outgrowth of the 1960s' SAGE ("Semi-Automated Ground Environment") air defense system of the USA's perimeter, was, despite being an "ideological fiction," a "contribution to and a visionary response to the emergence of a closed world." Edwards, "Military Command-Control Systems and Closed World Politics," in Thomas Y. Levin, Ursula Frohne, and Peter Weibel, eds, *CTRL SPACE. Rhetorics of Surveillance from Bentham to Big Brother* (Cambridge, MA: MIT Press, 2002), pp. 338–45, p. 345. On post-9/11 attempts to re-fortify the city for counterterrorism purposes, see Edward L. Glaeser and Jesse M. Shapiro, "Cities and Warfare: The Impact of Terrorism on Urban Form," *Journal of Urban Economics*, 51 (2002), pp. 205–24, p. 209; and Todd Swanstrom, "Are Fear and Urbanism at War?" *Urban Affairs Review*, 38.1 (2002), pp. 135–40.

38. See Blake, "Borderlands Under Stress," in Pratt and Brown, eds, *Borderlands Under Stress*, p. 8; and Anssi Paasi, "The Political Geography of Boundaries at the End of the Millennium: Challenges of the De-Territorializing World," in Eskelinen, Liikanen and Oksa, eds, *Curtains of Iron and Gold*, pp. 9–24, p. 15.

39. C.J. Chivers, "Eyeing Future Wealth, Russians Plant the Flag on the Arctic Seabed, Below the Polar Cap," *The New York Times* (3 August, 2007). Claims upon the maritime territory of Antarctica are held by Australia, France, New Zealand, Norway, the United Kingdom, Chile, and Argentina; land claims by the last three overlap.

40. See Liam O'Dowd, "From a 'Borderless World' to a 'World of Borders': 'Bringing History Back In'," *Environment and Planning D: Society and Space*, 29 (2010), pp. 1031–50. David Newman finds that the virtuality and permeability of postmodern borders notwithstanding, "they continue to provide the territorial compartment within which identities are formed at global, national and local levels, and within which life's activities continue to be played out." Newman, "Boundaries, Territory and Postmodernity: On the Territorial Demarcation of Lines," in Pratt and Brown, eds, *Borderlands Under Stress*, pp. 17–34, p. 31. Similarly, David M. Smith notes that while "space accessible to humankind is continuous," there is nonetheless "a need to control access and hence create partitions ... Geographical space must simultaneously be shared and divided." Smith, "Introduction," in Chisholm and Smith, eds, *Shared Space: Divided Space*, p. 1.

41. David Harvey, *Cosmopolitanism and the Geographies of Freedom* (New York: Columbia University Press, 2009), pp. 171, 172, 173, 190. Harvey refers here to Alfred North Whitehead's 1916 theory of relational places, of impermanent "permanences"; see Whitehead, "La théorie relationaliste de l'Espace," *Revue de métaphysique et de morale*, 23 (1916), pp. 423–54. See also Delaney, *Territoriality*; and Robert David Sack, *Human Territoriality: Its Theory and Its History* (New York: Cambridge University Press, 1986).

2
Berlin's Frontier City Legacy

When all the voids are filled up, and every Frontier is
defined, the problem will assume a different form.
(Lord Curzon of Kedleston, 1907)[1]

That the conflicted past of the city of Berlin occupies a key position
in any analysis of borders and bounded urban, individual, and collective identities is clear. In a sense, Berlin has known self-division right
from its onset: in the thirteenth and fourteenth centuries it emerged
from the coming together of two towns in 1307, Berlin and Cölln,
on the river Spree. The first known map of Berlin, by Johann Gregor
Memhardt in 1652, shows the city still essentially divided into its
two parts. When the city eventually expanded it seemed to "splinter"
rather than grow, as Werner Hegemann complained in his 1930 study,
citing the example of the seventeenth-century Dorotheenstadt that
was first situated outside the city gates.[2] Only in 1710 were the five
sections of the city – Berlin, Cölln, Friedrichswerder, Friedrichstadt,
and Dorotheenstadt – officially unified into one, with a customs wall
operating as of 1736.[3] Even when the city assumed the mantle of
belated Germany's capital in 1871, its rupturing border practices were
still keenly felt. Greater Berlin did not actually emerge until 1920,
when it finally absorbed its outlying areas – seven separate towns, 27
estate districts, and 59 rural communities – to become thirteen times
larger than before. Eventually, the Cold War lent the boldest forms to
this city's shape-shifting canvas, with the Berlin Wall functioning as
a synecdoche for the entire East-West line dividing Germany, Europe,
and the world. The partial scene of division in the Berlin cityscape
represented the whole-world system of the time, not just spatially and
geopolitically but in rhetorical and iconic terms as well.

Yet a more basic bordering of the city had been going on prior to actual division. Berlin had never enjoyed a pre-Wall status of bio- or geopolitical centrality for most Germans. Such a viewpoint has left Berlin on the eastern side of the mental map of Europe as far as most West Germans have been concerned – and this sense of often undisguised disdain was in place long before Cold War positioning came into effect.[4] The moving of the Polish border westwards after World War II to just some 50 miles from Berlin – less than an hour's drive today – hardly helped diminish this prejudice of Europe's West against Europe's East.

The lingering sense of unsatisfactory incompleteness for Berlin is not new, at least as far as the court of German public opinion concerned. Its uncertainties are mirrored, of course, by the pre-1871 lack of German nation-state history. In contrast to Berlin/Germany's "poor relation" or "parvenu" status, other European countries, in contrast, had been building on their post-Westphalian traditions of bordered nationalism. Especially since the French Revolution and the Napoleonic era, most Europeans were familiar with the right to protect their outer borders, as well as with such nationally controlled aspects of life as tax regimes, public health services, and nationalized educational regulatory boards.[5]

In contrast, modern Germany suffered from a rather uneasy self-image when it finally acceded to the elite ranks of the imperial powers. As a mirror to the fledgling nation, Berlin had been known, since Karl Scheffler's and then Ernst Bloch's designations of it in Wilhelmine and Weimar times respectively, as a city fated "*always to become and never to be.*"[6] Berlin as unifying German capital was long more of a promotion than a reality – an eternally sought but never reached castle in Kafka. This helps explain how, by the economic crisis of the late 1920s and early 1930s, disenchanted Germans nearing the end of their failing first democratic Weimar Republic were holding Berlin if not accountable for, then symptomatic of the country's troubles, and reading popular books like Hermann Ullmann's *Flucht aus Berlin* (*Escaping Berlin*): "We all suffer from 'Berlin,' not just those who have to live there."[7]

Using the capital to center the first German unification did not, then, prove effective. In contrast, it is true to say that Berlin's most enduring significance is based on its anti-status as a *frontier city*. The border-as-frontier occurred most forcefully in the American west. One of the most striking analyses of this phenomenon was provided over a century ago by the American historian Frederick Jackson Turner. In a watershed lecture of 1893, called "The Significance of the Frontier in American History," delivered in Chicago during its hosting of the Columbian

Exposition, Turner discerned that the USA was at its most American precisely where it was apparently least so, that is, on its continually moving, porous edge. It was the western frontier that had transformed purportedly free (Indian) lands throughout the nineteenth century, and this fact had distinguished the entire country from Europe. Turner conceptualized the frontier as the "outer edge of the wave – the meeting point between savagery and civilization."[8] In fact, the notion of the free, savage emptiness of the hinterland was a useful construct that facilitated the concepts of American heroism, unity, and democratic exceptionalism in the nineteenth century. The American frontier thesis also neglected to mention the large numbers of indigenous peoples already wiped out from contact with earlier white settlers.[9] Even against the backdrop of this devastating population loss, Turner's lasting contribution to white American cultural identity had to do with the figurative legacy of the frontier as something different from European borders. In US history, stated Turner, a border was not a site or place but a process, a moving line. In fact, Turner was writing about a wave so mutable that it had already broken: as Turner points out, the American Census Bureau of 1890 had announced that it literally could no longer chart the westward movement of the American frontier because there were too many pockets of settlement across the far west – demographic points that broke up any clear line of demarcation.

By contrast, Europe's borders have traditionally been considered to consist not of a moving frontier as in the USA but of, as Turner wrote, an immobile, "fortified boundary line" between populations – even when historical events have suggested otherwise.[10] West Europeans, in particular, are still prone to believe in their legacy of an expected and assumed border-stasis – despite all of Europe's warfare and despite the continually moving eastern edge, since the opening of the Wall, of what is considered to be European in the first place (namely, the ongoing decentering of Europe away from Paris, Rome, Frankfurt, Brussels, and London). In the West European psyche there is still a strong sense of stability in mono-cultural national identities upheld by borders that simply stayed as the maps dictated. Yet these expectations about the fixed boundaries of Europe were all forced and forged by post-conflict agreements like the Congress of Vienna (1815), the Congress of Berlin (1878), the Treaty of Versailles (1919), and the post-World War II treaties – which in the case of the 31 million eastern Europeans displaced within new borders by the Allies, had more to do with the tenets of Nazi geopolitics than most would care to admit. As Tony Judt cogently pointed out, after the First World War, Europe's borders were re-invented, and people stayed in place; whereas after the Second World War, peoples were re-invented, instead, and most state boundaries stayed where they were.[11]

The notion of a frontier opens up the concept of borders, even the European ones, to both expansionist and migratory patterns. The frontier offers up both positive possibilities (creative new opportunities) and negative consequences (the pioneering, plundering, imperialist tradition of one group determining the fate of another – yet also being changed by the colonized, as Turner clearly argued). Turner's frontier has a kinship with Bertolt Brecht's caricature of an American frontier-city in his musical drama *Rise and Fall of the City of Mahagonny (Aufstieg und Fall der Stadt Mahagonny*, 1928–29). Turner's phraseology is applicable to both: "[U]nrestraint is triumphant." Yet Brecht's satire of the downside to capitalist opportunity demonstrates, albeit unconsciously, the rampant vitalism of the frontier mentality and the anxiety that it inevitably provokes in more settled societies elsewhere. An illustration of this is Turner's adage about how first the English, and then the European-influenced East Coast establishment absolutely dreaded being outpaced by the American west. As Turner states: "The East [i.e., English society/ the East Coast] has always feared the result of an unregulated advance of the frontier, and has tried to check and guide it"[12] – and all in vain.

The positive flipside of the frontier mentality that Turner's text advocated and that Brecht's play provided as a cannibalizing burlesque can be identified in Scheffler's assessment, in 1910, of Wilhelmine Berlin on the imperial edge of German language and history as a frontier-town like American cities – but in geographical west-east reverse. Despite becoming the capital, Berlin hardly seemed so, at least in the opinion of Scheffler in his *Berlin: The Fate of a City (Berlin. Ein Stadtschicksal)*: "Berlin literally grew like a colonial town, the way that American and Australian towns emerged right out of the bush in the nineteenth century." Even its population appeared, he wrote, mixed like that of a colony. Berlin's boroughs or districts, Scheffler found, had been built suddenly, and with straight wide streets, like in American cities. He saw how this first New Berlin "is the pioneer of a new idea of work, one that incorporates new values about civilization, and destroys old values about culture." In contrast to the fate suffered by gold-hungry peasant-pioneers, like Brecht's protagonist Paul Ackermann, who come to Mahagonny and are condemned for lack of what they seek (namely money), Scheffler recognized that, as on the American frontier, modern Berlin's radical, basically un-German, mutational tendencies provide, in fact, a ripe "playground for unlimited opportunities."[13]

The very words used by Scheffler for Wilhelmine Berlin resemble the mixed feelings expressed by Europeans to this day about the USA: full of "vitality," economically "materialistic," "poor in culture but strong in willpower." Hence he essentially love-hated the place: "Berlin is one of the most horrible cities in Germany. It is to some degree the capital of all modern ugliness." Writing of the demographic explosion of Berlin in the early 1900s, Scheffler was cognizant of the fact that many of Berlin's "pioneers" had always come from its so-called "wild" eastern European side. In Turner-esque terms, he even went so far as to predict an era when eastern Europe will want its Berlin back in a "racial conflict" between the Slavic East and the European West: "There will come a time when the wave will flow back, when the fight for the East and for the old colonial country will start up again ... Berlin will be, at any rate, decisively influenced in its development by this wrestling."[14]

Scheffler's gold-digging frontier analogy was engaged by Hegemann's critique, in *Berlin in Stone* (*Das steinerne Berlin*), of the speculative boom-and-bust in 1870s Berlin, immediately following the country's initial unification and the city's first capitalization.[15] On the other hand, Scheffler's earlier moniker of transformational (re-)building for Berlin was deemed by Hegemann to have evolved into a useful component of the Bauhaus-style modernizing ethos of the mid-1920s.[16] The German capital of modernity heralded the era's negative and positive sides and was deemed a creative yet dangerously malleable place on that moving outer edge.[17] Overt border-characterizations of modern Berlin can be traced back to insecurity about the city and country as the very opposite: namely, as indications of border-*inadequacy*. Bloch's now-famous term, "groundlessness," for modern Berlin relates to the city's lack of bordered definition: it is built, he wrote, on "especially abstract ground" that "had not yet settled" on its literally sandy, swamp-like foundations.

The entire process of Berlin as a border-town began all over again in earnest after the fall of the Wall. Even though the Wall consists now only of remnants, the city is negotiating a present and a future out of its legacy as a divided frontier-city, oscillating between the European East and the European (as well as American) West. Certainly, it is no longer located along the sharpest edge of international disputes: world super-powers no longer define themselves by its boundaries; and illegal border crossers no longer die there. But in terms of socio-cultural innovation and urban design, Berlin's former border sites are combining with newer alternatives of what now constitute border zones, and often in creative, tangible ways.

The lines, then, of the post-Wall era continue to move, and Berlin serves as a microcosm of the shifts still underway in that greater European continental divide. During this post-*Wende*, post-millennial era of reunified Berlin's new "sobriety," the impact is still unfolding of the invasion of capitalism's money culture, a social and economic usurping of the formerly communist East by the ransacking West. The forces of the latter led the euphoric tide of urban transformation of Berlin in the early 1990s – but by the millennium, the dream was most definitely over. Despite the city's recently re-acquired capital status, global city status remains the desired but elusive goal. Berlin greeted the twenty-first century as a bankrupt, shabbily maintained shadow of the limitless ambitions articulated following reunification. The fortunes of plunderers and pioneers have risen and fallen since the city's initial building boom flipped into the bust of the mid-1990s and then limped toward the global recession a decade after.

Thus the late twentieth-century version of the equally short-lived California gold rush was enacted on the level of reclaiming (or rather, raiding) prime building sites not just in Berlin but across the former German Democratic Republic, as well as in other post-communist cities ripe for the picking, particularly Moscow, Warsaw, and Prague. The architectural "fortune seekers" mined whatever best suited them from Berlin's past urban imagery in order to clad the new structures.[18] The opportunities for building Berlin anew were driven by a combination of official planners (such as Wolfgang Nagel, former SPD Building Construction senator for Berlin who managed many of the land sale transactions in the wake of the Wall; and Hans Stimmann, Berlin's former director of urban planning, whose strict building codes determined much of what then followed), corporate developers (like Roland Ernst, who has since served time for fraud), architects (especially the late Josef Paul Kleihues, who first devised Critical Reconstruction for the International Building Exhibition [IBA] in the 1980s as an architectural blueprint for renewing the "European City"), and city marketers (like Volker Hassemer, former CDU Urban Development senator for Berlin, and founder of the marketing company Berlin Partner).[19] Far too much was also determined by the Treuhandanstalt, a governmental body convened to decentralize and sell off GDR-owned businesses. Riding on the coat-tails of the urban re-fashioning of the city's oldest central area that had been directly east of the Wall, self-styled pioneers from the West set out to "conquer" the old *Mitte* and make it over into the New World of the former communist East: high-tech start-up companies became ensconced along with new bars, restaurants, hotels, galleries, and apartments in trendily renovated pre-war tenements and factories. As soon as the boom of that era faded, these same ex-pioneers bemoaned the lost excitement – indeed, as if the "border lay between 1995 and 1996."[20]

Berlin's deeper – and at first sight less apparent – journey since the parting of the Iron Curtain has been toward the (new) conceptual-cultural East rather than toward the (old) West. Cultural historian Karl Schlögel sees Berlin's repositioning within central and eastern Europe both as a vital reunion and a re-beginning for the city.[21] A more satirical version of this has been iterated by Uwe Rada, editor at the Berlin *taz* newspaper, when he refers to the barbarian "Balkanization of Berlin," wherein today's Wild West is on the moving, exciting, but obviously also unnerving eastern edges of Berlin and Europe.[22] The New Berlin of the 1990s did not bring the West further East: rather, the countries from behind the former Iron Curtain have ended up pushing the line denoting cultural understandings of the West as their populations continue to migrate and expand into western Europe. These acts of coexistence and co-mingling amount to a reversal of who is meant to be colonizing whom in this unforeseen hybridization. Despite the emptying out of its own communist center, Berlin has been witness to its own eastern Europeanization.

The socio-cultural conquering by the purported victors of the Cold War has had, then, some unexpected turns. The radical changes affecting life in the continent's central and eastern parts are affecting the rest of Europe as well. Poland, for example, has been busy re-asserting its former democratic tradition and re-westernizing itself as a member of the European Union, but the presence of the communist East has lingered in Berlin's eastern part, in surrounding Brandenburg, and in the other "new federal states" for much longer than had been antici-pated. When a temporary natural gas shortage occurred in some west European nations in early 2006 (caused by Ukraine apparently siphoning off some gas during a price dispute with Russia), most inhabitants of the affected countries had been unaware of the degree to which they were dependent on Moscow for this resource (in Germany's case, over a third). The same point was driven home in early 2007: no crude oil was delivered to Germany when Russia shut down a pipeline as punishment for Belarus having illegally siphoned some off. Wishing to circumvent such natural resource interdependencies in the future, and asserting a new geopolitical hegemony that ignores the central and east European countries in between, Germany has struck a deal with Russia to receive its natural gas via the new Nord Stream pipeline directly along the seabed to Greifswald. The economic, infrastructural, and political power in the transcontinental "new topography" of post-Wall Europe is being re-charted, but not necessarily by those whom it affects most.[23]

In urban terms, the symbiotic process of the former communist East in the capitalist West is (rather perversely perhaps) entirely concurrent with efforts toward globalization and the Americanization of the New Berlin, particularly in retail, office, and entertainment architecture. It is the price to be paid for the city's efforts as a would-be "turn-table between East and West" (*Ost-West-Drehscheibe*).[24] As the West continues to erect its ostensibly conquering images and structures, easterners are boldly entering into formerly purely "western" sites and altering the status quo. Berlin's Brechtian Ackermann-types, then, are both Indian and trader: the new "pioneers" are just as often Easterners as Westerners, if not more frequently so.[25] One of Berlin's few enduring growth industries is the unofficial trade of the east European underground economy, that the government is struggling to partially legalize (for example, with underpaid Mini Jobs since 2003) because it cannot stop the flow.[26]

Berlin is not quite typical of the situations in which a border-city may find itself (at its best, a peripherally located site of unprecedented growth, transit, and trade that resists, subverts, and ultimately changes the power located at the center of the country). Rather, Berlin has remained the largest city in Germany (with a now stabilizing 3.4 million inhabitants, or 4.2 million if one includes the outlying areas) – and this despite the loss of more than a million people to death and flight as a result of World War II, despite the loss of capital-status to Bonn for its western half for the duration of the Cold War, despite all the advances in city-dominance made especially by Munich, Hamburg, and Frankfurt am Main under the West German federal system – and even despite the overall stalling of the German birth rate.

The removal of the Wall that had kept Berlin as an "edge city" in reverse (namely, the opposite of the American suburbanization process) has certainly created multiple layers of potential for bordered interaction.[27] But not all of them are taking place in Berlin. Urban geographer Stefan Krätke has cautioned against the illusory expectation that border development will occur in a narrow *linear* fashion in the border region itself.[28] In the case of East-meets-West in Europe, business initiatives with, for example, Poznań in Poland are mostly with West German or Italian firms, leap-frogging over poor Berlin. Occasionally, the border lands' expansion can be seen in operation: the Four Seasons hotel in Berlin decided to out-source its laundry straight to cheaper Poland, at a saving of

40 per cent in Berlin wage costs. This new direction of the German capital's services flooding eastwards has been dubbed a veritable "Russian River" of border crossings, but without Berlin's full participation.[29] A quarter of Poland's trade with Germany takes place in the Dortmund area alone. A telling illustration of Berlin's missed trade opportunities with the new East occurred when a Polish chain of gas stations bought up three per cent of the German market in 2003, but placed its German headquarters not in Berlin but in wealthy Hamburg.[30] These are hardly examples of a typical burgeoning border-city with nodal growth.

In other ways, Berlin is functioning as a new, post-Wall border-city – at least for Poles and Russians. While it took until the millennium for 40 per cent of West Berliners to have finally visited neighboring Poland, the East is already *in* the West, at least in Berlin: after the Turks, Poles are now the city's second largest immigrant group, at over 130,000; and 50 Polish firms are represented there. Many are Polish-born ethnic Germans who have moved to Berlin. Additionally, there are untold numbers working in the black market, especially in construction and domestic work – an extension, of sorts, of the *Polenmärkte* that were already a feature on the bombed-out voids of West Berlin in the late 1980s.[31] An alternative tourist guide is *The New Russian Berlin* (*Das neue russische Berlin*).[32] The guide re-establishes Berlin as a *novoi gorod*: in the 1920s, Vladimir Nabokov had already referred to Charlottenburg as Charlottengrad. In the high-end shopping mall along and underneath today's Friedrichstraße, one invariably hears its status-oriented visitors speaking Russian. Of the Russians who have immigrated to Berlin, most are not so socio-economically fortunate. The housing projects of East Berlin's outlying districts are in social transition; up to a third (28,000) of the inhabitants of Marzahn are "ethnic Germans" from the former Soviet Union.

One could make a list of all the as-yet-unfulfilled synonyms for reunification in the capital that have been used by planners and politicians in their post-Wall (sometimes fake, other times impatient, or else just idealizing) goodwill: "the 'getting closer' and 'growing together' of East and West, the closing of 'gaps' and 'wounds', the 'healing of scars'," as well as notions of "'opening gates' and 'building bridges'."[33] Indeed, the post-Wall years have been witness to planners' and politicians' myriad attempts to smooth out the border mentality and reality into an urbanism applicable for the entire nation. This vision of a new seamlessness has revealed a will imposed on the former East Berlin from without, and it has not corresponded to the experiences of those viewing the situation from within.

If the suturing of reunification could not be imposed by terminology and architecture alone, traces of the lingering border-city have been deemed by many to be both unwanted and unwarranted. "Forget Berlin!" cried one commentator in the Munich-based *Süddeutsche Zeitung*.[34] German responses have not been glowing concerning Berlin's persistence in retaining, even regaining, its borders after the Wall was meant to be long gone. As Rada laconically observes: "There are still a number of politicians who refuse to accept that Berlin is not a global city in the wings, but a disused industrial city: a metropolis at most for gold-diggers and adventurers (male and female), more saloon than salon, a wild mixture of Detroit and Lodz – a border town to the east, to be precise."[35] Berlin's faltering predicament is compounded by the emptying-out all around it in the former East German states, which have lost 1.5 million people since 1989. Demographers have predicted that cities like Leipzig and Dresden, which have already lost 10 per cent of their populations, could lose up to one third in the coming decades. There are already over one million empty apartments. Since 2003, high-rise residential blocks have been pulled down or creatively lowered as part of "scaling back/dismantling the East" (*Rückbau Ost*). Thus a literal emptying out has occurred of the reunified government's earlier renovations of the very same structures, as part of West Germany's massive economic reconstruction effort for the five eastern states.[36]

In order to help correct dismissive doom and gloom about the incomplete global relevance of the regained capital, as well as to move away from the simplistic border-fusion terminology too often invoked, the "Berlin Study" (*Berlinstudie*) was carried out, albeit more as a promotional tool than an analytical one. A series of expert findings funded by the EU and organized by the Berlin Senate from 1998 to 2000, in the manner of its predecessor the London Study of 1998, the Berlin Study focused on Berlin's unique "geopolitical position" on the new border as one of its leitmotifs or "strategies for the future."[37] As "an eastern city in the west, or a western city in the east," the report showed how Berlin should aim to serve as an "engine for European integration," particularly in the mid-east European region between the Baltic and the Black seas. Specifically, the Berlin Study called for a more open recognition of Berlin's unique situation, with more exchanges with eastern Europe, cross-border projects for employment opportunities, and networking between Berlin and eastern Europe in the key areas of infrastructural renewal and environmental sustainability.

To date, Berlin's economic inability to rise beyond the status of a border-town is not all that bad – a happy failure, so to speak. The good news – at least for the urban avant-garde of artists and writers, as well as for media industries – is that Berlin continues to fill a perennial need (creating, at its best, a non-exploitative pioneer spirit) for a space containing otherness into which one can go beyond one's current condition and parameters. The very crisis, flux, and ultimate permeability of Berlin's historical borders – whether as land of opportunity or as division delineating Cold War tensions – deliver a series of highly creative "threshold"-sites of urban transformation. Berlin serves, then, as a frontier that transforms those who engage its border condition. Turner, it is worth remembering, had praised what he called "this perennial rebirth, this fluidity of American life," a democracy born of an encounter with the "continually advancing frontier line" – where the engagement of the wilderness meant a transformation of self and state.[38] We may well wonder how long Berlin's border condition will be able to continue in the face of an official return to the "European City"-credo as the architectural expression of a political normalization for the reunified nation. Nonetheless, the re-formed yet recalcitrant Berlin still displays a "frontier anxiety"[39] – a sense of its own fragile exceptionalism even as its Wall-era has been paved over, an attempted cover-up of the city's repeated brokenness.

Notes

1. Lord Curzon of Kedleston, *The Romanes Lecture, 1907. Frontiers* (Oxford: Clarendon Press, 1907), Part 1, p. 7.
2. Werner Hegemann, *Das steinerne Berlin. Geschichte der größten Mietskasernenstadt der Welt* (Berlin: Gustav Kiepenheuer, 1930; repr. Frankfurt am Main: Ullstein, 1963), p. 45; see also Harald Bodenschatz, ed., *Renaissance der Mitte. Zentrumsumbau in London und Berlin* (Berlin: Verlagshaus Braun, 2005), pp. 167–73.
3. Berlin's customs wall replaced both its earlier fortification wall and its medieval city wall: a series of toll gates was created for tax purposes and to provide a check on deserting soldiers. Public spaces beyond the gates became Berlin's major squares, such as Alexanderplatz and Hackesche Markt. Industry, cemeteries, rail stations, prisons, breweries – all these tended to be built outside the city boundary and in the surrounding agglomerations like Moabit. Between 1866 and 1869, all remaining parts of Berlin's city wall were removed, leaving only the former customs portal, the Brandenburg Gate. See Philipp Oswalt, *Berlin: Stadt ohne Form: Strategien einer anderern Architektur* (Berlin: Prestel, 2000), pp. 73–79.
4. As Svetlana Boym remarks, in connection with the Slavic origin of the name Berlin in the root for "swamp" (*brl* – referring to the area's sandy soil and high water table): "For some the border between Europe and Asia did not pass through Russia but on the river Elbe" – which itself became part of the

inner German border of the Iron Curtain. Boym, *The Future of Nostalgia* (New York: Basic Books, 2001), p. 176.

5. Filmmaker and author Alexander Kluge spoke in the 1980s of the gap between Germany's historical and "imaginary" boundaries: those specified by the national anthem ("From the Maas to the Memel, from the Etsch to the Belt") have not been its borders; rather, "Germany ... must be understood in terms of its *lack* of boundaries." Kluge, "Rede über das eigene Land: Deutschland," in Stefan Heym et al., *Reden über das eigene Land* (Munich: Bertelsmann, 1983), p. 81. See also Malcolm Anderson, "The Transformation of Border Controls: A European Precedent?" in Peter Andreas and Timothy Snyder, eds, *The Wall around the West: State Borders and Immigration Controls in North America and Europe* (New York: Rowman & Littlefield, 2000), pp. 15–30, p. 18; and John Breuilly, "Sovereignty, Citizenship and Nationality: Reflections on the Case of Germany," in Anderson and Eberhard Bort, eds, *The Frontiers of Europe* (London: Pinter, 1998), pp. 36–67.

6. Karl Scheffler, *Berlin. Ein Stadtschicksal* (Berlin: Erich Reiss Verlag, 1910), p. 219, emphasis original; see also Ernst Bloch, "Estrangements II (Geographica)," in *Literary Essays*, trans. Andrew Joron (Stanford: Stanford University Press, 1998), pp. 354–86, p. 366.

7. Hermann Ullmann, *Flucht aus Berlin* (Jena: Eugen Diederichs Verlag, 1932), p. 9. In his review of the book, Siegfried Kracauer emphasizes that Ullmann still wanted Germans to stick with the capital, as if returning to a forgiven lover. Kracauer, "Berlin in Deutschland," *Frankfurter Zeitung*, 77.605 (14 August, 1932).

8. Frederick Jackson Turner, "The Significance of the Frontier in American History," in Turner, *The Frontier in American History* (New York: Henry Holt & Co., 1921), p. 3.

9. Ben Kiernan, *Blood and Soil: A World History of Genocide and Extermination from Sparta to Darfur* (New Haven: Yale University Press, 2007), pp. 310–63; Geoff King, *Mapping Reality: An Exploration of Cultural Geographies* (New York: St Martin's Press, 1996), pp. 104, 146; and Mike Davis, "Die Bedeutung der *Frontier*," in *Casino Zombies und andere Fabeln aus dem Neon-Westen der USA*, trans. Steffen Emrich and Britta Grell (Berlin: Schwarze Risse, 1999), p. 26.

10. Turner, "The Significance of the Frontier," p. 3. See also John Agnew, "The 'Civilisational' Roots of European National Boundaries," in David Kaplan and Jouni Häkli, eds, *Boundaries and Place: European Borderlands in Geographical Context* (Lanham: Rowman & Littlefield, 2002), pp. 18–33.

11. Tony Judt, *Postwar: A History of Europe Since 1945* (New York: The Penguin Press, 2005), pp. 22–32, p. 27; see also Sigmund Neumann, "The New Crisis Strata in German Society," in Hans J. Morgenthau, ed., *Germany and the Future of Europe* (Chicago: University of Chicago Press, 1951), pp. 31–32. Approximately half (15 million) of these "expellees" (*Vertriebene*) were ethnic Germans from the Sudetenland, Rumania, and Hungary (*Volksdeutsche*), as well as from Germany's eastern provinces (*Reichsdeutsche*). With the partition of postwar Germany came interzonal refugees into West Germany, as well other refugees who had fled the Soviet-controlled zone. About 13 million *Vertriebene* ended up in West Germany. The above figure does not include the numbers of "displaced persons" due to the Holocaust.

12. Turner admitted that the Western American frontier zone brought with it both an upside (the pragmatism and democratic opportunity contained within "individual liberty") and a downside ("all the manifest evils that follow from the lack of a highly developed civic spirit," and – referring to advocates of currency inflation, the Populists – "the worst forms of an evil currency"): in other words, it is both "strong in selfishness and individualism." Turner, "The Significance of the Frontier," pp. 38, 33, 32.

13. Scheffler, *Berlin*, pp. 16, 17, 230, 16.

14. Scheffler, *Berlin*, pp. 26, 235, 263, 200, 264.

15. See Chapter 26 of Hegemann, *Das steinerne Berlin*, pp. 243–57.

16. For a study of how the revolutionary transitions of Weimar German modernity were articulated in architecture, advertising, consumerism, fashion, and film, see Janet Ward, *Weimar Surfaces: Urban Visual Culture in 1920s Germany* (Berkeley: University of California Press, 2001).

17. This strategy is repeated in the artist George Grosz's grotesque-celebratory visions from 1916 of the urban cowboy in Berlin, such as *The Adventurer* or *The Golddigger*. Grosz's cartoon-like paintings are visual responses to Karl May's adventure stories of the American West, and suggest that, in Grosz's view, defiance and greed were better (more honest) than the German status quo. See Helen Adkins, "George Grosz and the American Dream," in Jean Clair, ed., *The 1920s: Age of the Metropolis* (Montreal: The Montreal Museum of Fine Arts, 1991), pp. 284–99.

18. Uwe Rada, *Berliner Barbaren. Wie der Osten in den Westen kommt* (Berlin: BasisDruck, 2001), p. 37. See also Heinrich Wefing's critique of the Berlin architects' "plundering of the past" in his essay "Berlin" in Stefan Bollmann, ed., *Kursbuch Stadt. Stadtleben und Stadtkultur an der Jahrtausendwende* (Stuttgart: Deutsche Verlags-Anstalt, 1999), pp. 143–59, esp. pp. 151–55.

19. For a critical who-was-who in rebuilding Berlin during the 1990s, see Eva Schweitzer, *Grossbaustelle Berlin. Wie die Hauptstadt verplant wird* (Berlin: Nicolai, 1996).

20. Anon., "Städtische Untote: Das 'Ende von Mitte'," *stadt.plan.mitte*, 7 (March 2003), p. 1.

21. Karl Schlögel, "Berlin und das Städtenetz im neuen Europa," in Bollmann, ed., *Kursbuch Stadt*, pp. 17–37, p. 19. In contrast, however, the more conservative Wolf Jobst Siedler, influenced by the reconfigured seat of the federal German government west of the Brandenburg Gate, theorizes in the other, westwards direction for the mentality of the New Berlin, as "perhaps an expression of the turn towards the west of Germany." Siedler, *Phoenix im Sand: Glanz und Elend der Hauptstadt* (Berlin: Propyläen Verlag, 1998), p. 223.

22. Rada, *Berliner Barbaren*, p. 50. See also Oswalt, *Berlin: Stadt ohne Form*, pp. 27–29.

23. Schlögel, "Berlin," in Bollmann, ed., *Kursbuch Stadt*, p. 34. Former Chancellor Gerhard Schröder certainly helped steer Germany's future when he cut a deal with Gazprom for the new Nord Stream gas pipeline project linking Germany and Russia by sea, just before leaving office in September 2005 – and went to work for the same Russian state-directed (and now the world's third largest) company immediately thereafter. See Andrew E. Kramer, "Eastern Europe Fears New Era of Russian Sway," *The New York Times* (13 October, 2009); *The New York Times* editorial (4 April, 2006); and Kramer and Steven Lee Myers,

"Workers' Paradise is Rebranded as Kremlin Inc.," *The New York Times* (24 April, 2006).

24. The promotional city language of the *Info Box* catalog (that accompanied its structural namesake at the construction site of Potsdamer Platz during the 1990s) spoke of Berlin as a "turn-table between western and eastern Europe." *Info Box. Der Katalog*, 3rd ed. (Berlin: Nishen, 1997), p. 260.

25. Schlögel, "Berlin," in Bollmann, ed., *Kursbuch Stadt*, pp. 36–37.

26. Journalist Evelyn Roll refers to Berlin's "border area of the shadow economy, East European smuggling, and the black market." Roll, "Raststätte 'Osteuropa'," *Süddeutsche Zeitung* (7/8 June, 2003).

27. Joel Garreau, *Edge City: Life on the New Frontier* (New York: Doubleday, 1991). See also Wolfgang Kil's critique of how post-Wall Berlin's periphery with Brandenburg succumbed to overly rapid suburbanization after all: Kil, "Berlin: Grenzenlos," in Thorsten Scheer, Josef Paul Kleihues, and Paul Kahlfeldt, eds, *Stadt der Architektur. Architektur der Stadt. Berlin 1900–2000* (Berlin: Nicolai, 2000), pp. 373–79, pp. 373–76.

28. See Stefan Krätke, "City of Talents? Berlin's Regional Economy, Socio-Spatial Fabric and 'Worst Practice' Urban Governance," *International Journal of Urban and Regional Research*, 28.3 (2004), pp. 511–29.

29. Carl Hanser, report for "Marketplace," National Public Radio (20 January, 2003).

30. Ulrich Zawatka-Gerlach, "Dortmund liegt Polen näher als Berlin," *Der Tagesspiegel* (10 October, 2003); and Claus-Dieter Steyer, "Der Adler ist gelandet," *Der Tagesspiegel* (7 June, 2003).

31. See Sandra Dassler and Serena Klein, "Die Polen kommen? Sie sind längst da!" *Der Tagesspiegel* (7 June, 2003); Alexander Tölle, "Berlin – eine mitteleuropäische Metropole in Grenzlage," in Barbara Breysach, Arkadiusz Paszek, and Tölle, eds, *Grenze – Granica: Interdisziplinäre Betrachtungen zu Barrieren, Kontinuitäten und Gedankenhorizonten aus deutsch-polnischer Perspektive* (Berlin: Logos Verlag, 2003), pp. 190–99, p. 197; and Schlögel, "Berlin," in Bollmann, ed., *Kursbuch Stadt*, p. 23.

32. Maria Chevrekouko and Ludmila Kusnezowa, *Das neue russische Berlin* (Berlin: Havel Spree Verlag, 2002).

33. Such a satirical list is compiled by Johannes Touché, "Vom Brückenschlagen. Eine Podiumsdiskussion zur Annäherung von Wedding und Prenzlauer Berg," *scheinschlag*, 10 (20 November–18 December, 2002), p. 4.

34. Johannes Wilms, "Vergesst Berlin! Die Hauptstadt als Dauerkostgänger der Republik," *Süddeutsche Zeitung* (6 June, 2001); see also Dieter J. Opitz, "Wer Ursache und Wirkung verdreht. Eine Replik auf eine Berlin-Polemik in der *Süddeutschen*," *Berliner Morgenpost* (9 June, 2001).

35. Uwe Rada, "Der barbarische Osten," in Albert Scharenberg, ed., *Berlin: Global City oder Konkursmasse? Eine Zwischenbilanz nach dem Mauerfall* (Berlin: Karl Dietz Verlag, 2000), pp. 129–33, p. 131; see also Kil, "Berlin: Grenzenlos," in Scheer et al., eds, *Stadt der Architektur*, pp. 376–77.

36. Notice the terminology shifts, from the earlier positive "Rebuilding the East" (*Aufbau Ost*) program to the "City Upgrade East" (*Stadtumbau Ost*) program in 2001 – which is itself a polite way of saying *Rückbau Ost*. Since 1990, the German government has applied €1.3 billion to restructure and prop up the still faltering former East German states. The initial hope that a "new

center" for the country would arise from the former German-German border region has since been replaced with an acceptance of the need to demolish and re-green the shrinking post-communist cities. See Alexandra Endges, "Aufbau Ost. In der Solidarpaktfalle." *Die Zeit Online* (18 May, 2010); Steffen Kröhnert, Franziska Medicus, and Reiner Klingholz, *Die demografische Lage der Nation. Wie zukunftsfähig sind Deutschlands Regionen?* Das Berlin Institut für Bevölkerung und Entwicklung (Munich: dtv, 2006); Bundesministerium für Verkehr, Bau- und Wohnungswesen, *Dokumentation zum Kongress "Zwei Jahre STADTUMBAU OST"* (Berlin, 2004); the governmental website www. stadtumbau-ost.info (date accessed 21 January, 2010); Arnold Bartetzky, "Nach der Expansion die Perforation. Städtebauliche Entwicklung in Ostdeutschland seit 1990: Das Beispiel Leipzig," in Vittorio Magnago Lampugnani and Matthias Noell, eds, *Stadtformem. Die Architektur der Stadt zwischen Imagination und Konstruktion* (Zürich: gta Verlag, 2005), pp. 310–19; Hartmut Häußermann, "Capitalist Futures and Socialist Legacies: Urban Development in East Germany Since 1990," *German Politics and Society*, 49.16.4 (1998), pp. 87–101; and Trevor Wild and Philip N. Jones, "Spatial Impacts of German Unification," *The Geographical Journal*, 160.1 (1994), pp. 1–16.

37. Der Regierende Bürgermeister von Berlin and Senatskanzlei, eds, "Die BerlinStudie. Strategien für die Stadt" (2000), at: http://zukunftscafe.de/berlinstudie (date accessed 3 March, 2010).

38. Turner, "The Significance of the Frontier," pp. 2–3.

39. See David M. Wrobel, *The End of American Exceptionalism: Frontier Anxiety from the Old West to the New Deal* (Lawrence: The University Press of Kansas, 1993).

3
Border Lands in the New Europe

Die Grenze verläuft nicht zwischen den Völkern, sondern zwischen oben und unten
(Former graffiti at the Köpi squathouse in
Berlin Mitte, on an external side [fire] wall)

Berlin, as a tale of two cities, is not alone in its tensions and transformations after the fall of the Wall. Without its Cold-War frontline function, it has gone back to operating within the wider continental framework within which it is situated: an east-west liminality in the (now New) Europe. Berlin's key position amongst all this jostling for position by European Union member states and non-EU states on both sides of the post-communist, economic Golden Curtain is made clear by the fact that Germany, now the largest European economy, is also the most involved country with Europe's Turneresque "outer edge."[1] Of all the old EU members, Germany has the most trade and investments with eastern Europe. This high degree of involvement can be ascribed to Germany's particularly unstable border history, and to the phenomenon of incoming migration that is still marked by the *jus sanguinis* rather than the *jus soli*.

We can illustrate the New Europe's spatial reconstruction, as it evolves out of and beyond the old and even the post-Wall boundaries, by means of a journey on the Saratov Express, a train that since 1993 has been shuttling every weekend between Saratov in Russia and Berlin.[2] The train ride amounts to a more than 46-hour endurance trek that provides clear evidence of the unstoppable cross-border pollinations now underway. On the move are (inter alia) clothes and edible delicacies that *commis-voyageur* Russians buy in Berlin and then take back with them to sell; Germans, who are marrying eastern Europeans and bringing them back to Germany; and on the return journey, Volga-Germans, who are giving away their houses and land before emigrating to Germany, along with multiple generations of their families, all on the basis of the blood-right that legally enables them to undertake this journey for a better life. This train is but one instance of a transcontinental frenzy of trade, a process that Karl Schlögel refers to as the unstoppable "drift" now moving back and forth across the former divide of the Iron Curtain – a force of commercial and cultural exchange forming and re-forming its own lines at will.[3]

Within such present-day expansion resides a utopianism of European unity with much older roots. The utopian hopes immediately following the end of the Cold War added fuel to the slogan originally attached to the 1986 Single European Act of a "Europe without Frontiers"; and we can trace a legacy of idealism in calls for European unity ever since Novalis's "Die Christenheit oder Europa" of 1799.[4] It was in fact Churchill who advocated a united postwar Europe in the hopes that the continent could then know happiness and honor in "limitless" measure; in a key sense, then, the Iron Curtain's descent that Churchill witnessed prompted the European unification movement into being.[5] Typically, however, it has been a movement that prefers top-down deregulating initiatives to the messiness of the informal market that is now coming in from the east. Since the 1990s, hundreds of laws have been passed by the European Commission, deregulating all kinds of internal borders in Europe for traffic by rail, water, air, and road; and for currency, trade, law, medical coverage, and even electricity. The European Union's cross-border cooperation programs (the INTERREG initiatives I, II, and III) funded a series of transnational programs, not just for contiguous EU states but for the EU's external borders as well.

So far, so good – or so it seems. But the post-Wall New Europe is not immune to our era's inherent contradiction of enhanced border openness alongside increased border controls. Here, the global north-south poverty divide also extends eastwards in a non-fixed, evolving boundary around the expanded member states of the European Union, which has taken over for itself the real-time significance of the term "Europe." Yet the directionality of the border has become even more diffuse than the moving line to the east and south. As Etienne Balibar has noted, post-Wall Europe has inadvertently brought a new aspect of the border (namely, the "13 million nationals of 'third' countries," the people migrating from beyond its edges) into all its cities.[6] The border lands of the New Europe are hence not peripheral but everywhere. The new arrival in Europe is the hybrid, yet undesired and often unofficial, unrecognized, and much resented post-Wall Other: the "transmigrant," either discriminated against as a second-class citizen/resident, or locked up in detention limbo.[7]

Fortress Europe with its multiple sites of migrant detention centers placed both at and just beyond its borders is still not capable of maintaining its ramparts. Filmmakers have attempted to humanize the situation – notably, Hans-Christian Schmid in *Lichter* (*Distant Lights*), a documentary that tracks unofficial border-crossings from Poland to Germany just before the former's accession to the European Union. The film shows how false promises are made to illegal migrants: a European "coyote" tells a group of hopeful Ukrainians, just before dropping them off in the woods at the Słubice border with Frankfurt (Oder): "Over there, where the lights are, that's Berlin." These migrants, like those crossing from South America to the USA, often become the unfortunate products of human trafficking. As such they constitute a degraded permutation of what used to be the Cold War's human smuggling networks, wherein westerners helped get people out of communist countries.[8]

The old EU did not need to wait until the present worldwide economic crisis to enter into its own identity problems. The loss of the postwar, Cold-War lines promoted a sense of destabilization, disuse, and unwelcome permeability. The essentially lost internal state-boundaries of the continental European Union are the focus of a two-part collection of photographs, entitled *Transition* (*Übergang*), by the Polish-born photographer Josef Schulz (Fig. 3.1).[9] Schulz's melancholic, lonely images are of disused customs houses as they stand today in total neglect along the former border checkpoints that once kept the European Union's member states officially apart from one another. This changed with the Schengen accords, which refer to the Luxembourg border town where they were first signed in 1985 and which since the end of 2007 have brought over 400 million citizens together in terms of border-free ground travel. The Schengen agreements make the act of marking national separateness by means of these customs points utterly meaningless.[10] Each empty customs-house image captures, then, a sense of this loss of function and power.

The fear exists among western, wealthier European nations that if EU internal borders open up entirely there will be no more Europe left. The global vision of a fully networked (urban) world, US-style, signifies danger for the "territorial anchoring of the [European] nation-state," as Jürgen Habermas has noted in his writings on postnational identity. Such a trend dissolves the differences between the nation-states within its capturing embrace, as it transforms fixed "boundaries" into unstable

Figure 3.1   Disused customs house at the Schengenized French-Spanish border. From "Transitions" (*Übergänge*), by Josef Schulz, 2005

"flows."[11] Habermas does not quite wish "border controls" to be so easily washed away, demolishing if not the geographical entity itself, then "the construct of the nation" (*das nationale Gebäude*) in the flood waters of free movement. A world in which the traditions of physical/ geographical and conceptual/socio-cultural expression are moving in tandem with globalizing influences can spell danger for the house of nationhood and beyond.

Extending this awareness of Europe's internal border erosion into the performative vein, the art project "BorderXing" (2002) by the British protest artist Heath Bunting (with Kayle Brandon) documents photographs and routes of a year's worth of hikes crossing these borders with total disregard for international law. Bunting's sense of fascination with what is, essentially, a series of broken, token borders is palpable here, and his online manual calls for emulation. Bunting proposes that "BorderXing" constitutes a "system of knowledge that can be used as a weapon."[12] Such encounters of artists with borders can create (web) sites where people wish they could go or fear to tread; they invite, if only virtually, acts of border-overcoming.

Of course, the playfully performative aspects of the broken internal borders of Schengenized, continental Europe only make sense for those already accepted and integrated within. All the official hype about a borderless Europe that has finally defeated the Iron Curtain has led not to the demise of European macro-spatial planning, but rather to its rise – witness the European Neighborhood Policy, in which the EU essentially offers funding to 16 of its non-EU neighboring states if they behave.[13] In short, the EU's efforts to regulate its economic edge-precipices are, in fact, part of a broader system of attempted control. The logic of continuing EU expansion seems to be proceeding along the lines of Catherine the Great's comment: "I have no way to defend my borders, except to extend them."[14] On one proactive level, future EU membership enticements can provide an encouragement for candidate countries to improve their own border disputes (such as Turkey's refusal to recognize Cyprus as a state; or Serbia's pan-Serbian contingent that still wants Kosovo back). But on another reactive level, Europe's moving eastern edge of purported contact and reform is even being partially re-sealed by the West. And so, while certain autonomies of the member nation-states are being removed, these same functions are being shifted to the level of institutional governance, and the external perimeter lines of the EU are becoming much more closely controlled since the demise of the Iron Curtain. Thus Europe's "outer edge," especially to the east, now serves as a sieve that attempts to control and sort human movement. A hard border for Europe's still evolving external perimeter has been confirmed, with strict visa (and soon biometric) controls, surveillance technologies, and sea patrols.[15]

The new EU, while marketed as a Europe without Frontiers, is in reality a "Europe of the Borders." For Alain Lipietz, this "sharp boundary" is "inconsistent with European ethics and dangerous for peace in Europe."[16] Hence the border lands are now heavily emphasized: Europe-Schengenland is all about entry/exit control, in an attempt to stem unwanted migration as well as human, drug, and weapons trafficking.[17] But the external border is nonetheless proving itself malleable and traversable. Since Lithuania's accession to the EU in 2004, for example, smuggling (of cigarettes, moonshine, vodka, and gasoline) from Russia's wedge of territory to the west and Belarus to the east has increased dramatically. Again, the all-too-porous border has prompted tighter controls: with EU help, electronic border sensors have been in place since 2006.[18] Long traffic delays occur while vehicles entering the EU are checked and searched, including using carbon dioxide sensors to identify people hiding in cargo containers. West Europeans' resentment against (and fear of) what they consider the unwelcome Easternization (read: criminalization) of "their" Europe is such that they are prepared to vote against Europe per se, as demonstrated by the French and Dutch referendums in 2005 and the Irish referendum in 2008, each rejecting a pan-European constitution.

Both sides of the new European divide are in several respects longing for the Iron Curtain of old.[19] The edge of Europe that used to exist in Germany is now on Russia's western side. In June 2003, President Putin asked the EU to lift its visa border between itself and Russia, referring to the restriction as another Berlin Wall. But at the same time, Russia fears a loss of identity without such demarcations. An example of such anxiety was acted out when Russia re-created a section of the old divide along a former Communist colony's border: new EU member Estonia found that its boundary line with Russia had been unilaterally fortified by the latter as a mock Iron Curtain, complete with barbed wire, guard towers, and a no-man's-land.[20] Putin's frustration is echoed by citizens of neighboring countries that are not (yet) members of the expanded Europe: they must now apply for visas to enter adjacent, former COMECON, but now new EU states. The danger here lies in the unintended anti-democracy sentiment that being left outside Schengenland may end up provoking. It is as if Oswald Spengler's (or indeed Samuel P. Huntington's) assumption of civilization and culture belonging solely to the West – even if its component countries differed over its articulation – were being made true.[21]

Nonetheless, critics of Schengenization's impact on the 3,000 miles of Europe's outer border neglect the dynamic, vital changes in the literal acts of bridging that are taking place across now-internal border lands that were basically closed off from each other during the Cold War. The Polish-German border, Germany's most important new boundary, is one such regional example. So hermetically sealed was this border, at least in the initial postwar period, that both the German Democratic Republic and Poland, between whom no love was lost, necessarily turned their backs on one another in order to build anew.[22] As a postwar punishment for Germany, the border marked forced mass migrations; it also imposed national identities for the populations on both sides of the line. Poles on the eastern side were forced to move there at the end of World War II from their own forfeited regions of eastern Poland (which became part of Belarus, Ukraine, and Lithuania). It may strike us today as odd that East Germans would have feared their border to the east as well as the one to the west, but such was indeed the case. Wolfgang Kil, recalling the landscape of his East German childhood, remarks that even though the river line between the GDR and Poland was known as the "Odra-Nysa Peace Border" (*Oder-Neiße-Friedensgrenze*), it was treated far more nervously by Germans than by Poles.[23] Streets and railway lines ended abruptly near the river. Not until the Berlin Agreement (Berliner Abkommen) of 1965 and the opening of the East German border with Poland in 1972 did the border region start to function as such, with 100 million border crossings during the 1970s, and shared cultural events in such border towns as Frankfurt-Słubice and Görlitz-Zgorzelec. In infrastructural terms, the softened border meant more sharing of electricity, gas, and water from the German to the Polish side.[24] But in 1980, the GDR tightened control over the human traffic due to contagion-fears about Solidarność. Hence the Odra-Nysa line remained, effectively, a sealed border for most of the Cold War era.

Nowadays, since Poland's accession to European Union status, this same line has become newly porous; and the problem of the EU border has been shifted to Poland's customs and borders guards to the east.[25] In the dynamic fusion of the now Schengenized former East Germany and Poland, cross-border traffic in the double town of Frankfurt-Słubice is enhanced by three bridges (highway, railway, and the new "city bridge"). The Odra river border itself is a waterway for western Europe. Poland's value-for-money is now being noticed by more than just East German motorists wanting to fill up their tanks across the border; German baked goods are often made from Polish wheat and sugar; and even the famous summer mushrooms (*Pfifferlinge*) are sold by German middlemen who buy them more cheaply from Poles; and the cross-border labor flow goes east as well as west. The E30, now a transit corridor from the German border to Poznań, has become dotted with a series of globalized service areas for cross-border Russian-German truck traffic.[26] Shared event culture is taking hold in the border region: in the summer of 2004, the Polish border town of Kostrzyn (Küstrin) hosted both a joint German-Polish exhibition, "Dialog Loci," on a formerly fortified island on the Odra river, as well as a massive international rock festival, dubbed the "Polish Woodstock." Another travelling exhibition in the spring of 2010 in the German-Polish border region detailed the cross-border cultural achievements of communities like Görlitz-Zgorzelec.[27]

These developments signify at least a beginning of a return of sorts to a pre-Nazi German-Polish interaction – minus, that is, the Jewish communities wiped out by the Third Reich. The long-term prognosis for the EU's internal borders east of the former Iron Curtain is a "cure": namely, fusion. In one of the first regional cooperation agreements of its kind, Görlitz-Zgorzelec symbolized Poland's entry to the EU with the building of a new bridge across the Nysa. The bus and streetcar transit system of the two cities of 100,000 joint inhabitants have been merged; and the school systems are open to children from both sides of the water. The lifting of cumbersome trade restrictions that were bound up with Poland's pre-EU status also transformed truck crossings that used to take up to three days due to border delays on the nearby autobahn. The twin cities stand a chance of emerging as a regional trade hub.[28] Indeed, from such fusion would come a much-needed *in*fusion of demographic youth. The aging German side of this border community, suffering from a drastic population loss of 24,000 since the *Wende* in search of jobs in Berlin and the western states of Germany, urgently needs the younger workforce and trade opportunities of its Polish neighbor, in order to help stem the westward post-Wall drain of population away from Germany's East. The xenophobic neo-Nazi attacks on non-whites are no longer just an acting-out of the mostly unemployed east German youth left behind, but have spread as regular occurrences across the continent.[29]

The steps toward border fusion of previously closed-off states in the New Europe can best be understood on the urban micro-levels, and are certainly backed up in long-term planning documents of the border cities themselves.[30] The most highly trafficked German-Polish border city is Frankfurt (Oder), a role that is rejuvenating this economically depressed town of 62,000 residents. Frankfurt (Oder) is becoming increasingly aware of its new role as a "transit-" or "through-city" (*Durchgangsstadt*), and is now referring to itself in tandem with its Polish sister-city (once its suburb) on the other side of the river, namely as Frankfurt-Słubice. Naturally hurdles of language and prejudice remain, even for Polish students studying at Frankfurt's Europa University Viadrina (20 per cent of the student body). And the brutal economic hurdle of border-difference is that residents on the Słubice side of the river earn one-quarter of the wages on the Frankfurt side; Poland is not expected to catch up with Germany in terms of earnings for the next 15 years. Political economists who care about the border region rather than just the German side can but hope that the US-Mexican *maquiladora*-effect will not end up replicating itself in the German-Polish border land.[31]

The above examples of transformational sites between Germany and Poland highlight how the New Europe's now-open internal border lands have enabled at least the initial stage in the re-integration of peoples and places not formerly considered even wholly "European." Balibar's wish to *"democratize the institution of the border"* toward a "universal right of *circulation* and *residency*" is coming true with respect to the *internal* if by no means the *external* edges of the New Europe.[32] Along related lines, if Ulrich Beck's concept of a "cosmopolitical," fully integrated Europe is going to happen as a continental unity that is nonetheless highly differentiated and locally democratic, it is to the internal border lands that we should turn to see its test-case scenarios, not just to the urban centers.[33]

Yet the changes affecting Europe have had unsettling and de-centering effects for the denizens of the Euro-zone (16 countries)/the Schengen-zone (24 countries)/the European Union (27 countries). A new acronym has emerged: "USE," the "Uncertain States of Europe." One thinks here of the documentary *The Middle* (*Die Mitte*) by Stanisław Mucha, in which various villages in the middle of a central European nowhere all lay insistent (and often unintentionally hilarious) claim to residing at Europe's geographical center.[34] At the end of the movie, student tourists who offer to help the director find Europe's navel with the aid of their GPS seem to lose both the center and themselves in the thick forest. Indeed, in these processes of continued uncertain fragmentation there emerges an almost schizoid identity for Europe, with contradictory projections of a removal of many of the internal boundaries between member states, as well as a solid perimeter border for Europe as a whole, and a shifting expansion of the EU eastwards. No matter how many laws and funds are put in place to attempt to stabilize the identity of the New European territorial land-grab, its spaces have become liquid and ripe for transformations.[35]

Hence postwar Europe's (western) sense of itself, not just the safely contoured nation-state, is now a threatened species. This explains Habermas's and Derrida's joint attempt to stem the tide in their manifesto for a new Europe, published in May 2003 in the *Frankfurter Allgemeine Zeitung*. In this article, Habermas (for Derrida was more a co-signatory than a co-author) challenged Europe to form a counterbalance to the "hegemonic unilateralism" of the USA.[36] Habermas's assertion marks how the political and cultural gulf that emerged between Europe and the USA, as a result of the US-Iraq war, emerged as a new border of sorts. Author Peter Schneider, referring to how Europeans have increasingly accused the Americans of betraying Enlightenment principles, seriously warned of a "new historic divide, comparable to the evolutionary split that occurred when a group of pioneer hominids thousands of years ago turned their backs forever on their African homeland."[37]

One reactive consequence of the decentralizing impact of post-Wall Europe could perhaps have been predicted. Habermas re-introduced Wolfgang Schäuble's 1994 term "core-Europe" (*Kerneuropa*) for a select few countries, which in practice amounts to a Franco-German power-alliance. Dissenter- and newcomer-nations would thus be relegated to the status of a new perimeter-Europe around this central "core." In short, he called for new fortifications, or borders, to replace the old ones that do not function meaningfully any more. Ironically, considering his critique of the United States, Habermas clearly desired a matching united territoriality for Europe (a new bordered zone from without). Habermas's desire for a select group of countries to determine international politics simply means an additional "hard-core" ring within the zone. He is clearly not alone in this logic. There has been a recent push for a core-Europe of states that do accept the 2007 Lisbon Treaty, versus those that do not.[38]

Not only do these suggested borders for such a "core" suggest a wished-for return to the first nation-members of the European community (from which Britain is also excluded), they are also a reactionary conceptual barricade against those former Eastern-bloc nations that recently received EU membership status – even if Habermas correctively claimed he could not imagine a Europe "without Prague, Warsaw, and Budapest."[39] Indeed, the latent intolerance perceived within Habermas's approach was compounded by historian Hans-Ulrich Wehler, who in 2003 warned of "fatal consequences" for Europe, and especially for Germany, if that other – Islamic – East, as represented by Turkey, ever succeeds in entering the EU.[40] The "deep furrows" of what Wehler calls the "cultural border" between European and Islamic identities should, according to this viewpoint, never be crossed, and Europe's "new borders to the East" should be drawn much more closely to home – instead of never having really been fixed in the first place. Similarly, French President Nicolas Sarkozy openly opposed Turkey's EU accession in his successful election campaign of 2007, claiming that Turkey just was not European in terms of culture and geography. In Wehler's and Sarkozy's definitions of Europe, Germany's own Turkish (Muslim), and France's North African (Muslim) populations, let alone Britain's Southeast Asian (Muslim, Hindu, and Sikh) peoples, do not appear to exist.

Poor "Old [West] Europe," indeed: the tides are rising over its Cold War borders, as US-globalization practices and mindsets come in from across the Atlantic, and new post-Wall migrants and their different *mores* enter from the Slavic as well as from the Muslim East. Habermas's main focus remains the unwelcome virtual presence of the United States in Europe – the flow that, as he sees it, would destroy previous lines of European difference into what he fears would be undemocratic sameness. Yet it is equally possible that the new East (both European and Islamic) is the silent symmetrical partner in his text, inadvertently assisting the USA to surround that which Habermas nostalgically wants to revive as the European Franco-German "core." After all, the directional flows of contemporary shifting territorial and cultural identities pertain, in Europe's case and especially in Berlin's, just as much to the post-Cold War East as to the pre- and now post-9/11 (American) West. Derrida, shortly after the fall of the Wall, had not lost this awareness when he wrote that Europe constitutes the ultimate border land of the West (that is, it is adjacent to what is *not* the West): "It is always in the figure of the Western heading and of the *final* headland or point that Europe determines and cultivates itself; it is in this figure that Europe identifies itself."[41] And Berlin shares, with Vienna, the role of being the European West's most eastern city.

Moreover, while Turner articulated a widespread anxiety accompanying the perceived closing of the American frontier in the late nineteenth and early twentieth centuries – a fear of the USA losing its uniqueness if it were to become more European (more staid, and hence less itself), now that it was losing the moving border line that had given its pioneering inhabitants their identity – today Habermas displays what could be termed a *mirror-anxiety* of the same. The dissolution of European borders vis-à-vis the USA is, for Habermas, the scariest concept of all. Habermas's stand indicates not simply a position against the US-led Iraq War, and former Secretary of Defense Donald Rumsfeld's jibe about old

Europe's political impotence (let alone feminization), but the extent to which a united Europe remains weak, and American mass cultural influence within (west) European space could rob European intellectual life of its former status. At the end of the nineteenth century in the wake of the closing of the frontier, many American intellectuals feared Europeanization: and now, in the decades ensuing the fall of the Wall, it is the other way around.

Locking the stable door after the horse has bolted will not amount to much. Let us hope that more critical attention can be paid to what is really going on in post-Wall Europe. Here more than anywhere else we are witnessing the border condition's creative energy, a stage of Zarathustran "crossing over" (*Übergang*) that is not beholden to nostalgia for a former era, but is full of new encounters between a plurality of Easts and Wests.[42] Perhaps, in Friedrich Nietzsche's sense of metaphorically crossing over to a new riverbank, the longer process of *Übergang* in Europe will not have to result in long-term fortifications after all.

Notes

1. Frederick Jackson Turner, "The Significance of the Frontier in American History," in Turner, *The Frontier in American History* (New York: Henry Holt & Co., 1921), p. 3.
2. The Berlin-Saratov route was the focus of a German television documentary directed by Klaus Schwagrzinna: *Der Zug der Träume – Von Berlin an die Wolga* (Westdeutscher Rundfunk / Norddeutscher Rundfunk, 2004). Compare the recently resumed train journey from Sarajevo to Belgrade: Nicholas Kulish, "Train Line across the Balkans Restitches a Wounded Region," *The New York Times* (11 January, 2010).
3. Karl Schlögel, "Berlin und das Städtenetz im neuen Europa," in Stefan Bollmann, ed., *Kursbuch Stadt* (Stuttgart: Deutsche Verlags-Anstalt, 1999), pp. 17–37, p. 32.
4. Novalis, *Werke II. Die Christenheit oder Europa und andere philosophische Schriften* (Cologne: Könemann, 2001).
5. For a critique of European unification, see "The History of an Idea: Special Report: European Unity," *The Economist* (3 January, 2004), pp. 38–40. See also Herbert Dittgen, "The End of the Nation-State? Borders in the Age of Globalisation," in Martin Pratt and Janet Allison Brown, eds, *Borderlands under Stress* (The Hague and Boston: Kluwer Law International, 2000), pp. 49–68, pp. 50, 58.
6. Etienne Balibar, *We, the People of Europe? Reflections on Transnational Citizenship*, trans. James Swenson (Princeton: Princeton University Press, 2004), p. 44, and see also p. 104; and Balibar, "Europe as Borderland," *Environment and Planning D: Society and Space*, 27 (2009), pp. 190–215.
7. Saskia Sassen has discussed how the wealthier European countries have been trying to rewrite their immigration laws and unsuccessfully attempting to refute the new paradigm of border-mutability. Sassen, *Globalization and Its*

Discontents (New York: The New Press, 1998), pp. 5–30. Indeed, as of 2008, illegal migrants can be banned from re-entering Europe for up to five years; see Caroline Brothers, "EU Votes to Unify Rules on Detention of Migrants," *International Herald Tribune* (18 June, 2008). See also Sassen's history of the geopolitics of European migration, *Guests and Aliens* (New York: The New Press, 1999; orig. German, 1996); and Karl Schlögel, *Die Mitte liegt ostwärts: Europa im Übergang* (Munich: Carl Hanser Verlag, 2002), pp. 65–123.

8. Hans-Christian Schmid, dir., *Lichter* (Munich: Claussen + Woebke + Putz Filmproduktion [Prokino Filmverleih], 2003). See, for example, Ulf Mann's *Tunnelfluchten. Grenzgänger. Verräter. Wühlmäuse* (Berlin: Transit, 2005) on the tunnels under the Berlin Wall along the Heidelberger Straße.

9. Josef Schulz, *Übergang*, with texts by Rolf Sachsse and Kerstin Stremmel (Cologne: Verlag schaden.com, 2007).

10. The Schengen Agreements of 1985 and 1990 became a convention in 1995, and part of the EU framework in the 1997 Treaty of Amsterdam, after having been implemented two years previously. They were originally signed by France, Germany, and the Benelux countries. Schengen III was signed in 2005. The United Kingdom and Ireland opted out of the Schengen border controls; Britain has joined in regarding the control of crime and trafficking (such as the Schengen Information System [SIS] and EUROPOL). New EU member states had the Schengen *acquis* come into effect a few years after joining (in Poland's case, in December 2007). The new External Borders Agency, which opened in 2005, has its operational headquarters in Warsaw. For an analysis of the impact of Schengen on Europe's borders, see William Walters, "Mapping Schengenland: Denaturalizing the Border," *Environment and Planning D: Society and Space*, 20 (2002), pp. 561–80.

11. Jürgen Habermas, "Die postnationale Konstellation und die Zukunft der Demokratie," in *Die postnationale Konstellation. Politische Essays* (Frankfurt am Main: Suhrkamp, 1998), p.103. Habermas refers to John Agnew's and Stuart Corbridge's observation about globalization's "trend from boundaries to flows." See Agnew and Corbridge, *Mastering Space: Hegemony, Territory, and International Political Economy* (New York: Routledge, 1995), p. 216; cited by Habermas, *Die postnationale Konstellation*, p. 104.

12. Elizabeth Bard, "How to Cross Borders, Social or Otherwise," *The New York Times* (27 October, 2004). Note, however, that Heath Bunting's "BorderXing Guide 2002–2003" can be read only by authorized users at www.tate.org. uk/netart/borderxing/ (date accessed 19 October, 2009).

13. European Commission, European Neighborhood Policy (ENP), at: http:// ec.europa.eu/world/enp/policy_en.htm (date accessed 18 May, 2010). The ENP appears to follow the tenets of Jean-François Drevet, who, referring to the moving edge of Turner's frontier, suggested that Europe's movement to the East be controlled by a series of metaphorical "canal locks." These canal locks (aka EU-funded incentives) can be applied to Europe's border regions, to help smooth out disparities between EU and adjacent non-EU countries' living standards as well as discontinuities in trade and infrastructure. But Thomas M. Wilson points out that the "bottom-up" construction of European eastern borderlands interacts with the "top-down" elites' influence, working against any homogenization brought about by the EU. Drevet, "The European Union and its Frontiers," in Andreas Faludi, ed., *European*

Spatial Planning (Cambridge, MA: Lincoln Institute of Land Policy, 2002), pp. 159–78, p. 166; and Wilson, "Sovereignty, Identity and Borders: Political Anthropology and European Integration," in Liam O'Dowd and Thomas M. Wilson, eds, *Borders, Nations and States: Frontiers of Sovereignty in the New Europe* (Aldershot: Avebury, 1996), pp. 199–219, pp. 200–6. See also O'Dowd and Wilson, "Frontiers of Sovereignty in the New Europe," in ibid., pp. 1–17, pp. 12–13.

14. Cited in Robert Cottrell, "Meet the Neighbours: A Survey of the EU's Eastern Borders," *The Economist* (25 June, 2005).

15. Sea patrols guarding entry into Sicily from Libya have become more efficient, but the migrants' rate of drowning has stayed stable, indicating that the trip is more dangerous than before. Ian Fisher, "For African Migrants, Europe Becomes Farther Away," *The New York Times* (26 August, 2007), p. 10.

16. A. Lipietz, "Social Europe, Legitimate Europe: The Inner and Outer Boundaries of Europe," *Environment and Planning D: Society and Space*, 11 (1993), pp. 501–12, p. 501.

17. See Luiza Bialasiewicz and John O'Loughlin on the transitional "crush zone" between Europe and Russia: "Galician Identities and Political Cartographies on the Polish-Ukrainian Border," in David H. Kaplan and Jouni Häkli, eds, *Boundaries and Place: European Borderlands in Geographical Context* (Lanham: Rowman & Littlefield, 2002), pp. 217–38, p. 219.

18. Steven Lee Myers, "For Europe's Sake, Spotting Moonshine among Swans," *The New York Times* (8 December, 2005).

19. As Svetlana Boym pointedly notes, the Iron Curtain itself was "not simply external; it is internalized in both the East and the West, and retraced by frustrated expectations and nostalgias for a common home." Boym, *The Future of Nostalgia* (New York: Basic Books, 2001), p. 241.

20. "Frontier Justice: Baltic Borders and the War," *The Economist* (7 May, 2005), p. 46; and Anderson, Bigo, and Bort, "Frontiers, Identity and Security," in Pratt and Brown, *Borderlands Under Stress*, p. 258.

21. Oswald Spengler, *The Decline of the West*, 2 vols, trans. Charles Francis Atkinson (New York: Alfred A. Knopf, 1928); orig. *Der Untergang des Abendlandes: Umrisse einer Morphologie der Weltgeschichte*, 2 vols (Munich: Beck, 1918); and Samuel P. Huntington, *The Clash of Civilizations and the Remaking of World Order* (New York: Simon and Schuster, 1996).

22. The Polish-German border reflects an extremely troubled history between the two countries. The boundary formed by the Odra and Nysa rivers between communist Poland and communist Germany was only as old as the end of World War II: it, too, helped prevent the slide of migrants westwards, as if it were an additional line of fortification for the Iron Curtain itself. Until 1949 the line between Poland and Soviet-controlled Germany was totally closed; an exception was (Polish) Gubin, which was permitted to use an electric power plant in its other urban half, (German) Guben. See Helga Schultz, "Schwierige Nachbarschaft an Oder und Neiße," in Barbara Breysach, Arkadiusz Paszek, and Tölle, eds, *Grenze – Granica: Interdisziplinäre Betrachtungen zu Barrieren, Kontinuitäten und Gedankenhorizonten aus deutschpolnischer Perspektive* (Berlin: Logos Verlag, 2003), pp. 36–48, p. 43.

23. Wolfgang Kil, *Land ohne Übergang. Deutschlands neue Grenze* (Berlin: ex pose verlag, 1992), pp. 11, 27.

24. Maria Rutowska, "Die regionale Zusammenarbeit in der deutsch-polnischen Grenzregion in den Jahren 1945–1989," pp. 42–48, and Helga Schultz, "Die Oderregion in wirtschafts- und sozialhistorischer Perspektive," pp. 79–113, pp. 108–10, both in Schultz and Alan Nothnagle, eds, *Grenze der Hoffnung: Geschichte und Perspektiven der Grenzregion an der Oder*, 2nd ed. (Berlin: Arno Spitz Verlag, 1999).

25. Siobhán Dowling, "Not So Quiet on the Eastern Front: Strikes, Protests and Gridlock at the Poland-Ukraine Border," *SpiegelOnline* (25 January, 2008).

26. Wilfried Hackenbroich, "Grenzraum. Border Space," in Regina Bittner, Wilfried Hackenbroich, and Kai Vöckler, *Transiträume. Transit Spaces. Frankfurt/ Oder – Poznan // Warschau // Brest // Minsk // Smolensk // Moskau* (Berlin: jovis Verlag, 2006), pp. 74–89; Kevin J. O'Brien, "For Jobs, Some Germans Look to Poland," *The New York Times* (8 January, 2004); and Martin Klesmann and Frank Herold, "Alles bleibt anders," *Berliner Zeitung* (31 July–1 August, 2004).

27. The exhibition "Grenze – welche Grenze? Menschen an Oder und Neiße" is detailed at www.eunop.eu/news/490/pi_menschen_an_oder_und_neisse_ d.pdf (date accessed 2 May, 2010).

28. See Mark Landler, "Divided European City Looks Toward a Reunion," *The New York Times* (20 April, 2003).

29. Uwe Rada, *Zwischenland. Europäische Geschichten aus dem deutsch-polnischen Grenzgebiet* (Berlin: bre.bra verlag, 2004), pp. 115–24. East German population loss is not new to the post-1989 years: German border towns, which were losing people even before World War II (mostly to Berlin, for jobs), took until the 1960s to regain their pre-war population. The double border-town of Guben-Gubin has lost over 10,000 on its German side since the *Wende*, but the population in its Polish half has stayed more constant. For a study of how informal, endogenous, predominantly German prejudices are still hampering cross-border activities in Guben-Gubin, see Ulf Matthiesen, "Transformational Pathways and Institutional Capacity Building: The Case of the German-Polish Twin City Guben/Gubin," in Göran Cars, Patsey Healey, Ali Madanpour, and Claudio de Magalhães, eds, *Urban Governance, Institutional Capacity and Social Milieux* (Aldershot: Ashgate, 2002), pp. 70–89; Matthiesen and Hans-Joachim Bürkner, "Antagonistic Structures in Border Areas: Local Milieus and Local Politics in the Polish-German Twin City Gubin/Guben," *Geojournal*, 54 (2001), pp. 43–50; and Rada, *Zwischenland*, pp. 125–36.

30. See the planning documents "Stadtkonzeption Frankfurt (Oder) 2010: Grenzenlos offen," at http://194.76.233.16/stadt/stkonz10/stk_inh.htm, and "Guben-Gubin: Stadt 2030," at www.guben-gubin-2030.de/de/index.html (date accessed 2 March, 2010).

31. Stefan Krätke, "Probleme und Perspektiven der deutsch-polnischen Grenzregion," in Schultz and Nothnagle, eds, *Grenze der Hoffnung*, pp. 162–203, p. 222.

32. Balibar, *We, the People*, p. 108, pp. 176–77 (emphasis original). See also Steffi Marung's discussion of the post-Wall "civilizational" border transformations in Poland. Marung, "Moving Borders – Competing Civilizing Missions: Germany, Poland, and Ukraine in the Context of the EU's Eastern

Enlargement," forthcoming in Marc Silberman, Karen E. Till, and Janet Ward, eds, *Walls, Borders, Boundaries: Spatial and Cultural Practices in Europe* (New York and Oxford: Berghahn Books, 2012).

33. On a new cosmopolitical European identity, see Ulrich Beck, "Europa neu denken," *Internationale Politik*, 60.7 (2005), pp. 6–12; and Beck and Edgar Grande, "Cosmopolitanism: Europe's Way Out of Crisis," *European Journal of Social Theory*, 10.1 (2007), pp. 67–85. See also Anssi Paasi, "Remarks on Europe's Transforming Meta-Geography," *Geopolitics*, 10.3 (2005), pp. 580–85.

34. Stanisław Mucha, dir., *Die Mitte* (strandfilm produktions GmbH, 2004).

35. For an analysis of the messy, creative "excess of political scenarios" in the New Europe, see Stefano Boeri, "Notes for a Research Program," in Rem Koolhaas, Boeri, and Sanford Kwinter, eds, *Mutations* (Bordeaux: ACTAR, 2000), pp. 356–77, p. 360: "This is the European territory as an archipelago, an accumulation of contexts, a cradle of diversity." Boeri suggests that European space on the local level can be defined in terms of its function as a *dispositif* for the ongoing mutation, modification, and reinterpretation of material space.

36. Jürgen Habermas and Jacques Derrida, "Nach dem Krieg: Die Wiedergeburt Europas," *Frankfurter Allgemeine Zeitung* (31 May, 2003). See also Habermas, "Der 15. Februar oder: Was die Europäer verbindet," in Habermas, *Der gespaltene Westen* (Frankfurt am Main: Suhrkamp, 2004), pp. 43–51; and Michael Heffernan, *The European Geographical Imagination* (Stuttgart: Franz Steiner Verlag, 2007), pp. 75–85.

37. Peter Schneider, "Across a Great Divide: Europe and America," *The New York Times* (3 March, 2004). In a podium discussion entitled "Europa wohin?" held at Berlin's Akademie der Künste on 27 June, 2003, Habermas vehemently denied any anti-Americanism in his article. For critical responses see, for example, Johannes Voggenhuber, who found that Habermas had missed the deeper relevance of the planning stage of the European constitution. Voggenhuber, "Der Philosoph in Pantoffeln: Habermas, von der Avantgarde zur Nachhut," *Die Zeit* (26 June, 2003).

38. Günter Grass, in a Deutschlandfunk radio interview of 29 June 2003, dismissed Habermas's "core Europe" concept for its underlying desire to become an institutionalized "driving force"; see "Grass attackiert Habermas in Diskussion über 'Kerneuropa'," *Der Tagesspiegel* (30 June, 2003). But see, for example, Theo Sommer, "Can I Speak for 27? Europe's Treaty Dilemma after the Irish Vote," *The Atlantic Times* (July 2008).

39. Habermas, "Europa wohin?" podium discussion; see also Caroline Fetscher, "Vision und Revision," *Der Tagesspiegel* (29 June, 2003).

40. Hans-Ulrich Wehler, "Die Türkei soll draußen bleiben. 90 Millionen Muslime, wachsender Islamismus: Darauf kann die EU verzichten," *Der Tagesspiegel* (27 June, 2003).

41. Jacques Derrida, *The Other Heading: Reflections on Today's Europe*, trans. Pascale-Anne Brault and Michael B. Naas (Bloomington: Indiana University Press, 1992), p. 25 (emphasis original).

42. Karl Schlögel has helpfully applied this term to the new Europe in his promotion of an inclusive, philo-Eastern attitude. Schlögel, *Die Mitte liegt ostwärts. Europa im Übergang* (Munich: Carl Hanser Verlag, 2002); and Schlögel, "Berlin," in Bollmann, ed., *Kursbuch Stadt*, p. 30.

Part II

Afterlives of the Wall: Reflections and Deflections

4
Agency at the Wall

Der Türhüter erkennt, daß der Mann schon an seinem Ende ist, und, um sein vergehendes Gehör noch zu erreichen, brüllt er ihn an: »Hier konnte niemand sonst Einlaß erhalten, denn dieser Eingang war nur für dich bestimmt. Ich gehe jetzt und schließe ihn.«

(Franz Kafka, 1915)[1]

Germany's Cold War borders could be said to be long gone, and the joined nation's regained capital, like the country, essentially fused. Yet the opposite is just as true. Berlin's Wall – the shadow it cast if no longer its full composition – is obviously still here more than two decades after the end of the German Democratic Republic. The capital city seems fully normalized; yet its emblem of difference is still extant, despite the Germans' rapid removal of the physical structure of the Wall itself. The Wall was dismantled during the euphoric *Wende*, yet it has endured as "the total German work of art," its fitting appellation in Günter Grass's novel *Too Far Afield*.[2] It is the *ex*-Wall (its remnants and consequences, its lines and projections, traces and stagings, in short: its inverse, imaginary status, like a photographic negative) that is still marking the city. This continuation of former geometries can be both positive and pathological in nature.

The Wall in its various afterlives is increasingly emerging, in fact, in a seemingly perverse role: as a barrier that was both hard and soft, both imposed on people from above and yet maintained by people from below, as a door and passageway like Kafka's Law "made only for you" (*nur für dich bestimmt*), Berlin/Germany. The Wall's spectral longevity provides a multivalent answer to Henri Lefebvre's question: "What is an ideology without a space to which it refers, a space which it describes, whose vocabulary and links it makes use of, and whose code it embodies?"

Lefebvre wondered whether "state socialism produced a space of its own" other than the "sterility" that would first confront the western visitor to socialist cities. The answer, essentially, was no, at least for Lefebvre – not a space that lived up to the promises of the Marxist and Leninist state. Perhaps this is why the Wall insists on lingering in the (west, central, and east) European collective imaginary as the most powerful monument of the Cold War, as the most significant urban trace in the afterlife of the East Bloc's political system. And the ex-Wall still has a role to play, a function today in the city of Berlin. Again, as Lefebvre saw: "No space ever vanishes utterly, leaving no trace. [...] Were it otherwise, there would be no 'interpenetration', whether of spaces, rhythms or polarities."[3] The Wall in its afterlife phase has ended up corresponding to more than just the ideology of the East, and to more than a space of destruction on urban soil. Only at the point beyond the Wall's physical extinction is it possible to assess its ultimate significance for Berlin; only now does it seem logical that the Wall that once divided has taken on shared meanings for the city. Thus we can find the continuity of the Wall's *dis*continuity for Berlin – and, by extension, for German identity.

During the twenty-eight-year existence of the Berlin Wall (1961–1989), and the eleven years of the closed inner German border that led up to it, the Wall's career appears to have been precisely as it was intended: the hardest, least permeable border in the Cold War world. The Wall, the Iron Curtain's most iconic section, was a desired-for, if never fully achieved, hermetic sealing. What was built as a necessity to the German Democratic Republic's viability as a country became a useful tool in the West's policy of containing the communist threat and marketing its own image as a champion of freedom. While the confrontation of the eleven-month Berlin Blockade (or *Luftbrücke*, from June 1948 to May 1949) is considered in retrospect to have been the midwife that gave birth to German division by forging West Berlin's dependency on the provisions and military of the Western Allies Britain and the USA, the West also took political advantage of the situation. The blockade permitted the USA to treat West Berlin as a projection of what Andreas W. Daum has termed its own "heroic narrative" in the world. In other words, when President John F. Kennedy so memorably identified himself in 1963 as a Berliner, what was really going on was that West Berliners were being made *paratactically synonymous* with Americans. West Berlin's borders became America's own. The seeds of the dream were sown that the city's full borders would one day be reinstated by the West, and thus "Berlin was regarded as a city of America."[4]

By the time the two most powerful leaders in the Cold War world met in Vienna in June 1961 during the height of the "Berlin Crisis," the hardening of the Berlin border as the last open spot in the Iron Curtain was beginning to feel inevitable for both sides. The Wall was effectively sketched out as a deal between the rhetorical lines insisted upon by East and West when Kennedy met Nikita Khrushchev. During their discussion, Khrushchev, repeating a position he had held since 1958, threatened that the postwar borders of eastern Europe needed firming up, and that this would entail "liquidating" the Allied occupation of West Berlin. Khrushchev declared that West Berlin constituted a "bone in the throat" of Communism, a "splinter," and worse still, an "abscess on the body of Europe" that needed to be removed.[5] Kennedy asked Khrushchev to "draw a line" between their opposing demands (namely, Kennedy's insistence on US-led troops remaining in West Berlin, and Khrushchev's insistence on a peace treaty with East Germany that would enforce his above threats). Well he might ask – as if in response to Kennedy's request, a three-dimensional line certainly *was* drawn up later that summer.

A closed intra-city border was becoming necessary from the viewpoint of the German Democratic Republic's Secretary General Walter Ulbricht, who had been writing to Khrushchev for advice and voicing concern at Warsaw Pact meetings about the need to stem the migration flood of East Germans to the West (up to three million).[6] At a news conference on 15 June, 1961, and in answer to a western journalist's question about the state boundary being erected at the Brandenburg Gate, Ulbricht responded that despite West German agitation for a wall to be built by East German construction workers, "no one has the intention to build a wall" (*Niemand hat die Absicht, eine Mauer zu errichten*). But Ulbricht was synonymous with this "no one." Constructing the wall became imminent the moment that Krushchev gave Ulbricht the green light to build "an iron ring around [West] Berlin"; but in an important sense it had been in the works ever since the first use of the term in the context of the Soviets' attempted blockade of Berlin.[7] According to a Soviet document released in 2009, Krushchev's order to build the Wall came on 1 August, 1961, just before a Warsaw Pact meeting at which the Soviet leader instructed the member states to support the closing of the GDR's border with the West; and where Ulbricht announced that his government had, in fact, been working ever since 1952 on a highly classified plan to close off East from West Berlin using first a fence and then an actual wall. The CIA had learned of the plan in 1958, however, dubbing it "Operation Chinese Wall."

These factors help explain why the desperate letter written to Kennedy by West Berlin's mayor Willy Brandt on 15 August 1961, just two days after the Wall went up, went essentially unheeded; and the manner in which the hard-border status of the Wall was swiftly accepted by the first generation of western critics.[8] Maurice Blanchot's comments written in the immediate wake of the Wall's construction focused on the "enforced political abstraction" it caused for Berlin. Blanchot made the Wall appear to be some kind of unavoidable fate when he referred to Cold War Berlin's universal condition of "fracture": "For everyone, Berlin is the problem of division. [...] Berlin is not only Berlin, but also the symbol of the division of the world." The entire city was made over into "this absent centre" of the Wall: "In this way, the wall succeeded in abstractly concretizing the division, to render it visible and tangible ..."[9]

Over the next decades, the East German government attempted to perfect the killer-barrier status of their Wall system. Indeed, the easing of Cold-War tensions thanks to the improvements encouraged by West German Chancellor Brandt's *Ostpolitik* as facilitator of the German-German détente of the 1970s – the Bonn-Moscow Treaty of 1970 that ratified the German-German border; the 1971–1972 Quadripartite Agreement; and the FRG-GDR Basic Treaty of 1972–1973, all landmarks of mutual recognition and normalization of relations between the two states – did not appear to apply to the Wall. Krushchev's metaphor of the iron grip of the Soviets encircling and strangling the city's western half seemed apt and instructive, especially when the West Berlin police learned that the East Germans were modernizing their border by dint of extended fortifications and military forces alike in a new "Ring around Berlin" (Fig. 4.1).[10] This was part of what *Time* magazine called the "grim improvements" resulting from the East Germans' multi-year, third-generation overhaul of the "Modern Border" (*Moderne Grenze*, 1967–1972) along its 858-mile course through Germany.[11] Hence détente was not interpreted as a softening of the closed border. Outside of Berlin the border had bunkers along with deadly mines: 60,000 SM 70 anti-personnel devices (*Selbstschußanlagen*) on its metal mesh fences and 1.3 million landmines (at least until the West German government bribed the GDR with a billion DM worth of loans in 1983 to remove them). East Germans tried nonetheless to cross it, and hundreds died trying. Estimates of actual fatalities among would-be Wall and German border-crossers still vary widely, with more recent estimates configuring an increasing number of deaths. A study by the Zentrum für zeithistorische Forschung indicates that 136 died crossing the Berlin Wall itself. More than 72,000 were imprisoned for wanting to illegally leave the GDR.[12]

Much seemed to depend on the purported impermeability of Krushchev's "iron ring," on forging over time the ever-improving image

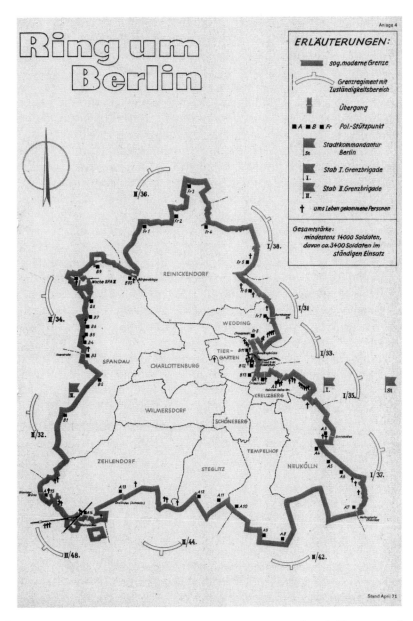

Figure 4.1 West Berlin police map of the East German military's "Ring around Berlin," April 1971

and status of the Wall as omniscient. The Wall's iconic (and the GDR's political) power quickly came to rest on this image of lethal perfection. It was in this apparent fairy-tale appearance that the "Good" and the "Bad" spatial halves of the Cold War could be most easily found, according to Rem Koolhaas: "The Wall was a masterpiece ... its psychological and symbolic effects were infinitely more powerful than its physical appearance." Despite the fact that it was "deadly," which Koolhaas certainly concedes, he articulates a yearning for the now-lost Wall that was so *"heartbreakingly beautiful* ... the most purely beautiful remnant of an urban condition." In this Faustian moment – "Tarry a while! you are so fair!" (*Verweile doch! du bist so schön!*) – we see a far more broadly reaching popular obsession with the fatal aesthetic of the Wall.[13] Using an eternal present tense for the Wall even after its fall, Koolhaas recalls its various stages of building, starting as a "line" and ending as a "zone":

> In its "primitive" stage the wall is decision, applied with absolute architectural minimalism: concrete blocks, bricked-in windows and doors ... In the next permutation, a second wall – this time of rough concrete slabs hurriedly piled on top of each other ... – is planned just behind the first. Only when this wall is finished is the first wall (the old houses) taken down. Sometimes, adding insult to injury, the street level – a portico, forever-empty shop windows, the striped poles of nonexistent barbers – is left as a kind of decorative pre-wall. This second wall is also unstable. It is continuously "perfected" through construction techniques ... the smooth, mechanical, *designed* wall is taken down 20 years later. Topped by an endless row of hollow concrete cylinders, it is impossible to grip for those who might want to escape.[14]

The reluctant admiration that can be detected in Koolhaas's art historical encounter with the Wall is echoed in Neil Leach's representation of the Wall as a *total* form of closure, one that reduced East Germans to living in a state as closed as Antigone's tomb. Windows and doors were blocked off in buildings whose façades happened to be situated along borough boundaries demarcating the Sectoral Border (*Sektorengrenze*) between the Soviets' and the Western Allies' chunks of Berlin. This was the case along the Bernauer Straße, where Ida Siekmann became the Wall's first casualty on 22 August 1961 when she jumped from an apartment window to her death on the West German sidewalk below (Fig. 4.2). The unnatural way in which the GDR border police blocked and walled off not just city streets but buildings on streets reminds Leach of the Greek myth

Figure 4.2 Memorial to Ida Siekmann, Bernauerstrasse, West Berlin (1962)

about Antigone's punishment to the death in a cave from which there was no escape. Antigone had transgressed against the law of the state (ruled by Creon) by insisting on giving her brother Polynices a proper burial. East Berlin thus became, for Leach, a "bridal chamber of death"; here the paradox regarding which part of the city was actually free makes itself apparent.[15] For people whose lives unfolded at the Wall, there seemed little room for human agency. This included members of the western Allied military forces, for example, for whom the inner German border was a no-go zone without prior authorization, and who received a highly choreographed series of border-crossing instructions when travelling between West Berlin and the Federal Republic.

Along the hard border, contradictions were to be erased. The Wall's emptying-out of the exit-entry functions of buildings' outer walls was followed by the ultimate demolition and erasure of any buildings considered too adjacent to and interruptive of the Wall zone. Symbolically, the Church of Reconciliation (*Versöhnungskirche*) in the no-man's-land on Bernauerstraße was demolished in 1985: this seemingly vindictive act of eradication was necessary from the GDR's perspective to finally rid that part of the terrain of any inconsistency with the Wall's three-dimensional function.[16] Indeed, the terrain of the Wall in Berlin seemed so impenetrable because it was made so be so very "thick" from east to west, following an age-old logic of repeated deterrence of height, depth, and human patrol: the inner wall, a fence, electro-optical and acoustic alarm devices, anti-vehicular steel or cement barriers and trenches, guard towers, lighting, raked sand, border patrol tracks, dogs, and finally, the outer Wall (the only one that the West really knew). Since the purpose of the Wall was to keep East Germans in rather than the western Other out, the process of "securing the hinterland" (*Hinterlandsicherung*) began early on. Far less obvious segments of Wall infrastructure began in East Berlin long before one would be able to encounter even the inner Wall – lamps daubed with coded colors to alert border guards of the imminent change in their urban scenery, indicating points beyond which even they were not allowed to venture without permission; cement seals over drain covers; and even large flower tubs designed to stop trucks.[17]

Thus the Wall as a material form operated horizontally: it was a terrain that became part of people's lives across miles of border zone across Germany; and it even existed beyond itself, surrounding a few of West Berlin's enclave communities. It also performed vertically, in ways not dissimilar to how Jerusalem's Wailing Wall, a remnant of the Second Temple's retaining wall, goes beyond its religious function in Judaism to serve as the geological foundation for the Dome of the Rock mosque above it; or how the Israeli separation barrier contains multiple "depth barriers" of extraterritorial Israeli islands cut out of Palestinian space, and even makes separate roads for Palestinians and Israelis at different elevation levels.[18] The Berlin Wall dictated not just which side owned infrastructural spaces like water, drains, railway tracks, bridges, and tunnels, but even the air between land and overhead structures – as happened with a bridge for the road that was built in 1972 from West Berlin to its inhabited enclave of Steinstücken between Wannsee and Potsdam.[19] To build the road that would re-link Steinstücken to the rest of the western world, the West and East Germans had successfully traded pieces of border land, but the East Germans could not trade "their" railway that ran under the bridge, and so the air and everything beneath the bridge was deemed GDR territory, while the bridge and the air above it belonged to West Berlin.

What were the overall costs of this bulwark's striving toward perfection? While the inner-German border certainly provided an "'economy of power'" for the GDR, it also cost so much that it damaged the East German economy (at a million East German marks per kilometer; or roughly 500 million East German marks in annual maintenance) and impacted the collective national psyche that defined itself in relation to its barrier and to the freedoms imagined on the western side.[20] The city paid a steep price, too, for the Wall's anti-urbanity: Brian Ladd has noted that the Wall behaved in ways that were "antithetical to the mobility and circulation characteristic of a modern city." One can (and the West did) form an interpretation of intentional anti-modernity by the communist East as an underlying rationale, wherein "the Berlin Wall of 1961 connoted an attempt, by political fiat, to reverse the growing economic and social mobility of the modern world."[21] Koolhaas rephrases the Wall's attempted temporal braking-effect in terms of the structure's design logic, deeming it an unwelcome, regressive reminder of modernity during an era that was defining itself increasingly under a newer aegis: *"[O]n the eve of postmodernism, here was unforgettable (not to say final) proof of the 'less is more' doctrine ..."*[22] Indeed, East German authors like Heiner Müller who were permitted to travel to the West experienced the border as a marker between two time zones. For Müller, the Wall was a "time-wall" (*Zeitmauer*) or "regulator" which stood between and seemingly forged the two different temporalities of the slowed-down East and the sped-up West.[23] Writing after reunification, Durs Grünbein has reflected on how division caused two distinct German types of human being to emerge, living according to "two times, two models, two ways of being as different from each other as those of natives and missionaries in the age of the voyages of discovery." The Wall was "a geographical-political-anatomical rift that no biography, no worldview, and no aesthetic project could escape."[24]

In all these acts of negation, then, the Wall became an identity source for city and world. While the Wall certainly halted and disfigured the Berlin polis's existing urban propinquities of exchange, communication, travel, and co-existence, the divided city managed to adapt. West Berlin also went beyond the Wall where absolutely necessary: for example, it paid East Berlin for the right to process its solid and water waste on East German terrain. A landfill agreement was painstakingly formalized for Großziethen, enabling West Berlin's household waste to be deposited there from 1973 to 1977 by means of a new, "enclosed" road crossing the death strip, accessible via an electric gate that was controlled by the East German border troops.[25] The Wall's impact was to force a re-channeling and re-forging of Cold War Berlin, in short, a transformation – but not the end – of its urban functions.

As a cement vitrine whose job it was to display the specular bipolarity of West and East, the Wall's image of impermeability became vitally necessary for the competing world systems to reflect themselves back to each other. It turns out that Antigone's cave-effect was taking place on both sides. Much to the chagrin of Cold Warrior remembrances, it is becoming increasingly difficult to romanticize a heroic status for the Cold War West.[26] The insider cover maps of postwar Germany that accompanied General Lucius D. Clay's account, *Decision in Germany* (1950), about his role as Military Governor of the US Occupation Zone in Germany and as "father" of the Berlin Airlift, clearly show West Berlin as a walled city well in advance of the fact. Yet it can be argued that such acts of collaboration prevented an all-out third world war. Both the West and the East, in a sense, created and maintained the Wall as an architectural manifestation of the ideological divide that existed between them. Despite the global border that it represented (and the deadly serious tanks, special ops forces, and nuclear arsenals that stood each side of it), the Wall proved to be co-scripted, and took on new meanings. In this light, the Wall amounted to an affect-ridden projection screen that both sides used in order to respectively articulate their own advantages and each other's relative misery.[27]

This does not undo the thesis that the Wall remained a "grotesque denial" of urban architecture.[28] Yet we have to contend with the fact that the Wall was ultimately adopted as a symbolic "zipper" that both joined and separated not just the city but West and East Germans as well.[29] The broken national fabric was thus able to do itself up, albeit forging two postwar identities thereby. As Ladd states, "both division and unity" were signified by the same Wall: for as long as it existed it created the illusion that East and West were still one people, even if two countries. When it came down, social differences between the two German systems became pronounced and disappointment rose, as if the "Wall had betrayed the hopes invested in it."[30] The implication of this metaphor is that without a zipper the two pieces or sides of cloth cannot be held together. The division seals, effectively.

We see from the above that the Wall's construction inadvertently helped "form" the postwar German people even as it divided them. In so forming, the Wall took on the functions of a membrane or filter for a living organism. This aspect of the German-German border opens it up from the catch-all realm of deadly aesthetic stasis toward an examination of its multiple phases and sluice-gate operations that kept the city of Berlin quite literally "going" – as in the multiple instances of the Wall's ultimate porosity, for example, regarding traffic, exchange of goods, and legal and illegal crossings. The Wall's hybridity pointed up some of its essential contradictions and absurdities. Collective faith in its hard-border status became increasingly unfixed and destabilized – resulting, ultimately, in the implosion of its purported barrier-function altogether on 9 November 1989, thanks to the peaceful activism of the East Germans.

New perspectives can be gained, then, concerning these evolutionary characteristics of the Wall that break open its "solid" reputation. Bruno Latour's concept of the oligopticon is useful in this regard. The oligopticon is not an absolute contradiction of the panopticon, as first described by Jeremy Bentham and as projected into modernity and beyond by Michel Foucault.[31] Rather, Latour develops an updated version of panoptic reciprocal potential that becomes evident in certain contexts. In a civil, liberal society, systems of oligoptic vision and control can enhance self-understanding on a mutual basis (and indeed this was the "cured" condition that Bentham intended his panopticon to work toward among the inmate populations); but in a dictatorship, such potential is sent underground. The East German Stasi system that placed informers (IMs) into all social networks of friends and family, and the populace's retreat-response into what is referred to as a "niche"-society, are testament to that.

The oligoptic reciprocity created by the Wall was neither intentional nor literal – after all, most East Germans were not allowed to gaze upon it in the first place since the terrain was blocked off with screening devices (*Sichtblenden*). Westerners enjoyed a partial, though one-sided gaze upon it, absorbing the international media's iconization of the Wall as a power structure.[32] Wall-tourist voyeurs saw somewhat more, peering across the outer barrier into the guarded border terrain beyond from the occasional vantage-point of specially erected viewing platforms (or even from a purpose-built tower, as in the Bavarian village of Zimmerau). Rather, the Wall's function as an oligopticon existed in the ways that it forged some unexpected, symmetrical responses between East and West Germans. As a porous, piecemeal entity, the Wall invited dynamic responses to itself. The Wall became part of a mutual system – not just a border maintained actively by both sides but a border that is impacted by people just as it impacts people. As opposed to the panoptic watch-towered perfectibility of its *design*, the Wall was an oligoptic system in *practice*. Hence it would be wrong to assume that the Wall's immensity precluded acts of cooperation and creativity, and even comfort and pleasure. Interactive agency and even a sense of identity could be found even at the Wall. As Marion in Wim Wenders' film *Wings of Desire* says: "Berlin. Here I'm a stranger, and yet everything is so familiar. At any rate you can't get lost, you just keep arriving at the Wall."[33]

While the GDR certainly became a barrier-state, people contributed to this barrier: it lived and breathed in them. Post-socialist studies in anthropology and cultural history by Daphne Berdahl and Edith Sheffer have pointed toward the ways in which border technologies, formidable as they were, could not succeed in forging passivity.[34] The Wall and inner German border alike cannot be reduced to their crisis points of harsh military opposition, as occurred in the face-off between Soviet and US tanks at Checkpoint Charlie (22–28 October, 1961), or with the permanent face-off of the watchtowers of both the US and Soviet militaries on each side of the border at the Fulda Gap, which was regarded as the most likely crossing-point of the inner German border if Soviet tanks were to attack Frankfurt am Main. The everyday truth of the border, however, was somewhat different. It was accepted and internalized in myriad ways. When the inner German boundary line was closed in 1952 with the help of Soviet soldiers, in most places it consisted only of barbed wire, and yet such as it was it produced a rapid drop in border crossings. East German border guards often married locally and thus became part of the community they were guarding. The moment the border was imposed on people, they started to make it their own, and have continued to do so even with the ex-border. Hence neither the actual Wall nor the "Wall in the head" can be reduced to something inert. Clearly, the borders of identity ran deeper than their physical nation-state manifestations, rather like strata, and thus could not be simply eradicated in the wake of 1989. During the Cold War, border communities bonded against their outside worlds just like villages have always done the world over, tending to dislike the ones on the other side (of the mountain, of the denominational or ethnic divide, and so on). In fact, border communities of adjacent Czechs and Austrians, Thuringians and Bavarians, East Germans and Poles respectively bonded by disliking each other long before the Cold War enforced remoteness between them. Recent micro-histories of border communities along the former Iron Curtain or other previously closed borders are revealing precisely the strength of these sentiments, yet also the ways in which the opened border lines are starting to enable cross-border social networking, commuting to work, infrastructural re-connections, intermarriages, and the co-education of children. Border travelogues by writers like Landolf Scherzer and ethnographically informed studies by Muriel Blaive and Thomas Lindenberger are bringing forth evidence not of empty blind prejudices of an unenlightened and passive East, but of currencies of community identities that were admittedly devalued by 1989, yet could not just be swept away along with state socialism.[35]

Moreover, both sides propped up the border in several ways. In the early days after the Wall went up, first as barbed wire and then as cement bricks, instability at the Wall was rampant. West Berliners came to gawk or throw stones at the new internal border: a 1961 police memo from Neukölln referred to them as a destabilizing bunch of "voyeurs" (*Schaulustige*). West Berlin's police force was in effect working to uphold the barrier by forbidding crowds of more than ten to congregate there.[36] Sometimes the West Berlin police helped keep protesters from their own "side" away from the Wall by hosing them down for good measure. The East German border guards, on the other hand, grenade-launched tear-gas at protestors as well. In the first year and a half of the Wall's existence, 401 incidents were recorded of the East German guards throwing a total of 1,935 tear gas canisters at protesters on the western side of the Berlin Wall.[37]

Border maintenance was elevated in 1972 to the status of a joint Border Commission, which was formed by both German militaries to solve boundary-related technical issues. The Border Commission was also utilized to sort out problems in border-line identification, such as at the Elbe. Sometimes a member of the West German public wanted to help (re)draw the line, too. In 1970 a schoolteacher, Mr Georg Frerichs of Oldenburg, wrote to the minister for Inner German Affairs to complain about discrepancies between what he had witnessed at the border on a school trip and what he had taught his children as it had been printed on border maps for the Elbe river between Lauenburg and Schnackenburg. In his response the minister had to admit that the FRG and GDR were still working out if the line was in the middle of the river, as the East Germans claimed and the West Germans let them stake, or whether West Germany in fact owned all its water along this stretch.[38]

As we look back at the Cold War we perceive more and more instances of these collaborative roles which helped in the formation not just of the infamous border-hardening around West Berlin in 1961, but, significantly, during the years that came before with the measures that increasingly firmed up the initial phase of the postwar "Green Border" across Germany (1945–1952) in order to facilitate a more orderly society on each side. Sheffer has suggested that the inner-German border between East and West has to be understood, particularly in its early years of formation, not as a "monolith" but as a "protagonist" of the Cold War itself.[39] The border became self-maintaining by both sets of governments and both sets of border populations, all desirous in some way or other of a stabilization effect with the closing of the line between them.

This human agency of the West regarding the Iron Curtain included making the border – and hence oneself – into what one wanted (it) to be. Kennedy's televised speech to Americans on 25 July 1961 contained a clever rhetorical sleight of hand that reversed the fear factor of the Berlin Crisis. Instead of appearing as the weakly guarded satellite trying to counter the Soviet bloc from within, West Berlin was hailed by Kennedy as a brave outpost of western freedom, a "frontier" before political barbarism: "Today, the endangered frontier of freedom runs through divided Berlin. We want it to remain a frontier of peace ... The Soviet government alone can convert Berlin's frontier of peace into a pretext for war."[40] Note how Kennedy was aiming to transform any sense of the Soviets' holding of West Berlin "hostage" into a frontier of opportunity, rendering West Berlin an enclave of freedom for the world.[41] Kennedy's speech also signaled that the USA was not going to seek to lay claim to East Berlin. By thus idealizing West Berlin he confirmed – to Ulbricht's and Krushchev's delight, and to Brandt's ultimate chagrin – the East German government's right to close the border around it. Thus did a circle of annihilative threat become a brave threshold of patriotic opportunity for the USA.

When borders exist, sometimes one has to deny them in order to maintain a sense of one's own agency. During its literal tenure it became human nature on both sides of the Wall to downplay it; essentially, it was forgotten, or "swept under the rug," as much as possible. This blanking-out of the Wall occurred in the minds of westerners, despite the appeal of Wall-tourism. The colorful graffiti by artists like Thierry Noir and Christophe Bouchet that was painted on the outer Wall (especially after its 1976 smooth-surface reincarnation) was ostensibly placed there as a postmodern counter-cultural act that highlighted the cruelty of the East. But on many parts of the Wall, especially by 1989, the graffiti was so overlaid as to be a mess (Fig. 4.3). It seemed all the paintwork was doing was to make the Wall more palpable as an urban icon, inadvertently propping up the complaisance of the West. Yet at least, as Ladd has noted, "[b]y making the Wall *visible*, the colorful graffiti (or art) also counteracted West Berliners' inclinations to ignore it."[42]

As far as the GDR was concerned the Wall constituted an official blind spot. The word "wall" was not used in the GDR to refer to the border; rather the term "Antifascist Defense Rampart" (*antifaschistischer Schutzwall*) was used to encourage the belief of needing to keep danger out, and often any mention of an actual boundary structure was avoided altogether. The *Sperrgebiet* (500m for the Wall; and 5km for the inner German boundary) meant that most East Germans simply did not have a mental picture of the border's layout. Many had been expelled from the border area in 1952.[43] In both East Berlin and East Germany, a topographical peripheralization was forged by the state: the terrain was cleared both of buildings and entire communities that were deemed too border-adjacent for comfort. Thus the "blanking out" was real enough. Most

Figure 4.3 The Berlin Wall near the Martin Gropius Bau (right) and what is now the Berlin city and state parliament building (left), 1989

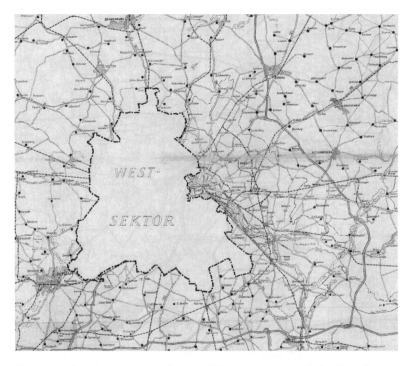

Figure 4.4   East German map showing West Berlin as a void, by Kloss (Berlin, c. 1951)

East Germans and East Europeans, as the target audiences of the politics of population containment that were literally kept in place by the hard border system separating the Soviet-satellite territories of postwar Europe from the West, were not permitted to freely discuss or even conceptualize these border structures and territories. It was, obviously, a forbidden boundary line. Most maps of Berlin drawn up by one "side" of the Iron Curtain purposefully did not portray each other in full (Fig. 4.4). East German border guards in training received city maps of West Berlin's edges – but nothing of its interior.[44] Author Peter Schneider's protagonist in *The Wall Jumper* (1982) meets an East European at Schönefeld airport, who laughs when shown the part of West Berlin in which the former lives on an East German map, because it is located in a void: "No streets, no houses, everything yellow! Desert!'"[45]

Schneider's satirical novel accuses both East and West of mutual prejudices and artifices about each other. He uses legal and illegal border-crossing examples as a means of undermining the mirroring techniques in which he observed both sides engage. Likewise, in her 2009 autobiography, Susanne Schädlich recalls having wondered as a child whether the "white patch" on the map for West Berlin meant that it was snowing there. Enduring a divided childhood as an unhappy East German in West Germany, and coming to terms with a distant, exiled father in the West and an IM-informant uncle in the East, Schädlich realizes that the forbidden "w" for "white" and "west" was a conceptual blindness that affected both East and West Germans.[46] For the two divided German cultures of the Cold War, let alone the two superpowers, it seemed that to know and identify oneself one just had to use the Wall in order to judge the Other. In *The Wall Jumper*, Schneider's narrator is critical of his fellow West Germans' self-absorption and of not truly looking to see the border for what it was but just as a reflective tool: "[F]or Germans in the West, the Wall became a mirror that told them, day by day, who was the fairest one of all." But East Germans, even and especially the intellectuals that he met, were doing the same, he finds. Each German state "acquired an identity in opposition to its other half."[47] In the German case, the Wall served as a collective identity-mechanism for postwar loss and retrieval.

This mirroring urge of Germans on both sides of the Wall to define themselves in relation to what they were not (their German Other) had to do with both German states' "negative identity" caused by World War II, as Stephen Brockmann has indicated. The two states end up caught up in a "psychopolitical endless loop": the Wall itself became the source of German identity rather than its negation, and jumping the Wall was thus more a personal odyssey of becoming who one needed to be, and not a political act. Brockmann, reading Schneider's opening paragraph of the novel, reminds us of the similarity on each side of the mirror-like Wall: arriving by plane, one crossed the Wall three times before landing in Tegel, and would be hard pressed as a non-native to tell the eastern from the western sides apart: "Precisely as a divided city, Berlin is a reminder of the lost German whole."[48] Schneider's thesis was applicable to urban planning, as well: the two Cold War Berlins resembled each other all the more when they attempted to outshine each other in their respective architectural exhibitions and emblematic displays of urban design. In terms of architectural rivalry, the two city halves kept a close eye on each other through a mesh-like "Nylon Curtain" rather than an Iron one.[49]

This competitive border condition of ape-like mirroring behaviors bore little resemblance to the socialist government's officially sanctioned stance toward its barrier. A 1961 poster depicts a young border guard protecting East Germans and asking them to STOP before the

Brandenburg Gate out of a sense of national loyalty. The only Berlin wall in GDR parlance, or on East Berlin maps, was the medieval one for Berlin-Cölln that was built between 1260 and 1300 (a remnant of which survives between the Littenstraße and Waisenstraße). Most maps of the GDR were purposefully empty beyond the border zones; only the military knew what was where as they built a defense line for the Warsaw Pact against the West. Moreover, the East Germans felt bordered in further to the East as well as to the West: Wolfgang Kil recalls a "borderland mentality of ordinance survey maps and bunkers on command, of military camps under camouflage and endless truck convoys"; in retrospect the entire GDR was nothing more than an "outpost" for the Soviets. According to Kil, all "borders" for East Germans signified "trauma": "The entire country of the GDR was trapped in the shadow of that one special border, which was far more than a physical structure: the WALL in Berlin or the merciless path [across Germany] ... THE BORDER was omnipresent in the talk, thoughts, feelings and dreams of GDR citizens."[50] It was a paranoia that affected how East Germans treated even the borders to the East.

Sometimes, however, the border had to be acknowledged and visited, even by the GDR. East German tour guides in the 1980s, for example, when taking officially invited visitors along the boulevard Unter den Linden in the GDR's capital were instructed by the state-run "Berlin-Information" office to explain the rather obvious presence of the Wall by such phrases as the necessary "safeguarding of the state border on 13 August 1961," a measure that had successfully "contained" western imperialist aggression, "saved" peace in Europe, scaled down Cold War tensions, and demonstrated the "power and decisiveness" of the Warsaw Pact countries to defend socialism.[51] There was even an Information Center explaining the need for the border, run by the National People's Army and housed in one of the gatehouses of the Brandenburg Gate (to which no regular GDR citizen could gain access). But no direct mention was to be made of the Wall that the visitors could see in front of them at the Brandenburg Gate.

Yet the East German media was fully capable of showing West Berlin as a visual entity to its readership if it suited the SED (Sozialistische Einheitspartei Deutschlands) regime's ideological needs: in 1965, for example, a map of the city's capitalist half was printed in the East German daily *Neues Deutschland*, showing the location of and naming the various Western "subversive centers and organizations" (including even the air corridors) that were out to undermine the GDR.[52] In East German infrastructural measurements, as well, West Berlin was permitted to make a guest re-appearance: a city government document surveying the terrain of the GDR capital included West Berlin's land mass in its assessments.[53] In a 1980 East German literary tourist guide to the GDR capital, the Wall is mentioned barely at all, but at least it is acknowledged initially in the book's introduction as a spatial entity that "runs through" the "divided city." But the Wall is still justified in temporal terms – by the moniker "13 August 1961" – as an event that stopped the West from "bleeding us to death."[54]

Occasionally, the GDR even had to publicly explain and define (albeit grudgingly) precisely the generally unspoken spatiality of the Warsaw Pact countries' border with the West. In 1975, following similar exhibitions promoting the East German capital in Prague and Warsaw, a Berlin exhibition took place in Iraq: "Berlin, Capital of the GDR, greets Baghdad." But this time, the exhibition organizers became aware that their hosts were curious precisely about the territoriality of the Wall, a topic officially absent from East German discourse. As one of the organizers of the exhibition noted, for the Iraqis the "problem of West Berlin is often still unclear (especially that it lies on the territory of the GDR)"; Iraqis were keen to learn more about the "status and the role of West Berlin and especially its location," all the more since the "role of the Antifascist Defense Rampart" was "still widely unknown" in Iraq. In other words, Berlin of the GDR was put in the unwelcome marketing position of having to explain itself and its shadowy western Other for the benefit of a non-Warsaw Pact country. So the exhibition organizers found themselves having to write back to Berlin to request a rush order of additional exhibit materials about West Berlin (but "not for distribution") to satisfy the Iraqis' interest.[55] What was shown at the Baghdad exhibit, in the end, was a map of the GDR that did in fact depict West Berlin. But the suggested curatorial text on the GDR's relation to its internal urban island of capitalism was cut to almost nil by the home-based GDR censors.[56]

This extreme malleability of the Wall and inner German border according to human need and context helps lift us out of the trap of architectural "technological determinism."[57] Simon Gunn, referring to Latour's actor-network theory (ANT), has reminded us how "history is frequently (perhaps always) the product of composite types of agency, human and non-human, that have conventionally been held apart."[58] Such blended happenings are typical of our interactive agency with the material and/or technological world. Due to this interaction, the Wall came into existence in the first place, and then its course and design kept changing in response to escape attempts, border re-contouring deals with the West, and simply because it literally could not stay erect as planned, but kept falling down.

The truth is that the Wall, indeed the country's entire barrier-system, was faulty. Those building the Wall, especially the men of the *Sicherheitskommando* (security commando) that was mobilized to construct the primitive version in 1961, along with the assistance of the paramilitary workers' groups in securing the streets, understandably had trouble following the very first map that guided them (Fig. 4.5). As Olaf Briese has recently demonstrated, behind what has become known as the various "generations" of the Wall's modernization (six in total, the last "high-tech" one still at the planning stages in 1989 and intended for completion by the year 2000), far more basic questions than sophisticated technological improvement were at stake.[59] To be sure, the Wall was born of process: as even the Wall-aesthete Koolhaas points out, the Wall was neither a "stable" nor a "single entity": it was "more a situation, a permanent, slow-motion evolution" improving its ability to close off, separate, and if necessary, kill.[60] But the reasons for this evolution are not in keeping with its reputation. We find, rather, plenty of indications for a de-demonization of the structure itself simply because it kept on becoming partly ruinous due to a variety of everyday factors: poor cement quality, for example, made the Wall collapse in places, even during its very first winter in January 1962.

Beyond its main "representative" areas many sections of the inner German border system were hardly impressive and proved extremely costly to maintain, let alone upgrade. A reporter for the *Frankfurter Allgemeine Zeitung* reported in 1969 that all it took was a helicopter trip near the inner German border for him to see that cement parts of the mostly metal fence had been removed in places (presumably because they had been needed at more vital points of the barrier, and materials were lacking). Along hundreds of miles along the border in Lower Saxony, he also observed that many of the anti-vehicular cement slab barriers had simply fallen down. It was clear to this West German reporter's eye that the GDR did not have the manpower to follow through and guard its Iron Curtain border section properly, despite all the modernization going on.[61] Across the entire length of the boundary zone, some of the guard towers were collapsing by the 1970s and had to be replaced.

Problems beset the maintenance of the most famous stretches of the Berlin Wall as well. In 1974 an internal report on the Wall's "reliability" by East Germany's 35th Border Regiment stated that between the Spree riverbank near the Reichstag and the Brandenburg Gate, not only was

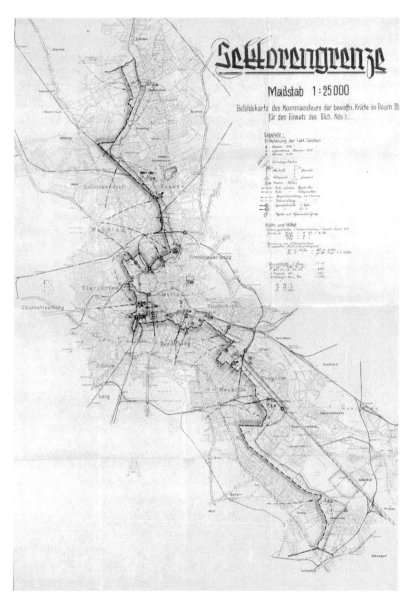

Figure 4.5 "Boundary of the Sectors." The first-ever map of the Berlin Wall, made for the East German People's Police and People's Army, 1961

the cement damaged in the outer wall's blocks, but its steel components were about to erode, and only the blocks' weight and the Wall's top pipe were keeping the upper five rows of wall blocks from falling down completely.[62] East German border guards' quality control concerns aside, the closed boundary that the Wall represented did not actually have to be impenetrable – it just had to look that way and project above all a "good structural-technical appearance."[63] The GDR government became increasingly aware that the Wall was the country's main export-image, and made efforts to streamline the Wall terrain's appearance in places where the western media would most likely observe it; it was as if the East was finally responding to the marketing message of the iconized hard Wall that had been so usefully enacted by the West.[64] Ultimately, what kept the Wall up and the East German people in was a whole lot of faith and fear concerning the border system (sustained by propaganda, socialization, and expectation). The structure itself, despite its modernization phases, could not live up to its reputation.

How can we reconcile this contradictory coexistence of the multiple, bottom-up imperfections and gaps that emerged in the Cold War's most famous border system with the top-down, ideological drive toward a closed perfectibility? First, it helps if we move toward a concept of all architecture (including the purportedly anti-circulatory Wall) as "flow architecture": in the study of spatial order, especially infrastructural kinds, we can learn much from failures and repair, as Stephen Graham and Nigel Thrift have suggested. Architecture's "morphogenetic figures" necessarily face ongoing cycles of decay-maintenance, or entropy-improvement.[65] Second, the concept of the border, even a hard one like the Wall, is best understood as a breathing membrane. Thrift denies that any truly bordered border exists as such – only as a porous, seeping skin. To make this point, Thrift draws an analogy with the image of the scanned body: we may look like containers therein but in fact we are continually "sloughing off pieces" of ourselves, we are leaky water vessels, leaving behind any number of traces like "discharges, memories, messages."[66] Thrift's metaphor can be related to Lefebvre's reading of the "living being"; the Wall can be seen as a membrane that protected the body of the socialist state even as it encased West Berlin, but it nonetheless had to absorb entry and exit in order to keep the urban organism(s) alive:

> A closure thus comes to separate within from without, so establishing the living being as a "distinct body." It is a quite relative closure, however, and has nothing in common with a logical division or abstract split. The membranes in question generally remain permeable,

punctured by pores and orifices. Traffic back and forth, so far from stopping, tends to increase and become more differentiated, embracing both energy exchange (alimentation, respiration, excretion) and information exchange (the sensory apparatus). The whole history of life has been characterized by an incessant diversification and intensification of the interaction between inside and outside.

Lefebvre's above comments can be read as one of the most instructive ways of understanding Berlin's Wall, more so than many geopolitical and technically correct definitions of a national border: "[E]very spatial envelope implies a barrier between inside and out," yet "this barrier is always relative and, in the cases of membranes, always permeable."[67] Viewing the Wall this way necessarily deflates its mythical reputation as having been the only thing between us and nuclear Armageddon.

One clear consequence of a border's porosity is the (usually filtered and controlled) frequency of border crossings. During the 1970s, the Wall's membrane function became more tangibly apparent thanks to détente, with an increase in legal German-German border crossings (direct family members from the East were permitted to visit relatives in the West for family events and birthdays starting with the 60th), easier telephone and postal connections, and infrastructurally improved street and rail links all coming into effect.[68] In its everyday functioning, the Wall continued to face fissures, absorb new textures, and accept its filtering role. In short, it had to be porous to let the city breathe – so to a certain degree, some of the "breaks" in the border were intentional.

But there were obviously illegal crossings, too. West Berliners dug tunnels to get a few East Berliners out from under; and in 1962 the US TV network NBC paid the builders of "Tunnel 29" 40,000 DM for the privilege of filming the lucky escapees' moments of arrival in the West.[69] (In 2000, Spiegel TV was on hand when this same tunnel was rediscovered.) The East German military dug four reconnaissance tunnels under the boundary with West Germany, discovered in 1983. During a six-year period (1974–1980), GDR border troops' internal records indicate that on average about a thousand people per year tried to get across the inner German border; even though 80 per cent of them were reported and stopped before they ever reached the fortified zone and about 150 would-be escapees were "captured" (or worse) per year in the border terrain itself, just under 50 per year on average did succeed in crossing over to the West.[70]

Some of the illegal German-German border crossings had nothing to do with civilian escape attempts. There were geopolitical challenges conducted in the air: in 1965, Soviet jets harassed western carriers flying in the Berlin Control Zone, and provoked fears of another blockade, this time in the air; diplomatic complaints were sent to Moscow by the USA, Britain, and France, reminding the Soviets of the need to adhere to the Allied Control Council agreements of 1945 and 1946 that had established the air zones to West Berlin. The German term, *Grenzverletzer*, for those who attempted to "violate" or "wound" the border by crossing it, is suggestive of a corporeal marker that can be hurt as easily as skin. The West German authorities used the term when referring to the territorial challenge of the East German military flying a helicopter into West German air space; or when the West German military responded by sending over propaganda balloons into the GDR.[71] From the East German point of view, the term *Grenzverletzer* bespoke an understanding of the Wall as a protective covering for the state organism, a defensive layer that could nonetheless be threatened, besieged, and opened, and thus must be guarded by state loyalists (the border patrol) with orders to shoot to kill. Nonetheless, more than 2,000 of the 50,000 border guards of the National People's Army (*Nationale Volksarmee*) and People's Marine (*Volksmarine*) became successful *Grenzverletzer* and defected. Hence even the guards could not be automatically trusted to uphold the border terrain and concomitant value system. The Stasi used informers (otherwise known as Volunteer Helpers of the Border Troops, or *Freiwillige Helfer der Grenztruppe*) to befriend and then determine border guards' reliability, and had guards sorted into categories of trustworthiness. So, according to this system of internal spying among border troops themselves, an "A" guard had to accompany a guard of a less reliable nature ("B" or "C") when on dual patrol. These categories even received the biotechnical nickname of "blood groups" (*Blutgruppen*).[72] Berlin's border guards had their little cement doors in the *Grenzmauer-75* slab version of the outer Wall to go make repairs or paint over graffiti on the side to the West (since the exterior side of the Wall was still on GDR territory). Yet these *Mauertore* caused no end of security headaches, with several keys from different officers needed just to open them and the ladders for repair-work kept at a distance – just in case a border guard tried to get away.[73]

Thus the Wall's piecemeal panopticism, its inability to prevent human inventiveness or subversion, let alone the GDR's problematic centralized production – all this caused holes, gaps, and rebuilding where necessary and made for a rather faulty global fault-line. The Wall was so full of punctured imperfections that one can begin to sense how a Kafkaesque paranoia could set in about unfinished building leading to the threat of invasion should collapse ensue. East German border guards conducted a series of stress-tests in 1974 on samples of the new, modernized version of the outer Wall. But the model slabs of the *Grenzmauer-75* did not fare very well. Of course the escape tests were rather theoretical since they were based on a would-be East German escapee being able to avoid the system of informants living in the border communities, penetrate through the entire border terrain and reach the outer Wall in the first place. Yet the tests' results showed that it was indeed possible to smash part of the Wall down with a truck; break through it with explosives, or scale it with a ladder.[74] On 8 April, 1978, a West German police car accident inadvertently proved the outer Wall's weaknesses; a photo taken by an East German border guard displays the flimsy nature of the world's barrier and the nonchalant curiosity of children who look as if they would have stepped into the no-man's-land if the border guard had not been standing there (Fig. 4.6).

Indeed, what the GDR government feared most about the West was that the latter's influence would keep coming in, uninvited: un-jammable West German radio and television, for example, kept on infiltrating most of the East German states, giving rise to a "second public" discourse.[75] Any border displaying such a closed-cum-permeable front would eventually produce its own level of schizophrenic absurdity. Schneider's narrator realizes that even if one crosses the Wall, as he does on his multiple visits to East Berlin, all one finds on the other side is a series of unwelcome resemblances. *The Wall Jumper* even spoofs Wall tourism for its competitive scopism: a tour group in the West starts waving at a tour group looking at them on the eastern side of the Wall, and the latter waves back. Even more ironically, the tour buses for both groups are run by the same travel company. Then both groups watch the watchtower guards in the middle watching them, all using their binoculars. Or again, when the narrator watches the TV news, he switches from West to East German coverage of the same events and finds mirror-language at work, each interpretation suiting the respective ideological system's needs. Again, ironically, the two male newscasters apparently have the same tie, haircut, and jacket.[76] The sheer reductionism of the mirroring detailed here is an urban version of the global one of the era: *Reader's Digest* narratives, especially from the late 1940s to the late 1960s, would shower the American public with representations of the Soviet Other as the sheer opposite of all American ideals – just in case anyone would ever figure out that they were not all that different, after all.[77]

The Wall's sad farce as a barrier is also pointed up by Herr Lehmann, the protagonist of the eponymous post-Wall novel by Sven Regener,

Figure 4.6   West German police car accident at the Wall, 8 April, 1978

when he lectures his West German parents for having expressed distaste for the idea of living in "all shut in" in West Berlin: "It's the other people in the East who have the problem. The idea of the thing [the Wall] is not that we can't get out, but that they can't get in. In which case, of course, for them, then, it would be getting out."[78] Ultimately it seemed that all the Wall really did was present a challenge that had to be crossed (even if only in the imagination), a transgression that must be enacted, not unlike the joke about the reason for the chicken crossing the road. Thus the firmer the barrier, the stronger becomes the human urge to conquer its law. This is seen in Schneider's anecdote about the compulsive Wall crosser, Herr Kabe, who admits as his rationale that "he had come for his own sake, that he had simply wanted to get to the other side" of the border. The narrator of *The Wall Jumper* even imagines what wall-crossers would talk about if they ever met: not so much the ideological whys and wherefores of jumping but, in all likelihood, the techniques needed for the feat, like mountaineers discussing ascent approaches. Schneider's narrator notes that even among East Berliners with no interest in jumping the Wall, "every improvement in the border system had spurred the creative drive to find a new loophole." It seemed, then, that "the urge to master the Wall" was as basic as the urge to climb a mountain: "[T]he Wall, like the mountain, was there; and the challenge would persist as long as the Wall remained standing."[79] A moment of Schneideresque absurdity came in 1988 at the Lenné Dreieck, a piece of land that had been excluded from the East German side of the Wall even though it was in that sector. When the Berlin Senate received the Dreieck in a border land exchange with East Germany, protesters from West Berlin camped out on it to prevent its use for a north-south freeway. To escape police, some of the protestors climbed over the Wall into East Berlin (and were sent back home again).[80]

The challenge of the Wall continued at its collapse, as well, with the physical engagement of the "Wall-peckers" (*Mauerspechte*) wanting to conquer it with a chisel or pick-axe and taking pieces of it away (and selling them). With Glasnost in the USSR, the porosity in the Wall's structure had finally entered its last phase of transformation. Signals were already being sent when President Ronald Reagan's speech at the Brandenburg Gate in June 1987 ("Mr. Gorbachev, tear down this wall") was matched by an utterance by USSR Secretary Gorbachev in March 1988, during a state dinner in Yugoslavia ("We are interested in eliminating the divisions of Europe").[81] In the last year of the GDR's existence more than 229,000 of its citizens fled the country via Hungary (whose border with Austria was opened in May) and Czechoslovakia (until the GDR shut the East German-Czech border in September after the West German embassy in Prague had been occupied by over 5,000 East Germans, who were allowed to go to the West in specially ordered "freedom trains"). The softening of the Polish-German border led to the burgeoning of unofficial cross-border trade at the so-called Polish Market (*Polenmarkt*) on West Berlin's Reichpietschufer near Potsdamer Platz.[82] Thus the Wall was coming to an end as it had begun, with a massive wave of out-migration from the East to the West.

It is in this context that we can best understand the comments of former GDR Major Peter Bochmann, employed in the passport control section at the border crossing point (*Grenzübergangsstelle*) Friedrichstraße/ Zimmerstraße (Checkpoint Charlie), as he recalls what happened at that border crossing in the fall of 1989. In one incident from mid-October, Bochmann encountered a would-be Wall crosser, a drunk East German male who simply wished, in effect, to feel as free as Schneider's Herr Kabe – but this was occurring right at the time of the massive, peaceful protest marches across East German cities, originating in Leipzig, and so the border was becoming something an inebriated young man could now challenge.[83] The man told Bochmann that he just wanted to "walk over to West Berlin" and then "return." Bochmann remonstrated with the man who "refused to go home and insisted on crossing the border immediately," whereupon Bochmann arrested him for a few hours until the man sobered up and apologized. A few weeks later on 9 November, however, alarm at the checkpoints was signaled to the border guards at 9.33pm. Thanks to Günter Schabowski's apparent slip-up during an answer to a journalist during a press conference two and a half hours earlier, regarding the timing of a new law permitting applications for East Germans to travel ("right now, without delay" [*sofort, unverzüglich*]), and the broadcast of his announcement on the evening TV news on both sides of the Wall, crowds were demanding entry to the West via all of Berlin's checkpoints. Yet rather than focus on the demand from his compatriots to cross over, Bochmann repeatedly refers to the possibility of Checkpoint Charlie being overwhelmed not by the East German crowds trying to get through to the West, but by what he deemed to be the larger crowds on the western side trying to come through to the East and goading GDR citizens to behave in disloyal ways; and they were now joined by East Berliners seeking re-entry, having already entered West Berlin via other checkpoints. In other words, before even the first person was allowed to cross through this particular gate into the West, its directionality had already become multiple, with East Berliners already on the other side. Bochmann and his fellow guards were put in the position of opening an essentially imploded gate, one that had become opened from other points in the city and thus had already lost its meaning. Not without a certain pride, Bochmann relates how he kept peaceful order and insisted that the crowds first obtain their exit visas from the local police station and then return to cross through the gate.[84] Nonetheless, agency at the Wall had finally become so strong that people could demand its opening.

We come to realize that to truly see Germany's border, then as now, is to sense its multivalent condition. In their ethnographic-photographic study *Here. Archived Time-Space* (*Hier. Archivierter Zeitraum*, 2006), Ulrike Brückner, Helga Kurzchalia, and Angelika Barz offer interviewee perspectives from all of Germany's multiple border communities, not just at the former Wall or along the former inner national divide, but along the lines that delineate Germany from the Czech Republic, Poland, Denmark, the Netherlands, Austria, Switzerland, Belgium, Luxembourg, and France.[85] Perhaps Ernst Bloch's analysis of the human territorial boundary can suggest best of all how the border challenged the city of Berlin, Berliners, and by extension Germans on each side of the Curtain to go beyond: "The border is simultaneously a separation and an opening: the initial place at the border is the antechamber of what lies beyond." For Bloch, this is why each and every border is to be differentiated one from another. The site of this antechamber itself can suffice, he states, to "open the door to an entire country" (*ein ganzes Land auftun*).[86]

Notes

1. Franz Kafka, "Vor dem Gesetz," *Selbstwehr. Unabhängige jüdische Wochenzeitschrift* 9.32 (1915), 2a-3, p. 3.
2. Günter Grass, *Ein weites Feld. Roman* (Göttingen: Steidl, 1995/ Munich: dtv, 1997), p. 11. Recommended secondary sources on the Berlin Wall and the inner German border include: Olaf Briese, forthcoming: *Steinzeit. Mauern in Berlin* (Berlin: Matthes & Seitz, 2011); Patrick Major, *Behind the Berlin Wall: East Germany and the Frontiers of Power* (New York: Oxford University Press, 2010); Deutsches Nationalkomitee für Denkmalschutz, ed., *Die Berliner Mauer. Vom Sperrwall zum Denkmal*, 76.1 (Bühl/Baden: KONKORDIA, 2009); Edgar Wolfrum, *Die Mauer. Geschichte einer Teilung* (Munich: C.H. Beck, 2009); Wieland Führ, *Berliner Mauer und innerdeutsche Grenze 1945–1990* (Petersberg: Imhof, 2008); Peter Bender, *Deutschlands Wiederkehr. Eine ungeteilte Nachkriegsgeschichte 1945–1990* (Stuttgart: Klett-Cotta, 2007); Hans-Hermann Hertle, *Die Berliner Mauer – Monument des Kalten Krieges* (Berlin: Ch. Links, 2007); Frederick Taylor, *The Berlin Wall: A World Divided, 1961–1989* (New York: HarperCollins, 2006); Maren Ullrich, *Geteilte Ansichten. Erinnerungslandschaft deutsch-deutsche Grenze* (Berlin: Aufbau Verlag, 2006); Axel Klausmeier and Leo Schmidt, *Mauerreste – Mauerspuren. Der umfassende Führer zur Berliner Mauer* (Berlin: Westkreuz Verlag, 2004); Roman Grafe, *Die Grenze durch Deutschland. Eine Chronik von 1945 bis 1990* (Berlin: Siedler, 2002); Thomas Flemming and Hagen Koch, *Die Berliner Mauer. Geschichte eines politischen Bauwerks* (Berlin: be.bra verlag, 1999); Dietmar Schultke,*"Keiner kommt durch". Die Geschichte der innerdeutschen Grenze, 1945–1990* (Berlin: Aufbau, 1999); Polly Feversham and Leo Schmidt, *Berliner Mauer heute: Denkmalwert und Umgang/The Berlin Wall Today: Cultural Significance and Conservation Issues* (Berlin: Bauwesen, 1999); Jürgen Ritter and Peter Joachim Lapp, *Grenze: Ein deutsches Bauwerk* (Berlin: Links, 1997); and Peter Wyden, *Wall: The Inside Story of Divided Berlin* (New York: Simon & Schuster, 1989).
3. Henri Lefebvre, *The Production of Space*, trans. Donald Nicholson-Smith (Cambridge, MA: Blackwell, 1991), pp. 44, 54, 164.

4. Andreas W. Daum, *Kennedy in Berlin. Politik, Kultur und Emotionen im Kalten Krieg* (Paderborn: Ferdinand Schöningh, 2003), pp. 8, 37.
5. See Wilfriede Otto, "Weichenstellung für den Mauerbau. Unterredung zwischen Nikita S. Chruschtschow und John F. Kennedy am 3. und 4. Juni in Wien," in Daniel Küchenmeister, ed., *Der Mauerbau. Krisenverlauf – Weichenstellung – Resultate* (Berlin: Berliner Debatte, 2001), pp. 116–43, pp. 127, 124.
6. On the mass emigration of East Germans in the 1950s and its enabling-impact on those who stayed, see Corey Ross, "Before the Wall: East Germans, Communist Authority, and the Mass Exodus to the West," *The Historical Journal*, 45.2 (2002), pp. 459–80.
7. Regarding Ullbricht's degree of antonomy in prompting Khrushchev's order, see Hope M. Harrison's *Driving the Soviets Up the Wall: Soviet-East German Relations, 1953–1961* (Princeton: Princeton University Press, 2003), pp. 139–223; and Matthias Uhl, "Mauerbau. Ein eiserner Ring um Berlin," *Die Zeit*, 24 (4 June, 2009). See also Manfred Wilke, *Der Weg zur Mauer. Stationen der Teilungsgeschichte* (Berlin: Christof Links Verlag, forthcoming in 2011).
8. In his memoirs, Willy Brandt related how news of the Wall was received as a "relief," or at least a "lesser evil," by the West. Brandt, *Erinnerungen* (Frankfurt am Main: Propyläen, 1989), p. 60.
9. Maurice Blanchot, "The Name Berlin," orig. 1961, trans. Aris Fiorestos, *Alphabet City*, 6 (1998): pp. 308–11, pp. 309, 308, 310.
10. Bundesarchiv Koblenz, B 137 6418, West Berlin police report (S Nr. 60/1971, Kommando 1, Schutzpolizei, April 1971). In the early 1970s the German Democratic Republic expanded its border area by an additional 26 per cent of adjacent communities; see Wilfriede Otto, "Spannungsfeld 13. August, 1961," in Küchenmeister, ed., *Der Mauerbau*, pp. 6–43, p. 39.
11. "The World: East Germany's Border Barriers," *Time Magazine* (22 January, 1973). The *Volksarmee*, an East German military magazine, had first outlined the forthcoming "modern securing of the border" in an article in volume 51 (1964); this was noticed by the West German government in the spring of 1965; Bundesarchiv Koblenz, "Grenze zur DDR (Demarkationslinie). Vorkommnisse an der Sektorengrenze in Berlin. Bd. 2: 1972–1977," B 137 8118. For an explanation of the modernization stages of the inner German border, see William E. Stacy, *U.S. Army Border Operations in Germany 1945–1983* (Military History Office, 1984), available at the US Army Center of Military History (CMH) website at: www.history.army.mil/documents/borderops/ch6.htm (date accessed 2 March, 2009).
12. For a list of Wall victims year by year see the website "Chronik der Mauer" of the Bundeszentrale für politische Bildung, at: www.chronik-der-mauer. de/index.php/opfer/Start/Index/id/593792 (date accessed 11 May, 2010). For comparative data on the still-varying statistics of victims of the German-German border (currently estimated between 270 and over 1,000), see Hans-Hermann Hertle and Gerhard Sälter, "Die Todesopfer an Mauer und Grenze," *Deutschland Archiv*, 39.4 (2008), pp. 667–76. According to the *Arbeitsgemeinschaft 13. August* organization (run by the Checkpoint Charlie museum), there were 1,065 crossing deaths overall at the Iron Curtain, including 484 at the GDR's border with the FRG; 65 deaths at its borders with socialist third countries like Czechoslovakia; and 181 drownings in the

Ostsee. See also Nicholas Kulish, "The Cold War's Back Door: Out of East Germany via Bulgaria," *The New York Times* (25 March, 2008).

13. Rem Koolhaas, "Field Trip," in Koolhaas and Bruce Mau, *S, M, L, XL* (New York: Monacelli Press, 1995), p 214–32, p. 222; emphasis original. Johann Wolfgang von Goethe, *Faust I* (orig. 1806–1829) (Frankfurt am Main: Fischer, 2008), line 1700.

14. Koolhaas, "Field Trip," in Koolhaas and Mau, *S, M, L, XL*, pp. 225, 219–220; emphasis original. On the Wall's stages toward perfection see Schultke, *"Keiner kommt durch"*, pp. 80–83.

15. Neil Leach, "Berlin 1961–89: The Bridal Chamber," in Leach, ed., *Architecture and Revolution: Contemporary Perspectives on Central and Eastern Europe* (New York: Routledge, 1999), pp. 209–18, p. 216.

16. See Gert Mattenklott, "Entgrenzungen. Die Mauer im Museum," in Markus Bauer and Thomas Rahn, eds, *Die Grenze. Begriff und Inszenierung* (Berlin: Akademie Verlag, 1997), pp. 255–59, pp. 255–56.

17. Stefan Jacobs, "Neue Grenzerfahrung: Jede Laterne ist verdächtig," *Der Tagesspiegel* (13 August, 2003).

18. See Eyal Weizman, *Hollow Land: Israel's Architecture of Occupation* (London and New York: Verso, 2007).

19. Steinstücken had been part of the borough of Wannsee since the formation of Greater Berlin in 1920, a clause which enabled the Federal Republic to insist to the Americans that it was worthy of keeping as part of West Berlin when initial US backing to keep the enclave seemed to waiver in June 1963. Bundesarchiv Koblenz, "Berlinfrage. Allgemeine Rechtslage, insbes. Berlin-Status, Mauerbau 13.8.61. 1962–1969," B 137 5906.

20. André Steiner, "Eine wirtschaftliche Bilanz der Mauer," in Hans-Hermann Hertle, Konrad Jarausch, and Christoph Kleßmann, eds, *Mauerbau und Mauerfall. Ursache – Verlauf – Nachwirkungen* (Berlin: Links Verlag, 2002), pp. 189–202, p. 198. See also Rüdiger Görner, *Mauer, Schatten, Gerüst. Kulturkritische Versuche* (Tübingen: Klöpfer & Meyer, 1999), p. 96; and Dietmar Schultke, *"Keiner kommt durch"*, pp. 93–94.

21. Brian Ladd, *The Ghosts of Berlin: Confronting German History in the Urban Landscape* (Chicago: University of Chicago Press, 1997), p. 19.

22. Koolhaas, "Field Trip," in Koolhaas and Mau, *S, M, L, XL*, p. 227; emphasis original.

23. Heiner Müller, "Walls/Mauern. Interview mit Sylvère Lotringer," in Müller, *Rotwelsch* (Berlin: Merve, 1982), pp. 9–87, p. 58.

24. Durs Grünbein, "Transit Berlin," trans. Andrew Shields, in Jean Stein, ed., *Grand Street 69*, 18.1 (New York: Grand Street Press, 1999; New York Foundation for the Arts), pp. 85–89, p. 87.

25. Bundesarchiv Militärarchiv Freiburg: GT 5778, Grenzkommando Mitte, Einrichtung einer Mülldeponie in Groß-Ziethen, June 1972–May 1974. That same landfill would later receive the waste from the construction of the new Potsdamer Platz. The landfill's contaminants and gases have since been painstakingly removed: "Sicherung der Altablagerung Großziethen. Ein Überblick," *Amtsblatt für den Landkreis Dahme-Spreewald*, 16.12 (1 July, 2009), pp. 1–2. See also Christof Ellger, "Berlin: Legacies of Division and Problems of Unification," *The Geographical Journal*, 158.1 (1992), pp. 40–46, p. 44.

26. On West Berlin's non-heroic, contrived state of normalcy, see David E. Barclay, "A 'Complicated Contrivance': West Berlin Behind the Wall, 1971–1989," forthcoming in Marc Silberman, Karen E. Till, and Janet Ward, eds, *Walls, Borders, Boundaries: Spatial and Cultural Practices in Europe* (Oxford and New York: Berghahn Books, 2012).

27. Edith Preuss, "The Wall You Will Never Know," *Perspecta*, 36 (2005), pp. 19–31.

28. Leach, "Berlin 1961–89," in Leach, ed., *Architecture and Revolution*, p. 216.

29. Lutz Rathenow and Harald Hauswald, *Ostberlin: Die andere Seite der Stadt in Texten und Bildern* (Munich: Piper, 1987), p. 154; cited by Ladd, *The Ghosts of Berlin*, p. 30, n. 18.

30. Ladd, *The Ghosts of Berlin*, pp. 30, 33.

31. Bruno Latour and Emilie Hermant, *Paris ville invisible* (Paris: La Découverte, 1998); Jeremy Bentham, *Panopticon: or, The Inspection-House: Containing the Idea of a New Principle of Construction Applicable to Any Sort of Establishment, in which Persons of Any Description Are to Be Kept under Inspection; and in Particular to Penitentiary-Houses, Prisons, Houses of Industry, Work-Houses, Poor-Houses, Manufactories, Mad-Houses, Lazarettos, Hospitals, and Schools*, in Bentham, *The Panopticon Writings* (New York: Verso, 1995); and Michel Foucault, *Discipline and Punish: The Birth of the Prison*, trans. Alan Sheridan (New York: Random House, 1991). On the oligopticon, see Chris Otter's landmark book, *The Victorian Eye: A Political History of Light and Vision in Britain, 1800–1910* (Chicago: University of Chicago Press, 2008), p. 5.

32. See Benjamin Drechsel, "The Berlin Wall from a Visual Perspective: Comments on the Construction of a Political Media Icon," *Visual Communication*, 9.1 (2010), pp. 3–24.

33. Wim Wenders and Peter Handke, *Der Himmel über Berlin. Ein Filmbuch* (Frankfurt am Main: Suhrkamp, 1987), p. 46; Wim Wenders, dir., *Der Himmel über Berlin* (Paris: Road Movies Berlin and Argos Films, 1987).

34. Daphne Berdahl showed these processes at work in the East German Thuringia border community of Kella: Berdahl, *Where the World Ended: Re-Unification and Identity in the German Borderland* (Berkeley: University of California Press, 1999). See also Edith Sheffer, forthcoming: *Burned Bridge: How East and West Germans Made the Iron Curtain* (Oxford University Press, 2011).

35. See Landolf Scherzer, *Der Grenz-Gänger* (Berlin: Aufbau-Verlag, 2005); and Muriel Blaive and Thomas Lindenberger, "Border Guarding as Spatial Practice: A Case Study of Czech Communist Governance and Hidden Transcripts," forthcoming in Silberman, Till, and Ward, eds, *Walls, Borders, Boundaries*.

36. Neukölln police file nr. 215, "Lagebericht PI Nk-/61" (22 September, 1961); cited in Ulf Mann, *Tunnelfluchten. Grenzgänger. Verräter. Wühlmäuse* (Berlin: Transit, 2005), pp. 54–56.

37. Pressedienst des Landes Berlin, "Die Situation an der Schandmauer. Ein Bericht des Senators Heinrich Albertz vor dem Abgeordnetenhaus" (15 November, 1962). Bundesarchiv Koblenz, B 137 5906, "Berlinfrage. Allgemeine Rechtslage, insbes. Berlin-Status, Mauerbau 13.8.61, 1962–1969." See also the USIA (United States Information Agency)'s propaganda documentary *The Wall* (directed by Walter de Hoog, 1962).

38. Bundesarchiv Koblenz, B 137 6418, "Grenze zur DDR (Demarkationslinie). Vorkommnisse an der Sektorengrenze in Berlin, 1966–1977."

39. Edith Sheffer, "On Edge: Building the Border in East and West Germany," *Central European History*, 40 (2007): pp. 307–39, pp. 307, 339.

40. For a recording of Kennedy's speech on the Berlin Crisis on 25 July 1961, see the website of the John F. Kennedy Library and Museum in Boston, at: www. jfklibrary.org (date accessed 11 February, 2010).

41. See, for example, John Mander, *Berlin: Hostage for the West* (Baltimore/ Harmondsworth: Penguin, 1962).

42. Ladd, *The Ghosts of Berlin*, p. 26; see also Ralf Gründer, ed., *Berliner Mauerkunst. Eine Dokumentation* (Cologne: Böhlau, 2007); Nicolas Whybrow, *Street Scenes: Brecht, Benjamin and Berlin* (Bristol: intellect, 2005), pp. 143–46; Major, *Behind the Berlin Wall*, pp. 271–73; and Tim Cresswell, *In Place/Out of Place: Geography, Ideology, and Transgression* (Minneapolis: University of Minnesota, 1996), pp. 31–61. On how the Wall and inner German border were depicted by East German artists, see Anke Kuhrmann, "Grenzsituationen – Die 'Berliner Mauer' in der Kunst," in Deutsches Nationalkomitee für Denkmalschutz, ed., *Die Berliner Mauer*, pp. 117–42; and April A. Eisman, "Painting the Berlin Wall in Leipzig: The Politics of Art in 1960s East Germany," in Philip Broadbent and Sabine Hake, eds, *Berlin, Divided City 1945–1989* (Oxford and New York: Berghahn Books, 2010), pp. 69–77.

43. In 1952, *Aktion Ungeziefer* moved 11,000 East Germans from their border communities further east, and thousands more were moved away in *Aktion Festigung* in 1961. The hardening of the border in 1952 also involved blocking 200 (i.e., more than two-thirds of the) roads leading from West Berlin into Brandenburg or East Berlin. See Inge Bennewitz and Rainer Potratz, *Zwangsaussiedlungen an der innerdeutschen Grenze: Analysen und Dokumente* (Berlin: Ch. Links Verlag, 2002).

44. Flemming and Koch, *Die Berliner Mauer*, pp. 102, 110.

45. Peter Schneider, *The Wall Jumper*, trans. Leigh Hafrey (New York: Pantheon Books, 1983), p. 10.

46. Susanne Schädlich, *Immer wieder Dezember. Der Westen, die Stasi, der Onkel und ich* (Munich: Droemer, 2009), pp. 15–16.

47. Schneider, *The Wall Jumper*, pp. 12, 72.

48. Stephen Brockmann, "Divided and Reunited Berlin in Peter Schneider's Fiction," in Carol Anne Costabile-Heming, Rachel J. Halverson, and Kristie A. Foell, eds, *Berlin: The Symphony Continues. Orchestrating Architectural, Social, and Artistic Change in Germany's New Capital* (New York: Walter de Gruyter, 2004), pp. 227, 227, 230.

49. György Péteri, ed., *Nylon Curtain: Transnational and Transsystemic Tendencies in the Cultural Life of State-Socialist Russia and East-Central Europe* (Trondheim: TSEECS nr. 18, 2006). See also Greg Castillo, "The Nylon Curtain: Architectural Unification in Divided Berlin," in Broadbent and Hake, eds, *Berlin*; and Brian Ladd, "Double Restoration: Rebuilding Berlin after 1945," in Lawrence J. Vale and Thomas J. Campanella, eds, *The Resilient City: How Modern Cities Recover from Disaster* (New York: Oxford University Press, 2005), pp. 117–34.

50. Wolfgang Kil, *Land ohne Übergang. Deutschlands neue Grenze* (Berlin: ex pose verlag, 1992), pp. 58, 59, 26.

51. R. Zeidler, "Politisch-Ideologische Konzeption für eine Lindenführung," Landesarchiv Berlin: Berlin Ost C. Rep. 737, Nr. 54, Indexnr. 87, "Berlin-Information."

52. "Subversive Zentren und Organisationen, die sich in den Nachkriegsjahren in Westberlin breitmachten," *Neues Deutschland* (20 July, 1965), cited in Ulf Mann, *Tunnelfluchten. Grenzgänger. Verräter. Wühlmäuse* (Berlin: Transit, 2005), p. 86.

53. The city's length across the "independent political entity of West Berlin" was assessed at almost 42km. In: "Territoriale Beschreibung der Hauptstadt der Deutschen Demokratischen Republik. Berlin," n.d. Landesarchiv Berlin, C. Rep. 114, Magistrat von Berlin, Abteilung Verkehr, Abt. Wissenschaft, Technik, und Investititionen, Nr. 737.

54. Klaus Walther, "Berlin für Anfänger," in Walther, Peter Abraham, and Werner Liersch, eds, *Berlin. Hauptstadt der DDR. Ein Reiseverführer* (Rudolstadt: Greifenverlag, 1980), p. 10.

55. Report and notes by organizer Kurt Fugger for the travelling city-exhibition "Berlin, die Hauptstadt der DDR, grüßt Baghdad" (1975). Landesarchiv Berlin, C. Rep. 737, Berlin-Information, Nr. 94.

56. Landesarchiv Berlin, C. Rep. 737, Berlin-Information, Nr. 81: Fläche 11.

57. Thomas J. Misa, "Retrieving Sociotechnical Change from Technological Determinism," in Merritt Roe Smith and Leo Marx, eds, *Does Technology Drive History? The Dilemma of Technological Determinism* (Cambridge, MA: MIT Press, 1994), pp. 115–42.

58. Simon Gunn, "Illuminating the Victorian City," *History and Technology*, 26.2 (2010), pp. 151–56, p. 154. See also Timothy Mitchell on the "mixed way that things happen." Timothy Mitchell, *Rule of Experts: Egypt, Techno-Politics, Modernity* (Berkeley: University of California Press, 2002), p. 52; cited by Gunn, "Illuminating the Victorian City," p. 154.

59. Olaf Briese, "Pfusch am Bau. Beiträge zur Baugeschichte der 'Berliner Mauer'," *Zeitschrift für Geschichtswissenschaft*, 57 (2009), pp. 613–36; and Briese, " Wartungsarm und formschön'. Zur Ästhetik der 'Berliner Mauer'," *Weimarer Beiträge*, 55.3 (2009), pp. 430–54.

60. Koolhaas, "Field Trip," in Koolhaas and Mau, *S, M, L, XL*, p. 219.

61. Peter Weigert, "Neue Türme, neue Zäune – und kaum noch Kontakte," *Frankfurter Allgemeine Zeitung* (27 May, 1969).

62. Bundesarchiv Militärarchiv Freiburg, GTÜ 007504: Grenzkommando Mitte; Analyse, Berichte und Protokolle über die Standfestigkeit der Grenzmauer und Sperranlagen, Februar 1974–April 1974.

63. Bundesarchiv Militärarchiv Freiburg, GTÜ 013244, Grenzkommando Mitte, Entwicklung und Erprobung einer Grenzmauer neuen Typs (Grenzmauer-75).

64. Briese, "Pfusch am Bau," p. 630. See also Wolfgang Rathje, *"Mauer-Marketing" unter Erich Honecker. Schwierigkeiten der DDR bei der technischen Modernisierung, der volkswirtschaftlichen Kalkulation und der politischen Akzeptanz der Berliner "Staatsgrenze" von 1971—1990*, 2 vols., PhD dissertation (Kiel: Department of Philosophy, Christian-Albrechts-Universität zu Kiel, 2001).

65. Stephen Graham and Nigel Thrift, "Out of Order: Understanding Repair and Maintenance," *Theory, Culture and Society*, 24.3 (2007), pp. 1–25, p. 6.

66. Nigel Thrift, "Raum," trans. Holger Steinmann and Daniel Seibel, in Jörg Döring and Tristan Thielmann, eds, *Spatial Turn. Das Raumparadigma*

in den Kultur- und Sozialwissenschaften (Bielefeld: transcript Verlag, 2008), p. 397.

67. Lefebvre, *The Production of Space*, p. 176. See also Whybrow, *Street Scenes*, p. 137.

68. Hans-Hermann Hertle, Konrad H. Jarausch, and Christoph Kleßmann, "Die fatale Stabilisierung. Einleitung," in Hertle, Jarausch, and Kleßmann, eds, *Mauerbau und Mauerfall*, pp. 9–18, p. 16.

69. The "great escape" tale was updated in the movie *Der Tunnel* directed by Roland Suso Richter (Teamworx for SAT.1/Beta Cinema, 2001).

70. Bundesarchiv Militärarchiv Freiburg, GTÜ 017790, Kommando der Grenztruppen, Meldung und Materialien zum Ausbau der Staatsgrenze, December 1982–June 1983.

71. Bundesarchiv Koblenz, B 137 / 6418, "Grenze zur DDR (Demarkationslinie). Vorkommnisse an der Sektorengrenze in Berlin. Bd. 1: 1966–1977."

72. Peter Joachim Lapp, "Grenzsicherung," in Küchenmeister, ed., *Der Mauerbau*, pp. 105–6. See also Schultke, *"Keiner kommt durch,"* pp. 121–24.

73. Report by Oberstleutnant Parche on 2 June 1980 to the commander of Berlin's Grenzkommando Mitte. Bundesarchiv Militärarchiv Freiburg: GTÜ 013245, Grenzkommando Mitte, Erprobungen der Grenzmauer-75, eines Mauertores und neuer Panzerhöcker, 1980.

74. Bundesarchiv Militärarchiv Freiburg: GTÜ 013245, Grenzkommando Mitte, Erprobungen der Grenzmauer-75, eines Mauertores und neuer Panzerhöcker, 1980.

75. Hertle, Jarausch, and Kleßmann, "Die fatale Stabilisierung," in Hertle, Jarausch, and Kleßmann, eds, *Mauerbau und Mauerfall*, pp. 16–17. See also Patrick Major, who considers the various border "loopholes" caused by West German radio and TV, as well as the pressure placed on the closed border system by would-be East German "emigrationists" in *Behind the Berlin Wall*, pp. 170–76, 188–93, 208–17.

76. Schneider, *The Wall Jumper*, pp. 12, 72, 26–27, 28; see also pp. 70–71.

77. John Agnew, *Geopolitics: Re-Visioning World Politics* (New York: Routledge, 2003), p. 106.

78. Sven Regener, *Herr Lehmann* (Frankfurt am Main.: Eichborn AG, 2001), p. 183. For reminiscences of West Berliners as border-crossers on the transit routes, see Jürgen Kleindienst, ed., *Mauer-Passagen. Grenzgänge, Flüchten und Reisen 1961–1989. 48 Erinnerungen aus Ost und West* (Berlin: Zeitgut Verlag, 2003).

79. Schneider, *The Wall Jumper*, pp. 31, 58–59, 59–60.

80. For a listing of all the exchanged areas along the Berlin-Berlin border, see Gerhard Kunze, *Grenzerfahrungen. Kontakte und Verhandlungen zwischen dem Land Berlin und der DDR 1949–1988* (Berlin: Akademie Verlag, 1999), pp. 490–91.

81. William F. Buckley, Jr., *The Fall of the Berlin Wall* (New York: Wiley, 2004), p. 139.

82. Uwe Rada, *Zwischenland. Europäische Geschichten aus dem deutsch-polnischen Grenzgebiet* (Berlin: bre.bra verlag, 2004), p. 82.

83. Gareth Dale, *Popular Protest in East Germany, 1945–1989* (New York: Routledge, 2005), pp. 151–67.

84. "Peter Bochmann's Commentaries. Thoughts Concerning the 9th of November." Peter Bochmann Archive (Wall/Checkpoint Collection), The Wende Museum and Archive of the Cold War, Los Angeles.

85. Ulrike Brückner, Helga Kurzchalia, and Angelika Barz, *Hier. Archivierter Zeitraum* (Rotterdam: Veenman Publishers, 2006).

86. Bloch, *Literary Essays,* trans. Andrew Joron et al. (Stanford: Stanford University Press, 1998), p. 445; Bloch, *Literarische Aufsätze*, Gesamtausgabe, vol. 9 (Frankfurt am Main: Suhrkamp, 1965), p. 502.

5
Post-Wall Resurrections

> *Pinkeln sich ein Ostberliner und ein Westberliner Hund an,*
> *sagt der eine zum anderen: »Komisch, da war doch früher*
> *irgend etwas zwischen uns.«*
> (German reunification joke, c. 2000)

Peter Schneider's (un)canny prediction about the longevity of the "Wall in one's head," a psycho-social and psycho-geographical condition lasting longer than any concrete entity, speaks to the condition of reunified Berlin and Germany.[1] We have seen that the Berlin Wall was in place before it was built, and not surprisingly it remains after it has been dismantled, at least for a while. The former Wall deserves to be studied with renewed emphasis for the way that people shaped it, rather than the other way around. Instances of all-too-human agency, frailty, and fallibility at this ultimately flimsy and mutable border terrain certainly provide a richer perspective on Wall history than can its endlessly recycled image of static monstrous monumentality.

However, post-Wall Berlin in the eradication of its Wall has willfully dislocated itself from its own recent history. Tourists arriving in Berlin, expecting to bring away perhaps their own piece of the Wall that fits in with the popular historical narrative they have received regarding the terror of the Cold War, do not find enough Wall remnants to convincingly signal a previous reign of terror. Despite the naivety of their questions, sometimes the tourists' gaze penetrates deeper than locals want to see. Berlin's tourists, when they arrive asking the perennial question "Where was the Wall", are at least posing a question about sites that reveal rather than hide the discontinuous, often traumatic (r)evolutions of the city's past.[2] Looking for and valuing Berlin's discordant layers caused by the hot and cold wars of the twentieth century corresponds well with the palimpsest-ideals of postmodern urban planning, which "looks at the city as the result of temporal accumulations in space, a sequence in which the latest intervention takes its place."[3] Berlin's history of this is more extreme than most, and therein lies its potency.

Berlin has not done a good job of promoting these space-time accumulations to itself and to outsiders. Once I was asked, by a young French tourist beside a lonesome chunk of the Wall that had been deposited at Potsdamer Platz just outside the S-Bahn station at the Beisheim Center, "which side [of the Wall] was East and which side was West?" He was right: it was hard to tell. Nowadays the memento has been extended to include additional slabs, information boards, and a tourist-trap chance to get a stamp of an East German visitor's visa: at least the vendor in East German border guard uniform sits on the East side of the cement slabs. How satisfying for tourists are these few remnants of the outer Wall? They appear clumsily provisional on the sidewalk, having been plopped down here to better mark the line marker in the ground that tracks the path of the former Wall in central Berlin (Fig. 5.1). Capitalism has built over Berlin's borders: the Marriott hotel at the Beisheim Center was constructed quite literally over the Wall-line. Disorientation abounds: apart from the four and a half miles of line-marker in the city's center, the path of the Wall is mostly obliterated. Its actual trajectory often comes as a complete surprise to visitors. Above all, many non-Berliners cannot get their heads around a dividing Wall that went around the western edges of the city, and not just through its center. The concept that East and West met at a western edge of a city is still hard for many to fathom. An American tourist standing for the first time on the Glienicke Bridge, famous as an exchange-site for Cold War spies, was astonished that this former border-point was not actually in the middle of Berlin, as a literal bridge between East and West.[4]

Germany's reunification is not necessarily a success that can be appended onto Cold Warrior narratives of victory over communism. A high school principal in Köpenick (former East Berlin) complained that his students no longer find the annual German Unity Day to be of any closer personal significance than World War II. Most young Germans' sense of togetherness, like any lingering sense of ongoing division among adult Germans, is based on ignorance of where the border was; but is this the best way forward?[5] The Berlin high school students' inability to care about their country's pre-1989 division is an indication of how German reunification moved too quickly. "Communicative memory," as cultural theorist Jan Assmann asserts in his Platonic memory model, is about immediacy and feeling; it is the

Figure 5.1 Slabs of the outer Wall (type UL 12.11 of the *Grenzmauer-75*) placed along the line-marker in the sidewalk, Potsdamer Platz, Berlin, 2010

form of "autopoetic" memory emphasized by Maurice Halbwachs. For Assmann, communicative memory usually comes before the more subsequent forms of "cultural memory," the displaced, mediated, institutionalized, and mythologizing rituals of the collective, which have both didactic and liberating functions, as Friedrich Nietzsche and Aby Warburg respectively noted. In most circumstances, forms of cultural memory are left to invoke – as Assmann says, "write" in the broadest sense of the word – the past after the first practitioners of communicative memory have contributed their piece as the most obvious, everyday players most closely connected to that history.[6] In Berlin's case after 1989, however, that first stage of urban collective memory, the communicative phase, was done away with too quickly. The former GDR was subsumed in its entirety, a move symbolized precisely in the felling of the Wall. Assmann states:

> Cultural memory, in contrast to communicative memory, encompasses the age-old, out-of-the-way, and discarded; and in contrast to

collective, bonding memory, it includes the noninstrumentalizable, heretical, subversive, and disowned. With the concept of cultural memory we have reached the furthest remove from our starting point: the individual memory in its neural and social conditioning factors.[7]

In short, while cultural memory is the much-needed archive, we still need communicative memory in all its lived immediacy. With the post-Wall phase of the Wall having removed the actual artifact too quickly, Berliners do not have as much to go on as they should have done. All that is left of the Wall is what can be made of it in that Platonic cave of representations. Cultural memory's distance from the Light is not at all a bad thing, however, since it fosters, at least theoretically, a sense of communal identity. Assmann perceives that "cultural memory disseminates and reproduces a consciousness of unity, particularity, and a sense of belonging among the members of a group." What happens in cultural memory is the "objectification, storing, reactivation, and circulation of meaning."[8]

In this way, when borders become officially obsolete their traces are sometimes unofficially still needed in one simulated guise or another. On 22 June, 1990, while the newly reunified Berlin was busily removing the physical traces of the Wall that had encircled the western half of the city, the American guardhouse at Checkpoint Charlie was hoisted up high by a crane and taken away on a flatbed truck. It was a telegenic scene: the staged dismantling of part of the Iron Curtain at one of its most highly charged crossing points. The ceremony was attended by the foreign ministers of the two German states and the four Allied countries of World War II. The East German guardhouse on the Communist side of the former border line was removed without world cameras half a year later. Yet by 2000, a copy of the Allied guardhouse was back in place: the popularity of Checkpoint Charlie for the purposes of what can now be understood as "communist heritage tourism" had necessitated its resurrection, or at least its simulacrum.[9] This second-generation replica hut is replete with sandbags and even student actors nonchalantly posing as Allied and East German border guards in return for a euro. The original structure stands somewhat forlornly in front of the Allied Museum in Berlin-Zehlendorf.[10] It would seem, then, that the degradation of Cold War border memory in the capitalistic service of Berlin's tourism trade is complete.

The ex-Wall is enjoying a thriving afterlife, at least as far as the tourist trade is concerned. Concomitantly, an overall academic and public interest in the contexts and practices of borders has been growing after the most severe territorial division of the industrialized world has been safely overcome. Yet it is a boom that did not come in time for even a respectable segment of fully preserved Wall terrain to be kept intact. By 1994 practically all the nation's border installations had been removed. In today's Berlin, traces of the Wall are not easy to find. Only twenty-six Wall sites are under the city's official protection, even though there are just under a thousand unprotected, often unrecognized and unrecognizable Wall remnants across the Berlin region.[11]

How did this happen? When the Wall was finally punctured and torn down, the last thing on most Berliners' and Germans' minds was keeping that eyesore line of Cold War memory. Just as all of Europe after World War II wanted to "forget the recent past and to forge a *new* continent," so too in the wake of the Wall negative, wounded memory was not what was wanted.[12] Daniel Libeskind, in a lecture given in 1997 at Humboldt University, uttered some wishful thinking with respect to bringing the Wall to mind in the re-building of Berlin. He spoke of the "peculiar site that is the seam between East and West" as an "emblem of a common ground and a confession – killing fields of a kind – framing the Brandenburg Gate"; his hope was that the "stratagems of architecture" could become "institutionalized on the principles of the transformation of being and recollection."[13]

Instead, the city sought out a different image for itself. A recent example of past ruptures being seamlessly smoothed over occurred in a TV commercial (*Imagespot*) about the city that was aired on CNN's international networks in the build-up to the twentieth anniversary of the fall of the Wall in November 2009. Even though the ad was designed to coincide with the anniversary celebrations, something was left out. The fall of the Wall was neither shown nor mentioned. Instead, in a somewhat reminiscent nod to the Blair government's rebranding of London as "Cool Britannia," scenes of the trendy New Berlin flashed by as the commercial's British-accented narrator described the German capital as "special ... the place to be"; "come and find out," he invites, "what we've made of our city."

If we examine the sediment at stake here (that is, what this ad leaves out), we find that the city's history of division and its ongoing Wall-legacy are the factors that still project themselves onto its contemporary fabric. They remain Berlin's deeper level of globalizing factors – stronger, indeed, than the pre-World-War II world-city status that the last two decades of rebuilding would like to recapture. The city that Berlin aspires to be in the contemporary global era is, inevitably, still tied as much to its divided era as to its "whole" era – to its role as cut-up pawn on the world stage of the Cold War; just as this significance is itself derived from what may be termed the German nation's perceived punishment in the bombed-out ruins in World War II. No wonder, then, that the TV ad, aiming at marketing Berlin as a city of eternal youth, left that out.

The swift destruction of the Wall terrain in 1989 and 1990 should give us pause. Its slabs were rapidly auctioned off and sold as mementos, as well as ground up and recycled for use in street works. It was dismantled by the same border troops who had guarded it. The energy and speed with which the Wall was removed from the city indicate how affect-ridden this last act of agency at the Wall really was. We can recall how GDR-dissident folk singer Wolf Biermann once reconfigured the Cold War's geopolitics in his homage to Heinrich Heine, "Germany, a Fairy Tale" (*Deutschland. Ein Wintermärchen*, 1964–1972). Divided Germany became, thanks to the Iron Curtain that ran through it, the "arse of the world," sang Biermann. And Berlin, the "hole" or rectum of that global divide signified by the two German states, was "divided within itself."[14] Biermann's song extends the metaphor right back to the original feces-"brown" of the Nazi movement that receives the blame for Germany having to serve in the first place as the stage for the excremental phenomena of Cold War politics. A post-(Wall-)script to Biermann – a release from this disgust, in a way – came with *Heroes Like Us* (*Helden wie wir*, 1995), a novel by Thomas Brussig. Here, magic realism dictates events as the East German hero Klaus effectively depoliticizes the Cold War, rendering thereby former enmities absurd and any guilt innocent. He achieves this by flashing his hugely enlarged penis at the border guards at the Wall on 9 November, 1989, causing them to remain stupefied while the crowds breach the checkpoint and enter West Berlin.[15] The "hero like us" has inadvertently caused the fall of the Berlin Wall as part of a Dionysian sexual rush of the masses.

Today there is more of the Wall outside of Berlin than in it.[16] Coffee-table books like *The Berlin Wall in the World* (*Die Berliner Mauer in der Welt*) showcase the ways in which the ex-Wall's cement slabs have come to take on afterlives in multiple commemorative contexts.[17] Las Vegas, my somewhat unusual university town, is no exception. In fact, we have two, of which only one is proper. One section of the Wall is exhibited at the Atomic Testing Museum, a recent Smithsonian affiliate that since 2005 has been inviting the public to re-visit not just the casinos but the immensely significant role of Nevada in planning the Cold War and the nuclear arms race. This (un)fortunate status for Nevada emerged, in part, due to the fact that 87 percent of the state's land is owned by the government. Notably, the Atomic Testing Museum's segment of the Wall is exhibited near a ruined beam fragment of the World Trade Center; their proximity suggests both the end of one Cold War and the beginning of another, as well as a neighboring interrelatedness in their symbolic remnants – and even, perhaps, a sense of hubris. The second piece of the Berlin Wall exhibited in Las Vegas appears to be much more in line with Biermann's or Brussig's indecent way of thinking. The Main Street Station Casino Hotel has slabs of it behind plexiglass located in the men's restroom – literally behind the urinals. In fact, one has little choice but to urinate "onto" the most famous Wall-divide in the world – or so I have been told.

Another case-in-point, less trendy and sexually charged but infinitely more family-oriented and cosy (*gemütlich*), was the "Fairy Tale for Berlin" (*Ein Märchen für Berlin*) enacted by giant puppets for the German Day of Unity on 3 October, 2009. The massive puppets of the French theater group Royal de Luxe rose up and "walked" a tale of Walled separation and post-Wall reunification for Berlin during the *Tag der Einheit* festivities. The puppets' sizes and genders (with the protective "uncle" in the West at more than twice the size of the "niece" in the East) reflected quite crassly upon the sizes of the two German populations at the time of the fall of the Wall (65 million West Germans; 16 million East Germans). They were, in fact, typical of an over-simplifying, strongly populist desire for closure and swift mythologization of even this recent past. This fairy-tale ending for reunified Germans (Uncle West had Niece East sitting on his knee at the Brandenburg Gate, after having lost her for so long on the other side of the urban Wall) lacks the scathing irony practiced by the German fairy tales favored by Heine, Biermann, and Brussig, and acted out by the Vegas casino restroom.

It is rather telling that the myriad citational Wall slabs that were sold and delivered worldwide do a better job of commemorating the geopolitical fault-line that the Berlin Wall once focalized (yes, even by peeing on it: at least that is interactive) than anywhere in Berlin today. A differently embodied commemoration of the Wall was planned for 9 November, 2009 by a British performance artist, Martin Butler, who invited 33,000 people to sign up online and stand in 330 groups along stretches of the former border separating West Berlin from the GDR and its capital. Unfortunately, the "Mauer Mob" project attracted more foreigners than Berliners, too few of whom actually bothered to volunteer.[18] This was rather like the forty-second anniversary of the building of the Wall which met with a desultory turn-out of participants willing to lie down in the road at Potsdamer Platz and represent what was thought to be the 899 East Germans who died trying to reach the West. Only one-tenth of the needed participants turned up.[19]

Instead, what Berliners were treated to on the twentieth anniversary of the fall of the Wall was another "giant" event: the "Domino Action." A domino-like falling down of the Berlin Wall recreated as mock-up slabs occurred as the highlight of the "Festival of Freedom" – 1,000 massive foam dominoes were toppled along a mile-long route of the former Wall next to the Brandenburg Gate. The dominoes had been painted by schoolchildren from Berlin and around the world as part of a "Wall Journey – the Wall in the World," a federally sponsored goodwill art project. It is possible that the marketing initiative behind this media-event quite consciously wished to give a new meaning to the phrase "domino effect" that used to be part of American foreign policy parlance during the Cold War. Even if it emerged initially as a coincidence, it makes sense that this particular metaphor of Cold War historical discourse could now morph into something new – all thanks to this admittedly sophomoric event that took place in the rain and caused former Solidarność founder Lech Walesa, who had been invited to push over the first domino, to suffer a spinal injury. Falling dominoes could from now on become associated with German reunification and peaceful border-opening, rather than with the need to contain the global threat of communism. At least the "Wall Project" festivities on 9 November, 2009 on Wilshire Boulevard in Los Angeles as organized by the Wende Museum used ten real Wall segments (the "longest stretch of the Wall outside Germany") along the street, in addition to an 80ft-long fake Wall bisecting it (the latter was subsequently dismantled by the party goers).[20] The commemorative barricade-party in LA can be compared to the swift police response that followed the 1962 blocking of Rue Visconti in Paris by Christo and Jeanne-Claude, when they erected a protest barricade of oil drums as a direct reaction to the building of the Berlin Wall: "Wall of Oil Barrels, Iron Curtain."

English dramatist David Hare has made a joke about Berlin's missing piece of history. He calls its absence a case of "bad marketing": namely, "the city of the famous Wall not actually having a wall."[21] This erasure makes for bad public history. To help us remember we need artifacts, signs, paths to tread, walls to touch, or voids that are at least still there: and, in the case of the Wall, at least some large segments of it that are relatively well maintained; and if that fails, just some rubble would do. Instead, all the public encounters of it is as a "shadow monument."[22] But can Wall remembrance be staged when next to no Wall is left for the public to visit? Most tourists see the messy, ruined stretch of the

Wall that is extant next to the Topography of Terror exhibition terrain, and are disappointed rather than elated at the damage that has been done to it (so much was removed, in fact, that the city put a fence on the Niederkirchnerstraße side of this Wall segment as early as 1990, and renewed the fence in 1999). Some post-Wall graffiti art on the last-remaining Wall panels near Potsdamer Platz in 2004 indicated an awareness of being erased, with bulldozers on one side and tanks on the other, and manga girls giving passers-by the cautionary tale about collective forgetting: "Don't Forget History" (Fig. 5.2). The New Berlin's boosterist forces (like Berlin Tourismus Marketing GmbH, and the marketing agency Berlin Partner) have realized this too late. But life must go on after the Fall. Thus the felling of the Wall can be likened not so much to being banished from Eden but to that which Nietzsche perceived as the intellectual conceptual killing off of God in the late nineteenth century and its unwelcome retribution: life's banality. Not so much the *fall* of the Wall as the *loss* of the ex-Wall could be seen as a loss for Berlin,

Figure 5.2 "Don't Destroy History." Post-Wall art on a last remaining original Wall remnant on the Stresemannstraße near Potsdamer Platz, Berlin, 2004

a plain reduction of its former unique and universal status to simply a banal city.

While the Wall's hasty removal was an understandable way of compensating for the trauma that it had inflicted, Svetlana Boym perceives that this demolition act has produced a "large psychic specter" that has produced a hard task: breaking down the Wall means "[b]reaking that invisible mirror or traveling through the looking glass to face cultural and economic differences."[23] For a sense of what this labored reconnection would feel like, Patrice-Loup Rifaux asks his French readers to imagine the impact on Paris of the loss of the Seine as a Cold War border. Upon reunification the two sides of the city would thus have to be "brutally reunited ... in a sort of monstrous kiss where the lips swallow each other up."[24] The *limes*, the edges, are, in Rifaux's sense, the most significant, and troubled, site of the city. But Berlin did not linger at the ex-border. Astonishingly, the city did not come up with a centralized plan regarding what to do with the urban land "wasted" by the Wall. Rather, the rebuilding of Wall-terrain by private developers was facilitated by a law passed in July 1996 that enabled the return of border land back to the former owners who could then sell it (with conditions permitting sensitive sites to be retained by the government).

Only by the year 2000 did the former Wall terrain (at least the 825 acres of the central death strip that had separated the city's two halves, but not the outer ring around West Berlin) start to be formally and separately assessed by the Berlin Senate Office for Urban Development.[25] At Potsdamer Platz, the last remaining watchtower was demolished at the end of 2000. The guard tower at Checkpoint Charlie was removed in early 2001 – it was considered too small to qualify for preservation. Recent German memory work regarding the Wall seems to have taken a step forwards and backwards at the same time: while the site of the largest border traffic crossing, the Marienborn Memorial to German Division (*Gedenkstätte Deutsche Teilung Marienborn*), opened in 2006, three years later, and just a few weeks after the twentieth anniversary of the fall of the Wall, sections of the former checkpoint at Bornholmer Strasse (specifically parts of a roof for a former parking lot) were being sold off over Ebay. And in September 2010 part of Berlin's Kontrollpunkt Dreilinden (the Allied Checkpoint Bravo's first of two sites, in operation from the 1950s until 1969) was sold at public auction, reaching a minimum asking price of only $58,000 (€45,000) for the terrain of 3.7 acres (15,000 sq m).[26]

It took a team of deconstructivist outsiders, the LA-based architects' team of Morphosis, to come up with an interactive, tactile memorial design that, if it had been built, might well have successfully "re-enacted" the Wall: a structured yet metaphorical space of pedestrian walkways that one would have entered into for an experience of the Wall as "a trench, a void, an inverted negative wall," "a mending wall of sorts." Originally intended as a "social conduit" for the divided city in 1986, Morphosis's "Berlin Wall Project" would have attracted cultural events, street theater, graffiti, and so on; after the Wall fell, Morphosis proposed it as an articulation of the city's need for a "living monument which would concretize and reconnect the fissure which is the Berlin Wall." Anthony Vidler has pointed out that the Morphosis concept was envisaged rather like Kafka's Great Wall of China as a series of piece-meal, fragmented architectural pieces, in homage to the extinct and extant pieces of the Wall.[27] Architect Jean Nouvel also wanted to revi-talize the ex-Wall, suggesting a light- and color-filled series of spaces for public consumption, flânerie, and entertainment in a project called "The Meeting Line." Nouvel wrote of his design: "As for the canyon that was once the Wall, we see a major opportunity to create a new core for public animation day and night. The lobotomy and mummi-fication of space that has played such a tragic role in the life of the city now seems irrelevant."[28]

What Berliners got, instead, was a Wall memorial (the *Gedenkstätte Berliner Mauer*) at the Bernauer Straße. While its location today is ill-fated in attracting tourists in search of the Wall, its choice was nonetheless serendipitous not just because the site happened to have an actual length of the Wall, but because of the way in which its buildings had been used as the literal line between the Soviet and French sectors in the first stages of the Wall's construction. An irony is that Bernauer Straße was the first section of the Wall to be officially dismantled in 1990 – yet it subsequently became the city's official site dedicated to post-Wall remembrance. The federally funded Wall Memorial, which opened in 1998, was designed by the firm of Kohlhoff & Kohlhoff of Stuttgart; a year later, the Wall Documentation Center opened opposite it.[29] The memorial, while indeed striking, is more an architectural commentary on the Wall than its actual commemoration. Indeed, such comme-moration far more meaningfully occurs in the Chapel of Reconciliation, an oval-shaped meditation chamber designed by Peter Sassenroth and Rudolf Reitermann (2000) on the site of where the sanctuary had stood in the demolished *Versöhnungskirche*. The chapel dedicates each day to an individual Wall victim in a monthly-alternating list.[30]

The design of the Kohlhoff & Kohlhoff Wall memorial, meanwhile, is gazed upon by tourists who climb the viewing tower next to the

Documentation Center on the other side of the road. The platform was added in 2003 when it became clear that tourists just were not "getting it" at ground level about the three-dimensional mock-up of the memorial's reconstructed Wall strip hidden in between its walls. The *simulated artifact* stepped in when the actual artifact was lacking. The memorial originally intended its visitors (those interested enough to discover it at ground level in the cemetery on the other side) to peer from the communist East toward the capitalist West (which is actually south-east to north-west, just to confuse visitors) through a slit in the inner wall and see the guarded terrain (a re-constituted sample piece of the death strip) between it and the outer Wall. The surfaces of these sections of the Wall had to first be repaired back to their working condition: what had happened to them post-1989 was not to be part of the memorial concept. Even more layered is the view through this slit beyond the outer Wall of a part of the poster affixed to the building of the Documentation Center that depicts the actual Wall being built in 1961, replete with border guards. Added to these various levels of artifice is the strong sense of déjà-*non*-vu, of a practical non-viewability: one's vantage-point through this slit in the inner wall is from the relatively impossible position of standing within the forbidden area (*Sperrgebiet*) on the eastern side. We cannot all share the perspective and position of Wim Wenders' angels who do indeed meander right through the no-man's-land and even the outer Wall in their invisible, omniscient status – but certainly, that is what this memorial is suggesting that we do in order to understand the Wall. This quasi-mystification of the Wall's urban landscape is intriguing as a piece of Wall sculpture – especially at the point where two rusty brown steel metal walls abut a resurrected cement Wall section at sharply inserted right-angles, thereby framing and closing the simulated Wall terrain off from public access. Perhaps the severity of these metal wall-sheets of wall that intersect with the reconstructed Wall-slabs and make the concoction into a "segment" are there to remind us of the original terrain's former power, or even just its ultimately finite nature. At the same time, if the visitor looks at the metal prop walls' inner side at the memorial, their intersection with the *Grenzmauer-75* brings both the vertical and horizontal lines of the slab and its round top-pipe into acute focus (Fig. 5.3). But this installation is too indirect, too abstract, to function as a major memorial by itself.

The most significant problem for the Wall Memorial and Documentation Center site has been the most obvious one: that not enough tourists were even bothering to visit the site in the first place, and it was therefore failing in its public history function. Memory studies experts

Figure 5.3   Berlin Wall Memorial by Kohlhoff & Kohlhoff, Bernauerstraße, Berlin, 1998

may be allergic to the Cold War "curiosity cabinet" of escape-attempt chronicles in home-made exhibits at the privately run Wall Museum House at Checkpoint Charlie.[31] This *Mauermuseum Haus am Checkpoint Charlie* was founded two years after the Wall's appearance by the late activist Rainer Hildebrandt (at Bernauer Straße, in fact). But attendance figures speak for themselves: with 850,000 visitors, the House at Checkpoint Charlie was the third most visited museum in the city in 2008. The more remotely located Wall Memorial, meanwhile, recorded 304,600 visitors and was languishing in 13th position.[32] Indeed the failure of Berlin to recall its division to itself and to the world, as a three-dimensional calling forth of collective memory, prompted the Checkpoint Charlie museum to go a few steps further than just the simulacrum of the guardhouse and the pretend border guards: in 2004, the museum director, Alexandra Hildebrandt, erected a controversial "Wall Crosses" (*Mauerkreuze*) memorial on an empty lot adjacent to the museum.[33] In 2005, a day after American Independence Day, this memorial was taken down by the city, ostensibly for its land-lease running out (as well as for making it look, according to the number of wooden crosses, as if 1,065 victims had died crossing Checkpoint Charlie, and for putting Wall slabs where the Wall had not stood). Practically the only good thing emerging from the public row over this ad hoc installation was the realization at top political levels that some significant Wall-memory improvements were needed in Berlin, as a way of meeting the tourists' desire for "more Wall," as well as preventing future outbreaks of non-city-sanctioned individual initiatives at memorializing the Wall.

With this aim in mind, in 2005 Berlin's Cultural Senator Thomas Flierl proposed something more ambitious in terms of the Bernauer Straße's actual urban topography. Recognizing that the Wall's erasure was "not thought through enough," Flierl realized that more of a reconstruction of the Wall was called for. The various dots in the city – up to fifty historically significant sites and events related to the former Wall – might yet become connected, via Flierl's *Mauergedenkkonzept* ("Wall Memorial Concept"), into what could hopefully be a re-staging of a decidedly non-vague section of the Wall. Flierl's plan included a re-creation of an entire stretch of the three-dimensional experience of the Wall (its outer and inner walls, and its entire terrain in between) along the relatively empty stretch along Bernauer Straße from Brunnenstraße to the Wall Park (Mauerpark).[34] Flierl and his urban planning colleagues ran into difficulties when they failed to fully consult with each other before this development strategy was announced. To achieve this reconnecting of lost death-strip-space, more than forty pieces of land would have to be united, half of which the city already owned, but the rest of which would be obtainable after arduous negotiation with various owners, including those still seeking compensation for their pre-war and pre-communist-era losses.[35] This last point proved to be an embarrassing one: the city-approved Flierl plan could not be carried out to its full extent. The subsequent development of a cluster of town-houses right next to the Chapel of Reconciliation became a prominent case in point, since they completely interrupt the visual axis for the recreated empty Wall terrain, as intended by Flierl.[36]

Despite such setbacks, the main site of the $50 million Wall re-development project at Bernauer Straße is scheduled for completion in time for the fiftieth anniversary of the construction of the Wall. Its focal points include both a new Information Pavilion near the

Nordbahnhof station and a "Window of Remembrance" (*Fenster des Gedenkens*) of victims along the former death strip (Fig. 5.4). It already enjoys a significant extension into the Wall-hinterland area of the Nordbahnhof's terrain just around the corner, which opened as a park in 2009. A design competition determined the future lay-out for the Wall Memorial's extended outdoor exhibit of nearly ten acres all the way to the Mauerpark (to enable this, the city is finally purchasing the remaining adjacent parcels of ex-Wall land – but too late to prevent the apartment-block development in the coming years of several ex-Wall sites right in the middle of the memorial terrain).[37] Rust-colored columns resembling the steel supports that once held the Wall's concrete together demarcate missing Wall segments and even a former guard tower. Thomas Klein, a speaker for the Wall memorial, echoed (hopefully consciously) Walter Ulbricht's famous line when he reassured the public that the reworking of the Bernauer Straße terrain through 2012 will not become a falsification or a commodification of memory, even though it still is a reconstruction: "No one intends to build a kind of Disney World here" (*Niemand hat vor, hier eine Art Disneyworld aufzubauen*).[38]

At the same time, the Wall most definitely sells, and it is not just lumps of purported Wall-cement any more. Berlin's imagery, such as its Wall art, can be co-opted for city-enhancement purposes, literally so in the case of the Iranian artist Kani Alavi's Wall piece that was given away by Wolfgang Thierse to the United Nations building in New York without the artist's permission.[39] For the internal German market, "GDR-soft" or a highly selective "nostalgia for the East" (*Ostalgie*) rules, from the popular film *Good Bye, Lenin!* to the rather fetching Ampelmann stores dotted around Berlin Mitte and the trendy Mondos Arts store in Friedrichshain with its GDR trinkets and mementos. In the initial days after the border's closure, border guard Conrad Schumann's wall-jumping moment across the barbed wire was immortalized by a West German photographer who happened to be at the right place on the Bernauerstraße. These days, visitors can get their photo taken for a fee while poking their head through a hole in a cardboard cut-out of this much-marketed image of Schumann as he discards his weapon in the middle of his leap. More than Schumann's face is absent, however, since this most famous of successful Wall crossers committed suicide in 1998.

Most tourists want to see a piece of Wall in the city's most prominent locations. So it makes good sense that the artist Ben Wagin's "Parliament of Trees" (*Parlament der Bäume*) – an installation that was configured

110

Figure 5.4 "Window of Remembrance" for Wall victims by ON architektur Christian Fuchs, Berlin Wall Memorial terrain, Bernauerstraße, 2010

immediately after the fall of the Wall by placing plants in front of Wall segments and arranging them in a calendar fashion in honor of Wall victims – has been partly re-integrated, minus trees, into the Parliamentary Library of the Bundestag (Marie-Elisabeth-Lüders-Haus) across the river from the Reichstag. On the other side of the river-bank close to the Reichstag is a reconstruction of another Wall-era victims' memorial, the "White Crosses." There is now a public exhibit of Wall-history on one of the levels of the Brandenburg Gate's new U-Bahn station, which opened in the summer of 2009. Other belated efforts to showcase the missing Wall include 31 plexiglass information boards which accompany the Wall's line-marker in the streets across central Berlin: an ensemble called the "History Mile Berlin Wall." (If the line stood out more – like the bright stripe in the ground mark-ing the Freedom Trail in Boston, for example – it might help.) Further, the city has installed ten rectangular, rust-colored "info-columns" (*Info-Säulen*) with the same height as the former outer Wall. And the Wall's disappearance is commemorated in more ways than one by the "Memorial to the Sunken Wall" (*Denkmal der versunkenen Mauer*): a neglected memorial (that is yet in plain view) by Christophe Girot (1997) on Invalidenstrasse at the junction with Luisenstrasse, between Mitte and Moabit. One of the latest additions to Wall-era commemo-ration, the privately run DDR-Museum at the Spree riverside opposite the Berlin Cathedral, rather adroitly reduces the material culture of the former state to a tactile theme park; its museum shop boasts a series of board games and playing cards to test your Ostalgie mettle.[40] The last 82ft/25m-long section of Wall that had stood near Potsdamer Platz along the Stresemannstrasse is being re-incorporated as a memory-line inside the new structure taking its place: ironically, the Federal Environment Ministry (BMU).[41] The former *Tränenpalast* (nicknamed the "Palace of Tears"), a customs hall where from 1962 to 1989 prima-rily westerners took leave of their East German loved ones before exit-ing the GDR at the Friedrichstraße station, is finally being renovated as a future "museum of division." And, as if from an attack of bad conscience, Sony donated to the city some segments of the Wall left over from its Potsdamer Platz development.

Given the paucity of display-worthy remnants, the current process of Wall memorialization is shifting gears from renovation (the East Side Gallery's hinterland Wall section and *Wende*-era art displays were partially renovated first in 2000 and then repainted in 2008 in time for the 2009 celebrations) to electronic formats of memory work. As part of his memorial concept, Flierl had wanted to install a series of six internet portals at significant sites of the ex-Wall, just in time for the visitors coming to Berlin for its hosting of the World Cup in the summer of 2006. It would have been a commemoration of the two Germanies' former boundedness by dint of a celebration of the web's boundary-free existence. The city is following through on the general idea. A high-tech hand-held "Mauerguide: Walk the Wall" that one can rent for €10 a day from information booths helps tourists walk or cycle the former Wall route and thus hopefully also reach the Wall Documentation Center in the first place. Thus a GPS device is helping to bring the path of the Wall back to life for the iPhone generation. The city's official website seems to be placing most of its hopes on the internet portal berlin.de/mauer in five (soon: six) languages as a means of "making visible" that which has been lost. Apart from their pedagogical effect, such internet sources on Wall history and memory need to be taken seriously in that they often include the best updates on surviving Wall artifacts and Wall commemorations.[42] Some of the most important public-access research has been conducted by Wall preservationist Leo Schmidt, who recorded all of Berlin's remaining border-sites via Google Earth maps; this site went online in 2009 as the "Memorial Landscape Berlin Wall."[43]

There have also been several attempts to provide digital mock-ups of the Wall, such as the CD-Rom *INTERZONE* by Franz John, who filmed the death strip from within before it was taken down (providing, finally, a Wenders angels' perspective of sorts). Inevitably, then, we are witnessing a nostalgic substitution of the ex-border for the high-tech "interface" – and so to this extent we are granting Paul Virilio his due, after all.[44] One recent film provides aerial tracking shots of the Wall terrain that no one ever saw, not even the guards in the watchtowers. *Walled In! Computer Animation of the German Border* (2009) is a virtual (and German/English bilingual) Wall film that is shown not just on the internet but on a constant loop to tourists visiting the Berlin Wall Memorial's new Information Pavilion.[45] Even though the film's narrator reminds the viewer several times that its camera perspective up and over the hinterland wall on the East side of the Bernauerstraße is an impossible one (since the *Sperrgebiet*, let alone the terrain between the inner and outer walls, was a place that "no normal GDR citizen could enter," but this is where the camera takes us), this seems to be the movie's entire point: finally we have gained what has been desired all along, namely the full panoptic visuality of the Wall's power from within and from above. Virtual memory reconstructions like this one seem intent on proving themselves scopically superior to the limited, pre-electronic human perspectives that existed during the tenure of the historical Wall.

What will be, then, in urban terms, the long-term legacy of the Germans' eradication of the Wall? By trying to make whole a patient who was not yet ready to be cured, by closing the communicative memory gap before it made sense in actual memory time to do so, the city clearly did itself a disservice. It took place during that radical time of the *Wende*, moreover, and as Andreas Huyssen has noted, there is such a thing as a repetition compulsion in Germany toward mythical re-beginnings "1945–1968–1989/90."[46] The too-rapid dismantling of the accidental monument of the Wall now neatly symbolizes the too-abrupt historical caesura that arose when East Germans voted for the dismantling of their political and social system and its absorption by the Federal Republic.

The city's reconstruction attempts – of itself, let alone of its Wall – have been criticized as a "montage of self-contradictory, ideological fragments."[47] The attacks on Berlin's new shapelessness have often been so ferocious as to warrant nostalgia for that (even if uncomfortably) defining line of the Wall. Yet one could also ask for patience for a city that is still regaining its unity and re-forming its post-Wall contours. True, more of the ex-Wall was needed as a defunct marker, just as more of the GDR's cultural-symbolic (if not political) way of life could and should have been retained; something that artists, writers, preservationists, and anthropologists knew in 1989. The founder of modern sociological theory, Georg Simmel, recognized that the "border is not a spatial fact with a sociological impact, but a sociological fact that shapes spatially."[48] Simmel's words help explain how Berlin's failure to hold on to parts of its Wall for long enough has been hindering its effort, in the global era, to develop a sense of its personality – to create its own new boundaries, the way an individual is formed by defining him- or herself against what he or she is not, or is no longer.[49]

Simply put: Berlin's identity was more tied up in the Wall than anyone could have projected. Searches now for the best Wall memorial project, or attempts to save or re-instate remaining Wall fragments, have become part of a greater need to create a public site or several sites at which the "unintentional" monument that the Wall eventually became can now serve as a memorial to its own overcoming.[50] This is why the federal government's decision, in 2007, to build a Unity memorial for the German capital is so out of place. The dismantled urban border is being partially preserved, and even re-created, in order for the long-term rituals of collective memory to be best served.

Notes

1. "It will take us longer to tear down the Wall in our heads than any wrecking company will need for the Wall we can see." (*Die Mauer im Kopf einzureißen wird länger dauern, als irgendein Abrißunternehmen für die sichtbare Mauer braucht.*) Peter Schneider, *The Wall Jumper*, trans. Leigh Hafrey (New York: Pantheon Books, 1983), p. 119; Schneider, *Der Mauerspringer. Erzählung*, orig. 1982 (Hamburg: Rowohlt, 1995), p. 110.
2. "Berliners Press for a Memorial to Remember History of the Wall," *The New York Times* (23 March, 2003).
3. Alan Colquhoun, "On Modern and Postmodern Space," in Joan Ockman, ed., *Architecture Criticism Ideology* (New York: Princeton Architectural Press, 1985), pp. 103–17, p. 116.
4. Michael Rutschky, "Das Reden von Berlin," in Jochen Schimmang, ed., *Zentrale Randlage. Lesebuch für Städtebewohner* (Cologne: DuMont, 2002), pp. 280–97, p. 285.
5. Nicholas Kulish, "With the Berlin Wall Just a Memory, German Divisions Fade," *The New York Times* (8 November, 2009).
6. Jan Assmann, *Das kulturelle Gedächtnis. Schrift, Erinnerung und politische Identität in frühen Hochkulturen* (Munich: Verlag C.H. Beck, 1997), p. 56; and Assmann, *Religion and Cultural Memory*, trans. Rodney Livingstone (Stanford: Stanford University Press, 2006), p. 95.
7. Assmann, *Religion and Cultural Memory*, p. 27.
8. Assmann, *Religion and Cultural Memory*, p. 38.
9. See Duncan Light, "Gazing on Communism: Heritage Tourism and Post-Communist Identities in Germany, Hungary and Romania," *Tourism Geographies*, 2.2 (2000), pp. 157–76.
10. On this issue, at least, the left and right agree: Britain's conservative newspaper *The Daily Telegraph* refers to the re-made Checkpoint Charlie site as disrespectful to the Cold War suffering it symbolized, citing Thomas Flierl's condemnation of it as a "'tasteless mockery'." Tony Paterson, "Berlin's Checkpoint Charlie Becomes Tourist Trap," *The Daily Telegraph* (16 August, 2008). Soon after the fall of the Wall, the US Department of Defense in its "Legacy Cold War Project" tried to indicate the need to preserve if not the physical structures then at least the legacy of Cold War military sites, as well as their future potential as resources and assets; see "Coming in from the Cold: Military Heritage in the Cold War" (June 1994), at: www.usmlm.org/home/coldwar/coldwar.html (date accessed 9 July, 2009). See also Leo Schmidt and Henriette von Preuschen, eds, *On Both Sides of the Wall: Preserving Monuments and Sites of the Cold War Era/Auf beiden Seiten der Mauer: Denkmalpflege an Objekten aus der Zeit des Kalten Krieges*, trans. Ralf Jaeger (Bad Münsterfeld: Westkreuz Verlag, 2005).
11. Catherine Schaer, "Berlin's Invisible Wall: Little is Left Today of the Cold War's Most Famous Monument," *Der Spiegel* (16 July, 2009).
12. Tony Judt, "The Past is Another Country: Myth and Memory in Post-War Europe," in Jan-Werner Müller, ed., *Memory and Power in Post-War Europe: Studies in the Presence of the Past* (New York: Cambridge University Press, 2002), pp. 157–83, p. 157.
13. Daniel Libeskind, *Daniel Libeskind: The Space of Encounter* (New York: Universe, 2000), p. 150.

14. www.lyriks.de/songtext/wolf-biermann/deutschland-ein-winterm-rchen-30393 (date accessed 25 October, 2009).

15. Thomas Brussig, *Helden wir wir* (Berlin: Volk & Welt, 1995).

16. Schaer, "Berlin's Invisible Wall."

17. Anna Kaminsky, ed., *Die Berliner Mauer in der Welt*, Bundesstiftung zur Aufarbeitung der SED-Diktatur (Berlin: Berlin Story Verlag, 2009). For a similar volume dedicated to the walls of world history, see Astrid Nunn, ed., *Mauern als Grenzen* (Mainz: Verlag Philipp von Zabern, 2009). Online versions of pictorial Wall memory can be found at, for example, www.brianrose.com/lostborder.htm; and www.grenzfoto.de/ (date accessed 1 May, 2010).

18. Five thousand (15 per cent of the needed number) participated on the night; twice that number had registered online. See Henning Onken, "Gebt uns die Mauer zurück – für 15 Minuten!" *Der Tagesspiegel* (1 November, 2009); and Kimberly Bradley, "Berlin Wall Returns, in Human Form," *The New York Times* (4 November, 2009).

19. "Liegen, wo die Mauer stand," *Der Tagesspiegel* (14 August, 2003).

20. On "The Wall Project," see www.wendemuseum.org/downloads/WallProject_JAN14_2010.pdf (date accessed 31 March, 2010).

21. David Hare, *Berlin/Wall* (London: Faber & Faber, 2009), p. 5.

22. Polly Feversham and Leo Schmidt, *Berliner Mauer heute: Denkmalwert und Umgang/The Berlin Wall Today: Cultural Significance and Conservation Issues* (Berlin: Bauwesen, 1999), p. 186. See also Anna Saunders, "Remembering Cold War Division: Wall Remnants and Border Monuments in Berlin," *Journal of Contemporary European Studies*, 17.1 (2009), pp. 9–19; and Joachim Schlör, "'It Has to Go Away, But at the Same Time It Has to be Kept': The Berlin Wall and the Making of an Urban Icon," *Urban History*, 33.1 (2006), pp. 85–105.

23. Svetlana Boym, *The Future of Nostalgia* (New York: Basic Books, 2001), p. 179. See also Jacques Derrida's comment on the post-Soviet ghost: "The specter, as its name indicates, is the *frequency* of a certain visibility. But the visibility of the invisible. And visibility, by its essence, is not seen, which is why it remains *epikeina tēs ousias*, beyond the phenomenon or beyond being." Derrida, *Specters of Marx: The State of the Debt, the Work of Mourning, and the New International*, trans. Peggy Kamuf (New York: Routledge, 1994), p. 100. Emphasis original.

24. Patrice-Loup Rifaux, *Berlin, fin de siècle* (Paris: L'Harmattan, 1998), p. 10.

25. Friedrich Bluth, Manfred Zache, and Helmut Zempel, *Stadtplanerisches Dokumentation zum ehemaligen Grenzstreifen der Mauer in Berlin* (Hohen Neuendorf: Z-Plan, 2000). This publication and other official reports on the former Wall terrain are discussed by Carolyn Loeb, "Planning Reunification: The Planning History of the Fall of the Berlin Wall," *Planning Perspectives*, 21.1 (2006), pp. 67–87.

26. Reinhart Bünger and Klaus D. Voss, "Kontrollpunkt Dreilinden wird versteigert," *Der Tagesspiegel* (21 August, 2010).

27. Morphosis, "The Berlin Wall," in Alan Balfour, ed., *Berlin* (London: Academy Editions, 1995), pp. 158–59, p. 159; Anthony Vidler, *Warped Space: Art, Architecture, and Anxiety in Modern Culture* (Cambridge, MA: MIT Press, 2000), pp. 213–14. See also http://morphopedia.com/projects/berlin-wall-competition-1 (date accessed 2 June, 2010).

28. Vittorio Magnago Lampugnani, ed., *Berlin Tomorrow* (London: Academy Editions, 1991), p. 71.
29. See Gerd Knischewski and Ulla Spittler, "Remembering the Berlin Wall: The Wall Memorial Ensemble Bernauer Strasse," *German Life and Letters*, 59.2 (2006), pp. 280–93.
30. Rudolf Stegers, "Transformation der Geschichte: Kapelle der Versöhnung," in Philipp Oswalt, *Berlin: Stadt ohne Form. Strategien einer anderen Architektur* (Berlin: Prestel, 2000), pp. 190–93.
31. David Ensikat, "Auf, auf zur Bernauer Straße!" *Der Tagesspiegel* (18 December, 2000).
32. See www.berlin.de/landespressestelle/archiv/2009/11/13/145973/index.html (date accessed 31 May, 2010).
33. Jennifer McScotts, "The Second Fall of the Berlin Wall: Examining the Hildebrandt Memorial at Checkpoint Charlie," *Future Anterior: Journal of Historic Preservation. History, Theory and Criticism*, 3.1 (2006), pp. 36–47.
34. Thomas Flierl, *Berlin: Perspektiven durch Kultur. Texte und Projekte* (Berlin: Theater der Zeit, 2007), p. 170.
35. "Bernauer Straße: Gedenkstätte wird später fertig," *Der Tagesspiegel* (23 December, 2005).
36. Thomas Rogalla, "Stadtvillen und Luftschlösser," *Berliner Zeitung* (29 September, 2005); and Nils Ballhausen, "Von Schussfeld zum Bauland," *Bauwelt*, 39–40 (2008), pp. 28–37.
37. For the design for the Berlin Wall Memorial terrain, see www.competitionline. de/beitraege/15077 (date accessed 31 March, 2010). The 2007 competition was won by Mola Winkelmüller with the landscape architecture team of sinai.Faust.Schroll.Schwarz and ON architektur. See also Friederike Meyer, "Erweiterung der Gedenkstätte Berliner Mauer," *Bauwelt*, 99.3 (2008), pp. 10–12.
38. GDR Secretary General Walter Ulbricht disingenuously announced to the international press in June 1961: "No one has the intention of building a wall" (around West Berlin: *Niemand hat die Absicht, eine Mauer zu errichten*). Thomas Klein, cited in Alexandra Maschewski, "Berlin-Touristen wollen mehr Mauer sehen," *Die Welt* (3 March, 2008).
39. "Alavi verliert. Prozess um Mauerbild," *Der Tagesspiegel* (25 May, 2007).
40. For example, Robert Rückel and Katrin Strohl, *Mauerquiz. Quizkarten rund um die Berliner Mauer* (Berlin: DDR Museum Verlag GmbH, 2009).
41. "Mauer-Rest im Zentrum weicht Neubau," *Der Tagesspiegel* (December 22, 2005).
42. See especially www.berlin.de/mauer/index.de.html; www.berliner-mauer-gedenkstaette.de/de/; www.chronik-der-mauer.de; www.grenzdenkmaeler. de/index.php?id=2; www.berlin.de/mauerdialog/; www.mauergeschichte. de/; and www.grenzerinnerungen.de/. See also the virtual reality artwork by Tamiko Thiel and Teresa Reuter (2009): www.virtuelle-mauer.de/; and in their *Werkbuch: Virtuelle Mauer/Reconstructing the Wall* (Berlin, 2009). The main Wall memory and preservation organization, the Berlin Wall Foundation (*Stiftung Berliner Mauer*, formed in 2008 and directed by Axel Klausmeier), runs both the Erinnerungsstätte Notaufnahmelager Marienfelde and the Verein Berliner Mauer – Gedenkstätte und Dokumentationszentrum e.V. at the Bernauer Straße, including the Chapel of Reconciliation

(www.berliner-mauer-dokumentationszentrum.de/; www.kapelle-ver-soehnung.de/bin/deutsch/index.php). Nonetheless, the privately run Mauermuseum Haus am Checkpoint Charlie (www.mauer-museum.com/) has remained the city's leader in attracting tourists' attention. A marked visitor increase has occurred at Berlin's former Stasi prison, Stiftung Gedenkstätte Berlin-Hohenschönhausen (http://en.stiftung-hsh.de/). Other border memorial sites include Checkpoint Bravo e.V. (the Dreilinden/Drewitz border crossing, www.checkpoint-bravo.de/); Gedenkstätte Deutsche Teilung Marienborn; Gedenkstätte Bautzen; Grenzlandmuseum Eichsfeld e.V.; and the "Green Belt," part of the "European Green Belt" initiative, a protected biotope area along the former Iron Curtain (www.europeangreenbelt.org/indoor.html). See also the post-Wall organization of Wall graffiti artists, the Künstlerinitiative East Side Gallery e.V. (www.eastsidegallery.com/deutsche.htm). (Date accessed 29 June, 2010). For an analysis of the museums and memorial sites along the former German-German border, including, for example, the divided village of Mödlareuth, see Anna Kaminsky, ed., *Orte des Erinnerns. Gedenkzeichen, Gedenkstätten und Museen zur Diktatur in SBZ und DDR* (Leipzig: Ch. Links Verlag, 2004).

43. Leo Schmidt, "Denkmallandschaft Berliner Mauer"/"Memorial Landscape Berlin Wall," at: www.denkmallandschaft-berliner-mauer.de / www.berlin-wall-map.com (date accessed 30 January, 2010). This builds on Schmidt's previous work with Axel Klausmeier, *Mauerreste – Mauerspuren. Der umfassende Führer zur Berliner Mauer* (Berlin: Westkreuz Verlag, 2004). See also Gerhard Sälter, *Mauerreste in Berlin/Relicts of the Berlin Wall*, trans. Miriamne Fields, 2nd ed. (Berlin: Druckerei Elsholz, 2007).

44. Paul Virilio, "The Overexposed City" (1984), in K. Michael Hays, ed., *Architecture Theory since 1968* (City of New York: The Trustees of Columbia University/Cambridge, MA: MIT Press, 1998), pp. 540–50, p. 543.

45. *Eingemauert! Computeranimation der deutschen Grenze* was directed by Max Hofmann and Christoph Lanz, and produced by Deutsche Welle (DW-World TV, 2009); see www.dw-world.de/popups/popup_single_mediaplayer/0,,4418575_type_video_struct_12313_contentId_4434532,00.html (date accessed 1 May, 2010).

46. Andreas Huyssen, *Present Pasts: Urban Palimpsests and the Politics of Memory* (Stanford: Stanford University Press, 2003), p. 147.

47. Philipp Oswalt, "Berlin, Stadt des 20. Jahrhunderts," *transition* 9 (July 2002), pp. 110–17, p. 110.

48. Georg Simmel, "Der Raum und die räumlichen Ordnungen der Gesellschaft," in Simmel, *Gesamtausgabe*, ed. Otthein Rammstedt, vol. 11, *Soziologie. Untersuchungen über die Formen der Vergesellschaftung* (Frankfurt am Main: Suhrkamp, 1992), pp. 687–790, p. 697.

49. Viviane von Orelli, "Stadtliebe. Das Zentrum als Ort der Gegensätze," in Maria Luise Hilber and Ayda Ergez, eds, *Stadtidentität. Der richtige Weg zum Stadtmarketing* (Zürich: Orell Füssli, 2004), pp. 189–94, p. 194.

50. Brian Ladd states that there are both "'intentional'" and "'unintentional'" monuments that signify a city's memory. Ladd, *The Ghosts of Berlin: Confronting German History in the Urban Landscape* (Chicago: University of Chicago Press, 1997), p. 12.

6
Alternative Border Zones in Berlin

Alle festen eingerosteten Verhältnisse ... werden aufgelöst ...
Alles Ständische und Stehende verdampft ...
(Karl Marx and Friedrich Engels, 1848)[1]

The Wall that is no longer physically manifest has become increasingly displaced by a whole host of representations. The naked, ruined tracts of land that the dismantled Wall first revealed to the New Berlin amounted to a visually powerful rendering of the psycho-spatial cost of the nation's unity. These voids certainly served to inspire the reunified city's obsession with building and becoming, but their first effect was that of creating an inverted topophilia. Reunified Berlin's obsession with the un-built and the possibilities but not the results of the re-built became a selling-point. It is the spatial version of the *arm aber sexy* ("poor but sexy") tagline for the city uttered by Mayor Klaus Wowereit. These disused spaces were not valued as sites of mourning and loss; they gained in significance as sites of play, transformation, danger, and discovery. The world came pouring into East Berlin and found many of these sites in locations unrelated to the Wall itself. The host of "alternative" post-Wall border zones for which post-Wall Berlin has become so famous demonstrates how people like to fetishize a sense of the uncontrollable urban. Berlin's multiple examples of land laid to waste, spaces of social marginalization, and sites that reveal traces of a now-lost historical era seem to transmit to us the unconscious of the city. Looking back, we can detect how they were even an antidote of sorts to the rushed removal of the Wall the moment it was deemed obsolete. Therefore these alternative border zones provided an experiential substitute for the initial phase of "communicative memory" concerning the Walled era that got lost in the *Wende*'s euphoria.[2]

118

The official plans for rebuilding post-Wall Berlin smoothed over the legacy of urban instabilities in a form of post-Wall "recovery as recovering." Yet Berlin's veiling-over of its unsteady forms is not as bad as it could be. Elsewhere, after all, entire cities like San Francisco are situated on quite literally unstable tectonic plates. Certainly, Berlin's own shifting identities do run down into the depths: witness an increasing public fascination with the hidden spaces, bunkers, and tunnels left behind by World War II and the Cold War. Underneath the Soviet memorial in the Tiergarten there are the remains of three tunnels built by the Nazis for the capital as "Germania," for example.[3] Sometimes it is as if the Nazi unconscious were lurking below ground: the SS drivers' bunker, discovered during preparations of the ex-Wall terrain for the Pink Floyd concert in 1990, was quickly covered up again.[4] On a regularly recurring basis, digging and demolition reveal unexploded bombs from World War II, prompting the evacuation of entire neighborhoods. But mostly, the subterranean instabilities of the city are best kept buried for city-boosterism purposes.

It did not, indeed, take a Wall to create Berlin's familiarity with "wounded" urban land. By the end of World War II, Berlin was the most bombed city in Germany. It had been Britain's top target, and as of March 1944 the Americans joined in, too.[5] By planner Hans Scharoun's estimates, there were 266,000 destroyed apartments and 410,000 semi-destroyed apartments, out of a prewar total of 1,562,000.[6] Berliners had as many housing units to rebuild as the English did in all their cities combined. Nature was, albeit temporarily, re-created out of the voids caused by war and then division. The ex-war, as well as the ex-border, gave rise to urban biotopes. Berlin's situation in the double voiding act by both the hot and cold wars made ideal conditions for what has been termed "biotopes of laziness."[7] Such unplanned fertility presented unexpected turns in German urban history. After the war, nature readily asserted itself out of the bombed and burned-out ruins, causing in Berlin and elsewhere a temporarily organic metropolis. This suited the Allies. The Morgenthau Plan for Germany, initially supported by Roosevelt himself, wanted to retain Germany's ruined urban cores, so as to make its people into an agricultural society, as a way of preventing a future rise to international power. The immediate Allied postwar reaction was iterated by Air Chief Marshal Sir Arthur Tedder in 1945 that the "ruins of Berlin should be preserved as a modern Babylon or Carthage – as a memorial to Prussian militarism and the Nazi regime. You can drive miles through smoking ruins and see nothing that is habitable. This city can never be rebuilt."[8] Even the Nazis had been prepared to move the surviving populations of several bombed cities elsewhere and just start again, following the *Gartenstadt* ("garden city") ideal. They had plans to vacate the burned-out eight square miles of the center of Hamburg, after the raid of July 1943, and relocate people to a brand new garden city on the periphery. According to such initiatives, Munich was to be moved to the Starnberger See, Dresden to the Heller, and Hannover to the Deister.[9] Ruined cities could thus be kept as broken cautionary tales, as urban spaces gone to seed, as empty monuments to the war.

The Allied campaign's indirect facilitation of a surprising collection of new plant species gave value (to botanists who could itemize them) to otherwise abandoned land. But the alarmist Mike Davis likes to invoke the *wildness* of human nature running amok at the same time as the *wilderness* of mother nature, by stressing the way World War II returned people's living conditions to the prehistoric era, likening starving Berliners in those first winters after the war to "doomed members of a huge forgotten Donner party," and even the weeds that grew up on bombsites to those that survived the last Ice Age.[10] Nature's rise was clearly visible for World War II-era witnesses of the radical undoing and wasting of the metropolis. W. G. Sebald, in his study *On the Natural History of Destruction*, offers childhood memories of German cities immediately after the war, not as structures but as accidental artifacts, "areas of waste land here and there ... mounds of rubble, cracked walls, and empty windows through which you saw the empty air."[11] But in the urban waste land, new functions arose. "Dig for Victory," went the British slogan: people in Europe's bombed cities grew food in allotment gardens carved out of destroyed, emptied lots or city parks and squares. The poet Gottfried Benn remarked on the "nettles tall as men" where Berlin's pavements used to be, and grass growing on the former road surfaces that people picked at night in order to feed their livestock animals.[12] The German "rubble mountains" (*Trümmerberge*) were subsequently landscaped into parks: the Teufelsberg (Devil's Mountain), for example, created out of 800 truckloads of rubble that were literally poured over a 22-year period on top of the site of Hitler's would-be military academy, became a place where young West Berliners eventually went skiing.[13] Warfare thus added interior open spaces to Greater Berlin's terrain, 42 percent of which (including its 82,000 allotment gardens, or *Kolonien*) is today either open space or water, more than in any other German city.[14] Only since the fall of the Wall has Berlin started to expand along its suburban belt (*Speckgürtel*), more in keeping with recent urban agglomeration trends elsewhere in the world toward the suburban "edge city."

Given this crisis-ridden heritage, of what, then, does Berlin's contemporary "urban nature" consist; what are its borders that continue after the Wall? The primary common denominator of these spaces is that they are both urban and empty: they offer sites of periphery and marginalization even though often geographically located within the city's central areas. Various uses of empty lots and unoccupied properties in Berlin and Eastern Europe have been unfolding since the fall of the Wall, inviting any number of *Zwischennutzungen* ("temporary applications") that are preferable to no uses at all. As alternative areas of urban difference and opportunity, they would appear to be, by their very nature, transitory. An example of unofficial, alternative urban land-use has been the bazaars that have cropped up in as-yet unplanned places across Eastern Europe. They provide evidence of the East's ongoing, bottom-up transformation of post-Wall capitalism. The Polish flea market at Potsdamer Platz constituted, according to Karl Schlögel, not just "that strange fall of the Wall before the fall of the Wall," but even the start of Berlin's rebirth.[15] Other functions for Berlin's seemingly discarded sites include the techno club scene; the popular beach bars along the Spree river; as well as art exhibitions and installations like the one by Irish artist Colin Ardley in a Schinkel ruin, the Sankt Elisabethkirche, in 2002; or the Skulpturenpark with its evolving installations on former Wall terrain.

Berlin's alternative border zones have also been emblematized by squathouses in semi-ruined buildings, a counter-cultural trend which began as part of the West German student movement in the 1970s and which has been ideally suited to *Wende*-era Berlin. The reunified capital's gentrification process has even made legal (somewhat non-transitory) tenants out of several of the squats: the Köpi (Köpenicker Straße 137 in Mitte), former East Berlin's first "West German" squathouse which was founded in early 1990, now has a multi-year rental agreement.[16] Other squats, like the *Wagenburg*-squat *Schwarzer Kanal* in Kreuzberg, have had to move on, because the owners (in this case, Hochtief) are developing the property. Given the fewer squat options left in Berlin than before, Schwarzer Kanal was not able to stay central; and so they were displaced further out to Neukölln.[17] It is unlikely they will be the focus of as much *dériviste* attention there.

To be sure, all cities have their alternative spaces (their "non-places," their *terrains vagues* or heterotopias, their "Thirdspace" or their "transurbanism") which are, precisely, *not* their architecture: places and urban processes that have been shut out, forbidden from the accepted public realm, and have taken on a life of their own.[18] As Greg Hise reminds us, "the void is an artifact also."[19] Berlin's voids are laden with more signification and contradiction than most.[20] The artist Christo, for example, has deemed Berlin the "site of the physical encounter of East and West," which gives it "the richest and most varied texture of any town in the world."[21] The Wall's demise created multiple such sites and not just those literally left behind on the actual site of the border.

Soviet-controlled Berlin and the entire German Democratic Republic became known by the derogatory term "the zone" (*die Zone*); but the phrase can now serve as praise for new kinds of outcast areas. These are not what, at first sight, they appear to be; derelict spaces are not necessarily just urban blight. They are not merely unsightly blots in the narrowly ameliorative path of the German capital's future. A group of unemployed East Berlin men who would sit chatting at the former death strip of the Wall at Brunnenstraße and Bernauerstraße at least made this place their own (Fig. 6.1). Some sites became examples of proactive urbanism and were transformed, quite literally, into urban playgrounds, as instantiated in the painstaking creation of the Winsstraße park in Prenzlauer Berg (1994–2006).[22] And a new major challenge is how best to create urban landscape uses out of the massive Tempelhofer Feld, now that its heritage-airport has been closed: Tempelhof locals, alternative counter-culturals (*Autonomen*), and the design elite alike are all interested parties with varying visions for its future.[23]

Berlin's new edge-zones could thus be experienced as something to cross and re-cross, as liminal regions of transformative opportunity. The former no-man's-land and a new entire half of a city were opened up to creativity. To be in these newly negated border zones forged a sense of transgressing, of truly living. Liberation could ensue: "Where there is nothing," Rem Koolhaas asserts, "everything is possible."[24] Berlin emerged from its immediate post-Wall phase with the potential, in the manner of Nietzsche's Zarathustra, of being able to endure, and perhaps even welcome, its post-Wall border zones as bridges across the abyss of urban transformations that the Wall itself stultified and forbade access to.

To bring Zarathustra up to date, we can refer to radical architectural theorist Lebbeus Woods. In a thinly veiled self-designation, Woods commented on the pioneers at the border zones of the world who engage the crisis of the frontier as an opportunity and who like to live on the (meta)physical borderline:

> There are always people who will come to inhabit the difficult spaces of the wall. They are the people of crisis, pushed usually unwillingly to confrontation with limits, borderline cases of every sort, adventurers, criminals, inventors, con artists, opportunists, people who cannot, or

Figure 6.1 Men sitting in the former "Death Strip" of the Wall at the intersection of Bernauerstraße and Brunnenstraße, Berlin, in 2005

have not been allowed to, fit in elsewhere. They are nomads of the body, refugees of the mind, restless, itinerant, looking without much chance of finding a sure way either forward or back. Instead, they turn the situation to an advantage, making uncertainty a virtue, and strangeness an ally.[25]

Regarding his "Walls" project for Sarajevo, Havana, and San Francisco in the 1990s, Woods sees walls as "metaphorical" or "literal" entities, revealing the "zones of crisis" that are kept hidden at the mainstream core. They are, as Woods states, "spaces 'between', zones where the norms and conventions of living on either side of the wall's divide do not, or, more likely, cannot apply."[26] His is an unfixed world where barriers and limits are broken through.

For Woods, creative excitement was expressed in the renewed spaces of the reunified German capital: "BERLIN HAUPTSTADT – Terra Nova."[27] Artist-architects like Woods have been instinctively drawn to depicting border zones, both for their creative transitions and for their closed-off dangers. Inspired by the fall of the Wall and the voids it exposed in its wake, Woods' visionary "Berlin Free-Zone" design project introduces the concept of a cybernetic "hidden city within the one now being shaped": an alternative urbanism of "freespaces ... conceived outside of any known building typologies." In this "free-zone" hidden within existing buildings, those who discover this *terra nova* are offered an "unlimited free access to communications and other ... networks." Woods thus employs the voidedness of Berlin's old center, its *Mitte* that was on the East side of the Wall, as a chance to implant a "heterarchy" or "new matrix" – a different way of conceiving architecture, away from its hierarchical, establishment-supporting mode. He abhors the process of what Mitte was already en route to becoming (via the GDR's Disneyesque reconstruction of the medieval Nikolaiviertel in the 1980s): a "creation of cultural theme parks – whose purpose is the codification of an older form of authority as well as lure to the masses."[28] In the building-site mania of 1990s Berlin, it seemed at least initially that some of Woods' call for a "free-zone" could be heeded, if only in the city's alternative border zones. But most unfinished sites constituted just the prenatal stage of overt, top-down urban planning; they only gave the illusion of hosting free experimentalism. The Dionysian "thrill of discontinuity" and fantasy of creative transience promised by these post-Wall building-sites was a fake one.[29]

The death strip of the Wall is not coincidentally represented as a birth scene in Wim Wenders' film from the approaching end of the

Cold War era, *Wings of Desire* (1987). Here, where no free human may live, the angel Damiel wants to escape his immaterial, infinite eternity (as he calls it, his "borderlessness," *Grenzenlosigkeit*) and thereby enter the realm of human existence in the world's most bordered city. When Damiel emerges into life it is literally *through* the outer structure of the Wall's terrain straight into the West. He is carried through the cement barrier by the other angel, Cassiel, directly from the side of death, the no-man's-land, alongside the oblivious pacing East German border guards. An existential birth is thus depicted by crossing one of the world's most closed thresholds. The first thing Damiel does is ask a passer-by about colors, which are now so visible on the graffitied Wall behind him. Now, as a mere mortal, he can create. The film switches to color to show off not just Damiel's new finite but deliciously tangible mortality, but also the possibilities of the unfettered West (albeit in an encircled West Berlin). He can now sense, see, taste, and feel the differences, textures, shapes, and forms that previously were not on his immortal, free-ranging radar. Damiel is now wholly "bordered," but ultimately far freer within the confines of his human perspectivism: his emotional fallibility, his terminally limited lifespan, his untrustworthy sensory and cognitive knowledge, his all-too-bordered city. Edward W. Soja has noted this birth-like characteristic of borders – they not only invite "paradoxical images and attracted opposites" but also a Foucauldian "transgression, a movement beyond the defined limits and enclosures of our lives to open new places and spaces, to search for reconciling alternatives, creative syntheses, resolving hybridities." The result is a "borderlands culture that resists enclosure and confinement."[30]

In Berlin, it is true that counter-cultural movements existed on both sides of the Wall (especially in Kreuzberg in the West and Prenzlauer Berg in the East). The removal of the Wall gave rise to a three-dimensional expansion and mutation of Berlin's existing double edge-culture, and to the more recent evolution of certain areas, like Friedrichshain, as a counter-cultural hub. The lifestyle boasts a refusal to assimilate and a preference for vectors where something new, unofficial, or unplanned begins to happen. The city's ephemeral sites have invited a reassessment of the city's Wall legacy; they point to an urban environment that can generate a greater number of ludic crucibles for frisson and change. However, lest one get too idealistic about such a condition for contemporary Berlin: this is a case of creativity born out of sheer necessity. Atypical sites in Berlin have arisen from World War II bombing, Cold War division, and overall poverty and neglect. Unused commercial and residential lots and buildings may be empty in the post-Wall era because of economic decline and population loss as East Germans upped and moved to the West. Unoccupied apartments are an East German malady affecting mostly the cement high-rises (*Plattenbauten*) from the 1960s and 1970s. Between 10 and 17 percent of residences across the "new federal states" are empty.[31] Another cause of disuse is due to post-Nazi and post-Communist contested ownership of property, with about 1,600 such disputes still lingering in Berlin.

We would therefore be wise to avoid too celebratory an air concerning the derelict spaces of Berlin; such caution has to do, somewhat perversely, with their very marketability. Local politicians have started to realize the cachet of these spaces as they draw the art and artists of *Zwischennutzung* to them. The inhabitants who come in to fill the voids can be literal (squatters or *Wagenbürger*) or representational (installation artists). In Berlin's center there are over 1,000 such spaces, both built and unbuilt. They total an area as geographically large as the Tiergarten park itself; Berlin's Mitte district alone boasts over 300 of them.[32] The Berlin Senate Department of Urban Development unashamedly advertises these vacant land parcels for sale online under the corporate rubric "Building Lot Management" (*Baulückenmanagement*).[33] The senate has even published a book in honor of the "Urban Pioneers" who will, they hope, rent out these oh-so-available spaces for clubs, festivals, and art shows; yet at the same time it insists on ultimate control of said places (witness the demolition fate of the *Zwischennutzung*-site par excellence, the East Germans' former Palace of the Republic [*Palast der Republik*, or PdR]).[34]

Hence what Berlin boasts is more a gloss or veneer of spontaneous and free urban terrain, rather than its actuality. A tell-tale sign of this control is contained in the fact that over two-thirds of all the creative users of Berlin's voids are recipients of some kind of public funding. And many *Zwischnutzung*-practitioners are merely stepping into a building or site during the gateway period to that property's (or neighborhood's) imminent gentrification. Even the shell of the gutted PdR became wholly commodified by the post-Wall city: as a "prestige- and PR-object" it became, pure and simple, "cultural capital."[35] So much, then, for liberal artistic subversion of the status quo! Indeed, author Durs Grünbein pours scorn on the new generation of Debordian *dérivistes*. Citizens of the ex-GDR may indeed have had their "life-worlds flattened" by the fall of the Wall but they have been outpaced by the new generation of Berlin hipsters, these "transit artists." Grünbein offers only scathing comments about the trendsetters of the Berlin's *terrains vagues* for not knowing or caring what the Wall really meant: "The no-man's-lands, the intermediate zones, the still unmarked areas – these, it seems, are now their hunting grounds. Here, clowns of the virtual, they cultivate the existence of someone living in a space of transit."[36]

Such caveats aside, one can still appreciate the alternative urban spaces and creative environments that Berlin's former and still ongoing bordered condition has had in abundance.[37] One must also factor in, as Koolhaas exaggerated in order to make a point about the romance of Berlin's ruins, how "large areas of the city have ended up in ruin simply because *they are no longer needed*" both during and after the Wall and without the once-expected rising population.[38] Witness here the longevity of Ernst Bloch's metaphor for modern Berlin as a series of *Funktionen im Hohlraum*, that is, processes in empty, hollow spaces.[39] For Philipp Oswalt, these aspects of Berlin have stressed the "temporary" to the point of influencing the city's self-understanding – as he states: "The city's central themes like emptiness, fragmentation, heterogeneity, multiplicity, temporality, formlessness, and subversion point to a high potential for innovation."[40] These pockets are occurring in the renewed capital city, which is, as the site of national government, in most places in the world the *de facto* hegemon. Berlin's case as a city emerging from its almost half-century division after World War II is different, however: hence the potential of these counter-hegemonic border zones.

To recognize the gift of these under-formed areas for a city does not necessarily mean that one wants to petrify or musealize them, or that one is against all commercial, office, or residential development. It is better, rather, to admit the coexistence, even symbiotic relationship, of the two urban drives – the urban subversive *homo ludens* and the urban regular *homo economicus* rely on one another.[41] Subversive sculpture can inhabit even the high-conformist spaces of the new Pariser Platz: Frank Gehry's DZ bank building (1999), for example, boasts a gigantic horse's head in-between the straightness of the front façade and glass-roofed atrium within, exploding through and above the roofline.

Given the circumstances of Berlin's post-Wall transformation, however, the "alternative" aspect of urban border zones has practically been granted endangered-species status, rather than being understood as a more natural hazard and happenstance of urbanism. In order to understand the fierce love that has been showered upon these sites by the various types of German cultural elite – intellectuals, left-leaning *Prominenten*, and actual *Sub-Kultur* practitioners alike – one has to place their over-reactions in the context of post-Wall Berlin's conservative building codes of Critical Reconstruction. As a result, a more significant valorization has been accrued by the often-marginalized spaces of post-Wall Berlin as opposed to similar sites in other cities, European or otherwise.

As Henri Lefebvre advocated in the *The Production of Space*, the value of the unconstructed or unfinished urban spaces (of which Berlin has often unexpected, sometimes exaggerated combinations) is contained in their *"prohibition"* power. Lefebvre writes:

> [W]alls, enclosures and façades serve to define both a *scene* (where something takes place) and an *obscene* area to which everything that cannot or may not happen on the scene is relegated: whatever is inadmissible, be it malefic or forbidden, thus has its own hidden space on the near or the far side of a frontier.[42]

Post-Wall Berlin novels have adapted this sentiment, reworking the country's long-held suspicions about its dubious capital. In Uwe Timm's *Johannisnacht* (1998), for example, Berlin is depicted as a shady place where social and moral laws simply do not apply.[43] In a similar Lefebvre-esque vein, Inka Parei, in her 1999 novel *The Shadow Boxing Woman* (*Die Schattenboxerin*), sets her dark novel of rape and recovery in the unofficial parts of East Berlin that are full of ruins, fissures, and illicit settlements for people to hide away in and live quite literally "in between" western post-industrial society's norms and expectations. The novel's plot pays particular attention to the south-east stretch of the Spree, near Baumschulenweg, where new office buildings stick out like sore thumbs and seem disconnected from the greater authenticity of urban ruin all around them. "Occasionally, new office buildings rear up between the demolition gaps and damaged walls of the houses. So gleaming, so complete, that it does not look as if they had any foundation here, more as if they came from far away, and landed here on a planet made of sand, soot, ruins and graffiti."[44]

Lefebvre's definition fits Berlin's Wall Park (Mauerpark), whose very messiness helps it achieve an acting-out of the no-man's-land that it once was: it now embodies the *border-as-park*. The terrain of the Mauerpark near the Schwedter Straße was once, in the immediate post-war years, part of both the French and Russian sectors before it became part of the Wall; its former functions included a Prussian military training ground and then a freight railway yard.[45] Today the Mauerpark's reputation as a *Subkultur*-outlet for Berlin youth is enhanced by its very own graffiti wall (remnant of the former *Hinterlandmauer*, or inner Wall). At night it hosts unofficial parties, bonfires, grills, beer-drinking and drug trades, activities that the police have had trouble controlling. Its very imperfections and ugliness, according to the tidy standards of what constitutes appropriate urban public space for the boosterist New Berlin, contribute to its alternative value. The original intention of the park's design by architect Gustav Lange has been already been realized – even as the park is still awaiting completion, since remaining sections of land intended for the park are owned by Vivico (for the federal railway).[46] Precisely because the Wall Park is a landscape "expression of the 'no-man's-land character' of the death strip" it has installed a sense of the uncomfortable past in the present that has so often been lacking in the city's other new projects.[47] The mutable border, then, can make insta-bilities and ugliness into something positive.

Other kinds of earthly, alternative fates have awaited non-urban sites of the German borderland. The inner German border assumed new identities, its very remoteness prompting both then and now a concomitant environmental as well as preservationist boosterism.[48] Landolf Scherzer, hiking the ex-German-German border, paints a broad canvas of the various, haphazard afterlives for the former border in Thuringia-Bavaria. Often, he finds neglect so complete that the border patrol path (*Kolonnenweg*) cannot be found, or only with navigational difficulty. Between the villages of Linden, Milz, and Mönchshof some remaining, decaying, and vandalized border watchtowers have become habitats for bats and owls. In one instance, near Behrungen, he could not find the boundary line because it had been ploughed over and made into a new Autobahn; in another, he finds a former border guard dutifully picking up trash around a massive, painted monument, the "Golden Bridge" (1996, by the artist Herbert Fell) at the former border crossing Eußenhausen/Henneberg, now a "sculpture park." Elsewhere, in Gompertshausen, Scherzer finds an example of a common practice across the former German border terrain: what used to be a barracks for GDR border guards had been turned into a home for 85 asylum-seekers from 13 countries.[49]

That Germany's unwanted asylum-seekers have been used to fill up these unwanted ex-border structures speaks volumes. One such border-barracks turned asylum-seekers' residence is in Stolpe Süd near Hennigsdorf (just outside of Berlin to the north-west). Renovated in 2002 by the engineering firm of Karin Hartmann, it currently houses just under 120 refugees and is one of about 40 similar sites in the region. Since asylum-seekers in Brandenburg are forced to use their *Wertgutscheine* (coupons) instead of cash and then only at certain stores, neo-Nazi groups can easily predict which streets they will be walking on and thus harass them. There is even a neo-Nazi store located precisely between the refugee house and the town center. Leftwing groups have tried to protest against the shop, and have held annual anti-racism protests in Hennigsdorf; and groups formed by churches (the *Hennigsdorfer Ratschlag*) or the Initiative Circle for the Asylum Seekers Home Stolpe Süd (*Initiativkreis zum Asylbewerberheim Stolpe Süd*) have tried to make a difference. The asylum-seekers themselves have protested against the food coupons when other German states permit cash for refugees' financial support. The local Hennigsdorf authorities want to redevelop the former military border land for single family homes, but for now are stuck with their refugees in situ.[50]

Thankfully, in some instances the erasure of the Wall has in some cases brought about an environmental reclamation of the earth. Efforts to "re-green" the border and restore what had been there before have brought about a positive, even heterotopic investment in various park and garden reclamation projects on sites that were once lost to the Wall.[51] Part of the Wall was superimposed on a former park, itself a palimpsest in the dry bed of the nineteenth-century Luisenstädtische Canal. It is now the product of urban revitalization and has been made over into a park again, and no trace of the Wall remains. It is where the British rock artist Joe Jackson positions himself, in his new life-role as a *Wahlberliner* in Kreuzberg, in a filmed interview about Berlin accompanying his *Rain* album (2007).[52]

In particular, there has been an aesthetically powerful transformation of Wall land in and around Babelsberger Park in Potsdam. Significantly, the border line next to Cecilienhof was the very first border area in Potsdam to be cleared by the border guards themselves, and hence reclaimed for the public. Landscape architect Peter Joseph Lenné's original plans were referred to in order to reconstruct as much as possible of the former lakeside path in the Babelsberger Park. It was this path, the *Uferweg*, that had served as the death strip of the border terrain, with a series of fences rather than a wall. Now it has been recreated as it used to be – a gradual transformative reclamation with the help of UNESCO funds that took almost fifteen years to complete. In some places, preservationists found that the contours of the original Lenné paths, as well as the clay, granite, and brick used for guiding water run-off, were still visible. A major challenge was that the landscape architectural rebuilding team had to put back earth where the GDR Wall-builders had removed it to forge a level surface next to the water for the Wall's fence system; and where they had not removed the earth, they had spread herbicides to clear the ground during the Wall's first two decades. At the foot of the Babelsberger Park's arbored "rose steps" (*Rosentreppe*), the earth had simply been dumped into the Lennésche Bucht, and so the architects retrieved it out of the water and restored the original inlet. The Babelsberger Park reclamation project also included undoing a considerable portion of the damage done by the Soviet KGB (then: NKWD/MWD), which had completely leveled the Pfingstberg of the Belvedere west of Cecilienhof for the formation of its own walled-in "Military Town Nr. 7." Overall, this initiative restored 89 acres of parkland, including Park Sacrow and the Neuer Garten of Sanssouci: at the latter location, a border area of 32 acres had completely destroyed the park, and so the landscape architects had to restore earth, paths, and plants alike.[53]

In fact, this instance of a post-Wall greening of Berlin's former death strip has been extended on a far larger scale across Europe's ex-Iron Curtain – by simply letting the environmental wilderness be, as soon as the border installations themselves had been taken away (all except, that is, the 33,000 mines that remain lost). This border-turned-biotope is home to many rare plants and species, and is a welcome legacy of the decades-long halted development along the line. It now constitutes the longest stretch of resurrected wilderness terrain in all of Europe. Initiatives by Germany's Friends of the Earth (BUND: *Bund für Umwelt und Naturschutz Deutschland*) led Mikhail Gorbachev, in his new role as president of Green Cross International, to propose a nature reserve for the former Iron Curtain from Finland to the Adriatic. A cycle route has also been created along its entire stretch.[54] For its part, Germany committed 85 per cent of undeveloped land left over from its internal borderscape to the park. As a result, Germany's Green Belt (*Grünes Band*) presently covers 861 square miles.[55]

The public spaces created out of the ex-Wall's zones have not always emerged smoothly, however. Particularly the issue of access to public space at freed-up sites along the former Wall zone have been argued over forcefully. The "Sink Media Spree" (*MediaSpree Versenken*) citizens' initiative, for example, has had a degree of success by winning a local referendum with their demand for at least 55 yards (50m) of public, pedestrian riverbank access despite all the Media Spree corporate development that is planned for the Osthafen docklands. Their rallying cry "Spree bank access for all" (*Spreeufer für alle*) has served as a mobilizing enabler of support for other groups in the city who have similarly grassroots/alternative (that is to say, non-corporate and non-gentrifying) visions for the future of their neighborhoods.[56]

Suburban versions of the access battles are also playing out. Along the idyllic banks of the Griebnitzsee lake in Babelsberg runs a section of the former border (the precise line of which was in the water itself). During the 1990s the southern riverbank was transformed into a lakeside walking path that literally followed in the steps, as at several other sections of the former urban border, of the path once paced by the East German border guards as they patrolled the death strip; this public access walk provided a direct link into the Babelsberg park's own path out of the former border-strip. But the Griebnitzsee section of the open path was closed off again in during 2008 and 2009 at several places by the new owners of the renovated villas whose extensive gardens were deemed by a series of Potsdam court decisions to belong to them, and not to the public (Fig. 6.2).[57] Between 2004 and 2009 there were 73 successful lawsuits brought against the city of Potsdam by landowners who wanted their waterfront properties to extend all the way down to the water's edge of the Griebnitzsee. Protesters placed a banner between two tree trunks at the water's edge telling the recalcitrant neighbor-homeowners to open up the pathway and tear down their walls: "Dear neighbors: Open the lakeside path! Tear down the walls!"

Figure 6.2   Griebnitzsee barricade built by a private homeowner in 2009, blocking a lakeside walking path built on former Berlin Wall terrain

(*Liebe Nachbarn, Öffnet den Uferweg wieder! Reisst die Mauern ein!*). The Potsdam city council placed information boards at the entrances to the partially blocked path promising that the land would be regained for public use, but it now appears to be retreating somewhat. To re-purchase the land of the lakeside border-path may cost the city of Potsdam about €3.2 million. Similar legally won strategies preventing the public use of newly instated lakeside versions of the ex-border path are being repeated nearby on the south bank of Potsdam's Groß Glienicker Lake, another former Wall strip along West Berlin's western-most border. In 2010, one of the Glienicke villa owners even blocked off his property down to the water's edge with none other than original border fencing.[58]

Unfortunately, such a series of incidents illustrates the very short shelf life of the refrain "We are the people" (*Wir sind das Volk*), the collective motto of the East Germans' Peaceful Revolution of 1989, and the focal point of at an outdoor exhibit at the Alexanderplatz for the twentieth anniversary of the Wall's fall. The temporarily empowered East German *Volk* that had taken to the streets is no longer wanted in terms of privately determined public space. The struggles over these riverbank paths or waterfront access sites along the former border provide unfortunate instances of corporate/socio-economic division and retrenchment. Landowners at these sites have seemed oblivious to any greater communal post-Wall significance of open public space at "their" newly purchased stretches of the former urban border.

Fighting to retain some spaces (even ones that must necessarily be transformed in these post-Wall times, just so long as they retain freedom of access for locals) has become a form of border lands discourse in (mostly East) Berlin that helps forge a sense of community and place in the resistance against the rapid tide of developers' change. East Germans have already lost so much in terms of sense of place. In Berlin, many architectural "markers" of the GDR's postwar modernity have been demolished; not just the Palace of the Republic but also the innocuous, innovative *Ahornblatt* (designed in 1973 by Ulrich Müther, and torn down in 2000). The loss of spatial and cultural sites that defined one's memories and identity has proven highly problematic for former East Germans. Such losses and devalorizations of their former lives have prompted a host of memory-oriented associations and an outpouring in East German literature.[59] Jana Hensel, in her autobiographical memoir *Children of the Zone* (*Zonenkinder*, 2002) admits to having "my own secret city border" that simply excludes certain parts of today's gentrified or commodified East Berlin.[60] She describes how she feels like an outsider in

Dussmann's mega-bookstore or the swish Galeries Lafayette department store on the Friedrichstraße. Or similarly, she visits the newly domed Reichstag but admits to greater feelings of German identity when at the Soviet war memorial in Treptow Park. She cannot locate the GDR of her childhood that she is trying to remember – it eludes her because most of its material signs have been demolished. But its immaterial signs are still everywhere in the behavioral patterns and expectations of its former citizens.

Certainly, West Berliners today are as guilty of *Westalgie* as the East Germans are of *Ostalgie*. However, these are differing nostalgias – by the mid-1990s, East Germans had lost 40 percent of their purchasing power, while West Berliners are yearning for the subsidy-filled era of the 1980s after détente had set in.[61] Overly protective stances toward the legacy of Berlin's bordered condition also contain more than a drop of nostalgia for the unformed spaces left behind by the dismantled Wall and before that, the war: for example, in Samira Gloor-Fadel's documentary film of 1998, *Berlin-Cinéma* (an overt homage to Wenders' vision of Berlin), we are shown immediate *Wende*-footage of children playing along the spaces of the voided *Mauerstreifen*, the ruined landscape where the Wall used to be.[62] Germans who were urban children in the immediate postwar years can, likewise, recall playing in the ruins as a vital experience of childhood. For Berlin intellectuals, the building-site furor that enveloped Berlin in the 1990s marks but a beginning of an end for the city's romance with ruins.[63]

Of course, the Wall has not disappeared conceptually: far from it. As John Bornemann noted, the two Berlins and two Germanies were not able to remove their interior inner border, the "45-year effort in state-orchestrated production of difference," quite as quickly as they could remove their Wall: "Creating a common semantics of space ... is a project in the reterritorialization of space, fraught with difficulties and burdened ... by the separate East and West traditions of all the dead and living generations, which now act like nightmares on the brain of the youth." German unity "has exacerbated rather than solved" Germany's postwar condition. "Far from eliminating division, unity has reformulated its terms" – a saga that has been playing itself out both in social and urban terms.[64] Division was indeed taken seriously by East German authors during the Cold War: for Heiner Müller it was as if "all dividing lines of the world" (*alle Trennlinien der Welt*) went through the GDR, creating a strong "pressure of experience" (*Erfahrungsdruck*), the veritable source of his creativity; and similarly, for Uwe Johnson, the Wall gave rise to a "literary category" capable of alienating the two German cultures on both its sides.[65]

German literary emphasis nowadays has shifted toward border- and Wall-crossings. Although this notable trend in post-Wall literary output is more subtle by far than the multiple, jumbled exhibits that practically over-document the daring escapes across the Wall in the Mauermuseum am Checkpoint Charlie, the two types of border-representation do share an obsessive "imagery of de-bordering (*Entgrenzung*): of subversion and infiltration, of transcending, transgressing and flying over, of disruption and of prizing open and breaking through."[66] But it took the Wall to fall for Wall- and border-literature to become such a dominant theme in German literary production. It is as if the Wall's overcoming in physical, political terms has demanded that literature pick up the lingering psycho-social slack – thus all the Wall traces emerging in contemporary German literature are yet the latest version of Blochian "non-simultaneity" (*Ungleichzeitigkeit*).[67] Recent literary reconstructions of Cold-War era life and of a divided Germany constitute contextualized and acutely felt demonstrations of acts of transit, separations, and border-crossings that tie right in with current globalized sensitivities.

Only a cautious optimism on this issue is forthcoming from a reality-check on Germany's ongoing East-West social divides offered by one of its best known Turkish-German authors, Zafer Şenocak. In a poem he defines his life in the schism of Turkish and (West) German cultural identities thus: "the border goes / through the middle of my tongue / I rattle it like a prisoner / the action on a wound" (*die Grenze verläuft mitten durch meine Zunge / ich rüttele daran wie ein Häftling das Spiel an einer Wunde*).[68] In Şenocak's book *Atlas of a Tropical Germany* we find a confident redrawing of the German map that includes those kept perennially outside of the now-reunified nation's borders: the approximately three million resident Turks who regardless of whether they have achieved citizenship are excluded from German cultural belonging. Şenocak points out that the post-Wall revival of Habermassian "constitutional patriotism" is but a useful shield for what is still an underlying strata of *jus sanguinis*. He effortlessly undermines the notion of the new multicultural Germany somehow coexisting with the reunified national sensibility. Germany's Islamic population is an "edge group," Şenocak states, kept on the "periphery" in a permanent interior borderland – indeed they are kept there by the self-distancing "power of [those in] the middle." These inner borders in Germany are what prevent those "so-called foreigners" who are already in the country from truly immigrating, from "arriving at the place where one is."[69] Şenocak's insight for German Turks in their borderland condition is the sense that the truer lived reality by now is the more hybrid, cross-border one of "syncretic ... mulattos, bastards."[70] Şenocak mocks both himself and his fellow Turks for their reactive retrenchment and for any acceptance of the marginalized location imposed upon them: "We are in the process of building islands for ourselves in Germany, we're digging ourselves in in our communities ... In Berlin, the city where I'm from, we live entirely according to the map. There are boroughs and areas that we'd better not enter."[71] Nonetheless, when the Wall came down, German Turks were among the first to open up stores in East Berlin.

An unintentional expression of Berlin-Turkish marginalization as a literal border zone, but asserting autonomy at the same time, happened when a Turkish immigrant and his family dared to build in unclaimed Cold War territory quite literally in the shadow of the Wall. A now-elderly Osman Kalin and his wife built a shack almost three decades ago on a triangular piece of forgotten land at the Mariannenplatz that was situated in West Berlin's Kreuzberg but outside of its jurisdiction in official GDR-territory (Fig. 6.3). The man's home and vegetable plot were belatedly "discovered" by the politicians and the press in 2004, when the district boundaries between Mitte and Kreuzberg were altered, officially shifting his unofficial residence and making a Kreuzberger of him at long last.[72] More generally, a significant architectural development in this history of enforced entrenchment within the margins of the city has been the recent spate of building permits for mosques that finally dare (in size and style) to look like mosques, like the one that opened in 2010 near the Görlitzer Bahnhof, the Umar-Ibn-Al-Khattab Mosque.[73] Finally, some of the city's 200,000 Muslims (mostly Turks who constitute 24.2 percent of all foreigners in Berlin, and who have had to pray in insignificant prayer halls) can attend larger mosques such as this one, a process which is starting the end of the marginalization of spaces of Muslim worship in Germany.

While the normalization of Muslim German mosque-building is desirable and overdue, there are other signs that Berlin's post-Wall maturation will signify some losses for the city's alternative spatial identities. One major contested site in Berlin has always, it seems, been the Alexanderplatz, particularly since the early twentieth century.[74] During the second decade of the twenty-first century the Alex will probably prove to be a final test-case of the limits of Berlin-type *dérivisme*, since the city's official aim for the square is to evacuate its long-term

Figure 6.3   Osman Kalin's self-built home and allotment garden at Mariannenplatz, Kreuzberg, in 2005

character of alterity, and to swap it for a mainstream, commercial public space instead. We should be leery of the over-planning of the New Berlin at the expense of older imprints of the city, including its grungier sections like the Alex, lest the city be reconfigured by technocrats into a city devoid of the "exchanges and collisions" between strangers, structures, and sites that together constitute the propinquity of the urban experience. Peter Fritzsche and more recently Gina Weszkalnys have advocated the importance of an anti-center for the New Berlin; in other words, the Alex as a site that has resisted, at least so far, the planning efforts of 1920s modernizing functionalism, GDR-socialism, and post-Wall Critical Reconstruction alike.[75] This is so because the Alex has been a jumbled juxtaposition of public spaces and structures as yet unwilling and unable to be fully subsumed within any single planning code. Yet in 1994, the Alexanderplatz was the focus of an architectural competition to help enable the city's globalizing rebirth-aspirations. The office of Hans Kollhoff and Helga Timmermann won the competition with a radical vision of thirteen high-rises (Fig. 6.4). The left reacted vehemently against these Alexanderplatz plans as overly ambitious examples of boosterism disconnected from reality.[76] There was also the fear, if completed, of the Alex becoming a "Mini-Manhattan."[77] It is as if the New Berlin has had to prove itself as a world city by the very "gigantomania" of these skyscrapers – but in fact, the "exorbitant growth euphoria of the early 1990s" may yet see another phase, since in 2010 the Alex became one of Berlin's hottest investment spots yet.[78] The next several years may end up making one of the last seemingly unconquerable outposts within the former-out-post city rather less like – well, Berlin.[79]

To conclude: Berlin's alternative border zones and their ongoing transitions that we have sketched out here as an inheritance of the post-Wall condition reflect, to some degree, Germany's ongoing dialogue with its problematic past. In 1985 Richard von Weizsäcker as President of West Germany memorably predicted that the "German question" would stay "open as long as the Brandenburg Gate is closed." Yet German non-resolution is still being acted out in post-Wall Berlin. Any blanket normalization of the new republic and the renewed capital is being postponed. We can apply here the insight of a Rumanian clergy-man, an ethnic German immigrant working as pastor to the former border village of Streufdorf in Thuringia: "You know, a border always opens, once it's opened up, many free spaces. It['s] just a question of what you fill them with."[80]

Figure 6.4 Winning master-plan design by Hans Kollhoff and Helga Timmermann for the Alexanderplatz competition, 1994

Notes

1. Karl Marx and Friedrich Engels, *Manifest der kommunistischen Partei*, Part I (1848), at: www.marxists.org/deutsch/archiv/marx-engels/1848/manifest/1-bourprol.htm (date accessed 4 June, 2010).
2. Jan Assmann, *Das kulturelle Gedächtnis. Schrift, Erinnerung und politische Identität in frühen Hochkulturen* (Munich: Verlag C.H. Beck, 1997), p. 56.
3. Dietmar and Ingmar Arnold, *Dunkle Welten. Bunker, Tunnel und Gewölbe unter Berlin* (Berlin: Ch. Links Verlag, 1997), p. 18.
4. Brian Ladd, *The Ghosts of Berlin: Confronting German History in the Urban Landscape* (Chicago: University of Chicago Press, 1997), pp. 132–33.
5. Reinhard Rürup, "Der Krieg und die Zerstörung," in Rürup, ed., *Berlin 1945. Eine Dokumentation* (Berlin: Verlag Willmuth Arenhövel, 1995), pp. 11–71, p. 11.
6. See Niels Gutschow, "Europa. Verbrannte Erde und Zukunft," in Jörn Düwel, Werner Durth, Niels Gutschow, and Jochen Schneider, eds, *1945. Krieg – Zerstörung – Aufbau. Architektur und Stadtplanung 1940–1960* (Berlin: Henschel Verlag, 1995), pp. 176–94, p. 192.
7. Heinrich Wefing, "Berlin," in Stefan Bollmann, ed., *Kursbuch Stadt. Stadtleben und Stadtkultur an der Jahrtausendwende* (Stuttgart: Deutsche Verlags-Anstalt, 1999), pp. 143–59, p. 143.
8. Arthur Tedder, quoted in Michael Mönninger, "City Islands in a Metropolitan Sea," *Deutschland*, English ed. (1 February, 1996), p. 44. Cited by Ladd, *The Ghosts of Berlin*, p. 174. See also Hans J. Morgenthau, ed., *Germany and the Future of Europe* (Chicago: The University of Chicago Press, 1951), p. v.
9. See Spiro Kostof, *The City Assembled: The Elements of Urban Form through History*, with Greg Castillo (Boston: Little, Brown, 1999), p. 261; Durth, "Stadt und Landschaft: Kriegszerstörungen und Zukunftsentwürfe," in *1945*, ed. Düwel et al., pp. 126–75, p. 154; and Gutschow, "Hamburg: the 'Catastrophe' of July 1943," in Jeffry M. Diefendorf, ed., *Rebuilding Europe's Bombed Cities* (New York: Palgrave Macmillan, 1990), pp. 114–30, pp. 118–20.
10. Mike Davis, *Dead Cities and Other Tales* (New York: The New Press, 2002), p. 384, 382.
11. W. G. Sebald, *On the Natural History of Destruction* (1999), trans. Anthea Bell (New York: Random House, 2003), p. 74.
12. Cited by Wolfgang Schivelbusch, *In a Cold Crater: Cultural and Intellectual Life in Berlin, 1945–1948*, trans. Kelly Barry (Berkeley: University of California Press, 1998), p. 14.
13. On the extent of Germany's rubble-clearance, see Jeffry M. Diefendorf, *In the Wake of War: The Reconstruction of German Cities after World War II* (New York: Oxford University Press, 1993), pp. 18–42.
14. Sabine Beikler, "Warum Berlin gut tut," *Der Tagesspiegel* (9 July, 2003).
15. Karl Schlögel, *Promenade in Jalta und andere Städtebilder* (Frankfurt am Main: Fischer, 2003), p. 202. These East European market spaces may be interpreted as sites of becoming, or as sites of abjection, or indeed both. Irina Novikova refers to markets like the one in Riga as "the place where 'Turkey' as the embodiment of cheap 'oriental' production meets 'Russianness' (or political 'aliens', posteriori migrants, and mainly women) as a cheap and socially inferior labor force and the space of abjection en route westwards."

Novikova, "Isaiah Berlin's City: Monuments and Shopping: Colours of White," *sinn-haft*, 14–15 (2003), pp. 25–33, p. 33.

16. Candice Novak, "Berlin's Last Squat Ends as Legit Housing Projects Flourish," *DW-World.de* (26 June, 2010); Stefan Berg and Marcel Rosenbach, "Häuserkampf. Die Autonomen und ihr 'Plutonium'-Deal," *Der Spiegel* (3 October, 2008); and "Autonomes Wohnprojekt Köpi unter dem Hammer," *Der Tagesspiegel* (8 May, 2007).

17. Isabell Jürgens, "Wagenburg muß weiterziehen," *Berliner Zeitung* (23 June, 2009).

18. See, for example: Quentin Stevens, *The Ludic City: Exploring the Potential of Public Spaces* (New York: Routledge, 2007); Marc Augé, *Non-Places: Introduction to an Anthropology of Supermodernity* (New York: Verso, 2005); Tim Edensor, *Industrial Ruins: Spaces, Aesthetics and Materiality* (New York: Berg, 2005); Nigel Thrift, "Transurbanism," *Urban Geography*, 25.8 (2004), pp. 724–34; Edward W. Soja, *Thirdspace: Journeys to Los Angeles and Other Real-and-Imagined Places* (Cambridge, MA: Blackwell, 1996); Tim Cresswell, *In Place/Out of Place: Geography, Ideology, and Transgression* (Minneapolis: University of Minnesota Press, 1996); and Michel Foucault, "Texts/Contexts. Of Other Spaces," *Diacritics*, 16.1 (1986), pp. 22–27. All are in some way or other responding to Guy Debord, "Theory of the Dérive," trans. Ken Knabb, at: www.cddc.vt.edu/sionline/si/theory.html (date accessed 12 June, 2010); originally published in *Les Lèvres Nues*, 9 (November, 1956).

19. Greg Hise, "Architecture as State Building: A Challenge to the Field," *Journal of the Society of Architectural Historians* (JSAH), 67.2 (2008), pp. 173–77, p. 173.

20. On Berlin's derelict spaces and their creative uses see, in particular, Kenny Cupers and Markus Miessen, *Spaces of Uncertainty* (Wuppertal: Müller + Busmann, 2002).

21. Dominique Laporte, *Christo* (New York: Pantheon, 1986), p. 83. Cited by Ladd, *The Ghosts of Berlin*, p. 82.

22. The creation of the Winsstraße park is detailed at www.werkstatt-stadt.de/en/projects/11/ (date accessed 11 March, 2010).

23. On the designs for the ex-airport's Tempelhofer Feld, see http://blogs.taz.de/architektur/tag/tempelhofer_feld/ (date accessed 29 June, 2010). On the complaints, see Anne Klesse, "Tempelhofer Feld. Die ungeliebte grüne Mitte," *Berliner Morgenpost* (6 May, 2010).

24. Cited by Philipp Oswalt, "Berlin, Stadt des 20. Jahrhunderts," *transition*, 9 (July 2002), pp. 110–17, p. 114.

25. Lebbeus Woods, *Radical Reconstruction* (New York: Princeton Architectural Press, 1997), p. 13.

26. Woods, *Radical Reconstruction*, p. 13. See also Woods and Ekkehard Rehfeld, eds, *Borderline* (New York: Springer, 1998).

27. Lebbeus Woods, journal entry, May 28–June 15, 1992; Getty Research Institute, Special Collection Lebbeus Woods, #970081, Box 1.

28. Lebbeus Woods, *Radical Reconstruction*, pp. 26, 27.

29. Franz Pröfener, "Flirting with Disaster: Zur Symbolgegenwart der 'Baustelle',", in Pröfener, ed., *Zeitzeichen Baustelle. Realität, Inszenierung und Metaphorik eines abseitigen Ortes* (Frankfurt am Main/New York: Campus Verlag, 1998), pp. 6–49, p. 13.

30. Edward W. Soja, "Borders Unbound: Globalization, Regionalism, and the Postmetropolitan Transition," in Henk van Houtum, Olivier Kramsch, and Wolfgang Zierhofer, eds, *B/ordering Space* (Aldershot: Ashgate, 2005), pp. 33–46, pp. 33–34. Soja refers to Michel Foucault, "A Preface to Transgression," in *Michel Foucault: Language, Counter-Memory, Practice: Selected Essays and Interviews*, trans. D. Bouchard and S. Simon (Ithaca: Cornell University Press, 1977), pp. 33–34.

31. Peter Jurczek and Bernhard Köppen, "Aufbau oder Abriß Ost? Konzeptionelle Überlegungen zur nachhaltigen Stadtentwicklung in den neuen Ländern," *Zukunftsforum Politik*, 63 (Sankt Augustin: Konrad-Adenauer-Stiftung, 2005), pp. 7–81, p. 10. See also Anette Freytag, "Bereit für die Brache? Städte und Landschaften im Kontext der Globalisierung," in Diethild Kornhardt, Gabriele Pütz, and Thies Schröder, eds, *Mögliche Räume* (Hamburg: Junius, 2002), pp. 136–46.

32. Katja Füchsel, "Die City liegt brach," *Der Tagesspiegel* (15 January, 2004).

33. See www.stadtentwicklung.berlin.de/bauen/baulueckenmanagement (date accessed 27 February, 2010).

34. Senatsverwaltung für Stadtentwicklung Berlin, *Urban Pioneers: Stadtentwicklung durch Zwischennutzung/Temporary Use and Urban Development in Berlin* (Berlin: Jovis Verlag, 2007). See also the comments of Berlin urban development senator Ingeborg Junge-Reyer, in Matthias Oloew, "Vorbild Palastruine – mit Kunst und Clubs gegen Leerstand," *Der Tagesspiegel* (3 April, 2005).

35. Nina Brodowski, "Geschichts(ab)riss," in Philipp Misselwitz, Hans-Ulrich Obrist, and Philipp Oswalt, eds, *Fun Palace 200X. Der Berliner Schlossplatz: Abriss, Neubau oder grüne Wiese?* (Berlin: Martin-Schmitz-Verlag, 2005), pp. 50–60, p. 59.

36. Durs Grünbein, "Transit Berlin," trans. Andrew Shields, in Jean Stein, ed., *Grand Street 69*, 18.1 (New York: Grand Street Press, 1999; New York Foundation for the Arts), pp. 85–89, p. 88.

37. See Phillipp Oswalt, *Berlin: Stadt ohne Form: Strategien einer anderern Architektur* (Berlin: Prestel, 2000), pp. 59–63.

38. Rem Koolhaas, "Imagining Nothingness," in Koolhaas and Bruce Mau, *S, M, L, XL* (New York: Monacelli Press, 1995), pp. 198–203, p. 200. Emphasis original.

39. Ernst Bloch, "Berlin: Funktionen im Hohlraum," *Erbschaft dieser Zeit* (Frankfurt am Main: Suhrkamp, 1973), pp. 212–18. Andreas Huyssen indicates how this phrase of Bloch's suggests a "bounded" void. Huyssen, *Present Pasts: Urban Palimpsests and the Politics of Memory* (Stanford: Stanford University Press, 2003), p. 168 note 3; orig. "The Voids of Berlin," *Critical Inquiry*, 24.1 (1997), pp. 57–81, p. 62 note 3.

40. Oswalt, "Berlin, Stadt des 20. Jahrhunderts," p. 117.

41. Mirko Pogoreutz, "Urban Intelligence," in Florian Haydn and Robert Temel, eds, trans. David Skog Ley and Steven Lindberg, *Temporary Urban Spaces. Concepts for the Use of City Spaces* (Boston: Birkhäuser, 2006), pp. 75–80, p. 77.

42. Henri Lefebvre, *The Production of Space*, trans. D. Nicholson-Smith (Cambridge, MA: Blackwell, 1991), pp. 35, 36.

43. Uwe Timm, *Johannisnacht* (Munich: dtv, 1998).

44 Inka Parei, *Die Schattenboxerin* (Frankfurt am Main: Fischer, 2001), p. 132.

45. Jesse Shapins and Johannes Touché, "Kein bürgerliches Idyll: Der Mauerpark wirkt als energievolles Stadtlandschaft," *scheinschlag*, 8 (2002), p. 5.

46. See www.mauerpark.info/politik/mehr-park (date accessed 2 January, 2010).
47. See Jesse Shapins, "Excavating the Mauerpark: Landscape Archaeology of a Berlin Open Space," senior thesis in Urban Studies (Columbia College, 2002), at: www.columbia.edu/cu/museo/jesse/thesis (date accessed 2 January, 2010).
48. Cold-War-era travelogues of the inner German border include B. Irmischer and D. Moldmann, *Am Deutsch-Deutschen Rand. Landschaft, Geschichte, Kultur, Wirtschaft entlang einer 1240km Reiseroute am östlichen Rand der Bundesrepublik* (Hamburg: Moldmann-Verlag, 1989). Post-Cold-War travelogues by westerners and easterners alike differ in tone but share a sense of *temps perdu*: see, for example, Oliver August, *Along the Wall and Watchtowers* (London: Flamingo, 2003); and Landolf Scherzer, *Der Grenz-Gänger* (Berlin: Aufbau-Verlag, 2005). On the environmental benefits of closed borderlands, see Alan Weisman, *The World without Us* (New York: Picador, 2007).
49. Scherzer, *Der Grenz-Gänger*, pp. 239, 253, 280, 233. The Gompertshausen *Asylantenheim* closed in 2007.
50. Ulrich Bergt, "Hennigsdorf stellt Nutzungskonzept für einstiges Militärgelände vor," *Märkische Allgemeine* (16 June, 2010); Markus Kavka, "Störungsmelder. Nö, stört uns nicht," *Zeit-Online* (13 December, 2007); and http://brandenburg.de/media_fast/5791/bericht_2002.pdf (date accessed 30 June, 2010).
51. On diversified, green open-space planning in post-Wall Berlin, see Sören Schöbel, *Qualitative Freiraumplanung. Perspektiven städtischer Grün- und Freiräume aus Berlin* (Berlin: Wissenschaftlicher Verlag, 2003).
52. Joe Jackson, *Rain* (Pokazuka Ltd; Sony/ATV Music Publishing, 2007).
53. In 2004, an exhibition dedicated to these reclamation efforts, entitled "Preußisch Grün," was held at Schloß Glienicke, and organized by the Stiftung Preußische Schlösser und Gärten Berlin-Brandenburg.
54. Greens politician Michael Cramer, who initiated the Berlin Wall cycling path, also proposed and organized the Iron Curtain cycle route. See Michael Cramer, *Europa Radweg. Eiserner Vorhang* (2009), at: www.ironcurtain-trail.eu (date accessed 3 May, 2010); and Cramer, *Berliner Mauer-Radweg* (Rodingersdorf: Esterbauer, 2001).
55. See the Central European Green Belt, www.greenbelteurope.eu (date accessed 1 May, 2010); and Tony Paterson, "From Iron Curtain to Green Belt: How New Life Came to the Death Strip," *The Independent* (17 May, 2009).
56. See www.ms-versenken.org/; and the Marthashof citizens' initiative (http://marthashof.info/?p=aktuell), which is protesting against an upscale condo development near the Oderbergerstraße in Prenzlauer Berg (date accessed 10 May, 2010); discussed by Christoph Scheuermann, "Developers and Dreamers Battle over Berlin Identity," *Spiegel Online International* (9 November, 2008).
57. "73 Prozesse zum Uferweg Griebnitzsee-Streit kostete Stadt bisher 325000 Euro," *Potsdamer Neueste Nachrichten* (24 June, 2009).
58. Sabine Schicketanz, "Der alte Grenzzaun steht wieder," *Der Tagesspiegel* (25 May, 2010); and Alexander Fröhlich, "Jetzt ist der Uferweg dicht," *Der Tagesspiegel* (6 July, 2009).
59. See Durs Grünbein's impassioned plea for East Germans to fare better with their life memories in his recent speech: "Unfreiheit. Rede in der Frauenkirche

zu Dresden am 6. Oktober 2009," *Deutschland-Archiv*, 42.6 (2009), pp. 983–92. GDR-memory organizations include the research institute Zentrum für Zeithistorische Forschung Potsdam e.V., but also many private citizens' associations like the Bund der Stalinistische Verfolgten e.V.; Bürger Büro e.V. Berlin (Verein zur Aufarbeitung von Folgeschäden der SED-Diktatur); Förderverein Gedenkbibliothek zu Ehren der Opfer des Stalinismus e.V.; Hannah-Arendt-Institut für Totalitarismusforschung (in Dresden); Stiftung zur Aufarbeitung der SED-Diktatur; and the Vereinigung der Opfer des Stalinismus e.V.

60. Jana Hensel, *Zonenkinder* (Hamburg: Rowohlt, 2002), p. 45.

61. Jens Schneider, "Mutual Othering: East and West Berliners Happily Divided?," in Carol-Anne Costabile-Heming, Rachel J. Halverson, and Kristie A. Foell, eds, *Berlin: The Symphony Continues. Orchestrating Architectural, Social, and Artistic Change in the New Capital* (Berlin: Walter de Gruyter, 2004), pp. 165–86, pp. 180–81.

62. Samira Gloor Fadel, dir., *Berlin-Cinéma* (Switzerland-France: Les Films de la Terrasse, 1998).

63. As Wolfgang Kil complains: "With every disappearing empty lot, a piece of uncertainty also disappears ... Instead come facts, all instantly complete. Berlin is becoming real. What is one still meant to dream of it?" Kil, "Vom Verschwinden des Himmels über Berlin," in Pröfener, ed., *Zeitzeichen Baustelle*, pp. 88–93, p. 93.

64. John Bornemann, "State, Territory, and Identity Formation in the Postwar Berlins, 1945–1989," *Cultural Anthropology*, 7.1 (1992), pp. 45–62, pp. 46, 58.

65. Heiner Müller, "Was ein Kunstwerk kann, ist Sehnsucht wecken" (1976), *Gesammelte Irrtümer 1. Interviews und Gespräche* (Frankfurt am Main: Verlag der Autoren, 1986), pp. 130–40, p. 135; and Uwe Johnson, "Berliner Stadtbahn" (1961), in Johnson, *Berliner Sachen. Aufsätze* (Frankfurt am Main: Suhrkamp, 1975), pp. 7–21, p. 19.

66. Gert Mattenklott, "Entgrenzungen. Die Mauer im Museum," in Markus Bauer and Thomas Rahn, eds, *Die Grenze. Begriff und Inszenierung* (Berlin: Akademie Verlag, 1997), pp. 255–59, pp. 258, 257. See, in this respect, Karl Jaspers' notion of asserting one's identity when rising to the challenge of a border-crossing: Jaspers, *Philosophie II. Existenzerhellung* (Berlin: Springer, 1973), pp. 201–54.

67. See especially the novels *Lagerfeuer* by Julia Franck (Cologne: Dumont, 2003) and *Aus der Geschichte der Trennungen* by Jürgen Becker (Frankfurt am Main: Suhrkamp, 1999). See also Katharina Gerstenberger, *Writing the New Berlin: The German Capital in Post-Wall Literature* (Rochester, NY: Camden House, 2008), pp. 124–29; Katharina Grätz, "Das Andere hinter der Mauer. Retrospektive Grenzkonstruktion und Grenzüberschreitung in Julia Francks 'Lagerfeuer' und Wolfgang Hilbigs 'Das Provisorium'," in Barbara Beßlich, Grätz, and Olaf Hildebrand, eds, *Wende des Erinnerns? Geschichtskonstruktionen in der deutschen Literatur nach 1989* (Berlin: Erich Schmidt Verlag, 2006), pp. 243–57, p. 256; Dieter Lamping, *Über Grenzen – Eine literarische Topographie* (Göttingen: Vandenhoeck & Ruprecht, 2001); and Edgar Platen and Martin Todthaupt, eds, *Grenzen, Grenzüberschreitungen, Grenzauflösungen. Zur Darstellung von Zeitgeschichte in deutschsprachiger Gegenwartsliteratur* (Munich: iudicium, 2004).

68. Zafer Şenocak, "Selling the Still of Morning at the Market" ("Verkauf der Morgenstimmung am Markt"), *Door Languages*, trans. Elizabeth Oehlkers Wright (Brookline: Zephyr Press, 2008), pp. 146–47. On German-Turkish post-reunification issues, see Hilary Silver, "Social Integration in the 'New' Berlin," *German Politics and Society*, 81.24 (2006), pp. 1–48.

69. Zafer Şenocak, *Atlas des tropischen Deutschland. Essays*, 2nd ed. (Berlin: Babel Verlag Hund & Toker, 1993), pp. 25–26, 41, 47.

70. Şenocak, *Atlas*, p. 42. In this context, see Stefano Allievi's work in favor of a "transnational Muslim space" in Europe. Migrants are the ultimate hybrid citizens, asserts Allievi, since "for them 'being globalized' is not only their job – it is their way of life." Allievi, "Islam in the Public Space: Social Networks, Media and Neo-Communities," in Allievi and Jørgen Nielsen, eds, *Muslim Networks and Transnational Communities in and across Europe* (Boston: Brill, 2003), pp. 1–27, pp. 7, 8. European Muslim culture is not entirely in favor with hybridity theories, however. See Ayse S. Caglar, "Hyphenated Identities and the Limits of 'Culture'," in Tariq Modood and Pnina Werbner, eds, *The Politics of Multiculturalism in the New Europe: Racism, Identity and Community* (New York: Zed Books, 1997), pp. 169–85. On Germany's blind spots, see Ruth Ellen Mandel, *Cosmopolitan Anxieties. Turkish Challenges to Citizenship and Belonging in Germany* (Durham, NC: Duke University Press, 2008).

71. Şenocak, *Atlas*, p. 88.

72. Fatina Keilani, "Sommerhaus rüber: Eine Hütte wechslet den Bezirk," *Der Tagesppiegel* (17 July, 2004), p. 12.

73. The empty lot filled by the Kreuzberg mosque dates from 1987, when a 1st of May arson attack destroyed a supermarket on that site. Lars von Tonne, "Berlin: Minarette über Kreuzberg," *Der Tagesspiegel* (21 May, 2007). See Patricia Ehrkamp's study of right-wing opposition against the building of prominent mosques, "Migrants, Mosques, and Minarets: Reworking the Boundaries of Liberal Democracy in Switzerland and Germany," forthcoming in Marc Silberman, Karen E. Till, and Janet Ward, eds, *Walls, Borders, Boundaries: Spatial and Cultural Practices in Europe* (Oxford and New York: Berghahn Books, 2012).

74. See Sabine Hake, *Topographies of Class: Modern Architecture and Mass Society in Weimar Berlin* (Ann Arbor: University of Michigan Press, 2008).

75. "It is from Alexanderplatz that I would start thinking about the metropolitan promise of Berlin between East and West"; see Peter Fritzsche, "A City of Strangers or a City of Neighbors? Berlin Confronts Metropolis," in Frank Trommler, ed., *Berlin: The New Capital in the East: A Transatlantic Appraisal* (Washington, DC: American Institute for Contemporary German Studies, 2000), pp. 23–36, pp. 32, 33. See also Gina Weszkalnys, *Berlin, Alexanderplatz: Transforming Place in a Unified Germany* (Oxford and New York: Berghahn Books, 2010); and Joan Copjec and Michael Sorkin, eds, *Giving Ground: The Politics of Propinquity* (London: Verso, 1999).

76. Resistance to developing the Alexanderplatz into a high-rise city occurred, for example, in an art exhibition at the DNA gallery in Mitte, "Whose Alexanderplatz?" and its accompanying discussion evening, which was organized by the "public space development" group in July 2002, on the topic of "Outpost of Mongolia? Or, What the Eastern Extension has to do with the Architecture of Berlin."

77. Wolfgang Ribbe, *Berlin 1945–2000. Grundzüge der Stadtgeschichte* (Berlin: Berliner Wissenschafts-Verlag, 2002), p. 187.

78. Erich Konter et al., "Papierbild einer Weltstadtcity: Der neue Alexanderplatz," in Harald Bodenschatz, ed., *Renaissance der Mitte. Zentrumsumbau in London und Berlin* (Berlin: Verlagshaus Braun, 2005), pp 249–61, p. 260. Ralf Schönball, "Alle wollen an den Alex," *Der Tagesspiegel* (29 June, 2010).

79. Paul Goldberger predicted that if Berlin "becomes only a new city, it will not be Berlin." Goldberger, "Reimagining Berlin," *The New York Times Magazine* (5 February, 1995).

80. Richard von Weizsäcker, *Von Deutschland aus. Reden des Bundespräsidenten* (Munich: Deutscher Taschenbuch Verlag, 1987) p. 54; Scherzer, *Der Grenz-Gänger*, p. 188.

Part III

German Geomancy: Power and Planning in Berlin

7
World City Planning in Weimar Berlin

Wenn dort das Grenzenlose als unüberwindliches Hindernis
erscheint, so setzt hier das Einfachbegrenzte beinahe noch
schwerer zu überwindende Hindernisse entgegen.
(Johann Wolfgang von Goethe, 1829)[1]

With just days to spare before the city's hosting of the soccer World Cup, Berlin's new central railway station opened in late May, 2006 after a spectacular laser light show. In this huge expansion, five Berlin railway stations and about 50 miles (80km) of new rail routes were opened, re-charting the infrastructural contours not just of post-Wall Berlin, but of the New Europe. When one considers Europe's railway stations in terms of their structure, as formalist creatures of iron and glass, as the urban transit palaces of the Industrial Revolution, one normally also thinks of them as great storehouses of urban, collective, and individual memories. W. G. Sebald certainly conceived of them thus in his novel *Austerlitz* (2001). In this novel, the eponymous protagonist is prompted into a Proustian retrieval of a repressed and painful past, when he stands as an adult in Liverpool Street station in London and remembers his arrival as a child in the British *Kindertransport* action of 1939 that saved him but not his Jewish parents.[2] In contrast, it would appear that in its attempt to build itself afresh, Berlin has created a main station (*Hauptbahnhof*) without memory.

Yet Berlin Central is, in fact, very much a part of the city's infrastructural history of multiple palimpsests. The station stands amidst a series of urban planning dreams and actualities that have, over time, determined the lines – not just the *outer* and but also the *inner* determining boundaries – of modern Berlin. In fact, Berlin's borders have been as much a question of the center as of the periphery. Berlin's contours have been the focus of intense planning discussions and attempted changes throughout the twentieth century. After all, a city's sense of itself and of its own relevance is often recognizable in terms of its infrastructural connections: its axialities, nodes, and grids. While in most major world cities, the key rail/air connections, road axes, natural boundaries, and public buildings all serve as anchors, grounding the signification of the city through the generations, Berlin has been forced to redesign its own contours so often that it has lost this stable tradition of space and identity. The various attempts to draw and redraw, to shape and re-shape the inner and outer boundaries of modern Berlin have played a significant role in how the city has tried to connect to itself, to the rest of Germany, and to the world at large. Berlin's infrastructural lines can be understood to be *in*trinsic as well as *ex*trinsic, (re-)defining as well as confining.

In order to understand how post-Wall Berlin has been busy reconcocting itself as a capital worthy of the name, we need to get a sense of how deeply destabilizing the myriad historical re-definitions of that city's inner core and infrastructural nodes actually were. We need to see how fixated Berlin's planners have been in their attempts at repositioning the city's circulatory functioning – be this for practical, aesthetic, or geopolitical reasons. Ultimately, the damage done to Berlin's genius loci by dint of the twentieth century's urban and political crises visited upon that city ended up creating boundary zones and lines within the center that differed fundamentally from the anchoring purpose served by other European capitals' downtown cores. Berlin's unsteady infrastructural forms can be said to have been literally "edgy" – up for grabs, liminally active, points at which something has been about to change or happen.

In the early decades of the twentieth century, the newly reached world city status of the German capital gave rise to an urgent need to re-shape urban communal identity – Berlin's *civitas* – according to the demands of the modern age and to resurrect a sense of German collective pride in the wake of the Versailles Treaty. Berlin's entry into the league of world cities was generally accepted after 1920, when its 74 various boroughs and districts were incorporated into one legal entity of 353 square miles (884 sq km), Greater Berlin (Groβ-Berlin), making Berlin's terrain larger than its competitors.[3] In the fifty years prior to the start of World War II, the number of Berliners grew from 1.89 million to 4.34 million. Interwar Berlin was (after London and New York) the world's third largest city, a major new cultural and industrial center for Europe and beyond. The radical swiftness of this transition is remarked on by Werner Hegemann, who, in his 1930 book *Berlin in Stone* (*Das steinerne Berlin*) contrasted the traffic of Potsdamer Platz, one of Europe's busiest intersections, with a bucolic sketch a hundred years previously by Karl Friedrich Schinkel, depicting Potsdamer Platz as a customs gate with the adjoining Leipziger Platz, and just five boys playing ball with their dog.[4]

Not all German reflections on the centering effect of the self-modernizing city were as welcoming. Oswald Spengler, in his dark interpretation of "The Soul of the City," blamed the emblem of the skyscraper for embodying the principle of un-German (American) "civilization," namely the cosmopolitan world city itself, which he abhorred:

> There arises the monstrous symbol and vessel of the completely emancipated intellect, the world-city, the center in which the course of a world-history ends by winding itself up ... [and] disfranchises and disvalues the entire motherland of its own Culture ... [...] The stone Colossus "Cosmopolis" stands at the end of the life's course of every great Culture. [...] This stony mass is the *absolute* city.[5]

Spengler uses Aristotle's term for urban densification's bringing together of differences, namely "synoecism" (Gr.: *synoikismos*), defined as the pull toward living together in the "densest nucleus," and the feeling of being in and of the urban fabric. But in Spengler's Cosmopolis, this coming together is not authentic. The "man of the world-cities" lives in a universe disconnected from the natural environs: "*the world of the upper floors*" is built on an "artificial footing." It is apparent from Spengler's dystopian sense of a disconnected and disconnecting metropolis, written on the eve of World War I and at the dawn of the Weimar Republic, that he was resistant to the social and design impact of high urban densification (*Verdichtung*) typically used to provide the modern nation's ultimate sense of (capital-city) place. We can find, in Spengler's attack on "*the world of the upper floors*," a critique of city lines (whether vertical skyscrapers, or horizontal technologized transportation systems) that literally divided people from the natural ground(ing) of the earth.[6]

In the urban sociologist Georg Simmel's "Bridge and Door" essay of 1909, we can locate an alternative perspective to that of Spengler. Indirect praise of urban planning can be found in this essay's focus on the necessary contiguity of space that focuses on (city) lines that join as well as break apart. Simmel's thematization of the spatial dialectics of *binden* (bind) and *lösen* (release), or *verbinden* (connect) and *trennen* (divide), are demonstrated by two built forms, the bridge and the door. Simmel recognizes that both forms point to humankind's ability to connect between two entities: in the case of the bridge, between two finite points, or in the case of the door, between the finite and the infinite (inside and outside). As Simmel sees it, we design these things because they reflect our physical and ontological condition: "things must first be separated from one another in order to be together. [...] [W]e are at any moment those who separate the connected or connect the separate. [...] [T]he human being is the connecting creature who must always separate and cannot connect without separating ... And the human being is likewise the bordering creature who has no border."[7]

In an important sense, modern planning history (and especially that of Berlin) reflects Simmel's detection of a symbiotic *frisson* between connection and division. That which Simmel calls "path-building" (*Wegebau*) – or specifically in the case of urban modernity, the re-definition of a city's center and its arteries – demonstrates humankind's ongoing dual need for joining the separated and defining separations within otherwise unified space. As Simmel states, "it ... [is] only in visibly impressing the path into the surface of the earth that places ... [are] objectively connected"; the "will to connection" (*Verbindungswille*) becomes a defining, a contouring, a "shaping of things" (*Gestaltung der Dinge*).[8] It is by defining difference (by highlighting separation) that, conversely, connection is forged for the whole spatial entity.

Simmel's spatial philosophy of modernity provides a useful antidote to the way in which modern urban planning has been generally depicted, especially in postmodern urban theory, as a malign fiction that went on to become a nightmarish reality. Nazi Germany's plans for its cities would certainly appear to be a case in postmodernist point. In his *Right to the City* (*Le droit à la ville*, 1967), Henri Lefebvre began the critique of how problems of modern capitalist society became transposed into planning ones, and how theories of "rationality and organization" turned into pathological "questions of space." In tandem with the avant-garde group, Situationist International, Lefebvre was reacting not so much to what had come before and with the Nazis, however, as against post-World War II planning as a top-down imposed order with rigid zoning. Rather than bring urban spaces together, modern (post-World War II) planning is, for Lefebvre, "an ideology which immediately divides up." He favors instead a socially integrative localization of planning efforts, and hence abhors "planning by extrapolation" for being overly "graphic and visual, tending toward meta-language," and for being pro-establishment.[9]

The conceptual evil of urban planning as a thought-and-deed-system would appear to originate in the fact that maps – and nowadays digital and satellite imaging, as well as virtual-reality models of cities and geographic information systems (GIS) – give us an illusion of controllable, designable, familiarized space. Certainly, the art of cartography has, since the age of exploration, been linked to shameless "territorial propaganda" that legitimized and facilitated acts of conquest.[10] Michel de Certeau, responding to the mistakes of postwar planning, offered his insight into these cartographical blind spots: "The map, a totalizing stage on which elements of diverse origin are brought together to form the tableau of a 'state' of geographical knowledge, pushes away ... as if into the wings, the operations of which it is the result or the necessary condition. It remains alone on the stage." De Certeau's landmark book of 1974, *The Practice of Everyday Life*, is aimed at resisting and undoing what he adopts from Michel Foucault as the spatial "grid of 'discipline'" inherent in modern institutions. In his project, de Certeau identifies and praises the "practices that are foreign to the 'geometrical' or 'geographical' space of visual, panoptic, or theoretical constructions" – he prefers to look at the daily activities of the ordinary *citadins* that prevail despite the "clear text of the planned and readable city." The enemy of such creative, metaphorical activity in the city (especially his favorite, *flânerie*) is clearly, he asserts, "the space planner urbanist, city planner or cartographer ... the voyeur-god." For de Certeau, planning creates but a "fiction": "The panorama-city is a 'theoretical' (that is, visual) simulacrum, in short a picture, whose condition of possibility is an oblivion and a misunderstanding of practices." Rather than remain within the unified demarcations of "topical," cartographical space, de Certeau embraces the possibilities of "topological" spatial arrangements that recognize the ways in which human input subverts all demarcation lines.[11]

The impact of Lefebvre and de Certeau on postmodern spatial theory has helped create a scholarly climate in which modern planning is held in very low esteem. Its cardinal sin is that it has been based on the systematic primacy of overseeable visuality: its totalizing, fixing tendencies damage contemporary sensitivities to spatial fluidity and the everyday tangibility of urban life. As a result, postmodern geographers and planning theorists have been seeking to deconstruct the modern map and its various power-contexts, bringing our attention to the hyper-real ways in which maps forge territories and cultural/bodily identities (and not the other way around).[12] As if seeking atonement for their discipline's past, they advocate post-Euclidean, de-centered, non-know-it-all planning that wants the involvement of the acted-upon (namely: real people).

Yet planning's origins, usually taken to coincide with the Renaissance, are less ominous than we might think: cartography's ideal of the Euclidean city has simply rested on the Ptolemaic grid of perspectivism.[13] This is how the architect (or more especially the planner/engineer) first assumed the role of urban inspector, or *surveillant*. The *Discourse on Method* itself promulgated an urban form which was, according to Descartes, "regularly laid out on a plain."[14] This plain was initially empty and hence it was open to the imagination of the Cartesian planner – yet the plain itself was not arbitrary.[15] The apparent world-wide power of planning and map-making is but an extension of the Renaissance and Enlightenment mission of universal emancipation within, as it was hoped, an ultimately discoverable, knowable plain of the world.

Of course, urban geomancy – defined as divination of and by a city's lines – has, to some degree, been with us ever since ancient times when divinity was constructed as a key part of the built environment. This is the cosmic form of planning, and applies to the ancient, medieval, baroque, as well as the Nazi city. The Greek origin of the term geomancy, *geomanteia (ge[o]* [ground] + *manteia*, from *mantikos* [divination]), serves to highlight de Certeau's and Lefebvre's discomfort concerning modern planning's intentions and its after-effects now that its original belief-system had, by the time of the Industrial Revolution, been emptied out. Originally, Egyptian, Greek, and Roman cities were geomantically shaped, that is, they were shaped according to their citizens' under-standing of their place in the universe. Roman cities were literally divided into four sections by two orthogonally intersecting axes: the *cardo* (the solar axis), which was crossed by the *decumanus* (the line of the equinox). Early Christian churches were often built on sites of former pagan temples; the churches, like the temples before them, were geomantically positioned as centering devices for the city as a whole. By the Baroque era, urban geomantics took the form of the radially planned city, which enhanced the visual power of the urban ruling caste, royal or otherwise: Pope Sixtus V built radial axes in Rome, for example, in order to augment public perception of his own proximity to the divine.[16]

However, the established space-time framework of this mission imploded under the impact of industrial modernity. David Harvey has demonstrated how the "annihilation of space through time" occurred through such late nineteenth- and early twentieth-century developments as radio transmission, Fordist mass production, advanced transportation networks, and the concomitant impact of Einstein's discovery of relativity. Harvey quotes Friedrich Nietzsche's will to power as the sum of all that was left in modernity's space-time compression. Nietzsche's exhilarating phrase of the post-Enlightenment world rings true as a "monster of energy, without beginning, without end. [...] Enclosed by 'nothingness' as by a boundary [...] set in a definite space as a definite force [...] as force throughout, as a play of forces and waves of forces..."[17] Modern planners and map-makers were left with the Cartesian plain, but it had been emptied out into a *tabula rasa*. Map-making was driven by a will to power based on principles of infinite expansion. The tools of modern planning and cartography filled in the plain, but without divine help. This is how rational(izing) man, as urban planner, substituted himself into God's role; one thinks here of Weimar artist George Grosz's functionalist-subversive sketch of 1921, *The New Man* (*Der neue Mensch*). In urban modernity, the planner became a geomancer, whether in terms of the city's proposed visual system of power, or the garden city's proposed social and environmental hygiene. While modern geomancy was not limited to the city, "world city" status could make or break geopolitical perceptions. Modernity's practice of geopolitics extended the lines of power from the metropolitan core to the entire state and its colonies.[18]

Nonetheless, what is generally understood to be the negative urban planning project of modernity needs to be revisited as an experiment in power. Bruno Latour's useful adjustment of Foucauldian theory suggests how urban modernity proffered oligoptic (rather than panoptic) systems of surveillance by which only partial (rather than total) control could be exercised at any given time.[19] Simmel's demonstration of how space is reconfigured by humankind into a sense of place, into lines that connect by dividing and divide by connecting, can be seen in terms of the industrial city's articulations of efficient circulation and nodal power. And it is really not as if this focus went away in the post-industrial, postmodern era. What we may term the foundational *lines of power* for Berlin – its streets, its infrastructure, its traffic and transportation network, its tempo, its internal and external connections – were formed according to the early twentieth century's demands, broken by modernity's two "hot" world wars and then its "cold" one, and are now being renewed for the twenty-first. These lines of power were planning's attempts to (re-)anchor and (re-)connect the at-first relatively unformed, then deformed (broken and divided), and now re-formed capital of Germany. Berlin's geomancy project, then, is still underway, and it should not be reduced to panopticism alone.

Putting Berlin on the map has always been an uphill struggle in terms of its reputation, at least among Germans. Observers in the Wilhelmine era assumed the new capital could not aspire to the urban cohesiveness and impressive vistas of more established world cities. We turn again to Karl Scheffler, Berlin's critical observer, who ascertained that Berlin had never grown organically out from the center, but rather had expanded haphazardly. These are its uncorrectable, "constitutional" failings, he says, which prevent ultimate "order, rhythm, and harmony." Writing in 1910, he contrasts "organic" (by which he means good, planned) growth with "arbitrary" (bad, unplanned) growth, unconsciously pointing up his era's association of planning as a plant-like, yet regularized growth-pattern. "The non-organic development of Berlin is apparent in how it did not swell evenly from the inside to the outside, but rather emerged piece-meal, in an almost arbitrary placement of sections next to each other." The result for Berlin: "a formless city shape [*ein formloser Stadtkörper*]: just by looking at the city map, one is amazed at the lack of clear structure."[20] The outline of a city tells you as much, Scheffler says, as do the rings of a felled tree. You can read the "original core" (*Urkern*) of a city that way.

So, we may indeed ask, just what was the complaining voice of Scheffler in search of? He was looking for axial main streets that indicate "buildable strength shining forth powerfully from the middle point," but he admits he could not find this trait in late Wilhelmine Berlin: "There's not a single street that cuts decisively through the city from north to south, or from east to west."[21] Of course there *were* shorter axes, especially the city's royal boulevard, Unter den Linden, built as the Great Elector's *via triumphalis* of the seventeenth century. By Scheffler's Imperial era, the dominant additional street lines were commercial ones: the north-south Friedrichstraße that crossed Unter den Linden, and the east-west Kurfürstendamm, its newer rival boulevard west of the Tiergarten park. But Scheffler faults most main streets for not intersecting consciously with the city's core, or forming important intersections, but ending in side streets or in the countryside. Unter den Linden was at least beginning to serve more as an artery thanks to its extension in the early 1900s further west beyond the Tiergarten, along the new Heerstraße. But Unter den Linden still had no symbolic or topographical relationship with the Kurfürstendamm. The city's various terminus train stations were gradually joined by the networks of the underground railway (U-Bahn, the first line of which was opened in 1902), and, after 1924, by the local rail system (the S-Bahn); but major road arteries remained deficient.

This frustrating situation was the inheritance of a city whose com-mercial life had moved "around" the existing Tiergarten and continually south-westwards beyond the old royal center in Mitte; thus the Tiergarten, formerly outside the city boundaries, accidentally ended up becoming the geographical middle, a doughnut hole around which the two actual centers in east and then west were formed. Barack Obama's speech at Berlin's Victory Column in July 2008 was held precisely in the middle of that doughnut hole. Having been refused the opportunity, by Chancellor Angela Merkel, to speak in former President Ronald Reagan's shadow at the Wall's most famous centerpiece, the Brandenburg Gate – a site considered too presumptuous for a US presidential candidate – Obama's next-best location at the Tiergarten's central point turned out to be, in fact, equally apt in terms of the city's past infrastructural dilemmas.

Wilhelmine Berlin's actual center possessed "nothing" of relevance, Scheffler continues, for the main streets. Scheffler blames this lack of "rhythm" on Berlin's non-contoured condition.[22] No matter how long you lived in the city, it could "confuse" you all over again. A source of the perceived problem was the lack of a standardized and rail-interlinked street network like that of the 85 miles of new roads for Paris designed between 1850 and 1870 by Seine prefect Georges-Eugène Haussmann. A further cause, Scheffler remarks, was the geographical inadequacy of the river Spree for not being enough of a "border- or orientation-concept" from west to east; as a result, unlike the Seine's relevance for Paris or the Thames for London, no one referred to whether he or she lived north or south of the Spree (and this is still the case today).[23]

It would have made Scheffler feel even more justified in his critique could he had known that Berlin would end up exiting the twentieth century just as it had entered it: with a problematic perception of itself as formless, lacking in contours and definition, with a weak center and a good-for-nothing river. Scheffler's views reflected a general assent that modern Berlin was in need of invasive, surgical planning if it was to catch up with its rivals on the world-city-stage. Perhaps as a result of this need, Foucault's claim that architects do not usually participate in the spatial-engineering realm of "territory, communication, and speed" does not apply to modern Berlin.[24] The city's multiple areas had proven hard to manage during the harsh war economy of World War I, but by 1918 planners were posing the question: *"How could we better define the borders of a future Greater Berlin?"*[25] The formation of a more unified Groß-Berlin in 1920 was seen as a response both to that crisis and the responsibilities that came with being a world city.

In particular, Martin Wagner, Berlin's Social Democrat director of urban planning (*Oberbaurat*) from December 1926 until his dismissal by the Nazis in 1933, fused the missions of architecture and planning in a strong vision of renewal for Berlin.[26] He aimed to reshape the center of the German capital via a streamlining of both architectural shape and infrastructural circulation. Wagner's reformist desire for roads was matched by the uniform Building Ordinance of late 1925, a first attempt at garden-city-oriented zoning aimed at decongesting the residential problem of the city: the infamously overcrowded back tenement apartments of the "rental barracks" (*Mietskasernen*).[27] Wagner operated amidst a general assent among his peer group of planners and architects of the Modern movement (*Neues Bauen*) that "axial plans," as derived from the Baroque era and as adapted by Haussmann, were the best way to forge a modern imprint upon the German metropolis, especially the capital.

For Wagner, Berlin was a mechanized operation or factory, to be molded into even more efficient motion, and he as chief planner was to be its orchestral "conductor" (*Dirigent*).[28] He wanted to apply the same mindset of urban musical machinery – a ceaseless harmony of composition and productivity – that is reflected in Walther Ruttmann's film of 1927, *Berlin, Symphony of a City* (*Berlin, Sinfonie der Großstadt*). It was as if Germany's first traffic light (installed at Potsdamer Platz at the end of 1924) had become the focal point around which urban design issues now circulated along with the vehicles. In 1929, Wagner designed a master plan for improving traffic flow at Potsdamer Platz, the westernmost portal to the old city center, with new buildings to match that wrapped themselves around the concepts of mechanized tempo and rationalized directionality. Indeed, this plan was part of Wagner's larger project with Ernst Reuter, who was in charge of Berlin's transportation, for opening up the capital's traffic arteries, especially those between Mitte in the east and the now more commercially fashionable Charlottenburg in the west.[29]

Wagner is speaking here the language of dynamic functionalist architecture for the commercial sphere made famous during the Weimar years by Erich Mendelsohn, whose ten-storey-high Columbus Haus at Potsdamer Platz was completed in 1932, as a direct inspiration for, as well as response to, Wagner's advocacy of the sheer energy of circulation revolving across that site. Wagner insisted that architecture and planning alike should follow the modern metropolis's most vital signs, namely traffic and consumerism. In fact, announced Wagner in a lecture during 1929, buildings should adapt their contours – their "*flow*" or "*flight* lines" (Flucht*linien*) – to the undulating "*directional* lines" (Gang*linien*) taken by would-be consumers. Particular attention should be paid, Wagner said, to the moments when the attention of people crossing the square, whether on foot or in vehicles (the "*moving* traffic," or Fließ*verkehr*), was caught by the actual attractions of the Stand*verkehr* (the "*stationary*" or "*frozen* traffic," so to speak) of powerful consumerist architecture. The goal, he declared, of building a "world city square" (*Weltstadtplatz*) fit for Berlin's capitalist modernity was to offer both a "stopping-point for consumer capacity and a through-passage for moving traffic." The role of building here was dual: as both consumer-entrapping spectacle (applying, he emphasized, the "*color, form,* and *light*" of electric advertising by night), and as traffic-circulation facilitator.[30]

Most of what Wagner wanted for his musical conducting of the Berlin factory-organism, however, did not get realized due to the stock market crash of 1929, which halted the post-inflation stabilization period of the Weimar Republic. Apart from Mendelsohn's Columbus Haus, the only actual impact on Potsdamer Platz by Wagner's philosophy of planning as a spectacle dedicated to circulation and shopping occurred in the improvement of the U-Bahn connections underneath the site. In 1929, thanks to an American loan of $15 million, Wagner supervised the building of the U-Bahn station under the Hermannplatz junction in Berlin-Neukölln, a connection which "fed" consumer-travelers directly into the new Karstadt department store above the station. Wagner remained a ceaseless capital-city promoter by means of planning Berlin into (modernity's) being, and his boosterist influence was enormously significant.[31]

Even though Wagner's New Berlin remained on the level of the "not yet," his Berlin-boosterism was eminently practical for the needs of reviving the psyche of a defeated Germany in the wake of the First World War. Wagner asserted: "The dynamic extension of our urban system seems to me to be far more important than sketching ideal city plans for the next century, and chasing an ideal phenomenon with hysterical worry whose ideal aspects do not last longer than a minute." Wagner illustrated this need to keep pace by citing the growth of automobiles in Berlin from 38,000 in 1925 to 82,000 in 1928.[32] Those who did not have access to cars went by tram, yet inevitably, car culture was on its way. Germany's urban fabric, Wagner realized after two study trips in 1924 and 1929 to a dozen US cities, would have to be "restructured" to absorb the unstoppable rise of the automobile, the experience of which would release people from "spatial and temporal fixedness." While obviously lagging behind metropolitan New York of the 1920s, where there was one car for every six people and a population of ten million, Berlin, he asserted, was nonetheless "well on the way to adapting to the American traffic revolution."[33] In the meantime, Berlin was becoming well acquainted with the negative side of this traffic revolution, experiencing a host of traffic accidents at its major intersections. Many planners understandably wished to untie the knot of inner Berlin. This need is illustrated by a "traffic-spider" image of Berlin in 1930 that is contrasted with that of London.[34] Weimar Berliners did not commute in from the outside green, like Londoners did and still do; rather, they traveled within the ring of what Werner Hegemann called the packed-in enclosure of the "city in stone." Wagner's aim remained a simple yet challenging one, that of combating the "moloch of 'transit'," the primacy of which shaped and determined all other considerations.[35]

This goal alone propelled such apparently domineering statements as: "A world city cannot be ruled and configured boldly and foresightedly enough."[36] In this situation of building new critical nodes and connectors into being, particularly during the Weimar Republic's brief years of economic and political stabilization (1924–1929), we can find the best illustration of the fact that modern German urban culture was an American capitalist apprentice, focusing on improving the circulatory system of the living transit-city. A second context was applied German nationalism: improving the capital's arteries and networks to the country and beyond served to bring about a perception that the various parts of a still non-cohesive Germany could be integrated.[37]

Wagner also focused his desire for infrastructural innovation on the Alexanderplatz, the old city center's eastern portal, which by the late 1920s had gained the city's largest underground and intercity rail stations, with twenty-three tram lines and nine bus lines running overground. Wagner published a clear set of guidelines for the redesign of the Alexanderplatz in *The New Berlin* (*Das Neue Berlin*) of 1929, a glossy publication that he co-edited with Adolf Behne, aimed at promoting Hans Poelzig's newly designed exhibition halls (the *Messegelände*) and Wagner's own aims for world-city transformations for Berlin (Fig. 7.1). Plans for the overhauling of the Alex went much further than just a boosterist coffee table book, however: in 1929, the poor residential area surrounding the Alex was razed, all in the spirit of commerce-oriented urban renewal. The 1928 design competition for the Alex was won by the Luckhardt brothers and Alfons Anker with a Mendelsohnian design of high-rise buildings, whose façades were adorned solely by horizontal bands of windows, undulating according to what were understood to be the curves of vehicular and ambulatory flow. It was this attention to a city's circulation, as the engine of modernity's wealth and growth, that would make an intersection like Alexanderplatz transform, in Wagner's words, from a "*small* town square" (Klein*stadtplatz*) to a "*world*-city square" (Welt*stadtplatz*).[38] And every quarter century, estimated Wagner, one would have to re-shape this world city's squares to accommodate the new needs of traffic flow. In the final analysis, the American investors for the Alex permitted only a partial rebuilding, not by the Luckhardts and Anker but by Peter Behrens, whose two matching office structures, the still extant Berolina Haus and Alexander Haus, were but the "gateway" part of Behrens' overall plan that likewise adhered to Wagner's Mendelsohnian principles.

Intriguingly, Ludwig Mies van der Rohe's design for the Alexanderplatz competition did not fit in with Wagner's prescription. Of the invited

Figure 7.1 Martin Wagner's master plan for the Alexanderplatz, Berlin, 1928

contributions, Mies's design was accorded last place, probably because it completely interrupted Wagner's Mendelsohnian tenets. Instead, it pronounced a new vision. The angles of Mies's solitaire glass high-rise boxes stand in direct opposition to the directions of traffic flow across the Alex: they would have served as incisions in the urban fabric, with an emptying-out effect in between the structures – an outright rejection of any Simmelesque awareness of the built environment serving as connecting "bridge" or "door." While Mies disliked Wagner's and Poelzig's redesign of the Berlin trade fair area for being too monumental, he seems not to have minded that his own re-conception of the Alex would have forged a new scale and form, one that purposefully avoided interacting with the traffic and people all around it.[39]

Equal to Mies in radical planning was Ludwig Hilberseimer, who publicly defended Mies's entry for the Alex against Wagner's traffic-lines-based prescription of architectural dynamism: "Previously," wrote Hilberseimer, "it was architecture that raped traffic. Today the reverse seems to be the case," he quipped as a way of shoring up Mies's traffic-negating approach.[40] Hilberseimer made the aim of his "high-rise city" quite clear: to remove the traffic-ridden chaos and pin down the essential design tenets for modernity – "theoretical systematization" that forges from contexts the "fundamental principles of urban planning."[41] Hilberseimer's new city blocks reflect the impact of Le Corbusier's project for the "Ville contemporaine pour 3 millions d'habitants" of 1922. In both models, center and radiality are replaced with separate zones of functional allocation that intend to make the modern city look like a Fordist factory. When we recall Hilberseimer's cellular planning, as witnessed in his 1929 design for the Friedrichstraße in Berlin, we may well doubt the wisdom of his own use of the "rape"-verb concerning what he would have done to regulate movement in this particular area of downtown, all in the name of his purified version of *Neues Bauen*. In point of fact, Hilberseimer, in 1963, later opposed his own former metropolis designs with the self-condemning term "necropolis."[42]

The *agon* between Wagner on the one hand, and Mies or Hilberseimer on the other, boils down to the fact that while Wagner, as an advocate of the streamlining of the 1920s city, certainly enjoyed the contrastive effects that the Mendelsohn-type dynamic buildings had in relation to the surrounding old Wilhelmine ornamentation and the city's lot-sizes set by the Hobrecht Plan (1862), he did not wish to totally negate them. In contrast, however, the erasure-designs by Mies and by Hilberseimer took the process of efficiency simply too far for Wagner as a planner of New Objectivity (*Neue Sachlichkeit*). In fact, such proposals were to await their eventual realization in the International Style of post-World War II USA and Europe. In the final analysis, it was the Miesian glass tower that ended up shaping downtown planning around itself in cities across the globe as an indicator of corporate strength.

Overall, then, Wagner's aims were decidedly more pedestrian – if one may say that of a car-obsessed German – in that he demonstrated an anti-idealistic and anti-monumental stance toward planning the capital, favoring an extension of Berlin's circulation needs in order to accentuate its world city role. Wagner's voice was one of many who articulated the urgency of solving Berlin's street jams and accidents. Most significantly, he was not trying to artificially stimulate, or create, a world role for Berlin – he was merely responding to the urgent actuality of Berlin's interwar status. Pro-active urban planning that conquered the former "'laisser faire laisser aller'" approach was made all the more necessary now that, as he categorically asserted, *"Berlin has become a world city."* His call for architects and clients to foster a quasi-Zarathustran "willpower to build a world city" articulated an autochthonous correspondence of Berlin's planning to Weimar Germany's position within early twentieth-century industrial modernity.[43]

Martin Wagner's vision for re-shaping Weimar Berlin teaches us an important contrastive lesson concerning decisions made for Germany's reunified capital. Hans Stimmann, the building director in office for most of the capital's post-Wall reconstruction period to date, attempted, like Wagner before him, to build into being an enhanced global relevance. But unlike Wagner, he approved a credo and image for Berlin that emanated from the still-intact modern city – the same city that Wagner regarded as a launch-pad for change and innovation. Approved by the city's Senate Department of Urban Development, Stimmann's policy of Critical Reconstruction went back to the pre-war city footprint as well as its building height and frontage – indeed its main goal has been restorative after the wounds of not just war and division, but of any historical chapters of architectural and ideological imprint upon the city since deemed undesirable (not just Nazi but communist and/or International Style).[44] In Critical Reconstruction's purported reach back into history or modernity, neither history nor modernity is brought forth. In the early twentieth century the new building style (*Neues Bauen*) not just reflected but even helped facilitate the ineluctable change of Berlin. By contrast, the Critical Reconstructionist policy for the post-Wall era has made certain showcase-parts of Berlin (the Friedrichstraße in particular) turn away from both contemporary architectural innovations as well as from a sustained engagement with the actual "historical ground" of Berlin.[45] Thanks to this, for example, streets have been narrowed that Wagner would have dearly wished to open up. An irony mentioned in the documentary film *Berlin's Hidden History* (dir. Brian Ladd and John Woods, 2002) is that in the pre-World War II era of modern Berlin, the new was being built, but that now in postmodern Berlin the old is being built back into the purportedly new urban fabric.[46]

We can conclude here with some advice that Daniel Libeskind offered regarding Berlin's relation to building not just upon but in fruitful relation to all its past identities, welcome or not:

> What is needed is a connection of Berlin to and across its own history. [...] The lost center cannot be reconnected like an artificial

limb to an old body, but must generate an overall transformation of the city. [...] The new vision for Berlin is not utopian in nature, rather it concretely envisions a place that has learned from its past and looks to the future. [...] Since even Orpheus did not succeed in walking backwards into the future.[47]

But "backwards into the future" has indeed been a determining factor in the Critical Reconstructionist platform. When the bottom fell out of the Weimar Berlin economy in the late 1920s, Wagner dedicated himself to different alternatives of urban design and to the needs of mass housing in a broader sense of *Wohnkultur*. Post-Wall Berlin meanwhile did not change course, even when it became clear that a reconstructed Berlin would not a world city make.

Notes

1. Goethe's quote from *Wilhelm Meisters Wanderjahre* (1829) is cited by Werner Hegemann in 1930 in an appeal for (American) frontier-crossing boldness in the urban planning of Berlin. Hegemann, *Das steinerne Berlin. Geschichte der größten Mietskasernenstadt der Welt* (Berlin: Gustav Kiepenheuer, 1930), p. 198.
2. W.G. Sebald, *Austerlitz*, trans. Anthea Bell (London: Hamish Hamilton, 2001), pp. 193–95.
3. Studies of the planning of modern Berlin include Helen Meller, *European Cities 1890–1930s: History, Culture and the Built Environment* (Chichester and New York: John Wiley & Sons, 2001); Brian Ladd, *Urban Planning and Civic Order in Germany, 1860–1914* (Cambridge, MA: Harvard University Press, 1990); and Horst Matzerath, "Berlin 1890–1940," in Anthony Sutcliffe, ed., *Metropolis 1890–1940* (Chicago: University of Chicago Press, 1984), pp. 289–319.
4. Hegemann, *Das steinerne Berlin*, p. 258.
5. Oswald Spengler, "The Soul of the City," from *The Decline of the West*, vol. II, trans. Charles Francis Atkinson (New York: Alfred A. Knopf, 1928); orig. *Der Untergang des Abendlandes: Umrisse einer Morphologie der Weltgeschichte*, vol. II (Munich: Beck, 1918). Repr. in *Classic Essays on the Culture of Cities*, ed. Richard Sennett (New York: Meredith Corporation, 1969), pp. 61–88, pp. 75, 76.
6. Spengler, "The Soul of the City," pp. 78–79. Emphasis original.
7. Georg Simmel, "Brücke und Tür," *Der Tag*, 683.216 (15 September, 1909), pp. 1–3; repr. in Simmel, *Brücke und Tür. Essays des Philosophen zur Geschichte, Religion, Kunst und Gesellschaft*, ed. Michael Landmann (Stuttgart: K.F. Koehler-Verlag, 1957), pp. 1–7, pp. 1–2, 6. Simmel, "Bridge and Door," in Neil Leach, ed., *Rethinking Architecture: A Reader in Cultural Theory* (New York: Routledge, 1997), pp. 66–69, p. 66, 69.
8. Simmel, "Brücke und Tür," p. 6; "Bridge and Door," p. 66.
9. Henri Lefebvre, *Writings on Cities*, trans. Eleonore Kofman and Elizabeth Lebas (Oxford: Blackwell, 1996), pp. 97–99, 152.

10. See, for example, Mark Monmonier, who underlines how "people trust maps": "A good propagandist knows how to shape opinion by manipulating maps. Political persuasion often concerns territorial claims, nationalities, national pride, borders, strategic positions, conquests, attacks, troop movements, defenses, spheres of influence, regional inequality, and other geographic phenomena conveniently portrayed cartographically." Monmonier, *How to Lie with Maps* (Chicago: University of Chicago Press, 1991), p. 87.

11. Michel de Certeau, *The Practice of Everyday Life*, trans. Steven Rendall (Berkeley: University of California Press, 1984), pp. 121, xiv, 93, 129.

12. Correctives include Eleonore Kofman and Elizabeth Lebas, "Recovery and Reappropriation in Lefebvre and Constant," in Jonathan Hughes and Simon Sadler, eds, *Non-Plan: Essays on Freedom, Participation, and Change in Modern Architecture and Urbanism* (Oxford: Architectural Press, 2000), pp. 80–89; Leonie Sandercock's call for contextualization in *Towards Cosmopolis: Planning for Multicultural Cities* (Chichester: John Wiley & Sons, 1998); and Michael J. Dear, *The Postmodern Urban Condition* (Malden and Oxford: Blackwell, 2000). On postmodern urban geography, see John Friedmann, "Toward a Non-Euclidian Mode of Planning," *Journal of the American Planning Association*, 59.4 (1993), pp. 482–85; John Pickles, *A History of Spaces: Cartographic Reason, Mapping, and the Geo-Coded World* (New York: Routledge, 2004); Geoff King, *Mapping Reality: An Exploration of Cultural Cartographies* (New York: St Martin's Press, 1996); and Iain Chambers, "Cities Without Maps," in Jon Bird, Barry Curtis, Tim Putnam, George Robertson, and Lisa Tickner, eds, *Mapping the Futures: Local Cultures, Global Change* (New York: Routledge, 1993), pp. 188–98.

13. See David Harvey, *The Condition of Postmodernity* (Cambridge, MA: Blackwell, 1989), pp. 240–59.

14. René Descartes, *Discourse on the Method* (1637), ed. David Weissman, trans. Elizabeth S. Haldane and G.R.T. Ross (New Haven: Yale University Press, 1996). In contrast with Descartes' legacy, the Asian city, asserts Ken-Ichi Sasaki, is traditionally conceived of more in user terms, namely sheer tactility. See Sasaki, "For Whom is City Design? Tactility versus Visuality," in Malcolm Miles, Tim Hall, and Iain Borden, eds, *The City Cultures Reader* (New York: Routledge, 2004), pp. 36–47, p. 37.

15. See Graham Macphee's discussion of Cartesian visuality in *The Architecture of the Visible* (London: Continuum, 2002), pp. 18–31.

16. On radiality and religion in urban form, see Kevin Lynch, *A Theory of Good City Form* (Cambridge, MA: MIT Press, 1981), p. 72; Lynch, "The Pattern of the Metropolis," and "The Visual Shape of the Shapeless Metropolis," in Tridib Banerjee and Michael Southworth, eds, *City Sense and City Design: Writings and Projects of Kevin Lynch* (Cambridge, MA: MIT Press, 1990), pp. 48–64, 65–86; and Spiro Kostof, *The City Shaped: Urban Patterns and Meanings Through History* (Boston and New York: Bulfinch [Little, Brown and Company], 1999), esp. pp. 174–95, 230–40, 271–75.

17. Harvey, *The Condition of Postmodernity*, p. 274.

18. Massimo Cacciari points to the "evolution from the *Stadt* [city] to the *Staat* [state]" in Max Weber's and Werner Sombart's analyses of rationalization as a process defining Western European urban modernity: "Creating a system, that is a State, from capitalism necessarily implies destroying the city liberties,

the guilds, the fraternitates, the coniuratio of the medieval city. It implies moving toward the realization of the State, as absolute rational ordo, but the city of this ordo is already the Metropolis." Cacciari, *Architecture and Nihilism: On the Philosophy of Modern Architecture*, trans. Stephen Sartarelli (New Haven: Yale University Press, 1993), p. 30. See also James C. Scott, "Authoritarian High Modernism," in Scott Campbell and Susan S. Fainstein, eds, *Readings in Planning Theory*, 2nd ed. (Malden and Oxford: Blackwell, 2003), pp. 125–41; and Lynda Nead's study of the ways in which mapping facilitated the modernization of London's water supply, drains, and sewers, in Nead, *Victorian Babylon: People, Streets and Images in Nineteenth-Century London* (New Haven: Yale University Press, 2000), pp. 13–26.

19. Bruno Latour and Emilie Hermant, *Paris ville invisible* (Paris: La Découverte, 1998).

20. Karl Scheffler, *Berlin. Ein Stadtschicksal* (Berlin: Erich Reiss Verlag, 1910), pp. 62, 45, 49.

21. Scheffler, *Berlin. Ein Stadtschicksal*, pp. 49, 50.

22. Scheffler, *Berlin. Ein Stadtschicksal*, pp. 50, 51. In this context, Scheffler even praises the generally maligned "rental barracks" which had spread through the city and are generally held responsible for turn-of-the-century Berlin's slum-city reputation. For Scheffler, the very uniformity of these structures goes at least some way to mending the city's "formlessness." See Scheffler, *Die Architektur der Großstadt* (Berlin: Bruno Cassirer Verlag, 1913), p. 13.

23. Scheffler, *Berlin. Ein Stadtschicksal*, pp. 52, 58.

24. Michel Foucault, "Space, Knowledge, and Power," in Paul Rabinow, ed., *The Foucault Reader* (New York: Pantheon, 1984), pp. 239–56, p. 244.

25. This was Fritz Beuster's call for lower-density city planning that could take advantage of Berlin's outlying areas and relieve the overcrowding of the tenement-blocks' infill, in *Groß-Berlin nach dem Kriege. Städtebau und Verwaltungsorganisation* (Berlin: Carl Heymanns Verlag, 1918), pp. 4, 5. Emphasis original.

26. On Wagner as urban planner of Weimar modernity, see Sabine Hake, *Topographies of Class: Modern Architecture and Mass Society in Weimar Berlin* (Ann Arbor: University of Michigan Press, 2008), pp. 39–50; David Frisby, *Cityscapes of Modernity. Critical Explorations* (Cambridge: Polity Press, 2001), pp. 270–302; Manfredo Tafuri, *The Sphere and the Labyrinth: Avant-Gardes and Architecture from Piranesi to the 1970s*, trans. Pellegrino d'Acierno and Robert Connolly (Cambridge, MA: MIT Press, 1987), pp. 197–233; and Ludovica Scarpa, *Martin Wagner und Berlin. Architektur und Städtebau in der Weimarer Republik*, trans. Heinz-Dieter Held (orig. 1983; Braunschweig: Friedr. Vieweg & Sohn, 1986).

27. On the changing fortunes in the reception history of the Berlin rental barracks, see Claus Bernet, "The 'Hobrecht Plan' (1862) and Berlin's Urban Structure," *Urban History*, 31.3 (2004), pp. 400–19.

28. Martin Wagner, "Städtebauliche Probleme der Großstadt" (orig. 1929); repr. in Klaus Homann, Martin Kieren, and Ludovica Scarpa, eds, *Martin Wagner 1885–1957. Wohnungsbau und Weltstadtplanung. Die Rationalisierung des Glücks* (Berlin: Akademie der Künste, 1985), pp. 102–7, p. 102. Wagner repeated this metaphor of the "planning conductor" in need of a good musical "score" in a text on the future of American urban planning that he

co-authored with Walter Gropius during World War II. Gropius and Wagner, "The New City Pattern for the People and by the People," in *The Problem of the Cities and Towns: Conference on Urbanism, March 5-6, 1942* (Cambridge, MA: Harvard University, 1942), pp. 95–96.

29. Marcel Breuer, better known for his Bauhaus furniture, adopted Wagner's tenets in a radical picture essay that detailed how to improve traffic flows at Potsdamer Platz, by fusing it with Leipziger Platz into an opened-up rectangle of traffic flow that avoided "cross-sections" and sent cross-traffic and pedestrians into tunnels. Breuer, "Verkehrsarchitektur – ein Vorschlag zur Neuordnung des Potsdamer Platzes," in Martin Wagner and Adolf Behne, eds, *Das Neue Berlin. Grossstadtprobleme* (Berlin: Verlag Deutsche Bauzeitung, 1929), pp. 136–41. Another version of rationally and completely separating pedestrians from traffic at Potsdamer Platz was offered by Werner Hegemann and Oskar Lange, whose design sought to remove the "fragmentation" of the square by keeping all foot traffic on new upper levels in order to free up the flow of vehicular traffic underneath. Hegemann, *Das steinerne Berlin*, pp. 271–72.

30. The rounded shape of the Haus Berlin, an unrealized design by the Luckhardt brothers in 1929 for Potsdamer Platz, entirely fits this "frozen traffic" appellation called for by Wagner. See Martin Wagner, first part of "Das Formproblem eines Weltstadtplatzes," in Behne and Wagner, eds, *Das Neue Berlin*, p. 37 (emphasis original). See also Wagner, "Städtebauliche Probleme der Großstadt," repr. in Homann et al., eds, *Martin Wagner 1885–1887*, p. 106 (emphasis original).

31. Tafuri critiques Wagner's position in the publication *Das Neue Berlin* because of the latter's boosterist persona: "There is no language for a 'neue Berlin' conscious that its elements exist only to attest to the 'not done' or the 'not possible' at the level of its national and international role." Tafuri recognizes here an "indefinite postponement of the requirements that Wagner can express solely on a theoretical level." Tafuri, *The Sphere and the Labyrinth*, p. 217.

32. Wagner, "Städtebauliche Probleme der Großstadt," in Homann et al., eds, *Martin Wagner 1885–1957*, pp. 104, 105.

33. Martin Wagner, *Städtebauliche Probleme in amerikanischen Städten und ihre Rückwirkung auf den deutschen Städtebau* (Berlin: special issue of *Deutsche Bauzeitung*, 1929), p. 5.

34. "Traffic-Spiders" (*Verkehrsspinnen*), in Hegemann, *Das steinerne Berlin*, p. 227.

35. Martin Wagner, "Weltstadt und Städtebauer," *Berliner Tageblatt*, 58.132 (19 March, 1929).

36. Wagner, *Städtebauliche Probleme*, p. 6.

37. Anthony McElligott has remarked of German modernity's emphasis on efficient traffic that "the smooth mobilization of goods and people into, from and within the city ... stood as a metaphor for capitalist circulation," all the more so for a participatory, post-World War I, "revived Germany." McElligott, *The German Urban Experience 1900–1945: Modernity and Crisis* (New York: Routledge, 2001), p. 184.

38. Wagner, "Das Formproblem eines Weltstadtplatzes," in Behne and Wagner, eds, *Das Neue Berlin*, p. 33; also Wagner, "Städtebauliche Probleme der Großstadt," in Homann et al., eds, *Martin Wagner 1885–1957*, p. 105. Emphasis original.

39. Ludwig Mies van der Rohe, *Städtebau*, 7 (1928), p. 138.

40. Ludwig Hilberseimer, second part of "Das Formproblem eines Weltstadtplatzes," in Behne and Wagner, eds, *Das Neue Berlin*, p. 39.

41. Ludwig Hilberseimer, *Groszstadtarchitektur* (Stuttgart: Verlag Julius Hoffmann, 1927), p. 13.

42. Ludwig Hilberseimer, *Entfaltung einer Planungsidee* (Berlin: Ullstein, 1963), p. 22.

43. Wagner, *Städtebauliche Probleme in amerikanischen Städten*, p. 5, emphasis original; and Wagner, "Städtebauliche Probleme der Großstadt," repr. in Homann et al., eds, *Martin Wagner 1885–1957*, p. 107.

44. Hans Stimmann's advocacy of a reconstruction of Berlin that would resurrect the city's former status on the world stage had the effect of antagonizing contemporary star architects and neutralizing less welcome chapters in Berlin's architectural history. Thus arose the "Architects' Debate" of the 1990s. See Florian Hertweck, *Der Berliner Architekturstreit* (Berlin: Gebr. Mann, 2010); Gavriel D. Rosenfeld, "The Architects' Debate. Architectural Discourse and the Memory of Nazism in the Federal Republic of Germany, 1977–1997," *History and Memory*, 9.1–2 (1997), pp. 189–225, pp. 208–16; and Stimmann, ed., *Physiognomie einer Großstadt. Berlin 1945–1953–1989–2000–2010* (Milan: Skira, 2000). For criticism of Stimmann's impact on Berlin, namely, his forcing of "an old Berlin that never was," see Peter Richter, "Unterm Sandstein wird geschinkelt," *Frankfurter Allgemeine Zeitung* (29 January, 2006).

45. Kurt W. Forster, "Berliner Balance," *Die Zeit*, 4 (28 January, 1994). See also Helmut Böttiger, "Das alte Chaos. Zeitreise in eine ganz andere Krise oder Warum die Sehnsucht nach den Zwanziger Jahren ein Missverständnis ist," *Der Tagesspiegel* (10 June, 2001). Wagner's modern transit-legacy can be seen, however, in the ongoing transformations at Alexanderplatz. See Dorothee Dubrau (former councilor for building and urban development in Berlin-Mitte), "Verkehrsmaßnahmen am 'Alex'," in Dubrau, ed., *Architekturführer, Berlin-Mitte*, Vol. 2 (Berlin: Dom Publishers, 2009), pp 600–01.

46. Brian Ladd and John Woods, dir., *Berlin's Hidden History* (Woods Productions/ EN Productions, 2002).

47. Daniel Libeskind, "Out of Line," *Daniel Libeskind: The Space of Encounter* (New York: Universe, 2000), pp. 143, 144.

8
Nazi (Ger)Mania

*[M]it großem starken Willen werden die Linien gezogen,
neue Straßen entstehen, großzügigere Gesichtspunkte als
bisher bedingen Linienführung und Ausgestaltung.*

(Fritz Todt, 1933)[1]

In the ongoing planning of the post-Wall German capital, echoes from
the infrastructural past are of course to some degree unavoidable – the
question is how such echoes are dealt with. The interrelationships
between these past planning stages are useful for understanding where
Berlin's geomancy has gone before and where it could still end up.
City planner Martin Wagner's boosterism of 1920s Weimar Berlin as a
world city of industrial tempo can be contrasted with the Nazis' own
re-centering of the city. Wagner's modernizing impact on Weimar urban
planning was *not*, on any official or subliminal level, building up to or
prefiguring Nazi megalomaniacal visions for Berlin as "Germania." Even
though Wagner was definitely planning Haussmannesque changes
for the center of Berlin, with future boulevards of up to two and a half
miles that would break through the existing downtown core, these were
not intended to promote any proto-Nazi static display of buildings'
might, spatial voids, or mass parades.

One bold reconfiguration appeared with the Weimar era's own unrealized design for a north-south axis through the center of Berlin, first
conceived of in 1908, officially proposed in 1917–1919, and published
in 1920 by the planner and theorist Martin Mächler (Fig. 8.1). It was
primarily intended to achieve two things. One: to improve the rail
and road circulation of the *arriviste* world city Berlin; and two: to symbolically center the government buildings as befitting such a world city.
Modern Berlin would then appear "as a natural organism," Mächler

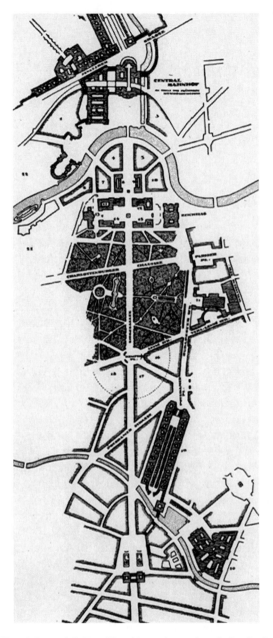

Figure 8.1 "Breakthrough" (*Durchbruch*) north-south axis for Berlin by Martin Mächler, 1920

wrote in anthropomorphic fashion, "as an ethnic-geographic individual, whose various members and organs can only function harmoniously when they are placed in the right spot."[2] The intended aim of Mächler's axis is reflected in its two names: it was to have been both infrastructural as a "Breakthrough" (*Durchbruch*), and governmental as a "Victory Avenue" (*Siegesallee*). In its first role, it would have re-centered Berlin's circulation with a new central rail station; and it would also have filled in the psychogeographical gap between the older eastern and the newer western commercial hubs (separated by the Tiergarten park). Mächler's overriding concern was to modernize Berlin by literally "opening it up."[3]

The whole point of Mächler's concept was a practical one, and was aligned with the philosophy of fellow planner Wagner – namely, to overcome Berlin's infamous "end-terminus" problem by building a brand new central rail station at the Humboldthafen, the docks north of the Spree river bend (*Spreebogen*) and of the Reichstag, and to use the north-south boulevard for connecting through rail traffic via an underground connector system. Traffic paths between the eastern and western parts of the city would also have been improved by Mächler's north-south axis; the Ministerial Gardens just west of the Wilhelmstraße, for example, would have made way for a new east-west street. In the 1920s, in fact, the east-west traffic artery problem for Berlin was discussed more than the north-south issue. Supporting Wagner's call for a dose of Haussmannization of Berlin due to the need to speed up traffic flow, Mächler highlighted, using an aerial photograph, how a total of six streets just dead-ended from east to west between Unter den Linden (south of the Brandenburg Gate) and the Leipziger Straße (north of Potsdamer Platz) (Fig. 8.2).[4]

Additionally, in Mächler's plan, the Königsplatz west of the Reichstag (which became the Platz der Republik during the Weimar years) would have been outlined and anchored with governmental buildings. Mächler wished to overcome how official buildings suffered from being "strewn about in an unplanned manner" (*planlos verteilt*) across Berlin-Mitte.[5] His proposed cluster of such buildings near the Reichstag would have corrected this state of disorganization unbecoming a new world city.[6] In this way, Mächler's north-south design plan would have functioned as a healing response to Germany's defeated morale after World War I. That re-aligning the city was to have had this effect is illustrated in a geomantic comment Mächler made in reference to the centralizing force of ancient Rome and its empire as an example of the paramount importance of "centralization-thinking" for victory, be this literal as in war or conceptual as in the post-World War I, peace-oriented "world

Figure 8.2 "Aerial view of the Wilhelmstraße area. Between 'Linden' and Leipziger Straße six streets run into dead-ends." Aerial photograph by Martin Mächler, 1929

newspaper" that he had in mind. His upbeat rhetoric emphasizes western culture's "continued blossoming" and the world city's role in successfully combating the danger of failure or "decay."[7] Mächler's north-south axis design, then, was positioned as a solution for Berlin's multiple lacks of cartographical definition, infrastructural efficiency, and national identity-granting contours.

Despite the fact that it was precisely the above aspects of Mächler's north-south axis design that were to prove inspirational for the Nazis, we should not subsume axiality itself, one of the major tropes of modern urban planning, within the fascist credo. The *pre*-Nazi attempts at axiality in Berlin planning cannot be lumped together as *proto*-Nazi precursors. Nor can axiality in planning be condemned as totalitarian per se, when one recalls how far back in time the geomantic desire extended in the shaping of cities and sites of worship. In ancient Greece, *axon* referred to that which connects an impulse or direction away from the center. This centrifugal focus of axiality lends itself well to the symmetrical representation in street design of royal or governmental power, or city-status.[8] In Haussmann's Paris, Daniel Burnham's City Beautiful plans for Washington DC (1905, 1901) and for Chicago (1909), as well as in the 1905 addition of Kingsway and Aldwych to the north side of the Strand in London, and the Fairmount Parkway axis cut into the Philadelphia cityscape in 1919, radial axes were regarded as a rational step toward the systematic modernization of the industrial metropolis. Otto Wagner also wished to design modern Vienna along radial lines, focusing on the concentric appeal of "nodes" (*Stellen*), namely the intersections of radial avenues with the new ring roads, which would enable a theoretically infinite, modular expansion of the city (and, by extension, of the Austro-Hungarian empire). The Nazis' axial project for Berlin followed in the wake of both Burnham and the City Beautiful movement (with its axiality and monumental public buildings), as well as Le Corbusier and the Charter of Athens that emerged from the CIAM IV conference of 1934 (with its focus on separating urban functions: work, leisure, circulation, and housing).[9]

Indeed, housed very much within this long and varied tradition of axial planning, the very first north-south axis proposals for Berlin had been designed by Peter Josef Lenné in 1839 and Karl Friedrich Schinkel in 1840. One can hardly accuse the great landscape artist and the even more renowned Berlin architect of being proto-Nazi – only pro-Prussian. At that time, the terrain for the axis – then a Prussian military drill ground just north and west of the Brandenburg Gate – was still outside the old city customs wall. Despite its desired corrective-compensatory role in the wake of World War I, Mächler's axial plan was *not* primarily dedicated to a massively static showcasing of state power via a procession of monumental buildings, in the vein of Hitler's and Albert Speer's later adaptation of the same concept.

The emphasis on traffic circulation in the planning praxis of Martin Wagner and in the planning theory of Mächler provides a crucial building-block for our understanding of how the Nazi regime adopted modern Weimar models of planning urban flow, but then applied them in the service of new goals. Clearly, the Nazis took up radial axiality for their own purposes, making Berlin's lines of power into highly politicized entities. The basic shift from Weimar to "Nazi modern," in terms of city planning, is generally understood to have been a break with urban modernity's dynamic, fluid directionality and an assumption of a display-oriented and hence static axiality.[10] Wagner, for all his dreams of the wholly rational city, remained an urbanist at heart, ever in tune with the pulse of the modern metropolis; he was promptly sacked from his post in 1933, went to Istanbul, and eventually landed a professorship at Harvard, thanks to Walter Gropius's intervention. Mächler, on the other hand, stayed behind to engage in unsuccessful bids to gain commissions from the Nazis. One can see – if not sympathize with – why Mächler was tempted. Thanks to Hitler's obsession with the importance of architecture as a vehicle for state power, city space became something to be completely controlled. Albert Speer, who rose to become the most powerful civilian Nazi in the Third Reich, was in a position like no previous German planner to see before him the Cartesian empty plain and to believe he could realize its potential. Hitler's famous phrase about the utility of architecture as a civilization's "word of stone" must be understood not only as a comment on the Nazis' preference for granite and marble in their outsized neo-classical public buildings (that is to say, as a question of style) but as a totalizing vision of city-formation and planning.[11]

For this vision to occur, Berlin was to be made over into a geomantic "World Capital Germania." Only nine months into his regime, Hitler stated at an urban planning meeting that the capital did not have enough monumental buildings: "Berlin is at present a non-systematic collection or a non-systematic assortment of residential and business structures"; hence the German capital needed to "catch up." Again, during a meeting in 1934 about plans for the new Tempelhof airport, Hitler declared he could not stand how the (formerly Jewish-owned) Karstadt department store, with its massive corner towers, was to date the most impressive building on the Berlin skyline.[12] It is believed that Hitler had most likely learned of the north-south axis at the Berlin Art Exhibition of 1927, which had re-displayed Mächler's project to the public. In his "Cultural Speech" at the 1935 party congress in Nuremberg, Hitler attacked the primacy of commercial skyscrapers, office buildings, hotels, and department stores in the modern city: "The great cultural-historical duty of National Socialism," he insisted, "consists precisely in departing from this tendency."[13] One year later, Hitler announced the re-formation of Berlin in his own image ("the new construction of Berlin as the capital of the German Reich").[14] The assignment of the General Building Inspectorate (Generalbauinspektion zur Neugestaltung der Reichshauptstadt, or GBI) that Speer was picked to lead was essentially an architectural *Gleichschaltung*: the strict unification and regulariza-tion of any "squares, streets and buildings that affect the city image."[15] Nor was the urban retooling limited to the capital: Berlin was one of several of the forty selected "Führer-cities" (with Hamburg, Munich, Nuremberg, and Linz) which were to be swiftly re-shaped as NSDAP-representations. New axialities were drawn up for each one, to emphasize a revised interpretation of public space that ran roughshod over the existing scale. The overall cost for Nazi Germany's urban planning efforts was to have been 100 billion Reichsmarks, an impossible sum even without the war.

In 1938, Speer's office announced plans for Berlin's North-South Axis and the extension of the existing East-West Axis. In fact, both axis plans had been desired by Hitler long before Speer's arrival on the scene, as part of the city of a future 10 million inhabitants. Unlike the unrealized North-South Axis, the East-West one was achieved under Nazi tenure, in part because its central feature, Unter den Linden, was already in place. The Berlin Olympics of 1936 caused the re-arranging of the existing E-W artery into a Nazified *via triumphalis*, extending the line of Unter den Linden all the way to the Reichssportfeld itself – a line of frozen display presenting a "monumental expression of the whole," of "world-wide Germanness," as a commemorative book on the Games proclaimed.[16] The Olympic stadium, seating 85,000, was built as an extension to the far west end of this axis (designed by Werner March and altered by Speer). At Schinkel's Lustgarten on Unter den Linden, conceived originally as a site of urban spectacle and agora from the perspective of the double stairway of his Altes Museum, the Nazis removed all the landscaping and paved it with granite so that the space could function as a *Gauforum*.[17] The Olympic flame (the bringing of which from Greece to the Games was a Nazi innovation) was carried from the opening ceremonies at the Pergamon altar on Museum Island and in the renovated Lustgarten, along Unter den Linden and the rest of the East-West Axis, to the stadium itself. In time for Mussolini's state visit in September 1937, Unter den Linden was re-modeled for the Italian fascist's open-car parade. The military march for the 1st of May holiday in 1937 also took place along the widened, lengthened avenue through the Tiergarten and beyond. By 1939, the widening of the East-West Axis was completed to a length of four and a half miles (7km) from the Brandenburg Gate to the Adolf-Hitler-Platz (now Theodor-Heuss-Platz). Eventual plans along the axis included a new technical university west of the Olympic stadium. Just in time for Hitler's 50th birthday, Speer gave a speech at the Brandenburg Gate to proudly announce its (temporary) completion.

The more infamous of the two axes for Berlin is the North-South one (Fig. 8.3). The Nazi plan for re-centering Berlin along the North-South Axis almost certainly would have killed off its existing centers. It would have overshadowed the aristocratic relevance of the former westernmost gateway to the city, the eighteenth-century Pariser Platz, by reducing it to a mere appendage on the south-east side of the Great Square (Großer Platz) in front of the Great Hall (Große Halle). It would have made the

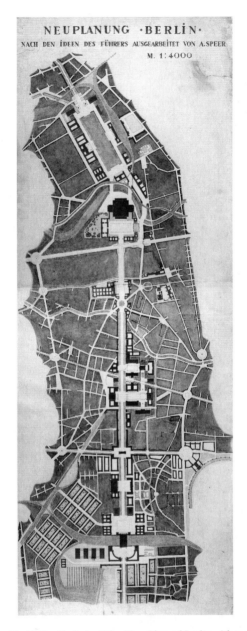

Figure 8.3 The North-South Axis: "The New Plan of Berlin, After the Ideas of the Führer. Prepared by Albert Speer," 1939

Brandenburg Gate – Berlin's most famous pre-Wall symbol – into an isolated traffic island at the intersection of the two axes. The Gate was to have been close to the intersecting point of the two Nazi axes, yet it would have been as good as eclipsed by their scale. In Speer's plan, the guard houses each side of the Gate would have been removed to facilitate east-west traffic flowing around and thus marooning the Gate on both sides.[18] Likewise, the Königsplatz, just west of the Reichstag, was to become palimpsested over by the Great Hall itself. Clearly, both the Reichstag and Brandenburg Gate would have been utterly dwarfed.[19] Moreover, the Nazi N-S axis would have all but destroyed not simply the buildings but also the commercial and nodal relevance of Potsdamer Platz, while nonetheless retaining Erich Mendelsohn's Columbus Haus of 1932 and the adjoining Leipziger Platz.

The Nazi government's careless treatment of existing city centers points up the fact that the significance of axial restructuring went further than just the city itself. Axiality was based on not just Hitler's will to imitate and out-build Burnham's rehabilitation of L'Enfant's Mall in Washington DC, or the Haussmannized Paris that he invaded, but moreover on the articulation of an urban geomancy for the entire Third Reich. The dream was to make Berlin-Germania into a new center of the universe. The former Weimar world city was to be reshaped into a "world capital city," as Hitler termed it, a place where latter-day divination could be experienced through the precise reorganization of the experience of urban space, both infrastructurally and architecturally – hence the projected positioning of Hitler's own tomb in the Great Hall, at the center of the axis.[20] The former significance of places like Stonehenge in Wiltshire, England, or Teotihuacán in Central Mexico was now to be resumed for all modern ethnic Germans (*Volksdeutsche*) across the globe, who could refer to Berlin-Germania as a conceptual pilgrimage-site as well as the literal organizing center of the world.

The mission of world-directed axiality as the ultimate use for Berlin's central node at the point where the North-South and East-West axes cross is suggested in Speer's assertion that "the center will be much more than the whole cross-axis itself." In an impassioned speech in 1939 that introduced the N-S Axis to the public, Speer spoke of the new "building willpower of our time" that would create the grand avenue's role as a new, post-Expressionistic "city-crown" (*Stadtkrone*) and highlight the city's "ruling effect."[21] Nazi spatial planning (*Raumplanung*) was specifically equated with German *Lebensraum*.[22] This combination of aims was amplified in 1942, when Speer assumed the duties, after the death of Fritz Todt, of both inspector-general of roads and minister for the entire war munitions effort.

Two comparative "before" and "after" shots from a 1942 issue of *Raumforschung und Raumordnung*, a Nazi planning journal, effectively illustrate this new world order.[23] The first is captioned: "Old Europe: Torn apart and dependent on England."[24] Here, the waning British Empire is depicted as an obviously messy, decadent ruler, permitting the threat of Russia to grow in the east. Nazi reconfigurations of the geopolitical map in favor of the Third Reich's *Lebensraum*-expansionism re-worked geographer Halford Mackinder's early twentieth-century model of the need for (then British) control of the rising Eurasian threat. Hitler made good mileage out of the threat of the (Soviet) East: for example, Speer's Nazi monument facing off against the Soviet pavilion at the 1937 Paris Exposition embodied this sense of the Third Reich as a last line of defense. In contrast, the "after"-shot of world infrastructural order imposed by Nazi Germany has Berlin at its radiating center of the entire map: "New Europe: A Free Organism." Any spatial disordering threats in the former map have been neatly overcome in the second Nazi version – in a manner resembling the Third Reich's overhaul of the national Autobahn system in the 1930s, the plans to build a wide-gauge railway all across the Crimea, as well as the function of Berlin as a clearing house for the central European trade system.[25] Such radiating initiatives of trade routes, road, and rail served to anchor Berlin as the core of the new order. During the 1930s, neighboring nations – especially Poland – watched how the Nazi Autobahn network of routes emanating from Berlin obviously represented an expansive desire of the German domain across Europe.

Nazi urban planning for Berlin was from the onset a microcosm of that regime's greater world-planning initiative. Let us not forget that by 1942, Hitler controlled a population of 250 million people across continental Europe – hence the focus on the forging of spatial order via new infrastructure. The "free organism"-quote accompanying the "after"-image is the opposite of what it really is. The map is linked by reverse logic to the one that appears in Fritz Hippler's infamous propaganda film of 1940, *The Eternal Jew* (*Der ewige Jude*), which seeks to portray cartographically the historical process of the infestation of Europe by Jews to become the Reich's "enemy within."

Hence the real "infestation" of Europe came from the Third Reich, and not just with its urban planning for Berlin as a hub. The poison was literally extended as a colonization effort across the conquered East, filling in the blanks between the lines of the new transportation network with its own people, who literally and biologically were to replace dead Jews in this newly acquired *Lebensraum*. Himmler predicted the settlement of the East by ethnic Germans by up to twenty million over the course of fifty to eighty years; this, asserted the SS leader, would push the Reich's eastern border ever further to the east.[26] And excluded from this new, purportedly cleansed realm – by dispossession, displacement, containment, and annihilation – were the European Jews. Speer's own role in the attempted erasure of Jews from the map of Berlin should not be overlooked: his GBI office was swift to make maps of each of the capital's "Jew-Free Areas" (*Judenreine Gebiete*). Thousands of Berlin Jews were forcefully evacuated by Speer's office – either by dint of being the predominant population of the demolished neighborhoods, or by having to give up their apartments to Germans who had been moved out of the terrain intended for the North-South Axis. Once homeless, they were deported to concentration camps from Berlin's Grunewald rail station.[27]

Despite such plans for world-dominating geomancy, Berlin was not destined to become Germania, after all. Not much of Nazi Berlin's North-South Axis ever existed except in maps and in architectural models. The Allied bombing raids first assisted Speer in land clearance for the Axis, but then prevented its fruition. Only the House of Tourism (Haus des Fremdenverkehrs) on the Runder Platz was actually built. As Speer wrote afterwards: "For five years I lived in this world of plans ..." Speer's own account tells how lights were shone onto the 1:50 "model city" of Germania in his GBI office (exhibition rooms in the Academy of the Arts, Pariser Platz 4) to simulate the movement of the sun upon real stone, or how spotlights cinematically lit up the models by night, awaiting Hitler's obsessive visits to them via the connecting tunnel from his new Chancellery building. Nazi model-mania was, in fact, a form of control – an attempt at controlling the visions of the future. Speer describes Hitler's boyish participatory excitement in leaning over a 1:1000 model of the N-S Axis in order to gain different street perspectives.[28]

We should not underestimate the relevance of the massive and multiple architectural models that were made for the impossibly expensive "new formation plans" (*Neugestaltungsplanungen*) for Berlin, Hamburg, Munich, Nuremberg, and beyond. They forged not the reality of public space in the Third Reich, but its psychological backdrop.[29] Not surprisingly, the models were included in propaganda films in which fountains of water were shown falling in front of the House of Tourism. In his writings Speer recalls how he helped shape an imaginary view through the frame of the massive Triumphal Arch that would capture the arriving traveler: this was exactly the vantage point that Hitler had been trying to achieve as he bent right down almost to his knees over his model city, namely "the point of view of the traveler emerging from the south station."[30] Again, as a present for Hitler's 50th birthday, Speer recounts how he gave him a model of the Triumphal Arch, thirteen feet high, that Hitler revisited multiple times during the night, like a child with a new toy.[31] A certain form of modeling mania, whether "Ger-mania" or not – was part and parcel of the modern urban experience.

Despite the sheer manic fiction of the Nazi geomantic vision for Berlin, we can ask, as architectural historian Iain Boyd White has done, a key question: "Was National Socialist Berlin ... a modern city?"[32] Could it have become one, if it had been built? The ultimate relevance of Speer may not reside in the absurdly vast scale of his neo-classical monumentalist architecture that mostly existed in models of wishful thinking but in his role as modern planner. As far as his intended post-war role as the head of the future Germania's rebuilding phase was concerned, the older, wiser Speer claimed that he would have applied the destruction of war not just to save on demolition efforts but to rectify any practical shortcomings of the North-South Axis. According to the later Speer's complaint about Hitler, the latter was not at all interested in the infrastructural consequences for the city fabric by the insertion of the Great Axis, envisioned at about two and a half times the length of the Champs-Elysées. In Speer's postwar account, the Große Achse is portrayed as having been part of a massive re-ordering of the city's circulation. In his purported desire to apply the soon-to-be-erased terrains of Hobrecht's nineteenth-century tenement lots toward massive modernizations of traffic flow, Speer portrayed himself as an efficient planner working on a "new urban concept" rather than as an anti-modern architect.[33] He positioned himself, in his postwar writings, as a continuous road/rail planning descendent of Martin Wagner's in the chain of German urban modernity.

Historians have reviewed Speer's planning role somewhat dubiously, unsure how to place it, especially given the generally accepted critical rejection of Nazi neo-classical architecture. While there have been recent efforts to reposition Nazi architectural monumentality alongside its international 1930s equivalents (such as in government structures in the Soviet Union or in the USA), urban planning parallels between Nazi plans and the interwar and postwar movements remain relatively under-drawn. The initial reaction has been that the North-South Axis would have been an aesthetic rather than a functional boulevard: a power line that would have defined the city but without channeling any of its infrastructural energy.[34] Such a view is lent credence by the fact that Speer struggled with the resistance put up by the mayor of Berlin, Julius Lippert (until his demotion in 1941), against the impact of the North-South Axis on Berlin. But increasingly, critics have been parsing apart the ways in which major aspects of Nazi urban planning, even in its axes, would have enhanced circulation and answered some of the Weimar era's concerns.[35] For the Berlin Olympics, for example, a modified version of the much desired underground north-south link was completed for the S-Bahn, if not for road or rail. A 1935 publication looked forward to the day when, thanks to the correction of this as-yet "missing connection" for Berlin, "travelers from Vienna, Cologne and Munich can travel to Copenhagen, Oslo and Stockholm without having to change trains."[36]

The somewhat heretical truth is that *efficiency in one area does not preclude efficiency in another*. Speer was wholly able to use modern urban planning in the services of war (and worse). Yet modern planning is not de facto totalitarian or inductively linked to the Holocaust. Nor is the opposite true: an assertion of Nazi planning's continuities with Weimar planning does not amount to any potential relativization, or risk of normalization, of the Nazi era and its massive crimes. Every time one approaches this era, one is, as a scholar, moved by a deeply ethical obligation to weigh any hermeneutical statement about Nazism in the light of the Holocaust. But this should not prevent a critical uncovering of aspects about Nazism that have been somewhat shielded from scrutiny – in this case, because of not fitting in with accepted notions about Nazi design. If twentieth-century urban planning in Germany and especially Berlin is marked more by continuities than discontinuities, despite the impact of the Nazi period, then this has to be assessed within the planning context itself.[37]

The double truth, then, is that Speer's hand in German modernization informed both urban infrastructure (mostly for the good) and the entire Reich (for the bad, in the cause of war and the Holocaust). In a 1943 speech given just moments before Goebbels' ravings at the Berlin Sport-Palast, Speer even boasted how improvements to the Reich railway system had improved the supply lines to the Front (and it was, as Raoul Hilberg consistently emphasized, the railway that serviced the system of the Final Solution).[38] Despite the fact, then, that we know the lesson against too much planning – namely that if you pay too much attention to systems of visual control and neglect the other ways in which urban space is explored and lived, you end up with the situation that Lefebvre once noticed: "the image kills"[39] – despite this fact, we cannot ignore the extent to which Berlin's rail and road systems alike would have undergone radical transformation in the new Germania (linking beyond city limits to the Autobahn and rail projects across Eastern Europe all the way to Moscow). The North-South Axis with its two new "through" rail stations would have removed the need for the existing terminus stations, and the leftover spaces of rail tracks would have been used as terrain for the Axis itself. This was seen by Speer as a welcome liberation. In a 1939 publication, Speer's plan for the Berlin railway was described as an "extension" of the S-Bahn by the Reichsbahn and other means (such as buses and densification of the U-Bahn stations) in order to build a new mass transit system for the city and forge the "freeing-up" (*Freimachung*) of the downtown from the tram system. The second main aim was to create new "tangential" rail links around the city's existing radial rail network and improve the links between Berlin and its "satellite towns." This vision of suburbanization based on a well-connected transit system was not really at odds with what Weimar planners had proposed.[40]

In fact, what we are witnessing as we look back over the stages of Berlin in terms of planning space is the sheer variety of *linked* strands that make it increasingly hard to isolate the Nazi era from what came before and after. The historical stumbling block has been that the Nazi GBI was in essence attempting to correct Berlin's perennial problem concerning its deficiency in lines of power, just as the interwar Weimar planners had wanted to do. Nazi planning gestures should be recalled within this broader context. For example, both the Nazis and today's New Berlin have responded to the Weimar-era's call for a north-south rail link.

As far as the complementary role of airports is concerned, it is not insignificant that their accessibility was planned in tandem with seventeen additional radial highways in Nazi Germania, each 200 feet wide, leading out from the center, with four new ring roads around the whole.[41] By 1938, in fact, Berlin's main outer ring highway of 115 miles (185km) was already two-thirds complete. The two Axes would have provided four access routes to the surrounding rings. Even the newly built Tempelhof airport would have been eventually supplanted by newer airports planned next to the four rail terminals surrounding the city, and Tempelhof itself was to have been transformed into a park (this is, ironically, one of its ongoing transformations).[42] And, for all the focus that has been paid by historians to the "evil = static" monumentality of the North-South Axis, there was to have been another, unexpected source of life along that unbuilt boulevard: shopping the Reich. Speer stressed, after the war, how Hitler had wanted the street to have lots of electric signs and function as a "continuous sales display of German goods," especially for foreign visitors.[43] Two-thirds of the building sites were intended for private businesses, especially at the south end, with store windows at ground level – even if the only way to actually cross the 400ft-wide road in safety would have been to use subterranean tunnels at subway entrances. Nor would the North-South Axis have dead-ended: Speer boasts how businesses were buying up additional terrain south of the Axis, in effect lengthening the boulevard. A residential area of 200,000 was planned for the south end.

Ultimately, we should ask ourselves how much urban and architectural historians have been obliged to "over-read" the Nazi plans for Berlin. The 1942 Master Plan for a postwar London by the English version of CIAM, the MARS Group (headed by two German refugee architects), demonstrates how a wholly new grid city plan can be as scary as any axial Germania, even without a totalitarian state funding it – indeed, perhaps more so, since this Master Plan for a new metropolis of 10 million would have created a radical modular city, molded only by the undulating presence of the Thames. Indeed, damage caused by the London Blitz facilitated a mindset for a future postwar capital that, had it been rebuilt as a *tabula rasa* city, would have symbolized a collective re-beginning at a time when preserving the past had never seemed so irrelevant.[44]

The uncomfortable question arises, then: can we accept that Speer, the reactionary advocate of obscenely sized totalitarian architecture, was simultaneously a modernizing urban planner, following in the wake of his avant-garde socialist predecessors from the 1920s? Can similar modernizing processes for the circulation of a city be identified that fit both the needs of the democratic government of the Weimar Republic and the Third Reich's *Blut und Boden* expansion and world domination plans? Also, can Speer serve as a point of continuity rather than discontinuity with post-World War II and post-Wall urban renewal projects in Berlin?[45] The social democratic insistence on modern communication, circulation, and speed in the Weimar era's New Berlin can be seen as a response to capitalism in order to control it (and transform it for the better), just as much as the Nazis attempted to model Berlin-Germania into a new obedient shape. Indeed we may dare to conclude that it would have ultimately been accepted as the Speerization of Berlin, just as now we speak of the Haussmannization of Paris as that which gave that city its circulatory efficiency and modern visual identity. Rather than isolate the Nazi planning era out of fear of contamination, we should instead acknowledge and contend with the things that link the Weimar, the Nazi, and the postwar/post-Wall planning phases together.

Notes

1. Fritz Todt, "Das Straßenbauprogramm Adolf Hitlers und die deutschen Ingenieure," *Deutsche Technik*, 1 (October 1933), pp. 53–54, p. 53.
2. Martin Mächler, "Ein Detail aus dem Bebauungsplan von Groß-Berlin," *Der Städtebau* 17.5/6 (1920); repr. in Ilse Balg, ed., *Martin Mächler – Weltstadt Berlin* (Berlin: Galerie Wannsee Verlag, 1987), p. 46.
3. This is how the expressionist-turned-functionalist architect Hugo Häring praised Mächler's axis design in an article of 1927. Häring, "Das Projekt Mächler," repr. in Balg, ed., *Martin Mächler*, p. 176.
4. See Mächler's response to Wagner's essay "Verkehr und Tradition," in Wagner and Adolf Behne, eds., *Das Neue Berlin. Grossstadtprobleme* (Berlin: Verlag Deutsche Bauzeitung, 1929), pp. 129–32.
5. Mächler, "Ein Detail aus dem Bebauungsplan," repr. in Balg, ed., *Martin Mächler*, p. 47.
6. Hugo Häring, Peter Behrens, and Hans Poelzig all designed government buildings for inclusion in Mächler's unrealized plan. See Wagner, "Der Platz der Republik," in Wagner and Behne, eds, *Das Neue Berlin*, p. 69; Lampugnani, "Berlin Modernism," in Terence Riley and Barry Bergdoll, eds, *Mies in Berlin* (New York: Museum of Modern Art/H.N. Abrams, 2001), pp. 34–65, pp. 61–63; and Carola Hein, ed., *Hauptstadt Berlin. Internationaler städtebaulicher Ideenwettbewerb 1957/58* (Berlin: Gebr. Mann, 1991), pp. 17, 19.
7. Martin Mächler, *Die Macht der öffentlichen Meinung. Studie zu einem Weltzeitungsplan* (Berlin: Gebhardt, Jahn & Landt, 1917), pp. 4, 5; Mächler, "Ein Detail aus dem Bebauungsplan," repr. in Balg, ed., *Martin Mächler*, p. 46.
8. For example, in a non-extant eighteenth-century Berlin painting of an ideal, unbuilt realization of the Belle-Alliance-Platz (now: Mehringplatz), an ideal trivium-arrangement modeled on Rome's Piazza del Popolo is indicated with the three radially extending streets; and the houses along the circular Platz are drawn so thinly they almost seem two-dimensional. Reproduced as Fig. 26 in Werner Hegemann, *Das steinerne Berlin. Geschichte der größten Mietskasernenstadt der Welt* (Berlin: Gustav Kiepenheuer, 1930).
9. Sir Peter Hall nearly neutralizes the work of Hitler's architect, Albert Speer, by reminding his readership how Speer, the nine international congresses of CIAM (1928–1953), and the City Beautiful movement alike can all be traced back to a shared ancestor, namely Haussmann. Hall, "Metropolis 1890–1940: Challenges and Responses," in Anthony Sutcliffe, ed., *Metropolis 1890–1940* (Chicago: University of Chicago Press, 1984), pp. 19–66, p. 56.
10. Peter Fritzsche, "Nazi Modern," *Modernism/Modernity*, 3.1 (1996), pp. 1–22. Speer applied axial principles in his famous "Cathedral of Light" (*Lichtdom*) for the Nuremberg Nazi Party Rally of 1934. On that occasion, 130 searchlights reached up 25,000 feet, turned inward from the vertical position to join each other in the middle and thus flood the red banners on the Zeppelin Field with light, and then returned to the vertical light-shaft position again. See Joachim Fest, *Speer: The Final Verdict*, trans. Ewald Osers and Alexandra Dring (New York: Harcourt, Inc., 2001), pp. 50–51; and Kathleen James-Chakraborty, *German Architecture for a Mass Audience* (New York: Routledge, 2000), pp. 87–94.

11. Adolf Hitler's speech of 22 January, 1938, at the Haus der Deutschen Kunst in Munich. Cited by Helmut Weihsmann, *Bauen unterm Hakenkreuz. Architektur des Untergangs* (Vienna: Promedia, 1998), p. 19.

12. These statements by Hitler on Berlin's failings are cited by Wolfgang Schäche, *Architektur und Städtebau in Berlin zwischen 1933 und 1945. Planen und Bauen unter der Ägide der Stadtverwaltung*, 2nd ed. (Berlin: Gebr. Mann Verlag, 1992), pp. 528, 550.

13. Cited by Rudolf Wolters in Albert Speer, ed., *Neue deutsche Baukunst* (Amsterdam/Berlin/Vienna: Volk und Reich Verlag, 1943), p. 9.

14. *Der Parteitag der Ehre vom 8. bis 14. September 1936. Offizieller Bericht über den Verlauf des Reichsparteitages mit sämtlichen Kongreßreden* (Munich: Zentralverlag der NSDAP, 1936), p. 69.

15. Cited in Schäche, *Architektur und Städtebau*, p. 575. *Gleichschaltung* occurred in building codes as well. See Ernst Neufert's *Bauordnungslehre*, an architectural standardization manual with a foreword by Albert Speer in which the latter advocates against "chance" measurements of any kind (Berlin: Volk und Reich Verlag, 1943).

16. Walter Richter et al., eds, *Olympia 1936. Die XI. Olympischen Spiele 1936 in Berlin und Garmisch-Partenkirchen*, vol. 2, Cigaretten-Bilderdienst Altona-Bahrenfeld (Bielefeld: E. Gundlach Aktiengesellschaft, 1936), pp. 6, 7.

17. On the Berlin Olympics, see David Clay Large, *Nazi Games: The Olympics of 1936* (W.W. Norton & Company, 2007); and Iain Boyd White, "Berlin, 1. Mai 1936," in Dawn Ades, Tim Benton, David Elliott, and Iain Boyd White, eds, *Kunst und Macht im Europa der Diktatoren 1930 bis 1945* (London: Hayward Gallery, 1996), pp. 43–49.

18. The Brandenburg Gate was built in 1789–93 by Carl Gotthard Langhans and its Quadriga by Johann Schadow, with guard houses constructed by Friedrich August Stüler in the mid-nineteenth century. It had already nearly been made into an isolated monument by Wilhelm II. The intended fate of the Gate's guard houses would have resembled that of the Victory Column (Siegessäule), moved by Speer from its Reichstag location to a separate island setting in the Tiergarten, offering a view for passing traffic. This also recalls how Mussolini cleared away buildings from around the Colosseum. See Albert Speer, *Architektur. Arbeiten 1933–1942* (Frankfurt am Main: Propylaen, 1978), p. 71.

19. According to the postwar Speer, Hitler intended to eventually demolish the Reichstag altogether and replace it with Speer and Waldemar Brinkemann's "Großdeutsche Reichstagsgebäude." Speer, *Architektur. Arbeiten 1933–1942*, p. 73.

20. Adolf Hitler, in Henry Picker, ed., *Hitlers Tischgespräche im Führerbunker: Hitler, wie er wirklich war* (Stuttgart-Degerloch: Seewald, 1976), p. 195.

21. Albert Speer, "Neuplanung der Reichshauptstadt," *Der Deutsche Baumeister*, 1 (January 1939), reprinted in Anna Teut, *Architektur im Dritten Reich 1933–1945* (Berlin and Frankfurt am Main: Ullstein, 1967), pp. 196, 199. Speer talks of the intersection of the two Axes as the city's chief "structure," and the N-S Axis as the "focal piece – a totally new site in the heart of the city." Speer's tone here contrasts rather strongly with his subsequent, post-war self-distancing from the same mission.

22. Wolters, in Speer, ed., *Neue deutsche Baukunst*, p. 9.

23. "Old Europe: Torn apart and dependent on England." "New Europe: A Free Organism." Nazi propaganda maps in *Raumforschung und Raumordnung* (1942); repr. in Werner Durth and Winfried Nerdinger, *Architektur und Städtebau der 30er/40er Jahre* (Bonn: Deutsches Nationalkomitee für Denkmalschutz, 1995), p. 32.

24. Sometimes such Nazi cartographies included depictions of the enemy (the British Empire; the Jewish influence) as an octopus with tentacles reaching across the nations of the world: see Karl Haushofer, *Grenzen in ihrer geographischen und politischen Bedeutung* (Heidelberg: Kurt Vowinckel Verlag, 1939), p. 137. Compare the World War I German BUFA propaganda film, *Das Saugetier* (1917), which depicts British expansionism as an ugly octopus taking over the European map.

25. On the spread of the Autobahn and how it promised to service as far as the Reich could extend, see Weihsmann, *Bauen unterm Hakenkreuz*, pp. 124–40; and White, "Der Nationalsozialismus und die Moderne," in Ades et al., eds, *Kunst und Macht*, pp. 258–69, pp. 266–68. On Berlin's world economic role in the Nazi system, see Anthony McElligott, "Reforging Mitteleuropa in the Crucible of War: The Economic Impact of Integration under German Hegemony," in Peter Stirk, ed., *Mitteleuropa: History and Prospects* (Edinburgh: Edinburgh University Press, 1994), pp. 129–59, pp. 140–41.

26. Heinrich Himmler, speech to SS leaders in Posen, 24 October, 1939; cited in Rolf-Dieter Müller, *Hitlers Ostkrieg und die deutsche Siedlungspolitik* (Frankfurt: Fischer Taschenbuch, 1991), pp. 119f.

27. On the "Jew-free" Berlin planned by Speer's GBI office, see Johann Friedrich Geist and Klaus Kürvers, "Tatort Berlin, Pariser Platz. Die Zerstörung und 'Entjudung' Berlins," in Jörn Düwel, Werner Durth, Niels Gutschow, and Jochen Schneider, eds, *1945. Krieg – Zerstörung – Aufbau. Architektur und Stadtplanung 1940–1960* (Berlin: Henschel Verlag, 1995), pp. 55–118, pp. 68–99; Fest, *Speer*, pp. 115–20; Susanne Willems, *Der entsiedelte Jude. Albert Speers Wohnungsmarktpolitik für den Berliner Hauptstadtbau* (Berlin: Edition Hentrich, 2002); and Paul B. Jaskot, *The Architecture of Oppression: The SS, Forced Labor and the Nazi Monumental Building Economy* (New York: Routledge, 2000). Jaskot notes that stones for the Berlin Axis plans and for autobahn-building across the Reich were quarried by concentration camp inmates.

28. Albert Speer, *Inside the Third Reich*, trans. Richard and Clara Winston (New York: Touchstone/Simon & Schuster, 1997), pp. 138, 132–33. The models were predominantly made in oak; they ranged in size from 1:500 to 1:1 (built life-size in a *Kleingarten*-colony on the Treptower Straße in Neukölln); and most were destroyed at the end of the war or used for firewood. See Weihsmann, *Bauen unterm Hakenkreuz*, pp. 27, 272.

29. For this reason, Wolfgang Schäche criticizes the Japanisch-Deutsches Zentrum, built in 1988, for being a precise "*1:1 model*" of the ruined Nazi-era Japanese Embassy, built on the same Tiergarten-perimeter site some fifty years previously. See Schäche, "Zur Funktion des Baumodells in der Architektur des 'Dritten Reiches'," *Der Architekt*, 4 (1989), pp. 204–23, p. 206 (emphasis original). Sometimes the Germania-*simulacrum* has even overcome architectural critics: Alan Balfour, for one, makes reference to the "dramatic photograph of the Great Hall viewed down the North-South Axis" as if it were, in fact, a view of an actual built environment. Balfour, *Berlin. The Politics of Order*

1737–1989 (New York: Rizzoli, 1990), p. 98. Another critic, Anna Teut, engages her reader in an imaginary perspectival "walk along the Nazi *via triumphalis.*" Teut, "Axis and Symmetry as a Medium of Subordination. Nazi Architecture Redivivus," *Daidalos*, 15 (1985), pp. 104–15, pp. 111–14.

30. Speer, *Inside the Third Reich*, pp. 135, 133.

31. Hitler and Speer were not alone in such modeling games: at the famed Futurama exhibit designed by Norman Bel Geddes for the 1939 New York World's Fair, 552 people at a time were conveyed in circular simulated flight around a massive model City of Tomorrow, planned for 1960. What impressed the public most was a "new type of 'aerialized spectatorship'," an "'aesthetics of ascension'." See Adnan Morshed, "The Aesthetics of Ascension in Norman Bel Geddes's Futurama," *Journal of the Society of Architectural Historians*, 63.1 (2004), pp. 74–99, pp. 78, 80.

32. Ian Boyd White, "Der Nationalsozialismus und die Moderne," in Ades et al., eds, *Kunst und Macht*, pp. 258–69, p. 258.

33. Speer, *Architektur. Arbeiten 1933–1942*, pp. 103, 104; Speer, *Inside the Third Reich*, pp. 77, 78.

34. See Barbara Miller Lane, "Interpreting Nazi Architecture: The Case of Albert Speer," in Börje Magnusson, Stefania Renzetti, Paolo Vian, and Sever J. Voicu, eds, *Ultra terminum vagari: Scritti in onore di Carl Nylander* (Rome: Edizioni Quasar, 1998), pp. 155–169; and Tim Benton, "Reden ohne Adjektive: Architektur im Dienst des Totalitarismus," in Ades et al., eds, *Kunst und Macht*, pp. 36–42. Wolfgang Schäche extends his architectural analysis onto the planning arena, stating how the North-South Axis was a "*via mortes,*" revealing "stone by stone, building by building, the imperial perspective of the intended world domination." Schäche, "Spurensuche am Pariser Platz: ein imaginärer Spaziergang," in Düwel et al., eds, *1945,* pp. 16–38, p. 31. Stephen D. Helmer agrees by implication, predicting that Hitler's Berlin would have failed infrastructurally: it would have become a "second, self-absorbed city ... severing vital links." Helmer, *Hitler's Berlin: The Speer Plans for Reshaping the Central City* (Ann Arbor: UMI Research Press, 1985), p. 24.

35. As Brian Ladd has noted: "[M]uch of the planning for Nazi Berlin shared the technocratic rationality of all modern urban societies." Ladd, *The Ghosts of Berlin: Confronting German History in the Urban Landscape* (Chicago: University of Chicago Press, 1997), p. 139. Helmut Weihsmann considers the North-South Axis to have been unlike the Nazis' anti-urban propaganda and in fact a "thoroughly urban," workable model. A tunnel would have gone under the lake at the north end for trucks. And yet Weihsmann does point out how the main square next to the Reichstag would have been closed to through traffic because of its role as a parade area. Weihsmann, *Bauen unterm Hakenkreuz. Architektur des Untergangs* (Vienna: Promedia, 1998), p. 275. Conservative architect Léon Krier's 1985 study on Speer defends the North-South Axis as "the central part of a coherent and readable metropolitan road pattern" – but even Krier, whose ardent defense of Speer's neo-classicism made his book appear reactionary, admits that in addition to the re-application of land used by the Reich railway, some 50,000 apartments would have been razed to make way for Speer's plan, with Jews the primary losers; even Haussmann only destroyed 20,000 houses. Krier, *Albert Speer. Architecture 1932–1945* (Brussels: Archives d'Architecture Moderne, 1985), pp. 50–51.

See also Schäche's critique of Krier's enhancements of Speer's architectural images, in Schäche, "Architektur und Stadtplanung des 'Dritten Reiches' im Spiegel der Bau- und Kunstgeschichte," *Deutsche Kunst und Denkmalpflege*, 47.1 (1989), pp. 5–14, pp. 10–11.

36. *Deutschland von heute* (Berlin: Terramare Office, 1935), p. 46.

37. On Berlin's planning continuities, see Wolfgang Sonne, "Specific Intentions – General Realities: On the Relation between Urban Forms and Political Aspirations in Berlin during the Twentieth Century," *Planning Perspectives*, 19.3 (2004), pp. 283–310.

38. Albert Speer and Josef Goebbels, *Tatsachen sprechen für den Sieg* (Berlin: Universum Verlag, 1943), p. 10. See Raul Hilberg, "German Railroads, Jewish Souls," *Society*, 14 (November-December, 1976), pp. 60–74.

39. Cited by Neil Leach, *The Anaesthetics of Architecture* (Cambridge, MA: MIT Press, 1999), p. 10.

40. Speer, *Inside the Third Reich*, p. 78. See also Reinhold Niemeyer, "Deutschland," in *Urbanisme et traffic local/Town Planning and Local Traffic/Städtebau und Nahverkehr*, XVII. International Housing and Town Planning Congress (Frankfurt am Main: Buchdruckerei & Verlag Kichler, 1939), pp. 1–22, pp. 8, 12; Hugo Häring, "Städtebauliche Probleme Groß-Berlins" (lecture, 30 June, 1927), repr. in Balg, ed., *Martin Mächler*, p. 194; and Werner Hegemann, who criticized the massive terrain wasted by the adjacent Potsdamer and Anhalter stations as a "indigestible alien body [*Fremdkörper*] in Berlin's intestines." Hegemann, *Das steinerne Berlin*, p. 227.

41. Speer, *Architektur. Arbeiten 1933–1942*, p. 103.

42. Karl Arndt, "Architektur und Politik," in Speer, *Architektur*, pp. 113–35, p. 130. On present and future plans for the use of the former Tempelhof airport, see www.stadtentwicklung.berlin.de/planen/tempelhof/de/aktuelles/index. shtml (date accessed 2 May, 2010).

43. Speer, *Inside the Third Reich*, p. 134.

44. A west-east traffic corridor would have determined all of central London, following the Thames' flow, with sixteen rectangular compartments north and south separated by green space; and three new through (non-terminus) railway stations and their links to the rest of Britain would have emanated along the grid of the west-east corridor and its radial strips. Like the Nazis' North-South Axis, this road for London would have held that city's prime governmental and commercial sites. Thankfully, the MARS Master Plan by Arthur Korn and Felix Samuely was swiftly rejected by the various professional and civic bodies. (Incidentally, it was only in 2008 that the UK's Crossrail Act authorized the construction of a direct west-east rail link underneath London, designed to bring Heathrow into better global-city contact with the financial district of Canary Wharf, and scheduled to open in 2017.) See John R. Gold's discussion of the Master Plan for London, in *The Experience of Modernism: Modern Architects and the Future City 1928–1953* (London: FN Spon, 1997), pp. 157–63; and Nicholas Bullock, *Building the Post-War World: Modern Architecture and Reconstruction in Britain* (New York: Routledge, 2002), pp. 39–40.

45. This sense of an interwar-to-postwar continuity runs counter to the argument of architectural continuity from the Bauhaus to Nazism. While I agree with Winfried Nerdinger's objection to Krier's attempted rehabilitation of Speer

into the canon of Schinkelesque neo-classicism, Nerdinger's thesis of matching Nazi futurism straight back to the Bauhaus is exaggerated. Certainly, some architects of the *Neues Bauen* – from Peter Behrens, Mies van der Rohe, and Gropius on down – tried to be active players in designing the new Reich, but that form of attempted continuity by designers is not the same as the historical causality of design. See Nerdinger, "Modernisierung, Bauhaus, Nationalsozialismus" and "Bauhaus-Architekten im 'Dritten Reich'," both in Nerdinger, ed., *Bauhaus-Moderne im Nationalsozialismus. Zwischen Anbiederung und Verfolgung* (Munich: Prestel, 1993), pp. 9–23, 153–78. See also Schäche, *Architektur und Städtebau in Berlin zwischen 1933 und 1945. Planen und Bauen unter der Ägide der Stadtverwaltung*, 2nd ed. (Berlin: Gebr. Mann Verlag, 1992), pp. 86–95, 146–48; and Durth and Nerdinger, *Architektur und Städtebau der 30er/40er Jahre*, pp. 34, 36.

9
Re-Centering Postwar and Post-Wall Berlin

Bonn Go Home

(Millennial graffiti in Berlin-Mitte's
Spandauer Vorstadt: an update of West
Berlin's Cold-War graffiti "Ami Go Home")

A telling fact in Berlin's tale of unexpected infrastructural continuities over the course of the twentieth century is that former Nazi planners simply continued their efforts in their new postwar jobs in the West. Urban historian Jeffry M. Diefendorf has asked: "Does it matter ... that so many of the leading planners and architects [of German reconstruction] had worked for the Nazis?"[1] Karl Bonatz, who had designed bunkers for Albert Speer's General Building Inspectorate, became Berlin's chief planner (*Stadtbaurat*) after Hans Scharoun (1947–1950). As Scharoun's conservative replacement, he defended "Berlin in stone" against the modernists, and planned a highway system for Berlin's uncertain future. Similar sets of uncomfortable continuities in planning history can be charted through the career of Hans Stephan. Like Speer an early NSDAP party member, Stephan worked as a department head at the GBI. Most histories of Nazi Germania include Stephan's well-known cartoon in 1942 of the path of the North-South Axis being shot through by a tank. He went more or less straight from his 1944 appointment, charged by Speer with the redesign of Berlin as Germania (excepting the North-South Axis, which Speer oversaw personally), to a key role in the planning for Berlin in the immediate post-war years. Stephan even became West Berlin's Building Senator (1956–59).

Indeed, only on paper was postwar Berlin to be reconstructed along wholly anti-Nazi lines. During his brief tenure (1945–46) as the Soviet-appointed *Stadtbaurat* for postwar Berlin, former Expressionist Scharoun

190

was able to design, if not build, a renewed metropolis out of the ashes in his Collective Plan of 1946.[2] Nazi geomantic axiality was thoroughly eclipsed therein.[3] In his ideal Plan based on the utopian grids of Hilberseimer and Le Corbusier, the "urban landscape" (*Stadtlandschaft*) concept, and the MARS plan for London, Scharoun envisioned for Berlin a rectangle of administrative buildings along a west-east axis following the river Spree. Indeed, the concept of the city's old core no longer played a role. As the streets cut the rectangle, so too were functions divided along those streets, such as banking or commerce. Residential areas were to be north and south of the rectangular arteries.

Significantly, Scharoun's design reacted against Speer's axial plan for Berlin, proposing instead a modular traffic system built around the Spree, replacing axes and rings through and round the existing city. Most intriguingly, his plan was intended to work for a *whole* city, while in fact it was quickly becoming clear that the Allies in the occupied city were behaving quite otherwise, according to sectoral lines already drawn up across the city before the war had even ended. In retrospect, it is clear to see that Scharoun's International Style was accepted because it was clearly not German, clearly not Nazi neo-classical, and clearly the opposite of radial axiality; and it fitted in with previous decades' desire to liberate the city from its cramped *Mietskasernen*. Scharoun's design has been deemed unduly influenced by the ideal of going beyond Germania – hence its radical negation of the city's historical substance.

Apart from Scharoun's Plan for Berlin, which sought to break with all historicism as well as the immediate Nazi past, it is possible to detect continuities not just between the technocracies of both Nazi and postwar planning, but also between the competing world-systems of the Cold War, as exemplified in the divided city of Berlin. From the 1950s onwards, main arterial roads were widened or created in both its East and West. The ideological differences between the two competing city halves masked their basic similarities that became most apparent by the 1960s and 1970s: open spaces, massive apartment blocks – the Ernst-Reuter-Platz in the West, for example, to more than match the Alexanderplatz in the East.[4] High-rise cement-slab housing projects practically indistinguishable in style (if not in construction quality) were erected in both the communist and the capitalist parts of Berlin.

At first, however, the two building styles could not have seemed further apart. A new postwar architecture of geopolitics was applied to each half of the city. As Brian Ladd has noted, this "double restoration" lasted up to the era of the construction of the Wall.[5] Moscow's influence clearly prevailed over East Berlin's postwar planning: already by

1950, the German Democratic Republic's Soviet-approved "Sixteen Principles of Urban Planning" were published for the new country's capital and beyond. It is generally accepted that the postwar planning trajectories for the two halves of Cold War Berlin were induced to follow a "polycentric" approach *à la* Athens Charter (in West Berlin) and a "monocentric" one *à la* Moscow Charter (in East Berlin).[6] Yet even with these overtly choreographed beginnings in opposite planning styles, there were mirror-image parallels between East and West as they both replicated certain aspects of Speer's geopolitical vision for the city. While West Berlin's Westtangente freeway project relied as much on Speer's earlier ring-road concept as on US functionalism, the Stalinallee formed, essentially, a continuation of the Nazi W-E axis.

The Stalinallee (1952–58) to the east of Alexanderplatz, designed by a half dozen architects including Hermann Henselmann, was intended as the main part of the Central Axis (Zentrale Achse) for East Berlin. As one of the planned *Magistralen* along radial-axial principles, it helped define and anchor the communist capital, pointing synchronically to Moscow in an effort to edge out the incipient functionalist style from the West. However, the people's uprising of 17 June, 1953, which spilled over in the new Stalinallee, put paid to any notion that axiality alone could enshrine top-down power.[7] Yet the belief persisted. In the same year, General Secretary Walter Ulbricht advocated the opening up of the terrain between the Schloßplatz and the Alexanderplatz to form communist parade grounds for the people to express their postwar "will to rebuild" (*Aufbauwille*).[8] Indeed, the GDR's eventual combination of its Alexanderplatz with the TV tower, the Marx-Engels-Forum, the Foreign Ministry building (demolished post-Wall, in 1996), and the Palace of the Republic (demolished 2006–08), were all intended to re-center the identity of Berlin-Mitte as the capital of the new communist state, and provide a new series of spaces for government-sponsored parades.

As the political differences between the Soviet and Western Allies became cemented in the rival physical forms of the occupied city of postwar Berlin, architecture and planning exhibitions became obvious tools for propagandistic display. The federally organized Interbau exhibition in West Berlin of 1957–58 was a reaction against the display avenue of the Stalinallee. It was a barely disguised political tool for the emerging Cold War, with the apartment blocks of the new Hansa quarter (Hansaviertel) in the Tiergarten constituting a showcase in the West's International Style.[9] Communist Berlin's response in the fall of 1958 was a competition for the "Socialist Transformation of the Center of the Capital City of the GDR" (*zur sozialistischen Umgestaltung des*

Zentrums der Hauptstadt der DDR), one that not surprisingly ignored the fact of West Berlin's existence. It was at this exhibition in 1958 that Henselmann first exhibited his design for the TV-tower, built at Alexanderplatz in the following decade.

When the decades of infrastructural severing of Berlin by the Cold War border of the Wall were taking effect, it was the Wall that provided the ultimate monument – and the most enduring line of demarcation – for Berlin. Ironically, the Wall's twenty-eight-year tenure granted Berlin that which the Nazis had wished for it, just in an unforeseen manner. The Wall forged what can be termed a *negative axis* of voided, inverted, seemingly impermeable, blocked-out space – a north-south axis through the center of the city as well as a ring around its western half. Indeed, the demolition of the Wall as the world's most famous border-barrier has meant that the city has been learning ever since how to define itself in relation to the (positive) absence of that marker, rather than in relation to its (negative) presence.

Since the Wall had anchored both West and East as a necessary outgrowth of the distance between the two world systems, the role of reconnection in Berlin has been of paramount importance because it stands not just for the normalization of the city, not just for the normalization of the country in its post-Holocaust guilt, but moreover of the re-alignment of the post-Cold War world. When the Wall was dismantled, it was as if that sense of inversion had to be quickly filled in for the city to succeed at its renewed self-definition. The aim has been to re-connect, bridge, join, and hence re-make the center of the city, and then re-make the re-centered Berlin into an infrastructural connecting point between other cities. In other words, the earlier planning discourses for Berlin are being resumed, reacted against, and extended upon.

Wall-less Berlin has created new icons or re-habbed existing ones as part of its political self-reinstatement and in tandem with the former West German federalist system's accommodation of the regained capital. In fact the re-dressing of Berlin in a capital's garb practically constitutes a self-regenerating, self-renewing source of energy, at least for political, cultural, and architectural ideologues. Chancellor Helmut Kohl certainly tapped into this tradition in his assertion of September 1997 at the foundation stone ceremony for the governmental quarter on the Spree river bend (Spreebogen). For Kohl, Berlin constituted the new "business card" of the German nation and, as an opportunity for such a new beginning, it was unparalleled by any other capital city.[10] Joining this wave of opportunity and opportunism during the 1990s' building "spree" all around Berlin's actual river Spree was Volker Hassemer, Senator of Development for Berlin prior to the fall of the Wall and founder of the city marketing company Berlin Partner. His enthusiasm typified voices that hailed this "great opportunity" to fill in the gap in the center of Berlin that had been laid to waste by the no-man's-land of the Wall and to "modernize it from the ground up."[11]

One building that was famously emptied out, purged as it were, and modernized from the ground up within its four exterior façade walls is the Reichstag (originally built between 1884 and 1894). The opening up of the building denotes its significance – up to one third of the interior was removed to make this possible.[12] With this act of phoenix-like resurrection, British architect Lord Norman Foster granted Berlin one of its best new candidates for a new Expressionist "city crown" (*Stadtkrone*).[13] Architectural judges like James S. Russell assessed the rebirth of the building, specifically the replacement high-tech glass dome neatly symbolizing the transparent workings of the reunified democracy, in terms of whether a building such as this really could "help a people remember the sins of the past and dedicate themselves to a less pathological future."[14] In 1999, when the renovated Reichstag was opened, the hope was that it indeed could and would. The double spiral of publicly accessible walking ramps affording views from within the famous cupola above the plenary chamber have helped reassert the building's nodality between the Brandenburg Gate and the new government quarter. Foster's dome was swiftly accepted as a leading symbol of the Berlin Republic – if not of Berlin itself – because of its qualities as a "readily marketable logo" for the nation.[15] Thanks to the dome, the building displays both itself and its view to tourists: its message is for its visitor-consumers to buy into technologized capitalism and buy into Germany. This is transparency incorporated, so to speak – as if Bonn's architectural credo has been remade for the Berlin highlife. In fact, the visiting public is able to catch no more than a glimpse through the dome's base of the politicians' deliberations beneath them. The public's gaze is directed outwards, bouncing off the dome's glass surfaces rather than into the parliamentary space below. Instead, the politicians are free to gaze upwards at the touring public, continually ascending and descending the dome above them (Fig. 9.1). The Reichstag's transparency-effect is really more one of *translucency*. The electric beacon of the Reichstag dome by night, alongside its commercially oriented neighbor at Potsdamer Platz, the Sony Center's dynamic circus-tent roof designed by Helmut Jahn, offers up a set of dialectically gleaming anchors for post-Wall Berlin that hearken back to the city's famed emphasis during the 1920s on *Lichtarchitektur* (the architecture of light).[16]

Figure 9.1   View of the dome from the plenary chamber in the Reichstag, Berlin (designed by Lord Norman Foster, 1999)

As part of the intense efforts to re-align and re-connect post-Wall Berlin, special emphasis has been accorded to the area around the Brandenburg Gate – Berlin's other famous monument – as a way of over-coming the legacy of the Wall. The Brandenburg Gate simply gained in significance as a stabilizing image for the city by dint of its frontline border position during the decades of division, as well as its memorable role as the effective herald of the opening of the Wall itself in November 1989. We can think here of Kohl's staged walk through the Gate a month after the opening of the Wall. Paul Virilio's vision of a post-modern borderless city (and specifically Virilio's question: "Where does the city without gates begin?") has been turned on its head by Berlin as it has sought to define itself without the Wall by reemphasizing its famous former custom's gate instead.[17] A telling image for Berlin's initial phase of post-Wall reunification could be found in the Telekom ad that covered the Brandenburg Gate during its renovation in 2001 (Fig. 9.2).

Figure 9.2 "We connect." Deutsche Telekom advertisement at the Brandenburg Gate during its renovation in 2001

This icon of Berlin used to stand tantalizingly out of reach to Westerners during the Cold War, just on the eastern side of the Wall. As a former symbol of the border, it now stood draped by Telekom's renovation-sponsoring rights: "We connect" (*Wir verbinden*). The Gate's pillars had even been pushed into a new position by the trompe d'oeil of the ad. In a sense, the Brandenburg Gate is Berlin's best *Stadtkrone* to date, reestablishing itself amidst its myriad new competitors because it shows itself off as a successful Simmelesque act of bridging at the Wall's most photographed site of separation and subsequent celebration at the Cold War's end.[18]

Next to the Gate and just south-east of the Reichstag, the re-built Pariser Platz now forms a closed spatial unit as it once did: one thinks here of Hans Stimmann's credo "Berlin must look like Berlin!"[19] The Pariser Platz's completion of all its bombed-out or demolished sides helps re-identify the true center of Berlin away from the city's modernist structures of the communist era. This is the architectural "war" on the eastern part of the city, against which Stimmann's Critical Reconstruction program has essentially been waged. It makes sense, then, that Pariser Platz is now also home to a Kennedy museum promoting the city's Cold War "outpost" values.

While it has been taking Berlin quite a while to come up with the best ways to commemorate the Wall as the negative axis that lent the city so much definition for much of the second half of the twentieth century, the city's focus on infrastructural renovation continues apace. New governmental and entertainment- and retail-oriented architecture has been erected to help boost the New Berlin, but long-term renewal must necessarily go beyond revitalization that is too reliant on iconic structures. One might look in vain, as architectural historian Max Page does, for the capital's "own Guggenheim Bilbao, its work of transcendent architecture."[20] Perhaps it always takes a crisis of immense proportions to clarify the significance of apparently *modern* infrastructural nodes, connectors, lines, and axes for a *post*modern city. This basic infrastructural level becomes exposed whenever history "ruptures" cities into a new set of spatial borders and collective needs. As Lower Manhattan faces this challenge since 9/11, or New Orleans since Hurricane Katrina, post-reunification Berlin faced in the 1990s (and is still confronting) a similar attempt to re-insert physical nodes of relevance and connectivity into its urban center, which was, essentially, a series of wastelands where the Cold-War Wall had previously stood.[21]

In short: Berlin's former inner-city border had to be made over into Berlin's new center. This could be achieved by the re-ignition of old and the creation of new nodes of contact, communication, exchange, and movement. Nodality is, in fact, part of what the centrality of a city means: the city is a city as such because it provides the definitions, edges, and connections between places both within and beyond the city itself. Berlin's infrastructural task has been more challenging than post-9/11 New York's, however, because its loss of urban center was far more extensive and was prolonged for decades – indeed, for so long that its very "voids" (like the no-man's-land of the Wall itself used to be) became some of its truest spatial denominators.

So when the Wall came down, architects started dreaming of what they could do with Berlin. In the initial euphoria after 1989, some star architects were immediately invited by the Deutsches Architektur Museum and the *Frankfurter Allgemeine Zeitung* to draw up designs for reunified Berlin (in the exhibition, "Berlin Tomorrow"). With high hopes they redesigned its emptied-out center, its Wall-spaces, its former border zones. They descended upon the failed eastern part of the city center in order to re-do it. Their dreams were certainly impractical – yet they were dreams that had every right to be articulated, given the unique moment that Berlin offered in terms of millennial re-conceptualizations of the city. And at least they *saw* the Wall (going against the trend of the eradication-oriented *Wende*) at the same time as seeing the need to join the city's two halves.

Most of the architects' entries in the "Berlin Tomorrow" exhibition were focused on the revitalizing art of axial bridging and mending for the city. Coop Himmelblau, for example, favored a "Berlin Crossing" boulevard-concept to bring the two halves of the city together, "a line between Theodor-Heuss-Platz and Fischerinsel" along the Leipziger Straße. Again, Josef Paul Kleihues (the father of Critical Reconstruction in Berlin) wanted a multi-lane "western thoroughfare."[22] Daniel Libeskind in his own contribution to the "Berlin Tomorrow" exhibition recognized the impact of infrastructural guidance for joining Unter den Linden to the western part of the city: "Only by breaking through the barriers of nineteenth-century planning and thought will the dam that held East separated from West (even before its political division) be breached, allowing the energies of Berlin to flood back freely into everyday life."[23]

A warning for Berlin came from fellow exhibition participant Lord Foster regarding the loss of the Wall: "To obliterate this area for ever, which is currently the presumed fate of the wall zone, would be to deny to future generations that this part of the history of the city ever existed." At the same time, however, Foster remained practical: "In rejoining

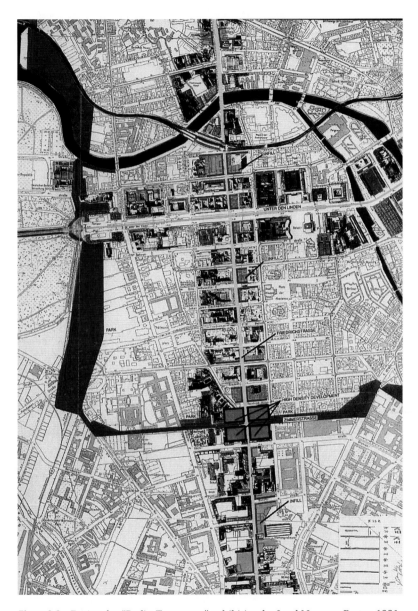

Figure 9.3 Design for "Berlin Tomorrow" exhibition by Lord Norman Foster, 1991

the two halves of the city it is essential that the street pattern is relinked across the wall zone."[24] Even with this circulatory re-connecting, Foster's suggestion of a city park for the entire Wall zone through central Berlin would have lent a new permanence to the city's internal border-wound (Fig. 9.3). Foster's point was taken up by Jacques Herzog, Pierre de Meuron and Remy Zaugg, who were cognizant of the fact that the Tiergarten is the "geometric centre" of Berlin, and that the two sides of the city remained irreparably "cut off" by the space of the park. Like Himmelblau, they wanted to link the city west-eastwards in a massive axis, from the Ku-Damm to Leipziger Straße, and provide a "double axis" just south of Strasse des 17. Juni and Unter den Linden. Their less promising idea was to insert four skyscrapers in rectangular formation – above, below, and on each side of the park, just to mark the center.[25] The relative outsiders from the US, Las Vegas experts Denise Scott Brown and Robert Venturi, wanted to link the Ku-Damm with the Alex via a grand boulevard just south of the Tiergarten. They also wanted a "Brandenburg Stair" that would have crossed across and over the eponymous Gate and basically hidden it from view.[26]

Amongst all these fanciful proposals, architect Christoph Langhof's "Delta City" (1995) vision for post-Wall Berlin rather stands out for its negation of the entire need to bring the city together. Rather, he proposed not a reunified terrain but an amplification of the two separate Berlins' political and social systems, by adding a third "Delta garden city" to the south of the city in Brandenburg, appending itself onto the existing infrastructure of rail, road, and air, and encouraging a polycentric understanding of Germany's reunification (Fig. 9.4). Langhof himself realized this was a "poetical interpretation," but for him the role of the architect is to help forge a "desired future," not repeat the status quo.[27] While these paper architecture ideas did not succeed in transforming post-Wall Berlin, at least they continued the dialogue with the past. In real time, Langhof's radical vision of ex-urbanizing Berlin has taken a somewhat more predictable path. The formerly sharp edges of West Berlin's periphery have become increasingly diffuse – namely, a suburbanization process is now occurring along its former western (formerly Cold-War bordered) as well as eastern edges. Berlin and Brandenburg are finally working together to create a measured tempo for such catch-up processes.[28]

Faced with the enormity of the task of reunifying the city, Berlin has in some respects been forcibly re-structured and re-centered. In 2001, its twelve boroughs were fused together out of the former twenty-three – an act that fused parts of the city that had been on both sides of the

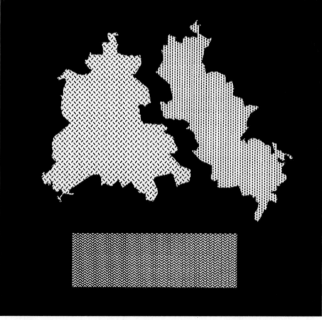

Figure 9.4 "Delta City" design for post-Wall Berlin by Christoph Langhof in "The Fever of the Architect," 1995

Cold War border. The maps of the very first post-Wall Land Use Plan (*Flächennutzungsplan*) of 1994 issued by the reunified capital's Senate Department for Urban Development gave the impression that the areas voided by the removal of the Wall had already all been uniformly re-constructed according to the era prior to division, indeed as if the Wall had never been.[29]

Berlin's re-centering process has also led to demotions in or demolitions of certain former icons. Against the signed protest of more than 100,000 West Berliners, the Zoologischer Garten train station has been demoted to a local portal after years of service as the national arrival and departure point for West German cities. Taking its place is the Hauptbahnhof, which lies in Berlin's regained center rather than in the center of West Berlin. The same forcible demotion in order to displace and replace the center applies to the fall 2008 closure of Tempelhof airport, this time despite even stronger organized protests from over 200,000 West Berliners in a referendum that failed to meet the minimum voting quota; and to the closure of West Berlin's Tegel airport, once the transformation of Schönefeld airport into Berlin Brandenburg International is complete in 2012.

Such acts of displacement are not limited to infrastructural nodes. The piece-by-piece demolition of the Palace of the Republic (Palast der Republik) might yet eventually be replaced with a baroque façade-version of what had stood there before, the City Palace (Stadtschloß, now being referred to as the future Humboldt Forum). Where once the Hohenzollern City Palace was deemed an unwelcome center that would have displaced the German Democratic Republic's desire for its capital's new socialist core, so too now the now-deconstructed Palace of the Republic was considered an obstacle or block for re-anchoring reunified Berlin. In the same vein of a programmatic re-enforcing of Berlin's national nodality, more of the six federal government ministries that had stayed in Bonn when others moved to Berlin in 1999 are now moving their headquarters to the capital, after all, gradually turning their Bonn locations into a mere formality.[30]

Some of the road changes, however, run counter to planning logic. Clearly, Weimar Berlin's chief planner Martin Wagner would not have been content with the attempted solutions of this century's New Berlin to bring the two halves of the city back together in terms of road arteries. Present-day Berlin has but two major west-east routes leading through Mitte. Inevitably, the Brandenburg Gate has made been into a pedestrian zone; and any emergency security arrangements for the newly rebuilt US Embassy next to the Gate will no doubt impact east-west traffic at some point.[31] The situation is compounded by the Inner

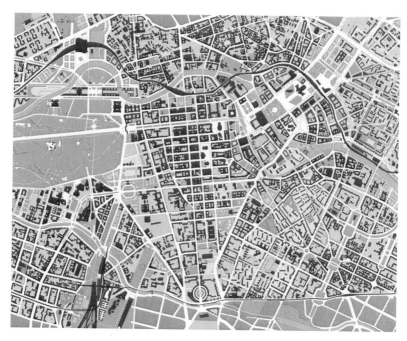

Figure 9.5 Excerpt from the "Inner City Master Plan" (*Planwerk Innenstadt*), as resolved by the State Parliament of Berlin in 1999

City Master Plan (*Planwerk Innenstadt*) – since expanded into the concurrent plans *Westraum*, *Nordostraum*, and *Südostraum*. Drafted in 1996 and started in 1999 by a group of exclusively West German planners, ostensibly as a way to bring together the city's centers in east and west, the *Planwerk Innenstadt* seemed at first to present an apparent return to the old Weimar-era debate about improving access between and within the western and eastern sections of the city (Fig. 9.5).[32] The program's changes impact Berlin's City-West (such as upgrading the postwar area of the Breitscheidplatz at the ruined Kaiser Wilhelm Memorial Church) even though its main agenda has been to infuse life and wealth into Mitte – a transfusion for the old city center that had sat in the communist East. Its proponents saw its revitalization program as a way of literally bringing the divided city back together, and as a way of enhancing and re-densifying the otherwise pedestrian-unfriendly traffic spaces of the 1960s and 1970s.

However, the *Planwerk Innenstadt* is more indicative of post-Wall Berlin's tendency to accidentally reverse the Weimar era's arterial linking need, all in the name of recreating a lost "European City" ideal that bespeaks Berlin's prewar density. Potsdamer Platz has been rebuilt as a confined series of narrow intersections; and Friedrichstraße has been narrowed at the same time as being gentrified and re-commercialized. The Plan also pumps perhaps too much artificial life into Mitte, such is its emphasis on recapitalizing the German capital. Further, it has been applied as a means of silencing proponents who wanted to retain prominent former GDR architecture and public, yet practically voided, spaces. Essentially, the Plan's too-transparent function has been to run roughshod over the physical landscape of former communist Berlin, and deny the eastern districts' particular history, for most of the second half of the twentieth century, of urban socialist development.

Where reunified Berlin has not been too busy eradicating or shielding itself from its communist traces, it has fared far better in its scenes of urban transformation. Two major projects have symbolically and infra-structurally joined that which was not connected before: the government quarter that crosses the "n" of the Spree river bend and its accompanying Hauptbahnhof (although it took until the summer of 2009 to link them to the city's subway system, the U-Bahn).[33] Both are indebted to the directions that Berlin has taken, or tried to take, in its past, as planners tried to lend it state-worthy empowerment.[34] This is what has been built back into post-Wall Berlin: as the renewed national capital, it now has at least the image of new lines of power that might seem to answer some of Karl Scheffler's, Martin Wagner's, and Martin Mächler's – let alone Albert Speer's or even Hitler's – earlier concerns.

The new West-East governmental axis designed by Axel Schultes with Charlotte Frank for the New Berlin's parliament, the winner of the Spreebogen Urban Design Competition, has not been able to, and has not wished to, escape Berlin's twentieth-century tale of geomantic axiality. The architectural competition for the Spreebogen site included the Humboldthafen's industrial area north of the Spree, and contained instructions specifying the role of axiality to bring the east and west of the city together. The Schultes-Frank winning design can be contrasted with the deconstructivist entry by Morphosis, which consisted of a series of undulating thin buildings along the curves of the riverbank. The Morphosis design entry for the German governmental quarter intended its fluidity to offer new kinds of "walls" for the reunified city: a "connective tissue," in fact.[35]

In contrast, and far more boldly than such a wave-effect would have offered, the Schultes-Frank concept for the Federal Chancellery and for the accompanying parliamentary buildings, entitled the Federal

Band (or Federal Ribbon: *Band des Bundes*), crosses the river just north of Foster's powerfully re-domed Reichstag at precisely the arc-location (the "n"-shape) of the river Spree. It ostensibly provides the formerly divided Berlin with a bridge across the former border of which Simmel could be proud. It is also a new node with its own underground station. In the end only the Chancellery, which opened in 2001, came from Schultes and Frank; the other government buildings in their master plan came from other architects; and the west-east axis was shortened. Nonetheless the axiality is powerful enough to pull one in: in particular, the Alsenblock (or Paul-Löbe-Haus) leaps dramatically across the Spree from west to east via a public footbridge to the Luisenblock (Marie-Elisabeth-Lüders-Haus) on the other side (Fig. 9.6). Both buildings repeat the circular "washing machine" motif that has been ascribed to the Chancellery itself.[36]

The Schultes design that boldly joins east and west crosses the memory of the infamous planned North-South Axis at a precise perpendicular angle, taking maximal advantage of the significance of the "n" shape in the riverbend, just as Hitler and Speer would have done in their placement of the Great Hall inside that same loop. That this is a conscious interaction is demonstrated by Schultes' own sketch of his Spreebogen design being superimposed at a perpendicular "so-there" angle upon Speer's imaginary model city (Fig. 9.7). Indeed, Schultes has come in for quite a bit of criticism over the degree of audacity in his rather obvious power line for the new German center of government.[37] Reasons for this critique are exacerbated not only by the Chancellery's solitaire-status and its raised fortress-garden, which is surrounded by a moat-like wall higher than the Berlin Wall ever was; but also by the series of underground tunnels protecting parliamentarians from the public. However, the German government's actual presence is, in fact, much more diffusely distributed across the fabric of the capital than one might think, given the effect of this new west-east axis.

The cartographical dialogue with the Nazi axial image for Berlin is being continued in a less self-conscious form by some of the government's own promotional images, which tilted Schultes' west-east axis. The effect of this half-rotation is such that the reunified German government's literal and metaphorical west-east procession across the Spree River still functions as a north-south echo of its ancestral Nazi imaginary. One can perhaps have some sympathy for what might otherwise appear to be this eternal re-run of the need to represent government structures along a strong axial line, even after the concept's ruination by the Hitler-Speer version. Schultes' governmental

Figure 9.6 "The Leap Across the Spree" footbridge at the Spree River Bend government quarter just north of the Reichstag, Berlin. East (left): the Luisenblock (Marie-Elisabeth-Lüders-Haus, 2003); and west (right): the Alsenblock (Paul-Löbe-Haus, 2001); both designed by Stephan Braunfels Architekten

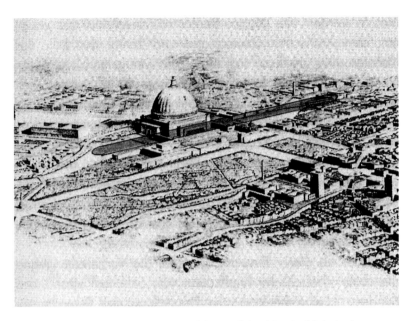

Figure 9.7 "The Federal Ribbon" (*Band des Bundes*), 1994: Axel Schultes' east-west response to Albert Speer's North-South Axis

axis that spans the Spree can be understood as a somewhat naive, yet symbolic, step in the direction of east-west healing, a welding together of that which the Wall had severed. And yet its deeper level of response still remains that of epitaph to the Nazis' wished-for axiality for Berlin's cityscape. In his defense of his vision for a government quarter that reaches "right across Speer's state axis," Schultes has complained that his original plan for a People's Forum was axed, as were other initiatives of his that would have linked the Chancellery to the other buildings and hence softened the lines.[38]

The government quarter certainly attests to the shortcoming of post-Wall Berlin's over-indulgence in new iconic architecture rather than in re-designing the tectonic fault-lines of infrastructure. Therefore the government quarter "stands for" more than it is. In key respects, then, the new Hauptbahnhof, situated just north east of the Chancellery and above the Spree river bend, is ultimately the more significant site-change (Fig. 9.8). As the largest cross-station in today's Europe, it alone can serve as a harbinger of future infrastructural shifts that could give Berlin new weighting. Rail travel, for Europeans, still goes right to the heart of metropolitan identity. Thus rail stations can bespeak a city's

Figure 9.8 Berlin Central Station (Hauptbahnhof), designed by von Gerkan, Marg and Partners, 2006

connectivity within the greater networked region of cities. Planners for post-Wall Berlin have made clear they share this approach: railway, not road or even air, still defines this polycentral city.[39]

Berlin Central was built by the architectural firm of von Gerkan, Marg and Partners on the site of the former Lehrter Bahnhof.[40] It clearly follows the legacy of the Mächler design and Speer's subsequent plan for the North-South Axis. Both Mächler and Speer planned a north-south rail link under their wished-for grand boulevard. As a result of this legacy, Meinhard von Gerkan's design was criticized early on for looking too megalomaniacal – in other words, too geomantic – for Berlin. But, as we have identified, the station really only followed what had long been wanted for the city. Despite fears of a renaissance of Nazi planning ideals, all we are really seeing is urban planning's clear continuities through all the historical ruptures and discontinuities that Berlin has known. There is no need, then, to fear the return of the (planning) repressed.[41]

The Hauptbahnhof serves as the central hub for the capital's "mushroom"- or "T"-shaped regional rail system (the *Pilzkonzept*), spread out across several refurbished and new rail stations.[42] The tracks of the Hauptbahnhof thus cross, north-south and underground, the west-east lines of the existing above-ground city rail system. Berlin Central finally offers an underground through (that is: non-terminus) station for continental rail traffic. Chancellor Kohl had immediately realized in the wake of the fall of the Wall that the "east-west [rail] connections" of both Germany and central Europe, stalled by the Cold War division, would henceforth, even if gradually, start to resume their former relevance.[43] Thus the "mushroom concept" of reunified Berlin's rail network was consciously aimed not just at Berliners re-navigating their way across their city, but at providing the infrastructural possibility of a future (regained) role for the capital at the heart of the new (again, regained) Europe. Moreover, the underground U55 line will, when it is eventually linked to the U5, provide a vital west-east link between the Hauptbahnhof and Alexanderplatz; and BBI airport will be directly linked to the station. To plan future key connections for the multiple types of rail network in Berlin, most of the work for the transit lines occurred underground on the north-south axis itself, and the river Spree even had to be re-canalized at great government cost from 1996 to 1998. After almost a decade of work, in 2006 the reunified capital finally received its direct north-south vehicular and rail (and future U- and S-Bahn) link of five and a half miles (9km), the underground rail part of which is tunneled underneath the Tiergarten for just over two miles (3.5km) between the river Spree in Moabit and the Landwehrkanal at Gleisdreieck.

The notion of north-south axiality (strictly speaking a north-west by south-east angle) is further highlighted by the two glass office "wing"-towers (*Bügelbauten*) flanking the Hauptbahnhof's symbolically named East-West Hall (*Ost-West-Halle*), which houses the local traversing rail connections.[44] The frames for the bridge-concourse between these towers were dramatically lowered into position in the summer of 2005, attracting an audience of 100,000.[45] Berlin's newly combined axiality was, in a sense, symbolized by this act. As von Gerkan has stated: "The two main elements, the huge glass roof and the station bridge that crosses over it, symbolize this crossing."[46] The "crossing" will be further accentuated in the near future when the end sections of the glass roof (already c. 390 yards [330m] in length) above the curving line of the west-east platform are extended according to von Gerkan's original architectural plans.[47] The station effectively houses both historical axialities of Berlin in one.

Berliners meanwhile need time to adjust, complaining with justification that the station is as yet far from adequately linked to their local transportation networks. Nonetheless the Hauptbahnhof as Europe's largest rail hub designed for 30-plus million passengers a year is more than just expensive three-dimensional window-dressing, in which the post-Wall capital certainly abounds. Admittedly, such boosterist-spectacular symbolism for Berlin is a resonant part of the Hauptbahnof. The arched glass roof echoes not just those of the industrial era's rail stations, as well as its glass palaces and shopping arcades; von Gerkan's design also clearly reverberates with nearby glass architectural icons of the New Berlin, particularly Foster's dome for the new Reichstag, or Helmut Jahn's canopy above the structures of the Sony Center at Potsdamer Platz. The station's additional role is as a mega-mall: a Virgin store serves as an anchor for eighty shops. Its experiential consumerist attractions are intended as a destination for the urban *flâneur*; the facilitating Gustav-Heinemann footbridge (2005) connects the Hauptbahnhof with the new Spreebogenpark and riverside path. Eventually, a privately funded mixed-use cultural, office, and residential development (the Lehrter Stadtquartier/Europacity) will cover the massive voided area surrounding the station: at 60 soccer fields in size it will be three times larger than the new Potsdamer Platz; but meanwhile the city is making do with such temporary land uses as a sand sculpture park.[48] Among the five architectural firms selected from 80 submissions for designing the Lehrter Stadtquartier, one is headed by a contemporary Albert Speer, none other than the architect son of the Nazi N-S Axis master planner on practically the same site. He was also chair of the selection committee for the Hauptbahnhof design itself.[49]

Such retail and future residential re-centering aside, the station has already been hailed as a new "compass" for Berlin, a "Brandenburg Gate for the twenty-first century."[50] Thanks to its new central and east European member states, the European Union's center is shifting eastwards, and that new center will, in all likelihood, be Germany, and one day Berlin. The delayed opening of Berlin Brandenburg Airport until 2012 has granted the German railway an unexpected opportunity to try to complete the airport's connections with the Hauptbahnhof. A new rail infrastructure is being planned to provide fully modernized links with the various branches of Germany's eastern railway: the Ostbahn with the Baltic states; the Stettiner, Frankfurter and Görlitzer Bahn with Poland; and the Dresdner Bahn with the Czech Republic, Slovenia, Slovakia, and Hungary, respectively.[51] The *transrapide* link for the Hauptbahnhof's western destinations is waiting to be added.

Thus the Simmelesque connections that divide and divisions that connect would appear to be well suited to defining the condition of re-forming an obviously still rather unfinished Berlin. But do Germans and Berliners believe in this infrastructural promise of renewal for their capital? Understandably, given the past of this city they often feel a sense of non-identification with or even deep distrust toward the ongoing changes in the contours of their cityscape – sentiments that have been reflected in novels about the reunification process of the German capital. In Peter Schneider's novel, *Edward's Return* (*Eduards Heimkehr*, 1999), all "infrastructural expansion" (*Ausbau der Infrastruktur*) in the capital appears to have fallen prey to a conspiracy theory, wherein the influx of (mis)guided capital is being financed by the Americans and their lackeys, the West Germans, and is even likened to the former colonization of India by the British or South America by the Spanish.[52] (What Schneider's protagonist would make of the fact that, in our globalized economy, Germany today is the second largest investor in Manhattan real estate, or has had to essentially bail out bankrupt Greece as the major contributor to the EU's stabilization package for the euro, is unclear.)

We should have some patience here: (German) intellectual cynicism that deflates centrality and symbolism on the national level is a highly useful protective shield against the horrors of the German extremist past, as well as against future disappointment. Whether consciously or not, and perhaps as part of a Halbwachsian collective memory, Scheffler's disbelieving anti-Berlin epithets of 1910 are being reiterated. For example,

in the novel *A Garden in the North* (*Ein Garten im Norden*, 1998) by
Michael Kleeberg – that is, before the emergence of the Hauptbahnhof –
it is asserted that the planning history of Berlin has not yet produced
a topography of power, despite the consecutive efforts of the likes of
Wagner, Speer, and now also Schultes. According to Kleeberg, for
all of Schultes' overt reconfiguring of the axial symbolism of the New
Berlin into the seat of German national government, today's reunified
capital still will not be able to compete with the accepted heritage of
Paris's radially orbiting "planetary system" of boulevard-linked monuments. It cannot hope, either, Kleeberg's narrator states, to equal the
"vertical striving" of the skyscrapers that so define the first world-city
of the twentieth century, namely New York. For Kleeberg, it is more
a case of poor old New Berlin: a city out of sync with itself, flowing
diffusely outwards like "lava" without real geographical definitions
(like hills, radial boulevards, or a grand river), and its "theoretical
center" of the seventeenth and eighteenth centuries too weak to hold
onto its renewed role, no matter how much post-Wall rehabbing it
receives. Here we see the perennial German suspicion toward Berlin is
still in full force. Welcome, then, to Germany's capital, where now that
the Wall is no longer there to hold in the "existential emptiness," the
"horror vacui functions as an architect."[53]

Perhaps, however, this otherwise justified criticism of the architectural
over-inscription of the New Berlin is only part of the post-1989 story.
Post-Wall Berlin appears not to have heeded Virilio's insistence that
the postmodern city is no longer concerned with being grounded:
"The localization and the axiality of the urban layout faded long ago ...
The representation of the contemporary city is ... no longer determined
by a ceremonial opening of gates ... nor by a succession of streets and
avenues."[54] Berlin seems not to have listened to Virilio's advice, at least
in certain areas, because in the post-Wall era it has embarked on a quest to
re-ground its center(s) and re-make its arteries. Hence it will take what
it can – here a piece of what ought to make a city global, there a piece
of what might help it look more like a capital city, and so on. Almost
instinctively, the markers of modernity that were left unfinished in its
broken planning history are being called upon again. The city is still
answering the planning questions set forth in the Weimar and Nazi eras.

The only way to fill the voids left by the Wall is an infrastructural
reconfiguration that not only knows the limits of Berlin's present
situation, but also predicts the city's future needs. Axiality and nodality,
the enablers of a city's centeredness, cannot be painted onto the face
of the city. Thus the new Hauptbahnhof, nestled in between and below

its two wing towers, will have a long wait for the centrality of Berlin to re-assert itself in order to approach anything close to the role once assigned to it by Wagner's collaborator Adolf Behne in 1929, when he defined Berlin's axiality as part of its mediating world-city role between Moscow and Paris: "Its essence is to be a bridge; it is twofold in its inception, it has two pillars, one on each side, east and west of the Spree" (*Sein Sinn ist, Brücke zu sein, und von Anfang an ist es zweihaft, hat es zwei Pfeiler, ein Hüben und Drüben, ein Östlich und Westlich der Spree*).[55] By the middle of the twenty-first century, when Berlin may well have recovered from its present bankruptcy, the Hauptbahnhof will be there smoothly connecting not just the city, but the European continental east, west, north, and south.

Notes

1. Jeffry M. Diefendorf answers his own question thus: "Neither 1933 nor 1945 marked a fundamental break in the history of German architecture and town planning." Diefendorf, *In the Wake of War: The Reconstruction of German Cities after World War II* (New York: Oxford University Press, 1993), pp. 279, 280, and 181. Werner Durth usefully identifies four points of continuity from pre-Nazi, Nazi, and post-Nazi eras: radical modernization; reactionary vernacular/neoclassical architecture; monumentalism; and an "opening up" of the city. Durth, "Stadt und Landschaft," in Jörn Düwel, Durth, Niels Gutschow, and Jochen Schneider, eds, *1945. Krieg – Zerstörung – Aufbau. Architektur und Stadtplanung 1940–1960* (Berlin: Henschel Verlag, 1995), pp. 126–75, pp. 151–53. See also Harald Bodenschatz, *Platz frei für das Neue Berlin! Geschichte der Stadterneuerung in der "größten Mietskasernenstadt der Welt" seit 1871* (Berlin: Transit, 1987); and Wolfgang Schäche, "Architektur für die Ewigkeit ...? Zur 'Theorie des Ruinenwertes' von Albert Speer und den Bauten des Reichsparteigeländes in Nürnberg," *Der Architekt*, 11 (1989), pp. 565–68, p. 567.
2. Scharoun's Plan for Berlin was shown at the 1946 exhibition, "Berlin plant, erster Bericht." Ironically, the future-oriented exhibition was held in a building that stood as a herald to the city's past: a non-bombed-out section of the soon-to-be-demolished City Palace (Stadtschloβ).
3. Scharoun's postwar Plan far exceeded his interwar renovations (like those planned for both pedestrian and traffic flows at the Berlin exhibition area). See "Messegelände Berlin," *Die Form* 1.1 (1925), pp. 83–84. On the postwar planning reaction against Speer, see Düwel, "Berlin. Planen im Kalten Krieg," in Düwel et al., eds, *1945*, pp. 195–234, p. 198; Gerrit Confurius, "Versuch eines gesamtdeutschen Neuanfangs. Ordnung zu schaffen in der verzweifelten Unordnung," in Thorsten Scheer, Josef Paul Kleihues, and Paul Kahlfeldt, eds, *Stadt der Architektur. Architektur der Stadt. Berlin 1900–2000* (Berlin: Nicolai, 2000), pp. 215–27, p. 222; Schäche, "Von der Stunde Null und der Legende des Wiederaufbaues," in Erich Konter, ed., *Wendezeiten in Architektur und Stadtplanung: Kontinuität oder Bruch in der Entwicklung nach 1945* (Berlin: Institut für Stadt- und Regionalplanung der Technischen Universität Berlin, 1986),

pp. 78–88, p. 80; and Harald Bodenschatz, "Stadterneuerung Berlin dies- und jenseits der Kapitulation 1945 – Warnung vor den Irrwegen disziplinär verengter bau- und planungsgeschichtlicher Diagnosen," in Konter, ed., *Wendezeiten*, pp. 89–99, p. 96. Bodenschatz also suggests that the anti-*Mietskasernen* discourse of postwar planners was a substitution for overcoming the more recent Nazi planning past. Bodenschatz, *Platz frei für das Neue Berlin*, p. 136.

4. Brian Ladd finds that from the aerial perspective one would have found much in common between West Berlin's Ernst-Reuter-Platz and East Berlin's Alexanderplatz: the International Style, or Brutalism, existed in both state systems. The GDR had, however, significantly more Brutalist housing projects (Hellersdorf, Hohenschönhausen, and Marzahn housed a third of all East Berliners). Ladd, *The Ghosts of Berlin: Confronting German History in the Urban Landscape* (Chicago: University of Chicago Press, 1997), pp. 189, 191. See also Roland Strobel's investigation of this phenomenon, specifically his conclusion that "competing political ideologies in East and West Berlin did not necessarily create different planning paradigms. [...] The greatest surprise is perhaps that the planning paradigm shifts came at the same time on both sides of the wall." Strobel, "Before the Wall Came Tumbling Down: Urban Planning Paradigm Shifts in a Divided Berlin," *Journal of Architectural Education*, 48.4 (1995), pp. 25–37, p. 35.

5. Brian Ladd, "Double Restoration: Rebuilding Berlin after 1945," in Lawrence J. Vale and Thomas J. Campanella, eds, *The Resilient City: How Modern Cities Recover from Disaster* (New York: Oxford University Press, 2005), pp. 117–34; see also Hanns-Uve Schwedler, "The Urban Planning Context in Berlin: a City Twice Unique," in William J.V. Neill and Schwedler, eds, *Urban Planning and Cultural Inclusion: Lessons from Belfast and Berlin* (Basingstoke and New York: Palgrave, 2001) pp. 24–41; and Greg Castillo, "Building Culture in Divided Berlin: Globalization and the Cold War," in Nezar Al Sayyad, ed., *Hybrid Urbanism: On the Identity Discourse and the Built Environment* (Westport: Praeger, 2001), pp. 181–205.

6. Schwedler, "The Urban Planning Context in Berlin," in Neil and Schwedler, eds, *Urban Planning and Cultural Inclusion*, pp. 24–25.

7. The role of the planned *Magistralen* is given in the "Grundsätze der Planung und Gestaltung sozialistischer Stadtzentren" (1960), repr. in Werner Durth, Jörn Düwel, and Niels Gutschow, eds, *Aufbau. Städte, Themen, Dokumente. Architektur und Städtebau der DDR*, vol. 2, 2nd ed. (Frankfurt am Main and New York: Campus Verlag, 1999), pp. 296–413; see also Peter Müller, *Symbolsuche – Die Ost-Berliner Zentrumsplanungen zwischen Repräsentation und Agitation* (Berlin: Gebr. Mann Verlag, 2005). On the uprising see Düwel, "Berlin," in Durth et al., eds, *Aufbau*, pp. 228–29.

8. Cited by Durth et al., eds, *Aufbau*, p. 84.

9. The Stalinallee and the Hansaviertel alike proved too expensive for both West and East Berlin to replicate across their respective halves of the city. See Schäche, "Der Hauptstadtbewerb 1957/58. Entwürfe gegen die Vergangenheit," in Scheer et al., eds, *Stadt der Architektur*, pp. 251–57.

10. "Berlin ist die Visitenkarte," *Die Welt* (27 September, 1997).

11. Interview with Volker Hassemer, "Informationstechnologie entlastet die Städte," in Christa Maar and Florian Rötzer, eds, *Virtual Cities: Die Neuerfindung*

der Stadt im Zeitalter der globalen Vernetzung (Basel: Birkhäuser Verlag, 1997), pp. 188–93, p. 188.

12. Michael S. Cullen, *Der Reichstag. Parlament, Denkmal, Symbol* (Berlin: be.bra verlag, 1999), p. 332.

13. Bruno Taut, *Die Stadtkrone* (Jena: Eugen Diedericks, 1919).

14. James S. Russell, "With his sleek, ecological design, Lord Norman Foster imbues the Reichstag with Germany's new self-image," *Architectural Record* (July, 1999), pp. 102–13, p. 103. These issues are further debated in excellent studies by Deborah Ascher Barnstone, *The Transparent State: Architecture and Politics in Postwar Germany* (New York: Routledge, 2005), esp. pp. 175–208 and 209–34; Eric Jarosinski, "Building on a Metaphor: Democracy, Transparency and the Berlin Reichstag," in Carol Anne Costabile-Heming, Rachel J. Halverson, and Kristie A. Foell, eds, *Berlin: The Symphony Continues. Orchestrating Architectural, Social, and Artistic Change in Germany's New Capital* (New York: Walter de Gruyter, 2004), pp. 59–76; Lutz Koepnick, "The Nation's New Windows," in *Framing Attention: Windows on Modern German Culture* (Baltimore: Johns Hopkins University Press, 2007), pp. 240–62 (orig. in *German Studies Review*, 24.2 [2001], pp. 303–23); and Peter Chametzky, "Rebuilding the Nation: Norman Foster's *Reichstag* Renovation and Daniel Libeskind's Jewish Museum Berlin," *Centropa*, 1.3 (2001), pp. 245–64, esp. pp. 253–55.

15. Jarosinski, "Building on a Metaphor," p. 64.

16. This auratic reworking of the Weimar era is suggested by Koepnick in *Framing Attention*, pp. 255–56. See also Janet Ward, *Weimar Surfaces: Urban Visual Culture in 1920s Germany* (Berkeley: University of California Press, 2001).

17. Paul Virilio, "The Overexposed City," in K. Michael Hays, ed., *Architecture Theory since 1968* (City of New York: The Trustees of Columbia University/ Cambridge, MA: MIT Press, 1998), pp. 540–50, p. 547.

18. Georg Simmel, "Bridge and Door" (1909), in Neil Leach, ed., *Rethinking Architecture: A Reader in Cultural Theory* (New York: Routledge, 1997), pp. 63–76.

19. Interview with Hans Stimmann, in Paul Goldberger, "Reimagining Berlin," *The New York Times Magazine* (5 February, 1995).

20. Max Page, "Berlin's Identity Crisis," *Architecture*, 93.9 (2004), pp. 25–27, p. 26.

21. Herbert Muschamp, reflecting on the needs of post-World Trade Center Lower Manhattan, called infrastructure a "city's central nervous system, an extruded form of social space in which the ideal of universal access is given both concrete and philosophical form." Muschamp, "Public Spirit, Private Money and a New New Deal," *The New York Times* (24 March, 2002). Referring to Manuel Castells' *The Informational City* (1989), Muschamp suggested that rebuilt Lower Manhattan could and should be composed as a "portal" or "Grand Central," both of industrial modernity's infrastructure of transportation, and of today's post-nation-state infrastructure of globally linked information. Muschamp's double infrastructural model implies that if Manhattan is to remain a global city for the electronic era, its profile must nonetheless also correspond with that of an urban center of modernity. New York's post-9/11 rebuilding is, quite apart from creating a meaningful

memorial to the event at the site, a matter of re-enforcing nodes of physical relevance – not just symbolic skyscraper structures but transportation systems and digital networks. Indeed, the most significant step so far is the Port Authority of New York and New Jersey's transit hub (designed by Santiago Calatrava) that will bring together subway, PATH, and the region. The modern city is, at least on the basic infrastructural level, still relevant.

22. Vittorio Magnago Lampugnani, ed., *Berlin Tomorrow: International Architectural Visions*, Architectural Design Profile 92 (London: Academy Editions, 1991), pp. 25, 57.

23. Daniel Libeskind, "Über den Linden," in Libeskind, *The Space of Encounter* (New York: Universe, 2000), p. 198.

24. Lampugnani, ed., *Berlin Tomorrow*, p. 31.

25. Lampugnani, ed., *Berlin Tomorrow*, p. 55.

26. Lampugnani, ed., *Berlin Tomorrow*, pp. 79–80.

27. Christoph Langhof, "The Fever of the Architect," in Alan Balfour, ed., *Berlin* (London, UK: Academy Editions, 1995), pp. 57–59, pp. 59, 57. Langhof's proposal is discussed by Rudolf Stegers, "Intensive Multiplizität: Gartenstadt Delta," in Philipp Oswalt, *Berlin: Stadt ohne Form: Strategien einer anderern Architektur* (Berlin: Prestel, 2000), pp. 296–99; and by Oswalt, "Berlin, Stadt des 20. Jahrhunderts," *transition*, 9 (July 2002), pp. 110–17, pp. 116–17.

28. See the Regional Development Plan of Berlin and Brandenburg (LEP B-B): http://gl.berlin-brandenburg.de/landesentwicklungsplanung/lepbb.html (date accessed 16 June, 2010).

29. See Carolyn Loeb, "Planning Reunification: The Planning History of the Fall of the Wall," *Planning Perspectives*, 21.1 (2006), pp. 67–87. For updated versions of the Land Use Plan, which has since been revised in 1998, 2004, and 2009, see the Berlin Senate's website www.stadtentwicklung.berlin.de/ planen/fnp/ (date accessed 3 June, 2009).

30. The Bonn-Berlin Act of 1994 is meant to maintain the special status of Bonn as a Federal City (*Bundesstadt*) in relation to Berlin, but public opinion doubts its longevity, and the number of Berlin's government employees has risen by over 1,100 since the millennium. See, for example, "Bonn-Berlin-Gesetz. Bundesregierung soll ganz nach Berlin ziehen," *Berliner Morgenpost* (22 November, 2008); "Bonn-Berlin-Gesetz. Mehrheit für Totalumzug nach Berlin," *Spiegel-Online* (29 April, 2007). On the government's move, see Max Welch Guerra, *Hauptstadt Einig Vaterland. Planung und Politik zwischen Bonn und Berlin* (Berlin: Verlag Bauwesen, 1999); and Michael Z. Wise, *Capital Dilemma: Germany's Search for a New Architecture of Democracy* (Princeton: Princeton University Press, 1998).

31. Traffic moving along the Straße des 17. Juni has to shift south around the Brandenburg Gate in order to reach the eastern half of the same artery, Unter den Linden; and the Leipziger Straße, the extension for eastbound traffic coming from Potsdamer Platz, is often clogged up. A new east-west option between the two, along the Französische Straße, was opened up in December 2009.

32. The four *Planwerke* for Berlin (Inner, North-East, South-East, West) are explained at www.stadtentwicklung.berlin.de/planen/planwerke/index.shtml (date accessed 14 July 2009). On the continuing future for Planwerk Innenstadt see Harald Bodenschatz and Thomas Flierl, eds, *Berlin plant. Plädoyer für ein Planwerk Innenstadt Berlin 2.0* (Berlin: Theater der Zeit, 2010). For advocacies of

the Plan see Hans Stimmann, ed., *Berliner Altstadt: Von der DDR-Staatsmitte zur Stadtmitte* (Berlin: Dom, 2009), and Dieter Hoffmann-Axthelm, "Planwerk Innenstadt Berlin," in Stimmann, ed., *1940–1953–1989–2000–2010. Physiognomie einer Großstadt* (Milan: Skira, 2000), pp. 23-25. See also Florian Urban, "Picture Postcards of Urbanity. Reflections on Berlin's Inner City and the 1999 Master Plan," *Journal of Architectural Education* (2003), pp. 68–73; Simone Hain, "Struggle for the Inner City – a Plan Becomes a Declaration of War," Schwedler, "The Urban Planning Context in Berlin," and Wolfgang Süchting and Patrick Weiss, "A New Plan for Berlin's Inner City: Planwerk Innenstadt," all in Neill and Schwedler, eds, *Urban Planning and Cultural Inclusion*, pp. 69–84, 24–41, 57–68.

33. The first part of the new U55, linking the Hauptbahnhof to the Brandenburg Gate, officially opened in August 2009; the next stage, by 2015, will extend the line to the Alexanderplatz. Peter Cook, in *The Architectural Review*, 221.1323 (2007), p. 34, rightly found the temporary lack of subway connection rather "funny," but delighted in the geometric celebration of the Hauptbahnhof's double rail directions that pass over each other.

34. Both sites bespeak the new "spatial presence of the state in the city," as Bodenschatz has noted. Bodenschatz, "Hauptstadtplanungen aus der Perspektive der Stadt," in Helmut Engel and Wolfgang Ribbe, eds, *Geschichtsmeile. Wilhelmstraße* (Berlin: Akademie Verlag, 1997), pp. 247–59, p. 247.

35. Balfour, "Morphosis: Spreebogen," in Balfour, ed., *Berlin*, pp. 120–21, p. 121.

36. Before the Wall fell, plans were ongoing in West Berlin to return the Spreebogen area to a residential site (using Hans Kollhoff's winning design of 1985 for the IBA competition). This redevelopment would have included Aldo Rossi's unrealized German History Museum (which is where the Chancellery now is). Already at this stage, Axel Schultes and Charlotte Frank submitted a follow-up entry to the same competition, in which they suggested a line of buildings on the "n"-shaped terrain forged by the Spree (but remaining, of course, within West Berlin territory and without crossing the river). The concept was thus typical "Schultes" in that it also resembled his design for the museum buildings in Bonn. See Heinrich Wefing, *Kulisse der Macht. Das Berliner Kanzleramt* (Stuttgart and Munich: Deutsche Verlags-Anstalt, 2001), pp. 40–77.

37. See Peter Marcuse, "Reflections on Berlin: The Meaning of Construction and the Construction of Meaning," *International Journal of Urban and Regional Research*, 22.2 (1998), pp. 331–38, p. 333.

38. Schultes states that his design was in tandem with the rail station's needs in terms of "harbour lines, grid direction and overall dimensions" – but that this cooperation was ignored in the ultimate plans for the latter. Schultes, "Berlin – The Belated Capital," in Balfour, ed., *Berlin*, pp. 38–47, p. 46; see also Matthias Oloew, "Die Raumgreifenden," *Der Tagesspiegel* (29 January, 2008).

39. Senatsverwaltung für Bauen, Wohnen und Verkehr, ed., *Verkehrskonzept für Berlin* (Berlin: Bloch & Co., GmbH, 1999), p. 11.

40. In 1871, the Lehrter Bahnhof became the rail link for Berlin with Lehrte (near Hannover) and then, as of 1884, with Hamburg. The adjoining Lehrter Stadtbahnhof (on a bridge over the concourse) opened in 1882 and linked the station to other connecting points in Berlin; by 1930, it became a station

for the S-Bahn. After World War II, only the S-Bahn station survived. In the spring of 2005 there was a top-down decision (by former Berlin Urban Development senator Peter Strieder and Deutsche Bahn chief executive Hartmut Mehdorn) to call the new super station built in these stations' stead the Berlin Hauptbahnhof, despite a 2003 poll showing Berliners' clear preference for the "Lehrter" name.

41. The return of the planning repressed in the Spreebogen area is read by Simon Ward as a sign not so much of any troubling Nazi nostalgia but of the sheer "obstinacy of Berlin's geography, the networks that have been laid over it" over the past one and a half centuries. Simon Ward, "'Neues, altes Tor zur Welt': The New Central Station in the 'New' Berlin," in Costabile-Heming, Halverson and Foell, eds, *Berlin*, pp. 77–92, p. 81.

42. As part of the "mushroom" shape centered by the Hauptbahnhof, Berlin's major train stations are now the new Papestraße (now renamed Südkreuz), the Ostbahnhof (formerly East Berlin's Hauptbahnhof, rebuilt by Becker Gewers and Kühn & Kühn, 1998–2000), Ostkreuz, Westkreuz, Spandau (redesigned by Gerkan, Marg & Partner (1996–98), the new Gesundbrunnen (*almost* renamed Nordkreuz), and the new subterranean station at Potsdamer Platz. The Traffic Projects German Unity (*Verkehrsprojekte Deutsche Einheit*) of 1991 and the Federal Plan for the Transportation System (*Bundesverkehrswegeplan*) of 1992 determined the kinds of infrastructural changes needed for both the reunified country and capital. Deutsche Bahn explains the new rail concept for Berlin at www.hbf-berlin.de/site/berlin__hauptbahnhof/en/start.html (date accessed 3 August, 2008).

43. Helmut Kohl, *Verhandlungen des Deutschen Bundestages, 11. Wahlperiode, Stenographische Berichte, 177. Sitzung* (28 November, 1989), pp. 13510–14. Cited in Simon Ward, "'Neues, altes Tor zur Welt'," in Costabile-Heming, Halverson, and Foell, eds, *Berlin*, p. 80.

44. Mounting costs for the Hauptbahnhof and north-south tunnel (together now officially estimated at €3.1 billion, shared between Deutsche Bahn and the government, and not including the cost of the U55 line) put these office towers in jeopardy for a while, and delayed other urban and regional railway improvements for Berlin. Deutsche Bahn moved its headquarters into the two towers in 2010. See Klaus Kurpjuweit, "Bummelzug im Prachtbahnhof," *Der Tagesspiegel* (12 September, 2004); and Kurpjuweit, "Hauptbahnhof wächst nun doch in die Höhe," *Der Tagesspiegel* (27 March, 2003).

45. The station's presence in Berlin has not been without incident. At the opening festivities in 2006, a disturbed man knifed over 40 people in the crowd; and in January 2007, a girder fell down during a severe storm. The shutdown and minimal functioning of the S-Bahn (as the Hauptbahnhof's link within the city) in the summer of 2009 hardly helped matters.

46. Richard Bernstein, "Just a Rail Hub? Or a New Sort of Compass for Europe?" *The New York Times* (9 March, 2006).

47. A court case awarded von Gerkan the legal right to the original length of the station's arched glass roof on the west-east platform, as well as the originally intended ceiling for the subterranean level of the station – both of which Deutsche Bahn CEO Mehdorn had unilaterally changed. This will entail closing the S-Bahn's section of the station for up to three months, and will cost DB about €53 million. See Jude Stewart, "Collision Course," *Metropolis*,

26.7 (2007), pp. 50–56; and Matthias Oloew, "Dacherweiterung führt zu erheblichen Einschränkungen," *Der Tagesspiegel* (29 June, 2008).

48. Up to 2,000 apartments will be built at the Humboldt Harbor basin's combined areas, the partial master plan for which was designed by Oswald Matthias Ungers. Berlin's mayor, Klaus Wowereit, is promoting a "Berlin Art Hall" (Berliner Kunsthalle) as a landmark for the project. Vivico, Deutsche Bahn's real estate company, is among those developing the site over the next two decades. Isabell Jürgens, "Stadtquartier, Berlins Europacity nimmt Gestalt an," *Berliner Morgenpost* (16 December, 2010); "Neues Quartier am Hauptbahnhof geplant," *Berliner Morgenpost* (14 November, 2009); and "Masterplan für das Lehrter Stadtquartier," *Der Tagesspiegel* (2 August, 2008).

49. Albert Speer & Partner (AP&S), based in Frankfurt am Main, is Germany's largest architectural company with over 90 architects and planners. It received the commission for the Hannover world trade fair (Expo 2000), and is currently building a new district of over 45 square miles in the Chinese city of Changchun.

50. Bernstein, "Just a Rail Hub? Or a New Sort of Compass for Europe?"; and Stefan Schomann, "Hauptbahnhof Berlin: Palast der Züge," *Geo-Magazin*, 6 (2006).

51. This future Europe makes clear just how intersecting were the roles, in the SPD-led government of Chancellor Gerhard Schröder, of Manfred Stolpe as both former Minister for the East (Ost-Beauftragter) and former Federal Traffic Minister. Michael Cramer, transportation expert for the Bündnis90/Greens party and founder of the hiking path along the former inner German border, makes this point in "Die Ost-Erweiterung braucht die Schiene nach dem EU-Referendum in Polen," *Der Taggespiegel* (10 June, 2003).

52. Peter Schneider, *Eduards Heimkehr* (Berlin: Rowohlt, 1999), p. 220.

53. Michael Kleeberg, *Ein Garten im Norden: Roman* (Berlin: Ullstein, 1998), pp. 145–47.

54. Virilio, "The Overexposed City," pp. 543, 544.

55. Adolf Behne, introduction to Behne, ed., *Berlin in Bildern: Aufnahmen von Sasha Stone* (Vienna and Leipzig: Verlag Dr Hans Epstein, 1929), p. 9.

Part IV

Holocaust Divides: Memorial Architecture in Berlin

10
Countermonument and Catastrophe

That nature, which condemns its origin,
Cannot be border'd certain in itself.

(William Shakespeare)[1]

The divided legacy of Berlin can be identified in arenas reaching beyond Berlin's ability to connect to itself, to Germany, and to the rest of Europe. When, in 2004, the former Israeli ambassador to Germany asked at a Berlin convention, "What does Germany want from Berlin?" he was asking because post-reunification Germans did not yet appear to have an answer.[2] One thing many Germans naturally hoped for in the New Berlin was, at long last, the very beginning at least of the overcoming of guilt for Nazi war crimes. "A Mastered Past" was the premature assertion of a *Spiegel* magazine's cover page for the fiftieth anniversary of the end of World War II – premature if only in the key sense that anti-foreigner attacks and anti-Semitic acts of vandalism have been rising steeply since reunification.[3] The reconstituted capital has brought with it duties that have outweighed some desires and new beginnings. These duties have arisen even if, as Peter Sloterdijk has tentatively predicted, we are now entering a normalization era when Germans will be able to finally "reap the benefits" of the Federal Republic's longstanding culture of repentance and "metanoethical efforts" concerning the Holocaust.[4] One obvious role for reunified Germany has been a renewed obligation to centralize its public declarations of responsibility for the Holocaust by means of major commemorative sites. We can chart the degree to which the public memorialization of the Holocaust has helped the German capital of the Berlin Republic mark a new era of healing and re-definition – assuming, of course, that such sites successfully reveal and reflect upon the wound of the Holocaust and thus actually achieve their memorializing task.

Metropolitan memory is the "deepest structure" of architecture. The late Italian postmodern architect Aldo Rossi asserted that "the city is the *locus* of the collective memory" of its people; "as certain artifacts become part of its memory, new ones emerge."[5] For a nation's capital this aspect of psychic-spatial accrual is paramount. Over time, our national monuments are conceived of and grow – or are shed and discarded – just like the objects of our consciousness. Here, Rossi is developing the theory of spatially induced social memory first proposed by the Durkheimian French sociologist Maurice Halbwachs (who died at Buchenwald in 1945). It is to Halbwachs that we owe the insight that memory is not, in fact, created in a purely individualistic way, except in the Freudian dreamwork; during waking hours, collective "frameworks" (whether language-, family-, class-, race- or place-based) are necessary to provide pressure and guidance in individual memory-formation. Indeed, entire systematic reconstructions must be made in the present, and these "landmarks" are perception-based in nature.[6] Rossi's application of Halbwachs' thesis onto the realm of architecture demonstrates how there is an ongoing dialectical union between people and the urban spaces they are transforming and being transformed by; as Rossi states, "memory becomes the guiding thread of the entire complex urban structure."[7]

In this way, we store our public memory (our heritage) in our cities' edifices – not only in historic or commemorative monuments but in various structures of urban achievement such as skyscrapers, bridges, airports, and train stations – all of which proceed to mold not just our group identities but also how we conceptualize the metropolis. Monuments can evolve accidentally or can be instilled from the outset with a sense of permanence, a condition that art historian Alois Riegl referred to a hundred years ago as an act of "art-volition."[8] The modern industrial age did not resist the role of urban monuments but rather incorporated such principles into a new transitory mode of building: Walter Gropius, for one, cited Riegl's *Kunstwollen*-principle of monument-creation as guiding his own work. Le Corbusier, in 1929, conceived of his destructive tower-buildings for the Voisin Plan in Paris not as anti-monuments but as, simply, the city's *new* monuments.[9] Erich Mendelsohn's photo album *Amerika* (1926) likewise focused on the latest technological achievements of skyscrapers and grain silos as the most daring monuments for the age.[10] Even Le Corbusier's Villa Savoye, emblematic of the anti-historical modern movement, found itself added to a historic preservation list in the postwar years.[11] Indeed, the plastic pop arts culture of the Independent Group in 1950s London found that monuments, museums, and a veritable "permanentization" of the past were becoming more, not less, important for people who live in an ephemeral culture based on serial (and soon digital) reproduction.[12]

Occasionally it is the city itself that is molded to alter and forge a specific form of collective memory. Berlin's fate was to nearly become a monumental "Germania." Hitler's architect Albert Speer was a keen admirer of the Washington model of the City Beautiful movement. Such admiration was not accidental: there is a certain irony that the people's capital of the United States should have ended up with the grandest, most imperial scale of European triumphalism, larger than any European capital could offer.[13] In the end, Berlin's most famous monument of recent times only subsequently emerged as an aesthetic-commemorative symbol in its own right: namely, the Wall (1961–1989), with a graffiti-art layer on its west side and a death strip (*Todesstreifen*) to the east.[14] When Berliners lost (or rather, chipped away at, dismantled) their Wall, they willfully lost their city's dominant image. Berlin's unique transitional condition since the fall of the Wall has brought with it new opportunities for expressing architecturally that which had, during the Cold War, been spatially as well as historically repressed. However whatever gets built will not alter the fact that Berlin is a "necropolis" that is literally "standing on its own grave."[15] As Berlin has emerged from the era of the Wall – the sign of the German nation's (actual) Cold War division and (perceived) post-Holocaust punishment – it has filled in many sites of its spatial wounds. But this filling-in is more than just architectural, and thus will continue into the foreseeable future. In the words of Brian Ladd: "In Berlin, Germany's wounds still lie open everywhere."[16]

This chapter undertakes a transect-course across some of Berlin's Holocaust-related *lieux de mémoire*.[17] These sites constitute a powerful visual code of the transmission of intergenerational memory through the representation of trauma: the word "monument," after all, has its origins in the Janus-faced verb *monere* (to exhort, warn, remember). The insertion of such monuments to mourning into the cityscape can be ideally regarded as the collective voice of the lost. Unlike Tombs to the Unknown Soldier, which, as Benedict Anderson has stated, generally evoke a sense of governmentally ordered, top-down national community and encourage a self-sacrificial readiness as the price of that collective belonging, Holocaust memorials are in a key sense meant to function in the opposite direction, and voice a certain *dis*continuity between denizens and statehood.[18] This bottom-up expression is launched into the public sphere by those who care enough that the trauma of the Shoah should continue to be articulated.

Before we consider such sites of mourning, however, it is worth noting that our current age is not necessarily changing the state-sanctioned, top-down memorialization and musealization of war as much as we might like to think. Certainly, in the contexts of national victory and pride, traditional state-glorifying monumentalism is still favored. A more obvious example of up-to-date monumentalism is the National World War II Memorial in Washington (2004): a Stonehenge-like gallery, inscribed with over 400,000 names of the fallen, consisting of 56 stone pillars (each 17 feet high) and two four-story-high triumphal arches, all on a 7.4-acre site that extends from one side of the Mall to the other, incorporating the Rainbow Pool into itself. This memorial by Austrian-American Friedrich St Florian dedicated to all the 16 million members of the US armed forces who saw active duty in the Second World War continues the neoclassicist monumental style that has loaned national symbolism to the Washington Mall. It follows in the style of building that has granted a collective identity to American visitors to the capital (as well as a symbolic Americanness for visitors from abroad).[19]

Small wonder, then, that in response to this rather uniform monumentality, an alternative architectural vocabulary has emerged.[20] A decidedly non-Speer-like style is evidently called for in the visual cultural context of mourning Holocaust victims and the German apology for Nazism. Holocaust architecture can be defined as a medium for maintaining or engendering the memory of catastrophe. As such it is a continuation in three-dimensional form of Sigmund Freud's suggestion in "Beyond the Pleasure Principle" (1920) that trauma could be repeated and controlled in dreams. Walter Benjamin, drawing on Freud, considered how shock is a necessary ingredient in the modern creative process and in the reception of art. Benjamin also conceived of historical time as a crisis, a "storm" of catastrophic history that masquerades as progress; this is the future into which the angel in Paul Klee's *Angelus Novus* painting is driven, while observing the incessant rubble of events as a "single catastrophe" piling up behind him.[21] What, by extension, can a similar form of architecture *qua* catastrophe do to create and steer the psychological and historical shock – to follow the Freudian dictum and "remember, repeat, and work through" the trauma – of the Holocaust? How can Holocaust architecture have a healing, yet also memory-sustaining, effect? Such healing or working through should not indicate the closure of amnesia: Benjamin favored "keep[ing] the wound open" over positive commemoration of the Great War, and the same can apply to Holocaust memory itself.[22] This challenge is complicated by the fact that nowadays the role of Holocaust architecture and other mourning-based monuments in our presentist, yet memory-obsessed age must first invoke the initial historical trauma to an otherwise immune public. Only when an invocation of the traumatic event has successfully occurred, that is, an affect-oriented invitation to partake of collective memory – in short, the creation of a space of mourning, usually by means of architectural inversion, voiding, negation: indeed, an architectural sublime – can any significant conversation with history on the part of the general public truly arise.

It is in this context that the veritable success story arose of the United States Holocaust Memorial Museum, situated adjacent to the Mall and between the Jefferson Memorial and Washington Monument. Since its opening in 1993, the massive 250,000-sq-ft museum has received more than two million visitors per year, and is, of the seven Holocaust museums in the US, the only one to have won worldwide recognition, its achievement forcing even Yad Vashem to embark on a complete architectural makeover.[23] In fact, it has spawned many more such museums and monuments: there are now two hundred memorials and museums to the Holocaust across North America and Europe, as well as the Holocaust Education Center in Fukuyama, Japan (1995) and one in Africa, the Cape Town Holocaust Centre (1999).[24] The success of the DC museum is due to several key factors, not least because its exhibition reinforces the heroic Allied tale of World War II (American soldiers liberating the camps, and specifically the film of Dwight Eisenhower's visit to the Ohrdruf camp, are the first materials that the public sees). Despite its distance from the sites of World War II, it is, as its name implies, a national museum for the US, having been conceived of in 1978 by President Jimmy Carter, who instigated a President's Commission on the Holocaust that was chaired by Holocaust survivor and activist Elie Wiesel.[25] But most importantly, the museum provides – with its astoundingly detailed collection of over 5,000 authentic materials with narrative and visual texts explaining the Holocaust's emergence, scope, and consequences – the clearest educational experience to date with which to refute the rising tide of Holocaust revisionism, at the historical moment when the event itself is passing into the memories of post-survivor generations. The Holocaust Memorial Museum thus offers the much-needed forging of a meditative sublime for the historical catastrophe that it teaches to the public.

Anyone who has visited the Holocaust Memorial Museum has witnessed its incredibly strong effect on mass tourists and educational groups, in other words, the most important target group of all – "people who don't even know what the Holocaust is," in the words of its German-born, Jewish-American architect James Ingo Freed (1930–2005).[26] It manages to make all levels of the public identify with what they are seeing, thanks to a skillful combination of both memory-inducing interior/exterior spaces and acutely experiential (even, at times, voyeuristic) exhibition contents. The DC museum exhibition is nothing if not practical: if it means having the public walk through a Treblinka railway freight car for them to empathize with those deported in such a manner to the death camps, then so be it. Such artifacts, even the personal belongings of actual victims, are necessary for the maintenance – indeed, creation – of collective memory concerning the Holocaust, despite Michael Sorkin's fears of this (or indeed any historical) exhibit's too-close proximity to the "mnemonics of the theme park."[27] In one well-known instance, the museum erred in showing too much of the real: nowadays, a mural-sized photograph of hair from shorn victims at Auschwitz hangs on the wall where the encased pile of human hair had originally been displayed when the museum first opened: actual human remnants proved too much to bear within the representational confines of the DC display, and hence a simulated image became preferable to the too-real, too-shocking thing itself.[28] Moreover, if the price to be paid for installing the Holocaust on the urban memory landscape of Washington has indeed been a conscious inclusion of the Shoah tragedy into the phenomenon now termed "heritage tourism," that is, a certain "packaging" of the historical event into an item made synchronous with a tourist's visit to the US nation's capital, then we as critics must weigh the cost of this inclusion against the obvious gains of retaining or creating Holocaust memory for future generations.[29]

As the catastrophe of Holocaust memory has become permanently mediated in memorial and museal form, one particularly successful type of architectural commemoration has been the trend toward counter-monuments that negate any sense of easy indifference in the observer. Here critics remain indebted to the work of James E. Young, who has delineated the material culture of Holocaust monuments worldwide as a memory against itself.[30] Aligned with Michel Foucault's concept of *counter-memory*, countermonuments stand against traditional state-supporting notions of what a monument should achieve. Indeed it may well have been the Holocaust that facilitated such a tidal change in the three-dimensional representation of memory – more specifically, as Rudy Koshar has suggested, when the US Army, under the leadership of General Patton, forced local citizens from Weimar to visit the "cadaver memorial" at Buchenwald. Koshar notes this was the beginning of the "end to traditional practices of the memory landscape."[31] The shocking or unexpected, even ironically suggestive visual (and often textual) rhetoric achieved by these countermonuments is often the best way to obtain the participatory involvement of passers-by in the historical message contained in the memorial.

One significant trait shared by countermonuments representing the Holocaust and fascism is that they explode any rhetoric of silence: passers-by become active participants, and reverence for the Holocaust now goes beyond mere sigetics to include cognition and communication. Holocaust catastrophe thus demands its own articulation. The monolithic grandeur achieved in Nathan Rapoport's Warsaw Ghetto Monument of 1948, styled in the victorious anti-fascist style of Socialist Realism, cannot be repeated these days without trespassing into the territory of overbearing kitsch. Its contemporary countermonumental opposite would be Rachel Whiteread's Holocaust monument on Vienna's Judenplatz (2000): a room-sized, concrete block of an inverted library, with the books' spines turned inwards and the doors forever impassable, and the names of Nazi concentration camps inscribed around the base. In Berlin, two of the most effective countermonuments work best because of their fragmented, embedded nature in the urban environment itself: by walking around neighborhoods, one discovers the street signs of the Bavarian Quarter memorial referencing the anti-Semitic laws of the 1930s ("Places of Remembrance," by Renata Stih and Frieder Schock, 1992–93), or Gunter Demnig's "Stumbling Stones" project (*Stolpersteine*, ongoing across Germany since 1995), whereby brass plates have been affixed to cobblestones underfoot to commemorate where victims of the Nazis used to live.[32] In each case, the memorials' texts insistently bring the past into the present: the Nazis' laws that were accepted by those whom they did not affect; the names of the persecuted in front of the homes they were forced to lose while their neighbors looked the other way.

Perhaps the arch-countermonumentalist is the Paris-based artist Jochen Gerz, who with his wife Esther Shalev-Gerz designed the Harburg-Hamburg Monument "Against Fascism, War, and Violence – and for Peace and Human Rights" (1986) that was gradually lowered into the ground as it was covered with graffiti contributed by the public, until it completely disappeared in 1993 (it is still visible behind a glass panel, underneath a flight of steps). Another instance of such inversion is Gerz's inscription in 1997 of the names of the 2,146 eradicated Jewish cemeteries in Germany underneath the cobblestones in the center of Saarbrücken, hence making it impossible to tell which were "marked" stones and which were not. In 2000 Gerz continued his unsettling dialogue with the Germans' Nazi past when he set up an installation of TV monitors in Berlin's former Nazi Air Ministry (Luftfahrtsministerium, now the federal Finance Ministry), screens that showed interviews with the civil servants working in the building and their reactions to the heritage of the place.

The recent trend toward countermonumentalism in commemorative architecture was first popularized by a non-Holocaust monument in a non-German context: the semi-subterranean Vietnam Veterans' Memorial on the Washington Mall. Designed by Chinese-American architect Maya Lin in 1982, it combines both a collective apology for a war that history has deemed anything but "good," with an honest, respectful commemoration of the American soldiers who died for it. Everything about this memorial is the opposite of bombastic. It is not even "straight": the line of its wall is angled or kinked in the middle to create two lines pointing toward the Washington Monument and the Lincoln Memorial, between which it resides. It descends into rather than rises from the ground, and the ground itself sinks in its center vertex in order to show a higher number of names of the war dead as the war continued. Its color is an inverted black granite, albeit one that reflects the viewer to him- or herself. It is an up-close, personal text in the Barthesian "writerly" sense that demands viewer engagement; even the font size for the inscribed names of the war dead is less than half an inch, an intimacy "unheard of in monument type sizing", as Lin explains. A constant feature of the Vietnam Memorial is how its very modesty of design brings its visitors together in inquiry and shared contemplation, sometimes to place objects at the foot of the wall as if it were a shrine – items that are then collected by the National Park Service. The architect stresses how she has never regarded her incredibly successful monument as a "wall" but rather as a rift, a boundary, a gash, an "edge to the earth, an open side" – hence a wound where mourning can occur on both private and public levels.[33]

Lest we forget the context, however: even as a monument against monumentalism, the Vietnam Memorial ultimately adds to, rather than detracts from, the Mall's self-glorification of the United States' capital city *qua* monument. The Vietnamese civilians who died are certainly not represented there: it remains, in essence, a monument of "good" (war-) conscience. Indeed, the importance of names has been a traditional motif in the state architecture of war ever since Sir Edwin Lutyens' massive memorial to the 100,000 missing British soldiers of the Great War's Battle of the Somme at Thiepval, France: Lin writes how it was the inscribed names on the Lutyens monument that she most wanted to emulate.[34] Jay Winter has noted how Lin's memorial, in its disarming honesty, finds a closer analogy in Lutyens' far simpler Cenotaph in Whitehall, which was dedicated in 1920 and immediately became "*the* permanent British war memorial," the single most powerful site of collective mourning for the British dead who were all left on the European continent from the 1914–1918 war; it is still the wreath-laying focus, every "Poppy" (Armistice) Day, of a nation's moment of silence.[35] Despite the parallelism with such classical forms of war commemoration, Lin's memorial was interpreted as doubting war; this latter tendency prompted the addition of two traditional sculptures in bronze to the same cause, namely Frederick Hart's "Three Fighting Men" (1984) and Glenna Goodacre's "Women's Memorial" (1993), which were installed nearby as representational augmentations (or rivals).[36]

The most intense recent debate concerning Holocaust representation in three-dimensional form occurred in the Berlin Republic's regained capital. Just at the point in history when the entire World War II generation of survivors and perpetrators alike is dying out, post-Wall Berlin ended up ensuring that the former divisive scar of the Wall was made visible again, this time in the form of a Holocaust memorial along the former Wall's death strip – as if in recognition of the unhealed wounds that were generated by the Shoah. Even though the axis of the Wall is no longer visible in today's Berlin, and even though its tenure was short-lived, the schism it represented originates in the underlying memory of Nazism. Hence the initial gesture toward building the Berlin Holocaust Memorial (first proposed in 1988 by TV-moderator Lea Rosh and historian Eberhard Jäckel after a visit to Yad Vashem) is, in and of itself, a countermonumental act, a re-gashing of a wound that most of the new capital's denizens would prefer to see (however superficially) healed.[37]

In its initial conception, the memorial and its debate were a response to what would have perhaps otherwise been deemed, at least in Israel and the US, as an untenable cover-up, indeed a deformation of capital identity, had post-Wall Berlin decided *not* to link its Phoenix-like rebirth with an official memorial of apology for Nazi mass murder. Cities tend to "grow according to the direction and meaning of their older artifacts": the point of the Berlin Holocaust Memorial could be, to adopt Rossi's words, a monument's chief skill, namely the "persistence" or "permanence" of a past being experienced right now in Germany, albeit in a belated format.[38] Jewish-German author Maxim Biller joked that the Holocaust has become the Germans' identity, just as much as it is the Jews'.[39] The memorial's impetus was thus to show the persistence of this difficult past; the very unsayability of this past for Germans might well have contributed to why a sculpturally formed memorial was wanted as the nation's new symbol of Holocaust atonement, and *not* a museum. By contrast, the DC Museum operates in a country without a Holocaust guilt-complex and thus caters to the simpler didactic requirement of keeping the Holocaust relevant for the present.

The "Memorial to the Murdered Jews of Europe," which opened in 2005 after seventeen years of debate, has since become one of the city's obligatory tour-bus stops. The memorial's foundation claims eight million visitors in the five years since its opening (although, since without charged admission, fixed entrance/exit, or security cameras, it is unclear to what degree the visitors actually visit, or just walk by the periphery). The catastrophic nature of this monument originates in its accidental location, which forced it to serve as a conceptually traumatized extension both of the Brandenburg Gate and the re-domed Reichstag, the center of government, directly to its north, as well as of the rebuilt Potsdamer Platz's skyscraper center of commerce and entertainment to its south. The layering of wound upon wound becomes clear when one considers that both former totalitarian regimes, as well as the Weimar-Wilhelmine governments that went before, are quite literally underneath it. Almost five acres (about 20,000 sq m) of nameless no-man's-land where the Wall had once stood were donated for this monument by Chancellor Helmut Kohl in 1994 – perhaps because this land had no official owner.[40] Its position is on the site of the former Ministerial Gardens – those of the destroyed buildings of the Foreign Office, the Reichspräsident's house, and the Ministry for Food and Agriculture along the eastern side, as well as partly on the site of a bunker that led to one of Joseph Goebbels' villas. Indeed, it is rather telling that German officials have felt the need not just to cover the archeological remains but also shield the precise locations of the Nazi bunkers in the vicinity of the Voß- and Wilhelmstraße from access and view, thereby prolonging the notion of an unsafe, best repressed national unconscious.[41] It is as if these bunker remains are a physical manifestation of what is lurking, as it were, beneath the rational ego of Habermassian "constitutional patriotism" (*Verfassungspatriotismus*), like a dangerous energy waiting for potential re-release after the fall of the Wall.[42] One thing is sure: when the Wall came down, only its "voids" were left, as Andreas Huyssen has remarked, and a massive one of these was set aside in those early days for the memorial.[43] Hence its excessive scale is a literal and accidental by-product of the Wall's demise.

During the years of debate before the Berlin Holocaust Memorial was even started, the desire to fill up the huge void of the site became a topic in and of itself. The chance fabrication of an entire city-block's worth of terrain led to a way to demonstrate to the world not so much the Germans' guilt but the burden of that guilt. The Berlin initiative became a very "German" memorial not so much for Jews as "for Germans."[44] German-Jewish commentator Henryk M. Broder ironically argued that the pride inherent in this "Germanization of the Holocaust" grew so great as to be assuaged only with a monument gigantic enough to cover all Berlin.[45] As a result of this automatic void-filling mentality, the Berlin Holocaust Memorial became a "super-memorial" (*Übermahnmal*) set to defeat countermonumentalism's basic tenets of modest negativity and thought-provoking implosion (*à la* Gerz or Lin). This was why artists Stih and Schnock had purposefully chosen an "anti-submission" in the first round of the memorial contest: in their "Bus Stop" proposal, the only structure devised for the site was indeed the *Bushaltestelle* for the vehicles that would then take people all over Europe to the concentration camp or other Holocaust-related site of their choice (Fig. 10.1).[46]

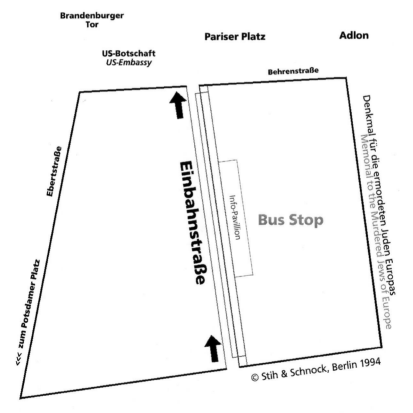

Figure 10.1   "Bus Stop. Project for a Holocaust Memorial in Berlin." Competition entry designed by Renata Stih and Frieder Schnock, 1994

Nonetheless, to keep the wound of history open, Berlin ended up with a monument that filled the huge ex-Wall space set apart for it. The showing became the telling of this memorial, and any healing and educational process ideally configured by catastrophe architecture of the Holocaust was not at the top of its agenda during the planning stages. The arguments among the political and cultural elites in the capital city of the former enemy concerning the Holocaust Memorial's ramifications led some critics to fear that the project was doomed, not because it failed to materialize after more than a decade of debate but precisely because it was built, and might well be demolished half a century from now anyway.[47] Nonetheless the project was called forth to serve, come what may, as a three-dimensional display of corrective collective memory, in order to show the world that the Berlin Republic has overcome its past – even if it has not, and even if average Berliners long stopped paying attention to the debate.

Notes

1. William Shakespeare, *King Lear* (1606), ed. R. A. Foakes (Arden Shakespeare Third Series, 1997), IV.ii, at: http://shakespeare.mit.edu/lear/lear.4.2.html (date accessed 2 July, 2010).
2. Quote by Avi Primor, cited in Guntram Doelfs, "Berlin ist das Gesicht des Bundes," *Berliner Morgenpost* (25 July, 2004).
3. "Bewältigte Vergangenheit. 8. Mai 1945–1995," illustration by Jochen Hein: cover page for *Der Spiegel*, 19 (1995). In 2008 there were over 14,000 neo-Nazi attacks across the country (especially in the east, including Berlin), with over 770 personal injuries. Overall, in 2008 there were nearly 20,000 acts of rightwing vandalism in Germany. This constituted a 15 percent rise over the previous year. "Anstieg rechtsextremer Straftaten," *Süddeutsche Zeitung* (19 May, 2009). In March 2010, Stefan J. Kramer, the Secretary General of the Central Council of Jews in Germany, called for a new federal ministerial position to address the rise in rightwing violence. See www.mut-gegen-rechte-gewalt.de/ (date accessed 14 May, 2010).
4. Peter Sloterdijk, *Theory of the Post-War Periods. Observations on Franco-German Relations since 1945*, trans. Robert Payne, foreword by Klaus-Dieter Müller, ed. Gerhard Blechinger (Vienna and New York: Springer, 2007), p. 36.
5. Aldo Rossi, *The Architecture of the City*, trans. Diane Ghirardo and Joan Ockman, intro. by Peter Eisenman (Cambridge, MA: MIT Press, 1982), p. 130.
6. Maurice Halbwachs, "The Social Frameworks of Memory," in Halbwachs, ed. and trans. Lewis A. Coser, *On Collective Memory* (Chicago: University of Chicago Press, 1992), pp. 37–40, 167–89.
7. Rossi, *The Architecture of the City*, p. 130. Appropriately enough, Rossi was selected as the designer of the new German Historical Museum that would have been built diagonally opposite the Reichstag, had the Wall not come down. That site is now the new German Chancellery. Rossi's relationship

with history is visible in his work elsewhere in the New Berlin, as in the Quartier Schützenstrasse, where he recreated the traditional façades of Wilhelmine block architecture built around inner courtyards, but in multiple colors. See Mathias Remmele, "Aldo Rossi's 'Quartier Schützenstrasse'," in Martina Düttmann and Felix Zwoch, eds, *Bauwelt Berlin Annual. Chronology of Building Events 1996 to 2001: 1997* (Berlin: Birkhäuser, 1997), pp. 32–39.

8. Alois Riegl, "Der moderne Denkmalkultus. Sein Wesen, seine Entstehung" (1903), in Riegl, *Gesammelte Aufsätze* (Berlin: Gebr. Mann, 1995); and Riegl, "The Modern Cult of Monuments: Its Character and Its Origin," trans. Kurt W. Foster and Diane Ghirardo, *Oppositions*, 25 (1982), pp. 21–50. Cited by Françoise Choay, *The Invention of the Historic Monument*, trans. Lauren M. O'Connell (New York: Cambridge University Press, 2001), pp. 12–13.

9. Walter Gropius, "Monumentale Kunst und Industriebau" (1911); see Mark Wigley, "The Architectural Cult of Synchronization," *October*, 94 (2000), pp. 31–61, pp. 46, 42.

10. Erich Mendelsohn, *Amerika. Bilderbuch eines Architekten* (Berlin: R. Mosse, 1926).

11. Wigley, "The Architectural Cult of Synchronization," p. 34; Wigley is referring to Nikolaus Pevsner's call to preserve the Le Corbusier villa in "Time and Le Corbusier," *Architectural Review*, 125.746 (1959), pp. 159–65.

12. Wigley, "The Architectural Cult of Synchronization," p. 50. Wigley cites John McHale's essay "The Plastic Parthenon" (1961) thus: "We seem to reconstruct and 'permanentize' the past as swiftly as we move forward into a more materially 'ephemeral' present and future." McHale, "The Plastic Parthenon," in Gillo Dorfles, ed., *Kitsch: The World of Bad Taste* (New York: Bell, 1969), pp. 98–110, p. 103.

13. Sir Peter Hall, *Cities of Tomorrow: An Intellectual History of Urban Planning and Design in the Twentieth Century*, updated ed. (Oxford: Blackwell, 1996), pp. 197–200; Alan Balfour, *Berlin: The Politics of Order, 1737–1989* (New York: Rizzoli, 1990), pp. 69–106; and James S. Russell, "Crowding the Mall: The National Memorial Dilemma," *Harvard Design Magazine* (Fall 1999), pp. 32–37, p. 35.

14. Brian Ladd cites Riegl's distinction, in "Der moderne Denkmalkultus," between "intentional" and "unintentional" monuments. Ladd, *The Ghosts of Berlin: Confronting German History in the Urban Landscape* (Chicago: University of Chicago Press, 1997), pp. 12, 247.

15. Kurt W. Forster, "Städtische Monumente der Endlichkeit," *Zeitschrift für schweizerische Archäologie und Kunstgeschichte*, 52.1 (1995), pp. 3–12, p. 10.

16. Ladd, *The Ghosts of Berlin*, p. 11.

17. Pierre Nora, "Between Memory and History: Les Lieux de Mémoire," trans. Marc Roudebush, *Representations*, 26 (1989), pp. 7–25.

18. Benedict Anderson, *Imagined Communities: Reflections on the Origins and Spread of Nationalism*, rev. ed. (London and New York: Verso, 1991), p. 23.

19. See Malte Lehming's comparison of the Berlin Holocaust Memorial debate and the controversy surrounding the US World War II Memorial, in "Wer will den Veteranen Kränze flechten?" *Der Tagesspiegel* (17 May, 2001). Parallels in the location battles over the World War II Memorial and the Berlin Holocaust Memorial are made clear in Michael S. Cullen, ed., *Das*

Holocaust-Mahnmal. Dokumentation einer Debatte (Zürich: Pendo, 1999), pp. 276–78.

20. See Janet Ward, "Sacralized Spaces and the Urban Remembrance of War," in Uta Staiger, Henriette Steiner and Andrew Webber, eds, *Memory Culture and the Contemporary City: Building Sites* (Basingstoke and New York: Palgrave Macmillan, 2009), pp. 145–60; Gavriel D. Rosenfeld, "Postwar Jewish Architecture and the Memory of the Holocaust," in Rose-Carol Washton Long, Matthew Baigell, and Milly Heyd, eds, *Jewish Dimensions in Modern Visual Culture: Antisemitism, Assimilation, Affirmation* (Waltham: Brandeis University Press, 2010), pp. 285–302; and Rosenfeld's forthcoming book, *Building After Auschwitz: Jewish Architecture and Jewish Memory since the Holocaust* (New Haven: Yale University Press, 2011).

21. Sigmund Freud, *Beyond the Pleasure Principle*, trans. James Strachey (New York: Norton, 1961); Walter Benjamin, "Theses on the Philosophy of History" (1939), in Benjamin, *Illuminations. Essays and Reflections*, ed. Hannah Arendt, trans. Harry Zohn (New York: Schocken, 1968), pp. 253–64, pp. 257–58.

22. Martin Jay, "Against Consolation: Walter Benjamin and the Refusal to Mourn," in Jay Winter and Emmanuel Sivan, eds, *War and Remembrance in the Twentieth Century* (New York: Cambridge University Press, 1999), pp. 221–39, p. 237.

23. The new Yad Vashem (2005) has more than tripled in size in a minimalist prism of a building, cut into the Mount of Remembrance by Israeli-Canadian architect Moshe Safdie. Andrea Oppenheimer Dean, "Moshe Safdie Offers a Memorial Journey through the Depths of a Jerusalem Hillside with his Yad Vashem History Museum," *Architectural Record*, 193.7 (2005), pp. 112–19; Chris McGreal, "'This is Ours and Ours Alone'," *Guardian Unlimited* (15 March, 2005); and Hillel Halkin, "Memory and Redemption Coexist as Yad Vashem Expands," *The Chronicle of Higher Education* (6 October, 2000).

24. Robert von Lucius, "Holocaust-Gedenkstätte in Afrika eröffnet," *Frankfurter Allgemeine Zeitung* (18 October, 1999).

25. See Isabelle Engelhardt's discussion of this aspect of "place" and "out-of-place" in "The Creation of an 'Artificial Authentic Place' – The United States Holocaust Memorial Museum in Washington, DC," in Luisa Passerini, ed., *Across the Atlantic: Cultural Exchanges between Europe and the United States* (Brussels: Peter Lang, 2000), pp. 141–51, pp. 143–45.

26. James Ingo Freed, "The United States Holocaust Memorial Museum," *Assemblage*, 9 (1989), pp. 58–79, p. 73.

27. Michael Sorkin, "The Holocaust Museum: Between Beauty and Horror," *Progressive Architecture*, 74 (1993), p. 74.

28. See Engelhardt, "'Artificial Authentic Place'," pp. 148–49.

29. See Anson Rabinbach, "From Explosion to Erosion: Holocaust Memorialization in America since Bitburg," *History and Memory*, 9.1/2 (1997), pp. 226–55, pp. 238, 241; Tim Cole's insightful reading of the DC museum in *Selling the Holocaust: From Auschwitz to Schindler* (New York: Routledge, 2000), pp. 146–71; and T. G. Ashplant, Graham Dawson, and Michael Roper, "The Politics of War Memory and Commemoration: Contexts, Structures and Dynamics," in Ashplant, Dawson, and Roper, eds, *The Politics of War Memory and Commemoration* (New York: Routledge, 2000), pp. 3–85, p. 70. On the universalization, indeed globalization, of the Holocaust, see Daniel

Levi and Natan Sznaider, "Memory Unbound: The Holocaust and the Formation of Cosmopolitan Memory," *European Journal of Social Theory*, 5.1 (2002), pp. 87–106.

30. James E. Young, *At Memory's Edge: After-Images of the Holocaust in Contemporary Art and Architecture* (New Haven: Yale University Press, 2000), pp. 90–119.

31. Rudy Koshar, *From Monuments to Traces: Artifacts of German Memory, 1870–1990* (Berkeley: University of California Press, 2000), p. 210, 266.

32. See www.stolpersteine.com (date accessed 18 July, 2009). On the Schöneberg memorial by Stih and Schnock, see Karen E. Till, *The New Berlin: Memory, Politics, Place* (Minneapolis: University of Minnesota Press, 2005), pp. 154–60.

33. Maya Lin, *Boundaries* (New York: Simon & Schuster, 2000), pp. 4.14, 4.11.

34. Lin, *Boundaries*, pp. 4.09–12.

35. Jay Winter, *Sites of Memory, Sites of Mourning: The Great War in European Cultural History* (New York: Cambridge University Press, 1995), pp. 104–05. See also Koshar, *From Monuments to Traces*, p. 109; and Katie Trumpener, "Memories Carved in Granite: Great War Memorials and Everyday Life," *PMLA*, 115.5 (2000), pp. 1096–103. On German World War I monuments, see Jürgen Tietz, "Monumente des Gedenkens," in Rainer Rother, ed., *Die letzten Tage der Menschheit. Bilder des ersten Weltkrieges* (Berlin: Ars Nicolai, 1994), pp. 397–408.

36. For critiques of the neoconservative Reagan era's desire to revise the Lin memorial, see Erika Doss, *Spirit Poles and Flying Pigs: Public Art and Cultural Democracy in American Communities* (Washington, DC: Smithsonian Institution Press, 1995), pp. 29–31; and Russell, "Crowding the Mall," p. 34.

37. Referring to the first competition's winning designs by Christine Jackob-Marx and Simon Ungers, Hans-Ernst Mittig noted how the effect would have created not a "memorial" (*Denkmal*) but a "woundorial" (*Wundmal*). Mittig, "Von der Schuld zur Verantwortung," *Freitag* (18 April, 1997).

38. Rossi, *The Architecture of the City*, p. 59.

39. Maxim Biller, "Heiliger Holocaust," *Die Zeit*, 49 (1996). See also Jörn Rüsen on how "the Holocaust constitutes German identity by catastrophe." Rüsen, "Holocaust Memory and Identity Building: Metahistorical Considerations in the Case of (West) Germany," in Michael S. Roth and Charles G. Salas, eds, *Disturbing Remains: Memory, History, and Crisis in the Twentieth Century* (Los Angeles: Getty Research Institute, 2001), pp. 252–70, p. 259.

40. One-sixth of the terrain did in fact belong to the city council of Berlin-Mitte, but was transferred in late 1992 to Lea Rosh's foundation that was in charge of the memorial project. See Michael S. Cullen, "Geist und Ungeist eines Ortes. Ein Versuch über die Ministergärten," in Riki Kalbe and Moshe Zuckermann, eds, *Ein Grundstück in Mitte. Das Gelände des künftigen Holocaust-Mahnmals in Wort und Bild* (Göttingen: Wallstein, 2000), pp. 32–37, p. 37.

41. Alan Cowell, "Underground History Surfaces Again in Berlin," *The New York Times* (8 April, 1998). The same attitude has been demonstrated toward other Nazi bunkers: for example, when even the *Führerbunker* itself was rediscovered in 1999 during construction work on government buildings, Building Senator Peter Strieder (SPD) refused to open it to the public; and it was Daniel Goldhagen who in vain suggested putting the various bunkers under UNESCO protection and using them to educate the public about the Nazi era. Wolfgang Bayer and Steffen Winter, "Unesco-Schutz für Hitlers

Bunker?" *Der Spiegel*, 46 (15 November, 1999), pp. 80–82. Dietmar Arnold, founder of Berlin Underworlds (*Verein Berliner Unterwelten*), has called for the preservation of Nazi bunkers as an effective means of ensuring an open public memory of the Third Reich. One small measure of Arnold's success is that in 2006, Berlin Underworlds was permitted to erect a sign marking the spot of Hitler's bunker, just a couple of hundred yards from the Holocaust Memorial. For a map of the Nazi bunkers' locations, see Dietmar Arnold and Ingmar Arnold, *Dunkle Welten. Bunker, Tunnel, Gewölbe unter Berlin* (Berlin: Ch. Links Verlag, 2000), p. 141); see also Dietmar Arnold, *Der Potsdamer Platz von unten* (Berlin: Ch. Links Verlag, 2001).

42. The term originated with Dolf Sternberger and was adopted by Habermas in his writings as a critical neutralization of nationalism. See Aleida Assmann and Ute Frevert, *Geschichtsvergessenheit, Geschichtsversessenheit. Vom Umgang mit deutschen Vergangenheiten nach 1945* (Stuttgart: Deutsche Verlags-Anstalt, 1999), p. 67.

43. Andreas Huyssen, "The Voids of Berlin," *Present Pasts: Urban Palimpsests and the Politics of Memory* (Stanford: Stanford University Press, 2003), pp. 49–71; orig. *Critical Inquiry*, 24.1 (1997), pp. 57–81.

44. Benjamin Korn, "Der Mensch, die Maschine des Vergessens," *Die Zeit* (22 November, 1996); see also Silke Wenk, in "Der Wettbewerb um das zentrale 'Denkmal für die ermordeten Juden Europas' als soziologisches Experiment," in Leonie Baumann, Rainer Hörmann, et al., eds, *Der Wettbewerb für das 'Denkmal für die ermordeten Juden Europas'. Eine Streitschrift* (Dresden: Verlag der Kunst, 1995), pp. 163–68.

45. Henryk M. Broder, *Volk und Wahn* (Hamburg: Spiegel Buchverlag, 1996), p. 220.

46. On Stih and Schnock's "Bus Stop" entry for the Holocaust memorial competition, see Till, *The New Berlin*, pp. 180–86.

47. Roger Cohen remarked on how "this large hole in the heart of Berlin" that was becoming "increasingly conspicuous" was also "prompting occasional exasperated suggestions that the best memorial would be simply to leave the site vacant." Cohen, "Berlin Mayor to Shun Holocaust Memorial Event," *The New York Times* (18 January, 2000). Julius Schoeps, director of the Moses-Mendelssohn-Zentrum in Potsdam, said the government would probably demolish the monument after fifty years. Cited by Thomas Lackmann, "Wir sind das Opfer. Die 'Zukunft des Gedenkens': eine Diskussion in Berlin," *Der Tagesspiegel* (19 October, 2000).

11
Eisenman's Cement Graveyard

Es ist dem Menschen im Tiefsten wesentlich, daß er sich
selbst eine Begrenzung setze, aber mit Freiheit, d. h. so, daß
er diese Begrenzung auch wieder aufheben, sich außerhalb
ihrer stellen kann.

(Georg Simmel, 1909)[1]

What has Berlin's Memorial to the Murdered Jews of Europe, designed by Peter Eisenman and opened to the public in 2005, actually inscribed upon the reunified capital's identity? Before its construction had even commenced it was hoped that the memorial's very lack of function, its role and status as symbolic architecture, would augment its ability to represent the New Berlin to itself, to the country, and to the international community. Significantly the philosopher Julian Nida-Rümelin, in his brief role as federal (and federalist) Cultural Minister, had spoken out against the rebuilding of a replica of the former city palace (Stadtschloß) on the site of East Germany's Palace of the Republic, precisely in order to cancel out any possible role of the palace as an overly positive, overly proud symbol of a new national identity based on an idealized, selective public memory.[2] In this way, the Holocaust memorial became indirectly freed up to become a superimposed mirror of Germany's negative collective identity, instead.

Collective memory is, however, always a cunning construct. As Edward Said states, in an age where religious rituals matter little to most people, more attention than ever is being placed on the ersatz-symbol of collective memory:

The art of memory for the modern world is both for historians as well as ordinary citizens and institutions very much something to be used, misused, and exploited, rather than something that sits inertly there for each person to possess and contain. [...] People now look to this refashioned memory, especially in its collective forms, to give themselves a coherent identity, a national narrative, a place in the world, though ... the processes of memory are frequently, if not always, manipulated and intervened in for sometimes urgent purposes in the present.[3]

The Holocaust Memorial Museum in DC, while containing information on all the victim groups of the Nazis, was built only when the country was mature enough (and especially when the American Jewish community was ready) for the memories that it would display and create concerning Jewish identity.[4] By inverse relation, Germans have until now not been truly ready to build their own memorial or museum on the national level, and have had to have their most powerful stimulants of Holocaust memory foisted upon them by the same imported American memory source.[5] In the States, of course, different collective blind spots are still waiting for their resolution in memorial terms. There is, after all, no Hiroshima-Nagasaki monument in DC; one can only but imagine that resistance to it would still be at least as fierce as that which was mounted against the ill-fated Enola Gay exhibit (1994–1995).[6]

In the memory-and-erasure game that post-Wall Berlin is currently playing with itself, it was perhaps too much to ask for a meaningful Holocaust memorial amongst all the pasting-together, via buildings, of capital city identity that has often belied and denied Germany's multicultural, transnational present and divided, crisis-ridden past. On the other hand, it is not as if there were not any Holocaust and/or anti-Nazism memorials at all in Germany – the Bundeszentrale für politische Bildung counted up to 2,000, from structures to plaques.[7] Indeed, many such memorials have sprouted up in Berlin since the fall of the Wall. It is as if Holocaust architecture in the re-centralized Berlin is compensating for what could not be articulated so well in collective memory before reunification. Witness the memorials in the city center, such as the Neue Wache on Unter den Linden; the concentration camp signs at Wittenbergplatz U-Bahn Station; the Euthanasia Memorial next to the Berlin Philharmonic on the site of the former Tiergarten 4 ("T4") address where the first gassings were planned; or the sculptures (by Ingeborg Hunzinger) on the Rosenstraße near the Alexanderplatz depicting the German women who protested in that street in 1943 against the imprisonment of their Jewish husbands; and anti-Nazi memorials like the German Resistance Memorial (Gedenkstätte deutscher Widerstand) in Tiergarten;

the Bebelplatz' underground "Library" monument (by Israeli artist Micha Ullman) commemorating the 1933 book-burning that took place on that spot; and the Topographie des Terrors exhibition long housed in temporary quarters on the site of the former Gestapo headquarters.[8] In various other parts of the city we can find the Rainbow Column (Regenbogenstele) at Nollendorfplatz to commemorate homosexual victims; the Wannsee Conference Memorial villa; the Mirror Wall of names of locally deported Jews near the Steglitz town hall (designed by Wolfgang Göschel, Joachim von Rosenberg, and Hans-Norbert Burkert, and completed in 1995); and the Grunewald S-Bahn station memorial to deported Jews (a combination of a cement wall, designed in 1991 by Polish sculptor Karol Bronitowski, and the metal engravings on the platform by the Saarbrücken architects Nikolaus Hirsch, Wolfgang Lorch, and Andreas Wandel).[9] Outside Berlin itself are the signs indicating the routes of death marches, or the actual concentration camps Ravensbrück and Sachsenhausen, both of which have received renewed attention since reunification. Even the Israeli Embassy in Berlin-Zehlendorf, opened in the spring of 2001, incorporates (albeit non-public) memorial architecture into itself by featuring a row of six stone slabs (designed by the Tel Aviv architect Orit Willenberg-Giladi), each in memory of one of the six million murdered Jews.[10]

The CDU response to the Berlin Holocaust Memorial debate of the 1990s and beyond was to voice the fear of creating an unsightly Holocaust "memorial mile"[11] of various victim groups in Berlin's city center – an inverted, negative version of the Washington Mall. While German conservatives might prefer to have monuments only to the immigrant-phobic sensibility of *Leitkultur*, as Friedrich Merz (CDU) termed it, it is also true that the current trend toward memorial-proliferation is a phenomenon not limited to Germany alone. To repeat the insights of McHale and the Independent Group: we are living in an overly musealized age, where the artifacts or monuments are increasingly needed to convince us of the existence of a non-digital real – actual material contents that we then proceed to discard anyway, in favor of the simulated products on sale in the museum (online) store. We can speak of a rise in "memorial, or *museal*, sensibility," even as actual *historical* sensibility, some would argue, is on the wane. The case of post-Wall Germany's "relentless monument mania ... commemorating ... the one world of organized destruction and genocide," to use Andreas Huyssen's words on post-Wall Germany's belated, obsessive rush to acknowledge its wartime guilt in art form, is but an exaggeration of a preexisting condition in which we all participate.[12]

Despite these inauspicious conditions for memory, it was always possible that the Berlin Holocaust Memorial's central location in the new capital and its disruptive proximity to the arch-symbols of Berlin (the Brandenburg Gate and the Reichstag) might have facilitated a new focalization in both Berliners' and visitors' minds, even amidst the recent plethora of Holocaust memorials in the city. Such a memorial could have introduced a tone of self-questioning when contrasted with the apparently complete, reconstituted formats of the Pariser Platz and the new governmental Spreebogen area, as well as of the commercial Americanism of the rebuilt Potsdamer Platz. As a centralized post-Wall wound, it could have helped people enter into a sense of participatory mourning for and presence with the absent victims. But the originally praiseworthy and countermonumental impetus to provide a visual cut into German memory lapses regarding the Holocaust on the reunified cityscape gave rise to a memorial that both *over-* and *under-*corrects.

One obvious way in which the Berlin Memorial under-corrects is in its narrowness of mission: namely, its exclusivity for Jewish victims alone and, consequently, its forcing other victim groups to create their own memorials nearby. This move realigned Jews dangerously close to Nazi techniques of categorization, as historian Reinhart Koselleck cautioned, cementing Jews in their condition of prime victims of Nazism and representatives of the German "culture of suffering" (*Leidkultur*) at the expense of the memory of all other Nazi-persecuted groups: homosexuals, Jehovah's Witnesses, the mentally and physically disabled, Sinti and Roma, and other political and religious dissenters (let alone the other large victim groups of the Nazis: civilian Poles, Russians, and Soviet prisoners of war).[13] The Holocaust Memorial's narrowness of mission prompted into being new neighboring monuments, like the memorial to gay victims persecuted and murdered by the Nazis, which is located directly across the street in the Tiergarten. Another excluded-group memorial, to the Sinti and Roma victims of the Nazis, is underway near the Reichstag.[14]

In inverse relation to the Holocaust Memorial's exclusion of non-Jewish victim groups, another memorial in Berlin committed a faux pas for including too many. Chancellor Kohl, in his glory days of *Wende*-government, opted to redesign the Neue Wache on Berlin's Unter den Linden as the "Central Memorial of the Federal Republic of Germany for the Victims of War and Tyranny." A former Prussian guardhouse, this neo-classical Schinkel building of 1818 with an interior designed in 1931 by Heinrich Tessenow had already been used during the Weimar and Nazi eras to commemorate the fallen soldiers of the Great War, and also in turn by the East Germans to commemorate the dead of World War II, both soldiers and camp victims. German liberals were swift to blame Kohl's 1993 revision of the Neue Wache for a representational sin in its blending of the memory of the Jewish dead with the other Nazi victims. Their anger was itself a transference of the general embarrassment felt when Kohl and former US President Reagan had visited Bitburg cemetery together in 1985, a site where SS soldiers lay buried. The Neue Wache's inscription,"To the victims of war and tyranny" (*Den Opfern von Krief und Gewaltherrschaft*), the same as the inscription on the earlier Bonn memorial to the same, was not deemed guilty enough, even though bronze plaques were subsequently added specifying Jewish, Gypsy, and homosexual victims with a text based on a 1985 speech by West German President Richard von Weizsäcker.[15]

Most damning was how the "new" Neue Wache's large-size version of Käthe Kollwitz' 1937–38 statue, "Mother with Dead Son" (*Mutter mit totem Sohn*), was interpreted not as the universal figure of pacifist mourning that Kollwitz had first intended it to be – a lesson she had personally learned after having let her son volunteer for the Great War and die in it – but as an overly transparent copy of a Catholic *pietà* and therefore wholly inappropriate to fully embrace Jewish memory.[16] The countermonumentalism of inserting an anti-war statue into the official war commemoration site of the Neue Wache slipped into the shadows. This rejection by German and Jewish-German intellectuals alike of the mother figure's symbolic role as a forgiving bridge-effect, while on the surface demonstrating a welcome anti-nationalistic solidarity with the interests of Holocaust victims, constitutes what is probably a permanent refusal of shared mourning between Germans and Jews. In short, retaining victimhood-status for Jews still makes continued diplomatic sense for Germany's international reputation; the Neue Wache memorial was not to be permitted to offer any redemptive escape for the perpetrator nation. Thus Peter Eisenman's design of the Berlin Holocaust Memorial has become the abstracted distillation of this scarred (and by now sacred) German/Jewish *agon*. The critics' outcry in Germany over the Neue Wache represents a rejection of the possibility of a truly reunited memory, one that would indeed signify a new stage in the mourning process between the perpetrator-nation and its principal victim-group. Despite all the representational controversy, however, the Neue Wache since its dedication by Kohl in 1994 has nonetheless functioned as a national commemorative site to World War II, and international leaders have followed protocol in placing their wreaths there on official visits to the German capital (a role not originally envisioned by the Foreign Ministry for the Holocaust Memorial).[17]

The Holocaust Memorial's most obvious form of overcorrection is in its vastness of scale. How, then, did the Berlin Republic come to be so out of sync, so *unzeitgemäss*, that it facilitated a memorial of monumental proportions? Commentators on both the left and the right flip-flopped on their acceptance and rejection of the various versions of the design stages. The first step toward harmful confusion arose when Kohl vetoed the first competition-winning design entry by Berlin architects Christine Jackob-Marx (with Hella Rolfes, Hans Scheib, and Reinhard Stangl) in 1995 – but he only did so after Ignatz Bubis (1927–99) as the head of Germany's Central Jewish Committee (*Zentralrat der Juden*) had told him the gargantuan design was absolutely untenable. Indeed, after the controversial failure of the first design competition a fully fledged debate arose concerning the possible relocation of the memorial to a less prominent place and size: no fewer than eleven displacement-locations were discussed, but in the end the original site was retained.[18]

Jackob-Marx's actual design, nicknamed the "gravestone slab" (*Grabplatte*), was to have been as large as the city block itself, tilted high at one end, with a gradual, post-construction inscription of approximately 4.4 million known names of murdered Jews (from archives at Yad Vashem). These names, however, would not have been visible from street level, not touchable like those on Lin's Vietnam Veterans Memorial, but absorbable only by some godlike eye. Cultural Minister Michael Naumann (SPD) entered office in 1998 waving a carte blanche to substitute the planned monument for a museum *à la* the Holocaust Museum in DC, but was later forced to backtrack to the position of appending the latter onto the former.[19] The "spiritual arson" accusation that Bubis made of author Martin Walser's attempt, in 1998, to say out loud what most Germans were thinking – namely that to build such a thing would be to create an enslaving, permanent monster, a "monumentalization of shame"[20] – ended up achieving a level of resigned obligation, by the SPD and the new Chancellor Gerhard Schröder, to build the memorial no matter what, and hence the Bundestag vote was passed in June 1999.[21] At least the former mayor of Berlin, Eberhard Diepgen (CDU) of the West Berlin old guard, was consistent in his populist condemnation of the monument, and in his tactless refusal to attend the annual on-site ceremony on the national Holocaust commemoration day (held since 1995 on 27 January, the date of the Soviet liberation of Auschwitz).

The second design competition of 1997 awarded first prize to New York-based architect Peter Eisenman (and also sculptor Richard Serra, who subsequently withdrew). Eisenman's design went through several stages but was eventually constructed at an official cost of €27.6 million paid by the government, with €2.5 million raised by the memorial foundation. The original Eisenman-Serra design was an uncompromisingly aggressive graveyard labyrinth of 4,200 cement pillars (termed the *Stelenfeld*, from the Greek *stele* for free-standing column). Wolf Biermann voiced the opinion of many German intellectuals and the general thinking public alike when he published a poem in the *Frankfurter Allgemeine Zeitung* in which he parodied how "the Führer himself would have been pleased" with such a "megalomaniacal monument."[22] In 1998, Eisenman heeded mounting criticism and produced "Eisenman II," wherein the number of pillars in the grid-like maze was cut to the still mammoth number of 2,750 (and eventually to 2,711) but on the same-sized terrain. Originally to have been more than 23 feet (7m) tall, the rectangular structures were changed to varying heights and angles, with some of them reaching up to over 15 feet (4.8m.) and the flatter ones resembling tombs or sarcophagi, all in a wave-like formation of height differential.[23] For the columns' actual material, Eisenman applied a metallic shimmer to a bluish-gray cement.[24] The ground of the memorial resembles that of a shallow lake floor, sloping somewhat deeper in the middle than at the outer edge – not symmetrical at any point, but varying in elevation just like the columns themselves. The three-foot gap between the structures is wide enough for a single person to walk through (but the 945,000 cobblestones underfoot certainly make it hard for the walking impaired; and one visitor died of a head injury after slipping on the winter ice there in February 2009).

It should have come as no surprise that such a design has invited forms of participation from the public that are not necessarily in tune with Holocaust remembrance. To date, the dominant mode of visitor participation has been neglectful or ludic, but not reflective. The *taz* referred to the memorial as a "playing field of memory"; and *Der Spiegel* complained of the stench caused by certain members of the public using it as an unofficial urinal. If anything the "field of columns" serves as a lure for this kind of behavior. No signage exists except for a rather admonishing plaque set in the ground telling visitors not to run, make noise, play music, walk their dogs, roller blade, cycle, smoke, drink, sun themselves – or "dirty the field of stelae" (Fig. 11.1). Temporary buildings erected across a side-street have provided toilets, but also the distractions of beer and sausage. Most tourists descending from the tour

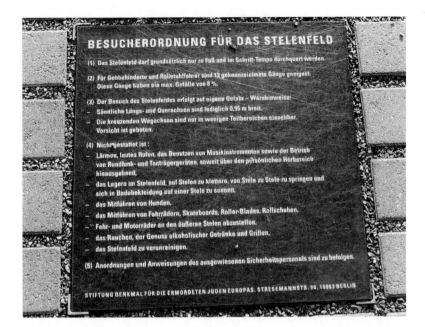

Figure 11.1 "Visitor Ordinance for the Field of Stelae" at Berlin's Memorial to the Murdered Jews of Europe (*Denkmal für die ermordeten Juden Europas*), by Peter Eisenman, 2005

buses or strolling from the Brandenburg Gate along the Ebertstraße down to Potsdamer Platz do not wander deeply into the maze of stones, but hover around its edges. Younger visitors play, recline on, or jump between the stelae; or simply climb up on impulse in order to pose for pictures or get a better view of the Reichstag (Fig. 11.2). In this regard the prediction of Salomon Korn, architect and head of the Jewish community in Frankfurt am Main and who served on the first jury for the memorial, was an accurate one: for Korn, the monument field is "essentially harmless," that is to say, almost *significans*-free, meaning little to those too young or too foreign to understand its portent.[25]

Yet the memorial's open-target nature remains worrying. This is exacerbated due to its adjacency, immediately to its north, to the rebuilt US Embassy, the anti-terrorist perimeter-regulations for which necessitated a negotiated re-alignment of the Behrenstraße between the two sites, taking 39 feet (12m) away from the memorial terrain. The barrier fence around the sides of the US Embassy is comprised of thin metal columns that inadvertently "speak to" the stelae of the memorial across the street (Fig. 11.3). Despite having such an important neighbor, the memorial

Figure 11.2   Berlin's Memorial to the Murdered Jews of Europe, by Peter Eisenman, 2005

Figure 11.3 Security fence at the southwest corner of the US Embassy Berlin, with the Memorial to the Murdered Jews of Europe in the background

itself relies on relatively low security.[26] The little shack that used to stand on the Ebertstraße advertising the memorial was daubed withanti-Semitic graffiti in the summer of 2001. Even without the fifteen incidents of vandalism on the memorial in its first three years, or even without the risk of an anti-US/anti-Jewish terrorist attack on the embassy and memorial combined, there still remains the danger of children straying out of sight once inside the vast terrain (205,300 sq ft / 19,070 sq m) that is filled by the field of columns.

If we are not that concerned about the relative unchartability and unguardability that Eisenman's oversized memorial causes on an everyday basis, we should, as *New Yorker* journalist Jane Kramer reminded us, avoid giving credence to the view that "the right number of stone slabs ... will possess a memory for mass death." Eisenman's design surely scores just as highly on the Richter scale of monstrous (a.k.a.: Speer-like) monumentalism as did the vetoed, slanted slab of Jackob-Marx.[27] Good intentions have thus re-ghettoized the (dead) Jews. In an age of counter-monumentalism, of Lin's "feminine" Vietnam Wall, Berlin has received a mass death-equivalent of a Prussian nationalist monument – and from Eisenman, a famed deconstructivist avant-garde architect, to boot. In his book, *At Memory's Edge* (2000), James E. Young, as the only Jewish member of the second round's selection committee, gives detailed yet neutral praise to the Eisenman design, while subtly indicating in retrospect (and even though he voted for Eisenman) that a different countermonumental direction would have been, in fact, the wiser path to take.[28] As if allaying such concerns, the brochure published in late 2000 by the memorial's foundation found it necessary to reassure the public that future visitors, in passing through the rows of pillars, "will not feel overawed or reduced to insignificance."[29] Nonetheless, this massive cemetery is what the supporters of Eisenman's cement graveyard wanted. Aleida Assmann sees in the Eisenman memorial "a kind of replacement cemetery for the cemeteries that do not exist" (for the six million Jewish victims). For this reason she hopes that its centrality and size might outdo all the other buildings of the post-Wall capital to become a "founding myth" of the Berlin Republic, in a manner related to the Holocaust's (or Yad Vashem's) function within Israel's own national mythos.[30]

Eisenman himself, in the text accompanying his memorial design, offers a disavowal of "sentimental nostalgia" in commemorative architecture, particularly in the context of the Holocaust. His memorial, he writes, presents "no aim, no end, no way in or out ... no remembrance of the past." Eisenman thus takes countermonumentalism to an ahistorical conclusion with respect to the Shoah. By enhancing the power of postmodern architecture and re-carving it without any religious motifs whatsoever, Eisenman hopes that the Berlin Holocaust Memorial will signify nothing but the "living memory of individual experience" of itself to the visitor: an absolutist, purpose-built "living condition."[31] But this assertion does leave one wondering just how many visitors to the memorial can think that way.

Public history is accountable in terms of the effectiveness of what it teaches and presents, and a Holocaust memorial is of course heavily charged with a public history function. Does Eisenman's memorial provide an adequate stage for Holocaust remembrance in the public sphere? With his emphasis on unsettling and removing all that is "anthropocentric" from the building process, by refusing history in all its "stable," meta-narrative faults (his version of Jacques Derrida's attack on the "metaphysics of presence"), Eisenman's abstraction was perhaps not the ideal architectural partner.[32] Can the human, can the religious ever be made totally absent in an architecture of absence? The true significance of the Holocaust as an act of commemoration is in danger of being emptied out thereby. Eisenman's abstract, digitized building style, his post-Cartesian recognition of what he terms "figurative space," could be said to simply contain within itself an ersatz structure of the religious motifs it wishes to replace.[33] A high public level of engagement, an involuntary participatory witnessing of the dead, as achieved by both the list of war dead on Lin's Vietnam Memorial and the photographed families lining the walls of the DC Museum's Tower of Faces, has been made much harder for visitors walking in the purposefully de-personalized, voided spaces between Eisenman's stelae in Berlin. Jürgen Habermas sensed this when he suggested that an "abysmal rupture" appended onto and into the Bundestag parliament building in Berlin would have been a far more succinct method of Holocaust commemoration than Eisenman's, one that would have directly engaged all who entered and exited the building.[34]

In growing recognition of the future Berlin Holocaust Memorial's defectively open-ended signification, a supplemental Place of Information (*Ort der Information*) was appended onto the memorial design; this clause subsequently became part of the Bundestag vote.[35] After the official request for a museum-addition Eisenman designed "Eisenman III," with a new glass structure to house the exhibit-to-be; but this was subsequently dismissed as far too costly a venture. So in the summer of 1999 Eisenman obtained the Berlin memorial foundation's acceptance of a structure that would be built underneath his "Eisenman II." As a result, the south-east corner of the site contains a small underground museum structure, to assist where the memorial falls short. Education has thus been brought in to fill the gap, in the form of a compensatory show-and-tell that is barely visible from the outside. Each of the main four rooms of the exhibit takes up the somewhat meager space of 1,500 square feet (150 sq m). When Eisenman visited in 2010 to mark the fifth anniversary of his memorial, the small size of the exhibition rooms was his one complaint.[36]

Since the *Ort der Information* could not hope to display artifacts on the level of the DC exhibit (which received far more than it could possibly show from Auschwitz and Yad Vashem), emphasis has been placed on personalized narratives, instead.[37] The designer Dagmar von Wilckens prepared exhibits for the rooms: a "space of dimensions," a "space of families," a "space of names," and a "space of places," respectively.[38] The information center (essentially, "Eisenman IV") certainly enhances what its architect terms the "geometrical continuity'" of the columns above ground, several of which hang like stalactites from the ceiling of part of the exhibition area, or reappear as horizontal benches for sitting. While sculptural, such efforts do help link the memorial and the pedagogical messages contained within the museum.[39] The main viewing room of the *Ort der Information* has three echoed models of bench-like stelae, and more 2-D flat stelae shining out of the floor, containing first-person testimony of victims/survivors. It is as if the voices of the fallen are coming out of their graves of light. Finally, in this key instance, the stelae actually seem to "speak" to the visitors. Their inscriptions educate and move. Significantly, Chancellor Merkel brought the Israeli Prime Minister Benjamin Netanyahu to the memorial's information center during his visit to Berlin in January 2010.

Yet the exhibit area's hidden status – that of being underground and far away from the Goebbels bunker, which explains why it was placed in the remotest corner from the main pedestrian access points on the Ebertstraße between the Brandenburg Gate and Potsdamer Platz – is certainly indicative of its basic problem of having been an add-on in the planning process. Despite the fact that tour guides, understandably, have made the memorial an obligatory stop on the Berlin history itinerary, not everyone who gets out of the bus finds his or her way to the information center. Only 3,000 people gave witness to Holocaust Memorial Day at the site of the memorial on 27 January, 2001, yet over 50,000 Berliners attended the "Long Night of the Museums" just a few days later. Or again: the *Topographie des Terrors* – the mission of which, from its inception by a private initiative over twenty years ago, has been quite literally to dig up knowledge about the perpetrators of the Third Reich – has higher visitor volume than the Holocaust Memorial's information center. As the eighth and ninth most visited cultural sites in the city (520,000 and 456,000 visitors in 2008, respectively), the *Topographie des Terrors* and the *Ort der Information* have become rivals in the city's collective memory of Nazism and the Holocaust; but it is probable that with its new exhibition building, the Topographie will henceforth attract more.[40]

Moreover, the controversial issue of building a museum into what is perceived to be infected earth did not go unnoticed: the *Frankfurter Allgemeine Zeitung* voiced a certain hesitance, absent in Eisenman's own plans, at putting a meditative, educational place down into a space that remains part of the "contaminated ground" of Goebbels' villa and bunker, as if the "hellish ambience" of the site might thereby interfere with the exhibition's ability to function.[41] Indeed, a related instance of uncanny, unwelcome ground-stirring arose with the Berlin Senate's contract (with the Munich-based firm of Wöhr + Bauer GmbH) to build a parking garage for the State Opera House under the Bebelplatz and hence around the book-burning memorial. Ullman had to suffer the indignity of his underground artwork becoming a structural part of a parking garage that was built quite literally around and beneath it. While tourists view the empty bookshelves from above just as before, the structure of the memorial itself has been made part of the garage's uppermost floor, hidden inside a walled cube. Martin Jay's analysis of Benjamin's "trope of troubled burial" holds true here: ground that has been as good as dedicated to those who were initially robbed of the right to their own burial earth should not afterwards be disturbed, for such a disruption indicates a disrespectful end to the symbolic memory-digging that the memorial represents.[42] Berlin's former building senator Peter Strieder had no conception of this nuance: his spokesperson blithely stated that "the Bebelplatz is not a cemetery, and the memorial is not an altar." Only after several years of growing complaints did Berlin's politicians finally realize, for example, that it was impolitic to continue to erect a tent for the annual Mercedes Fashion Week completely over the Bebelplatz memorial.[43]

Clearly, the Berlin Holocaust Memorial has not been in need of any additional levels of absurd coincidence coming its way. Yet its foundation launched a poster campaign in 2001 that was meant to assist with public donations: disastrously, the poster used an unwitting take on Jean Baudrillard's phrase about the Gulf War's always-mediated status – the slogan ran: "The Holocaust Did Not Take Place," and resulted in the memorial foundation itself being accused by a survivor of Auschwitz living in Berlin of illegal *Volksverhetzung* ("incitement of hatred by the people").[44] Perhaps the worst moment of unintentional absurdity in the fate of the Berlin Memorial arose when it was reported in 2003 that Degussa AG, the corporation selected to produce an anti-graffiti chemical coating (Protectosil) for each of the memorial's stelae, was the parent of the infamous Degesch company that had made Zyklon-B for the Nazi death camps' gas chambers. Absurdity thus extended seamlessly into the horrifyingly grotesque. It was subsequently revealed that the very foundation of the entire Memorial contains products from both Degussa and Bayer; while Degussa's guilt extended to the reworking of gold stolen from Jewish victims, Bayer had been equally involved, via IG Farben, in the production of Zyklon-B.[45] Eisenman's own attempt to calm the resulting furor was far from successful: after a bad joke to the Memorial committee linking Degussa with gold teeth extractions, he was (as a Jew) accused of anti-Semitism. But one cannot assign absurd coincidence to the fact that five years after the memorial's opening day, there are cracks in 2,200 of the stelae, and the memorial's foundation has insufficient money to fix the problem. Already during the construction phase, the cement used for the demo stelae was far too soft and easily scratched. Eisenman explained the cause of the cracks as an insufficient amount of steel in the columns, but blamed the federal government's advisors to the project, as well as his engineers.[46] We see, then, that gigantic scale does not alone "permanence" make.[47]

Above and beyond such a tragic-comedy of errors, the lingering question regarding the Berlin Holocaust Memorial remains: do we not have a case here of the memorial being simultaneously too much (in scale and scope) and too little (too late, too artificial, too superimposed) for Berlin? It has ended up as a product of what some perceive to be the Holocaust Industry, an externally applied pressure and voyeuristic mechanism of mass-shaming of the Germans, rather than an internally desired and locally driven inspiration to mourn and recognize collective guilt.[48] Berliners were handed their Holocaust Memorial, despite all the elites' debates, as a fait accompli. As the indie rock group "Wir sind Helden" (We Are Heroes) sang satirically in 2005: "They've built us a memorial ... we're forever united in cement and bliss." Pierre Nora himself, originator of the *lieux de mémoire* concept, has voiced concern over the theme-parking of memory sites, and referring to Friedrich Nietzsche's history essay has called for an almost exorcising "duty to history."[49] The commemoration of the past via the Berlin Holocaust Memorial would thus appear to be almost perversely blending with the fêting of urban identity in order to enact Berlin revivalism. German war guilt can now be expressed architecturally and so that the tourists come – *und damit basta.*

Notes

1. Georg Simmel, "Brücke und Tür," *Der Tag*, 683.216 (15 September, 1909), pp. 1–3; repr. in Simmel, *Brücke und Tür. Essays des Philosophen zur Geschichte,*

Religion, Kunst und Gesellschaft, ed. Michael Landmann (Stuttgart: K.F. Koehler Verlag, 1957), pp. 1–7, p. 4.

2. "Under no circumstances may a palace be the architectural symbol of the third German Republic," stated Nida-Rümelin categorically. "Nida-Rümelin ist gegen Nachbau des Schlosses," *Der Tagesspiegel* (8 March, 2001). Andrei S. Markovits and Simon Reich critiqued the Berlin Holocaust Memorial debate and other Holocaust commemorations in Germany as attempts at "liberat[ing] the new Berlin Republic from the burdens that shackled its Bonn predecessor." Markovits and Reich, *The German Predicament: Memory and Power in the New Europe* (Ithaca: Cornell University Press, 1997), p. 205.

3. Edward W. Said, "Invention, Memory, and Place," *Critical Inquiry*, 26 (2000), pp. 175–92, p. 179.

4. Peter Novick in *The Holocaust in American Life* (New York: Houghton Mifflin, 1999) traces the postwar development in attitudes among American Jews toward the Shoah, from initial neglect and suppression to the more recent "institutionalization of Holocaust memory" that the Washington Holocaust Museum incorporates (p. 276).

5. See, for example, the Broadway play of *The Diary of Anne Frank* (performed in Germany in the late 1950s); Marvin Chomsky's *Holocaust* TV series (screened on German TV in 1981); Steven Spielberg's movie *Schindler's List* (released in Germany in 1994 and seen by three and a half million Germans in the first seven weeks); Daniel Goldhagen's *Hitler's Willing Executioners* (Goldhagen went on a tour of Germany in 1996); and the right-wing sympathies with Normal G. Finkelstein's exposé book, *The Holocaust Industry: Reflections on the Exploitation of Jewish Suffering* (New York: Verso, 2000).

6. On the failed Enola Gay exhibition at the Smithsonian Air and Space Museum see Michael J. Hogan, "The Enola Gay Controversy: History, Memory, and the Politics of Presentation," in Hogan, ed., *Hiroshima in History and Memory* (New York: Cambridge University Press, 1996), pp. 200–32; and Edward T. Linenthal and Tom Engelhardt, eds, *History Wars: The Enola Gay and Other Battles for the American Past* (New York: Holt, 1996). Although the bombing of Hiroshima and Nagasaki is not memorialized in Washington, the modest National Japanese American Memorial (2001) located near the Capitol commemorates the Japanese American civilians interned during the war as well as the military service of Japanese Americans. In contrast, recent attempts to better incorporate African American identity on the Mall have succeeded, with the new National Museum for African American History and Culture, headed by Lonnie G. Bunch, opening in 2015; and the planned Martin Luther King Jr National Memorial is to be a piece of landscape architecture with a 24ft-high "stone of hope" near the FDR memorial.

7. Reinhard Rürup, "Ideologisierter Holocaust? Was Norman Finkelsteins Vorwurf für die deutschen Gedenkstätten bedeutet," *Die Zeit*, 34 (2000).

8. The best interpretive history of the Topographie des Terrors is given by Karen E. Till in *The New Berlin*. Because of escalating costs, a proposed museum for the Gestapo headquarters site by Swiss architect Peter Zumthor was halted in 2000 after construction had already started. A second, less costly alternative design by Ursula Wilms opened in 2010; see Stiftung Topographie des Terrors, ed., *Gelände Rundgang: Topographie des Terrors. Geschichte des historischen Orts* (Weißenhorn: Mareis Druck GmbH, 2010); and Thomas E. Schmidt,

"Grauwert der Geschichte," *Die Zeit*, 19 (6 May, 2010). While the Berlin Jewish Museum and Holocaust Memorial have received mostly federal funding, the cost of the museum for the Topographie des Terrors was shared equally between the government and the debt-ridden city of Berlin.

9. For a listing of such memorials, see Andrew Roth and Michael Frajman, *Das jüdische Berlin heute. Ein Wegweiser*, trans. Elisabeth Seligmann (Berlin: Quadriga, 1999), pp. 93–131.

10. See Falk Jaeger, "Ein Stück Jerusalem in Berlin," *Der Tagesspiegel* (9 May, 2001).

11. Cited by Uwe Lehmann-Brauns, CDU speaker for cultural-political issues. "Streit um Mahnmal für Sinti und Roma," *Der Tagesspiegel* (26 July, 2000).

12. Andreas Huyssen, "Monument and Memory in a Postmodern Age," in James E. Young, ed., *The Art of Memory: Holocaust Memorials in History* (New York: Prestel, 1994), pp. 9–17, p. 11.

13. Reinhart Koselleck, "Erschlichener Rollentausch. Das Holocaust-Denkmal im Täterland," *Frankfurter Allgemeine Zeitung* (9 April, 1997), repr. in Michael S. Cullen, ed., *Das Holocaust-Mahnmal. Dokumentation einer Debatte* (Zürich: Pendo, 1999), p. 99. Henryk M. Broder was punning on the conservatives' use of the term *Leitkultur* (which refers to German "dominant culture" in an anti-multicultural sense): Broder, *www.Deutsche Leidkultur.de* (Augsburg: Ölbaum-Verlag, 2001); see also Broder, "Rent a Jew," *Der Tagesspiegel* (25 January, 2001).

14. The Sinti and Roma memorial, scheduled for completion in 2011, is designed by Israeli artist Dani Karavan. The Memorial to Gays Persecuted during National Socialism (2008), a concrete block – a stele, in fact, echoing the memorial across the street, and housing an alternating video feed of two gay men or two gay women kissing – was designed by Ingar Dragset and Michael Elmgreen (based in Berlin, and originally from Norway and Denmark). Several months after its opening the memorial was severely vandalized.

15. The full text is given in Peter Reichel, *Politik mit der Erinnerung. Gedächtnisorte im Streit um die nationalsozialistische Vergangenheit* (Frankfurt am Main: Fischer, 1999), p. 208. See also Richard von Weizsäcker, "Der 8. Mai – 40 Jahre danach," *Von Deutschland aus. Reden des Bundespräsidenten* (Munich: Deutscher Taschenbuch Verlag, 1987), pp. 11–35.

16. See Reinhart Koselleck, "Stellen uns die Toten einen Termin? Die vorgesehene Gestaltung der Neuen Wache wird denen nicht gerecht, deren es zu gedenken gilt," *Frankfurter Allgemeine Zeitung* (23 August, 1993); repr. in Michael Jeismann, ed., *Mahnmal Mitte: Eine Kontroverse* (Cologne: DuMont, 1999), pp. 44–53. At least Frankfurt's Jewish leader, Salomon Korn, while uncomfortable with the previous German regimes' legacy of the Neue Wache, agreed that all victims should be commemorated there. See Korn, interview with Marion Pietrzok, "Es gilt, gegen die Herrschaft dumpfer Gefühle anzukämpfen," in Thomas E. Schmidt et al., eds, *Nationaler Totenkult. Die Neue Wache. Eine Streitschrift zur zentralen deutschen Gedenkstätte* (Berlin: Kramer Verlag, 1995), pp. 101–03, p. 103; Christoph Stölzl, "Schwierigkeit zu trauern. Gespräch zur Zukunft der Neuen Wache," in Jörg Fessmann, ed., *Streit um die Neue Wache. Zur Gestaltung einer zentralen Gedenkstätte* (Berlin: Akademie der Künste, 1993), pp. 55–81; and Dirk Verheyen, *United City, Divided Memories? Cold War Legacies in Contemporary Berlin* (Lanham: Lexington Books, 2008), pp. 41–48.

17. See the Foreign Ministry's explanation of protocol at the Neue Wache for visiting dignitaries, at: www.auswaertiges-amt.de/EN/AAmt/Abteilungen/ Protokoll_node.html (date accessed January 18, 2009); and Thomas Lackmann, "Dann wird von uns Programm gefordert'," *Der Tagesspiegel* (18 November, 2000).

18. One of these alternative sites was the originally suggested site of 1988, namely the terrain of the Topographie des Terrors. See "Exkurs Standort," in Ute Heimrod, Günter Schlusche, and Horst Seferenz, eds, *Der Denkmalstreit – das Denkmal? Die Debatte um das "Denkmal für die ermordeten Juden Europas."* *Eine Dokumentation* (Berlin: Philo Verlag, 1999), pp. 769–830. It was also briefly suggested by Andreas Nachama (director of the Topographie des Terrors, a rabbi, and at the millennium the leader of Berlin's Jewish community) that all non-Jewish memorials to the Holocaust, instead, could be shunted off to that site. See Gerd Nowakowski, "Wie der NS-Zeit gedenken. Der Ort der Täter soll nicht zum Ort der Opfer werden," *Der Tagesspiegel* (6 June, 2000).

19. Petra Kipphoff, "Der Abenteuerer," *Die Zeit*, 31 (1998). György Konrád, President of Berlin's Akademie der Künste, influenced Naumann into suggesting yet another deflection, a pleasant-sounding "memorial garden" (*Gedenkgarten*) next to the museum where children could play. See Jörg Lau, "Die Angst vorm Symbol. Zum Holocaust-Mahnmal gibt es keine Alternative," *Die Zeit*, 53 (12 December, 1998).

20. The uproar was caused by Martin Walser's speech upon receiving the Peace Prize of the German Book Trade. See Walser, "Die Banalität des Guten," *Frankfurter Allgemeine Zeitung* (12 December, 1998); Aleida Assmann and Frevert, *Geschichtsvergessenheit*, pp. 69–72; and Jan Assmann, *Religion and Cultural Memory*, trans. Rodney Livingstone (Stanford: Stanford University Press, 2006), pp. 21–22.

21. Former SPD leader and West Berlin mayor Hans-Jochen Vogel published his pro-memorial opinion shortly before the Bundestag's vote, citing Chancellor Willy Brandt's 1990 demand for Germany to have an "unmistakable statement" (*unübersehbarer Ausdruck*) in memory of Europe's murdered Jews. Vogel, "Es bedarf eines deutlichen Zeichens," *Der Tagesspiegel* (8 June, 1999). For the text summarizing the government's decision to build the monument, see Lea Rosh, ed., *"Die Juden, das sind doch die anderen." Der Streit um ein deutsches Denkmal* (Berlin: Philo, 1999), p. 152.

22. Wolf Biermann, "Güterbahnhof Grunewald," *Frankfurter Allgemeine Zeitung* (6 July, 1998). See also Huyssen's designation of Eisenman's memorial as "a monumental memory sore." Huyssen, "Twin Memories: Afterimages of Nine/Eleven," *Present Pasts*, p. 159; orig. in *Grey Room*, 7 (2002), pp. 8–13, p. 9.

23. Eisenman Architects, "Realisierungsentwurf. Engeres Auswahlverfahren zum Denkmal für die ermordeten Juden Europas", brochure, trans. Ingeborg Rocker and Dr Günter Schlusche (Berlin: Deutsches Historisches Museum, 1998); Heimrod et al., eds, *Der Denkmalstreit – das Denkmal?*, pp. 1111–14; Lothar Heinke, "Holocaust-Gedenkstätte. Das Mahnmal vor meinem Fenster," *Der Tagesspiegel* (18 July, 2001); and www.stiftung-denkmal.de (date accessed 3 January, 2009).

24. Torsten Hampel, "Blaugrau, mit feinen Poren. Die ersten Probe-Stelen für das Berliner Mahnmal," *Der Tagesspiegel* (19 May, 2001).

25. Olga Kapustina, "Spielfeld der Erinnerung," *taz* (5 May, 2010); "Public Disrespect: Berlin Holocaust Memorial Used as Toilet," *Der Spiegel* (29 January, 2007); "Oktoberfest am Holocaust-Mahnmal," *Der Tagesspiegel* (20 October, 2008); and interview with Salomon Korn, "'Was uns trennt, das verbindet uns auch,'" *Der Tagesspiegel* (1 November, 1999). See also Gerhard Ullmann, "Das Holocaust-Mahnmal in Berlin: Ort des Gedenkens oder urbaner Freiraum?" *Garten + Landschaft*, 116.11 (2006), pp. 36–37.

26. Minimal lighting at the Berlin Holocaust Memorial is all that aids a private security service. In November 2000 the Bundestag had authorized DM7 million (€3.5 million) for a security plan for the memorial. While there is an electronic check at entry to the underground *Ort der Information*, there is no camera surveillance of the open-air memorial. "Keine Kameras für Berliner Mahnmale," *Der Tagesspiegel* (1 September, 2008); Jola Merten and Dirk Westphal, "Ungeschütztes Holocaust-Mahnmal," *Berliner Zeitung* (17 November, 2000).

27. Jane Kramer, "Living with Berlin," *The New Yorker* (5 July, 1999), pp. 50–64, p. 54. Upon entering office, cultural minister and Memorial-skeptic Michael Naumann declared that the very concept of a centralized national Holocaust memorial had "something bureaucratic, Albert-Speer-monumental, ...[and] oppressive" about it. "Naumann: Vieles wird älter aussehen als ein neues Stadtschloβ," *Der Tagesspiegel* (21 July, 1998).

28. James E. Young, *At Memory's Edge: After-Images of the Holocaust in Contemporary Art and Architecture* (New Haven: Yale University Press, 2000), pp. 209–16. See also Max Bächer's comment in 1995 that "the actual problem is the senseless size, which instead of producing legitimate monumentalism (in the sense of *monere* = to exhort, to remember) almost involuntarily provokes a want of proportion." Bächer, "Der ganze Wettbewerb war ein Miβgriff. Phrasenhafte Ausschreibung, falscher Standort: So muβ das Holocaust-Mahnmal scheitern," in Jeismann, ed., *Mahnmal Mitte*, pp. 116–21, p. 118.

29. Stiftung Denkmal für die ermordeten Juden Europas, "The Memorial to the Murdered Jews of Europe" (October 2000). The phrase was not included in subsequent editions of the brochure.

30. "Niemand lebt im Augenblick," interview with Jan Assmann and Aleida Assmann, *Die Zeit*, 50 (3 December, 1998). See also Aleida Assmann, *Der lange Schatten der Vergangenheit: Erinnerungskultur und Geschichtspolitik* (Munich: Beck, 2006).

31. Eisenman Architects, "Realisierungsentwurf."

32. See Jeffrey Kipnis' analysis of Peter Eisenman and Jacques Derrida in "Twisting the Separatrix," Kipnis and Thomas Leeser, eds, *Chora L Works. Jacques Derrida and Peter Eisenman* (New York: The Monacelli Press, 1997), pp. 137–60, p. 138. Mary McLeod finds fault with Eisenman's "formal hermeticism" for referring to itself and for retreating from "social processes" and from the "urban context," for not seeking "possibilities of reconstituted community." McLeod, "Architecture and Politics in the Reagan Era: From Postmodernism to Deconstructivism" (1989), in K. Michael Hayes, ed., *Architecture Theory Since 1968* (Cambridge, MA: MIT Press, 1998), pp. 678–707, p. 692, 693.

33. Eisenman, cited in Ralf Schönball, "Peter Eisenman im Gespräch," *Der Tagesspiegel* (17 March, 2001). Herbert Muschamp critiqued the "elimination of self-expression from the architectural object" of Eisenman's Wexner

Center for the Arts on the Ohio State University campus, in "Who's That Peering Out of the Grid?," *The New York Times* (18 March, 2001). See, however, Johan Åhr's attempt to insert faith into the Berlin memorial, in his "Memory and Mourning in Berlin: On Peter Eisenman's Holocaust-Mahnmal," *Modern Judaism*, 28.3 (2008), pp. 283–305.

34. Jürgen Habermas was referring to Salomon Korn's idea. See Habermas, "Der Zeigefinger: Die Deutschen und ihr Denkmal," *Die Zeit*, 14 (1999).

35. Michael Naumann, as Cultural Minister, pushed this clause through. Walter Mayr, "Sprengsatz auf zwei Beinen," *Der Spiegel* 52 (12 December, 1998), pp. 30–31; and Michael Sontheimer, "'Alleingang verhindern'," *Der Spiegel,* 52 (12 December, 1998).

36. Claudia Keller, "Bürgerfest am Stelenfeld," *Der Tagesspiegel* (5 May, 2010).

37. Naumann invited the Shoah Visual History Archive (Los Angeles) to provide the contents for the Berlin memorial's Place of Information. This idea was shelved when Spielberg's archive became involved in planning the exhibits for Libeskind's Jewish Museum. A second idea to import copies of the archives of the Leo Baeck Institute in New York was tabled for the same reason. See "Pilotprojekt," *Der Tagesspiegel* (18 October, 2000), p. 28. Finally, the names of all known Holocaust victims, as archived by Yad Vashem, were provided.

38. The four "named" rooms were suggested by Andreas Nachama, Reinhard Rürup, and Eberhard Jäckel. See Thomas Lackmann, "Im Keller," *Der Tagesspiegel* (8 July, 2000); see also Lackmann, "Konzentrationsraum." This concept is obviously over-indebted to Jochen Gerz's own competition entry for the Berlin Holocaust Memorial (second round): Gerz had suggested rooms of "memory," of "answers" (in response to the "why did this happen?" question), and of "silence." See "Jochen Gerz. Paris," Heimrod et al., eds, *Der Denkmalstreit – das Denkmal?* pp. 883–86, pp. 883–84.

39. Moritz Müller-Wirth, "Das Wort des Architekten," *Frankfurter Allgemeine Zeitung* (8 July, 2000).

40. Berlin's top four museums in order of attendance rates are the Pergamonmuseum, the Egyptian Collection (now in the Neues Museum), the Haus am Checkpoint Charlie, and the Deutsches Historisches Museum. See the Berlin Senate's museum statistics for 2008, announced in late 2009 at: www.berlin.de/landespressestelle/archiv/2009/11/13/145973/index.html (date accessed 16 February, 2010).

41. Ulrich Raulff, "Die Tiefe. Entscheidung beim Mahnmal," *Frankfurter Allgemeine Zeitung* (8 July, 2000).

42. Martin Jay, "Against Consolation: Walter Benjamin and the Refusal to Mourn," in Jay Winter and Emmanuel Sivan, eds, *War and Remembrance in the Twentieth Century* (New York: Cambridge University Press, 1999), p. 229.

43. See the Initiative Bebelplatz which aims to protect Ullman's memorial: www.bbk-kulturwerk.de/cms/site/side1310.html (date accessed 31 May, 2010); Sabina Beikler, "Initiative will Models vom Bebelplatz fernhalten," *Der Tagesspiegel* (17 January, 2010); Franz Wegener, "Vor der Geschichte verpflichtet, 'auf den Platz acht zu geben'," *Der Tagesspiegel* (23 May, 2001); "Bebelplatz Skulptur: Kein Kompromiss: Ullman korrigiert Strieder," *Der Tagesspiegel* (29 June, 2001); and Petra Reetz, cited in Nils Meyer, "Krieg unterm Altar," *Der Tagesspiegel* (31 July, 2001).

44. See "Holocaust Poster. Stilwechsel," *Der Tagesspiegel* (20 July, 2001); "Plakat-Aktion. Rosh: Spendenaufruf erfolgreich," *Der Tagesspiegel* (24 July, 2001); and Frank Jansen, "Holocaust-Plakat: Ermittlungen wegen Volksverhetzung," *Der Tagesspiegel* (1 August, 2001).

45. Dagmar Rosenfeld, "Degussa darf am Holocaust-Mahnmal weiterbauen," *Der Tagesspiegel* (14 November, 2003); "Kartell des Todes," *Der Tagesspiegel* (11 November, 2003); and Richard Bernstein, "Holocaust Legacy: Germans and Jews Debate Redemption," *The New York Times* (29 October, 2003). After a temporary halt to the building process, Degussa's participation in the project was continued. The scandal was a contributing factor in the resignation of the Memorial foundation's manager, Sybille Quack, who was replaced by Hans-Erhard Haverkampf in 2004.

46. Interview with Peter Eisenman, "Warum man am Holocaust-Mahnmal spielen darf," *Berliner Morgenpost* (5 May, 2010). The structural engineering firm for the project was Happold Ingenierbüro.

47. Aleida Assmann, *Der lange Schatten der Vergangeneit*, p. 240.

48. Assmann and Ute Frevert have demonstrated in their study of German postwar memory *Geschichtsvergessenheit – Geschichtsversessenheit* that the West German (and originally Allied) tactic of inducing collective guilt by means of a "culture of shame" (*Schamkultur*) created only an official, governmental discourse and politics of atonement, with an underlying, and unacknowledged, tone of private resentment; while in the German Democratic Republic, Nazi guilt was immediately transferred away from home turf onto imperialist fascists, or re-channeled into an alternative sublimating set of Communist victory-imagery. The clash of these two cultures' memory-sets since reunification has been described by Jürgen Habermas as the "*double* past," or psychological burden, of two totalitarian regimes that still have to be worked through. See Assmann and Frevert, *Geschichtsvergessenheit, Geschichtsversessenheit*, pp. 88–96; and Habermas, "What Does 'Working Off the Past' Mean Today?" (orig. 1992), *A Berlin Republic: Writings on Germany*, trans. Steven Rendall, introduction by Peter Uwe Hohendahl (Lincoln: University of Nebraska Press, 1997), pp. 17–40, p. 40 (emphasis original). See also Karl Heinz Bohrer's account of the failure of the cultures of both guilt and shame in "Schuldkultur oder Schamkultur. Und der Verlust an historischem Gedächtnis," *Neue Zürcher Zeitung* (12/13 December, 1998), repr. in Jeismann, ed., *Mahnmal Mitte*, pp. 300–12.

49. Pierre Nora, "Gedächtniskonjunktur. Pflicht zur Erinnerung. Wie Nietzsche vor der 'Historie' müsste man heute vor dem 'Gedächtnis' warnen," *Freitag* (8 March, 2002). Awareness of these dangers is illustrated by William J. Neill, "Marketing the Urban Experience: Reflections on the Place of Fear in the Promotional Strategies of Belfast, Detroit and Berlin," *Urban Studies*, 38 (2001), pp. 815–28; Caroline Gay, "The Politics of Cultural Remembrance: The Holocaust Monument in Berlin," *International Journal of Cultural Policy*, 9.2 (2003), pp. 153–66; and Chapter 3 of Hans-Georg Stavginski, *Das Holocaust-Denkmal: Der Streit um das "Denkmal für die ermordeten Juden Europas" in Berlin (1988–1999)* (Paderborn: Ferdinand Schöningh Verlag, 2002).

12
Siting the Holocaust in Libeskind's Jewish Museum

Lector, si monumentum requiris, circumspice
(Epigraph on Sir Christopher Wren's tomb,
St Paul's Cathedral, London)

There is an unintended Holocaust memorial in Berlin that fits the criteria that the city's Memorial to the Murdered Jews of Europe and its debate failed to actualize. It is ranked as the city's fifth most popular museum (with just under 759,000 visitors in 2008). The Jewish Museum, designed by Daniel Libeskind as an invited entry in the 1988 competition for a new Jewish extension of the baroque-style Berlin Museum in Berlin-Kreuzberg, was to be a postwar West Berlin substitute for the original Jewish Museum that existed for five years behind the synagogue in the Oranienburger Straße and was closed one year after *Kristallnacht* (and is now reopened as the Centrum Judaicum, with two-thirds of the original artwork).[1] Libeskind's extension building opened in 1999 in an exhibition-less condition, and has been functioning (albeit without the architect's official blessing) as a substitute Holocaust memorial ever since. The museum closed temporarily in December 2000 for various service-related overhauls and again during 2001 for the preparation of its exhibition contents; 348,700 people came to see the empty building between January 1999 and January 2001, a figure which translates (given the closings) to an initial annual rate of 500,000. The radical building was designed without contents as an artwork in an open terrain. It made its worldwide statement during those pre-exhibition years, devoid of any predestined series or sequence except the narrative placed on it by a tour guide. It was rescued in 2001 from the ongoing financial crisis of Berlin's cultural institutions by its upgrade to federal status (a far cry from the early 1990s, when Libeskind's wife Nina had to launch an all-out media campaign to prevent the conservative Mayor Diepgen from shutting off city funding during the museum's building stages).[2] It is now the fully funded Stiftung Jüdisches Museum Berlin.

While addressing the chasms created on the urban landscape by the forced departure of Berlin's Jews, Libeskind's museum is an ode to the entirety of Jewish existence in Berlin.[3] It is hence more than a monument to this population's tragic alterity in German history – just as it is relieved of any criticism for not including non-Jewish victims of Nazi atrocities. For this building, remarkable for its myriad spatial and metaphorical techniques of criss-crossing, Libeskind was awarded the German Architecture Prize in the fall of 1999. Andreas Huyssen has recognized that "Libeskind's expansion of the Berlin Museum may be a better memorial to German and Jewish history, the history of the living and of the dead, than any official funereal Holocaust monument could possibly be." Anthony Vidler extends such praise, explaining how Libeskind's building "manages to hold the visitor in spatio-psychological suspense, the closest experience to what I imagine a religious experience of architecture to be."[4]

As creator of a building that illustrates the fractured history of Jewish life and death in the new German capital, Libeskind has become the contemporaneous architect of German-Jewish memory and crisis. He achieved this reputation by engaging the same basic countermonumental principle of negative building, of rupture across, above, and into the ground applied so well in Lin's Vietnam Veteran's Memorial, or Gerz's Harburg-Hamburg Monument Against Fascism. His construction of zinc-clad cement and steel uncannily documents the sense of Jewish presence in, and disarticulated absence from, the Berlin cityscape. The zig-zagged building with its diagonal slashes of windows is based on the "irrational matrix" of a "compressed and distorted" Star of David, and the whole is spliced by the famed, straight-line series of black-painted interior towers of empty space, termed "voids" by the architect himself.[5] The rubble that only Walter Benjamin's/Paul Klee's angel can see is contained, so to speak, within these emptied islands of spatial and historical crisis (and indeed, Libeskind acknowledges Benjamin as one of his conceptual inspirations for the building). Libeskind's tower-voids include the one that is located in the (now former) Berlin Museum's Kollegienhaus, with a stairwell taking the visitor from the old building into the new (designed as a transition from the history of Berlin to the history of Jewish life and death in Germany). Another void contains a floor-art installation of thousands of plate-iron faces ("Fallen Leaves" [*Shalakhet*], by the Israeli artist Menashe

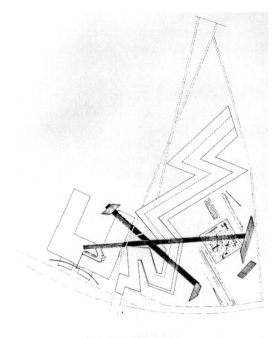

X - Museum, 'interchange station', Jewish-Berlin collection

Figure 12.1 "X – Museum, 'interchange station'." Design sketch for the Jewish Museum Berlin by Daniel Libeskind, 1999

Kadishman). The Holocaust Tower is separated from the rest of the building: it is unlit and unheated, with a single unreachable window up high, and a threatening heavy door whose hinge is on a tilt so as to keep it swinging shut behind all those who enter the dark chimney-like, 89ft-high (27m) chamber. A reviewer was so impressed he thought he had found post-Wall Berlin's "soul" in that Holocaust void.[6] Essentially the towers are without recourse to any historical information on the Holocaust; the architect scrapped his original idea of inscribing the names of deported Berlin Jews inside the voids.[7] The visitor's journey through the building as a whole occurs along three inclined corridors that one reaches via the "interchange station" of the stairs between the Kollegienhaus and the Extension (Fig. 12.1). One follows different line-axes that lead to the Holocaust Tower, the Garden of Exile outside, or a main Staircase of Continuity leading to the jagged exhibition areas upstairs. Thus one can select from alternative narrative "ends" for Jewish culture and history.

Figure 12.2   Garden of Exile, Jewish Museum, Extension to the Berlin Museum, by Daniel Libeskind, 1999

The building's interior voids are re-presented in exteriorized format on the terrain outside the museum. In the Garden of Exile, also called the E. T. A. Hoffmann Garden (Hoffmann used to work in the Kollegienhaus), is a square area of 49 concrete columns of four times human size (each 23ft [7m] high), inclining toward the building's outer wall as the terrain itself slants away from the same: a veritable mini-labyrinth that connects the disoriented walker among them only to the sky above, with olive trees (a sign of hope) growing out of the tops of the pillars (Fig. 12.2).[8] Anyone wishing further proof that Peter Eisenman's later design, itself rather too much like Libeskind's garden (as Libeskind has complained), is hard to police should try navigating even this comparatively tiny sculpture.[9] Despite their Derridean affinities, Libeskind's museum jumps out of the fixed spatial equation engaged in by Eisenman's memorial, that of Holocaust memory as calamity that necessarily numbs cognition. Instead, Libeskind's building by marking the "erasure of [Jewish] history" in Berlin and Germany demands a "future to that history."[10] In fact, Libeskind blends a dose of practical Brechtianism with his regular Heideggerianism in his conviction that the museum-form in general frees one from the memorial-form's frequent danger of remaining trapped in a solely "catastrophe"-way of reconstructing the Holocaust; people should, rather, be encouraged to engage the topic in an "explanatory and knowledgeable manner."[11]

The result of the unprecedented success of the Jewish Museum is presenting a certain conundrum for Berlin. As far back as the museum competition jury's comments, it was hoped (in vain, as it turned out) that the power of Libeskind's building would not allow it to "become an architectural memorial and obliterate the needs of the museum."[12] The public alone decided this issue, visiting the empty museum in 1999 and 2000 as if it were in its entirety a memorial to the Jewish experiences of the Holocaust. Small wonder is it, then, that some thought the museum should remain empty, such is its efficacy.[13] Like both his critics and his admirers, Libeskind is well aware that his museal forms, rather than the contents, are what draw the crowds; and while it may be said that his No Exit Museum (Museum ohne Ausgang) in Osnabrück (1998) for the art of Holocaust artist Felix Nussbaum competes with the pictures within, it has also undeniably generated a significant rise in Nussbaum's value on international art markets. MGM Mirage was hoping to reap similar benefits of a consumerist sort when it invited Libeskind to design the Strip-fronting luxury mall that anchors the new City Center in Las Vegas (2009). The international Libeskind-effect thus adds a certain karat to any collection, the Jewish Museum's or otherwise.[14]

So far, then, we have in Berlin a museum whose attraction is that it functions more as Holocaust architecture than as the space of its exhibits, and a memorial that offers its public less than a Holocaust monument ought to give. Those who want a more moving experience will in all likelihood go to the Jewish Museum, the exhibits of which, even if permanently out-designed by Libeskind's architecture, still present a representative picture of Jewish death *and life* in Germany. Defending Eisenman's memorial as a "portal" that could lead people onwards to the Jewish Museum or the Topography of Terror hardly seems to help one's assessment of the former's actual contribution.[15] In fact, perhaps the most important function of the Jewish Museum is, despite its Holocaust pathos, to go beyond what has been termed the "Horror Marketing Attraction" of post-Wall Berlin as world capital of Nazi relics.[16] The Jewish Museum's exhibit of Jewish life in Germany from Roman times to the present contributes to a *"new era* in respect to Germany's recent past," whereby the Holocaust can be integrated "into a larger panoramic narrative about German-Jewish history."[17] The Jewish Museum has in fact been busy diversifying into a significant cultural venue for Jewish life in Berlin today: the recent addition of the Glass Courtyard (2007), again by Libeskind, offers a sheltering glass canopy (*sukkah*) for concerts and events between the wings of the Kollegienhaus. In 2010 Libeskind also announced plans for a third new part of the ensemble: a tilted cube of a building to be built to house the future Jewish Museum Berlin Academy, intended for educational programs.

Nonetheless, the uncanny expression of the Holocaust via architecture is the chief factor in why people go to and revisit the Jewish Museum. Libeskind's design performs a radicalization of the restraint involved in Freed's building in DC, and a comparison of the two certainly benefits Libeskind's bravado. Yet one should not understand this as a critique of the DC Museum, which performs a different task in a different context than does the Jewish Museum in the capital city causally linked to the Holocaust. Libeskind, of course, was given carte blanche, and did not have Washington's Commission on Fine Arts to work against. While the Tower of Faces in the DC Holocaust Memorial Museum provides a well-crafted use of verticality, in that the visitor revisits the photographs of the lost people of the Lithuanian *shtetl* of Ejszyszki on lower levels, in Libeskind's building we have nothing but a continuous play on angle, slant, divide, disconnection, and reconnection of lines. The single diagonal light fissure in the floor of the Hall of Witness in Freed's building, a line that is at the same angle as the ridge in the skylight above the hall (13 degrees), contains a "tension … splitting the space in two": and this act of diagonal fissuring is the premise for the entire structure of Libeskind's museum.[18] The sample first names of victims and lists of their former communities in Europe that are carved into the glass walls on the west side of the third- and fourth-floor bridges joining the two structures of Freed's museum find their counterpart in the text-covered base of Libeskind's early model for the Berlin museum (and displayed in the museum itself), where alphabetically ordered Berlin Jews' names line the outer bases of the model. The dark constrained spaces of the DC Museum's exhibit areas, as they contrast with the light, open sense of the bridges, the Hall of Witness, and the Hall of Remembrance, provide a light-dark dialectic that is, in turn, fully expanded by Libeskind, who bases the interior experience of his structure on the interaction of white color, natural and electric light, and lines of light architecture traversing plain surfaces, with the occurrence of black (the tower voids). Freed's bridges take the visitor to the next stage in the Holocaust history being narrated and displayed; while Libeskind's *Caligari*-esque, diagonally crossing corridors with tilting walls and floors are there as aesthetic lines of anti-directionality. Even the Jewish Museum's Staircase of Continuity (in its proportions reminiscent of the Mauthausen concentration camp's infamous quarry steps) does not just go upstairs to the exhibition areas, but leads literally to a wall (Fig. 12.3).

Figure 12.3 Staircase of Continuity, Jewish Museum, Extension to the Berlin Museum, by Daniel Libeskind, 1999

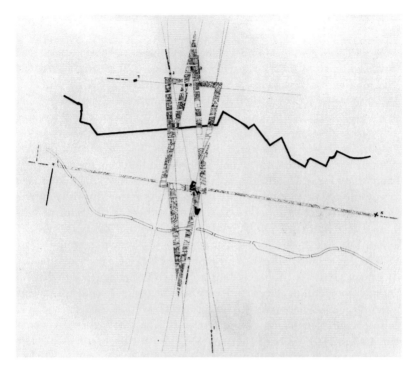

Figure 12.4 "Urban Scheme: Star of David." Design sketch for Jewish Museum Berlin by Daniel Libeskind, 1999

Yet despite this radicalism, Berlin's Jewish Museum is grounded in Berlin in more ways than one – unlike Eisenman's columnar grid that appears antagonistic to senses of history and place.[19] Early design sketches show that Libeskind envisaged a map of Berlin marking the addresses of former Jewish cultural leaders over the centuries, and these coordinates were overlaid with a Star of David. He abstracted these constellations into a series of intersecting ellipses across the city; and the Berlin Wall also featured as a schism overriding the urban terrain out of which emerged the museum (Fig. 12.4).[20] Libeskind's very title for the museum, "Between the Lines," is suggestive of a Jewish history for the entire city that resides between the divisions and in the voids of historical loss, rupture and trauma. Indeed, Libeskind shows in his frequent writings on Berlin a keen sense of the presence and then absence of the Wall (his design stage for the museum began with the Wall still up), even altering parts of his designs in order to reflect the city's radical new conditions for building. Whereas once the Jewish Museum had been in close proximity to Checkpoint Charlie in the former literal edge-borough of neglected Kreuzberg adjoining the Wall, now it stands in the city's new center, a short walk from the Friedrichstadtpassagen's retail glamour in the reconstructed Mitte. In a response to Jacques Derrida's commentary on his museum, Libeskind stated: "My enemies told me I was no longer a deconstructivist, because I had straightened the walls. But I did it because I felt the project was no longer protected by the kind of schizophrenia developed out of the bilateral nature of the city. It had to stand and close itself off in a different way."[21]

At the heart of the conceptual (and political) debate over the Berlin Memorial for the Murdered Jews of Europe exists that which Libeskind refers to as the importance of creating *thing-ness* in such an entity: by this he means not empty monumentalism, but rather the concrete, material nature of a Holocaust-symbolizing structure in the actual, centralized, urban location of the former perpetrators, that is, its ongoing status as a highly contextualized "'thing' in the city" (*"Ding" in der Stadt*).[22] His own words on the rebuilding of post-Wall Berlin (specifically, his rejected competition entries for Potsdamer Platz and Alexanderplatz) consistently remind the reader that reconstruction should be in accordance with the city's own history and sense of place, not a glossing over of uncomfortable aspects of the past: for the Alex, he wanted to retain even the ugly GDR prefabs so as to show the history of the square as a "ruin of time"; and for the combination of a former Cold War edge-site and a pre-World War II city center that Potsdamer Platz presents, he proposed a "site-as-puzzle," as a measure of keeping "Humpty Dumpty" broken because such fragmentation is that site's true history. At the same time, his suggestion for renewing Berlin's Unter den Linden was to free the street from its function as a "dam" between East and West, and unblock it with new architecture.[23] The appendage of Libeskind's Jewish Museum to the Berlin Museum stands – along with his designs, inter alia, for the Contemporary Jewish Museum in San Francisco, the Extension to the Denver Art Museum, Manchester's Imperial War Museum North, and the master plan for the World Trade Center site ("Memory Foundations"), as well as his latest incision of a massive "arrow" into Dresden's Military History Museum – as an example of his belief that historical metamorphosis through the act of building "must be incorporated in an urban framework which encourages the creation of unpredictable, flexible and hybrid architectures."[24]

This art of inserting into architecture a dialogue with localized time and place is visible in Libeskind's own runner-up design, "Stonebreath" (*Steinatem*), for the second competition for the Berlin Holocaust

Memorial. In Libeskind's memorial design, amidst a mostly voided space on the five-acre lot, "footprints" of the Reichstag and Brandenburg Gate would have formed the dimensions of the memorial's concave ground; and a precise visible axis ("channel"), along which would have been built a series of six towers ("solidified voids," one for each million Jewish dead), would have pointed to the precise location of the Wannsee Villa southwest of the city center.[25] But the jury disliked Libeskind's self-referentiality of shamelessly exhibiting the voids from his own Jewish Museum, and even daring to point to this building with another axis in the ground.

By stressing the crucial urban *sitedness* of good Holocaust representation, Libeskind provided an indirect message to the entire Berlin Memorial debate. Eisenman's monument lacks a necessary core connected to this same notion of *situs*. It ultimately stumbles over its own artifice, namely, its conscious disconnectedness from both the materiality of historical exhibit and the materiality of historical place. Eisenman's declared preference for a topos of "fluctuation," his "continuous blurring" of place, scale and time, differs from Libeskind's more phenomeno-logically based "contextualism," which gives value to what exists on the historical and spatial context of the site (itself a reaction against modernist architecture's tendency of total erasure).[26] It is interesting to note that Eisenman's entry for the Viennese Holocaust memorial competition was, like Libeskind's for Berlin, highly cognizant of place and time: by means of a rupture into the ground of the square into which it would have been placed, it would have included a map of the terrain of Auschwitz, the railway lines that led there, and maps of the former Jewish ghettos of Vienna: all refreshingly "referential" for Eisenman. However, unlike Whiteread's winning design, the massive scale of Eisenman's self-overlaying, multiple structure for Vienna would have completely destroyed the *Judenplatz*'s function as public square.[27]

By contrast, Libeskind's "thing-ness"-theory is further articulated in his assertion that the best thing for Berlin would be to invest not so much in a separate monument to the Holocaust but in maintaining Ravensbrück and Sachsenhausen, because as actual concentration camps they are not the "invented memory" of an "artificial memorial."[28] Libeskind's idea of maintaining authentic Holocaust sites is however a highly discursive, interactive one: with his "Hope Incision" design for Sachsenhausen, for example, he continued his meditation-technique of exteriorized yet abstracted commemoration of atrocity by adding, from above, a diagonal series of steel-girded jagged slices onto the concentration camp's actual terrain.[29] Libeskind's design, excluded from the memorial site's original competition that wanted architects to design apartments there, purposefully did *not* adhere to the guidelines in order to maintain the site's legacy as camp and avoid the anti-historicity of residential dwelling at this place. Yet neither was "Hope Incision" a static use of Sachsenhausen's terrain.[30] Libeskind's design aimed at reinvigorating the site as a memorial but also at providing for transformative land-uses – such as building facilities on former SS-land next to the camp for training local Oranienburgers in new high-tech office skills as well as artisan work, or for human rights organizations. Libeskind wanted the site to "retain a strong memory" and, simultaneously, facilitate "the dawn of a new Mourning."[31]

What we have seen of Libeskind's work shows his endeavor to reconstruct heterogeneous urban memory that is the de facto opposite of the conservative vision of the past that has determined former building director Hans Stimmann's Critical Reconstruction project for post-Wall Berlin. Libeskind's concern is that any Holocaust memorial should as a landscape of memory remain essentially an icon in the "here," a "space of lived experience," and not be obliterated by the landscape of the present (which itself may be a pastiche of past styles).[32] This wish for obliteration was inadvertently expressed by a journalist writing on the pre-groundbreaking ceremony at the Holocaust Memorial site on 27 January, 2000. Bernhard Schulz provided what he considered to be an optimistic future scenario of Eisenman's monument "fitting in" with the rest of the new and old buildings of the German capital. Ironically, Schulz now appears to have been right in his prediction that the memorial would simply blend into the background, with his comment that it would be successfully "posited within an urban system of references where Foster's glass dome of the reworked Reichstag will shine forth over it, as will the Piano-, Kollhoff- and Jahn-skyscrapers of Potsdamer Platz."[33] What a lot of effort to go to: to spend so many years arguing over and building a monumental monument that you would then prefer to see turn into a comfortable piece of urban furniture and hence be as good as erased from the horizon!

Of all the star architects operating in post-Wall Berlin, Libeskind took the strongest stance against the erasure of subversive urban memory, arguing for a reconstruction that re-included the Wall as an absent presence, and for the pluralistic *genius loci* of the urban in general as a "spatial and temporal network." Libeskind's combinatory architectural blend of postmodernism with humanism, of abstraction with narrative, can express for the maintenance of Holocaust memory that which Eisenman's less interactive abstraction cannot. Libeskind may be both a romantic and a revolutionary, navigating as he himself admits between the "Scylla of nostalgic historicism and the Charybdis of totalitarian tabula rasa," but he has given ample material form to his belief that avant-garde architecture can indeed be humanistic, that it can provide more than the language of Jencksian postmodern signs, to include the "equation of a city's soul."[34]

As such, the overriding need is for an autochthonous Holocaust architecture that is accurately sited within the memory landscape of its community. The Jewish Museum by Libeskind is consciously planted "between the lines" of Jewish memory in Berlin that are laid out temporally through and spatially across the city. The axialities of Jewish life in Berlin are layered over the victims' absences. It joins other rooted sites of Holocaust memory in the capital that succeed in revealing the traces of what has gone before – as, for example, at the literal tracks of Platform 17 (Gleis 17), the Grunewald deportation memorial.[35]

Indeed, the sitedness of these other sites of traumatic memory in the city is abstractly exemplified, even guided and re-oriented, by Libeskind's Jewish Museum extension. In terms of the conceptual/ethical awakening that such memory sites ideally enact upon their viewers, we can extend Rolf Goebel's discussion regarding the sites of "architectural citation" to further ponder the combined remembrance in Berlin of the Holocaust, Nazism, and World War II: how do past events like these fare in this multiply rebuilt city, and can the on-site urban representation of these traumas still interrupt any apparent "linearity of history"?[36] Huyssen sees in the "disparate city-text" of re-made Berlin a palimpsest that does show its previous penmanship: "Berlin as palimpsest implies voids, illegibilities, and erasures, but it offers also a richness of traces and memories, restorations and new constructions that will mark the city as lived space."[37]

It is to be hoped, then, that despite all the rebuilding, as many layers have been revealed as hidden, that seamlessness has not resulted everywhere, and that interactive segmentations are continuing – at least as far as the work of public history is concerned. This certainly appears to be the case at the exposed intersection of space and time that occurs where the ruined cellar walls of the Gestapo headquarters at the Topography of Terror meet what is probably the most-visited remnant of the Berlin Wall on the Niederkirchnerstraße, with the former Nazi Air Ministry behind them both. In past practice, however, far too many tourists here have been totally confused regarding the respective roles of the two walls, inadvertently seeking a causal correspondence between the two, instead of recognizing their apparent fusion as illusory and as just the spatial coincidence of two consecutive totalitarian regimes. It

Figure 12.5 The Topography of Terror Documentation Center's new outdoor exhibit, 2010: remnant of the Wall above the excavated cellar ruins of the Gestapo headquarters, with the former Nazi Air Ministry (now Finance Ministry) in the background, Niederkirchnerstraße, Berlin

is a site-layering quagmire that the new Topography outdoor exhibit, redesigned by Heinz W. Hallmann and opened in 2010 along with the new museum, now seeks to explain better to visitors (Fig. 12.5).

In the long term, the challenge facing Berlin's Jewish Museum, the Memorial to the Murdered Jews of Europe, and the city's other trauma-related sites of memory is consistent with, as Fredric Jameson has argued, the challenge of the "repression of historicity" endemic to post-modern culture: "The building can ... only serve as a history lesson if its public and its viewers still have a sense of history; it cannot provide them with one if that organ has atrophied." Berlin is, in this sense, closer to the climate of North American postmodernity than it is to other East European cities such as Warsaw undergoing post-socialist reconstruction. The post-Wall city remains the problem child, hence the ideal case-study as iterated by Libeskind of "the need [for us to apply architecture] to resist the erasure of history, the need to respond to history, the need to open the future: that is, to delineate the invisible on the basis of the visible" and thus keep alive the "memory of the city ... the time in which it dwells, and ... the freedom it represents."[38] His Jewish Museum, an architectural postmodernism of hope rather than of nihilism, will continue its trajectory as the ultimate "overturning" (the original meaning of *katastrophē*) – the enduring dramatic turn in the tragedy that Holocaust architecture can call forth.

Notes

1. Hermann Simon, *Das Berliner Jüdische Museum in der Oranienburger Straße.* Geschichte einer zerstörten Kulturstätte (Berlin: Hentrich & Hentrich, 2000).
2. Daniel Libeskind Papers (Getty Research Institute), Series 4 (Press Clippings 1990–1992), Box 30; and Series 3 (Correspondence), Box 28.1–7.
3. A Nazi census of June 1933 indicates a Jewish population in the German capital of 160,000; this amounted to one-third of all Jews in Germany. By 1939, only 80,000 Jews remained in Berlin; the rest had fled. During the Final Solution three-quarters of these remaining Jews were deported from Berlin to the concentration/death camps. See www.ushmm.org/wlc/en/article. php?ModuleId =10005450 (date accessed 4 August, 2010).
4. Andreas Huyssen, "The Voids of Berlin," *Present Pasts: Urban Palimpsests and the Politics of Memory* (Stanford: Stanford University Press, 2003), pp. 49–71, p. 71; orig. *Critical Inquiry*, 24.1 (1997), pp. 57–81, pp. 80–81. Anthony Vidler, "'Building in Empty Space': Daniel Libeskind's Museum of the Voice," in Libeskind, *Daniel Libeskind: The Space of Encounter* (New York: Universe, 2000), pp. 222–24, p. 222.
5. Libeskind, "Between the Lines: Opening Speech, Berlin, 1999," in *Daniel Libeskind: The Space of Encounter*, pp. 23–29, p. 26.
6. Herbert Muschamp, "The New Berlin – Building on the Rubble of History; Once Again, a City Rewards the Walker," *The New York Times* (11 April, 1999).
7. Daniel Libeskind Papers (Getty Research Institute), Series 1–0, Roll 96**, Working Plans 1990.
8. Francesca Rogier, "The E.T.A. Hoffmann Garden of Daniel Libeskind," *Daidalos*, 65 (1997), pp. 110–13.
9. Both Libeskind and Gerz accused Eisenman of plagiarizing their respective entries in the second round of the Holocaust Memorial competition. Libeskind stated: "My columns are the same height and stand at the same distance from each other as the columns in Eisenman's new design, only that he wants to put up many more of them." See "Mahnmal: Regierung wehrt sich gegen Plagiatsvorwürfe," *Der Tagesspiegel* (2 February, 1999).
10. Libeskind, "Between the Lines," in *Daniel Libeskind: The Space of Encounter*, p. 25.
11. Libeskind, "Das Erinnern kann man nicht erfinden," *Berliner Zeitung* (17 July, 1995); cited in Ute Heimrod, Günter Schlusche, and Horst Seferenz, eds, *Der Denkmalstreit – das Denkmal? Die Debatte um das "Denkmal für die ermordeten Juden Europas". Eine Dokumentation* (Berlin: Philo Verlag, 1999), p. 472.

12. Rolf Bothe (director of the Berlin Museum at that time), quoted in Volker Heise and Susanne Holstein, eds, *Realisierungswettbewerb. Erweiterung Berlin Museum mit Abteilung Jüdisches Museum. Voraussetzungen, Verfahren, Ergebnisse* (Berlin: Senatsverwaltung für Bau- und Wohnungswesen, 1990), pp. 55, 166–67.

13. Susanna Sirefman states that Libeskind's Jewish Museum "is a brilliant monument; it is not a museum, and would do best to remain empty." Likewise, Vidler finds that as a "paradoxical statement of the twentieth-century monumental problem," it will always assert "the primacy of its own spaces as the exhibited work." Sirefman, "Formed and Forming: Contemporary Museum Architecture," *Daedalus. Journal of the American Academy of Arts and Sciences*, 128.3 (1999), pp. 297–320, p. 315; Vidler, "Building in Empty Space'," in Libeskind, *Daniel Libeskind: The Space of Encounter*, p. 224.

14. In 1998, Michael Blumenthal hired Jeshajahu Weinberg, who had created the narrative model of the Holocaust Memorial Museum's permanent exhibit in Washington, DC, but Weinberg died at the start of 2000. His replacements were author Nigel Cox and anthropologist-cum-museum-planner Ken Gorbey, whose previous experience with the Te Papa Museum in New Zealand included the organization of a high-tech exhibit, complete with roaring dinosaurs. The Jewish museum's exhibition space was thus organized with awareness of the American (as some have said: Disneyesque) interactive model, a wake-up call for Germany's more devout sensibilities regarding Judaism and the Holocaust. See the exhibition's vision statement and related documents released by *Die Welt* (29 July, 2000); "Pilotprojekt," *Der Tagesspiegel* (18 October, 2000); and Thomas Lackmann, *Jewrassic Park. Wie baut man (k)ein Jüdisches Museum in Berlin* (Berlin: Philo Verlag, 2000), pp. 174–75, 182–83. Gorbey defended his talents in Roger Cohen's "A Jewish Museum Mired in Dissent Struggles to Be Born in Berlin," *The New York Times* (15 August, 2000). See also Jan Okatar Fischer, "Full Disclosure: Invoking the Past in Recent German Exhibition Design," *Harvard Design Magazine*, 19 (2003/04), pp. 1–9, pp. 1–4.

15. Jörg Lau, "Erinnern ohne Masterplan," *Die Zeit* (4 May, 2000).

16. Thomas Lackmann, "Der letzte Schrei," *Der Tagesspiegel* (5 April, 2001). Lackmann came up with eight "theses" about the Jewish Museum's exhibits as a "museum of the present," a "museum of the world of Berlin," a "museum of questions of identity," and so on. Lackmann, *Jewrassic Park*, pp. 193–95.

17. Tom L. Freudenheim (the Jewish Museum's former assistant director), "Confronting Memory and Museums," in Todd Herzog and Sander L. Gilman, eds, *A New Germany in a New Europe* (New York: Routledge, 2001), pp. 143–65, p. 161.

18. James Ingo Freed, "The United States Holocaust Memorial Museum," *Assemblage*, 9 (1989), pp. 58–79, p. 71. In 1959, Oskar Hansen proposed a monument for Birkenau at Auschwitz of a granite path slashing diagonally across the camp. Freed originally wanted to include two symbolic cracks or fissures, and asked Richard Serra to help in the design, but changed his mind. See Adrian Dannatt, *United States Holocaust Memorial Museum. James Ingo Freed* (London: Phaidon, 1995), p. 15.

19. Daniel Abramson does not see this fundamental difference between Eisenman's and Libeskind's conceptual styles in his comment that both architects design (Holocaust) monuments of "little coherence" that "discourage

debate and paralyze action." Abramson, "Make History, Not Memory," *Harvard Design Magazine*, 9 (Fall 1999), pp. 78–83, p. 82.

20. Libeskind's design phase for the Jewish Museum constitutes an embedding of the lines of "no permanent structure" for such paper architecture projects as the Heraclitean *Chamber Works* (1983). Libeskind, "Unoriginal Signs," in Libeskind, *Chamber Works. Architectural Meditations on Themes from Heraclitus* (London: Architectural Association, 1983), p. 5. It is a work that goes too far into abstraction even for Eisenman, who in a commentary essay to the folio refers to it as "non-architecture'" (p. 6).

21. Libeskind, *radix-matrix. Architecture and Writings* (Munich and New York: Prestel, 1997), p. 113. See also Libeskind, "Global Building Sites – Between Past and Future," in Uta Staiger, Henriette Steiner and Andrew Webber, eds, *Memory Culture and the Contemporary City: Building Sites* (Basingstoke and New York: Palgrave Macmillan, 2009), pp. 69–81.

22. Libeskind, in Bernhard Schneider, *Daniel Libeskind. Jüdisches Museum Berlin* (Berlin and New York: Prestel, 1999), p. 33. See also Walter Benjamin's reference, in *One-Way Street* (*Einbahnstraße*, 1928), to the creative "world of things" (*Dingwelt*) of children at play with material items. Benjamin, *Gesammelte Schriften*, ed. Rolf Tiedemann and Hermann Schweppenhäuser (Frankfurt am Main.: Suhrkamp, 1972), vol. 4.1, p. 93.

23. Libeskind, *radix-matrix*, pp. 10, 26, 96.

24. Libeskind, "Traces of the Unborn," in Neil Leach, ed., *Architecture and Revolution: Contemporary Perspectives on Central and Eastern Europe* (New York: Routledge, 1999), pp. 127–29, p. 127.

25. See Libeskind, "Steinatem," in Heimrod et al., eds, *Der Denkmalstreit – das Denkmal?* pp. 887–88; Libeskind, "Stonebreath," in Libeskind, *The Space of Encounter*, pp. 159–60.

26. This is, in fact, how Eisenman differentiates his jointly designed project with Derrida for Bernard Tschumi's Parc de la Villette in Paris, from both modernism and Colin-Rowe-inspired postmodernism in architecture. Eisenman, "Separate Tricks," in Jeffrey Kipnis and Thomas Leeser, eds, *Chora L Works. Jacques Derrida and Peter Eisenman* (New York: The Monacelli Press, 1997), p. 135.

27. See Lucas Gehrmann and Marianne Greber, eds, *Judenplatz Wien 1996. Wettbewerb, Mahnmal und Gedenkstätte für die jüdischen Opfer des Naziregimes in Österreich 1938–1945* (Vienna: Folio, 1996), pp. 42–49. It is also worth noting that the Ground Zero master plan by Libeskind for New York has both a supertower (the monument) and the bathtub memorial park (the countermonument). In this instance, pride and loss work together – not guilt and loss, as in the German context of commemorating the Holocaust.

28. Libeskind, "Das Erinnern kann man nicht erfinden," in Heimrod et al., eds, *Der Denkmalstreit*, p. 472.

29. Harald Olkus, "Die Schatten der Vergangenheit," *Der Tagesspiegel* (4 December, 1999). Reichel recounts how Libeskind gave up his earlier design that included the underwater submerging of SS buildings at Sachsenhausen; Reichel, *Politik mit der Erinnerung*, pp. 114–17.

30. For some Brandenburg officials, Libeskind's design for Sachsenhausen was less a re-formation of the past than an "over-formation." A revised version ("Libeskind-II"), which was nonetheless approved by both the Stiftung

Brandenburgische Gedenkstätten and the federal government as the official plan for the area, was placed on hold for lack of funds. Eventually the design "Station Z" by HG Merz Architekten was completed in 2006, instead, for the camp's execution site. Alexander Pajević, "Landesdenkmalschützer gegen Libeskind-Plan für Sachsenhausen," *Der Tagesspiegel* (16 March, 2001); Kerstin Decker, "KZ-Sachsenhausen. Erinnern ist das Gegenspiel aus Nähe und Distanz," *Der Tagesspiegel* (17 March, 2001); Decker, "Gedenkstättenleiter: Libeskind-Plan soll verwirklicht werden," *Der Tagesspiegel* (18 March, 2001); and Elisabeth Plessen, "Gedenkstätte Sachsenhausen 'Station Z'," *Deutsche Bauzeitung*, 140.6 (2006), pp. 28–37.

31. In "Hope Incision," a superimposed displacement of the "former monumental central axis" of the camp was intended to combine history with hope: in short, a functional land use to "rehabilitate," even "reconsecrate," the infamous terrain. Libeskind, *radix-matrix*, p. 102.

32. Neil Leach, "Introduction," in Leach, ed., *Architecture and Revolution*, pp. 1–10, p. 7.

33. Bernhard Schulz, "In Sichtweite der Politik," *Der Tagesspiegel* (27 January, 2000). See also Ulrike Kunkel's review of the completed memorial as "discrete" and "blend[ing] in well." Kunkel, "Mahnmal. Mahnmal für dier ermordeten Juden Europas. Architekten: Eisenman Architects," *Deutsche Bauzeitung*, 140.6 (2006), pp. 66–68, p. 66.

34. Libeskind, "Traces of the Unborn," in Leach, ed., *Architecture and Revolution*, p. 129, 128, 129; see also Libeskind, *radix-matrix*, p. 10; and Libeskind, *The Space of Encounter*, p. 195.

35. The Grunewald memorial brings home the executioner-function of the deportation trains deployed by the Third Reich, as first emphasized by Raul Hilberg. There were 44 tracks to Auschwitz alone; 1,000–2,000 deportees were forced into each train, with 80–100 per freight car moving at 30 miles per hour. In 2008, a travelling exhibition of the Reichsbahn's involvement with the Holocaust, the "Train of Commemoration" (*Zug der Erinnerung*), symbolically re-enacted the fate of the 11,400 Jewish children deported from France, via a train that visited over 40 stations across Germany on its way to Auschwitz (after touring French cities a few years previously). Deutsche Bahn's director Hartmut Mehdorn reluctantly permitted a concurrent "Special Trains to Death" (*Sonderzüge in den Tod*) exhibition at Potsdamer Platz station. See Hilberg, "German Railroads/Jewish Souls," *Society*, 14.1 (November/December 1976), pp. 60–74; Simone Gigliotti, *The Train Journey: Transit, Captivity, and Witnessing in the Holocaust* (New York and Oxford: Berghahn Books, 2009); Alfred C. Mierzejewski, "A Public Enterprise in the Service of Mass Murder: The Deutsche Reichsbahn and the Holocaust," *Holocaust and Genocide Studies*, 15.1 (2001), pp. 33–46; and Leoni Wild, "Holocaust-Opfer in der Scham-Ecke," *Spiegel-Online* (23 January, 2008).

36. Rolf Goebel, "Berlin's Architectural Citations: Reconstruction, Simulation, and the Problem of Historical Authenticity," *PMLA*, 118.5 (2003), pp. 1268–89, pp. 1287, 1276.

37. Huyssen, *Present Pasts*, pp. 81, 84; orig. "After the War: Berlin as Palimpsest," *Harvard Design Magazine* (2000), pp. 70–75.

38. Fredric Jameson, "History Lessons," pp. 69–80, p. 74, and Libeskind, "Traces of the Unborn," p. 127, both in Leach, ed., *Architecture and Revolution*.

Part V

Rebranding Berlin: Global City Strategies for the Twenty-First Century

13
Berlin Borders – New Global City Orders

> *[A]nd it came to pass, when ... the people shouted with a*
> *great shout, that the wall fell down flat, so that the people*
> *went up into the city, every man straight before him ...*
> (Joshua 6.20, *The Holy Bible*, King James Version)

The Cold War, like the earlier world-system of colonialism (if beheld, that is, from a western vantage-point), provided a simplified ideology, a two-part model with which to explain the world. The urban centers of colonialism and the Cold War were, in a key sense, inverted images of each other. While Victorian London constituted a global distributional trading hub for British Imperial power, the post-World War II division of Berlin forged a "negative" metropolis with relevance far beyond the two German national identities. Walled Berlin was a world city all right, but hardly the kind that bestows the right flavor of wealth and centrality. The era of division inverted the city's existing urbanity and isolated its western section within the communist bloc, forcing each of its two parts to reinvent itself as an artificially holistic entity with a symbolic identity for each of the two major players of the Cold War. Berlin's ruptured spaces and flows displayed in everyday urban terms precisely where one world-system abruptly ended and another began.

By the time the Wall came down in 1989, globalization was well underway, and neither city nor nation-state existed in the form they once did. The impact of globalization on urban form has indeed been the "fundamental phenomenon" that Henri Lefebvre once recognized, one that pluralizes city centers while nonetheless insisting on new acts of centering.[1] The question emerges whether the notion of capital city collapses as well – and if so, this occurred at the precise point in time when Germany was reinstating Berlin as something resembling what it once was or promised Germans it might yet become. Some have gone so far as to believe that nowadays any city (that is, not just Berlin) "has lost its obligation to represent the nation"; today's capitalism "forces us to seek a balance between the former idea of the capital and the city as a commodity, as a product of technology and commercialism." Others question the need for capitalization in the context of (West) Germany's position as a world-export leader with a multi-polar metropolitan system.² Hence the reclamation of Berlin's capital status and the re-branding of Berlin's image on the urban, regional, and international levels have been (at times uneasy) partners since reunification. Moreover whether one likes it or not, the process of re-capitalizing a city for its national audience nowadays necessarily involves at least a staging of the globalizing turn in order to catch up with other leading capitals and global cities.

In terms of urban transformation, the cliché of the global city suggests a form that rises above social and territorial borders toward a new, wholly interconnected condition. The ideal global city is the virtual metropolis without walls, the city *sans frontières*. As architects Michael Gallis and James S. Russell have declared of globalization's impact: the "*connectivity*" that the information society makes possible has created "a new kind of urbanity. [...] In these networks, cities are the hubs for making, for distributing, and for consuming."³ Politicians, developers, and investors alike have subscribed to building the structures that best suit this vision of a limitless transformation of urban form in the electronic age. Only now, during a worldwide recession in the early twenty-first century, do the limitations of urban speculation seem all too apparent. Nonetheless, the dream of the city without borders still brings with it the promise of a new type of urban power. Saskia Sassen has emphasized how global cities are most often "postindustrial production sites" that re-centralize and reconsolidate between themselves the command functions of the world economy. Hence, for those cities capable of being fully integrated into the global network, this means the very opposite of the geographic "drift" sensed by Paul Virilio, that is, the purported death of the city brought about by the information superhighway.⁴ Yet Virilio's vision remains applicable in the ways in which new media form an essential part of inter-urban self-promotion and boosterist growth, and post-Wall Berlin has been no small player in these stakes.

Berlin's conquered borders certainly opened up as a realm of new "world order[s]" and psychological possibilities. While the concept of a borderless Berlin sounded tempting in the heady days of the *Wende* in the early 1990s, it clearly did not prove that practical. The advances in information technology notwithstanding, urban space cannot be turned into an ageographical entity – or its very inverse, a "universal conurbation," as Lewis Mumford predicted of the "de-materialization, or etherialization" caused by the "removal of limits" in the "Invisible City." William J. Mitchell declared in his update of Mumford's terms: "The network is the urban site before us, an invitation to design and construct the City of Bits (capital of the twenty-first century)." In fact, neither Mumford's nor Mitchell's McCluhanesque vision of cyberspace heralds the total demolition of urban context; after all, people still remain very much "bound to location."[5] Rather, the virtual realm of high tech is transferring itself onto our vision of the urban, and hence also onto the entities once represented by the urban.

These entities were first articulated by Aristotle in book VII of his *Politics*, specifically in his expectation that state territory should have clearly defined, controllable borders. These borders were, for Aristotle, symbolized in urban contexts by the formation of national capitals and the government buildings that the latter contain. Aristotle defined the borders of his ideal state as being of moderate size yet big enough for productive self-sufficiency, facilitating ease of exit but not alien access, and located on surveyable land with good transportation by sea and road, and near to agricultural lands and raw materials for manufacturing. Thus Aristotle's ideal bordered state is the opposite to the dream (or nightmare) of the virtual city as "uncontrolled territory," as Mitchell suggests, given the risk of cyberattack: "[T]he great power struggles of cyberspace will be over network topology, connectivity, and access – not the geographic borders and chunks of territory that have been fought over in the past."[6] But still, the more mundane truth for today's cities lies somewhere in between Mitchell's freewheeling City of Bits and Aristotle's totally bordered-in state. Any aspirations toward border-free status are usually articulated purely in the service of some form of desired Aristotelian control, especially an enhancement of the visibility of the urban setting – and for capital cities, that of the nation as well.

This *apparent* freedom or appeal of global city status featured strongly in the discourses involving Berlin after that city was voted, by the mere seventeen-vote majority of the Bundestag in 1991, as the reclaimed seat of government for the reunified Germany. The temporal-spatial trajectory for Berlin's self-reinvention effort corresponded with international post-communist celebration and with the "hot" global city theories of the 1990s. Berlin was now, it seemed, set to engage in competitive bidding on the hierarchical listings of what constitutes, or does not constitute, a global city. It is, after London, demographically the number two city within the European Union as measured by actual population within city limits (albeit dwarfed by the far more populous megacities of the broader European continent, Moscow and Istanbul). But according to a 2008 GaWC inventory of the top three tiers of 125 contemporary global cities – which ranks cities according to their representation by advanced producer services in law, accounting, banking/finance, and advertising – Berlin is nowhere near "alpha" global-city status. It fits squarely within the middle range of the "beta" globals; and yet even this is an advance, since in the 1990s it was still only deemed a "gamma" global, at a time when the most that Sassen was initially predicting for post-Wall Berlin is that it would be part of a "regional, yet transnationally oriented urban system," or city-circuit, in central Europe.[7]

Berlin may indeed be trying in vain to join the top tier of a club that is recognizable by what Manuel Castells has termed global "network-architecture" that replicates itself in certain key cities.[8] However, such networks tend to reproduce a First World agenda that has little to do with the broader truth that by now all cities are to some degree globalized or "globalizing."[9] As participants in global distribution and cospolitical connections, less-than-world cities are being impacted by the effects, both actual and predicted, of globalization, and they are changing their planning goals as a result.

Moreover, what came to really matter in this failed global-city bid were image and nostalgia, rather than substance. Understandably enough, Berlin's politicians and boosters wanted the once heavily bordered city of the Cold War era to embrace the opposite ideal of unfettered global freedom, hankering after an overhauled equivalent of the world city label that Berlin of the 1920s not only attained but exemplified.[10] The architectural transformations of Berlin during the Weimar Republic once underlined, both consciously and unconsciously, the urgency, visibility, and tactility of the city's world city status. Could the level of that era be attained again? That this belief in a city of densification (*Verdichtung*) went dormant rather than died is attested by the great boosterist emphasis placed on regaining and rehabbing Berlin's lost center(s). Promoters and planners for Berlin in the 1990s intended that the city's identity be enhanced by dint of re-centered, renovated, and reconnected boroughs, into an updated Proustian version of *temps retrouvé* – that is, into what it is remembered and more importantly marketed as having used to be.

Nonetheless, in the case of Berlin, postmodern urban planning still had to respond to the traumas wrought upon the city during the twentieth century. The Allied air war had voided the Nazi plans for the capital as "Germania," and then the Cold War era of the divided city had necessarily made any separate planning for the respective halves not as effective as planning for the whole would have been. The boundary-free "atomization and disintegration" that Virilio looked forward to was precisely *not* what took over the New Berlin in the 1990s, despite the city's embrace of the global city epithet.[11] This apparently contradictory tale fits in well with globalization practices that have produced a paradoxically increased focus on localized identities. To some degree, we can find a blend of the new virtual and the old territorial in any postmodern city-building trajectory. Thus alongside the globalization marketing wave for the reunified capital, Berlin's planners made use of re-territorializing strategies whereby the rebuilt center bespeaks "images of locality and historicity," in short a "reinscription of national legacies and subnational identifications," as Lutz Koepnick has observed: "... it is Berlin's drive toward the global that produces locality and historical particularity in the first place."[12] The desired goal of a renewed concentric center for Berlin that reinvigorates the presence of a corporate and governmental elite, strengthens the European-cum-German ideal of the old town (*Altstadt*), signifies urban historical continuity and community, and achieves a better recognition of capital-city status within the strong federalist system of Germany, and by extension within Europe itself – all this still remains an incomplete process.

Whatever Berlin's long-term achievements will finally be in terms of its renewed sites of *genius loci*, we must also situate them within the millennial skepticism that sees urban identities, no matter how overwritten and tended to, at permanent risk of losing out to today's myriad, globalized "non-places" like malls, freeways, and airports that no longer take the history and the locality of the city – even the European city – into consideration.[13] On some level, every single instance of post-Wall re-urbanization (like the gentrification of 1980s and 1990s London, Baltimore, or New York) risks producing a series of "urbane disguises," a "city of simulations" superseding the historical city.[14] Worse yet, the renewal of a city's image can forge lures that are overly controlling in terms of who can be there, and what may occur there (in short, the "bread and circuses" thesis).[15] What city developers ostensibly aim for is, therefore, not always what the residents on the receiving end will get.

None other than David Harvey has come to the defense of these processes that he terms "urban entrepreneurialism." Berlin is but one of the more visible and dramatic participants in a broader evolution of and by cities toward a competitive realm of the virtual in which image-city competes against image-city. Sometimes a city tries to copy another city's good idea (for example, Berlin may yet succeed in building its own version of the London Eye ferris wheel in the Tiergarten). Other times, cities use their specific localities to forge unique paths of identity-renewal (such as in Hamburg's ongoing renewal of its harbor as the new *HafenCity* and the re-development of its port islands known as the "Leap Across the Elbe").[16] Harvey defines this shift toward urban entrepreneurialism as an inevitable and distinguishing feature of the service economy in the post-Fordist (essentially, post-1970s) era. The irony here is that place and identity (if not Proustian time) *can* be regained thereby. When city boosters remake their city's image they sometimes in fact do provide precisely the solidarity and communal sense of identity so sorely needed by the mixed groups of urban dwellers today. Harvey points out: "[W]hen an urban terrain is opened for display, fashion and the 'presentation of self' in a surrounding of spectacle and play," it is possible that "everyone ... can participate in the production of an urban image through their production of urban space," and "all can at least feel some sense of belonging to that place." [17] Place-remaking can achieve new urban identities, even though it remains a risky business prone to the future economic climate into which it is necessarily projected, and even though it is never over and always unfolding.

As a caveat, Harvey has emphasized the destructively zero-sum consequences to such games of wealth-creation in the name of *genius loci*, as undertaken by urban governments who often compete at each other's expense. His critical take on the postmodern service era's effect on cities rather resembles an update of film director Fritz Lang's disturbing scene of Joh Fredersen as the ultra-modern capitalist in apparently total control of the city in *Metropolis* of 1927. And yet Harvey refuses to totally demonize the ongoing hegemony of urban entrepreneurialism, indicating rather that its most frequent crime, that of the "triumph of image over substance," remains a relatively innocuous house of cards.[18]

We should therefore bear in mind that the rebranding of Berlin and of other cities brings with it some important illustrations for our current condition of post-1989 urban globalization. The New Berlin's market-driven transformations over the last two decades have, theoretically at least, offered both new and native Berliners an opportunity to become active agents, not just those who have been acted upon. Berlin, in the manner of cities like Warsaw, Budapest, Prague, and Moscow, has been busily engaged in the boosterist activities of promotion and construction that – for all their imported faults from the West, as well as temptations of the all-too-human kind – nonetheless together constitute the first stage in the journey toward the regenerative direction of *civitas*. East

Berlin's (re)turn toward capitalism has been a globalizing turn, but it has not yet been one that bequeaths top global city status. It has more to do with what Karl Schlögel perceives to be a post-Iron Curtain re-opening and repositioning of any number of borders, a process underway across the entire continent: the reworking of boundaries in interurban European competition and centrality, infrastructure and distribution, migrant traffic and networking. For cities of the former Eastern Bloc, this amounts to a re-growth period for what were the "de-urbanized wastelands" of cities under communism. Close observers of these ongoing urban transformations like Schlögel have noted that the central and East European urban system is in the midst of creating many new and complex center-periphery relationships: a re-shaping, post-socialist "reforesting" process that cannot be judged according to exclusively western expectations of success.[19]

Moreover, no matter which side of the former Iron Curtain a city is on, and no matter how left-wing an urban government happens to be, these days all major municipalities are induced to behave like entrepreneurial neo-conservatives and engage in interurban, competitive city-marketing, with a constant investment focus on the regeneration of the downtown through heritage tourism, infrastructural upgrades (in rail, air, highway, and telecommunications), and the reproduction of certain urban structures shown to be highly effective in staging spectacular ephemera – such as convention centers, stadiums, malls, and museums by star architects. For cities in the five new (formerly East German) federal states in particular, self-reinvention, especially the improvement of "locational quality" (*Standortqualität*), has become a basic necessity after the harsh impact of de-industrialization and unemployment, the two by-products of reunification and the Treuhand's privatization efforts.[20]

Indeed, manufacturing is often duty bound to behave like an urban entertainment industry in order to lure product buyers: one of Germany's major tourist attractions has emerged in the West German city of Wolfsburg, which used to be relatively neglected due to its proximity to the Iron Curtain. Since 2000, however, Wolfsburg has boasted the *Autostadt*: a luxury theme park on over 60 acres, built to induce an average of two million annual visitors to purchase Volkswagen automobiles (the city's main industry since its founding during the Third Reich). Such is the hold of the automobile brand over the city that the latter temporarily changed its name to Golfsburg in the fall of 2003 to assist the launch of the latest model. Its corporate glass headquarters, designed by Gunter Henn, were featured in Tom Tykwer's film, *The International*

(2009), but not as anything remotely connected to a people-friendly brand. Instead, it housed the evil think-tank of a global bank conspiracy – an all-seeing corporate eye turned on the little man from Interpol (played by Clive Owen) who tried to fight back. Thus in this post-Wall filmic case at least, transparency in architecture means opacity despite all the glass curtain walls.

Tykwer's film depicts western capitalism-run-amok without making recourse to the particular temptations that arose in the wake of communism. Yet Harvey's urban entrepreneurial model, predicated as it is upon an expectation of common decency, may have found its limit-case not just in post-Wall Berlin but in central and East Europe's cities offering massive post-socialist temptation to all-out gain. Castells acknowledged that while the incorporation of cities in the ex-Soviet bloc amounted to the "last frontier" for capitalism's expansion of the global economy, it is highly unlikely that most of the 400 million potential denizen-consumers in these cities will personally reap any of the rewards in the foreseeable future.[21]

Given this chance to conquer, we can better understand how the initial drive to fill in reunified Berlin became so aggressive. Public and private development in Berlin rose from under $5 billion in 1990 to over $15 billion by the end of the decade. By the end of the 1990s, Berlin had 300 major construction sites (50 large-scale ones in Mitte alone, the downtown area most obviously affected by real estate's investment in the East after the fall of the Wall).[22] Real estate speculation caused Berlin office space to expand twenty times. For a while in the 1990s, building volume was at DM27 billion, essentially making Berlin the largest building site in the world.

The investment in post-Wall Berlin had unique connotations – as a declaration of intent from Chancellor Gerhard Schröder's inaugural speech of 1998 made clear: "For some people, 'Berlin' still sounds too Prussian, authoritarian, too centralistic. We intend to oppose this image with our completely unaggressive vision of a 'republic of the new center [*Mitte*]'... symbolically, this new center is taking shape in Berlin – at the center of Germany and the center of Europe."[23] Answering the call from on high, the boosters variously devised a capital city that was to become a house made of Critical Reconstructionist cards, an "ideological super-structure" of overly rushed international and federal investment.[24] The "New Berlin" phrase that was adopted by the capital's own marketing company hearkens back to the 1920s' use of the term. The recycled moniker represented an irresistible opportunity to rebuild and to re-form the face of Germany for the post-Cold War era.

As part of this initial idealism, euphoria, and greed of building the Berlin Republic into being, tax breaks and city loans were given far too readily to real estate developers who promptly over-built and over-renovated both on the commercial and residential levels, and then waited during most of the 1990s for a reluctant government to relocate. In 2001, the Berlin Senate Office for Urban Development reported that in terms of its 20 million square yards of office space, post-Wall Berlin was now ranked third in line next to such "alpha" European globals like Paris and London (with their respective 37+ and 32+ million square yards of office space). In other words, Berlin literally constructed for itself, in terms of commercial architecture, the shape of a European world city. There was just one (not insignificant) problem with this picture: Europe and the world have yet to respond to the invitation. Berlin fell prey to urban capitalism's weak underbelly tendency of credit-financed overbuilding, and quite literally over-produced itself. Understandably, then, Berlin's development management during the last decade of the twentieth century has been deemed a case of "'worst practice' urban governance."[25]

The sheer volume of empty residential and office space in East Germany arose because until 1998, billions of DM in tax breaks (granted by the now-infamous *Fördergebietsgesetz* that permitted first 50 per cent, and then in 1997 and 1998 25 per cent of tax breaks on new buildings in the East) were offered to West German companies that built or renovated offices and apartments that did not fill with tenants.[26] Commercial architecture (stores and restaurants at ground level, offices upstairs) was used as a tool by which Berlin would surely, somehow, become the metropolis boosters wanted it to be. Consideration given to demand was lacking, as it was with the top-down urban planning exacted on renewing residential downtowns of East Germany. The federal, state, and local government planners could not make people want to live in East German downtowns when they needed to move west to find work, no more than the Berlin senate and city boosters could make corporations relocate their main offices to the new capital. Thus the West German federalist system has been holding out on Berlin. The city is now more than $90 billion (€62 billion) in debt, mostly due to such deals that were simply not based on the economic reality of the place in which they occurred.

Dreams of a borderless, globally significant Berlin receded as economic opportunities fell short for the rejoined city, and the New Berlin got the building-site blues. Evelyn Roll blamed the "gobbledygook" blathered on and on by the capital's "inventors of stimulation" (*Erregungsfabrikanten*) for the resulting stagnation.[27] One of the country's largest building concerns, Philipp Holzmann, which invested billions of euros in post-Wall projects in East Germany, went bankrupt in 2002 – so the consequences of overproduction of real estate in East Germany finally reached its originators.[28] Thus building-site ruins and voids began to de-form the New Berlin. It took fifteen years, for example, for the twelve-storey-high Landsberger Arcades, a massive complex on Landsberger Allee in Lichtenberg designed by the late Aldo Rossi, to be completed. Eventually the structure, which had gained the informal name *Rossi-Ruine*, was opened as the business-oriented Andel's Hotel. Another example of Berlin's stalled commercial development, this time in West Berlin, has been the "Zoo Window," the much-anticipated renovation of a triangular lot on Hardenbergplatz, diagonally across from the Zoo train station. After over a decade of an embarrassingly empty building site at the heart of City-West, the 36-storey *Zoofenster* skyscraper is finally going up. The tower's completion may help fill newly developed empty office and retail space nearby, such as in the adjacent City Light House. But it will certainly dominate both its neighbors, the Zoo station to the immediate north and the Kaiser Wilhelm Memorial Church on Breidscheidplatz to the east, especially since its construction necessitated the demolition of the (in)famous Schimmelpfeng Haus that had stood in between, a bridge-structure in the 1960s-style of Le Corbusier's "machine for living."[29]

A representative caesura marking the city's dashed hopes came as early as 1993 when Berlin lost to Sydney in its bid to host the 2000 Olympics.[30] (At least this sports industry blow to the capital's place-marketing efforts was compensated for when Berlin hosted the soccer World Cup in 2006.) A more recent illustration of this deflation of expectations would be the case of eBay, which opened up its German base at Europarc Dreilinden – in other words, an actualization of borderless capitalist exchange now operating in one of Berlin's new business parks, located at (of all places) a former Cold War "control point" (*Kontrollpunkt*), a checkpoint known by the American military as Checkpoint Bravo, for West German traffic entering and leaving West Berlin along the GDR-transit route. But in a reverse move in early 2010, in the midst of the global recession, 360 eBay employees had to be let go.

In the globalization rush for the German capital, post-communist urban transformations have affected both the infrastructural *base* and the architectural *superstructure* (or visage). One can imagine Aristotle looking favorably on the way in which post-Wall Berlin, in order to proceed up the global urban ladder, has sought to re-introduce a high degree of nodal relevance and efficiency – in air, rail, and highway links, as well as in telecommunications infrastructure. A still-significant problem for Berlin is that its geographical position during the Cold War made it into a subsidized "outpost" from which most companies had fled westwards. Surrounded and cut in two for twenty-eight years by the Wall, Berlin was shut out from the trade corridor that continues to extend across western Europe between London and Milan. This corridor, known for its shape as the metaphorical "Blue Banana," has encouraged polarization between cities in Europe.[31] While the conurbations within this central business corridor do include two West German areas, the Rhein-Main and Rhein-Ruhr regions, Berlin is situated too far to the east, and thus still remains outside its scope. As Sassen succinctly noted, the New Berlin found itself "definitely on the periphery."[32]

As if to illustrate Sassen's point, at the millennium the German capital even temporarily lost its direct transatlantic flights. Re-introduced by Lufthansa in the spring of 2001 after a gap of four years, the Berlin-Washington, DC flight was regarded as a symbolic boosterist gesture rather than a financially viable one, and it was cancelled again less than two weeks after 9/11. At this time, Berlin had no direct flights to either the American or the Asian continent – but it did have a quick two-hour Aeroflot one to Moscow. (Berlin's rail connections are also still very much a part of the communist past: in ninety hours, one can travel via western Europe's longest direct rail route to the Siberian city of Novosibirsk over three thousand miles away.) By 2005, after a three-year gap, Berlin-Tegel airport regained two transatlantic connections with Delta/Air France and Continental to New York; but the US ambassador to Germany still cannot take a direct Berlin-DC flight. The situation is slowly improving: in 2008, Berlin-Tegel became the fourth German airport to have a direct route to Beijing with Hainan Airlines.

The admittedly still rather second-rate air transportation connections for the reunified German capital have hampered the city's few global players. Indeed, precious few corporations (Deutsche Bahn AG; one of Siemens' two main offices; and pharmaceuticals Bayer Schering-Pharma, Sanofi-Aventis, and Pfizer) have moved their headquarters or at least their European representations to Berlin since reunification. Further, the governmental subventions for West Berlin should not have been eradicated as swiftly as they were after the Wall; otherwise Germany might have fared better at holding onto, or attracting, companies that decided to relocate production to the newly available, cheaper eastern European countries or to Asia. Even the major investors for the new Potsdamer Platz have not displayed much Berlin-loyalty. Sony sold its own Sony Center in 2008, just eight years after its opening, to Morgan Stanley and other US-German investment companies, at a loss of €150 million; and in 2010 the landmark structure designed by Helmut Jahn passed hands again at a loss, this time to the South Korean pension firm NPS. Daimler, the second major investor in Potsdamer Platz, sold its share of retail and corporate space in 2007 to SEB, a Frankfurt-based asset management group.

One can but hope that Berlin will be able to escape its relatively isolated condition within one generation of planning. Due to the ongoing development of high-tech communications and high-speed rail and highway systems, an ever more rapid networking of European cities with each other is emerging. In the case of Europe, "time-space maps" are being applied to help predict the future rankings of cities: these are non-topographical, literally "warped" maps that show the shrinking of distances between cities according to time-units of travel. Geographers have predicted that ongoing and future infrastructural improvements will, if completed, cut in half most travel times from the German capital to cities within Europe by 2020, which would significantly condense the time-space map for the Berlin region.[33] Examples of these projects include the seven new highways built by the federally owned company DEGES, and Berlin's new Central Rail Station (2006). What applies here to Berlin is even more crucial for peripherally located East European nations that have recently joined the European Union. This kind of "time-space" accessibility of cities *vis-à-vis* their distribution of trade and telecommunications thus becomes a vital planning consideration for luring advanced producer services to those locations.

Most significantly, the new Berlin Brandenburg airport (designed by a group of architects including Meinhard von Gerkan) is presently scheduled to open a year late in 2012, at a cost of over €2.5 billion, as a massive extension of the existing Schönefeld airport. Originally termed Berlin Brandenburg International (BBI), and now with the additional moniker "Willy Brandt Airport," it will market its advantage of an hour's less travel time between western and eastern Europe as well as Asia, and could feasibly start a new chapter in postwar/post-Wall Berlin's thwarted global connectivity. Such is at least the planners' goal. Businesses are also betting on it, with four industrial parks already emerging in the vicinity of the airport's construction site, and the nearby Adlershof high-tech center already housing over 800 companies and 14,000 employees.[34] Yet such a chapter will not start immediately, since Lufthansa has insisted all along that it will not move its hubs from Frankfurt am Main and Munich to the new BBI. Certainly, Berlin's current air traffic flying into Tegel and Schönefeld is full of low-cost tourism carriers (most prominently Air Berlin, which is nonetheless Germany's second-largest airline), not the multiple business flight connections upon which an airline builds any decision to relocate its hub(s). In short, BBI, with its two runways and passenger traffic about half that of Frankfurt, is destined to open only as Germany's third-busiest airport – with room to expand. For a decade, many Berliners thought the airport would never get built: anti-development lawsuits on behalf of 4,000 members of the citizens' protest group *Bürgerverein Brandenburg-Berlin* reached, in the end unsuccessfully, the Leipzig federal court level in 2006.[35] As one of Germany's three "city-states," Berlin may enjoy state-like powers unto itself, but has no jurisdiction in Brandenburg, where the airport is partly located. Yet popular interest in the airport has evidently grown: over 50,000 members of the public attended an open day for the "topping off" of the terminal's *Infotower* in May 2010.

Compared to the enormity of re-centering Berlin's infrastructural relevance for the world, re-capitalizing Berlin purely on the super-structural level seemed a far easier route for the quicker production of surface results. Iconic replacements or inventions of structures by star architects have certainly added to the city's (inter)national prominence. Essentially this has been achieved by commodifying the city's public and commercial spheres. Privately sponsored architecture more than publicly funded government buildings has provided a post-Cold War facelift; commercial architecture including office space exerted a "considerable influence on the new face of Berlin."[36] Most of the structures for the governmental presence have simply not been able to compete.[37] When it comes to the re-branding of a now fully or still nascent demo-cratic city, new commercial sites often outnumber governmental ones in both quantity and effect.

We should, however, suspect that Berlin's rushed architectonic facelift is hiding something – all the debates concerning the structural style of the New Berlin amount to a form of commercial cladding that conveniently lets the other decisions continue to be made in private and shielded from public input – in other words, "power and its uses, wealth and its uses," as Peter Marcuse conspiratorially wrote in a Berlin-specific adaptation of Harold Lasswell's maxim of "who gets what, when, how."[38] In the early 1990s developers were making a start-ling profit of 40 per cent off the reunified capital. In many instances, Berlin's municipal governments used a cartel of building firms, and the nobly named "Central Office for Fighting Corruption" (*Zentralstelle Korruptionsbekämpfung*) must have felt like it was chasing windmills when faced with the myriad cases of building corruption – 119 in the first half of 1998 alone, its first year of operation in the city's legal department. The KOAI (*Koordinierungsausschuß für innenstädtische Investitionen*, or Coordination Committee for Inner City Investments) functioned rather like a secret society to remake the Friedrichstrasse from a socialist into capitalist retail landscape, but using a few large plots instead of the original multiple-lot footprint.[39] One of its founders, a building senator called Wolfgang Nagel, moved in 1996 over to the Fundus Group, a real estate development company whose projects included Quartier 206, part of the multi-level Friedrichstadtpassagen mall that extends along the Friedrichstraße as a rival "street." The other KOAI founder, building senate member Hanno Klein, was murdered by a letter bomb in 1991.[40]

Another instance that undermined the potential of urban entrepreneurialism to do any communal good whatsoever in post-Wall Berlin has been the infamous Bankgesellschaft Berlin, which was founded in 1994 by the city's CDU leader Klaus-Rüdiger Landowsky with the agreement of the entire coalition-based Berlin Senate. Landowsky was a former law partner of the then Mayor Eberhard Diepgen (likewise CDU). The Bankgesellschaft Berlin encouraged real estate investments from which a few became very rich; and it proceeded to camouflage the city's descent into bankruptcy by the end of the decade. As a result of "risk prevention regulation" (*Risiko-Abschirmungs-Gesetz*), the city's massive debt is now being paid for by Berlin's taxpayers and by reductions in a range of city services (such as parks upkeep, or snow clearance during extreme winter weather conditions), even as certain members of the city's elite have profited from their guaranteed investments. Worse yet, given the federal tax write-off for offices without tenants, Berlin's insolvency would have existed even without being compounded many times over by the corrupt bank, the scandal surrounding which brought about a change of Berlin's government.[41] Even though post-Wall Berlin's rebranding as a would-be global city should not be made over into a overly reductive story of secret investments and fraud, there were clearly great perils in letting big business dictate the direction of planning in any former central or east European city (a denomination to which Berlin also belongs) without heed to the societal after-effects, let alone the erasure of important monuments.[42]

We see, then, that the reunified German capital has been host to an extreme experiment. With a current monetary building volume of €14.7 billion ($18.8 billion), Berlin's transformation has been a process with upsides and especially downsides caused by the multiple concerted efforts at speeding up the urban processes of globalized, capital-inducing, nodal relevance.[43] This brings us to the question: why after all do we insist on building for power and display? Not just for a nation's might or for higher urban international rankings, one might say, but for the psychological well-being of the city's denizens: to claim in three-dimensional terms that its genius loci (even if it is remade) is one of permanence. Certainly, candidates for Berlin's ultimate post-Expressionistic *Stadtkrone*, or "city crown," abound – be this completed projects like the entertainment areal of the rebuilt Potsdamer Platz or the re-domed Reichstag; still ongoing projects such as the "Mediaspree" corporate development along the riverbank at the Osthafen; as well as future re-urbanization plans for the areas around Berlin's Central Station (the Lehrter Stadtquartier / Europacity) and the Alexanderplatz.[44] The conundrum is that these days re-centering the city amounts to urban self-endangerment: the stronger, wealthier city is in fact far more at risk in the post-9/11 era. The greater the number of critical iconic points, the more places there are that can be attacked.[45] Global, nodal cities become the most at risk – thus all the attempts to re-chart this era's Berlin as a city beyond borders may yet lead to further impermanence.

Notes

1. Henri Lefebvre, *Writings on Cities*, trans. Eleonore Kofman and Elizabeth Lebas (Oxford: Blackwell, 1996), p. 208.
2. See, respectively, Arata Isozaki, in Hans Stimmann, ed., *Babylon, Berlin etc. Das Vokabular der europäischen Stadt* (Basel: Birkhäuser, 1995), pp. 160–67, p. 163; and Dieter Läpple, "The German Metropolis System – An Alternative to the Global City? A Trend Reversal in Urban Development," in Oliver Hamm and IBA Hamburg, eds, *Metropolis: Reflections* (Berlin: Jovis Verlag, 2007), pp. 162–71, p. 165.
3. Michael Gallis and James S. Russell, "World City: Why Globalization Makes Cities More Important than Ever," *Architectural Record*, 3 (2002), pp. 70–73, p. 72.
4. Saskia Sassen, *The Global City: New York, London, Tokyo* (Princeton: Princeton University Press, 1991), p. 126; Paul Virilio, "The Overexposed City," in K. Michael Hays, ed., *Architecture Theory since 1968* (Cambridge, MA: MIT Press, 1998), pp. 540–50, p. 544.
5. Lewis Mumford, *The City in History: Its Origins, Its Transformations, and Its Prospects* (New York: Harcourt Brace & Co., 1989, orig. 1961), pp. 540, 563, 540; William J. Mitchell, *City of Bits: Space, Place, and the Infobahn* (Cambridge, MA: MIT Press, 1995), p. 24; and Joseph Rykwert, *The Seduction of Place: The History and Future of the City* (New York: Vintage, 2002), p. 158.
6. See Mitchell, *City of Bits*, pp. 155, 150; and Aristotle, *Politics*, in *Aristotle in 23 Volumes*, vol. 21, trans. H. Rackham (Cambridge, MA: Harvard University Press; London: William Heinemann Ltd., 1944), VII.1327a–1331a, at: www.perseus.

tufts.edu/hopper/text?doc=Perseus%3Atext%3A1999.01.0058%3Abook%
3D7%3Asection%3D1327a (date accessed 20 June, 2010).

7. In the 2008 rankings of the Globalization and World Cities Research Group
    and Network, Frankfurt am Main is Germany's highest ranked global city,
    with "alpha minus" status; Berlin and Hamburg both receive "beta" rankings;
    Munich and Düsseldorf "beta minus"; and Stuttgart "gamma plus." See
    www.lboro.ac.uk/gawc/world2008t.html (date accessed 9 August, 2010);
    J.V. Beaverstock, P.J. Taylor, and R.G. Smith, "A Roster of World Cities," *Cities*,
    16.6 (1999), pp. 445–58, p. 456; and Saskia Sassen, *Metropolen des Weltmarkts. Die
    neue Rolle der Global Cities* (Frankfurt am Main: Campus Verlag, 1996), p. 62.

8. Manuel Castells, "Space Flow – der Raum der Ströme," in Stefan Bollmann,
    ed., *Kursbuch Stadt. Stadtleben und Stadtkultur an der Jahrtausendwende*
    (Stuttgart: Deutsche Verlags-Anstalt, 1999), pp. 39–81, p. 43.

9. See Andreas Huyssen, "Introduction: World Cities, World Cultures," in
    Huyssen, ed., *Other Cities, Other Worlds: Urban Imaginaries in a Globalizing
    Age* (Durham: Duke University Press, 2008), pp. 1–25, pp. 10–11; Saskia
    Sassen, ed., *Deciphering the Global: Its Scales, Spaces and Subjects* (New York:
    Routledge, 2007); Peter Marcuse and Ronald van Kempen, eds, *Globalizing
    Cities: A New Spatial Order?* (Malden: Blackwell, 2000); Doreen Massey, "A
    Global Sense of Place," *Marxism Today* (June 1991), pp. 24–29; and Anthony
    D. King, *Urbanism, Colonialism, and the World Economy* (New York: Routledge,
    1990), p. 82.

10. See Janet Ward: *Weimar Surfaces: Urban Visual Culture in 1920s Germany*
    (Berkeley: University of California Press, 2001).

11. Virilio, "The Overexposed City," p. 549.

12. Lutz Koepnick, *Framing Attention: Windows on Modern German Culture*
    (Baltimore: Johns Hopkins University Press, 2007), pp. 241, 242. See also Virag
    Molnar, "The Cultural Production of Locality: Reclaiming the 'European
    City' in Post-Wall Berlin," *International Journal of Urban and Regional Research*,
    34.2 (2010), pp. 281–309.

13. See Marc Augé, *Non-Places: Introduction to an Anthropology of Supermodernity*
    (New York: Verso, 2008); Keller Easterling, *Enduring Innocence: Global Architecture
    and Its Political Masquerades* (Cambridge, MA: MIT Press, 2005); Iain Sinclair,
    London Orbital: A Walk Around the M25 (London: Granta, 2002); and Hans
    Ibelings, *Supermodernism: Architecture in the Age of Globalization* (Rotterdam:
    NAi, 1998).

14. Michael Sorkin, "Introduction: Variations on a Theme Park," in Sorkin, ed.,
    Variations on a Theme Park: The New American City and the End of Public Space
    (New York: Hill & Wang, 1992), pp. xi–xv, p. xiv.

15. David Harvey, *Spaces of Capital: Towards a Critical Geography* (Edinburgh:
    Edinburgh University Press, 2001), p. 364; and Gerry Kearns and Chris Philo,
    "Culture, History, Capital: A Critical Introduction to the Selling of Places,"
    in Kearns and Philo, eds, *Selling Places: The City as Cultural Capital, Past and
    Present* (New York: Pergamon Press, 1993), pp. 1–32, p. 5.

16. Jörn Walter, "Perspectives of the Metropolis. The Internationale Bauausstellung
    in the Context of Hamburg's Urban Development," in Hamm and IBA
    Hamburg, eds, *Metropolis: Reflections*, pp. 12–31.

17. David Harvey, *Spaces of Capital*, pp. 345–68, p. 364.

18. Harvey, *Spaces of Capital*, p. 365.

19. Karl Schlögel, "The Comeback of the European Cities," *International Review of Sociology*, 16.2 (2006), pp. 471–85, p. 481.
20. Jutta A. Helm, "Introduction. German Cities between Globalization and Unification," *German Politics and Society*, 16.4 (1998), pp. 7–17, p. 8; see also Harvey, *Spaces of Capital*, p. 349.
21. Manuel Castells, *The Rise of the Network Society*, vol. 1 of Castells, *The Information Age: Economy, Society and Culture* (Cambridge, MA: Blackwell, 1996), pp. 136–37. Recent scholarship on the ongoing capitalist transformations of post-communist European cities is finding that these cities' paths to capitalism have produced varied new hybridities not entirely subsumable within western patterns. See Florian Koch and Marianne Rodenstein, eds, *Die europäische Stadt in Transformation: Stadtplanung und Stadtentwicklungspolitik im postsozialistischen Warschau* (Wiesbaden: VS Verlag, 2009); Kiril Stanilov, ed., *The Post-Socialist City. Urban Form and Space Transformations in Central and Eastern Europe after Socialism* (Dordecht: Springer, 2007); and F.E. Ian Hamilton, Kaliopa Dimitrovska Andrews, and Natasa Pichler-Milanovic, eds, *Transformation of Cities in Central and Eastern Europe: Towards Globalisation* (Tokyo/New York/Paris: United Nations University Press, 2005).
22. Heinrich Wefing, "Berlin," in Bollmann, ed., *Kursbuch Stadt*, pp. 143–59, p. 144; and Stephan Lanz and Jochen Becker, *Metropolen* (Hamburg: Rotbuch Verlag, 2001), p. 75.
23. Chanceller Gerhard Schröder's inaugural speech, "Because We Have Faith in Germany's Strength" (10 November, 1998). Quoted by Jochen Becker, "Planet Berlin. In the History Park of the New Center," in Dave Hullfish Bailey, *Union Pacific. Berlin's Neue Mitte and the Fringes of Las Vegas* (Berlin: Vice Versa Verlag, 1999), pp. 1–14, p. 2.
24. Uwe Rada, *Berliner Barbaren. Wie der Osten in den Westen kommt* (Berlin: BasisDruck, 2001), p. 56. See also Hartmut Häußermann's and Elizabeth Strom's accurate Cassandra-call in "Berlin: The Once and Future Capital," *International Journal of Urban and Regional Research*, 18.2 (1994), pp. 335–46.
25. Stefan Krätke, "City of Talents? Berlin's Regional Economy, Socio-Spatial Fabric and 'Worst Practice' Urban Governance," *International Journal of Urban and Regional Research*, 28.3 (2004), pp. 511–29.
26. See Stefan Krätke and Renate Borst, *Berlin: Metropole zwischen Boom und Krise* (Opladen: Leske + Budrich, 2000), p. 143.
27. Evelyn Roll, "Raststätte 'Osteuropa'," *Süddeutsche Zeitung* (7/8 June, 2003).
28. Edmund L. Andrews, "Big Builder in Germany is Bankrupt," *The New York Times* (22 March, 2002).
29. The *Zoofenster* skyscraper is designed by Christoph Mäckler: see www.chm.de/de/zoofenster.html (date accessed 2 June, 2010). Ground was first broken in 1999 for a new skyscraper hotel to re-anchor the Ku'Damm area known as City-West. But when investors withdrew in 2002, Hilton also stepped back. New investment from Abu Dhabi (Harvest United Enterprises) enabled Hilton to step back in, however, with Waldorf Astoria (a member of the Hilton chain) as the major tenant of the new tower. See Cay Dobberke, "Jede Woche eine Etage. Zoofenster-Hochhaus," *Der Tagesspiegel* (22 June, 2010); and Nikolaus Bernau, "Fenster zum Zoo," *Berliner Zeitung* (6 May, 2009).
30. Harald Bodenschatz, *Städtebau in Berlin. Schreckbild und Vorbild für Europa* (Berlin: Dom Publishers, 2010), p. 107.

31. See Michael Wegener, Klaus R. Kunzmann, and Klaus Spiekermann, "Wachsendes Europa – schrumpfender Kontinent," *arch +*, 122 (1994), pp. 238–33, p. 29; and Andreas Faludi, ed., *European Spatial Planning* (Cambridge, MA: Lincoln Institute of Land Policy, 2002), pp. 24, 52, 89.

32. Saskia Sassen, "Ausgrabungen in der 'Global City'," in Albert Scharenberg, ed., *Berlin: Global City oder Konkursmasse? Eine Zwischenbilanz zehn Jahre nach dem Mauerfall* (Berlin: Karl Dietz Verlag, 2000), p. 17. Overcoming Berlin's peripheral position also dominates the assessment of Karl Lenz's "Berlin: Hauptstadt zwischen Vergangenheitsbewältigung und Neuorientierung," in Rita Schneider-Sliwa, ed., *Städte im Umbruch. Neustrukturierung von Berlin, Brüssel, Hanoi, Ho Chi Minh Stadt, Hongkong, Jerusalem, Johannesburg, Moskau, St. Petersburg, Sarajewo und Wien* (Berlin: Reimer, 2002), pp. 11–45.

33. Wegener, Kunzmann, and Spiekermann, "Wachsendes Europa," p. 32.

34. Nicholas Kulish, "2 Sides to Berlin's New Airport: Some See Shining Beacon, Some a Waste of Money," *The New York Times* (9 March, 2010); IHK Berlin, press announcement (3 November, 2009), at: www.berlin.ihk24. de/servicemarken/presse/presseinfo/archiv/Presseinformationen_2009/ Presseinformationen_von_Oktober_bis_Dezember_2009/BBI_Chancen_ regionale_Wirtschaft.jsp (date accessed 1 February, 2010).

35. The Leipzig-based Federal Administrative Court ruled against the citizens' initiative in favor of BBI on 16 March 2006. See the ruling at: www.bverfg. de/pressemitteilungen/bvg08-031.html. See also the citizens' association Bürgerverein Brandenburg-Berlin's website www.bvbb-ev.de; and citizens' initiatives against BBI's flight routes, http://bbi.flugrouten.de (date accessed 10 March, 2010).

36. Annegret Burg, "The Commercial Building: An Urban Component," in Burg and Hans Stimmann, eds, *Berlin Mitte. Die Entstehung einer urbanen Architektur* (Basel: Birkhäuser, 1995), pp. 24–29, p. 25.

37. Hartmut Häußermann, "Sichtbarkeit und Unsichtbarkeit von Macht im Zentrum von Berlin – Vom Kaiserreich bis zur Gegenwart," in Wolfgang Eichwede and Regine Kayser, eds, *Metropolen im Wandel. Berlin-Moskau* (Berlin: Jovis Verlag, 2003), pp. 120–30, p. 128.

38. Peter Marcuse, "Reflections on Berlin: The Meaning of Construction and the Construction of Meaning," *International Journal of Urban and Regional Research*, 22.2 (1998), pp. 331–38, p. 334; and Harold Lasswell, *Politics: Who Gets What, When, How* (New York: P. Smith, 1936). Marcuse continues this line of inquiry in his "Tradition in a Global City?," *Traditional Dwellings and Settlements Review*, 17.2 (2006), pp. 7–18.

39. Karin Lenhart, *Berliner Metropoly. Stadtentwicklungspolitik im Berliner Bezirk Mitte nach der Wende* (Opladen: Leske + Budrich, 2001), pp. 13–14, 131–53; Thomas Winter and Klaus Schmidt, "Berliner Power Circles," *Forbes*, 2 (1992), pp. 62–69; and "Korruption am Bau," *Süddeutsche Zeitung* (3 September, 1998).

40. On Klein's death and the development of Friedrichstraße, see Eva Schweitzer, *Grossbaustelle Berlin. Wie die Hauptstadt verplant wird* (Berlin: Nicolai, 1996), pp. 55–68, 32–50.

41. See Krätke, "City of Talents"; Matthew D. Rose, *Eine ehrenwerte Gesellschaft. Die Bankgesellschaft Berlin* (Berlin: Transit Verlag, 2003); Ralf Schönball, "Steuerzahler müssen zahlen, die Aubis-Chefs verdienen," *Der Tagesspiegel*

(20 May, 2001); and Ulrich Zawatka-Gerlach, "Berlin wäre auch ohne Bankprobleme im Sommer zahlungsunfähig," *Der Tagesspiegel* (31 May, 2001).

42. Neil Leach, "Introduction," in Leach, ed., *Architecture and Revolution: Contemporary Perspectives on Central and Eastern Europe* (New York: Routledge, 1999), pp. 1–10, p. 4.

43. See the property market research company BulwienGesa AG's "Property Developments 2010 in German A-Cities: Berlin, Düsseldorf, Frankfurt am Main, Cologne, Munich and Stuttgart," *Quarterly* (July 2010), pp. 1–2, p. 2.

44. For city-wide, up-to-date developments on these multiple projects, see the website of Berlin's Senate Department for Urban Development: www.stadtentwicklung.berlin.de/planen (accessed 14 June, 2010).

45. See Mike Davis, *Dead Cities and Other Tales* (New York: The New Press, 2002), pp. 361–99.

14
Las Vegas on the Spree: The Americanization of the New Berlin

www.lasvegasfreedom.com: Was Sie wollen. Wann Sie wollen.
Der RTL-Sommer. Die Besten bleiben hier.
(Two billboard advertisements at Berlin's former Checkpoint Charlie, 2001)

"Las Vegas" has become, among its other meanings, a metaphor of city-creation – that is to say, the Strip is known as a site of instant architectural *bricolage*, of ahistorical fabrication and unashamed self-invention, of a hyperreal so strong that it has become substantial. Vegas' "architecture of seduction" not only influenced urban design worldwide in the direction of the "tourist city," but gave rise by the millennium to one of the United States' fastest paced areas of urban agglomeration.[1] Because it stands for Americanization in its most blatant, populist, and vulgar sense, particularly the urban practices of the ever-growing American West, the Vegas metaphor has long inspired a neurotic "fear and loathing" among the cultural-intellectual elite, particularly those whose raison d'être is provided by cities established in modern industrial times.

Increasingly, however, the pervasive reach of the Vegas metaphor of commodification extends into the root of all architectural practice. Architect Rem Koolhaas and his Harvard students have mused how the whole world seems to have become a mall, with shopping the "last remaining form of public activity ... The traditional European city once tried to resist shopping, but is now a vehicle for American-style consumerism ... Perhaps the end of the twentieth century will be remembered as the point where the city could no longer be understood without shopping." It is in the context of this latest urban condition

298

that Las Vegas, postmodernity's infamous fantasy destination for middle-America and purveyor of the Baudrillardian simulacrum, modified itself again into a supra-reality, this time of "substance" and "sheer mass."[2]

Indeed, there is now also such a thing as a Berlin metaphor for Vegas: artist Dave Hullfish Bailey proposed that Berlin would be worth copying by Las Vegans intent on designing new theme-architecture, because Berlin is the only city that has followed the Strip casinos' three main tenets: namely, nostalgia, exoticism, and futurism. Hilariously, Bailey suggested a *Scholle Vaterland*-themed casino that could help transform a neglected part of North Las Vegas; the basic theme of such a hotel project would be Berlin's insignia of an unfinished demolition-cum-building-site.[3] Such a casino would help stave off gaming boredom by being themed or predicated upon on Berlin's strongest identificatory principle, that of a voided building site; and Thunderbird planes would handily "bomb" the building site into existence on opening day. The New Berlin, then, might even be a model for the world's simulacrum-experts, the Las Vegans.[4]

Now that the colonialized postwar era of West Berlin as both literally and figuratively an "American city" is over, the new Americanism of reunified Berlin is no longer a prop or shield for western-style democracy.[5] Rather, it has provided the very engine of rebuilding the city – but with highly negative connotations. Andreas Huyssen pinpoints the cynical nature of this problematic: "The issue in central Berlin, to use Venturi, Scott Brown, and Izenour's by now classic postmodern terms from *Learning from Las Vegas* in this very different context, is how best to decorate the corporate and governmental sheds to better attract international attention: not the city as multiply coded text to be filled with life by its dwellers and its readers but the city as image and design in the service of displaying power and profit."[6] Formerly public properties were sold to privately owned investor groups, that is to say: the market decided what should go up where.[7] This latter condition does not apply solely to the renewed capital, of course. In 2006, Dresden eradicated its public debt by selling all its 48,000 units of public housing to an American private equity investor, Fortress Investment Group.

These days, however, the connotation made with the USA tends to be related to the money-making that occurred during the first, rabid reconstruction phase of reunified Germany, and especially Berlin. Indeed, one cautionary tale of over-development seemed to have met another during a recent exhibition in Berlin of Nicole Huber and Ralph

Stern's photo collection, "Urbanizing the Mojave Desert: Las Vegas."[8] About one-third of the new development in Berlin has had American backing.[9] The CDEC (Central European Development Corporation), which is run by cosmetics billionaire Ronald S. Lauder, developed almost five acres (100,000 sq m) of property at Checkpoint Charlie.[10] By 2008, however, the CEDC encountered stiff resistance when Lauder tried to re-tool the dying airport Tempelhof for his own vision of a luxury clinic and gateway for private jets of the super-wealthy arriving in the city.

Meanwhile, most German critics both on the right or the left would never admit openly or willingly to any complicity in the increasing degree of Americanization (or globalization) in their own urban design, even as they bemoan the start of "big box" or "container" architecture on the suburban fringes, especially in the former East Germany and along the periphery of Berlin with Brandenburg. The electronically enhanced cinematic billboard on the new C&A store on the Ku'Damm – part of the overall revamping of the chic retail mile of the city's western half, to catch up with the innovations in the city's east – certainly appears as effective as those in Singapore or Vegas (Fig. 14.1).[11] American fast food and drink chains have had an impact, with Starbucks cropping up all across the city's central areas, even at the entrance to the Hackesche Höfe; and there are over 40 McDonald's in Berlin. Yet German and US retailing laws and socio-cultural perceptions about consumerism remain substantially different, which is understandable given the fact that, according to the International Council of Shopping Centers (ICSC), Germany has 1.3 square feet of shopping center space per capita for Europe's 4 and the USA's 23. Germany has about 465 shopping centers (half of which opened in the opportunistic era between 1990 and 1997); Europe has 5,700, and the USA 105,000. Germans' dislike of (and German law's restrictions upon) large-scale mass retail caused the world's largest employer, Wal-Mart, to withdraw from the German market in 2006. Nonetheless, the sheer rapidity of real estate development in the former East German states is an indication for Hartmut Häußermann that they are now the most "American" parts of Germany; economic necessity has led East German municipal governments to grant to real estate developers the same essential powers as urban planners.[12]

On what, though, is the anti-American metaphor really based? The "case" of the Critics vs. Americanized New Berlin is in several respects a reflection of the recent fall-out against American-style globalization. In an article for *Le Monde*, just a couple of months after the 9/11 attacks, Jean Baudrillard irresponsibly blamed the Islamic terrorist acts on an

Figure 14.1 C&A department store at the Ku-Damm Corner (Ku'damm-Eck), Kurfürstendamm, Berlin (by von Gerkan, Marg & Partner, 2001)

American suicidal desire, a self-destructive capacity wrought by a form of globalizer's guilt. This sentiment subsequently became compounded by most Europeans' far more rational resistance to the US-led War in Iraq. German venting about the USA led ex-Cultural Minister Michael Naumann in an editorial article for *Die Zeit* to take the growing number of German anti-Americanists to task. Henryk Broder, writing for *Der Spiegel* online, found himself in politically incorrect trouble when he hazarded the guess that at this rate, German anti-Americanism (and its accompanying undercurrent of anti-Semitism) would end up siding with the Islamic extremist terrorists.[13]

Nonetheless, German anti-Americanism concerning the New Berlin should ultimately be understood as less political than symbolic: specifically, as expressions against urban rebranding when it errs in the directions of poor taste, sameness, and careless speed. From *brand* to *bland* is just one short step in the serialized reproduction of global city structures. Lord Norman Foster's signature effect of transparency and technology, while effective in the domed Berlin Reichstag, has led to a "Fosterization" of the City of London, such is its over-use there.[14] Berlin has its Niketown – just like the Niketowns in other leading cities worldwide, of course – but does that necessarily help build the city's global image? Being American is not a prerequisite for these building sins, of course. As part of a group exhibition the month before German unity formally came into effect in October 1990, conceptual artist Hans Haacke, responding to the under-market price paid by the then Daimler Benz for land at Potsdamer Platz, sounded a note of satirical alarm about the instant rebranding of Berlin by placing a Mercedes-Benz sign atop a defunct watchtower in the former no-man's-land of the Wall near the Heinrich-Heine checkpoint (Fig. 14.2). For good measure Haacke combined the Benz insignia, famous for having branded West Berlin's own capitalist era during the Cold War as an emblem atop the Europa Center, with a remodeling of the watchtower's windows in the manner of the bronze reflective façade of the GDR's Palace of the Republic. But

Figure 14.2 "Freedom is now simply going to be sponsored – out of petty cash." Hans Haacke's installation on a former Wall watchtower, as part of the group exhibition "The Finiteness of Freedom," Berlin, 1990

Haacke's ultimate target was Daimler-Benz's selling (out) Berlin in the present, and how that echoed Benz's vast profits from Nazi slave labor in the not-so distant past.[15]

Further, the New Berlin has become for Koolhaas "a Chinese city," as well.[16] Koolhaas, who knows of what he speaks with his OMA firm's involvement in rapidly designing a new global-urban Asia, believes that any city that builds beyond a certain speed ends up sacrificing a certain form of authenticity. The changes in the demographics of Berlin's trendiest and now most transformed Mitte borough reflect this sense of an overnight (American/Chinese) selling-out of its identity. Mitte has traded its former East German locals for the ministerial, chattering, and entrepreneurial classes, who are often West German or indeed foreign (of all Berlin's districts, Mitte has the highest proportion of foreigners, at 28.7 percent) – as well as the young subculture-seeking generation, until gentrified rents pushed them away from the new center.[17] Particularly these young bohemians (dubbed the "urban pioneers," or "Generation Berlin") became the popular embodiment of the way in which hip Berlin conjures up the possibility of rejuvenating the German psyche.[18] Even bohemians get older, however: in 2010, high rents and complaints by family-oriented neighbors prompted Knaack and Magnet, two of Prenzlauer Berg's trademark nightclubs, to move on to the better (cheaper) *Szene* near the Spree river in a still-dingy part of Kreuzberg. Yet the city's enduring poverty in relation to West Germany – with one in five adults and one in three children on welfare, joblessness at its recent "improved" rate of 14 per cent (cushioned by work subsidies, but still nearly double the national rate), and only 13 per cent home ownership – makes for a sobering re-grounding of the initial projections for population growth and wealth for building the New Berlin.[19] Berlin's population even shrank from pre-*Wende* levels to below 3.4 million as residents moved out to fulfill their suburban dreams in new homes built on the affordable Brandenburg periphery. Nonetheless, since 2005 the suburbanization trend has been weakening and Berlin's population is stabilizing. Opportunities to move to semi-urban communities on the capital's edge (like Neu-Karow, Adlershof, Bornstedter Feld, or Kirchsteigfeld) are becoming matched by new developments along Berlin's waterways (such as Wasserstadt Oberhavel and Rummelsburger Bucht). In the first few years of the twenty-first century Berlin's out-migration was outpacing its in-migration, but that direction is now halting, if not reversing (and a similar phenomenon can be seen in Leipzig and Dresden).

Most infamously, the transformations of Berlin's center have produced a tide of demographic displacement of the poor to other, less fashionable parts of the city (in the west: Neukölln, Tiergarten, and Wedding; and in the east, Marzahn and Hellersdorf). In Spandauer Vorstadt and Prenzlauer Berg, luxury apartments have been built in a latter-day version of American-style conquest that since reunification has granted a German layer of meaning to the frontier metaphor. Gentrified rents and social exclusion are now on the rise even in parts of Kreuzberg, a part of West Berlin traditionally known for its Turkish Germans, *Autonomen*, and former Wall-adjacent state of neglect.[20] An unofficial politics of exclusion has gone on in the rebuilding of Berlin.[21] The urban renewal of Spandauer Vorstadt in particular is generally regarded as Berlin's most successful to date: at what has been referred to as the "undeniable middle" of the "renaissance of the center" are the *flânerie*-inspiring Hackesche Höfe, with their courtyard façades now in all the original colors, as first designed by August Endell in 1906.[22] But the area gained more restaurant seating than actual inhabitants; what it is now also gaining is hotels and tourist-oriented retail. Realtors essentially drew up a new set of boundaries for the gentrified area, re-naming it *Quartier Hackescher Markt* in order to sell their properties more easily to investors (and not just foreign ones) put off or confused by the name Spandauer Vorstadt. East German citizens' groups complained that they were gentrified out of an increasingly alien "Boomtown-Mitte," as evacuated renters could not afford to live in their former, newly reno- vated apartments, selling for up to €3,000 per sq m, and renting for up to twice the earlier rate. In the most fashionable locations near the Hackescher Markt, formerly residential buildings were renovated using public subsidies intended to retain apartments as such, straight into future office and retail space (creating oversized pseudo-apartments that had, for instance, three toilets but no bathroom).[23]

Overall, then, certain sections of the populace – the unemployed (especially East Germans), minimum-wage earners, and immigrants with language and education barriers (mostly Turks) – have been the most displaced, whether physically or culturally, by the urban planning discourses of the New Berlin. The stores and restaurants of Prenzlauer Berg's Oderbergerstraße, for example, are undeniably hip, but the street's original East German residents are long gone. Within the hegemonic framework of architectural repair and renewal, Berlin's poor have been regarded for the most part as representational accidents that are best dis- possessed or suppressed. We are indeed witnessing Berlin's architectural self-recreation, but it is an image meant for privileged, "included" groups only. The remapping of Berlin's public stage was intended to create a new interrelated cohesiveness, suggesting national strength both to the world and above all to the reunified Germany, but what has been projected inevitably clashed with the city's (and country's) actual demographics, its dwelling and working norms. Only recently have Berlin's boosters begun to adjust their global visions to include a more diverse mission statement for the capital, or *Leitbild*. Since 2004, Berlin's Office of Migration and Integration boasts a multicultural motto: BĘŘŁŸÑ.[24]

This has not been the first time that construction frenzy ever spread across the city. The "Founders' Crash" of 1873 (*Gründerkrach*), prompted by an international banking system collapse and the refusal of construction credit, stalled the first unified German era's attempt to expand the new capital. But memories were (and are) short. "In twenty years, Berlin will have four million inhabitants, and it will be Chicago," predicted the French journalist Jules Huret in 1909.[25] A year later, Karl Scheffler was complaining that "[a]ll of new Berlin is owned by the developers."[26] A Weimar-era tourist guide to Berlin found it "the most restless and nervous capital in the world," yet was proud of "its constant fluctuation and transformation."[27] And in his 1933 book, the geographer Friedrich Leyden referred to the American boomtown of Berlin as a "fast-grown world city, proud of its dizzily steep ascent." Leyden (who met his death a decade later in the Theresienstadt ghetto) spoke of the "similarity of Greater Berlin with American world cities, whose size is also of recent origin and without the ballast of historical tradition are placed, seemingly rootless, into their surrounding environment." Full of people from someplace else, the modern Berlin that Leyden knew had an "unfinished, improvisational quality" about it.[28] These comments tend to match rather closely the pulse of the 1990s that brought people flocking to Berlin to experience its construction and becoming: in short, to become observers and virtual co-participants its very acts of (in)completion. In effect, then, Berlin, which has been going through a second "Founders' Era" (*Gründerzeit*), has as many critics today of the process as it obviously had the first time around. For Axel Schultes, who wishes his entire master plan for the government quarter could have been realized, this is a time full of as much architectural "'botching'" as Theodor Fontane witnessed in Berlin of the 1870s.[29]

Hence hyping, visiting, photographing or otherwise depicting, distributing, and thus re-enacting the *act of building* has served both to overwrite Berlin's bordered condition, and to signal a global city status to the international community (Fig. 14.3). The New Berlin's love affair with constant construction became so strong that "what is being constructed is an image": the "new character of the city" (and by extension

Figure 14.3   Building-site Berlin: view of the Reichstag from the Swiss Embassy, 1998

not just this city), asserted Peter Marcuse, is henceforth contained within "construction *per se*."[30] Images of the cranes filling the sky over Berlin filled the magazines, and seemed to serve as strong indicators that the city's disunity and global inconsequence were being overcome. Out of the enormous *Baustelle* was thus born a great *Schaustelle*, a phrase that the entire city adopted as a self-celebratory outdoor exhibit of itself and its own transformational construction sites in the summer of 2003: "Display Site Berlin: Discover What's Behind It" (*Schaustelle Berlin: Entdecken, was dahinter steckt*) – but not many really tried; most tourists were content to just enjoy the exciting surface-effects of the *Baustelle*-oriented events and tours.

In many instances development becomes an urban contagion of sorts. Where development begins in an area it encourages more development right next door. On the Chausseestraße in Mitte, there is a building site of global significance: offices for the 6,000 employees of the German Foreign Intelligence Agency, the Bundesnachrichtendienst (BND), which is moving from the Munich area to be closer to governmental power. Ironically it is being built on what before 1989 was a rather different form of globality – namely, the land of the GDR's World Youth Stadium

Figure 14.4   Derelict property for sale, Chausseestraße, Berlin, 2009

(Stadion der Weltjugend). The site became available after being razed in the city's failed bid for the 2000 Olympic Games. On the other side of the street from the future German spies HQ is one of Berlin's all-too-familiar promises over the last two decades: a developer's attempt to cash in on the frenetic building activity going on opposite, and render upscale what is a derelict slum (Fig. 14.4).

These multiple acts of building into, over, and out of the city's former border condition are both celebrated and critiqued in Hubertus Siegert's documentary film *Berlin Babylon*, which documents the capital's multiple building-site transformations from 1996 to 2001, including the opening of Potsdamer Platz.[31] Berlin's frenzy of building and renewal is certainly doubted during the exchange in the film between architects Werner Dürth and Günter Behnisch as they wander through their assignment, the as-yet un-reconstructed Academy of the Arts on Pariser Platz, full (especially for Behnisch) of the Nazi architectural ghosts of Speer's GBI office. It is also doubted during the film's narrative interlude, its "Angel of History" scene. Here, the camera-eye perspective is in one of the channels or tunnel entryways at the Hauptbahnhof's construction site, and as Angela Winkler narrates Walter Benjamin's famous lines from the "Theses on the Philosophy of History," a hushed, forgotten temporality of change and rupture is suggested by the fast time-lapse photography of the clouds overhead. The filmmaker himself has tended to emphasize the Angel's melancholic critique of forced, ignorant (urban) progress: "What is lost is lost."[32]

Yet *Berlin Babylon*'s strength as a movie lies in how the energy of the editing techniques simultaneously belies the urban melancholy that it acknowledges. Viewers focus the exciting processes of building on, over, and under the former voids of Berlin. The Berlin of the 1990s is celebrated by the film for its constant building-cum-demolition; sometimes the city is seen at rest but most often it is filmed at sites of perpetual construction-motion – such as when construction workers donned deep-sea diving gear to build the foundations of the new Potsdamer Platz many feet underwater, in round-the-clock shifts. Accompanying the film as both elegy and energizer is the industrial soundtrack of the band Einstürzende Neubauten (Collapsing New Constructions); indeed, the music seems to resonate better than do the some of the opportunistic comments of the architectural and planning elite inter-viewed in the film. Despite the machinic-organic metaphor which clearly links Siegert's film to *Symphony of a Great City* (*Sinfonie der Großstadt*), the 1927 Berlin documentary by Walther Ruttmann, Berlin appears here as an entity that has been brought back to life from dormancy or death – Sleeping Beauty, Snow White, or Frankenstein, depending on how generous one feels. Siegert's *Berlin, Babylon*'s sustained and simple focus is on the city that has somehow outlived its curse of death and division, and is now reliving and rebuilding again.

As it tried to stand on its own two reunified feet but in imported clothes, Berlin appeared to be outpacing even Vegas in the process of self-commodification, especially with the development of Potsdamer Platz, Europe's largest building site of the 1990s. The site exemplified and emboldened that which Ute Lehrer has referred to as a hugely influential "spectacularization of the building process."[33] The Potsdamer Platz's Info-Box (1995–2001), erected for people to ascend and behold planners' visions for Berlin and the building work going on all around, was pedagogical in scope. Such a degree of educating the public about Potsdamer Platz was deemed necessary given that it had been so laid to waste as a bombed-out, emptied field of nostalgia; its only remaining functions for westerners seemed to consist of flea-market bargaining and tourist gazes upon the infamous Wall terrain. It was, in short, the epitome of the (West) German postwar condition, and as such remained unrecognizable for the old man, Homer, who wanders like Odysseus while yearning for the intersection's pre-World War II days in Wim Wenders' film *Wings of Desire*: "But I won't give up until I have found Potsdamer Platz!"[34]

The entire area was sold for a song to Daimler and Sony in the immediate post-Wall era of unbounded optimism.[35] Today, its three modest high-rise towers by Renzo Piano, Hans Kollhoff, and Helmut Jahn are marketed as signifying a compensatory power of regained centrality and function; indeed, they serve as a beacon for what boosterist commercialism has achieved for Berlin. Completing the ensemble are the adjoining Lenné-Dreieck (Beisheim Center) and the octagonal reconstruction of the Leipziger Platz. Even though claims were made that the Daimler terrain in particular followed the building styles of the European City model (in comparison, that is, with the glass-walled Sony Center opposite), all of Piano's alleys and side streets serve to frame such rather "American" locales as the casino or the Potsdamer Arkaden mall, which rather puts that theory to rest. Potsdamer Platz's strongest statement is surely Jahn's Sony Center atrium, with its transparent roof linking the encircling buildings and attracting (according to Sony) eight million visitors per year. This permanent circus-tent of privately monitored "public" space that is both outside and inside has become a new square in its own right – despite the traditional understanding of what a space for *flânerie* ought to be (namely, non-corporate).[36] The Sony Center's suspended roof bears an obvious resemblance not just to the interior "cone" of Jean Nouvel's Galeries Lafayette department store on the Friedrichstraße; it is also echoed in the interior view of Lord Foster's dome for the Reichstag, an accidental similarity which only helps point up the functional kinship of these two arenas in helping to provide new centers for Berlin on the commercial and governmental levels, respectively (Fig. 14.5; compare Fig. 9.1).

If we recall the unfulfilled skyscraper competition of 1922 to build a tower on the Friedrichstraße, we can see how this dream has now been brought to a belated fruition (even if not at that particular site itself, home since 2009 to a disappointingly gloomy office high-rise). If anywhere so far, Potsdamer Platz is where Berlin has finally realized its modernist wish to build a mini-Manhattan. But in so doing it became a mini-Vegas, a citational package that comes with its simulacrum of Europe's first traffic light "tower" installed there in the mid-1920s; as well as entombed remains of the Kaisersaal and the front façade of the Hotel Esplanade within the Sony complex. Essentially, Potsdamer Platz bears the hallmarks of the New Berlin's most "American sector." It encapsulates the post-Wall process whereby the former *Spree-Athen* of

Figure 14.5   Roof of the Sony Center, Potsdamer Platz, by Helmut Jahn, 2000

Frederick the Great tried to catch up and became, instead, an instantly created "Vegas on the Spree." As a result, German intellectual reactions to this constructed intrusion that postdated the 1994 withdrawal of the bulk of US troops from German soil have been predominantly harsh.

While Piano has referred to the city-in-the-city as a phoenix (but not Phoenix, AZ) arising from the "desert," Werner Sewing has called it, less charitably, a "test-tube city."[37] Similarly, Frank Roost critiqued Potsdamer Platz's monocorporate development for masquerading as multiplicity, especially in Piano's "superficial collage of elements of European old town quarters (alleys, squares, side streets, steps to entrances)" which only "serves the cliché" and "does not create any real urban variety, but functions only as a decorative frame around the shopping mall and the office center."[38] For Roost, there can be no authentic urbanity arising from such a staging of urban tourism as the backbone for metropolitan renewal and economic prosperity.

Let us take a closer look, however, at one of the epicenters of Potsdamer Platz, the indoor mall Potsdamer Arkaden, which opened in 1998 (Fig. 14.6). East Berliners in particular have been honing their post-*Wende* consuming "citizenship" skills there.[39] The Potsdam Arcades became one of Germany's first clones (now one of a dozen in Berlin alone) of a US-style mall with regular prices – that is, it stands for successful low-end commercialism, unlike the Friedrichstadtpassagen or the Ku'Damm. Its success has been duplicated by the massive Alexa mall at Alexanderplatz (2007), which attracted twelve million shoppers in its first year. The Potsdam Arcades mall was developed by ECE Projektmanagement, which has also developed the new mall at Leipzig's main train station as well as sixty other shopping centers across Germany, especially in the eastern states, and across central and eastern Europe. Critics may hate to hear this, since they seem to forget Potsdamer Platz's original commercial function, but the success of Potsdamer Arkaden is the nearest equivalent to one of the original square's main mass cultural attractions, Haus Vaterland, the Weimar Republic's own people's palace.[40] It is an unfortunate academic tendency to feel somehow superior to commerce and to despise the mass culture of consumerism (and consumers themselves, for that matter). The title for the German edition of a collection of Mike Davis's essays makes the case against *Casino Zombies*.[41] Is the fate for an Americanized, commercialized Berlin that of casino-cultural "zombification," or is the time long overdue for a more balanced assessment? After all, those zombie-consumers keep coming back to the mall, movie theaters, hotels, casino, and restaurants of the new Potsdamer Platz.

Architect Daniel Libeskind recognized an underlying problem raised by Potsdamer Platz, despite its relative success. Highly skeptical of the ability of Potsdamer Platz to transform the city's image for itself and

Figure 14.6 Potsdam Arcades mall at Berlin's Potsdamer Platz, by ECE Projektmanagement, 1998

abroad, he denigrated the use of this site for the promotion of millennial architectural commodity fetishism: "I believe that Berlin, like any city which deserves to be called that, is no commodity. It is not something which can be bought in a store like a refrigerator, washing machine, or computer. A city is something which you really need, like the air we breathe. That quality is something which you can't always say of commodities." We might well prefer to imagine what would have been had Daniel Libeskind been permitted to build his own master plan for Potsdamer Platz – a fantasy land of zigzagging structures celebrating the site's Cold War status of voids and divisions, and leaving untouched the destroyed street plan of old, with a "one kilometer long wilderness ..., in which everything," states Libeskind, "can remain as it is."[42] However, this "as is" is suspect: it neglects Potsdamer Platz as it actually used to be before it was bombed, cut in two, and leveled as a no-man's-land. It seems that all post-Wall imaginings concerning Potsdamer Platz, whether arguing for its refashioning as a commercial city or for its memorialization as a broken monument, have arisen from an imagined original condition of urban fullness and completeness. This imaginary fullness is what is most missed in the new Potsdamer Platz, even if it was never there. As Gerwin Zohlen states, the busy traffic junction of Potsdamer Platz was rather the very opposite of presence, "the non-form [*Un-Form*] ... the non-square [*Un-Platz*] par excellence," careening full of tempo, traffic, and Einsteinian relativity.[43]

Even the apparent opposite of the new Potsdamer Platz, namely the Kunsthaus Tacheles, has become a victim of its own commodification. Initiated by squatters during the *Wende*, this countercultural arts initiative in a ruined Wilhelminian arcade building (the Friedrichstraßen-Passage) on East Berlin's Oranienburger Straße rose to fame for its alternative installations and performance art and for epitomizing the voice of a more honest engagement with Berlin's disunity.[44] After being purchased by Fundus in 1998, the structure's crumbling, ruinous condition was literally propped up. Fundus planned to turn both Tacheles and the mostly empty city block on which it stands into a massive neo-traditional New Urbanism project by Andres Duany and Elizabeth Plater-Zyberk (better known as the American architects of Seaside, Florida). Fundus wanted to rename this area the Johannisviertel, a mixed-use collection of retail, offices, penthouses and a hotel, all clustered around *flânerie*-inducing courtyards and squares. In late 2008 the decade-long agreement between Fundus and the Tacheles association with its symbolic 1 DM (50 euro cents) rent per month came to an end, and Tacheles became a squat once more.[45] For critics like Sewing and Roost, the New Urbanist plans for the site would have amounted to an inauthentic Disneyfication on the level of the *Truman Show* movie (which was filmed in Duany and Plater-Zyberk's Seaside). Had this project not been tabled, it is possible that the Tacheles artists would have ended up by now as lone sub-culturals amidst a sea of New Urbanism, like exotic animals in a "natural" habitat at the zoo, on show for the visiting thrill-seekers. But in a sense, however, this is what they have already become. Certainly they appear to be losing out to a recently inserted next-door neighbor, a branch of the upscale Lutter & Wegner restaurant trying its best to look like it has been there forever in the downstairs front section of the building. Currently, the Tacheles artists are – unironically – seeking a transition to public funding status: a bid that they find justified by their role in serving as an "economic cornerstone" for the city and attracting so many tourists to that part of Berlin.[46] The artists' future, however, remains as unclear as that of the now-broke Fundus group, which wants to auction off the property.

Several key sites of Berlin's boosterist make-over have needed time to take hold. In the attempt to make the Friedrichstraße into an Oxford Street alternative to the Regent Street of the Ku'Damm, the risk was in creating something far greater than Friedrichstraße had ever been before (in the 1920s, for example, it was an entertainment and retail district with a decidedly seedy reputation at night). Along the dozen or so small blocks between its eponymous train station and the former Checkpoint Charlie at Zimmerstraße, the new Friedrichstraße has had to contend with a high ratio of empty commercial spaces, including offices in the three glamorous Quartier buildings built by Jean Nouvel, Pei Cobb Freed & Partners, and O. M. Ungers above the Friedrichstadtpassagen. Entire buildings (both new and renovated ones) on blocks of the Friedrichstraße further south of this trio have had to await occupancy according to the ascending cocktail-mix of retail, office, and residential occupants. The late Aldo Rossi's city block building, Quartier Schützenstraße (1997), just east of Checkpoint Charlie, had about a 50 percent occupancy rate during its first decade, and ended up partly becoming hotel space. One of the four intersecting corners of Charlottenstraße and Schützenstraße, situated at the northwest side of the Rossi building, remains undeveloped twenty years after the fall of the Wall, despite its status as prime commercial real estate (Fig. 14.7). Even the flagship new building designed by Josef Paul Kleihues at the now-eradicated site of Checkpoint Charlie, next to the commemorative photo billboards of Soviet and US soldiers designed by artist Frank Thiel, had trouble finding tenants.

To what degree is the crisis-ridden brokenness that constitutes the undeniable richness of the Berlin cityscape being made over into

Figure 14.7 Empty city block, intersection of Charlottenstraße and Schützenstraße, near Checkpoint Charlie, Berlin, in 2009

a seamless simulation of historical continuity? So strong has been the impulse to make Berlin into its previous images – especially in Wilhelmine-Weimar days, when huge sections of the city were built to accommodate a population boom from two to four million between the 1900s and the 1920s – that the city has stood accused of becoming its own theme park. Critical Reconstruction's highly selective historical re-codification has especially affected the most transformed area of all, Mitte. Berlin has been merging simulacra with its layers of war- and Wall-torn architectural and infrastructural palimpsests; too often, the reconstructions resemble a pastiche. Officially promoted "beauty" has been built next to and over sites where the less officially noticed historical "beast" still lingered – and won. While the many bars and restaurants installed in Mitte and Prenzlauer Berg certainly boast instances of architectural-historical layering, theirs are often invented ones. Heine may have enjoyed his wine with E. T. A. Hoffmann at Lutter & Wegner, but they certainly were not at the new "fake old" branches of the restaurant that have popped up east of the former Wall – dining experiences with uncannily close parallels to Las Vegas's Red Square restaurant at Mandalay Bay hotel, with its aged interior and a "forged" statue of a headless Lenin. Other instances include the Pariser Platz's Haus Sommer and Haus Liebermann, designed by Kleihues, adjoining the Brandenburg Gate; and the Fundus company's neoconservative reconstruction of the Adlon Hotel nearby, much derided by critics yet *the* address for rich tourists and visiting dignitaries. In this way, any emulation of the prewar world-city effect in Berlin is destined to fall short, lacking as it does the modern era's ability to engage the processes of industrial modernization back upon itself in terms of design and function.

This is why the well-intentioned application of Critical Reconstructionist tenets – re-hashing the old street plan, lot sizes, façade materials, and building height limits of 72 feet (22m) for cornice lines, and 98 feet (30m) for rooftops – has led to an instant-history "stage-set" impression of fake spatial completion and historical cohesion that reunified Berlin will simply have to live with. The result of the transformation of the central business and government quarter of Berlin has ultimately become a homogenizing one. Indeed, when it came time for the German press to take stock of Berlin's accomplishments during the twenty-year celebrations of the fall of the Wall, one commentator poured out (so to speak) his physical nausea at the expanses of new dreary sameness born of the Stimmann-effect of Critical Reconstruction: "Whoever has moved through the newly constructed areas of Berlin for a few days starts to experience the right-angled stone grid of the new buildings' façades – which by now cover large sections of the city – as a corporal punishment ..."[47] Evidently, this excoriating vitriol is not something one would feel like saying today about the Haussmann-effect on Paris, even though the latter was far stricter regarding the uniform appearance of that city's center. Again, the conceptual error in Berlin's case resides in the mimetic rule-following not so much of a building code but of an imagined urban identity-creating code of a previous era. Indeed, Brian Ladd has cautioned that the "1890s or 1920s cannot be restored, except as a stage set for tourists."[48] This is in line with Paul Virilio's observation about the post-Wall German capital:

> As with the reconstruction of Warsaw in the 1950s, behind the desire to wipe out the past there lurks an incredible transformation of

history into a mere STAGE SET, *a transformational stage set* capable of including everything and anything. ... [T]here is the urge to destroy, to wipe out not only what is really ugly, but anything which spoils the prospect of a glorious globalization.[49]

Commercial and non-commercial sites alike have been or are being reconstructed to fit the now-requisite stage-set appeal that alone today seems to guarantee economic growth for urban centers. If only Berlin's selected stage-set could have been something more in tune with its immediate bordered past, much of the recent critical agonizing over the capital's architectural condition could have been avoided.

Other prominent examples of Berlin's stage-set ambience include structures once lost to World War II and the GDR's reconstruction of East Berlin as its own capital, but now regained in actuality or in future plans: the rebuilt Kommandantur on Unter den Linden (as the head-quarters for the media company Bertelsmann); Schinkel's Bauakademie, currently a painted scaffold but set to be reconstructed to match the desires of Berlin's architectural elite; and, especially, the city palace (Stadtschloß), the need for the return of which has been not just promoted but practically created by the initiative called Gesellschaft Historisches Berlin. The Humboldt Forum, if indeed there is ever enough federal money and popular support to build it (since 80 percent of polled Berliners now apparently reject the concept), would, according to the winning design by Francesco Stella (2008), have palace-replica outer walls encasing exhibition rooms designed along contemporary guidelines, and a rather token-sized dome. Also, a perilously absurd situation seems inevitable: one of the City Palace portals on the Humboldt Forum façade will find its original right across the road, preserved and built into the Staatsratsgebäude by the GDR to honor Karl Liebknecht's call for the socialist republic in 1918 (supposedly from the very balcony where the Kaiser had initiated World War I in 1914). No matter – the Staatsratsgebäude is now an American-style MBA academy. Thus the Humboldt Forum would surely provide as much of a *mélange* through architectural time and taste as can be found by Vegas' urban tourists as they walk within (or go on foot or by monorail from and to) ancient Egypt, skyscraper New York, and Haussmannized Paris on the Strip.[50] In the meantime, adjacent to the on-site, marketing-oriented Humboldt-Box, a grander yet still "temporary" version of the same is being constructed (Fig. 14.8).

Most crucially, then, the impetus of Berlin's Critical Reconstruction has let in the American bogeyman by mistake. This is all the more ironic since Hans Stimmann once defined the European City model's main aim

Figure 14.8 Promotional "Humboldt-Box" marketing the rebuilding of Berlin's City Palace as the future Humboldt Forum; behind it, a bigger information center being built for the same purpose, in 2010

as that of warding off such American icons as malls.[51] The Stimmann-effect is proving to be, most inadvertently, a "Vegasizing" one. The battle lines were being drawn even as they were already crossed and transgressed: Vegas is already in Berlin. Commercial interests ended up "planning" the New Berlin (rather than any slower-moving governmental agency), because key areas were rebuilt according to the highest bidders who conformed with the Critical Reconstructionist regulatory building and zoning styles. Berlin's speculative building boom of the early 1990s only strengthened the inadvertent parallelism of Critical Reconstructionist Berlin to the USA's style of market-driven urban planning. As political scientist Elizabeth A. Strom has emphasized, *"capitalist urban development doesn't require the mobilization of political support."*[52]

Are, then, the redone commercial sites of post-Wall Berlin doomed to offend against democratic urban space? Richard Sennett, in *The Spaces of Democracy*, has rejected the "all-at-once, massive development of urban centers" and defines the space of democracy as a decentralized collage, instead, in the fashion of Aristotelian *"synoikismos –* a coming together of differences."[53] Certainly, the open-market operative in Berlin has been at risk of a spatial "over-encoding": too stark a boundary emerges at the point where the developed area abruptly ends and the older existing fabric of the city edges up to the new. Such differences are not, of course, the kind of synoecism that Sennett had in mind. By "over-encoding" I refer to a process of socio-geographical mapping through which too many adjoining sites are developed too swiftly and homogeneously, producing a rigid network of fixed urban interfaces that remain too bounded and separate from each other. This is what remains as a possible danger for Berlin. Such is the composition, most obviously, of Potsdamer Platz, of the incoming Mediaspree project at the Osthafen area between Friedrichshain and Kreuzberg, and the future Lehrter Stadtquartier/EuropaCity development next to Berlin Central; it also applies to new-old Mitte, now a downtown equivalent of master-planned community planning. For the immediate future they will stand most for their separateness from the existing Berlin fabric all around them.

But we cannot halt this urban process of void-filling, only steer its style and speed. Françoise Choay, in her book *The Invention of the Historic Monument* (2001), notes that the general urban phenomenon of building up a void is indeed part of the very "modernization" of a city's "ancient urban tissue" – a renewing process that "is brought about by filling existing voids, or voids created for the purpose." In this sense, then, post-Wall Berlin might be more easily forgiven for fulfilling, if in too rushed a fashion, an age-old tendency in urban transformation.[54] This is what critics of all the void-filling – and of New Urbanism, of Critical Reconstruction, and the rest – have been missing out on. It may well be symptomatic to repeatedly attempt to fill up the strange emptiness of which postwar Berlin was full (full of marks and traces of its former structures and movements), and yet we cannot hold on to such voids and wounds in a state of eternal petrification. They are all but impossible to memorialize as such, indeed to do so would work against urban life, not assist it. After all, the radical voidedness of Ground Zero, the destroyed site of the World Trade Center, can and should be cited in a memorial to the thousands crushed and burned at the spot, but for the sake of New York City and beyond, the entirety of this site *qua* catastrophe cannot be maintained in stasis. Such is the fallacy behind Werner Sewing's otherwise entirely justified complaint that "50 years of recent history are being completely ignored: the divided city, the Wall-city, the city of the Cold War."[55] Again, there is more than a dose of petrified stasis in the nostalgic longing for German urban-cum-collective homelessness in the character of Eduard, the protagonist in Peter Schneider's post-Wall Berlin novel of 1999, *Eduards Heimkehr* (*Edward's Return Home*). Eduard bemoans the lack of city-identity or *Stadtbild* that once was Potsdamer Platz, yet feels distrustful of the overly radical surgical changes underway there to reincarnate the closure that this new center will entail.[56]

The general intrusion of the commodification of architecture, whether for retail or for tourism theme-park purposes, into the urban fabric of Berlin is part of what architecture now does and what cities now do, even if this means building in the image of a former urban identity (now: myth). Critics' melancholic nostalgia over the demise of Berlin's voids is based on a somewhat selective memory of a dreamed-of authenticity and cohesion for the urban past – not only of the very patchiness and walled up separations of Cold War Berlin, but also of the city's pre-Wall (and especially, interwar pre-Nazi) era of rapid modernization. A balanced view needs to be found that does not condemn in advance infrastructural and superstructural renovation. Commercial development will have to accompany the city's long journey to growth.

Yet reactions against the American-style methods used in the rebuilding of Berlin have been voiced on the US side of the Atlantic as well. After the initial celebrations of transformational building, around the millennium it became fashionable to castigate poor New Berlin's bid to remake itself as a global player, rather than to indicate the more patient path of waiting a decade more for the city's long-term post-Wall identity to start to emerge. One such example is *The New York Review of Books'* attack on post-Wall Berlin's "lost" architectural "opportunities": the critique is based on a condemnatory citing of American urban and consumer practices as the root of Berlin's diseased condition. In this review essay, Berlin's vast, spread-out terrain is cause for the author, Martin Filler, to pinpoint Berlin's affinity to Los Angeles more "than any other European capital"; Potsdamer Platz is singled out by Filler for its inward-turn of public space by means of "atriums and multilevel shopping malls as anti-urban as anything on the American roadside strip"; the Sony Center is decried as a "glitzy, glass-skinned shopping and entertainment center better suited to L.A. or Las Vegas"; and the view from the (incidentally pre-post-Wall) Kulturforum, complains Filler, "might as well be in Texas as in Brandenburg." The Vegas-gaming metaphor pops up yet again between the lines in Filler's concluding condemnation of the "grotesque speculative frenzy of the classic boomtown" that "overwhelmed all other impulses in 1990s Berlin."[57] In short, Filler claims that Berlin has failed because it has become, or (more mysteriously) always already was, simply too American – even though a considerable part of his negative reaction is obviously an East Coast reaction to the growing economic and social influence of the American West. In point of fact, in his attack Filler approaches the historical truth of Berlin's identity. Berlin of the 1920s owed much of its world stature to a massive post-Versailles Treaty shift toward Americanism in business and consumer practices (in the shape of Fordism, Taylorization, New Objectivity, and the Hollywood-Babelsberg connection).

Despite judgments like Filler's, the globalizing development of Berlin is continuing, and its focal points are still moving, prompting new "hot spots" to emerge in construction site energy, private investment, citizens' initiatives, and architectural debate. One line of Berlin's shifting inner-city borders moved further east to fresher terrain near the Ostbahnhof. In particular, the presence, since 2001, of the world's largest record company, Universal Music Group, in a converted warehouse (first built in 1928 for food refrigeration purposes) next to the Oberbaumbrücke, is part of a transformational synaesthetic clustering in that entire area of dead docklands once adjacent to the Wall. While London's financial center has been effectively moved eastwards by the 1980s development of Canary Wharf out of once-deserted docks, Berlin's ongoing transformation of the Osthafen area is perhaps no less ambitious. Universal's relocation led MTV Deutschland to move from Munich to an Osthafen warehouse in 2004; other media companies like the music TV station VIVA followed suite. Germany's music industry now considers Berlin the nation's music capital.

Part of the Mediaspree project is the business area Oberbaum City, just north and east of the Oberbaumbrücke: an entire media/IT area in the converted former Osram electric company's headquarters from a hundred years ago. Its most symbolic building is an office tower, a former light-bulb factory built in 1907, which now presents a new glass façade and five additional stories. It stands as an impressive architectural merger of Berlin's Wilhelmine manufacturing glory days and the hopes of wedding the New Berlin to the New Economy. But as an early arrival among the newcomers to the MediaSpree area, Oberbaum City has had to endure remoteness from central Berlin and a wait for the snowball-effect of clustering to take effect.[58] A more dramatic change for the area has been the O2 World Arena (2008). Its developers were AEG, the Denver-based Anschutz corporation, which required that a 130ft-long piece of the East German hinterland Wall at the riverside East Side Gallery be broken in front of the adjacent arena, permitting visual and boat access to the Spree.[59] The 17,000-capacity O2 Arena has helped bring Berliners together in its role as home to the champion *Eisbären* ice hockey team (formerly for Stasi players only); and in 2009 it hosted the MTV Europe Music awards. It will, appropriately enough, be the venue for Roger Waters on the Berlin stop of his worldwide concert tour of Pink Floyd's *The Wall* in 2011 – an update of the one he staged at the former Wall terrain of Potsdamer Platz in the heady summer of 1990. Over the next couple of decades, the entire surrounding area along the Spree between Friedrichshain and Kreuzberg will be dramatically transformed, covering a terrain twice the size of the Potsdamer Platz development.

Clearly, the link and then legacy between the United States and Berlin forged by the postwar decades has played a key role in post-Wall intuitions and perceptions about the city's commodified self-reinvention, as well. "The war over Europe is indeed over. People power won. We can stand down – pass the donuts."[60] Thus spoke journalist Thomas L. Friedman when marking the twentieth anniversary of the fall of the Berlin Wall, referring in the same breath to both the end of the Cold War and to the Dunkin' Donuts chain outlet which can now be found at the capital's reconstructed Pariser Platz. The New Berlin can be summed up, quite literally it seems, as a sell-out in the name of democratic-capitalistic freedom – *und das ist auch gut so.*

Notes

1. Neil Leach, *The Anaesthetics of Architecture* (Cambridge, MA: MIT Press, 1999), pp. 76–78.
2. Rem Koolhaas, coordinator of "Shopping. Harvard Project on the City" with Tae-Wook Cha, Chuihua Judy Chung, Jutiki Gunter, Daniel Herman, and Hiromi Hosoya et al., in Koolhaas, Stefano Boeri, and Sanford Kwinter, eds, *Mutations* (Bordeaux: ACTAR, 2000), pp. 124–83, pp. 125, 127, 165. See also Dennis R. Judd and Susan S. Fainstein, eds, *The Tourist City* (New Haven: Yale University Press, 1999); Ada Louise Huxtable, *The Unreal America: Architecture and Illusion* (New York: The New Press, 1997); and Sharon Zukin, *Landscapes of Power: From Detroit to Disney World* (Berkeley: University of California Press, 1991).
3. Dave Hullfish Bailey, *Union Pacific. Berlin's Neue Mitte and the Fringes of Las Vegas* (Berlin: Vice Versa Verlag, 1999), pp. 7, 19.
4. Ulf Meyer cited this aspect of my "Las Vegas on the Spree" presentation at the UIA XXI congress in Berlin in 2002, in Meyer, "Die Eroberung des Himmels. Ministädte, Megacities: Heute endet der Weltkongress der Architektur in Berlin," *Der Tagesspiegel* (26 July, 2002); as did Peter Yeadon, "Bau Wow: Shall We Bark or Bite?", *Canadian Architect*, 47.10 (October 2002), pp. 42–43; and Catherine Slessor, "Vegas on the Spree," *Architectural Review*, 212.1267 (2002), pp. 28–29.

5. Andreas Daum, "America's Berlin 1945–2000: Between Myths and Visions," in Frank Trommler, ed., *Berlin: The New Capital in the East. A Transatlantic Reappraisal* (Washington, DC: AICGS, 2000), pp. 49–73, p. 50.

6. Andreas Huyssen, *Present Pasts: Urban Palimpsests and the Politics of Memory* (Stanford: Stanford University Press, 2003), p. 63; orig. "The Voids of Berlin," *Critical Inquiry*, 24.1 (1997), pp. 57–81.

7. Hartmut Häußermann, "U-Bahn und Urban. Wie die europäischen Städte immer amerikanischer werden," *Süddeutsche Zeitung* (30 June, 2000).

8. Nicole Huber and Ralph Stern, *Urbanizing the Mojave Desert: Las Vegas* (Berlin: Jovis, 2008).

9. Stefan Krätke and Renate Borst, *Berlin: Metropole zwischen Boom und Krise* (Opladen: Leske + Budrich, 2000), p. 92.

10. See Ulf Meyer, "'Wo bitte geht's zum Checkpoint Charlie?'" in Architektenkammer Berlin and Lothar Juckel, eds, *Architektur in Berlin. Jahrbuch 1997* (Hamburg: Junius Verlag, 1997), pp. 64–69.

11. The C&A store and Swissôtel at the Ku'Damm-Eck opened in 2001 and were designed by Meinhard von Gerkan. The low-lying video wall is over a thousand square feet (100 sq m) in size and was the cause of complaints from drivers during its first weeks of operation for being too blinding. See "Neues Ku'Damm-Eck blendete Autofahrer," *Der Tagesspiegel* (15 June, 2001); and Gerwin Zohlen, "Metropole als Metapher," in Gotthard Fuchs, Bernhard Moltmann, and Walter Prigge, eds, *Mythos Metropole* (Frankfurt am Main: Suhrkamp, 1995), pp. 23–34, p. 23.

12. Hartmut Häußermann, "Von der Stadt im Sozialismus zur Stadt im Kapitalismus," in Häußermann and Reiner Neef, eds, *Stadtentwicklung in Ostdeutschland* (Opladen: Westdeutscher Verlag, 1996), pp. 5–47, p. 27. Philipp Oswalt points out that over 50 percent of retail in the former East Germany has been on the suburban fringes, in contrast to about 25 percent in West Germany; Oswalt, *Berlin: Stadt ohne Form: Strategien einer anderern Architektur* (Berlin: Prestel, 2000), p. 79. On the rise of "big box architecture" outside German city centers, see Dieter Hoffmann-Axthelm, "Das Einkaufszentrum," in Gotthard Fuchs, Bernhard Moltmann, and Walter Prigge, eds, *Mythos Metropole* (Frankfurt am Main: Suhrkamp, 1995), pp. 63–71; Klaus Kleine and Thomas Offermanns, "In Deutschland geplante Factory Outlet Center," *Raumforschung und Raumordnung*, 58.1 (2000), pp. 35–46; and Günter Heinritz and Jürgen Rauh, "Gutachterliche Stellungnahmen über Factor Outlet Center. Eine kritische Betrachtung," *Raumforschung und Raumordnung* 58.1 (2000), pp. 47–54.

13. Jean Baudrillard, *The Spirit of Terrorism and Requiem for the Twin Towers*, trans. Chris Turner (New York: Verso, 2002); Henryk Broder, *Kein Krieg, nirgends. Die Deutschen und der Terror* (Berlin: Berlin Verlag, 2002); and Michael Naumann, "Seid nicht so German," *Die Zeit*, 40 (2001). See also Russell A. Berman, *Anti-Americanism in Europe: A Cultural Problem* (Stanford: Hoover Institution Press, 2004).

14. See Marc Gobé, *Emotional Branding* (New York: Allworth Press, 2001), p. 143; and Anna Klingman, *Brandscapes: Architecture in the Experience Economy* (Cambridge, MA: MIT Press, 2007), pp. 265–68.

15. Hans Haacke, "Freedom Is Now Simply Going to Be Sponsored – Out of Petty Cash," in Jean Stein, ed., *Grand Street 69*, 18.1 (New York: Grand Street Press, New York Foundation for the Arts, 1999), pp. 178–81.

16. Rem Koolhaas, "Die chinesische Stadt," conversation with Hans Ulrich Obrist, in Miriam Wiesel, ed., *Berlin/Berlin, Katalog der ersten Berlin Biennale* (Ostfildern: Cantz Verlag, 1998), p. 57; cited by Oswalt, *Berlin. Stadt ohne Form*, p. 101.

17. See Christian Helge Röfer, "Das Wohnen in der Stadt wird immer attraktiver," *Der Tagesspiegel* (18 October, 2005); Jochen Becker, "Neue Mitte/Helle Mitte. Jumpcuts zwischen Hackeschem Markt und Platte," *Widersprüche. Zeitschrift für sozialistische Politik im Bildungs-, Gesundheits- und Sozialbereich*, 20 (2000), pp. 69–83, p. 70; and Lothar Heinke, "Trittin an der Käsetheke, Müntefering beim Joggen. Begegnungen in Mitte," *Der Tagesspiegel* (12 September, 2000).

18. Klaus Overmeyer and Senatsverwaltung für Stadtentwicklung Berlin, eds, *Urban Pioneers. Berlin Stadtentwicklung durch Zwischennutzung/Temporary Use and Urban Development in Berlin* (Berlin: Jovis, 2007); and Heinz Bude, *Generation Berlin* (Berlin: Merve, 2001). For a discussion of Bude's term see Katharina Gerstenberger, *Writing the New Berlin: The German Capital in Post-Wall Literature* (Rochester, NY: Camden House, 2008), pp. 12–13; and Margit M. Sinka, "Heinz Bude's Defining Construct for the Berlin Republic: the *Generation Berlin*," in Carol-Anne Costabile-Heming, Rachel J. Halverson, and Kristie A. Foell, eds, *Berlin: The Symphony Continues. Orchestrating Architectural, Social, and Artistic Change in the New Capital* (Berlin: Walter de Gruyter, 2004), pp. 187–204.

19. Boosters and even the official land use plan of 1994 were predicting (erroneously as it turned out) an annual growth rate of 40,000 new Berliners with an ultimate increase for the city of 300,000 inhabitants. Hanns-Uve Schwedler, "The Urban Planning Context in Berlin: a City Twice Unique," in William J. V. Neill and Schwedler, eds, *Urban Planning and Cultural Inclusion: Lessons from Belfast and Berlin* (Basingstoke: Palgrave, 2001), pp. 24–41, p. 32.

20. Lars Dittmer, "Anwohner im Graefkiez fürchten Verdrängung," *Der Tagesspiegel* (1 July, 2010).

21. See Doreen Massey's advocacy of urban hybridity and "coeval others," in Massey, *World City* (Cambridge: Polity, 2007), p. 216; and Neil Smith, *The New Urban Frontier: Gentrification and the Revanchist City* (New York: Routledge, 1996). See also studies of the gentrification of Prenzlauer Berg by Andrej Holm, *Die Restrukturierung des Raumes. Stadterneuerung der 90er Jahre in Ostberlin: Interessen und Machtverhältnisse* (Berlin: Transcript Verlag, 2006); and Matthias Bernt, *Rübergeklappt. Die "Behutsame Erneuerung" im Berlin der 90er Jahre* (Berlin: Schelzky & Jeep, 2003).

22. Harald Bodenschatz, *Städtebau in Berlin. Schreckbild und Vorbild für Europa* (Berlin: Dom publishers, 2010), p. 129. See August Endell, *Die Schönheit der großen Stadt*, orig. 1908 (Berlin: Archibook, 1984); and Gerhard Ullmann, "Insel der Urbanität. Zur Renovierung der Hackeschen Höfe in Berlin-Mitte," *Deutsche Bauzeitung*, 6 (1997), pp. 53–59.

23. On these developments, see Matthias Oloew, "Zu viele feine Adressen in Mitte," *Der Tagesspiegel* (8 August, 2008); Christian van Lessen, "Abschied von der Szene," *Der Tagesspiegel* (13 July, 2008); Klaus Ronneberger, Stephan Lanz, and Walther Jahn, *Die Stadt als Beute* (Bonn: Dietz, 1999), pp. 79–81; Jochen Becker, "Hype Park," in Stadtrat, ed., *Umkämpfte Räume* (Hamburg, Berlin, and Göttingen: Assoziation A, 1998), pp. 179–90; Johannes Touché,

"Mentalitätswechsel? – Nie! Die Krise der behutsamen Stadtentwicklung," *scheinschlag*, 11 (2002), p. 3; Ulrike Steglich, "Noch schlechtere Nachrichten," *sanierung im mitte: sanierungsbeilage im scheinschlag* (16 May–26 June 2002), p. 5; and Steglich's assessment of the renovation of the building at Große Präsidentenstraße 10/Hackescher Markt 4, owned by Nippon Development Corporation: Steglich, "... da waren's nur noch zehn. Wie ein Investor mit Hilfe des Bezirkamts Wohnungen zu Büros umwandeln will," *stadt.plan.mitte* (Mitte) (4 December 2002), p. 6.

24. See www.berlin.de/lb/intmig/ (date accessed 3 September, 2009); and Stephan Lanz, *Berlin aufgemischt: abendländisch – multikulturell – kosmopolitisch? Die politische Konstruktion einer Einwanderungsstadt* (Bielefeld: transcript Verlag, 2007).

25. Jules Huret, *En Allemagne: Berlin* (Paris: Bibliothèque-Charpentier, 1909), p. 32. For one origin of the phrase "Chicago on the Spree," see Walther Rathenau, *Die schönste Stadt der Welt*, orig. 1899 (Berlin/Vienna: Philo, 2002), p. 23.

26. Karl Scheffler, *Berlin. Ein Stadtschicksal*, 2nd ed. (Berlin: Erich Reiss Verlag, 1910), p. 187.

27. Max Osborn, ed., *Kennen Sie Berlin?/How to See Berlin* (Stettin: F. Hessenland, 1928), p. 25.

28. Friedrich Leyden, *Groß-Berlin. Geographie der Weltstadt*, orig. 1933 (Berlin: Gebr. Mann Verlag, 1995), pp. 170, 173, 184.

29. Axel Schultes, "Berlin – The Belated Capital," in Alan Balfour, ed., *Berlin* (London: Academy Editions, 1995), pp. 38–47, p. 39.

30. Peter Marcuse, "Reflections on Berlin: The Meaning of Construction and the Construction of Meaning," *International Journal of Urban and Regional Research*, 22.2 (1998), pp. 331–38, p. 331.

31. Hubertus Siegert, dir., *Berlin Babylon* (Berlin: S.U.M.O. Film, 2001). The film's closest affine is Volker Sattel's *Unternehmen Paradies* (*Enterprise Paradise*, 2002), which observes the structures and denizens of the New Berlin from alienating angles. Siegert's film can also be regarded as occupying a midway position between the far more critical documentary, *Die leere Mitte* (directed by Hito Steyerl in 1998), focusing on the marginalized groups who built Berlin's intended center – the foreign, often illegal labor force that was employed at Potsdamer Platz – and the much less critical Ruttmann-echo directed by Thomas Schadt, *Berlin: Sinfonie einer Großstadt* (2002), which depicts a mosaic in an eventful year (2001) in the life of the city as opposed to Ruttmann's 24-hour cycle of Weimar urban life.

32. Hubertus Siegert, in Siegert and Ralph Stern, "Berlin. Film and the Representation of Urban Reconstruction Since the Fall of the Wall," in Joan Ockman, ed., *Out of Ground Zero: Case Studies in Urban Reinvention* (New York: Prestel, 2002), pp. 116–31, p. 129. Walter Benjamin, *Illuminations: Essays and Reflections*, ed. Hannah Arendt, trans. Harry Zohn (New York: Schocken Books, 1968), pp. 257–58.

33. Ute Lehrer, "Zitadelle Innenstadt: Bilderproduktion und Potsdamer Platz," in Albert Scharenberg, ed., *Berlin: Global City oder Konkursmasse? Eine Zwischenbilanz zehn Jahre nach dem Mauerfall* (Berlin: Karl Dietz Verlag, 2000), pp. 95–110, p. 110; and Lehrer, "Reality or Image? Place Selling at Potsdamer Platz," in Raffaele Paloscia, ed., *The Contested Metropolis. Six Cities at the Beginning of the 21st Century* (Basel and Boston: Birkhäuser, 2004), pp. 45–52,

p. 46. See also Karen E. Till, "Construction Sites and Showcases: Mapping 'The New Berlin' through Tourism Practices," in Stephen P. Hanna and Vincent J. Del Casino, Jr., eds, *Mapping Tourism* (Minneapolis: University of Minnesota Press, 2003), pp. 51–78.

34. *Aber ich gebe so lange nicht auf, bis ich den Potsdamer Platz gefunden habe!* Wim Wenders and Peter Handke, *Der Himmel über Berlin. Ein Filmbuch* (Frankfurt am Main: Suhrkamp, 1987), p. 59; Wim Wenders, dir., *Der Himmel über Berlin* (Paris: Road Movies Berlin and Argos Films, 1987).

35. Finally, the EU stepped in after the Potsdamer Platz acquisition deals with the then-Daimler Benz (68,000 sq m), Sony (25,000 sq m), ABB, and Metro. In 1991 Daimler was told to pay an additional third of the original DM90 million purchase price in the 1990 deal with then-mayor Walter Momper. See Elizabeth A. Strom, *Building the New Berlin: The Politics of Urban Development in Germany's Capital City* (Lanham: Lexington Books, 2001), pp. 188–190; Rolande Enke on fears of "Potsdaimler Platz" in "Missed Opportunities? The Re-Creation of Potsdamer Platz – Planning, Competitions and Construction," in Yamin von Rauch and Jochen Visscher, eds, *Der Potsdamer Platz. Urban Architecture for a New Berlin* (Berlin: Jovis, 2000), p. 32; and Heinrich Wefing, *Der Neue Potsdamer Platz. Ein Kunststück Stadt* (Berlin: be.bra verlag, 1998), pp. 48–49.

36. On the Sony Center's function as a branding center for Sony's interests rather than for those of the city of Berlin, see Frank Roost, *Branding Center: Über den Einfluß globaler Markenkonzerns auf die Innenstädte* (Wiesbaden: Vs Verlag für Sozialwissenschaften, 2008), pp. 97–172, esp. pp. 170–71.

37. Werner Sewing, "Heart, Artificial Heart, or Theme Park? Trying to Make Sense of Potsdamer Platz," in von Rauch and Visscher, eds, *Der Potsdamer Platz*, pp. 47–58, p. 47.

38. Frank Roost, "Die Disneyfizierung Berlins. Stadtumbau nach den Wünschen der Entertainmentindustrie," *scheinschlag*, 11.2 (22 February–21 March, 2001), p. 5.

39. See Daphne Berdahl's study of the intertwined lessons learned by former East Germans regarding (West German) national citizenship and mass consumerist patterns of behavior: Berdahl, "The Spirit of Capitalism and the Boundaries of Citizenship in Post-Wall Germany," *Society for the Comparative Study of Society and History*, 47 (2005), pp. 235–51.

40. Haus Vaterland's rounded corner is in fact echoed in a new building at the south point of Potsdamer Platz, on the site of the original structure (designed by general architect Giorgio Grassi and Schweger + Partner, Berlin).

41. Mike Davis, *Casino Zombies und andere Fabeln aus dem Neon-Westen der USA* (Berlin: Schwarze Risse, 1999).

42. Daniel Libeskind, "Potsdamer Platz," *radix-matrix. Architecture and Writings* (Munich and New York: Prestel, 1997), pp. 160–63, pp. 161, 162.

43. Gerwin Zohlen, "Erblast des Mythos. Das Verfahren Potsdamer/Leipziger Platz. Rückblick nach vier Jahren," in Vittorio Magnago Lampugnani and Romana Schneider, eds, *Ein Stück Großstadt als Experiment. Planungen am Potsdamer Platz in Berlin* (Stuttgart: Verlag Gerd Hatje, 1994), pp. 14–23, p. 17.

44. See Janet Stewart, "Das Kunsthaus Tacheles: The Berlin Architectural Debate of the 1990s in Micro-Historical Context," in Stuart Taberner and Frank Finlay, eds, *Recasting German Identity: Culture, Politics, and Literature in the Berlin Republic* (Rochester, NY: Camden House, 2002), pp. 50–66.

45. Joel Atlas, "Iconic Berlin Squat Receives Eviction Notice," *The New York Times* (7 January, 2009).
46. See the "Tacheles Reset" initiative: http://super.tacheles.de/cms/ (date accessed 3 May, 2010).
47. Gottfried Knapp, "Wurst, Steine, Tränen," *Süddeutsche Zeitung* (9 November, 2009).
48. Brian Ladd, *The Ghosts of Berlin: Confronting German History in the Urban Landscape* (Chicago: University of Chicago Press, 1997), p. 231.
49. Paul Virilio, "Open Skies over Berlin," in Kathrin Becker and Urs Stahel, eds, *Remake Berlin* (Winterthur: Steidl Verlag, 2001), pp. 150–55, p. 154; emphasis original.
50. The latest prediction is a construction start date of 2014; see "Schloßplatz. Wowereit hält Stadtschloß-Verschiebung für Armutszeugnis," *Der Tagesspiegel* (7 June, 2010). For the official update on the future of the Humboldt Forum, see the Federal Ministry of Transport, Building and Urban Development website at www.bmv.de/en/artikel-,1872.1007758/Reconstruction-of-the-Berlin-R.htm; and for some citizens' design alternatives see the "Mind the Gap, Berlin" initiative http://zukunft-schlossplatz.de (date accessed 17 June, 2010). On the intense debates raised by the palace specter, see Beate Binder, *Streitfall Stadtmitte: der Berliner Stadtschloß* (Cologne: Böhlau, 2009).
51. Haus Stimmann, "New Berlin Office and Commercial Building," in Annegret Burg and Stimmann, eds, *Berlin Mitte. Die Entstehung einer urbanen Architektur* (Basel: Birkhäuser, 1995), pp. 6–23, p. 17.
52. Strom, *Building the New Berlin*, p. 235; emphasis original.
53. Richard Sennett, *The Spaces of Democracy* (Ann Arbor: University of Michigan Press, 1998), pp. 41, 19. Aristotle stresses synoecism as the non-tribal cohabitation of different groups within the institutions of the *polis*. Edward W. Soja also adapts the term to designate a collection of urban energies caused by the "purposeful clustering and collective cohabitation of people in space." Soja, "Putting Cities First: Remapping the Origins of Urbanism," in Gary Bridge and Sophie Watson, eds, *A Companion to the City* (Cambridge, MA: Blackwell, 2000), pp. 26–34, p. 28; see also Soja's Part 1 of *Postmetropolis: Critical Studies of Cities and Regions* (Cambridge, MA: Blackwell, 2000).
54. Françoise Choay, *The Invention of the Historic Monument*, trans. Lauren M. O'Connell (New York: Cambridge University Press, 2001), p. 154.
55. Werner Sewing, "Schöne neue alte Stadt," *scheinschlag*, 5 (17 May–14 June, 2001), 6.
56. Peter Schneider, *Eduards Heimkehr* (Hamburg: Rowohlt, 1999), p. 164.
57. Martin Filler, "Berlin: The Lost Opportunity," *The New York Review of Books* (1 November, 2001), pp. 28–31, pp. 29, 28, 31.
58. Dieter Hoffmann-Axthelm, "Schweigsame Oberbaum City," *Bauwelt*, 93.9 (2002), pp. 14–17.
59. See Nicholas Kulish, "Ice Hockey Helps Raze Berlin Wall in the Mind," *The New York Times* (9 November, 2008); and Klaus Kurpjuweit, "Anschutz baut – wenn die Rendite stimmt," *Der Tagesspiegel* (28 June, 2003).
60. Thomas L. Friedman, "The Power in 11/9," *The New York Times* (18 October, 2009).

15
Building for Real in Virtual Berlin

From this hour, I ordain myself loosed of limits and imaginary lines!

(Walt Whitman, 1856)[1]

The dream of the global city rises above borders, but it remains a dream. There are no actual global cities by the above criterion, yet it is this criterion that sustains the myth of urbanized globalization. Berlin's participation in this dream framework is nonetheless not so far-fetched. Hardly a lead player in the hierarchy of cities today, Berlin's self-(re)presentation continues as one of the most vigorously imagined and maintained world cities. Its fictitious status as a networked city, as a virtually conceived version of itself, gets more vibrantly touted. Urban identities – of cities, of parts of cities, and of actual people as denizens of those cities – have been ineradicably altered ever since televisual space effectively replaced the metropolitan street-scene as the major site of consumerist display and social exchange. Ironically, however, the same electronic technologies that have been blamed for diminishing so many of the major public spaces (or three-dimensional faces) of the modern city are themselves the building blocks of how cities are now planning their future growth. There seem, then, to be other gains going on for the post-industrial city, which is not necessarily losing out to the electronic post-urban condition in the manner of the countryside's earlier loss of social relevance in relation to the industrialized city. Perhaps the long-term good news is that branding in the virtual realm can, surprisingly, help build a new economic reality into being. Even Berlin's much-faulted boosterism now has a key practical role to play in combating the city's debt mountain, which costs millions of euros annually in interest alone: for a positive image of Berlin must necessarily be hawked and marketed by Berlin credit managers so as to lure potential investors.

The German capital's artifice of becoming, made more acute by early euphoric planning hopes of the *Wende* and then a prolonged period of post-party disillusionment, is, however, certainly not a new tendency for this city. Rather, it corresponds to a Berlin tradition of creating a virtual metropolis as a substitute for perceived deficiencies, past and present. The entire twentieth century contains instances of Berlin's self-aggrandizing staging, particularly by means of architectural exhibitions. Indeed, Berlin's needs have been amply illustrated through the decades via architecture's projective capacity to encapsulate the collective aspirations for a city. Early instances of this trend included the Greater Berlin urban planning exhibition of 1910; the Weimar era's competitions for Alexanderplatz in 1928 and for Potsdamer Platz the following year; the Nazis' Berlin Olympics of 1936; and, ultimately, Albert Speer's and Hitler's plans for Berlin, as the reborn "Germania," to host a world trade fair in 1950. During the decades after World War II, architectural exhibitions and competitions were used as a stabilizing means of promoting the rebuilding of (West) Berlin and of demoting its "outpost" status, and for confirming East Berlin as the new GDR's national capital: for example, the International Building Exhibition (*Interbau*) of 1957; the (West's) *Hauptstadt Berlin* ("Berlin Capital") competition of 1958 that willfully ignored the division of the city, and the competition "for the Socialist Redesign of the Center of the GDR Capital" (*zur sozialistischen Umgestaltung des Zentrums der Hauptstadt der DDR*) the following year; West Berlin's International Building Exhibition (*Internationale Bauausstellung*, or IBA) of 1987, and the official 750th anniversary of the city in the same year with rival celebratory efforts both sides of the Wall; as well as the fêting of West Berlin as the *Kulturhauptstadt* ("cultural capital") of Europe in 1988, the city's penultimate year as Cold War symbol.

German reunification brought about an understandable surge in this habitual self-staging of Berlin. Peaking around the millennium, a significant number of architectural exhibitions reflected their organizers' boosterist hopes, including "e.g., Berlin" (*z.B. Berlin*) in 2000 at the Postbahnhof; "City of Architecture – Architecture of the City" (*Stadt der Architektur – Architektur der Stadt*), organized by Josef Paul Kleihues and Paul Kahlfeldt in 2000 at the Neues Museum; *Berlin – Stadtmodelle* ("Berlin – City Models") in 2001 in an ex-warehouse at the Oberbaumbrücke; *Große Projekte. Berlin* ("Large-scale Projects: Berlin") at the Postbahnhof in 2002, with models of more than a dozen buildings; *Die Hand des Architekten* ("The Hand of the Architect") historical exhibition of sketches and models for planning the capital, held at the Altes Museum in 2002; not to mention the ongoing exhibition of Berlin models at the Senate Department for Urban Development. Berlin's planning achievements, plans, and dreams have been continually shown to the public in a series of self-obsessed displays of the city's current and future shape, such as the outdoor "Places on Display – 20 Years of a Changing Berlin" (*Schauplätze – 20 Jahre Berlin im Wandel*) that celebrated the twentieth anniversary of the fall of the Wall by showcasing several sites of urban renovation.[2] In line with this obsessive architectural self-representation, a permanent home for such exhibitions, dubbed a *Haus der Architektur*, was suggested in 2001 as a possible use for the GDR's Staatsratsgebäude; the idea has since shifted over to be the contents of the future Bauakademie, if it is ever rebuilt. Signs of (albeit fleeting) world attention occurred with Berlin's hosting of two of the largest conferences in architecture and urbanism, the "Urban 21" World Cities conference in 2000, and the UIA World Conference of Architecture in 2002.

Ad campaigns for the post-Wall city have often been merged with these exhibition venues, especially *Schaustelle Berlin* in 2003. For the two summers before and after the millennium, the Berliner Festspiele and the Architektenkammer Berlin made the city's self-referentiality entirely transparent with a series of architectural tours and publications around the theme "Berlin, Open City: The City as Exhibition."[3] The motto *Das Neue Berlin* morphed in the hands of the city marketing company Partner für Berlin (now: Berlin Partner) into a product in and of itself. Beyond the need to exhibit Berlin as a permanent exhibition, promotional imaging for the capital also featured strongly in a host of German architectural publications during the 1990s. The city financed boosterist venues for convincing the public of the New Berlin's actuality beyond virtuality, such as with the events-series *Stadtforum* and the magazine *Foyer*. The growing tendency to view the city through the appealing, virtual lens of an axonometric model became city policy with the evolving maps of Stimmann's *Planwerk Innenstadt* initiative. Architectural and panorama maps became fashionable. Huyssen wondered at Berlin's self-staging: "From void ... to mise-en-scène and to image, images in the void: *Berlin wird* ... Berlin becomes image."[4] The sheer plethora of these image-events certainly leads one to suspect that there might be something else afoot – perhaps a wished-for transformation of collective identity on behalf of all Germans, far broader than just for the city itself. However, as Peter Sloterdijk has surmised, in the ongoing re-make of Berlin there is as yet no therapeutic process that will enable Germans to "become something other than what they are."[5]

As a result of serving as a piece of Play-Doh for post-Wall planning commissions, architectural organizations, and speculative investors and developers, much of Berlin-Mitte appears as a work of art on display as reality and vice versa. Slavoj Žižek has satirized this condition, confessing how he once mistook street work for an artwork when he beheld the various brightly colored utilities pipes exposed on and above Berlin streets and thought they were "another one of those postmodern art events, the aim of which was ... to make visible the belly, the hidden inner machinery of the city." Or again, conversely, Žižek recounts how, during a crane-show staged at Potsdamer Platz, some passers-by misunderstood the spectacle as cranes actually at work (albeit in a rather synchronized fashion). It is in this way that the "commercialization of culture" has produced its opposite, namely the "'culturalization' of the market economy."[6]

Hence it is not so surprising that, representationally speaking, virtual Berlin has entered toy-land. The Legoland Discovery Centre at the Sony Center or Berlin's own Model Park in Marzahn are just some of the larger examples of the trend. In a move that illustrates the architectural experience's increasing proximity to children's games and adventures, the city is for sale as an architectural cardboard pop-up in models of buildings that one associates with East Berlin's lost *mythos*: for example, *faltplatte.de* has produced an eponymous foldable GDR-era residential high-rise, as well as one of the "people's palace" (the *Volkspalast*, or *Palast der Republik*), and another of the Stalinallee (now Karl-Marx-Allee). There is also, of course, a pop-up model of the Berlin Wall itself.[7] With the image of Berlin counting for more than any actual street-level experience, a fitting microcosmic example was a pop-up book depicting the architectural events since reunification: *Das Berlin-Paket* (2001).[8]

Perhaps this trend started with wanting to emulate the canvas mock-up of the City Palace in 1993 and 1994, by Goerd Peschken and Frank Augustin; and Christo and Jeanne-Claude's Wrapped Reichstag in 1995. Visitors to the capital can buy *berlinerluft.org* postcards of a wide range of Berlin's architectural icons, from the Brandenburg Gate to the New Synagogue and the GDR's TV Tower, that give instructions on how to cut along the dotted lines and create miniature building models (Fig. 15.1). Thanks, then, to an overloaded impetus toward urban transformation, architectural boosterism in Berlin has become an infinitely self-replicating process. It has also become therapeutic. These Berlin model toys are reminiscent of the needs met by the Freudian *fort/da*

332

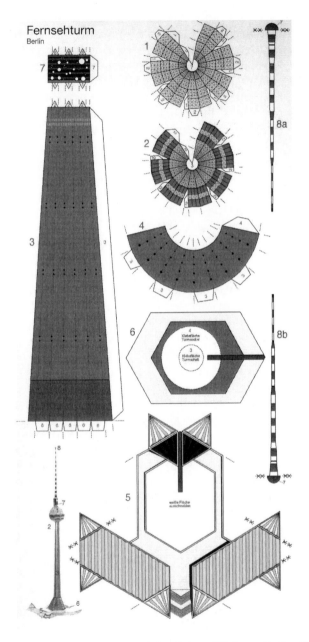

Figure 15.1   Postcard cut-out model of the GDR-era TV Tower, Berlin, 2004

process: one is invited to consume in order to partake of the powers of constructing and deconstructing a city whose identity has been morphing faster than it is reasonable or comfortable for its denizens to accept. Clearly, Volker Hassemer, founder of Berlin Partner, has experienced some frustration at people's inability to deal with post-Wall Berlin's rapidity of change, since he refers to the "building site in the heads" of Berliners (*Baustelle in den Köpfen*).[9]

Yet this web of models and simulations, while often amusingly virtual, cannot be so easily discounted. This is because it plays a major role in the only industries that stand a chance of helping to make Berlin global: the socially connected growth areas of (city- or place-) marketing, sports, culture, entertainment, and the service economy. Saskia Sassen, in considering the ways in which telematics is always "inflected by the cultures, the material practices, the imaginaries that take place outside cyberspace," remains cognizant that there is such a thing as the reality of the virtual realm: "Digital space is embedded in the larger societal, cultural, subjective, economic, imaginary structurations of lived experience and the systems within which we exist and operate."[10] In this vein, electronic Berlin maps tend to appeal to the desire to recapture the glorious lost city of pre-World War II years, as well as the romantically disused "otherspace" of the Cold War's Wall. Views of a digitized Berlin are now available on interactive CD-ROM, with aerial shots at important junctures in the twentieth century. Berlin "online" also exists in 360-degree panoramic perspectives, often in real time, at favorite sites like Potsdamer Platz or the view from the roof of the renovated Reichstag. When the Friedrich-Carré was being built near the Friedrichsstraße train station, passers-by were offered a live-cam shot of the building process on 15 screens along its construction fence. The same fascination applies to demolition as well: people worldwide watched, via stop-motion video, the step-by-step demolition of the Palace of the Republic (2006–8). The voyeurism can also be pedagogically creative in scope: a UCLA-based "Hypermedia Berlin" project, developed by Todd Presner, calls out to the "new media flâneur" to interactively re-encode the city and be as innovative regarding Berlin's urbanism as Walter Benjamin's *Arcades Project* was in suggesting a modern, multidimensional understanding of Paris.[11] Virtual Berlin can of course simply be practical as well: the various news and city-marketing websites that emerged in the late 1990s, like those of *tagesspiegel.de, meinberlin. de, zitty.de* (all owned by Urban Media GmbH), as well as *BerlinOnline.de* and the city's official *berlin.de* (both owned by Gruner + Jahr AG & Co., Bankgesellschaft Berlin AG, and Berliner Volksbank) function not simply as tourism portals but as multi-service city information systems.

One may well also inquire as to the degree of satirical self-awareness in these multiple self-stagings of the German capital. There have indeed been some reflective responses: virtual multiplications in city-building were made the subject of a 2003 exhibition at Düsseldorf's Kunsthalle. Here, architectural theorists Sybil Kohl, Philipp Oswalt, and Albrecht Schäfer scathingly depicted three categories about urbanism, predominantly in the former East Germany, that do not exist except in the virtual realm and are hence even more worthy of recording – *Verlassene Stadt* ("Deserted City"), *Ersatzstadt* ("Substitute City"), and *Ungebaute Stadt* ("Unbuilt City"), respectively.[12] In this photo-album trilogy of urban non-form, readers learn, in turn, about the all-too-real myriad empty sites caused by the selling-off of GDR companies and the exodus of former East Germans to the West German states; about the instant architecture born of the speculation wave; and finally about those projects doomed to remain forever stuck at the design or competition stage. In another instance, the real estate market in general and the Fundus company in particular were parodied in poster format at the Prater beer garden in Prenzlauer Berg. The poster announced: "To be built here: 10,000 m^2 fulfillment of all wishes under one roof – Glass-roofed atrium in a courtyard garden – Retail spaces, consumer terrorism – Underground garages on two levels – Designer hotel suites with fitness and anti-aging center – Culture for passers-by in restored historic Prater room – Events for the whole family – Eight luxury apartments with panoramic view of Prenzlauer Berg. Completion 2008. Fungus-Group: We encourage art as we buy it selflessly."[13] Artist Stefanie Buerkle, whose Berlin-based painting "Construction Gaps" (*Baulücken*) graces the cover of this book, posed for several days as a real estate agent promoting an illusory luxury development, complete with an equally illusory billboard that she had designed and placed next to an empty lot in Neukölln: *Luxe, plaisir et liberté* ("Luxury, Pleasure, and Liberty").[14]

The rising sense of unreality in the New Berlin's aspirations has also been charted cinematically. Berlin's indeterminate virtuality has perhaps been best captured by the Tom Tykwer film *Run Lola Run* (1999), where the plot turns around various possible arbitrary outcomes of life and death akin to an interactive video game. The heroine Lola is shown alternately as a human and as a cartoon video-game protagonist, and the Berlin streets that she continually runs through, while appearing realistic (non-virtual), bear little resemblance to direction and topography on any actual map of the reunified city. A literary articulation of the risks inherent in Berlin's infinite self-representability can be found in Normann Ohler's novel, *Mitte* (2001), which depicts an impermanent virtual reality within the rotting *Altbau*-fabric of the former East German capital: here, urban degeneration among the frenzied capitalist gentrification all around the Hackescher Markt area occurs in both the electronic and physical realms. We can recall here the famous building-site representations of Berlin's earlier modernity, as detailed in Alfred Döblin's montage visions of the interwar capital in *Berlin Alexanderplatz* (1929), in which cinematic perspectives were spliced into the novel, such as the pile-driver in violent operation, the subway tunneling, or the street work at Rosenthaler Platz. In Ohler's novel in contrast, rebuilding Berlin has forged not so much an infectious modern urban energy of renewal as a damaged environment which has sold its authentic Faustian soul en route to a desired era of post-Wall rehabbing and a vainly sought-after world-ranking among cities.[15] In Ohler's (or his protagonist Klinger's) world, a seismic fault seems to lurk underneath post-Wall Berlin's attempt to refurbish its streets with the pre-Wall capital city's identity. Cracks will appear in the New Berlin's structures because the new is make-believe old.[16]

It took a while for any sense of ludic, literary irony about Berlin's image to reach local governance levels. The city's ad campaign for the summer of 2003, *Mir geht's Berlin*, was a poster launched in 70 German cities, intended to promote a sense of Berlin's unique individuality, as in the sense of "How are you?" – "I'm feeling Berlin, thank you" – which made it sound as if the Berlin experience was akin to catching a cold. But then, later that year, Klaus Wowereit responded to an interviewer's question that his city was indeed "poor, but sexy." All of a sudden Berlin had from its mayor an ideal, if accidental, brand slogan; the city's cultish, youth-oriented identity was essentially saved by the much-quoted *arm aber sexy* moniker. (Not surprisingly, a flipside to such posturing of Berlin as the place for youth to seek out life-defining experiences is that a mainstay of the tourism trade is now the binge-drinking pub crawls – even bike pub crawls – of Mitte.) Moreover, since 2008, *seiberlin.de* ("beberlin") has been promoted by Wowereit and Berlin Partner as a city campaign to further essentialize and extend that same sense of place-based cultishness into as many realms as possible: the city's history, its focus on research and development, its multiculturalism, and so on. In this way (or so it is hoped) the city's "hard-branding" is being accelerated in ways that bypass unwanted truths and offer benefits from the symbolic economy instead.[17]

So "beberlin" is not so unrealistic, after all. While the legacy of Berlin's former border status has refused to move out of the way in the city's bid for relevance in the global economy, it is in the realm of virtual urbanism that Berlin has been able to pick up the slack. This phenomenon is of course happening in myriad metropolitan centers as a technique of postmodern place-marketing. But in Berlin's case we find a specific kind of virtual topophilia providing far more than just a compensatory role for the city's long litany of urban failures.[18] Beyond the ironic gap projected between actual material conditions and the image, urban or otherwise, the self-stagings of this city have in fact ended up having a concrete effect on Berlin's ability to progress beyond its backwater status, and move toward the mere possibility of a future world-citydom befitting the postmodern era. Thus in post-Wall Berlin's case, image really is almost everything.

Marketing an image of Berlin for tourists according to the value of its inherited imagery, especially as the "capital city of knowledge and culture," according to one of its slogans, would appear to be working well.[19] Berlin's tourism industry is growing faster than in any other German city, and the annual visitor rate to the capital is fast approaching eight million a year. The power of Berlin to lead other cities culturally was accidentally enhanced by its decades of having had to provide double everything as a divided city: witness present-day Berlin's seven universities, twenty technical colleges, eighty research institutes, three opera houses, fifty theaters, and over one hundred and seventy museums. As if to illustrate this, in 2005 Berlin received a UNESCO "City of Design" Award specifically for its strength in fostering cultural industries. *The New York Times*, for one, is buying the product, recently calling Berlin a "cultural capital not just of Europe, but of the world"; and *The Economist* praised Berlin for its central role in establishing Germany's dance boom.[20]

Berlin's most significant cultural *grand projet* is the long-term re-conceptualization of the Museum Island in Mitte, which consists of five structures built between 1830 and 1920, all in a state of disrepair or even ruin when the city reunified.[21] The Prussian Cultural Heritage Foundation (Stiftung Preußischer Kulturbesitz) is currently re-centralizing Berlin's art collections that were scattered across seventeen state museums in the city, products of war and division. Not surprisingly, making the Museumsinsel whole again in terms of its structures and art holdings holds tremendous significance for the post-Wall city, even if it is one that is not yet fully actualized and made visible. Voltaire and the Crown Prince Friedrich first aspired that Berlin should become an "Athens on the Spree" in their correspondence of 1737; and it was by means of a national art culture that the nineteenth-century Prussian capital wished to both conceptually ground and pragmatically market itself.

At least one cultural "Wall in the head" evaporated when another head (the ancient Egyptian bust of Princess Nefertete) was moved from its West Berlin location in Charlottenburg first to the Altes Museum in 2005 and then into a prime spot in the newly renovated Neues Museum in the fall of 2009. By helping to re-center the city's art collections, Nefertete as icon also assisted in the sense of Berlin's and Germany's reunification just in time for the twentieth anniversary of the fall of the Wall.[22] And the celebrations regarding Nefertete's return were not the first. The 2001 re-opening of the renovated Alte Nationalgalerie (originally built in 1876) was regarded as a bringing together, indeed a reunification, of German heritage from that comparatively innocent era – a final resting place for the wandering works of art by Karl Friedrich Schinkel and Caspar David Friedrich that had been previously divided between East and West Berlin.[23] The media celebrated the opening as the refound *Mitte* for the whole nation, enacting thereby a succinct elision of the Wall's former role as the literal "middle" of Berlin. Indeed, the renovation of all of Museum Island will be one of the last major federally funded building works intended to reunify the capital. The business of Berlin's museum culture functions, then, in much the same way as does the culture of business provided by Potsdamer Platz: both represent, by means of the reunified artworks or the reconstructed site of Potsdamer Platz once split by the Wall, "turntable" (*Drehscheibe*) sites that provide the successful capital-cultural evidence of joining and fusing the city.

Beyond tourism and the intangible added-value of high cultural significance, can any economic successes be charted in so much hyping of the Berlin image? It would appear to be so. Where post-Wall Berlin has had its clearest case of economic success thus far has been at the interface between the cultural and the virtual economy, in the globalized network of new content industries like multimedia. Berlin has become a "city of talents" that can build on its accepted strengths: cultural and media production, bio-sciences, the software industry, marketing, sports, entertainment, and the service sector. In fact, most of the new companies arriving or starting in Berlin every year come from those categories. Thus despite being just a second-tier global city Berlin actually ranks as a first-tier "global *media* city," according to Stefan Krätke's ranking of cities according to their level of networked media company clusters, just as global cities are typically defined by their level of advanced producer services.[24] As a global multimedia city in today's culture industry Berlin is thus able to challenge Hamburg's or Munich's leadership in that area.

Intriguingly, in this virtual industry realm urban locality and urban imaging go hand in hand. Krätke has demonstrated in a study of multimedia-company clustering that there is a strong interrelationship between the product-services of such companies and their location within the gentrifying parts of former East Berlin, including sites along the former Wall.[25] The Chausseestraße area in Mitte, in particular, attracted a strong presence of multimedia firms and gained the epithet "Silicon Alley." Clearly, the Mediaspree's site location has become a desired part of the newly arrived companies' brand image, and the firms, in turn, are interdependent on one another's proximity in these shared arenas in order to build up networked nodes, affording the city a new "space of opportunities'" for its creative class.[26] A certain synergy between locality and globalization can thus be witnessed in such instances of clustering. As Sassen has argued, in this imbrication the local can serve as a "'microenvironment with global span' insofar as it is deeply internetworked." Thus Berlin's brand image in the global cultural economy continues to gain in status through the "soft power" reach of the city as coercive lure and come-hither attraction for those skill-sets. A city like Berlin, with this high degree of cultural capital, is needed for such companies to flourish in the first place; and in return, the activity of such enterprises regenerates the city, offering a "new idea of ... urbanity."[27]

Our remaining product, then, is rebranded Berlin, which despite all the errors made along the way seems to be having an increasingly positive effect. In spring 2007, *Der Spiegel* (itself no stranger to dramatic cover pages depicting the travails and transformations of the German capital since the fall of the Wall) hailed Berlin in an ironic *New Yorker*-style image as the "Comeback of a World City" (Fig. 15.2). More empirically and less ambitiously, Karl Schlögel also hails Berlin as a "comeback" city but includes it as one site among many in the ongoing "revolution of urbanity" that has superseded the liberating civil revolutions of eastern Europe in 1989–1990.[28]

Today's Berlin is, then, an urban-comeback-kid, whose chance of success can be said to revolve around the notion of whether it ultimately succeeds in identifying the "ghost of a better future" over the memories of its past. This is Ernst Bloch's phrase of 1932 as he ploughed the metaphor of Berlin's unfinished condition and "'newly constructed' feel" into his vision of an improved German democratic landscape, hoping in vain for better things beyond the stock market crash, economic depression, and rising unemployment that ultimately led German voters to Hitler.[29] Certainly, we can reflect on the degree to which Bloch's assessment of modern Berlin's fertile mutability has been overtaken by more recent takes on Berlin's postmodern condition as being

Figure 15.2 "Berlin: Comeback of a World City." Cover of *Der Spiegel*, 12 (19 March, 2007)

beyond repair to anything approaching its former value. Wolf Jobst Siedler, for example, certainly touched a postwar nerve in his demotion of the city as "no more than a burnt out memory of itself," a position which risks disconnecting all post-Wall reconstruction efforts from the global marketplace and short-circuiting them upon the city's past "inspirational strength."[30] Yet Bloch's words can nonetheless provide a conceptual bridge that optimistically links the old Berlin, in its world-city function of modernity, with a Berlin for our (still new) century:

> This unreal Berlin, in the humor of its emptiness and the seriousness of its mutability [*Beweglichkeit*], is one of the most genuine of all cities accursed and elected to existence in these times … This city's

mutability [*Wendigkeit*] makes it a site of least resistance to turning points [*Wende*] – the ones that truly bring change – and to the renovation of the world ... Other cities are often mere ghosts of a better past; hollow Berlin is possibly – there is no choice – the ghost of a better future.[31]

Will Bloch's lessons for Berlin ever be heeded? For example, if Berlin rebuilds its City Palace on the site of the East German Palace of the Republic that it destroyed for destroying the former, it may well become stuck with a prominent ghost of its (selective) better past, rather than the center of the center that is intended thereby. Wolfgang Kil hit the nail on the head: if the improvisational *Zwischennutzung* phase of the Palace of the Republic had been allowed to continue – that is, if the communist building had not been demolished piece by piece and the artists had been permitted to stage their work there – Berlin might have accidentally gained the veritable "republican Forum" that Axel Schultes had originally wanted next to his Chancellery building.[32] An alternative border zone of permanent subculture would have been officially anointed by the city of Berlin. But we can see how this would have been an impossibility – had the ruined shell of the *PdR* been thus anointed, it would have lost its edge.

Supporters of the City Palace substitute, the planned Humboldt Forum, believe that this structure will fill what is deemed the much-needed, unifying agora for Berlin. Yet the ironies are still there: apart from the baroque-style façade itself, such a center would consist of two voids, both the covered courtyard (the recreation of the former *Eosanderhof*) and an adjoining open one (the *Schlüterhof*), around which the total structure of 260,000 square feet (24,000 sq m) would extend. While defining Berlin, it is hoped that this agora-function of the rebuilt palace would also serve as a "'portal to the world'" because of all the various museal holdings to be brought across the city from Berlin's Asian and ethnological museums.[33] "The result of visual, decentralized democracy should be," if we heed Richard Sennett's advice, "to shatter those images which attempt to represent the city as a whole."[34] But that is the heavy burden the future Humboldt Forum, if it is ever built, is intended to carry. Berlin has been attempting and will go on to attempt again and again new formations of an urban agora that somehow answers all the needs inherent to the city's attempted recentralization. But who knows? Perhaps the green grassy space that now awaits rebuilding after the demolition of the GDR Palace will start beating with the pulse of the agora, after all (Fig. 15.3).

Figure 15.3 Berlin's agora? The lawn that replaced the demolished Palace of the Republic on the site of the former City Palace in 2009

We have seen that in the memory-and-erasure game that Berlin has been playing with itself, the net result is the pasting-together, via buildings, of accidentally amassed capital-city dreams and nation-state fantasies that for the most part attempt to belie and deny the German nation's multicultural presence and the capital's traumatic, divided past. Yet perhaps Berlin's better future may well have been more accurately assessed by its boosters than the city's doomsayers would suggest. A leading global city status may be remote indeed after Berlin's litany of failures, but it should be recalled that such ranking really can be artificially created. West Germans have a particularly short memory in this regard: after all, Frankfurt am Main in the immediate post-World War II era was the focus of a carefully controlled and hyped urbanization program, one that sought to prove that city's world-metropolitan status to the outside world. The "New Frankfurt" and its surrounding urban region, nowadays awarded "alpha" global-city status by the GaWC inventory for its position in today's international money economy, was in fact carefully steered into becoming such by the Americans' *deus ex machina*, the Marshall Plan. This is how the made-over "Mainhattan von Deutschland" emerged with a status and function that is taken for granted today.[35] Frankfurt as a global city is an export product that served as an *insta-fix* for the postwar West German democratic economy, optimally linked to the world via its stock exchange, trade fairs, road and rail connections, and Lufthansa hub. If the next generation of Berliners is lucky, some of the better remodeling of Berlin might just stick in a similar way.

Furthermore, for having hyped itself as that which it wishes to resemble, however far out of reach, post-Wall Berlin deserves to be forgiven, at least from the point of view of the American experience of city-building. After all, both promises of the future and substitutions of an urban historical past (borrowed from other established cities) have been a fundamental part of regional and urban boosterism. Some of the most influential historical applications of boosterism can be found in the mid-nineteenth- and early twentieth-century creation of the American midwest and West, with promoters' myriad promises to potential migrants back East and to potential immigrants in Europe.[36] Of course, boosterist images cannot be applied to any city indefinitely without adapting to actual material conditions. The prototypical boosterist city of Los Angeles at the beginning of the twenty-first century is now as aging as was New York at the beginning of the twentieth, and hence has to see itself more clearly along its own trajectory. These two decades of Berlin's post-Wall reconstruction, despite their heavy dependency on virtual projections of globalization rather than economic manifestations of the latter, may be considered a malleable step in this direction – but only a first. It is as if the city were still learning to design the interface that will ultimately best fit its post-Wall visage: that which Berlin will ultimately "be."

"What remains," then, of the German capital's self-reinvention efforts? *Was bleibt* is not just Christa Wolf's reflection about a life lived in Berlin and how one lives the rest of it, but moreover a final question for the future of the city.[37] Perhaps, indeed, some selected elements of the rebranded capital will become permanent after being city-marketed as products of virtual volition. A commentator for *Die Zeit* once remarked that it seemed as if there were a giant screen on the Spree's river curve onto which Berliners were busy "predicting and projecting the urban future."[38] That screen is still there, full of Schopenhauerian will and representation. For the rules of projection, however, we can leave a last word with Jacques Derrida, who returned to Bloch's concerns soon after Berlin's reunification, and presciently urged the city to acknowledge its incomplete non-identity not as a failure but as a precondition for its ultimate success: "the impossibility to draw the limits and the borders for a city is a categorical imperative. [...] We must at the same time vigorously program and leave some place for play, for things to be open to what is to come."[39] Let us, in turn, encourage the trajectory of Berlin adapting to its failure to become a paint-by-numbers global city, and also better valuing the heritage of brokenness that is an integral part of its urban fabric. In this way, Berlin's identity can be sought via the contradictory spaces that are truly its own. In terms of its evolution for the twenty-first century, this city is not yet done with bordering.

Notes

1. Walt Whitman, "Poem of the Road" (later "Song of the Open Road") in *Leaves of Grass*, 2nd ed. (Walt Whitman/Fowler and Wells, 1856).
2. See www.mauerfall09.de/portal/schauplaetze/schauplaetze.html (date accessed 20 March, 2010).
3. Roland Enke, Reinhard Alings, Bernhard Schneider, and Gerwin Zohlen, with Berliner Festspiele, eds, *Berlin: Open City* (*The City on Exhibition. The Guide*, vol. 1; and *Renewal Since 1989*, vol. 2) (Berlin: Nicolai, 1999).
4. Andreas Huyssen, *Present Pasts: Urban Palimpsests and the Politics of Memory* (Stanford: Stanford University Press, 2003), p. 64; orig. "The Voids of Berlin," *Critical Inquiry*, 24.1 (1997), pp. 57–81.
5. Uwe Rada, *Hauptstadt der Verdrängung: Berliner Zukunft zwischen Kiez und Metropole* (Berlin: Verlag Schwarze Risse, 1997), p. 8.
6. Slavoj Žižek, "Wer naiv fragt, wird schockiert. Fragen wir also naiv!" *Die Zeit* 50 (9 December, 1999).

7. Andreas Seidel and Jürgen Schnirch, *The Berlin Wall* (2003), www.xzcute.com (date accessed 2 May, 2010).

8. M. Lewitscharoff, ed., *Das Berlin-Paket* (Munich: ars Edition, 2001), which was subjected to withering commentary in *Die Zeit*, 50 (6 December, 2001).

9. Volker Hassemer, "Stadtentwicklung und Stadtmarketing nach 1990 – die Perspektive eines kommunalen Verantwortungsträgers," in Thomas Biskup and Marc Schalenberg, eds, *Selling Berlin: Imagebildung und Stadtmarketing von der preußischen Residenz bis zur Bundeshauptstadt* (Stuttgart: Franz Steiner Verlag, 2008), pp. 335–44, p. 340.

10. Saskia Sassen, "Reading the City in a Global Digital Age: Between Topographic Representation and Spatialized Power Projects," in Linda Krause and Patrice Petro, eds, *Global Cities: Cinema, Architecture, and Urbanism in a Digital Age* (New Brunswick: Rutgers University Press, 2003), pp. 15–30, p. 19.

11. Todd Presner, "The City in the Ages of New Media: From Ruttmann's *Berlin: Die Sinfonie der Großstadt* to Hypermedia Berlin," in Lutz Koepnick and Erin McGlothlin, eds, *After the Digital Divide? German Aesthetic Theory in the Age of New Media* (Rochester, NY: Camden House, 2009), pp. 167–85, p. 177.

12. Sybil Kohl, Philipp Oswalt, and Albrecht Schäfer, *Architektur-Stadtführer Ostdeutschland* (Cologne: Verlag der Buchhandlung Walther König, 2003).

13. "Bauplakat," *scheinschlag*, 6.2 (2003).

14. Stefanie Buerkle, "Architecture as Scenography, the Building Site as Stage," in Uta Staiger, Henriette Steiner, and Andrew Webber, eds, *Memory Culture and the Contemporary City: Building Sites* (Basingstoke and New York: Palgrave Macmillan, 2009), pp. 181–90, pp. 188–89.

15. Alfred Döblin, *Berlin Alexanderplatz. Die Geschichte von Franz Biberkopf* (Munich: dtv, 1988); and Norman Ohler, *Mitte* (Berlin: Rowohlt, 2001), p. 222.

16. Cracks in the new cement and/or rain leaks have, in fact, appeared in several prominent new structures of the New Berlin, notably the Chancellery, the Bundestag buildings Paul-Löbe-Haus and Jakob-Kaiser-Haus (its tunnel to the Reichstag), the DZ-Bank, the Academy of Arts, and the Holocaust Memorial.

17. Sabine Beikler, "Wowereits Vision: Da ist noch Luft drin," *Der Tagesspiegel* (14 June, 2009); see also Graeme Evans, "Hard-Branding the Cultural City – From Prado to Prada," *International Journal of Urban and Regional Research*, 27.2 (2003), pp. 417–40, p. 418.

18. See Allan Cochrane and Andrew Jonas, "Reimagining Berlin: World City, National Capital or Ordinary Place?" *European Urban and Regional Studies*, 6.2 (1999), pp. 145–64.

19. See, for example, www.berlin.de/international/berlin_a-z/capital_city/index.en.php (date accessed 11 March, 2010).

20. Sam Sifton, "Berlin, the Big Canvas," *The New York Times* (22 June, 2008); "On Top of the World: Dance," *The Economist* (12 August, 2006).

21. The focal point of the *Museumsinsel* will be, in addition to an underground "archeological promenade," a new visitor center, the James Simon Galley (named after one of Berlin's major art benefactors to the museum, the Jewish-German magnate Henri James Simon). Both additions have been designed by David Chipperfield; their common purpose will be to guide tourist traffic and protect the fabric of the existing structures. The James Simon Gallery will be a glass palimpsest of sorts, built to fit the dimensions

of Schinkel's Packhofgebäude which used to stand on that site. See www. museumsinsel-berlin.de/index.php?lang=en&page=1_1 (date accessed 2 December, 2009).

22. At the same time, Nefertete symbolizes the latest case in a series of open-border challenges regarding the provenance of cultural treasures. See Judy Dempsey, "A 3,500-Year-Old Queen Causes a Rift Between Germany and Egypt," *The New York Times* (20 October, 1989).

23. Journalists and critics celebrated the renovated Alte Nationalgalerie's reopening as a (post-Nietzschean) re-"birth of the nation out of the spirit of art." See, for example, Peter-Klaus Schuster, "Die Geburt der Nation aus dem Geist der Kunst. Zur Wiedereröffnung der Alten Nationalgalerie," in Angelika Wesenberg and Eve Förschl, eds, *Die Nationalgalerie. Das XIX. Jahrhundert* (Leipzig: E.A. Seemann Verlag, 2002), pp. 9–38.

24. Stefan Krätke has advocated the phrase "city of talents" as an "urban *marketing formula*" for the German capital. More recently he has emphasized how the "metropolisation" effect caused by knowledge-cultural industries is on the long-term rise in the urban areas of eastern and central Europe. Krätke, "City of Talents? Berlin's Regional Economy, Socio-Spatial Fabric and 'Worst Practice' Urban Governance," *International Journal of Urban and Regional Research*, 28.3 (2004), pp. 511–29, p. 511 (emphasis original); and Krätke, "Metropolisation of the European Economic Territory as a Consequence of Increasing Specialisation of Urban Agglomerations in the Knowledge Economy," *European Planning Studies*, 15.1 (2007), pp. 1–27, p. 19. See also Sassen, "Ausgrabungen in der 'Global City'," in Albert Scharenberg, ed., *Berlin: Global City oder Konkursmasse? Eine Zwischenbilanz zehn Jahre nach dem Mauerfall* (Berlin: Karl Dietz Verlag, 2000), pp. 14–26, p. 18; Philip Cooke, *Knowledge Economies: Clusters, Learning and Cooperative Advantage* (New York: Routledge, 2002), pp. 130–56; Erwin Riedmann, "Global City Berlin? Illusionen und die Ironie der Geschichte," *dérive. Zeitschrift für Stadtforschung*, 20 (2005), pp. 34–37; Bastian Lange, "Culturepreneurs in Berlin: Orts- und Raumproduzenten von Szenen," in Alexa Färber et al., eds, *Hotel Berlin. Formen urbaner Mobilität und Verortung* (Münster: LIT Verlag, 2005), pp. 53–64; Martina Löw, *Soziologie der Städte* (Frankfurt am Main: Suhrkamp, 2008); and Ulrich Zawatka-Gerlach, "Berlin zieht an," *Der Tagesspiegel* (2 October, 2009).

25. Stefan Krätke, *Medienstadt. Urbane Cluster und globale Zentren der Kulturproduktion* (Opladen: Leske + Budrich, 2002).

26. Krätke, "City of Talents," p. 518. Krätke is referring to Richard Florida, *The Rise of the Creative Class: And How It's Transforming Work, Leisure, Community and Everyday Life* (New York: Basic Books, 2002).

27. Sassen, in Krause and Petro, eds, *Global Cities*, p. 20; and Sassen, "Ausgrabungen in der 'Global City'," in Scharenberg, ed., *Berlin*, p. 19. See also Jeannot Simmen and Thorsten Heinze, *berlin-2010.eu* (Berlin: Edition Club Bel Etage, 2010); and Joseph S. Nye, *Soft Power: The Means to Success in World Politics* (New York: Public Affairs, 2004).

28. Karl Schlögel, "The Comeback of the European Cities," *International Review of Sociology*, 16.2 (2006), pp. 471–85, p. 471.

29. Ernst Bloch, "Berlin, as Viewed from the Landscape" (1932), in *Literary Essays*, trans. Andrew Joron et al. (Stanford: Stanford University Press, 1998), pp. 361–71, pp. 371, 370.

30. Wolf Jobst Siedler, "Das immerwährende Berlin I," *Die Welt* (14 September, 1999). Siedler's thought is an outgrowth of his 1964 book attacking the *tabula rasa* methods of postwar rebuilding, *Die gemordete Stadt. Abgesang auf Putte und Straße, Platz und Baum* (Berlin: Siedler, 1993).

31. Bloch, "Berlin," in *Literary Essays*, pp. 370–71; Bloch, "Berlin aus der Landschaft gesehen," in *Literarische Aufsätze, Gesamtausgabe*, vol. 9 (Frankfurt am Main: Suhrkamp, 1965), pp. 408–20, p. 419.

32. Wolfgang Kil, "Chronik eines angekündigten Todes," in Amelie Deuflhard, Sophie Krempl-Klieeisen, Philipp Oswalt, Matthias Lilienthal, and Harald Müller, eds, *Volkspalast. Zwischen Aktivismus und Kunst* (Berlin: Theater der Zeit, 2006), pp. 154–60, p. 158. The rationale for saving the Palace of the Republic from demolition is also discussed in a volume by Philipp Misselwitz, Hans Ulrich Obrist, and Philipp Oswalt, eds, *Fun Palace 200X – der Berliner Schlossplatz: Abriß, Neubau, oder grüne Wiese?* (Berlin: Martin Schmitz Verlag, 2005).

33. On the Humboldt Forum's agora, see Andreas Kilb, "Schloßdebatte. Im Palast der Replik," *Frankfurter Allgemeine Zeitung* (9 March, 2009); and Klaus-Dieter Lehmann, "Weltort für Kunst und Kultur – Berlins Mitte," in Stiftung Preussischer Kulturbesitz, ed., *Jahrbuch Stiftung Preußischer Kulturbesitz 2005* XLII (Berlin: Verlag Dietrich Reimer/Verlag Gebr. Mann, 2006), pp. 115–28, pp. 119, 120.

34. Richard Sennett, *The Spaces of Democracy* (Ann Arbor: College of Architecture + Urban Planning, The University of Michigan, 1998), p. 41. See also Uwe Rada's preference for Berlin's neighborhood (*Kiez*)-filled poly-centrality, in Rada, *Hauptstadt der Verdrängung*, pp. 49–52.

35. Roger Keil and Klaus Ronneberger, "The Globalization of Frankfut am Main: Core, Periphery and Social Conflict," in Peter Marcuse and Ronald van Kempen, eds, *Globalizing Cities: A New Spatial Order?* (Malden: Blackwell, 2000), pp. 228–48; J.V. Beaverstock, P.J. Taylor, and R.G. Smith, "A Roster of World Cities," *Cities*, 16.6 (1999), pp. 445–58, p. 456; and Klaus Ronneberger, Stephan Lanz, and Walther Jahn, *Die Stadt als Beute* (Bonn: Dietz, 1999), pp. 25–29.

36. Greg Hise, *Magnetic Los Angeles: Planning the Twentieth-Century Metropolis* (Baltimore: Johns Hopkins University Press, 1999); David M. Wrobel, *Promised Lands: Promotion, Memory, and the Creation of the American West* (Lawrence: University Press of Kansas, 2002); and Stephen V. Ward, *Selling Places: The Marketing and Promotion of Towns and Cities 1850–2000* (New York: Routledge, 1998), pp. 9–28.

37. Christa Wolf, *Was bleibt* (Frankfurt am Main: Luchterhand, 1990), p. 103; *What Remains and Other Stories*, trans. Heike Schwarzbauer and Rick Takvorian (New York: Farrar, Straus, and Giroux, 1993), p. 295.

38. Thomas Assheuer, "Das Deutschlandspiel. Viel Abschied, wening Ankunft – Der Streit um die Deutung einer Berliner Republik," *Die Zeit*, 37 (1998).

39. Jacques Derrida, in Derrida, Kurt Forster, and Wim Wenders, "The Berlin City Forum," *Architectural Design*, 62.11/12 (1992), pp. 46–53, p. 49.

Selected Bibliography

Part I: Berlin and the Bordered Condition

Agnew, John A. *Geopolitics: Re-Visioning World Politics* (New York: Routledge, 1998).

———— "The Territorial Trap: The Geographical Assumptions of International Relations Theory," *Review of International Political Economy*, 1 (1994), pp. 53–80.

Agnew, John, Katharyne Mitchell, and Gearóid Ó Tuathail, eds, *A Companion to Political Geography* (Malden, MA: Blackwell Publishers Ltd, 2003).

————, and Stuart Corbridge, *Mastering Space: Hegemony, Territory and International Political Economy* (New York: Routledge, 1995).

Albert, Mathias, David Jacobson, and Yosef Lapid, eds, *Identities, Borders, Orders: Rethinking International Relations Theory* (Minneapolis: University of Minnesota Press, 2001).

Anderson, Benedict, *Imagined Communities: Reflections on the Origin and Spread of Nationalism*, 2nd ed. (New York: Verso, 1991).

———— "The New World Disorder," *New Left Review*, 193 (1992), pp. 3–13.

Anderson, Malcolm, *Frontiers: Territory and State Formation in the Modern World* (Malden, MA: Blackwell/Polity Press, 1996).

————, and Eberhard Bort, eds, *The Frontiers of Europe* (London: Pinter, 1998).

Andreas, Peter, and Timothy Snyder, eds, *The Wall around the West: State Borders and Immigration Controls in North America and Europe* (New York: Rowman & Littlefield, 2000).

Antonsich, Marco, Vladimar Kolossov, and M. Paola Pagnini, eds, *Europe Between Political Geography and Geopolitics* (Rome: Società Geografica Italiana, 2001).

Ash, Timothy Garton, *Free World: Why a Crisis of the West Reveals the Opportunity of Our Time* (New York: Allen Lane, 2004).

Balibar, Etienne, "Europe as Borderland," *Environment and Planning D: Society and Space*, 27 (2009), pp. 190–215.

———— *We, the People of Europe? Reflections on Transnational Citizenship*, trans. James Swenson (Princeton: Princeton University Press, 2004).

Barth, Fredrik, ed., *Ethnic Groups and Boundaries: The Social Organization of Culture Difference* (Boston: Little, Brown, and Co., 1969).

Bauman, Zygmunt, *Liquid Modernity* (Cambridge: Polity Press, 2000).

Beck, Ulrich, "Europa neu denken," *Internationale Politik*, 60.7 (2005), pp. 6–12.

———— *Cosmopolitan Vision*, orig. 2004 (Cambridge, UK and Malden, MA: Polity, 2006).

————, and Edgar Grande, "Cosmopolitanism: Europe's Way Out of Crisis," *European Journal of Social Theory*, 10.1 (2007), pp. 67–85.

Berezin, Mabel and Martin Schain, eds, *Europe without Borders: Remapping Territory, Citizenship and Identity in a Transnational Age* (Baltimore: Johns Hopkins University Press, 2003).

Bittner, Regina, Wilfried Hackenbroich, and Kai Vöckler, *Transiträume. Transit Spaces. Frankfurt/Oder – Poznan // Warschau // Brest // Minsk // Smolensk // Moskau* (Berlin: Jovis Verlag, 2006).

Boym, Svetlana, *The Future of Nostalgia* (New York: Basic Books, 2001).

Brenner, Neil, "Beyond State Centrism? Space, Territoriality, and Geographical Scale in Globalization Studies," *Theory and Society*, 28 (1999), pp. 39–78.

Breysach, Barbara, Arkadiusz Paszek, and Alexander Tölle, eds, *Grenze – Granica: Interdisziplinäre Betrachtungen zu Barrieren, Kontinuitäten und Gedankenhorizonten aus deutsch-polnischer Perspektive* (Berlin: Logos Verlag, 2003).

Brown, Wendy, *Walled States, Waning Sovereignty* (New York: Zone Books, 2010).

Buchanan, Allen, and Margaret Moore, eds, *States, Nations, and Borders: The Ethics of Making Boundaries* (New York: Cambridge University Press, 2003).

Buck-Morss, Susan, *Dreamworld and Catastrophe: The Passing of Mass Utopia in East and West* (Cambridge, MA: MIT Press, 2000).

——— *Thinking Past Terror: Islamism and Critical Theory on the Left* (New York: Verso, 2003).

Bundesministerium für Verkehr, Bau- und Wohnungswesen, *Dokumentation zum Kongress "Zwei Jahre STADTUMBAU OST"* (Berlin, 2004).

Cars, Göran, Patsey Healey, Ali Madanpour, and Claudio de Magalhães, eds, *Urban Governance, Institutional Capacity and Social Milieux* (Aldershot: Ashgate, 2002).

Castells, Manuel, *The Rise of the Network Society* (Cambridge, MA: Blackwell, 1996).

Chevrekouko, Maria, and Ludmila Kusnezowa, *Das neue russische Berlin* (Berlin: Havel Spree Verlag, 2002).

Chisholm, Michael, and David M. Smith, eds, *Shared Space: Divided Space. Essays in Conflict and Territorial Organisation* (London: Unwin, 1990).

Curzon of Kedleston, Lord, *The Romanes Lecture, 1907. Frontiers* (Oxford: Clarendon Press, 1907).

Deger, Petra, and Robert Hettlage, eds, *Der europäische Raum: Die Konstruktion europäischer Grenzen* (Wiesbaden: VS Verlag für Sozialwissenschaften, 2007).

Delaney, David, *Territory: A Short Introduction* (Cambridge, MA: Blackwell Publishing, 2005).

Deleuze, Gilles, and Félix Guattari, *A Thousand Plateaus: Capitalism and Schizophrenia*, trans. Brian Massumi (Minneapolis: University of Minnesota Press, 1987).

Demko, George J., and William B. Wood, eds, *Reordering the World: Geopolitical Perspectives on the Twenty-First Century*, 2nd ed. (Boulder: Westview Press, 1999).

Derrida, Jacques, *The Other Heading: Reflections on Today's Europe*, trans. Pascale-Anne Brault and Michael B. Naas (Bloomington: Indiana University Press, 1992).

Diener, Alexander C., and Joshua Hagen, eds, *Borderlines and Borderlands: Political Oddities at the Edge of the Nation-State* (Lanham: Rowman and Littlefield, 2010).

Donnan, Hastings and Thomas M. Wilson, *Borders: Frontiers of Identity, Nation and State* (Oxford and New York: Berg, 1999).

Dumont, Gérard-François, and Pierre Verluise, *Géopolitique de l'Europe* (Paris: Sedes, 2009).

Dwork, Debórah and Robert Jan Van Pelt, *Auschwitz, 1270 to the Present* (New York: Norton, 1996).

Ellis, Steven G., and Lud'a Klusáková, eds, *Imagining Frontiers, Contesting Identities* (Pisa: Edizioni Plus/Pisa University Press, 2007).

Eskelinen, Heikki, Ilkka Liikanen, and Jukka Oksa, eds, *Curtains of Iron and Gold: Reconstructing Borders and Scales of Interaction* (Aldershot: Ashgate, 1999).

Faludi, Andreas, ed., *European Spatial Planning* (Cambridge, MA: Lincoln Institute of Land Policy, 2002).

Forrester, Zaborowska, and Elena Gapova, eds, *Over the Wall/After the Fall: Post-Communist Cultures Through an East-West Gaze* (Bloomington: Indiana University Press, 2004).

Foucault, Michel, *Security, Territory, Population: Lectures at the Collège de France, 1977–1978*, ed. Michel Senellart, trans. Graham Burchell (New York: Palgrave Macmillan, 2007).

Fulbrook, Mary, *History of Germany 1918–2000: The Divided Nation*, 2nd ed. (Malden, MA: Blackwell, 2002).

Ganster, Paul and David E. Lorey, eds, *Borders and Border Politics in a Globalizing World* (Lanham: SR Books, 2005).

Garreau, Joel, *Edge City: Life on the New Frontier* (New York: Doubleday, 1991).

Geisen, Thomas, and Allen Karcher, eds, *Grenze: Sozial – Politisch – Kulturell: Ambivalenzen in den Prozessen der Entstehung und Veränderung von Grenzen* (Frankfurt am Main: IKO – Verlag für Interkulturelle Kommunikation, 2003).

Genz, Julia, Mirjam Schneider, and Sebastian Wogenstein, eds, *An Grenzen: Literarische Erkundungen* (Hannover: Wehrhahn Verlag, 2007).

Glaeser, Edward L., and Jesse M. Shapiro, "Cities and Warfare: The Impact of Terrorism on Urban Form," *Journal of Urban Economics*, 51 (2002), pp. 205–24.

Graham, Stephen, ed., *Cities, War, and Terrorism: Towards an Urban Geopolitics* (Malden, MA: Blackwell Publishing, 2004).

Habermas, Jürgen, *Der gespaltene Westen* (Frankfurt am Main: Suhrkamp, 2004).

——— *Die postnationale Konstellation. Politische Essays* (Frankfurt am Main: Suhrkamp, 1998).

Häußermann, Hartmut, "Capitalist Futures and Socialist Legacies: Urban Development in East Germany Since 1990," *German Politics and Society*, 49.16.4 (1998), pp. 87–101.

Harvey, David, *Cosmopolitanism and the Geographies of Freedom* (New York: Columbia University Press, 2009).

——— *The Condition of Postmodernity: An Enquiry into the Origins of Cultural Change* (Cambridge, MA: Blackwell, 1989).

Haushofer, Karl, *Grenzen in ihrer geographischen und politischen Bedeutung* (Heidelberg: Kurt Vowinckel Verlag, 1939, orig. 1927).

Heffernan, Michael, *The European Geographical Imagination* (Stuttgart: Franz Steiner Verlag, 2007).

——— *The Meaning of Europe: Geography and Geopolitics* (New York: Hodder Arnold, 1998).

Hegemann, Werner, *Das steinerne Berlin. Geschichte der größten Mietskasernenstadt der Welt* (Berlin: Gustav Kiepenheuer, 1930; repr. Frankfurt am Main: Ullstein, 1963).

Heym, Stefan, et al., *Reden über das eigene Land* (Munich: Bertelsmann, 1983).

Hoffmann, Heinrich, and A. R. Marsani, *Deutscher Osten. Land der Zukunft* (Munich: Heinrich Hoffmann, 1942).

Herles, Helmut, ed., *Die Hauptstadt-Debatte: der stenographische Bericht des Bundestages* (Bonn: Bouvier, 1991).

Huntington, Samuel P., *The Clash of Civilizations and the Remaking of World Order* (New York: Simon and Schuster, 1996).

Judt, Tony, *Postwar: A History of Europe Since 1945* (New York: The Penguin Press, 2005).

Kaplan, David, and Jouni Häkli, eds, *Boundaries and Place: European Borderlands in Geographical Context* (Lanham: Rowman and Littlefield, 2002).

Kiernan, Ben, *Blood and Soil: A World History of Genocide and Extermination from Sparta to Darfur* (New Haven: Yale University Press, 2007).

Kil, Wolfgang, *Land ohne Übergang. Deutschlands neue Grenze* (Berlin: ex pose verlag, 1992).

King, Geoff, *Mapping Reality: An Exploration of Cultural Geographies* (New York: St Martin's Press, 1996).

Kirby, Kathleen M., "Thinking Through the Boundary: The Politics of Location, Subjects, and Space," *Boundary 2: An International Journal of Literature and Culture* 20.2 (1993), pp. 173–89.

Klauser, Francisco R., "Splintering Spheres of Security: Peter Sloterdijk and the Contemporary Fortress City," *Environment and Planning D: Society and Space*, 28.2 (2010), pp. 326–40.

Kolossov, Vladimir, "Theorizing Borders: Border Studies: Changing Perspectives and Theoretical Approaches," *Geopolitics*, 10 (2005), pp. 606–32.

————, and John O'Loughlin, "New Borders for New World Orders: Territorialities at the Fin-de-Siècle," *Geojournal*, 44.3 (1998), pp. 259–73.

Koolhaas, Rem, Stefano Boeri, and Sanford Kwinter, eds, *Mutations* (Bordeaux: ACTAR, 2000).

Krätke, Stefan, "City of Talents? Berlin's Regional Economy, Socio-Spatial Fabric and 'Worst Practice' Urban Governance," *International Journal of Urban and Regional Research*, 28.3 (2004), pp. 511–29.

Kröhnert, Steffen, Franziska Medicus, and Reiner Klingholz, *Die demografische Lage der Nation. Wie zukunftsfähig sind Deutschlands Regionen?* Das Berlin Institut für Bevölkerung und Entwicklung (Munich: dtv, 2006).

Ladd, Brian, *The Ghosts of Berlin: Confronting German History in the Urban Landscape* (Chicago: University of Chicago Press, 1997).

Lampugnani, Vittorio Magnago, and Matthias Noell, eds, *Stadtformem. Die Architektur der Stadt zwischen Imagination und Konstruktion* (Zürich: gta Verlag, 2005).

Large, David Clay, *Berlin* (New York: Basic Books, 2000).

Lefebvre, Henri, *The Production of Space*, trans. Donald Nicholson-Smith (Cambridge, MA: Blackwell, 1991).

Levin, Thomas Y., Ursula Frohne, and Peter Weibel, eds, *CTRL SPACE. Rhetorics of Surveillance from Bentham to Big Brother* (Cambridge, MA: MIT Press, 2002).

Lipietz, A., "Social Europe, Legitimate Europe: The Inner and Outer Boundaries of Europe," *Environment and Planning D: Society and Space* 11 (1993), pp. 501–12.

Maier, Charles S., *Dissolution: The Crisis of Communism and the End of East Germany* (Princeton: Princeton University Press, 1997).

Matthiesen, Ulf, and Hans-Joachim Bürkner, "Antagonistic Structures in Border Areas: Local Milieux and Local Politics in the Polish-German Twin City Gubin/Guben," *Geojournal*, 54 (2001), pp. 43–50.

Morgenthau, Hans J., ed., *Germany and the Future of Europe* (Chicago: University of Chicago Press, 1951).

Mucha, Stanisław, dir., *Die Mitte* (strandfilm produktions GmbH, 2004).

Muir, Richard, *Political Geography: A New Introduction* (New York: John Wiley & Sons, Inc., 1997).

Newman, David, "The Lines that Continue to Separate Us: Borders in Our 'Borderless' World," *Progress in Human Geography*, 30.2 (2006), pp. 143–61.

Niedermüller, Peter, and Bjarne Stoklund, eds, *Europe: Cultural Construction and Reality* (Copenhagen: Museum Tusculanum Press, 2001).

O'Dowd, Liam, "From a 'Borderless World' to a 'World of Borders': 'Bringing History Back In'," *Environment and Planning D: Society and Space*, 29 (2010).

———, and Thomas M. Wilson, eds, *Borders, Nations and States: Frontiers of Sovereignty in the New Europe* (Aldershot: Avebury, 1996).

Ó Tuathail, Gearóid (Gerard Toal), *Critical Geopolitics* (Minneapolis: University of Minnesota, 1996).

———, Simon Dalby, and Paul Routledge, eds, *The Geopolitics Reader* (New York: Routledge, 1998).

Ozment, Steven, *A Mighty Fortress: A New History of the German People* (New York: HarperCollins, 2004).

Paasi, Anssi, "Europe as a Social Process and Discourse. Considerations of Place, Boundaries and Identity," *European Urban and Regional Studies*, 8.1 (2001), pp. 7–28.

——— "Remarks on Europe's Transforming Meta-Geography," *Geopolitics*, 10.3 (2005), pp. 580–85.

Pavlakovich-Kochi, Vera, Barbara J. Morehouse and Doris Wastl-Walter, eds, *Challenged Borderlands: Transcending Political and Cultural Boundaries* (Aldershot: Ashgate Publishing, 2004).

Pellow, Deborah, ed., *Setting Boundaries: The Anthropology of Spatial and Social Organization* (Westport: Bergin & Garvey, 1996).

Pratt, Martin, and Janet Allison Brown, eds, *Borderlands under Stress* (The Hague and Boston: Kluwer Law International, 2000).

Rada, Uwe, *Berliner Barbaren. Wie der Osten in den Westen kommt* (Berlin: BasisDruck, 2001).

——— *Die Oder: Lebenslauf eines Flusses* (Berlin: Gustav Kiepenheuer Verlag, 2005).

——— *Zwischenland. Europäische Geschichten aus dem deutsch-polnischen Grenzgebiet* (Berlin: bre.bra verlag, 2004).

Ratzel, Friedrich, "Der Lebensraum. Eine biogeographische Studie," in Karl Bücher, ed., *Festgaben für Albert Schäffle zur siebenzigsten Wiederkehr seines Geburtstages am 24. Februar 1901* (Tübingen: Laupp, 1901), pp. 103–89.

Richie, Alexandra, *Faust's Metropolis: A History of Berlin* (New York: HarperCollins, 1998).

Rupnik, Jacques. "Europe's New Frontiers: Remapping Europe." *Daedalus*, 123.3 (1994), pp. 91–114.

Sack, Robert David, *Human Territoriality: Its Theory and Its History* (New York: Cambridge University Press, 1986).

Sahlins, Peter, *Boundaries: The Making of France and Spain in the Pyrenees* (Berkeley: University of California Press, 1989).

Sassen, Saskia, *Globalization and Its Discontents* (New York: The New Press, 1998).

——— *Guests and Aliens* (New York: The New Press, 1999; orig. German, 1996).

Schallmayer, Egon, *Der Limes – Geschichte einer Grenze*, 2nd ed. (Munich: C.H. Beck, 2007).

Scheffler, Karl, *Berlin. Ein Stadtschicksal* (Berlin: Erich Reiss Verlag, 1910).

Schlögel, Karl, *Die Mitte liegt ostwärts: Europa im Übergang* (Munich: Carl Hanser Verlag, 2002).

——— "Oder, Odra, Oderstromland," *Lettre International. Europas Kulturzeitung*, 50 (2000), pp. 19–23.

————— *Promenade in Jalta und andere Städtebilder* (Munich: Carl Hanser Verlag, 2001).

Schmid, Hans-Christian, dir., *Lichter* (Munich: Claussen + Woebke + Putz Filmproduktion [Prokino Filmverleih], 2003).

Schmitt, Carl, *Der Nomos der Erde im Völkerrecht des Jus Publicum Europäum* (Berlin: Duncker & Humblot, 1950).

————— *Völkerrechtliche Großraumordnung, mit Interventionsverbot für raumfremde Mächte. Ein Beitrag zum Reichsbegriff im Völkerrecht* (Berlin: Deutscher Rechtsverlag, 1939).

Schroer, Markus, *Räume, Orte, Grenzen: Auf dem Weg zu einer Soziologie des Raumes* (Frankfurt am Main: Suhrkamp, 2009).

Schultz, Helga, ed., *Grenzen im Ostblock und ihre Überwindung* (Berlin: Arno Spitz Verlag, 2001).

—————, and Alan Nothnagle, eds, *Grenze der Hoffnung: Geschichte und Perspektiven der Grenzregion an der Oder*, 2nd ed. (Berlin: Arno Spitz Verlag, 1999).

Schulz, Josef, *Übergang*, with texts by Rolf Sachsse and Kerstin Stremmel (Cologne: Verlag schaden.com, 2007).

Schulze, Hagen, *Germany: A New History*, trans. Deborah Lucas Schneider (Cambridge, MA: Harvard University Press, 1998).

Schwagrzinna, Klaus, dir., *Der Zug der Träume – Von Berlin an die Wolga* (Westdeutscher Rundfunk/Norddeutscher Rundfunk, 2004).

Schweitzer, Eva, *Grossbaustelle Berlin. Wie die Hauptstadt verplant wird* (Berlin: Nicolai, 1996).

Scribner, Charity, *Requiem for Communism* (Cambridge, MA: MIT Press, 2003).

Siedler, Wolf Jobst, *Phoenix im Sand: Glanz und Elend der Hauptstadt* (Berlin: Propyläen Verlag, 1998).

Silberman, Marc, ed., *The German Wall: Fallout in Europe* (New York and Basingstoke: Palgrave Macmillan, forthcoming in 2011).

—————, Karen E. Till, and Janet Ward, eds, *Walls, Borders, Boundaries: Spatial and Cultural Practices in Europe* (New York and Oxford: Berghahn Books, forthcoming in 2012).

Sloterdijk, Peter, "Geometry in the Colossal: The Project of Metaphysical Globalization," trans. Samuel A. Butler, *Environment and Planning D: Society and Space*, 27.1 (2009): pp. 29–40.

————— *Sphären: Mikrosphärologie*, 3 vols. (Frankfurt am Main: Suhrkamp, 1998–2004).

Soja, Edward W., *Postmodern Geographies: The Reassertion of Space in Critical Social Theory* (New York and London: Verso, 1989).

Sorkin, Michael, ed., *Indefensible Space: The Architecture of the National Insecurity State* (New York: Routledge, 2008).

Soysal, Yasemin Nuhoğlu, *Limits of Citizenship: Migrants and Postnational Membership in Europe* (Chicago: University of Chicago Press, 1995).

Spengler, Oswald, *Der Untergang des Abendlandes: Umrisse einer Morphologie der Weltgeschichte*, 2 vols. (Munich: Beck, 1918).

————— *The Decline of the West*, 2 vols., trans. Charles Francis Atkinson (New York: Alfred A. Knopf, 1928).

Stöber, Georg, and Robert Maier, eds, *Grenzen und Grenzräume in der deutschen und polnischen Geschichte: Scheidelinie oder Begegnungsraum?* (Hannover: Verlag Hahnsche Buchhandlung, 2000).

Strassoldo, Raimondo, "The Study of Boundaries: A System-Oriented, Multidisciplinary Bibliographical Essay," *The Jerusalem Journal of International Relations*, 2:3 (1977), pp. 81–107.

Swanstrom, Todd, "Are Fear and Urbanism at War?" *Urban Affairs Review*, 38.1 (2002), pp. 135–40.

Taylor, Peter, "The State as Container: Internationality, Interstateness, Interterritoriality," *Progress in Human Geography*, 19 (1995), pp. 1–15.

Turner, Henry Ashley, Jr., *Germany from Partition to Reunification*, rev. ed. (New Haven: Yale University Press, 1992).

Turner, Frederick Jackson, *The Frontier in American History* (New York: Henry Holt & Co., 1921).

Ullmann, Hermann, *Flucht aus Berlin* (Jena: Eugen Diederichs Verlag, 1932).

Van Houtum, Henk, Olivier Kramsch, and Wolfgang Zierhofer, eds, *B/ordering Space* (Aldershot: Ashgate, 2005).

Virilio, Paul, "The Overexposed City" (1984), in K. Michael Hays, ed., *Architecture Theory since 1968* (City of New York: The Trustees of Columbia University/ Cambridge, MA: MIT Press, 1998), pp. 542–50.

Walters, William. "Mapping Schengenland: Denaturalizing the Border," *Environment and Planning D: Society and Space* 20 (2002), 561–80.

Ward, Janet, "Berlin-Mahagonny and the Re-Shaping of Post-Wall Borders," *The Brecht Yearbook*, 29 (2004), pp. 406–19.

Wenders, Wim, dir., *Der Himmel über Berlin* (Paris: Road Movies Berlin and Argos Films, 1987).

———, and Peter Handke, *Der Himmel über Berlin. Ein Filmbuch* (Frankfurt am Main: Suhrkamp, 1987).

Whitehead, Alfred North, "La théorie relationaliste de l'Espace," *Revue de métaphysique et de morale*, 23 (1916), pp. 423–54.

Wild, Trevor, and Philip N. Jones, "Spatial Impacts of German Unification," *The Geographical Journal*, 160.1 (1994), pp. 1–16.

Wilson, Thomas M., and Hastings Donnan, eds, *Border Identities: Nation and State at International Frontiers* (New York: Cambridge University Press, 1998).

Wright, Patrick, *Iron Curtain: From Stage to Cold War* (New York: Oxford University Press, 2007).

Wrobel, David M., *The End of American Exceptionalism: Frontier Anxiety from the Old West to the New Deal* (Lawrence: The University Press of Kansas, 1993).

Zaiotti, Ruben, *Cultures of Border Control: Schengen and the Evolution of European Frontiers* (Chicago: University of Chicago Press, forthcoming in 2011).

Part II: Afterlives of the Wall: Reflections and Deflections

Allievi, Stefano, and Jørgen Nielsen, eds, *Muslim Networks and Transnational Communities in and across Europe* (Boston: Brill, 2003).

Anderson, Susan C., "Walls and Other Obstacles: Peter Schneider's Critique of Unity in *Der Mauerspringer*," *German Quarterly*, 66.3 (1993), pp. 362–71.

Arand, Manuela, and Thomas Knuth, eds, *Berlin 1989 – 2009. Eine Bilanz in 12 Gesprächen* (Berlin: Berlin Story Verlag, 2009).

Arnold, Dietmar, and Ingmar Arnold, *Dunkle Welten. Bunker, Tunnel und Gewölbe unter Berlin* (Berlin: Ch. Links Verlag, 1997).

Ash, Timothy Garton, *In Europe's Name: Germany and the Divided Continent* (New York: Random House, 1993).

Assmann, Jan, *Das kulturelle Gedächtnis. Schrift, Erinnerung und politische Identität in frühen Hochkulturen* (Munich: Verlag C.H. Beck, 1997).

——— *Religion and Cultural Memory*, trans. Rodney Livingstone (Stanford: Stanford University Press, 2006).

Augé, Marc, *Non-Places: Introduction to an Anthropology of Supermodernity* (New York: Verso, 2005).

August, Oliver, *Along the Wall and Watchtowers* (London: Flamingo, 2003).

Baker, Frederick, "The Berlin Wall and the Bastille: Tearing Down Walls and Building Myths," *European Review of History*, 1.2 (1995), pp. 157–67.

——— "The Berlin Wall: Production, Preservation and Consumption of a 20th-Century Monument," *Antiquity* 67.257 (1993), pp. 709–33.

Bauer, Markus, and Thomas Rahn, eds, *Die Grenze. Begriff und Inszenierung* (Berlin: Akademie Verlag, 1997).

Bauwelt, special issue: "Stadtbauwelt 154" (UIA World Congress 2002), 93.24 (2002).

Becker, Jürgen, *Aus der Geschichte der Trennungen* (Frankfurt am Main: Suhrkamp, 1999).

Beinhauer-Köhler, Bärbel, and Claus Leggewie, *Moscheen in Deutschland. Religiöse Heimat und gesellschaftliche Herausforderung* (Munich: C.H. Beck, 2009).

Bender, Peter, *Deutschlands Wiederkehr. Eine ungeteilte Nachkriegsgeschichte 1945–1990* (Stuttgart: Klett-Cotta, 2007).

Bennewitz, Inge, and Rainer Potratz, *Zwangsaussiedlungen an der innerdeutschen Grenze: Analysen und Dokumente* (Berlin: Ch. Links Verlag, 2002).

Bentham, Jeremy, *The Panopticon Writings* (New York: Verso, 1995).

Berdahl, Daphne, *Where the World Ended: Re-Unification and Identity in the German Borderland* (Berkeley: University of California Press, 1999).

Beßlich, Barbara, Katharina Grätz, and Olaf Hildebrand, eds, *Wende des Erinnerns? Geschichtskonstruktionen in der deutschen Literatur nach 1989* (Berlin: Erich Schmidt Verlag, 2006).

Bienert, Michael, *Stille Winkel an der Berliner Mauer* (Hamburg: Ellert & Richter Verlag, 2009).

Blanchot, Maurice, "The Name Berlin," orig. 1961, trans. Aris Fiorestos, *Alphabet City*, 6 (1998), pp. 308–11.

Bloch, Ernst, *Erbschaft dieser Zeit* (Frankfurt am Main: Suhrkamp, 1973).

——— *Literarische Aufsätze, Gesamtausgabe*, vol. 9 (Frankfurt am Main: Suhrkamp, 1965).

——— *Literary Essays*, trans. Andrew Joron et al. (Stanford: Stanford University Press, 1998).

Bluth, Friedrich, Manfred Zache, and Helmut Zempel, *Stadtplanerisches Dokumentation zum ehemaligen Grenzstreifen der Mauer in Berlin* (Hohen Neuendorf: Z-Plan, 2000).

Bornemann, John, *After the Wall: East Meets West in the New Berlin* (New York: Basic Books, 1990).

——— *Belonging in the Two Berlins: Kin, State, Nation* (New York: Cambridge University Press, 1992).

——— "State, Territory, and Identity Formation in the Postwar Berlins, 1945–1989," *Cultural Anthropology*, 7.1 (1992), pp. 45–62.

Brandt, Willy, *Erinnerungen* (Frankfurt am Main: Propyläen, 1989).

Briese, Olaf, "Pfusch am Bau. Beiträge zur Baugeschichte der 'Berliner Mauer'," *Zeitschrift für Geschichtswissenschaft*, 57 (2009), pp. 613–36.

———— *Steinzeit. Mauern in Berlin* (Berlin: Matthes & Seitz, forthcoming in 2011).

———— "'Wartungsarm und formschön'. Zur Ästhetik der 'Berliner Mauer'," *Weimarer Beiträge: Zeitschrift für Literaturwissenschaft, Ästhetik und Kulturwissenschaften*, 55.3 (2009), pp. 430–54.

Broadbent, Philip, and Sabine Hake, eds, *Berlin, Divided City 1945–1989* (Oxford and New York: Berghahn Books, 2010).

Brockmann, Stephen, "Germany as Occident at the Zero Hour," *German Studies Review*, 25.3 (2002), pp. 477–96.

Brussig, Thomas, *Helden wir wir* (Berlin: Volk & Welt, 1995).

Brückner, Ulrike, Helga Kurzchalia, and Angelika Barz, *Hier. Archivierter Zeitraum* (Rotterdam: Veenman Publishers, 2006).

Buckley, William F., Jr., *The Fall of the Berlin Wall* (New York: Wiley, 2004).

Bürkle, Stephanie, and Thomas Sakschewski, *Beirut–Berlin* (Berlin: Vice Versa Verlag, 1997).

Cooke, Paul, and Jonathan Grix, eds, *East Germany: Continuity and Change* (Amsterdam: Rodopi, 2000).

Copjec, Joan, and Michael Sorkin, eds, *Giving Ground: The Politics of Propinquity* (London: Verso, 1999).

Costabile-Heming, Carol Anne, Rachel J. Halverson, and Kristie A. Foell, eds, *Berlin: The Symphony Continues. Orchestrating Architectural, Social, and Artistic Change in Germany's New Capital* (New York: Walter de Gruyter, 2004).

Cramer, Michael, *Berliner Mauer-Radweg* (Rodingersdorf: Esterbauer, 2001).

Cresswell, Tim, *In Place / Out of Place: Geography, Ideology, and Transgression* (Minneapolis: University of Minnesota Press, 1996).

Cupers, Kenny, and Markus Miessen, *Spaces of Uncertainty* (Wuppertal: Müller + Busmann, 2002).

Dahn, Daniela, *Wehe dem Sieger! Ohne Osten kein Westen* (Hamburg: Rowohlt, 2009).

Dale, Gareth, *Popular Protest in East Germany, 1945–1989* (New York: Routledge, 2005).

Daum, Andreas W., *Kennedy in Berlin. Politik, Kultur und Emotionen im Kalten Krieg* (Paderborn: Ferdinand Schöningh, 2003).

Davis, Mike, *Dead Cities and Other Tales* (New York: The New Press, 2002).

Debord, Guy, "Théorie de la derive," *Les Lèvres Nues*, 9 (November 1956); repr. in *Internationale Situationniste*, 2 (December 1958), pp. 19–23.

Derrida, Jacques, *Specters of Marx: The State of the Debt, the Work of Mourning, and the New International*, trans. Peggy Kamuf (New York: Routledge, 1994).

Deutsches Nationalkomitee für Denkmalschutz, ed., *Die Berliner Mauer. Vom Sperrwall zum Denkmal*, 76.1 (Bühl/Baden: KONKORDIA, 2009).

Diefendorf, Jeffry M., *In the Wake of War: The Reconstruction of German Cities after World War II* (New York: Oxford University Press, 1993).

————, ed., *Rebuilding Europe's Bombed Cities* (New York: Palgrave Macmillan, 1990).

Diers, Michael, *Schlagbilder. Zur politischen Ikonographie der Gegenwart* (Frankfurt am Main: Fischer, 1997).

Diewald, Martin, Anne Goedicke, and Karl Ulrich Mayer, eds, *After the Fall of the Wall: Life Courses in the Transformation of East Germany* (Stanford: Stanford University Press, 2006).

Döring, Jörg, and Tristan Thielmann, eds, *Spatial Turn. Das Raumparadigma in den Kultur- und Sozialwissenschaften* (Bielefeld: transcript Verlag, 2008).

Drechsel, Benjamin, "The Berlin Wall from a Visual Perspective: Comments on the Construction of a Political Media Icon," *Visual Communication*, 9.1 (2010), pp. 3–24.

Dullau, Michael, *Grenzland* (Mammendorf: pro literatur Verlag, 2005).

Edensor, Tim, *Industrial Ruins: Spaces, Aesthetics and Materiality* (New York: Berg, 2005).

Elkins, T. H., and B. Hofmeister, *Berlin: The Spatial Structure of a Divided City* (New York and London: Methuen, 1988).

Ellger, Christof, "Berlin: Legacies of Division and Problems of Unification," *The Geographical Journal*, 158.1 (1992), pp. 40–46.

Faber, Richard, and Barbara Naumann, eds, *Literatur der Grenze – Theorie der Grenze* (Würzburg: Königsberg & Naumann, 1995).

Feversham, Polly, and Leo Schmidt, *Berliner Mauer heute: Denkmalwert und Umgang / The Berlin Wall Today: Cultural Significance and Conservation Issues* (Berlin: Bauwesen, 1999).

Fischer, Jaimey, and Barbara Mennel, eds, *Spatial Turns: Space, Place and Mobility in German Literary and Visual Culture* (Amsterdam and New York: Rodopi, 2010).

Flemming, Thomas, and Hagen Koch, *Die Berliner Mauer. Geschichte eines politischen Bauwerks* (Berlin: be.bra verlag, 1999).

Flierl, Thomas, *Berlin: Perspektiven durch Kultur. Texte und Projekte* (Berlin: Theater der Zeit, 2007).

Foucault, Michel, *Discipline and Punish: The Birth of the Prison*, trans. Alan Sheridan (New York: Random House, 1991).

——— "Texts/Contexts. Of Other Spaces," *Diacritics*, 16.1 (1986), pp. 22–27.

Franck, Julia, *Lagerfeuer* (Cologne: Dumont, 2003).

Führ, Wieland, *Berliner Mauer und innerdeutsche Grenze 1945–1990* (Petersberg: Michael Imhof Verlag, 2008; Eng. trans. 2009).

Gerstenberger, Katharina, *Writing the New Berlin: The German Capital in Post-Wall Literature* (Rochester, NY: Camden House, 2008).

Goodbody, Axel, Pól Ó Dochartaigh, and Dennis Tate, eds, *Dislocation and Reorientation: Exile, Division and the End of Communism in German Culture and Politics* (Amsterdam: Rodopi, 2009).

Göktürk, Deniz, David Gramling, and Anton Kaes, eds, *Germany in Transit: Nation and Migration, 1955–2005* (Berkeley: University of California Press, 2007).

Görner, Rüdiger, *Mauer, Schatten, Gerüst. Kulturkritische Versuche* (Tübingen: Klöpfer & Meyer, 1999).

Grafe, Roman, *Die Grenze durch Deutschland. Eine Chronik von 1945 bis 1990* (Berlin: Siedler, 2002).

Graham, Stephen, and Nigel Thrift, "Out of Order: Understanding Repair and Maintenance," *Theory, Culture and Society*, 24.3 (2007), pp. 1–25.

Grass, Günter, *Ein weites Feld. Roman* (Göttingen: Steidl, 1995/Munich: dtv, 1997).

——— *Unterwegs von Deutschland nach Deutschland. Tagebuch 1990* (Göttingen: Steidl Verlag, 2009).

Grathwol, Robert P., and Donita M. Moorhus, *American Forces in Berlin: Cold War Outpost, 1945–1994* (Washington, DC: Department of Defense, Legacy Resource Management Program, Cold War Project, 1994).

Grünbein, Durs, "Unfreiheit. Rede in der Frauenkirche zu Dresden am 6. Oktober 2009," *Deutschland-Archiv*, 42.6 (2009), pp. 983–92.

Gründer, Ralf, ed., *Berliner Mauerkunst. Eine Dokumentation* (Cologne: Böhlau, 2007).

Gunn, Simon, "Illuminating the Victorian City," *History and Technology*, 26.2 (2010), pp. 151–56.

Hare, David, *Berlin/Wall* (London: Faber & Faber, 2009).

Harrison, Hope M., *Driving the Soviets Up the Wall: Soviet-East German Relations, 1953–1961* (Princeton: Princeton University Press, 2003).

Haydn, Florian, and Robert Temel, eds, *Temporary Urban Spaces. Concepts for the Use of City Spaces*, trans. David Skog Ley and Steven Lindberg (Boston: Birkhäuser, 2006).

Hensel, Jana, *Zonenkinder* (Hamburg: Rowohlt, 2002).

Hertle, Hans-Hermann, *Die Berliner Mauer – Monument des Kalten Krieges* (Berlin: Ch. Links, 2007).

————, and Gerhard Sälter, "Die Todesopfer an Mauer und Grenze," *Deutschland Archiv*, 39.4 (2008), pp. 667–76.

————, Konrad Jarausch, and Christoph Kleßmann, eds, *Mauerbau und Mauerfall. Ursache – Verlauf – Nachwirkungen* (Berlin: Links Verlag, 2002).

————, and Maria Nooke, *Die Todesopfer an der Berliner Mauer 1961–1989: Ein biographisches Handbuch* (Berlin: Ch. Links Verlag, 2009).

Hesse, Janet, *Befriedet: Vergessene Orte an der Innerdeutschen Grenze* (Edel: momenti Verlag, 2009).

Hise, Greg, "Architecture as State Building: A Challenge to the Field," *Journal of the Society of Architectural Historians*, 67.2 (2008), pp. 173–77.

Hoffmann, Andreas, *Verschwundene Orte. Prominente Abrisse in Berlin* (Berlin: Transit, 1997).

Hofmann, Max, and Christoph Lanz, dir., *Eingemauert! Computeranimation der deutschen Grenze* (Deutsche Welle / DW-World TV, 2009).

Hofmann-Axthelm, Dieter, and Ludovico Scarpa, *Berliner Mauern und Durchbrüche* (Berlin: Verlag Ästhetik und Kommunikation, 1987).

Holland-Moritz, D., and Gabriela Wachter, eds, *War jewesen: West-Berlin 1961–89* (Berlin: Parthas Verlag, 2009).

Irmischer, B., and D. Moldmann, *Am Deutsch-Deutschen Rand. Landschaft, Geschichte, Kultur, Wirtschaft entlang einer 1240km Reiseroute am östlichen Rand der Bundesrepublik* (Hamburg: Moldmann-Verlag, 1989).

Johnson, Uwe, *Berliner Sachen. Aufsätze* (Frankfurt am Main: Suhrkamp, 1975).

Jurczek, Peter, and Bernhard Köppen, "Aufbau oder Abriß Ost? Konzeptionelle Überlegungen zur nachhaltigen Stadtentwicklung in den neuen Ländern," *Zukunftsforum Politik* 63 (Sankt Augustin: Konrad-Adenauer-Stiftung, 2005), pp. 7–81.

Kaluza, Stephan, *Die unsichtbare Mauer / The Invisible Wall / Le mur invisible*, trans. Patrick B. Kremer, Alexandra Skwara, Marie-Liesse Zambeaux (Cologne: DuMont, 2009).

Kaminsky, Anna, ed., *Die Berliner Mauer in der Welt*, Bundesstiftung zur Aufarbeitung der SED-Diktatur (Berlin: Berlin Story Verlag, 2009).

————, ed., *Orte des Erinnerns. Gedenkzeichen, Gedenkstätten und Museen zur Diktatur in SBZ und DDR* (Leipzig: Ch. Links Verlag, 2004).

Klausmeier, Axel, and Leo Schmidt, *Mauerreste – Mauerspuren. Der umfassende Führer zur Berliner Mauer* (Berlin: Westkreuz Verlag, 2004; Eng. trans. 2004).

Kleindienst, Jürgen, ed., *Mauer-Passagen. Grenzgänge, Flüchten und Reisen 1961–1989. 48 Erinnerungen aus Ost und West* (Berlin: Zeitgut Verlag, 2003).

Knischewski, Gerd, and Ulla Spittler, "Remembering the Berlin Wall: The Wall Memorial Ensemble Bernauer Strasse," *German Life and Letters*, 59.2 (2006), pp. 280–93.

Koolhaas, Rem, and Bruce Mau, *S, M, L, XL* (New York: Monacelli Press, 1995).

Kornhardt, Diethild, Gabriele Pütz, and Thies Schröder, eds, *Mögliche Räume* (Hamburg: Junius, 2002).

Kunze, Gerhard, *Grenzerfahrungen. Kontakte und Verhandlungen zwischen dem Land Berlin und der DDR 1949–1988* (Berlin: Akademie Verlag, 1999).

Küchenmeister, Daniel, ed., *Der Mauerbau. Krisenverlauf – Weichenstellung – Resultate* (Berlin: Berliner Debatte, 2001).

Lamping, Dieter, *Über Grenzen – Eine literarische Topographie* (Göttingen, Vandenhoeck & Ruprecht, 2001).

Latour, Bruno, and Emilie Hermant, *Paris ville invisible* (Paris: La Découverte, 1998).

Leach, Neil, ed., *Architecture and Revolution: Contemporary Perspectives on Central and Eastern Europe* (New York: Routledge, 1999).

Ledanff, Susanne, *Hauptstadtphantasien: Berliner Stadtlektüren in der Gegenwartsliteratur 1989–2008* (Bielefeld: Aisthesis, 2009).

Le Carré, John, *The Spy Who Came in from the Cold* (New York: Pocket Books / Simon & Schuster, 1963).

Leuenberger, Christine, "Constructions of the Berlin Wall: How Material Culture Is Used in Psychological Theory," *Social Problems*, 53.1 (2006), pp. 18–37.

Light, Duncan, "Gazing on Communism: Heritage Tourism and Post-Communist Identities in Germany, Hungary and Romania," *Tourism Geographies*, 2.2 (2000), pp. 157–76.

Maier, Julia, *Raumlaborberlin: Acting in Public* (Berlin: Jovis Verlag 2008).

Major, Patrick, *Behind the Berlin Wall: East Germany and the Frontiers of Power* (New York: Oxford University Press, 2010).

Malzahn, Claus Christian, *Über Mauern, oder, Warum das Leben im Schatten des Schutzwalls eine sonnige Sache war* (Berlin: WJS Verlag, 2009).

Mandel, Ruth Ellen, *Cosmopolitan Anxieties. Turkish Challenges to Citizenship and Belonging in Germany* (Durham, NC: Duke University Press, 2008).

Mander, John, *Berlin: Hostage for the West* (Baltimore and Harmondsworth: Penguin, 1962).

Mangani, Sunil, *Image Critique and the Fall of the Berlin Wall* (Bristol: Intellect, 2008).

Mann, Ulf, *Tunnelfluchten. Grenzgänger. Verräter. Wühlmäuse* (Berlin: Transit, 2005).

McScotts, Jennifer, "The Second Fall of the Berlin Wall: Examining the Hildebrandt Memorial at Checkpoint Charlie," *Future Anterior: Journal of Historic Preservation. History, Theory and Criticism*, 3.1 (2006), pp. 36–47.

Meinhof, Ulrike H., and Dariusz Galasinski, "Photography, Memory, and the Construction of Identities on the Former East-West German Border," *Discourse Studies*, 2.3 (2000), pp. 323–53.

Meyer, Friederike, "Erweiterung der Gedenkstätte Berliner Mauer," *Bauwelt*, 99.3 (2008), pp. 10–12.

Mews, Siegfried, "The Desire to Achieve 'Normalcy': Peter Schneider's Post-Wall Berlin Novel *Eduard's Homecoming*," *Studies in Twentieth- and Twenty-First Century Literature*, 28.1 (2004), pp. 258–85.

Misa, Thomas J., "Retrieving Sociotechnical Change from Technological Determinism," in Merritt Roe Smith and Leo Marx, eds, *Does Technology Drive History? The Dilemma of Technological Determinism* (Cambridge, MA: MIT Press, 1994), pp. 115–42.

Misselwitz, Philipp, Han-Ulrich Obrist, and Philipp Oswalt, eds, *Fun Palace 200X. Der Berliner Schlossplatz: Abriss, Neubau oder grüne Wiese?* (Berlin: Martin-Schmitz-Verlag, 2005).

Modood, Tariq, and Pnina Werbner, eds, *The Politics of Multiculturalism in the New Europe: Racism, Identity and Community* (New York: Zed Books, 1997).

Müller, Heiner, *Gesammelte Irrtümer 1. Interviews und Gespräche* (Frankfurt am Main: Verlag der Autoren, 1986).

——— *Rotwelsch* (Berlin: Merve, 1982).

Müller, Jan-Werner, ed., *Memory and Power in Post-War Europe: Studies in the Presence of the Past* (New York: Cambridge University Press, 2002).

Novikova, Irina, "Isaiah Berlin's City: Monuments and Shopping: Colours of White," *sinn-haft*, 14–15 (2003), pp. 25–35.

Nunn, Astrid. ed., *Mauern als Grenzen* (Mainz: Verlag Philipp von Zabern, 2009).

Ockman, Joan, ed., *Architecture Criticism Ideology* (New York: Princeton Architectural Press, 1985).

Oswalt, Philipp, "Berlin, Stadt des 20. Jahrhunderts," *transition*, 9 (July 2002), pp. 110–17.

——— *Berlin: Stadt ohne Form: Strategien einer anderern Architektur* (Berlin: Prestel, 2000).

Otter, Chris, *The Victorian Eye: A Political History of Light and Vision in Britain, 1800–1910* (Chicago: University of Chicago Press, 2008).

Parei, Inka, *Die Schattenboxerin* (Frankfurt am Main: Fischer, 2001).

Péteri, György, ed., *Nylon Curtain: Transnational and Transsystemic Tendencies in the Cultural Life of State-Socialist Russia and East-Central Europe* (Trondheim: TSEECS nr. 18, 2006).

Platen, Edgar, and Martin Todthaupt, eds, *Grenzen, Grenzüberschreitungen, Grenzauflösungen. Zur Darstellung von Zeitgeschichte in deutschsprachiger Gegenwartsliteratur* (Munich: iudicium, 2004).

Preuss, Edith, "The Wall You Will Never Know," *Perspecta*, 36 (2005), pp. 19–31.

Pröfener, Franz, ed., *Zeitzeichen Baustelle. Realität, Inszenierung und Metaphorik eines abseitigen Ortes* (Frankfurt am Main and New York: Campus Verlag, 1998).

Rathenow, Lutz, and Harald Hauswald, *Ostberlin: Die andere Seite der Stadt in Texten und Bildern* (Munich: Piper, 1987).

Rathje, Wolfgang, *"Mauer-Marketing" unter Erich Honecker. Schwierigkeiten der DDR bei der technischen Modernisierung, der volkswirtschaftlichen Kalkulation und der politischen Akzeptanz der Berliner "Staatsgrenze" von 1971–1990*, 2 vols., PhD dissertation (Kiel: Department of Philosophy, Christian-Albrechts-Universität zu Kiel, 2001).

Regener, Sven, *Herr Lehmann* (Frankfurt am Main: Eichborn AG, 2001).

Rifaux, Patrice-Loup, *Berlin, fin de siècle* (Paris: L'Harmattan, 1998).

Ritter, Jürgen, and Peter Joachim Lapp, *Grenze: Ein deutsches Bauwerk* (Berlin: Links, 1997).

Rivatz, Dominique de, *Endlosschleife, Der Berliner Mauerweg / The Never-Ending Wall: The Berlin Wall Trail / San début ni fin: le chemin du Mur de Berlin* (Bern: Benteli, 2009).

Rose, Brian, *The Lost Border: The Landscape of the Iron Curtain* (New York: Princeton Architectural Press, 2004).

Ross, Corey, "Before the Wall: East Germans, Communist Authority, and the Mass Exodus to the West," *The Historical Journal*, 45.2 (2002), pp. 459–80.

Rott, Wilfried, *Die Insel: eine Geschichte West-Berlins 1948–1990* (Munich: C.H. Beck, 2009).

Rottman, Gordon L., *The Berlin Wall and the Inner-German Border 1961–1989* (Oxford: Osprey, 2008).

Saunders, Anna, "Remembering Cold War Division: Wall Remnants and Border Monuments in Berlin," *Journal of Contemporary European Studies*, 17.1 (2009), pp. 9–19.

Sälter, Gerhard, *Mauerreste in Berlin / Relicts of the Berlin Wall*, trans. Miriamne Fields, 2nd ed. (Berlin: Druckerei Elsholz, 2007).

Schädlich, Susanne, *Immer wieder Dezember. Der Westen, die Stasi, der Onkel und ich* (Munich: Droemer, 2009).

Schätzlein, Gerhard, Bärbel Rosch, and Reinhold Albert, *Grenzerfahrungen*, 3 vols. (Hildburghausen: Verlag Frankenschwelle, 2002–2005).

Scherzer, Landolf, *Der Grenz-Gänger* (Berlin: Aufbau-Verlag, 2005).

Schimmang, Jochen, ed., *Zentrale Randlage. Lesebuch für Städtebewohner* (Cologne: DuMont, 2002).

Schivelbusch, Wolfgang, *In a Cold Crater: Cultural and Intellectual Life in Berlin, 1945–1948*, trans. Kelly Barry (Berkeley: University of California Press, 1998).

Schlögel, Karl, *Promenade in Jalta und andere Städtebilder* (Frankfurt am Main: Fischer, 2003).

Schlör, Joachim, "'It Has to Go Away, But At the Same Time It Has to be Kept': The Berlin Wall and the Making of an Urban Icon," *Urban History*, 33.1 (2006), pp. 85–105.

Schmidt, Leo, and Henriette von Preuschen, eds, *On Both Sides of the Wall: Preserving Monuments and Sites of the Cold War Era / Auf beiden Seiten der Mauer: Denkmalpflege an Objekten aus der Zeit des Kalten Krieges*, trans. Ralf Jaeger (Bad Münsterfeld: Westkreuz Verlag, 2005).

Schneider, Peter, *Der Mauerspringer. Erzählung*, orig. 1982 (Hamburg: Rowohlt, 1995).

——— *The Wall Jumper*, trans. Leigh Hafrey (New York: Pantheon Books, 1983).

Schöbel, Sören, *Qualitative Freiraumplanung. Perspektiven städtischer Grün- und Freiräume aus Berlin* (Berlin: Wissenschaftlicher Verlag, 2003).

Schultke, Dietmar, *"Keiner kommt durch". Die Geschichte der innerdeutschen Grenze, 1945–1990* (Berlin: Aufbau, 1999).

Schumann, Ludwig, and Hans-Wulf Kunze, *Grenze: Verletzte Landschaften* (Mageburg: Blaue Äpfel Verlag, 1999).

Schurer, Ernst, Manfred Keune, and Philip Jenkins, eds, *The Berlin Wall: Representations and Perspectives* (New York: Peter Lang, 1996).

Sebald, W.G., *On the Natural History of Destruction* (1999), trans. Anthea Bell (New York: Random House, 2003).

Senatsverwaltung für Stadtentwicklung Berlin, *Urban Pioneers: Stadtentwicklung durch Zwischennutzung / Temporary Use and Urban Development in Berlin* (Berlin: Jovis Verlag, 2007).

Şenocak, Zafer, *Atlas des tropischen Deutschland. Essays*, 2nd ed. (Berlin: Babel Verlag Hund & Toker, 1993).

———— *Door Languages*, trans. Elizabeth Oehlkers Wright (Brookline: Zephyr Press, 2008).

Shapins, Jesse, "Excavating the Mauerpark: Landscape Archaeology of a Berlin Open Space," senior thesis in Urban Studies (Columbia College, 2002).

Sheffer, Edith, *Burned Bridge: How East and West Germans Made the Iron Curtain* (New York: Oxford University Press, forthcoming in 2011).

———— "On Edge: Building the Border in East and West Germany," *Central European History*, 40 (2007), pp. 307–39.

Simmel, Georg, "Der Raum und die räumlichen Ordnungen der Gesellschaft," in Simmel, *Gesamtausgabe*, ed. Otthein Rammstedt, vol. 11, *Soziologie. Untersuchungen über die Formen der Vergesellschaftung* (Frankfurt am Main: Suhrkamp, 1992), pp. 687–790.

Silver, Hilary, "Social Integration in the 'New' Berlin," *German Politics and Society*, 81.24 (2006), pp. 1–48.

Soja, Edward W., *Thirdspace: Journeys to Los Angeles and Other Real-and-Imagined Places* (Cambridge, MA: Blackwell, 1996).

Stacy, William E., *U.S. Army Border Operations in Germany 1945–1983* (Military History Office, 1984).

Stein, Jean, ed., *Grand Street 69*, 18.1 (New York: Grand Street Press, 1999; New York Foundation for the Arts).

Stevens, Quentin, *The Ludic City: Exploring the Potential of Public Spaces* (New York: Routledge, 2007).

Taberner, Stuart, ed., *Contemporary German Fiction: Writing in the Berlin Republic* (New York: Cambridge University Press, 2007).

————, and Frank Finlay, eds, *Recasting German Identity: Culture, Politics, and Literature in the Berlin Republic* (Rochester, NY: Camden House, 2002).

Taylor, Frederick, *The Berlin Wall: A World Divided, 1961–1989* (New York: HarperCollins, 2006).

Theweleit, Klaus, *Das Land, das Ausland heißt. Essays, Reden, Interviews zu Politik und Kunst* (Munich: Deutscher Taschenbuch Verlag, 1995).

Thrift, Nigel, "Transurbanism," *Urban Geography*, 25.8 (2004), pp. 724–34.

Timm, Uwe, *Johannisnacht* (Munich: dtv, 1998).

Trommler, Frank, ed., *Berlin: The New Capital in the East: A Transatlantic Appraisal* (Washington, DC: American Institute for Contemporary German Studies, 2000).

Ullrich, Maren, *Geteilte Ansichten. Erinnerungslandschaft deutsch-deutsche Grenze* (Berlin: Aufbau Verlag, 2006).

Verheyen, Dirk, *United City, Divided Memories? Cold War Legacies in Contemporary Berlin* (Lanham: Lexington Books, 2008).

Vidler, Anthony, *Warped Space: Art, Architecture, and Anxiety in Modern Culture* (Cambridge, MA: MIT Press, 2000).

Walther, Klaus, Peter Abraham, and Werner Liersch, eds, *Berlin. Hauptstadt der DDR. Ein Reiseverführer* (Rudolstadt: Greifenverlag, 1980).

Webber, Andrew J., *Berlin in the Twentieth Century: A Cultural Topography* (New York: Cambridge University Press, 2008).

Wegmann, Nicholas, "Die Mauer 1961–1989," *Weimarer Beiträge: Zeitschrift für Literaturwissenschaft, Ästhetik und Kulturwissenschaften*, 47.1 (2001), pp. 104–23.

Weisman, Alan, *The World Without Us* (New York: Picador, 2007).

Weizman, Eyal, *Hollow Land: Israel's Architecture of Occupation* (London and New York: Verso, 2007).

Weszkalnys, Gisa, *Berlin, Alexanderplatz. Transforming Place in a Unified Germany* (New York and Oxford: Berghahn Books, 2010).

Wolfrum, Edgar, *Die Mauer: Geschichte einer Teilung*, 2nd ed. (Munich: C.H. Beck, 2009).

Woods, Lebbeus, *Radical Reconstruction* (New York: Princeton Architectural Press, 1997).

————, and Ekkehard Rehfeld, eds, *Borderline* (New York: Springer, 1998).

Whybrow, Nicolas, *Street Scenes: Brecht, Benjamin and Berlin* (Bristol: intellect, 2005).

Wilke, Manfred, *Der Weg zur Mauer. Stationen der Teilungsgeschichte* (Berlin: Christoph Links Verlag, forthcoming in 2011).

Wolf, Christa, *Parting from Phantoms: Selected Writings, 1990–1994*, trans. Jan van Heurck (Chicago: University of Chicago Press, 1997).

Wolfrum, Edgar, *Die Mauer. Geschichte einer Teilung* (Munich: C.H. Beck, 2009).

Wyden, Peter, *Wall: The Inside Story of Divided Berlin* (New York: Simon & Schuster, 1989).

Part III: German Geomancy: Power and Planning in Berlin

Abrams, Janet, and Peter Hall, *Else/Where: Mapping* (Minneapolis: University of Minnesota Design Institute, 2006).

Ades, Dawn, Tim Benton, David Elliott, and Iain Boyd White, eds, *Kunst und Macht im Europa der Diktatoren 1930 bis 1945* (London: Hayward Gallery, 1996).

Arbeitsgruppe Berlin-Wettbewerbe, and Felix Zwoch, eds, *Hauptstadt Berlin Stadtmitte Spreeinsel Internationaler Städtebaulicher Ideenwettbewerb 1994* (Berlin and Boston: Birkhäuser, 1994).

Åman, Anders, "What Do Buildings and Cities Tell and How Do They Do It?", *International Review of Sociology*, 16.2 (2006), pp. 379–94.

Balfour, Alan. ed., *Berlin* (London: Academy Editions, 1995).

———— *Berlin. The Politics of Order 1737–1989* (New York: Rizzoli, 1990).

Balg, Ilse, ed., *Martin Mächler – Weltstadt Berlin* (Berlin: Galerie Wannsee Verlag, 1987).

Banerjee, Tridib, and Michael Southworth, eds, *City Sense and City Design: Writings and Projects of Kevin Lynch* (Cambridge, MA: MIT Press, 1990).

Barnestone, Deborah Ascher, *The Transparent State: Architecture and Politics in Postwar Germany* (New York: Routledge, 2005).

Benjamin, Walter, *Beroliniana* (Munich and Berlin: Koehler & Amelang, 2001).

Bernet, Claus, "The 'Hobrecht Plan' (1862) and Berlin's Urban Structure," *Urban History*, 31.3 (2004), pp. 400–19.

Beuster, Fritz, *Groß-Berlin nach dem Kriege. Städtebau und Verwaltungsorganisation* (Berlin: Carl Heymanns Verlag, 1918).

Bird, Jon, Barry Curtis, Tim Putnam, George Robertson, and Lisa Tickner, eds, *Mapping the Futures: Local Cultures, Global Change* (New York: Routledge, 1993).

Blockmans, Wim P., "Reshaping Cities: The Staging of Political Transformation," *Journal of Urban History*, 30.1 (2003), pp. 7–20.

Bodenschatz, Harald, *Platz frei für das Neue Berlin! Geschichte der Stadterneuerung in der "größten Mietskasernenstadt der Welt" seit 1871* (Berlin: Transit, 1987).

————— *Städtebau in Berlin. Schreckbild und Vorbild für Europa* (Berlin: Dom, 2010).

—————, ed., *Renaissance der Mitte. Zentrumsumbau in London und Berlin* (Berlin: Verlagshaus Braun, 2005).

—————, Hans-Joachim Engstfeld, and Carsten Seifert, eds, *Berlin. Auf der Suche nach dem verlorenen Zentrum* (Hamburg: Junius Verlag, 1995).

—————, and Thomas Flierl, eds, *Berlin plant. Plädoyer für ein Planwerk Innenstadt Berlin 2.0* (Berlin: Theater der Zeit, 2010).

Bullock, Nicholas, *Building the Post-War World: Modern Architecture and Reconstruction in Britain* (New York: Routledge, 2002).

Briesen, Detlef, *Berlin, die überschätzte Metropole. Über das System der deutschen Hauptstädte von 1850 bis 1940* (Bonn: Bouvier, 1992).

Buddensieg, Tilmann, *Berliner Labyrinth, neu besichtigt. Von Schinkels Unter den Linden bis Fosters Reichstagskuppel* (Berlin: Wagenbach, 1999).

Bundesministerium für Raumordnung, Bauwesen und Städtebau, Bundesministerium für Innerdeutsche Beziehungen, Bund Deutscher Architekten BDA, Bundesarchitektenkammer, Deutsches Architekturmuseum, eds, *Ideen, Orte, Entwürfe: Architektur und Städtebau in der Bundesrepublik Deutschland / Ideas, Places, Projects: Architecture and Urban Planning in the Federal Republic of Germany* (Berlin: Ernst, 1990).

Cacciari, Massimo, *Architecture and Nihilism: On the Philosophy of Modern Architecture*, trans. Stephen Sartarelli (New Haven: Yale University Press, 1993).

Campbell, Scott, and Susan S. Fainstein, eds, *Readings in Planning Theory*, 2nd ed. (Malden, MA, and Oxford: Blackwell, 2003).

Castillo, Greg, "Building Culture in Divided Berlin: Globalization and the Cold War," in Nezar AlSayyad, ed., *Hybrid Urbanism: On the Identity Discourse and the Built Environment* (Westport: Praeger, 2001), pp. 181–205.

Chametzky, Peter, "Rebuilding the Nation: Norman Foster's *Reichstag* Renovation and Daniel Libeskind's Jewish Museum Berlin," *Centropa*, 1.3 (2001), pp. 245–64.

Collins, Christiane Crasemann, *Werner Hegemann and the Search for Universal Urbanism* (New York: W.W. Norton, 2005).

Costabile-Heming, Carol Anne, Rachel J. Halverson, and Kristie A. Foell, eds, *Berlin: The Symphony Continues. Orchestrating Architectural, Social, and Artistic Change in Germany's New Capital* (New York: Walter de Gruyter, 2004).

Cullen, Michael, *Der Reichstag. Parlament, Denkmal, Symbol* (Berlin: be.bra verlag, 1999).

—————, and Uwe Kieling, *Das Brandenburger Tor. Ein deutsches Symbol* (Berlin: Edition, 1999).

Czaplicka, John J., Nida Gelazis, and Blair A. Ruble, eds, *Cities After the Fall of Communism: Reshaping Cultural Landscapes and European Identity* (Baltimore: Johns Hopkins University Press, 2009).

Dangschat, Jens S., "Berlin and the German Systems of Cities," *Urban Studies*, 30.6 (1993), pp. 1025–51.

Dear, Michael J., *The Postmodern Urban Condition* (Malden, MA and Oxford: Blackwell, 2000).

Debuschewitz, Peter, Ulrich Naumann and Dietmar Bartholome, eds, *Berlin Hauptbahnhof 1994–2006. Lehrter Bahnhof* (Berlin: Luftbildverlag, 2007).

de Certeau, Michel, *The Practice of Everyday Life*, trans. Steven Rendall (Berkeley: University of California Press, 1984).

Descartes, René, *Discourse on the Method* (1637), ed. David Weissman, trans. Elizabeth S. Haldane and G.R.T. Ross (New Haven: Yale University Press, 1996).

Diefendorf, Jeffry M., *In the Wake of War: The Reconstruction of German Cities after World War II* (New York: Oxford University Press, 1993).

Dubrau, Dorothee, ed., *Architekturführer Berlin-Mitte*, 2 vols. (Berlin: DOM publishers, 2009).

Durth, Werner, Jörn Düwel, and Niels Gutschow, eds, *Aufbau. Städte, Themen, Dokumente. Architektur und Städtebau der DDR*, vol. 2, 2nd ed. (Frankfurt am Main and New York: Campus Verlag, 1999).

Durth, Werner, and Winfried Nerdinger, *Architektur und Städtebau der 30er / 40er Jahre* (Bonn: Deutsches Nationalkomitee für Denkmalschutz, 1995).

Düwel, Jörn, Werner Durth, Niels Gutschow, and Jochen Schneider, eds, *1945. Krieg – Zerstörung – Aufbau. Architektur und Stadtplanung 1940–1960* (Berlin: Henschel Verlag, 1995).

Engel, Helmut, and Wolfgang Ribbe, eds, *Geschichtsmeile. Wilhelmstraße* (Berlin: Akademie Verlag, 1997).

Fest, Joachim, *Speer: The Final Verdict*, trans. Ewald Osers and Alexandra Dring (New York: Harcourt, Inc., 2001).

Flierl, Bruno, *Berlin baut um – Wessen Stadt wird die Stadt?* (Berlin: Verlag für Bauwesen, 1998).

Foucault, Michel, "Space, Knowledge, and Power," in Paul Rabinow, ed., *The Foucault Reader* (New York: Pantheon, 1984), pp. 239–56.

Freisleben, Antje, and Johannes Modersohn, eds, *Kritische Würdigung der Kritischen Rekonstruktion* (Munich and Berlin: Deutscher Kunstverlag, 2006).

Friedmann, John, "Toward a Non-Euclidian Mode of Planning," *Journal of the American Planning Association*, 59.4 (1993), pp. 482–85.

Frisby, David, *Cityscapes of Modernity. Critical Explorations* (Cambridge: Polity Press, 2001).

Fritzsche, Peter, "Nazi Modern," *Modernism/Modernity*, 3.1 (1996), pp. 1–22.

Gittus, E. J. "Berlin as a Conduit for the Creation of German National Identity at the End of the Twentieth Century," *Space and Polity*, 6.1 (2002), pp. 91–115.

Goebbels, Joseph, *Kampf um Berlin. Der Anfang* (Munich: Frz. Eher Nachf., 1932).

Gold, John R., *The Experience of Modernism: Modern Architects and the Future City 1928–1953* (London, UK: FN Spon, 1997).

Gropius, Walter, and Wagner, Martin, "The New City Pattern for the People and By the People," in *The Problem of the Cities and Towns: Conference on Urbanism, March 5–6, 1942* (Cambridge, MA: Harvard University, 1942), pp. 95–116.

Guerra, Max Welch, *Hauptstadt Einig Vaterland. Planung und Politik zwischen Bonn und Berlin* (Berlin: Verlag Bauwesen, 1999).

Hake, Sabine, *Topographies of Class: Modern Architecture and Mass Society in Weimar Berlin* (Ann Arbor: University of Michigan Press, 2008).

Hall, Peter, *Cities of Tomorrow: An Intellectual History of Urban Planning and Design in the Twentieth Century*, 3rd ed. (Malden, MA: Blackwell, 2002).

Hall, Thomas, *Planning Europe's Capital Cities: Aspects of Nineteenth-Century Urban Development* (London: E. & F.N. Spon, 1997).

Harley, J. B., *Le pouvoir des cartes* (Paris: Economica, 1995).

Hayes, K. Michael, *Modernism and the Posthumanist Subject: The Architecture of Hannes Meyer and Ludwig Hilberseimer* (Cambridge, MA: MIT Press, 1992).

Hård, Mikael, and Thomas J. Misa, eds, *Urban Machinery: Inside Modern European Cities* (Cambridge, MA: MIT Press, 2008).

Häußermann, Hartmut, and Rainer Neef, eds, *Stadtentwicklung in Ostdeutschland. Soziale und räumliche Tendenzen* (Opladen: Westdeutscher Verlag, 1996).

Hein, Carola, Helmut Geisert, and Doris Haneberg, eds, *Hauptstadt Berlin. Internationaler städtebaulicher Ideenwettbewerb 1957/58* (Berlin: Gebr. Mann, 1991).

Heinrich, Max, "Die Entwicklung der Reichshauptstadt durch den Ausbau ihrer Ost-West-Achse," *Stadtbaukunst*, 8 (20 June, 1927), pp. 55–58.

Hegemann, Werner, *Das steinerne Berlin. Geschichte der größten Mietskasernenstadt der Welt* (Berlin: Gustav Kiepenheuer, 1930).

Helmer, Stephen D., *Hitler's Berlin: The Speer Plans for Reshaping the Central City* (Ann Arbor: UMI Research Press, 1985).

Hilberg, Raul, "German Railroads, Jewish Souls," *Society*, 14 (November–December, 1976), pp. 60–74.

Hilberseimer, Ludwig, *Entfaltung einer Planungsidee* (Berlin: Ullstein, 1963).

——— *Groszstadtarchitektur* (Stuttgart: Verlag Julius Hoffmann, 1927).

Homann, Klaus, Martin Kieren, and Ludovica Scarpa, eds, *Martin Wagner 1885–1957. Wohnungsbau und Weltstadtplanung. Die Rationalisierung des Glücks* (Berlin: Akademie der Künste, 1985).

Huber, Nicole, "Center or Nexus: Berlin's 'New' Politics of Belonging," *Journal of Urban History*, 32.1 (2005), pp. 82–103.

Hughes, Jonathan, and Simon Sadler, eds, *Non-Plan: Essays on Freedom, Participation, and Change in Modern Architecture and Urbanism* (Oxford: Architectural Press, 2000).

James-Chakraborty, Kathleen, *German Architecture for a Mass Audience* (New York: Routledge, 2000).

Jarosinski, Eric, "Architectural Symbolism and the Rhetoric of Transparency: A Berlin Ghost Story," *Journal of Urban History*, 29.1 (2002), pp. 62–77.

Jaskot, Paul B., *The Architecture of Oppression: The SS, Forced Labor and the Nazi Monumental Building Economy* (New York: Routledge, 2000).

Kil, Wolfgang, *Gründerparadiese. Vom Bauen in Zeiten des Übergangs* (Berlin: Verlag Bauwesen, 2000).

King, Geoff, *Mapping Reality: An Exploration of Cultural Cartographies* (New York: St Martin's Press, 1996).

Kleeberg, Michael, *Ein Garten im Norden: Roman* (Berlin: Ullstein, 1998).

Kleihues, Josef Paul, and Christina Rathgeber, eds, *Berlin–New York: Like and Unlike* (New York: Rizzoli, 1993).

Klemek, Christopher, *The Transatlantic Collapse of Urban Renewal: Postwar Urbanism from New York to Berlin* (Chicago: University of Chicago Press, forthcoming in 2011).

Klemm, Thomas, and Kathleen Schröter, eds, *Die Gegenwart des Vergangenen. Strategien im Umgang mit sozialistischer Repräsentationsarchitektur* (Leipzig: Meine Verlag, 2007).

Koepnick, Lutz, *Framing Attention: Windows on Modern German Culture* (Baltimore: Johns Hopkins University Press, 2007).

Konter, Erich, ed., *Wendezeiten in Architektur und Stadtplanung: Kontinuität oder Bruch in der Entwicklung nach 1945* (Berlin: Institut für Stadt- und Regionalplanung der Technischen Universität Berlin, 1986).

Kostof, Spiro, *The City Shaped: Urban Patterns and Meanings Through History* (Boston and New York: Bulfinch [Little, Brown and Company], 1999).

Krajewski, Christian, and Wolfgang Schumann, eds, *Berlin, Stadt-Entwicklungen zwischen Kiez und Metropole seit der Wiedervereinigung* (Münster: Arbeitsgemeinschaft Angewandte Geographie Münster, 2006).

Krier, Léon, *Albert Speer. Architecture 1932–1945* (Brussels: Archives d'Architecture Moderne, 1985).

Krier, Rob, and Christoph Kohl, *Potsdam, Kirchsteigfeld: Eine Stadt entsteht / The Making of a Town / La naissance d'une ville* (Bensheim: awf, 1997).

Ladd, Brian, "Double Restoration: Rebuilding Berlin after 1945," in Lawrence J. Vale and Thomas J. Campanella, eds, *The Resilient City: How Modern Cities Recover from Disaster* (New York: Oxford University Press, 2005), pp. 117–34.

———— *Urban Planning and Civic Order in Germany, 1860–1914* (Cambridge, MA: Harvard University Press, 1990).

————, and John Woods, dirs., *Berlin's Hidden History* (Woods Productions/EN Productions, 2002).

Lampugnani, Vittorio Magnago, ed., *Berlin Tomorrow: International Architectural Visions*, Architectural Design Profile 92 (London: Academy Editions, 1991).

Land Berlin für die Auslober des Internationalen Städtebaulichen Ideenwettbewerbs, and Felix Zwoch, eds., *Hauptstadt Berlin: Parlamentsviertel im Spreebogen: Internationaler Städtebaulicher Ideenwettbewerb, 1993* (Berlin and Boston: Birkhäuser, 1993).

Lane, Barbara Miller, "Interpreting Nazi Architecture: The Case of Albert Speer," in Börje Magnusson, Stefania Renzetti, Paolo Vian, and Sever J. Voicu, eds, *Ultra terminum vagari: Scritti in onore di Carl Nylander* (Rome: Edizioni Quasar, 1998), pp. 155–169.

Large, David Clay, *Nazi Games: The Olympics of 1936* (W.W. Norton & Company, 2007).

Latour, Bruno, and Emilie Hermant, *Paris ville invisible* (Paris: La Découverte, 1998).

Leendertz, Ariane, *Ordnung schaffen: Deutsche Raumplanung im 20. Jahrhundert* (Göttingen: Wallstein, 2008).

Lefebvre, Henri, *Writings on Cities*, trans. Eleonore Kofman and Elizabeth Lebas (Oxford: Blackwell, 1996).

Lenger, Friedrich, ed., *Towards an Urban Nation. Germany Since 1780* (New York: Berg, 2002).

Loeb, Carolyn, "Planning Reunification: The Planning History of the Fall of the Berlin Wall," *Planning Perspectives*, 21.1 (2006), pp. 67–87.

Luescher, A., "Refashioning No-Man's-Land: Urban Image Politics and the Visual Dimensions of Democracy," *Cities*, 19.3 (2002), pp. 155–60.

Lynch, Kevin, *A Theory of Good City Form* (Cambridge, MA: MIT Press, 1981).

Macphee, Graham, *The Architecture of the Visible* (London: Continuum, 2002).

Marcuse, Peter, "Not Chaos, but Walls: Postmodernism and the Partitioned City," in Sophie Watson and Katherine Gibson, eds, *Postmodern Cities and Spaces* (Cambridge, MA: Blackwell, 1995), pp. 243–53.

———— "Reflections on Berlin: The Meaning of Construction and the Construction of Meaning," *International Journal of Urban and Regional Research*, 22.2 (1998), pp. 331–38.

Matschenz, Andreas, ed., *Stadtpläne von Berlin: Geschichte vermessen* (Berlin: Gebr. Mann, 2006).

Mächler, Martin, *Die Macht der öffentlichen Meinung. Studie zu einem Weltzeitungsplan* (Berlin: Gebhardt, Jahn & Landt, 1917).

McElligott, Anthony, ed., *The German Urban Experience 1900–1945: Modernity and Crisis* (New York: Routledge, 2001).

Meller, Helen, *European Cities 1890–1930s: History, Culture and the Built Environment* (Chichester and New York: John Wiley & Sons, 2001).

Miles, Malcolm, Tim Hall, and Iain Borden, eds, *The City Cultures Reader* (New York: Routledge, 2004).

Monmonier, Mark, *How to Lie with Maps* (Chicago: University of Chicago Press, 1991).

Müller, Peter, *Symbolsuche – Die Ost-Berliner Zentrumsplanung zwischen Repräsentation und Agitation* (Berlin: Gebr. Mann Verlag, 2005).

Müller, Rolf-Dieter, *Hitlers Ostkrieg und die deutsche Siedlungspolitik* (Frankfurt am Main: Fischer, 1991).

Neill, William J.V., and Hanns-Uve Schwedler, eds, *Urban Planning and Cultural Inclusion: Lessons from Belfast and Berlin* (New York and Basingstoke: Palgrave Macmillan, 2001).

Nerdinger, Winfried, ed., *Bauhaus-Moderne im Nationalsozialismus. Zwischen Anbiederung und Verfolgung* (Munich: Prestel, 1993).

Neufert, Ernst, *Bauordnungslehre*, foreword by Albert Speer (Berlin: Volk und Reich Verlag, 1943).

Pabsch, Matthias, *Pariser Platz, Architektur und Technik. Vom manuellen zum digitalen Zeitalter* (Berlin: Reimer, 2002).

Page, Max, "Berlin's Identity Crisis," *Architecture*, 93.9 (2004), pp. 25–27.

Pickles, John, *A History of Spaces: Cartographic Reason, Mapping, and the Geo-Coded World* (New York: Routledge, 2004).

Ratenieks, A., *Was bringt die Neuordnung Europas den europäischen Völkern?* (Dresden: Gesellschaft für europäische Wirtschaftsplanung und Grossraumwirtschaft, 1942).

Ribbe, Wolfgang, *Berlin 1945–2000. Grundzüge der Stadtgeschichte* (Berlin: Berliner Wissenschafts-Verlag, 2002).

Riley, Terence, and Barry Bergdoll, eds, *Mies in Berlin* (New York: Museum of Modern Art / H. N. Abrams, 2001).

Ring, Kristin, ed., *Emerging Identities – East! Berlin, Bratislava, Budapest, Ljubljana, Prague, Tallinn, Vilnius, Warsaw* (Berlin: Jovis Verlag, 2006).

Rogier, Francesca, "Growing Pains: From the Opening of the Wall to the Wrapping of the Reichstag," *Assemblage*, 29 (1996), pp. 44–71.

Rosenfeld, Gavriel D., "The Architects' Debate. Architectural Discourse and the Memory of Nazism in the Federal Republic of Germany, 1977–1997," *History and Memory*, 9.1–2 (1997), pp. 189–225.

Russell, James S., "With His Sleek, Ecological Design, Lord Norman Foster Imbues the Reichstag with Germany's New Self-image," *Architectural Record* (July, 1999), pp. 102–13.

Rürup, Reinhard, ed., *Berlin 1945. Eine Dokumentation* (Berlin: Verlag Willmuth Arenhövel, 1995).

Sandercock, Leonie, *Towards Cosmopolis: Planning for Multicultural Cities* (Chichester: John Wiley & Sons, 1998).

Scarpa, Ludovica, *Martin Wagner und Berlin. Architektur und Städtebau in der Weimarer Republik*, trans. Heinz-Dieter Held (orig. 1983; Braunschweig: Friedr. Vieweg & Sohn, 1986).

Schäche, Wolfgang, "Architektur für die Ewigkeit…? Zur 'Theorie des Ruinenwertes' von Albert Speer und den Bauten des Reichsparteigeländes in Nürnberg," *Der Architekt*, 11 (1989), pp. 565–68.

———— "Architektur und Stadtplanung des 'Dritten Reiches' im Spiegel der Bau- und Kunstgeschichte," *Deutsche Kunst und Denkmalpflege*, 47.1 (1989), pp. 5–14.

———— *Architektur und Städtebau in Berlin zwischen 1933 und 1945. Planen und Bauen unter der Ägide der Stadtverwaltung*, 2nd ed. (Berlin: Gebr. Mann Verlag, 1992).

———— "Zur Funktion des Baumodells in der Architektur des 'Dritten Reiches'," *Der Architekt* 4 (1989), pp. 204–23.

Scheer, Thorsten, Josef Paul Kleihues, and Paul Kahlfeldt, eds, *Stadt der Architektur. Architektur der Stadt. Berlin 1900–2000* (Berlin: Nicolai, 2000).

Scheffler, Karl, *Berlin. Ein Stadtschicksal* (Berlin: Erich Reiss Verlag, 1910).

Schneider, Peter, *Eduards Heimkehr* (Berlin: Rowohlt, 1999).

Schmaling, Sebastian, "Masked Nostalgia, Chic Regression: The 'Critical' Reconstruction of Berlin," *Harvard Design Magazine*, 23 (2006), pp. 24–30.

Schorske, Carl E., *Thinking with History: Explorations in the Passage to Modernism* (Princeton: Princeton University Press, 1998).

Schwarz, Karl, *Utopischer Ort Berlin. Historische Topographie*, vol. 3 of *Die Zukunft der Metropolen: Paris, London, New York, Berlin* (Berlin: Dietrich Reimer Verlag, 1984).

Sebald, W.G., *Austerlitz*, trans. Anthea Bell (London: Hamish Hamilton, 2001).

Senatsverwaltung für Bauen, Wohnen und Verkehr, ed., *Verkehrskonzept für Berlin* (Berlin: Bloch & Co., GmbH, 1999).

Senatsverwaltung für Stadtentwicklung, Umweltschutz und Technologie, ed., *Planwerk Innenstadt Berlin. Ergebnis, Prozeß, Sektorale Planungen und Werkstätten* (Berlin: Kulturbuch Verlag, 1999).

Siedler, Wolf Jobst, *Die gemordete Stadt* (Berlin: Herbig, 1964).

———— *Phoenix im Sand: Glanz und Elend der Hauptstadt* (Berlin: Propyläen Verlag, 1998).

Simmel, Georg, "Berliner Gewerbeausstellung," *Die Zeit* (Vienna), 7.91 (July 25, 1896); "The Berlin Trade Exhibition," trans. Sam Whimster, *Theory, Culture & Society*, 8 (1991), pp. 119–23.

———— *Brücke und Tür. Essays des Philosophen zur Geschichte, Religion, Kunst und Gesellschaft*, ed. Michael Landmann (Stuttgart: K.F. Koehler Verlag, 1957).

———— "Bridge and Door," in Neil Leach, ed., *Rethinking Architecture: A Reader in Cultural Theory* (New York: Routledge, 1997), pp. 66–69.

Sonne, Wolfgang, "Specific Intentions – General Realities: On the Relation between Urban Forms and Political Aspirations in Berlin during the Twentieth Century," *Planning Perspectives*, 19.3 (2004), pp. 283–310.

Speer, Albert, *Architektur. Arbeiten 1933–1942* (Frankfurt a.M.: Propylaen, 1978).

———— *Inside the Third Reich*, trans. Richard and Clara Winston (New York: Touchstone / Simon & Schuster, 1997).

————, ed., *Neue deutsche Baukunst* (Amsterdam / Berlin / Vienna: Volk und Reich Verlag, 1943).

————, and Joseph Goebbels, *Tatsachen sprechen für den Sieg* (Berlin: Universum Verlag, 1943).

Spengler, Oswald, *Der Untergang des Abendlandes: Umrisse einer Morphologie der Weltgeschichte*, 2 vols (Munich: Beck, 1918).

———— *The Decline of the West*, 2 vols, trans. Charles Francis Atkinson (New York: Alfred A. Knopf, 1928).

Stiftung Denkmalschutz Berlin, ed., *Das Brandenburger Tor: Weg in die Geschichte, Tor in die Zukunft* (Berlin: Jovis, 2003).

Stimmann, Hans, ed., *Berliner Altstadt. Von der DDR-Staatsmitte zur Stadtmitte* (Berlin: Dom, 2009).

———, ed., *Berlin 1945–1953–1989–2000–2010: Physiognomie einer Großstadt* (Milan: Skira, 2000).

———, and Martin Kieren, eds, *Die Architektur des Neuen Berlin* (Berlin: Nicolai, 2000).

Stirk, Peter, ed., *Mitteleuropa: History and Prospects* (Edinburgh: Edinburgh University Press, 1994).

Strobel, Roland, "Before the Wall Came Tumbling Down: Urban Planning Paradigm Shifts in a Divided Berlin," *Journal of Architectural Education*, 48.4 (1995), pp. 25–37.

Sutcliffe, Anthony, *Towards the Planned City: Germany, Britain, the United States, and France, 1780–1914* (New York: St Martin's Press, 1981).

———, ed., *Metropolis 1890–1940* (Chicago: University of Chicago Press, 1984).

Szambien, Werner, *Berlin. Une ville en suspens* (Paris: Norma Editions, 2003).

Taberner, Stuart, and Paul Cooke, eds, *German Culture, Politics, and Literature into the Twenty-First Century* (Rochester, NY: Camden House, 2006).

Tafuri, Manfredo, *The Sphere and the Labyrinth: Avant-Gardes and Architecture from Piranesi to the 1970s*, trans. Pellegrino d'Acierno and Robert Connolly (Cambridge, MA: MIT Press, 1987).

Taut, Bruno, *Die Stadtkrone* (Jena: Eugen Diedericks, 1919).

Teut, Anna, *Architektur im Dritten Reich 1933–1945* (Berlin and Frankfurt am Main: Ullstein, 1967).

——— "Axis and Symmetry as a Medium of Subordination. Nazi Architecture Redivivus," *Daidalos*, 15 (1985), pp. 104–15.

Urban, Florian, *Neo-Historical East Berlin: Architecture and Urban Design in the German Democratic Republic 1970–1990* (Burlington and Farnham: Ashgate Publishing, 2009).

——— "Picture Postcards of Urbanity. Reflections on Berlin's Inner City and the 1999 Master Plan," *Journal of Architectural Education* (2003), pp. 68–73.

Wagner, Martin, *Städtebauliche Probleme in amerikanischen Städten und ihre Rückwirkung auf den deutschen Städtebau* (Berlin: special issue of *Deutsche Bauzeitung*, 1929).

——— "Weltstadt und Städtebauer," *Berliner Tageblatt*, 58.132 (19 March, 1929).

———, and Adolf Behne, eds, *Das Neue Berlin. Grossstadtprobleme* (Berlin: Verlag Deutsche Bauzeitung, 1929).

Ward, Janet, "Re-Capitalizing Berlin," in Marc Silberman, ed., *The German Wall: Fallout in Europe* (New York: Palgrave Macmillan, forthcoming in 2011), pp. 79–97.

Wefing, Heinrich, *Kulisse der Macht. Das Berliner Kanzleramt* (Stuttgart and Munich: Deutsche Verlags-Anstalt, 2001).

Weihsmann, Helmut, *Bauen unterm Hakenkreuz. Architektur des Untergangs* (Vienna: Promedia, 1998).

Willems, Susanne, *Der entsiedelte Jude. Albert Speers Wohnungsmarktpolitik für den Berliner Hauptstadtbau* (Berlin: Edition Hentrich, 2002).

Williams, John Alexander, ed., *Berlin Since the Wall's End: Shaping Society and Memory in the German Metropolis* (Newcastle: Cambridge Scholars, 2008).

Wise, Michael Z., *Capital Dilemma: Germany's Search for a New Architecture of Democracy* (Princeton: Princeton Architectural Press, 1998).

Wolters, Rudolf, *Neue deutsche Baukunst* (Prague: Volk und Reich Verlag, 1943).

Zachau, Reinhard, ed., with Rolf Goebel and Sabine Hake, *Topography and Literature: Berlin and Modernism* (Göttingen: V&R Unipress, 2009).

Zohlen, Gerwin, *Auf der Suche nach der verlorenen Stadt* (Berlin: Nicolai, 2002).

———, ed., *Stadtbau. Die Stimmann-Dekade. Berlin 1991–2006* (Berlin: Internationale Bauakademie, 2006).

Part IV: Holocaust Divides: Memorial Architecture in Berlin

Abramson, Daniel, "Make History, Not Memory," *Harvard Design Magazine*, 9 (Fall 1999), pp. 78–83.

Arnold, Dietmar, *Der Potsdamer Platz von unten* (Berlin: Ch. Links Verlag, 2001).

———, and Ingmar Arnold, *Dunkle Welten. Bunker, Tunnel, Gewölbe unter Berlin* (Berlin: Ch. Links Verlag, 2000).

Ashplant, T.G., Graham Dawson, and Michael Roper, eds, *The Politics of War Memory and Commemoration* (New York: Routledge, 2000).

Assmann, Aleida, *Der lange Schatten der Vergangenheit: Erinnerungskultur und Geschichtspolitik* (Munich: C.H. Beck, 2006).

———, and Ute Frevert, *Geschichtsvergessenheit, Geschichtsversessenheit. Vom Umgang mit deutschen Vergangenheiten nach 1945* (Stuttgart: Deutsche Verlags-Anstalt, 1999).

———, and Sebastian Conrad, eds, *Memory in a Global Age: Discourses, Practices and Trajectories* (New York and Basingstoke: Palgrave Macmillan, 2010).

Assmann, Jan, *Religion and Cultural Memory*, trans. Rodney Livingstone (Stanford: Stanford University Press, 2006).

Åhr, Johan, "Memory and Mourning in Berlin: On Peter Eisenman's Holocaust-Mahnmal," *Modern Judaism*, 28.3 (2008), pp. 283–305.

Ball, Karyn, *Disciplining the Holocaust* (Albany: SUNY Press, 2008).

Bathrick, David, Brad Prager, and Michael D. Richardson, eds, *Visualizing the Holocaust: Documents, Aesthetics, Memory* (Rochester, NY: Camden House, 2008).

Baumann, Leonie, Rainer Hörmann, et al., eds (Neue Gesellschaft für Bildende Kunst), *Der Wettbewerb für das "Denkmal für die ermordeten Juden Europas". Eine Streitschrift* (Dresden: Verlag der Kunst, 1995).

Benjamin, Walter, "Theses on the Philosophy of History" (1939), in Benjamin, *Illuminations. Essays and Reflections*, ed. Hannah Arendt, trans. Harry Zohn (New York: Shocken, 1968), pp. 253–64.

Broder, Henryk M., *Volk und Wahn* (Hamburg: Spiegel Buchverlag, 1996).

——— www.*Deutsche Leidkultur.de* (Augsburg: Ölbaum-Verlag, 2001).

Carrier, Peter, *Holocaust Monuments and National Memory Cultures in France and Germany since 1989: The Origins and Political Function of the Vél d'Hiv' in Paris and the Holocaust Monument in Berlin* (New York and Oxford: Berghahn Books, 2005).

Choay, Françoise, *The Invention of the Historic Monument*, trans. Lauren M. O'Connell (New York: Cambridge University Press, 2001).

Cole, Tim, *Selling the Holocaust: From Auschwitz to Schindler* (New York: Routledge, 2000).

Crinson, Mark, ed., *Urban Memory: History and Amnesia in the Modern City* (New York: Routledge, 2005).

Cullen, Michael S., ed., *Das Holocaust-Mahnmal. Dokumentation einer Debatte* (Zürich: Pendo, 1999).

Dannatt, Adrian, *United States Holocaust Memorial Museum. James Ingo Freed* (London: Phaidon, 1995).

Daum, Andreas, and Christof Mauch, eds, *Berlin–Washington, 1800–2000: Capital Cities, Cultural Representation, and National Identities* (New York: Cambridge University Press, 2005).

Dean, Andrea Oppenheimer, "Moshe Safdie Offers a Memorial Journey through the Depths of a Jerusalem Hillside with his Yad Vashem History Museum," *Architectural Record*, 193.7 (2005), pp. 112–19.

Demps, Laurenz, Eberhard Schultz, and Klaus Wettig, *Bundesfinanzministerium: ein belasteter Ort?/The Federal Ministry of Finance: Can History Taint a Building?* (Berlin: Parthas, 2002).

Doss, Erika, *Spirit Poles and Flying Pigs: Public Art and Cultural Democracy in American Communities* (Washington, DC: Smithsonian Institution Press, 1995).

Eghigan, Gregg, and Matthew Paul Berg, eds, *Sacrifice and National Belonging in Twentieth-Century Germany* (College Station: Texas A&M University Press, 2002).

Eisenman Architects, "Realisierungsentwurf. Engeres Auswahlverfahren zum Denkmal für die ermordeten Juden Europas" (brochure), trans. Ingeborg Rocker and Dr. Günter Schlusche (Berlin: Deutsches Historisches Museum, 1998).

Eisenman, Peter, "Peter Eisenman: Memorial to the Murdered Jews of Europe, Berlin, Germany 1998–2005," *A + U: architecture and urbanism*, 8.419 (2005), pp. 36–53.

Enders, Kilian, "Enormity of the Banal: Eisenman's Memorial of Order and Chaos," *Architecture Today*, 161 (2005), pp. 78–80, pp. 83–84, p. 87.

Engelhardt, Isabelle, "The Creation of an 'Artificial Authentic Place' – The United States Holocaust Memorial Museum in Washington, DC," in Luisa Passerini, ed., *Across the Atlantic: Cultural Exchanges between Europe and the United States* (Brussels: Peter Lang, 2000), pp. 141–51.

Evans, Martin, and Ken Lunn, eds, *War and Memory in the Twentieth Century* (New York and Oxford: Berg, 1997).

Fessmann, Jörg, ed., *Streit um die Neue Wache. Zur Gestaltung einer zentralen Gedenkstätte* (Berlin: Akademie der Künste, 1993).

Fischer, Jan Okatar, "Full Disclosure: Invoking the Past in Recent German Exhibition Design," *Harvard Design Magazine*, 19 (2003–2004), pp. 1–9.

Forster, Kurt W., "Städtische Monumente der Endlichkeit," *Zeitschrift für schweizerische Archäologie und Kunstgeschichte*, 52.1 (1995), pp. 3–12.

François, Etienne, and Hagen Schulze, eds, *Deutsche Erinnerungsorte* (Munich: C.H. Beck, 2001).

Freed, James Ingo, "The United States Holocaust Memorial Museum," *Assemblage*, 9 (1989), pp. 58–79.

Frei, Norbert, *1945 und wir. Das Dritte Reich im Bewußtsein der Deutschen* (Munich: C.H. Beck, 2005).

Freud, Sigmund, *Beyond the Pleasure Principle*, trans. James Strachey (New York: Norton, 1961).

Freudenheim, Tom L., "Confronting Memory and Museums," in Todd Herzog and Sander L. Gilman, eds, *A New Germany in a New Europe* (New York: Routledge, 2001), pp. 143–65.

Gay, Caroline, "The Politics of Cultural Remembrance: The Holocaust Monument in Berlin," *International Journal of Cultural Policy*, 9.2 (2003), pp. 153–66.

Gehrmann, Lucas, and Marianne Greber, eds, *Judenplatz Wien 1996. Wettbewerb, Mahnmal und Gedenkstätte für die jüdischen Opfer des Naziregimes in Österreich 1938–1945* (Vienna: Folio, 1996).

German Politics and Society, 17.3 (1999), special issue on "The Dilemmas of Commemoration: German Debates on the Holocaust in the 1990s."

Geyer, Michael, "The Place of the Second World War in German Memory and History," *New German Critique*, 71 (1997), pp. 5–40.

Gigliotti, Simone, *The Train Journey: Transit, Captivity, and Witnessing in the Holocaust* (New York and Oxford: Berghahn Books, 2009).

Goebel, Rolf, "Berlin's Architectural Citations: Reconstruction, Simulation, and the Problem of Historical Authenticity," *PMLA*, 118.5 (2003), pp. 1268–89.

Grenzer, Elke, "The Topographies of Memory in Berlin: The Neue Wache and the Memorial for the Murdered Jews of Europe," *Canadian Journal of Urban Research*, 11.1 (2002), pp. 93–110.

Habermas, Jürgen, "What Does 'Working Off the Past' Mean Today?" (orig. 1992), in *A Berlin Republic: Writings on Germany*, trans. Steven Rendall, intro. Peter Uwe Hohendahl (Lincoln: University of Nebraska Press, 1997), pp. 17–40.

Halbwachs, Maurice, *On Collective Memory*, ed. and trans. Lewis A. Coser (Chicago: University of Chicago Press, 1992).

Hampton, Mary N. and Douglas C. Pfeifer, "German Memory Sites and Foreign Policy," *German Studies Review*, 30.2 (2007), pp. 371–90.

Hartman, Geoffrey, ed., *Holocaust Remembrance: The Shapes of Memory* (Cambridge, MA and Oxford: Blackwell, 1994).

Hayes, K. Michael, ed., *Architecture Theory Since 1968* (Cambridge, MA: MIT Press, 1998).

Hebbert, Michael, "The Street as Locus of Collective Memory," *Environment and Planning D: Society and Space*, 23.4 (2005), pp. 581–96.

Heckner, Elke, "Berlin Remake: Building Memory and the Politics of Capital Identity," *The Germanic Review*, 77.4 (2002), pp. 304–25.

Heimrod, Ute, Günter Schlusche, and Horst Seferenz, eds, *Der Denkmalstreit – das Denkmal? Die Debatte um das "Denkmal für die ermordeten Juden Europas". Eine Dokumentation* (Berlin: Philo Verlag, 1999).

Heise, Volker, and Susanne Holstein, eds, *Realisierungswettbewerb. Erweiterung Berlin Museum mit Abteilung Jüdisches Museum. Voraussetzungen, Verfahren, Ergebnisse* (Berlin: Senatsverwaltung für Bau- und Wohnungswesen, 1990).

Herf, Jeffrey, *Divided Memory: The Nazi Past in the Two Germanys* (Cambridge, MA: Harvard University Press, 1997).

Hogan, Michael J., ed., *Hiroshima in History and Memory* (New York: Cambridge University Press, 1996).

Hoss, Christiane, and Martin Schönfeld, eds, *Gedenktafeln in Berlin: Orte der Erinnerung an Verfolgte des Nationalsozialismus 1991–2001* (Berlin: Verein Aktives Museum, 2002).

Huyssen, Andreas, *Present Pasts: Urban Palimpsests and the Politics of Memory* (Stanford: Stanford University Press, 2003).

Jeismann, Michael, ed., *Mahnmal Mitte: Eine Kontroverse* (Cologne: DuMont, 1999).

Jenkins, David, ed., *The Reichstag Graffiti/Die Reichstag Graffiti* (Berlin: Jovis, 2003).

Jordan, Jennifer A., *Structures of Memory: Understanding Urban Change in Berlin and Beyond* (Stanford: Stanford University Press, 2006).

Kalbe, Riki, and Moshe Zuckermann, eds, *Ein Grundstück in Mitte. Das Gelände des künftigen Holocaust-Mahnmals in Wort und Bild* (Göttingen: Wallstein, 2000).

Kipnis, Jeffrey, and Thomas Leeser, eds, *Chora L Works. Jacques Derrida and Peter Eisenman* (New York: The Monacelli Press, 1997).

Kirsch, Jan-Holger, *Nationaler Mythos oder historische Trauer? Der Streit um ein zentrales "Holocaust-Mahnmal" für die Berliner Republik* (Cologne: Böhlau, 2003).

Knischewski, Gerd, and Ulla Spittler, "Remembering in the Berlin Republic: The Debate about the Central Holocaust Memorial in Berlin," *Journal of Contemporary Central and Eastern Europe*, 13.1 (2005), pp. 25–42.

Koepnick, Lutz, "Forget Berlin," *The German Quarterly*, 74.4 (2002), pp. 343–54.

Koseleck, Reinhart, and Michael Jeismann, eds, *Der politische Totenkult. Kriegerdenkmäler in der Moderne* (Munich: Wilhelm Fink Verlag, 1994).

Koshar, Rudy, *From Monuments to Traces: Artifacts of German Memory, 1870–1990* (Berkeley: University of California Press, 2000).

Koss, Juliet, "Coming to Terms with the Present," *Grey Room*, 16 (2004), pp. 116–31.

Kramer, Jane, "Living with Berlin," *The New Yorker* (5 July, 1999), pp. 50–64.

———— "The Politics of Memory," *The New Yorker* (14 August, 1995), pp. 48–65.

Kunkel, Ulrike, "Mahnmal. Mahnmal für dier ermordeten Juden Europas. Architekten: Eisenman Architects," *Deutsche Bauzeitung*, 140.6 (2006), pp. 66–68.

Laboulbenne, Xavier, ed., *Fraktur: Gespräche über Erinnerung in der Berliner Republik* (Berlin: B-Books, 2008).

Lackmann, Thomas, *Jewrassic Park. Wie baut man (k)ein Jüdisches Museum in Berlin* (Berlin: Philo Verlag, 2000).

Ladd, Brian, *The Ghosts of Berlin: Confronting German History in the Urban Landscape* (Chicago: University of Chicago Press, 1997).

Landsberg, Alison, "America, the Holocaust, and the Mass Culture of Memory: Towards a Radical Politics of Empathy," *New German Critique*, 71 (1997), pp. 63–86.

Leach, Neil, ed., *Architecture and Revolution: Contemporary Perspectives on Central and Eastern Europe* (New York: Routledge, 1999).

Levi, Daniel, and Natan Sznaider, "Memory Unbound: The Holocaust and the Formation of Cosmopolitan Memory," *European Journal of Social Theory*, 5.1 (2002), pp. 87–106.

Libeskind, Daniel, *Chamber Works. Architectural Meditations on Themes from Heraclitus* (London: Architectural Association, 1983).

———— *Daniel Libeskind: The Space of Encounter* (New York: Universe, 2000).

———— *radix-matrix: Architecture and Writings* (Munich and New York: Prestel, 1997).

Lin, Maya, *Boundaries* (New York: Simon & Schuster, 2000).

Linenthal, Edward T. and Tom Engelhardt, eds, *History Wars: The Enola Gay and Other Battles for the American Past* (New York: Holt, 1996).

Long, Rose-Carol Washton, Matthew Baigell, and Milly Heyd, eds, *Jewish Dimensions in Modern Visual Culture: Antisemitism, Assimilation, Affirmation* (Waltham: Brandeis University Press, 2010).

Maier, Charles S., *The Unmasterable Past: History, Holocaust, and German National Identity* (Cambridge, MA: Harvard University Press, 1988).

Mangos, Simone, *A Monumental Mockery: The Construction of the National Holocaust Memorial in Berlin* (Berlin: dissertation.de, 2007).

Markovits, Andrei S., and Simon Reich, *The German Predicament: Memory and Power in the New Europe* (Ithaca: Cornell University Press, 1997).

Mierzejewski, Alfred C., "A Public Enterprise in the Service of Mass Murder: The Deutsche Reichsbahn and the Holocaust," *Holocaust and Genocide Studies*, 15.1 (2001), pp. 33–46.

Milton, Sybil, *In Fitting Memory: The Art and Politics of Holocaust Memorials* (Detroit: Wayne State University Press, 1991).

Mittig, Hans-Ernst, *Gegen das Holocaustdenkmal der Berliner Republik* (Berlin: Kramer, 2005).

Naumann, Michael, *Die schönste Form der Freiheit. Reden und Essays zur Kultur der Nation* (Berlin: Siedler Verlag, 2001).

Nora, Pierre, "Between Memory and History: Les Lieux de Mémoire," trans. Marc Roudebush, *Representations*, 26 (1989), pp. 7–25.

———— "Gedächtniskonjunktur. Pflicht zur Erinnerung. Wie Nietzsche vor der 'Historie' müsste man heute vor dem 'Gedächtnis' warnen," *Freitag* (8 March, 2002), p. 16. Complete version published as "Gedächtniskonjunktur," trans. Grete Osterwald, *Transit*, 22 (2001–2002), pp. 18–31.

Neill, William J., "Marketing the Urban Experience: Reflections on the Place of Fear in the Promotional Strategies of Belfast, Detroit and Berlin," *Urban Studies*, 38 (2001), pp. 815–28.

Niven, Bill, *Facing the Nazi Past: United Germany and the Legacy of the Third Reich* (New York: Routledge, 2002).

Novick, Peter, *The Holocaust in American Life* (New York: Houghton Mifflin, 1999).

Plessen, Elisabeth, "Gedenkstätte Sachsenhausen 'Station Z'," *Deutsche Bauzeitung* 140.6 (2006), pp. 28–37.

Rabinbach, Anson, "From Explosion to Erosion: Holocaust Memorialization in America since Bitburg," *History and Memory*, 9.1/2 (1997), pp. 226–55.

Rauterberg, Hanno, *Holocaust Memorial Berlin: Eisenman Architects*, trans. Ishbel Fiett (Baden: Lars Müller Publishers, 2005).

Remmele, Matthias, "Aldo Rossi's 'Quartier Schützenstrasse'," in Martina Düttmann and Felix Zwoch, eds, *Bauwelt Berlin Annual. Chronology of Building Events 1996 to 2001: 1997* (Berlin: Birkhäuser, 1997), pp. 32–39.

Reichel, Peter, *Politik mit der Erinnerung. Gedächtnisorte im Streit um die national-sozialistische Vergangenheit* (Frankfurt am Main: Fischer, 1999).

Riegl, Alois, "Der moderne Denkmalkultus. Sein Wesen, seine Entstehung" (orig. 1903), *Gesammelte Aufsätze* (Berlin: Gebr. Mann, 1995), pp. 144–93; "The Modern Cult of Monuments: Its Character and Its Origin," trans. Kurt W. Foster and Diane Ghirardo, *Oppositions*, 25 (1982), pp. 21–50.

Robin, Régine, *Berlin Chantiers. Essai sur les passés fragiles* (Paris: Editions Stock, 2001).

Rogier, Francesca, "The E.T.A. Hoffmann Garden of Daniel Libeskind," *Daidalos*, 65 (1997), pp. 110–13.

Rosenfeld, Gavriel D., *Building after Auschwitz: Jewish Architecture and Jewish Memory Since the Holocaust* (New Haven: Yale University Press, 2011).

———— "The Architects' Debate. Architectural Discourse and the Memory of Nazism in the Federal Republic of Germany, 1977–1997," *History and Memory*, 9.1–2 (1997).

————, and Paul B. Jaskot, eds, *Beyond Berlin: Twelve German Cities Confront the Nazi Past* (Ann Arbor: University of Michigan Press, 2008).

Rosh, Lea, ed., *"Die Juden, das sind doch die anderen." Der Streit um ein deutsches Denkmal* (Berlin: Philo, 1999).

Rossi, Aldo, *The Architecture of the City*, trans. Diane Ghirardo and Joan Ockman, intro. by Peter Eisenman (Cambridge, MA: MIT Press, 1982).

Roth, Michael S., and Charles G. Salas, eds, *Disturbing Remains: Memory, History, and Crisis in the Twentieth Century* (Los Angeles: Getty Research Institute, 2001).

Rother, Rainer, ed., *Die letzten Tage der Menschheit. Bilder des ersten Weltkrieges* (Berlin: Ars Nicolai, 1994).

Rürup, Reinhard, ed., *Topographie des Terrors: Gestapo, SS und Reichssicherheitshauptamt auf dem "Prinz-Albrecht-Gelände." Eine Dokumentation* (Berlin: Willmuth Arenhövel, 1989).

Russell, James S., "Crowding the Mall: The National Memorial Dilemma," *Harvard Design Magazine* (Fall 1999), pp. 32–37.

Said, Edward W., "Invention, Memory, and Place," *Critical Inquiry*, 26 (2000), pp. 175–92.

Schmidt, Thomas E., Friedrich Diekmann, Hans-Ernst Mittig, Vera Böhm, et al., eds, *Nationaler Totenkult. Die Neue Wache. Eine Streitschrift zur zentralen deutschen Gedenkstätte* (Berlin: Kramer Verlag, 1995).

Schneider, Bernhard, *Daniel Libeskind. Jüdisches Museum Berlin* (Berlin and New York: Prestel, 1999).

Schwepphäuser, Gerhard, and Jörg H. Gleiter, eds, *Wegschauen? Weiterdenken! Zur Berliner Mahnmal-Debatte* (Weimar: Bauhaus Universität Weimar, 1999).

Simon, Hermann, *Das Berliner Jüdische Museum in der Oranienburger Straße. Geschichte einer zerstörten Kulturstätte* (Berlin: Hentrich & Hentrich, 2000).

Sirefman, Susanna, "Formed and Forming: Contemporary Museum Architecture," *Daedalus. Journal of the American Academy of Arts and Sciences*, 128.3 (1999), pp. 297–320.

Sloterdijk, Peter, *Theory of the Post-War Periods. Observations on Franco-German Relations since 1945*, trans. Robert Payne, foreword by Klaus-Dieter Müller, ed. Gerhard Blechinger (Vienna and New York: Springer, 2007).

Sorkin, Michael, "The Holocaust Museum: Between Beauty and Horror," *Progressive Architecture*, 74 (1993), p. 74.

Staiger, Uta, Henriette Steiner and Andrew Webber, eds, *Memory Culture and the Contemporary City: Building Sites* (New York and Basingstoke: Palgrave Macmillan, 2009).

Stavginski, Hans-Georg, *Das Holocaust-Denkmal: Der Streit um das "Denkmal für die ermordeten Juden Europas" in Berlin (1988–1999)* (Paderborn: Ferdinand Schöningh Verlag, 2002).

Stiftung Topographie des Terrors, ed., *Gelände Rundgang: Topographie des Terrors. Geschichte des historischen Orts* (Weißenhorn: Mareis Druck GmbH, 2010).

Till, Karen E., *The New Berlin: Memory, Politics, Place* (Minneapolis: University of Minnesota Press, 2005).

Trumpener, Katie, "Memories Carved in Granite: Great War Memorials and Everyday Life," *PMLA*, 115.5 (2000), pp. 1096–103.

Ullmann, Gerhard, "Das Holocaust-Mahnmal in Berlin: Ort des Gedenkens oder urbaner Freiraum?", *Garten + Landschaft*, 116.11 (2006), pp. 36–37.

Verheyen, Dirk, *United City, Divided Memories? Cold War Legacies in Contemporary Berlin* (Lanham: Lexington Books, 2008).

Ward, Janet, "Monuments of Catastrophe: Holocaust Architecture in Washington and Berlin," in Andreas Daum and Christof Mauch, eds, *Berlin – Washington,*

1800–2000: Capital Cities, Cultural Representation, and National Identities (New York: Cambridge University Press), pp. 155–200.

———— "Sacralized Spaces and the Urban Remembrance of War," in Uta Staiger, Henriette Steiner and Andrew Webber, eds, *Memory Culture and the Contemporary City: Building Sites* (Basingstoke and New York: Palgrave Macmillan, 2009), pp. 145–60.

Ward, Simon, "Material, Image, Sign: On the Value of Memory Traces in Public Space," in Silke Arnold-de Simine, ed., *Memory Traces: 1989 and the Question of German Cultural Identity* (Bern: Peter Lang, 2005), pp. 281–308.

Weizsäcker, Richard von, "Der 8. Mai – 40 Jahre danach," *Von Deutschland aus. Reden des Bundespräsidenten* (Munich: Deutscher Taschenbuch Verlag, 1987), pp. 11–35.

Wiedmer, Caroline, *The Claims of Memory: Representations of the Holocaust in Contemporary Germany and France* (Ithaca: Cornell University Press, 1999).

Wigley, Marc, "The Architectural Cult of Synchronization," *October*, 94 (2000), pp. 31–61.

Winter, Jay, *Sites of Memory, Sites of Mourning: The Great War in European Cultural History* (New York: Cambridge University Press, 1995).

————, and Emmanuel Sivan, eds, *War and Remembrance in the Twentieth Century* (New York: Cambridge University Press, 1999).

Young, James E., *At Memory's Edge: After-images of the Holocaust in Contemporary Art and Architecture* (New Haven: Yale University Press, 2000).

———— *The Texture of Memory: Holocaust Memorials and Meaning* (New Haven: Yale University Press, 1993).

————, ed., *The Art of Memory: Holocaust Memorials in History* (New York: Prestel, 1994).

Zelizer, Barbie, ed., *Visual Culture and the Holocaust* (New Brunswick: Rutgers University Press, 2001).

Part V: Rebranding Berlin: Global City Strategies for the Twenty-First Century

Bailey, Dave Hullfish, *Union Pacific. Berlin's Neue Mitte and the Fringes of Las Vegas* (Berlin: Vice Versa Verlag, 1999).

Baudrillard, Jean, *Simulacra and Simulation*, trans. Sheila Faria Glaser (Ann Arbor: University of Michigan Press, 1994).

———— *The Spirit of Terrorism and Requiem for the Twin Towers*, trans. Chris Turner (New York and London: Verso, 2002).

Beaverstock, J.V., P.J. Taylor, and R.G. Smith, "A Roster of World Cities," *Cities*, 16.6 (1999), pp. 445–58.

Becker, Jochen, "Hype Park," in Stadtrat, ed., *Umkämpfte Räume* (Hamburg, Berlin, and Göttingen: Assoziation A, 1998), pp. 179–90.

———— "Neue Mitte/Helle Mitte. Jumpcuts zwischen Hackeschem Markt und Platte," *Widersprüche. Zeitschrift für sozialistische Politik im Bildungs-, Gesundheits- und Sozialbereich*, 20 (2000), pp. 69–83.

Becker, Kathrin, and Urs Stahel, eds, *Remake Berlin* (Winterthur: Steidl Verlag, 2001).

Berdahl, Daphne, "The Spirit of Capitalism and the Boundaries of Citizenship in Post-Wall Germany," *Society for the Comparative Study of Society and History*, 47 (2005), pp. 235–51.

Berger, Dick, Ingo Müller, and Sandra Siewert, *Von der Partei zur Party 1969–2003. Der Berliner Fernsehturm als grafisches Symbol* (Berlin: s.wert design, 2003).

Berman, Russell A., *Anti-Americanism in Europe: A Cultural Problem* (Stanford: Hoover Institution Press, 2004).

Bernt, Matthias, *Rübergeklappt. Die "Behutsame Erneuerung" im Berlin der 90er Jahre* (Berlin: Schelzky & Jeep, 2003).

Binder, Beate, *Streitfall Stadtmitte: der Berliner Stadtschloß* (Cologne: Böhlau, 2009).

Biskup, Thomas, and Marc Schalenberg, eds, *Selling Berlin: Imagebildung und Stadtmarketing von der preußischen Residenz bis zur Bundeshauptstadt* (Stuttgart: Franz Steiner Verlag, 2008).

Bloch, Ernst, *Literarische Aufsätze, Gesamtausgabe*, vol. 9 (Frankfurt am Main: Suhrkamp, 1965).

———— *Literary Essays*, trans. Andrew Joron et al. (Stanford: Stanford University Press, 1998).

Bollmann, Stefan, ed., *Kursbuch Stadt. Stadtleben und Stadtkultur an der Jahrtausendwende* (Stuttgart: Deutsche Verlags-Anstalt, 1999).

Brenner, Neil, "Review Essay. Berlin's Transformations: Postmodern, Postfordist … or Neoliberal?" *International Journal of Urban and Regional Research*, 26.4 (2002), pp. 635–42.

————, and Roger Keil, eds, *The Global Cities Reader* (New York: Routledge, 2006).

Bridge, Gary, and Sophie Watson, eds, *A Companion to the City* (Cambridge, MA: Blackwell, 2000).

Broder, Henryk, *Kein Krieg, nirgends. Die Deutschen und der Terror* (Berlin: Berlin Verlag, 2002).

Bude, Heinz, *Generation Berlin* (Berlin: Merve, 2001).

Burg, Annegret, and Hans Stimmann, eds, *Berlin Mitte. Die Entstehung einer urbanen Architektur* (Basel: Birkhäuser, 1995).

————, ed., *Neue Berlinische Architektur: Eine Debatte* (Berlin, Basel and Boston: Birkhäuser, 1994).

Bürkle, Stefanie, *Home: Sweet: City 1997–2007* (Berlin: Vice Versa Verlag, 2007).

Castells, Manuel, *The Rise of the Network Society*, vol. 1 of *The Information Age: Economy, Society and Culture* (Cambridge, MA: Blackwell, 1996).

Cochrane, Allan, and Adrian Passmore, "Building a National Capital in an Age of Globalization: The Case of Berlin," *Area*, 33.4 (2001), pp. 341–52.

————, and Andrew Jonas, "Reimagining Berlin: World City, National Capital or Ordinary Place?" *European Urban and Regional Studies*, 6.2 (1999), pp. 145–64.

Cooke, Philip, *Knowledge Economies: Clusters, Learning and Cooperative Advantage* (New York: Routledge, 2002).

Davis, Mike, *Casino Zombies und andere Fabeln aus dem Neon-Westen der USA*, trans. Steffen Emrich and Britta Grell (Berlin: Schwarze Risse, 1999).

Dear, Michael J., *The Postmodern Urban Condition* (Malden, MA and Oxford: Blackwell, 2000).

Derrida, Jacques, Kurt Forster, and Wim Wenders, "The Berlin City Forum," *Architectural Design*, 62.11/12 (1992), pp. 46–53.

Deuflhard, Amelie, Sophie Krempl-Klieeisen, Philipp Oswalt, Matthias Lilienthal, and Harald Müller, eds, *Volkspalast. Zwischen Aktivismus und Kunst* (Berlin: Theater der Zeit, 2006).

Döblin, Alfred, *Berlin Alexanderplatz. Die Geschichte von Franz Biberkopf,* orig. 1929 (Munich: dtv, 1988).

Easterling, Keller, *Enduring Innocence: Global Architecture and Its Political Masquerades* (Cambridge, MA: MIT Press, 2005).

Eichwede, Wolfgang, and Regine Kayser, eds, *Metropolen im Wandel. Berlin-Moskau* (Berlin: Jovis Verlag, 2003).

Ekici, Didem, "The Surfaces of Memory in Berlin: Rebuilding the Schloß," *Journal of Architectural Education,* 61.2 (2007), pp. 25–34.

Endell, August, *Die Schönheit der großen Stadt,* orig. 1908 (Berlin: Archibook, 1984).

Enke, Roland, Reinhard Alings, Bernhard Schneider, and Gerwin Zohlen, with Berliner Festspiele, eds, *Berlin: Open City,* 2 vols. (Berlin: Nicolai, 1999).

Evans, Graeme, "Hard-Branding the Cultural City – From Prado to Prada," *International Journal of Urban and Regional Research,* 27.2 (2003), pp. 417–40.

Färber, Alexa, et al., eds, *Hotel Berlin. Formen urbaner Mobilität und Verortung,* Berliner Blätter: Ethnographische und ethnologische Beiträge (Münster: LIT Verlag, 2005).

Faludi, Andreas, ed., *European Spatial Planning* (Cambridge, MA: Lincoln Institute of Land Policy, 2002).

Finney, Gail, ed., *Visual Culture in Twentieth-Century Germany* (Bloomington: Indiana University Press, 2006).

Fischer, Joachim, and Michael Makropoulos, eds, *Potsdamer Platz. Soziologische Theorien zu einem Ort der Moderne* (Munich: Wilhelm Fink Verlag, 2004).

Flierl, Thomas, and Hermann Parzinger, eds, *Humboldt-Forum Berlin: Das Projekt* (Berlin: Theater der Zeit, 2009).

Florida, Richard, *The Rise of the Creative Class: And How It's Transforming Work, Leisure, Community and Everyday Life* (New York: Basic Books, 2002).

Förderverein Berliner Stadtschloss e.V., Berlin, with Technische Universität Berlin and Architektenbüro Stuhlemmer, eds, *Berliner Stadtschloss. Rekonstruktion zweier Fensterachsen. Photogrammetrische Rekonstruktion* (Berlin: Förderverein Berliner Stadtschloss e.V., 2000).

Fuchs, Gotthard, Bernhard Moltmann, and Walter Prigge, eds, *Mythos Metropole* (Frankfurt am Main: Suhrkamp, 1995).

Gallis, Michael, and James S. Russell, "World City: Why Globalization Makes Cities More Important than Ever," *Architectural Record,* 3 (2002), pp. 70–73.

Gobé, Marc, *Emotional Branding* (New York: Allworth Press, 2001).

Goebel, Rolf, "Forget Hermeneutics? A Response to Lutz Koepnick," *The German Quarterly,* 75.2 (2002), pp. 197–200.

Grech, John, "Empty Space and the City: The Reoccupation of Berlin," *Radical History Review,* 83 (2002), pp. 115–42.

Grésillon, Boris, *Kulturmetropole Berlin* (Berlin: Berliner Wissenschafts-Verlag, 2004).

Grumeth, Pia, ed., *Berlin Topografiefreunde 15, ein alternativer Stadtführer* (Berlin: solid earth, 2003).

Häußermann, Hartmut, and Andreas Kapphan, *Berlin: von der geteilten zur gespaltenen Stadt? Sozialräumlicher Wandel seit 1990* (Opladen: Leske+Budrich, 2000).

———, Andrej Holm, and Daniela Zunzer, *Stadterneuerung in der Berliner Republik. Modernisierung in Berlin-Prenzlauer Berg* (Opladen: Leske+Budrich, 2002).

————, and Elizabeth Strom, "Berlin: The Once and Future Capital," *International Journal of Urban and Regional Research*, 18.2 (1994), pp. 335–46.

————, and Reiner Neef, eds, *Stadtentwicklung in Ostdeutschland* (Opladen: Westdeutscher Verlag, 1996).

Hamilton, Ian, F. E., Kaliopa Dimitrowska Andrews, and Natasa Pichler-Milanovic, eds, *Transformation of Cities in Central and Eastern Europe: Towards Globalisation* (Tokyo, New York, and Paris: United Nations University Press, 2005).

Hamm, Oliver, and IBA Hamburg, eds, *Metropolis: Reflections* (Berlin: Jovis Verlag, 2007).

Hanna, Stephen P., and Vincent J. Del Casino, Jr., eds, *Mapping Tourism* (Minneapolis: University of Minnesota Press, 2003).

Harvey, David, *Spaces of Capital: Towards a Critical Geography* (Edinburgh: Edinburgh University Press, 2001).

Haxthausen, Charles W., and Heidrun Suhr, eds, *Berlin: Culture and Metropolis* (Minneapolis: University of Minnesota Press, 1990).

Heinritz, Günter, and Jürgen Rauh, "Gutachterliche Stellungnahmen über Factor Outlet Center. Eine kritische Betrachtung," *Raumforschung und Raumordnung*, 58.1 (2000), pp. 47–54.

Helm, Jutta A., "Introduction. German Cities between Globalization and Unification," *German Politics and Society*, 16.4 (1998), pp. 7–17.

Hennet, Anna-Inès, *Die Berliner Schlossdebatte im Spiegel der Presse* (Berlin: Braun, 2005).

Hertweck, Florian, *Der Berliner Architekturstreit* (Berlin: Gebr. Mann, 2010).

Heßler, Martina, and Clemens Zimmermann, eds, *Creative Urban Milieus. Historical Perspectives on Culture, Economy, and the City* (Frankfurt am Main: Campus Verlag, 2008).

Hilber, Maria Luise, and Ayda Ergez, eds, *Stadtidentität. Der richtige Weg zum Stadtmarketing* (Zürich: Orell Füssli, 2004).

Hise, Greg, *Magnetic Los Angeles: Planning the Twentieth-Century Metropolis* (Baltimore: Johns Hopkins University Press, 1999).

Hoffmann, Andreas, *Luftschlösser. Berlins unvollendete Bauten* (Berlin: Transit Buchverlag, 2003).

Hoffmann-Axthelm, Dieter, "Schweigsame Oberbaum City," *Bauwelt*, 93.9 (2002), pp. 14–17.

Holfelder, Moritz, *Palast der Republik. Aufstieg und Fall eines symbolisches Gebäudes* (Berlin: Ch. Links, 2008).

Holm, Andrej, *Die Restrukturierung des Raumes. Stadterneuerung der 90er Jahre in Ostberlin: Interessen und Machtverhältnisse* (Berlin: Transcript Verlag, 2006).

Huber, Nicole, and Ralph Stern, *Urbanizing the Mojave Desert: Las Vegas* (Berlin: Jovis, 2008).

Huret, Jules, *En Allemagne: Berlin* (Paris: Bibliothèque-Charpentier, 1909).

Huyssen, Andreas, *Present Pasts: Urban Palimpsests and the Politics of Memory* (Stanford: Stanford University Press, 2003).

————, ed., *Other Cities, Other Worlds: Urban Imaginaries in a Globalizing Age* (Durham: Duke University Press, 2008).

Huxtable, Ada Louise, *The Unreal America: Architecture and Illusion* (New York: The New Press, 1997).

Ibelings, Hans, *Supermodernism: Architecture in the Age of Globalization* (Rotterdam: NAi, 1998).

Internationale Bauakademie Berlin, ed., *Humboldt-Forum. Symposion zu Fragen der Rekonstruktion und der räumlichen Konzeption des Berliner Schlosses für das Humboldt-Forum* (Bad Langensalza: Druckhaus "Thomas Müntzer" GmbH, 2007).

Judd, Dennis R., and Susan S. Fainstein, eds, *The Tourist City* (New Haven: Yale University Press, 1999).

Kapphan, Andreas, *Das arme Berlin. Sozialräumliche Polarisierung, Armutskonzentration und Ausgrenzung in den 1990er Jahren* (Opladen: Leske+Budrich 2002).

Kearns, Gerry, and Chris Philo, eds, *Selling Places: The City as Cultural Capital, Past and Present* (New York: Pergamon Press, 1993).

King, Anthony D., *Urbanism, Colonialism, and the World Economy* (New York: Routledge, 1990).

Kleine, Klaus, and Thomas Offermanns, "In Deutschland geplante Factory Outlet Center," *Raumforschung und Raumordnung*, 58.1 (2000), pp. 35–46.

Klingman, Anna, *Brandscapes: Architecture in the Experience Economy* (Cambridge, MA: MIT Press, 2007).

Koch, Florian, and Marianne Rodenstein, eds, *Die europäische Stadt in Transformation: Stadtplanung und Stadtentwicklungspolitik im postsozialistischen Warschau* (Wiesbaden: VS Verlag, 2009).

Koepnick, Lutz, "Forget Berlin," *The German Quarterly*, 74.4 (2001), pp. 343–54.

———, and Erin McGlothlin, eds, *After the Digital Divide? German Aesthetic Theory in the Age of New Media* (Rochester, NY: Camden House, 2009).

Kohl, Sibyl, Philipp Oswalt, and Albrecht Schäfer, *Architektur-Stadtführer Ostdeutschland*, 3 vols. (Cologne: Verlag der Buchhandlung Walther König, 2003).

Koolhaas, Rem, Stefano Boeri, and Sanford Kwinter, eds, *Mutations* (Bordeaux: ACTAR, 2000).

Krätke, Stefan, "City of Talents? Berlin's Regional Economy, Socio-Spatial Fabric and 'Worst Practice' Urban Governance," *International Journal of Urban and Regional Research*, 28.3 (2004), pp. 511–29.

——— *Medienstadt. Urbane Cluster und globale Zentren der Kulturproduktion* (Opladen: Leske + Budrich, 2002).

——— "Metropolisation of the European Economic Territory as a Consequence of Increasing Specialisation of Urban Agglomerations in the Knowledge Economy," *European Planning Studies*, 15.1 (2007), pp. 1–27.

———, and Renate Borst, *Berlin: Metropole zwischen Boom und Krise* (Opladen: Leske + Budrich, 2000).

Krause, Linda, and Patrice Petro, eds, *Global Cities: Cinema, Architecture, and Urbanism in a Digital Age* (New Brunswick: Rutgers University Press, 2003).

Kuhrmann, Anke, *Der Palast der Republik: Geschichte und Bedeutung des Ost-Berliner Parlaments- und Kulturhauses* (Petersberg: Imhof, 2006).

Ladd, Brian, *The Companion Guide to Berlin* (Rochester, NY and Woodbridge: Boydell & Brewer, 2004).

Lampugnani, Vittorio Magnago, and Romana Schneider, eds, *Ein Stück Großstadt als Experiment. Planungen am Potsdamer Platz in Berlin* (Stuttgart: Verlag Gerd Hatje, 1994).

Lanz, Stephan, *Berlin aufgemischt: abendländisch – multikulturell – kosmopolitisch? Die politische Konstruktion einer Einwanderungsstadt* (Bielefeld: transcript Verlag, 2007).

——— "Powered by Quartiersmanagement: 'Füreinander Leben im Problemkiez'," *dérive: Zeitschrift für Stadtforschung*, 31 (2008), pp. 28–31.

————, and Jochen Becker, *Metropolen* (Hamburg: Rotbuch Verlag, 2001).

Lasswell, Harold, *Politics: Who Gets What, When, How* (New York: P. Smith, 1936).

Leach, Neil, *The Anaesthetics of Architecture* (Cambridge, MA: MIT Press, 1999).

Lehmann, Klaus-Dieter, "Weltort für Kunst und Kultur – Berlins Mitte," in Stiftung Preußischer Kulturbesitz, ed., *Jahrbuch Stiftung Preußischer Kulturbesitz 2005*, XLII (Berlin: Verlag Dietrich Reimer/Verlag Gebr. Mann, 2006), pp. 115–28.

Lenhart, Karin, *Berliner Metropoly. Stadtentwicklungspolitik im Berliner Bezirk Mitte nach der Wende* (Opladen: Leske + Budrich, 2001).

Lepik, Andres, and Staatliche Museen zu Berlin Preußischer Kulturbesitz, eds, *Masterplan Museumsinsel Berlin. Ein europäisches Projekt* (Berlin: G + H Verlag, 2000).

Leyden, Friedrich, *Groß-Berlin. Geographie der Weltstadt*, orig. 1933 (Berlin: Gebr. Mann Verlag, 1995).

Lewitscharoff, M., ed., *Das Berlin-Paket* (Munich: ars Edition, 2001).

Löw, Martina, *Soziologie der Städte* (Frankfurt am Main: Suhrkamp, 2008).

Maar, Christa, and Florian Rötzer, eds, *Virtual Cities: Die Neuerfindung der Stadt im Zeitalter der globalen Vernetzung* (Basel: Birkhäuser Verlag, 1997).

Maciuika, John V., "Castles in the Sand: The Politics of Architecture at the Heart of Berlin" (work in progress).

Marcuse, Peter, "Reflections on Berlin: The Meaning of Construction and the Construction of Meaning," *International Journal of Urban and Regional Research*, 22.2 (1998), pp. 331–38.

———— "Tradition in a Global City?" *Traditional Dwellings and Settlements Review*, 17.2 (2006), pp. 7–18.

————, and Ronald van Kempen, eds, *Globalizing Cities: A New Spatial Order?* (Malden, MA: Blackwell, 2000).

Maron, Monika, *Bitterfelder Bogen. Ein Bericht* (Frankfurt am Main: Fischer Verlag, 2009).

Massey, Doreen, "A Global Sense of Place," *Marxism Today* (June 1991), pp. 24–29.

———— *World City* (Cambridge: Polity, 2007).

McCormack, R.W.B., *Mitten in Berlin. Feldstudien in der Hauptstadt* (Munich: C.H. Beck, 2000).

McRobbie, Angela, "Reflections on Precarious Work in the Cultural Sector," in Bastion Lange, Ares Kalandides, Birgit Stöber, and Inga Wellmann, eds, *Governance der Kreativwirtschaft. Diagnosen und Handlungsoptionen* (Bielefeld: transcript Verlag, 2009), pp. 123–39.

Meyer, Ulf, "'Wo bitte geht's zum Checkpoint Charlie?'," in Architektenkammer Berlin and Lothar Juckel, eds, *Architektur in Berlin. Jahrbuch 1997* (Hamburg: Junius Verlag, 1997), pp. 64–69.

Michel, Karl Markus and Ingrid Karsunke, eds, *Berlin. Metropole*, Kursbuch 137 (Berlin: Rowohlt, 1999).

Misselwitz, Philipp, Hans Ulrich Obrist, and Philipp Oswalt, eds, *Fun Palace 200X – der Berliner Schlossplatz: Abriß, Neubau, oder grüne Wiese?* (Berlin: Martin Schmitz Verlag, 2005).

Mitchell, William J., *City of Bits: Space, Place, and the Infobahn* (Cambridge, MA: MIT Press, 1995).

Molnar, Virag, "The Cultural Production of Locality: Reclaiming the 'European City' in Post-Wall Berlin," *International Journal of Urban and Regional Research*, 34.2 (2010), pp. 281–309.

Morris, E., "Heritage and Culture: A Capital for the New Europe," in G.J. Ashworth and P.J. Larkham, eds, *Building a New Heritage: Tourism, Culture, and Identity in the New Europe* (New York: Routledge, 1994), pp. 229–59.

Mumford, Lewis, *The City in History: Its Origins, Its Transformations, and Its Prospects*, orig. 1961 (New York: Harcourt Brace & Co., 1989).

Ockman, Joan, and Salomon Frausto, eds, *Architourism: Authentic, Escapist, Exotic, Spectacular* (Munich: Prestel, 2005).

Osborn, Max, ed., *Kennen Sie Berlin?/How to See Berlin* (Stettin: F. Hessenland, 1928).

Oswalt, Philipp, ed., *Shrinking Cities*, 2 vols. (Ostfildern-Ruit: Hatje Cantz/New York: D.A.P, 2005).

Overmeyer, Klaus, and Senatsverwaltung für Stadtentwicklung Berlin, eds, *Urban Pioneers. Berlin Stadtentwicklung durch Zwischennutzung/Temporary Use and Urban Development in Berlin* (Berlin: Jovis, 2007).

Paloscia, Raffaele, ed., *The Contested Metropolis. Six Cities at the Beginning of the 21st Century* (Basel and Boston: Birkhäuser, 2004).

Presner, Todd, "Digital Geographies: Berlin in the Ages of New Media," in Jaimey Fisher and Barbara Mennel, eds, *Spatial Turns: Space, Place, and Mobility in German Literary and Visual Culture* (Amsterdam: Rodopi, 2010).

Puchta, Dieter, Friedrich Schneider, Stefan Haigner, et al., eds, *The Berlin Creative Industries: An Empirical Analysis of Future Key Industries* (Wiesbaden: Gabler Verlag, 2010).

Rada, Uwe, *Hauptstadt der Verdrängung: Berliner Zukunft zwischen Kiez und Metropole* (Berlin: Verlag Schwarze Risse, 1997).

Rathenau, Walther, *Die schönste Stadt der Welt*, orig. 1899 (Berlin and Vienna: Philo, 2002).

Richter, Dagmar, "*Spazieren* in Berlin," *Assemblage*, 29 (1996), pp. 72–85.

Riedel, Raimo, *Der Traum von der Metropole. Ein Vergleich der Prozesse der Metropolisierung von Chicago nach 1871 und Berlin nach 1989 in Diskurs und Realität* (Hamburg: Diplomica Verlag, 2007).

Riedmann, Erwin, "Global City Berlin? Illusionen und die Ironie der Geschichte," *dérive. Zeitschrift für Stadtforschung*, 20 (2005), pp. 34–37.

Roll, Evelyn, *Nun soll endlich Glanzzeit sein. Berliner Beobachtungen* (Vienna: Picus Verlag, 2000).

Ronneberger, Klaus, Stephan Lanz, and Walther Jahn, *Die Stadt als Beute* (Bonn: Dietz, 1999).

Roost, Frank, *Branding Center: Über den Einfluß globaler Markenkonzerns auf die Innenstädte* (Wiesbaden: Vs Verlag für Sozialwissenschaften, 2008).

——— *Die Disneyfizierung der Städte: Großprojekte der Entertainmentindustrie am Beispiel des New Yorker Times Square und der Siedlung Celebration in Florida* (Opladen: Leske + Budrich, 2000).

Rose, Matthew D., *Eine ehrenwerte Gesellschaft. Die Bankgesellschaft Berlin* (Berlin: Transit Verlag, 2003).

Rosenfeld, Gavriel D., "The Architects' Debate. Architectural Discourse and the Memory of Nazism in the Federal Republic of Germany, 1977–1997," *History and Memory*, 9.1–2 (1997), pp. 189–225.

Rothman, Hal K., and Mike Davis, eds, *The Grit Beneath the Glitter: Tales from the Real Las Vegas* (Berkeley: University of California Press, 2002).

Rykwert, Joseph, *The Seduction of Place: The History and Future of the City* (New York: Vintage, 2002).

Sassen, Saskia, *Metropolen des Weltmarkts. Die neue Rolle der Global Cities* (Frankfurt am Main: Campus Verlag, 1996).

———— *The Global City* (Princeton: Princeton University Press, 1991).

————, ed., *Deciphering the Global: Its Scales, Spaces and Subjects* (New York: Routledge, 2007).

Schadt, Thomas, *Berlin: Sinfonie einer Großstadt* (Berlin: Nikolai, 2002).

Scharenberg, Albert, ed., *Berlin: Global City oder Konkursmasse? Eine Zwischenbilanz nach dem Mauerfall* (Berlin: Karl Dietz Verlag, 2000).

Schlögel, Karl, "The Comeback of the European Cities," *International Review of Sociology*, 16.2 (2006), pp. 471–85.

Schneider, Peter, *Eduards Heimkehr* (Hamburg: Rowohlt, 1999).

Schneider-Sliwa, Rita, ed., *Städte im Umbruch. Neustrukturierung von Berlin, Brüssel, Hanoi, Ho Chi Minh Stadt, Hongkong, Jerusalem, Johannesburg, Moskau, St Petersburg, Sarajewo und Wien* (Berlin: Reimer, 2002). Translated as *Cities in Transition: Globalization, Political Change and Urban Development* (Dordrecht: Springer, 2006).

Schweitzer, Eva, *Großbaustelle Berlin: Wie die Hauptstadt verplant wird* (Berlin: Nicola, 1996).

Senatsverwaltung für Stadtentwicklung, ed., *z.B. Berlin. Zehn Jahre Transformation und Modernisierung. Begleitbuch zur Ausstellung* (Berlin: Edition Foyer, 2000).

————, and Bundesministerium für Verkehr, Bau und Wohnungswesen, eds, *Historische Mitte Berlin. Schlossplatz. Ideen und Entwürfe 1991–2001* (Berlin: Ruksaldruck GmbH + Co., 2001).

Senatsverwaltung für Stadtentwicklung, Umweltschutz und Technologie, ed. *Internationale Expertenkommission. Historische Mitte Berlin. Materialien* (Berlin: Brandenburgische Universitätsdruckeri und Verlagsgesellschaft, 2002).

Sennett, Richard, *The Spaces of Democracy* (Ann Arbor: University of Michigan Press, 1998).

Sewing, Werner, *Bildregie: Architektur zwischen Retrodesign und Eventkultur* (Basel and Boston: Birkhäuser/Verlag für Architektur, 2003).

Siegert, Hubertus, dir., *Berlin Babylon* (Berlin: S.U.M.O. Film, 2001).

————, and Ralph Stern, "Berlin. Film and the Representation of Urban Reconstruction Since the Fall of the Wall," in Joan Ockman, ed., *Out of Ground Zero: Case Studies in Urban Reinvention* (New York: Prestel, 2002), pp. 116–31.

Simmen, Jeannot, and Thorsten Heinze, *berlin-2010.eu* (Berlin: Edition Club Bel Etage, 2010).

Sinclair, Iain, *London Orbital: A Walk Around the M25* (London: Granta, 2002).

Slessor, Catherine, "Vegas on the Spree," *Architectural Review*, 212.1267 (2002), pp. 28–29.

Smith, Neil, *The New Urban Frontier: Gentrification and the Revanchist City* (New York: Routledge, 1996).

Soja, Edward W., *Postmetropolis: Critical Studies of Cities and Regions* (Cambridge, MA: Blackwell, 2000).

Sorkin, Michael, ed., *Variations on a Theme Park: The New American City and the End of Public Space* (New York: Hill & Wang, 1992).

Sperling, James, "Neither Hegemony nor Dominance: Reconsidering German Power in Post Cold-War Europe," *British Journal of Political Science*, 31 (2001), pp. 389–425.

Stanilov, Kiril, ed., *The Post-Socialist City. Urban Form and Space Transformations in Central and Eastern Europe after Socialism* (Dordecht: Springer, 2007).

Stein, Jean, ed., *Grand Street 69*, 18.1 (New York: Grand Street Press/New York Foundation for the Arts, 1999).

Stewart, Janet, *Public Speaking in the City: Debating and Shaping the Urban Experience* (New York and Basingstoke: Palgrave Macmillan, 2009).

Stimmann, Hans, ed., *Babylon, Berlin etc. Das Vokabular der europäischen Stadt* (Basel: Birkhäuser, 1995).

Strom, Elizabeth A., *Building the New Berlin: The Politics of Urban Development in Germany's Capital City* (Lanham: Lexington Books, 2001).

Sundermeier, Jörg, Verena Sarah Diehl, and Werner Labisch, eds, *Mittebuch* (Berlin: Verbrecher Verlag, 2003).

Swoboda, Hannes, ed., *Der Schlossplatz in Berlin. Bilanz einer Debatte* (Berlin: Bostelmann & Siebenhaar, 2002).

Taylor, Ronald, *Berlin and Its Culture: A Historical Portrait* (New Haven: Yale University Press, 1997).

Tietz, Jürgen, *Berliner Verwandlungen. Hauptstadt / Architektur / Denkmal* (Berlin: Verlag Bauwesen, 2000).

Ullmann, Gerhard, "Insel der Urbanität. Zur Renovierung der Hackeschen Höfe in Berlin-Mitte," *Deutsche Bauzeitung*, 6 (1997), pp. 53–59.

Venturi, Robert, Denise Scott Brown, and Steven Izenour, *Learning from Las Vegas* (Cambridge, MA: MIT Press, 1972).

von Beyme, Klaus, *Hauptstadtsuche: Hauptstadtfunktionen im Interessenkonflikt zwischen Bonn und Berlin* (Frankfurt am Main: Suhrkamp, 1991).

von Boddien, Wilhelm, and Helmut Engel, *Die Berliner Schlossdebatte: pro und kontra* (Berlin: Berlin Verlag, 2000).

von Rauch, Yamin, and Jochen Visscher, eds, *Der Potsdamer Platz. Urban Architecture for a New Berlin* (Berlin: Jovis, 2000).

Wagner, David, *In Berlin* (Berlin: Nicolai, 2001).

Ward, Janet, "Berlin, the Virtual Global City," *Journal of Visual Culture*, 3.2 (2004), pp. 239–56.

———— "City Branding," in Gert Wingårdh and Rasmus Waern, eds, *Crucial Words: Conditions for Contemporary Architecture* (Basel and Boston: Birkhäuser Verlag, 2008), pp. 26–29.

———— "Las Vegas on the Spree: Americanization in the New Berlin," in Gail Finney, ed., *Visual Culture in Twentieth Century Germany: Text as Spectacle* (Bloomington: University of Indiana Press, 2006), pp. 83–100.

———— *Weimar Surfaces: Urban Visual Culture in 1920s Germany* (Berkeley: University of California Press, 2001).

Ward, Stephen V., *Selling Places: The Marketing and Promotion of Towns and Cities 1850–2000* (New York: Routledge, 1998).

Wefing, Heinrich, *Der Neue Potsdamer Platz. Ein Kunststück Stadt* (Berlin: be.bra verlag, 1998).

Wegener, Michael, Klaus R. Kunzmann, and Klaus Spiekermann, "Wachsendes Europa – schrumpfender Kontinent," *arch +*, 122 (1994), pp. 238–43.

Wesenberg, Angelika, and Eve Förschl, eds, *Die Nationalgalerie. Das XIX. Jahrhundert* (Leipzig: E.A. Seemann Verlag, 2002).

Wiesel, Miriam, ed., *Berlin/Berlin, Katalog der ersten Berlin Biennale* (Ostfildern: Cantz Verlag, 1998).

Wilhelm, Karin, and Gregor Langenbrinck, eds, *City-Lights. Zentren, Peripherien, Regionen. Interdisziplinäre Positionen für eine urbane Kultur* (Vienna: Böhlau Verlag, 2002).

Wolf, Christa, *Was bleibt* (Frankfurt am Main: Luchterhand, 1990); *What Remains and Other Stories*, trans. Heike Schwarzbauer and Rick Takvorian (New York: Farrar, Straus, and Giroux, 1993).

Wrobel, David M., *Promised Lands: Promotion, Memory, and the Creation of the American West* (Lawrence: University Press of Kansas, 2002).

Yeadon, Peter, "Bau Wow: Shall We Bark or Bite?", *Canadian Architect*, 47.10 (October 2002), pp. 42–43.

Zohlen, Gerwin, Berliner Festspiele, and Architektenkammer Berlin, eds, *Berlin: offene Stadt*, 2 vols. (Berlin: Nikolai, 1999).

Zukin, Sharon, *Landscapes of Power: From Detroit to Disney World* (Berkeley: University of California Press, 1991).

Index

Bold page numbers indicate figures.